WORKS BY GEOFFREY PERRETT

History

AMERICA IN THE TWENTIES: A HISTORY

DAYS OF SADNESS, YEARS OF TRIUMPH: THE AMERICAN PEOPLE 1939–1945

A DREAM OF GREATNESS: THE AMERICAN PEOPLE 1945–1963

Fiction

EXECUTIVE PRIVILEGE

AMERICA
IN THE
TWENTIES
A HISTORY

Geoffrey Perrett

A TOUCHSTONE BOOK
Published by Simon & Schuster, Inc.
NEW YORK

First Touchstone edition, 1983
Published by Simon & Schuster, Inc.
Simon & Schuster Building
Rockefeller Center
1230 Avenue of the Americas
New York, New York 10020
TOUCHSTONE and colophon are registered trademarks
of Simon & Schuster, Inc.

Designed by Eve Kirch

Manufactured in the United States of America

1 3 5 7 9 10 8 6 4 2
1 3 5 7 9 10 8 6 4 2 Pbk.

Library of Congress Cataloging in Publication Data

Perrett, Geoffrey.
America in the twenties.
Bibliography: p.
Includes index.
1. United States—History—1919-1933.
I. Title
E784.P44   973.91   81-21259
                               AACR2

ISBN 0-671-25107-4
ISBN 0-671-25108-2 Pbk.

For Anne
Now. Always.

Contents

8 *Contents*

PART III: BELSHAZZAR'S FEAST

PART IV: PURPLE TWILIGHT

Introduction

Everyone knows the Twenties: flappers, jazz bands, the Charleston, tea-cups filled with bathtub gin—one long party and everyone had a hangover (known as the Depression) in the morning. The Twenties are both the most derided decade in American history and the most glamorous. It has been a pleasant experience to be told "How interesting" when people wanted to know what I was writing. They often elaborated with remarks such as "What a wonderfully decadent time!" or "That was the last time Americans really knew how to enjoy themselves." Almost without exception the hundred or more people who've asked me about this book had a firm, unshakable idea of what the period was like. I had begun with much the same idea myself. I thought of the Twenties as a period that had been "done"—to a turn.

Like most people who've read about it, my reading began with Frederick Lewis Allen's *Only Yesterday*. I swallowed the entire book at a gulp, on a tingling crisp day in Berkeley in the spring of 1970. I literally couldn't stop reading it until I'd finished. "Delightful," I said, putting it down. There was one phrase, though, which stuck in my mind, a phrase which encouraged certain doubts even as I read.

In the preface to the 1957 edition I was reading, Allen remarked, "I should confess that in the effort to highlight the trends of the nineteen-twenties—and to enliven the book—I illustrated the book with rather extreme, though authentic, examples of odd or excited behavior." Then, several years later, I came across *The Big Change*. In the preface to this Allen made a more substantial admission: "During the years 1930 and

1931, when I had been at work on *Only Yesterday* . . . my best sources had been the daily papers and magazines of the period; the books of reportage or appraisal *which I really needed to consult* could have been ranged on a single shelf." (My italics.)

That revived my earlier doubts, and I thought of the handicaps he had faced. On the one hand, the cut-and-paste approach allowed him to write an entertaining, impressionistic account which undoubtedly captured some of the feverish, hectic nature of the period. But on the other hand, there were no reliable biographies of the major thinkers, scientists, reformers, politicians and writers of the Twenties for him to turn to. There were hardly any reliable studies of the country's art, health, education, sex life and cities. At least half the population lived in poverty, yet that half virtually never appears in *Only Yesterday*.

Allen nonetheless set the mold in which every general account of the Twenties has been put for the past fifty years. *Only Yesterday* virtually created popular social history in the English-speaking world. In its modest way it has proved to be one of the most influential books of the century. Yet there were those gaps. I hoped, by writing this book, to provide the first complete account of the one period everyone knows.

By allowing myself more scope than Allen and his disciples, I've been able to adopt a different approach. In the "informal" history major characters or important events are nearly always crammed into a few pages, sometimes a few paragraphs. There is no room for them to develop as the period develops. Such books usually consist of highlights. The reader of this book, however, will find many characters who are threaded through various chapters like the characters in a novel. A major event will begin in one chapter, be untouched for more than a hundred pages, to be taken up and developed further, only to be resolved at the end of the book. To me, it is a method that comes closer to the flow of life, to the way things really happen. It took seven years, for example, for Sacco and Vanzetti to move from conviction to execution. It took about two years for the Depression to take hold and write finis to the Twenties.

Finally, on interpretation (an area Allen shunned) I discovered a duality I'd never expected. I had assumed the Twenties were the first decade of the twentieth century, with the Great War serving as the death agony of the nineteenth. And so they were. That is why the period can seem so familiar to us, even to those like myself who were born in the Forties. What I'd not expected to find were large areas of American life still in the grip of the Victorian/Puritan/Frontier past.

It was the struggle between these two worlds that gave tension and shape to what would otherwise have been formless and futile. All across

American life there was a deep break in continuity, with the sense of release that liberation brings, along with all the anxiety occasioned by the unknown. It made for an exciting time.

PART I

NORMALCY

I. Of Pestilence and Peace

I

The autumn of 1918 might have been a presentiment of the end of the world. Along an arc reaching from Flanders to Vladivostok men armed with bayonets, rifles, and machine guns were mutilating one another in the clinging mud of autumn rains, to the flash and roar of high explosives. Most were markedly older or younger than those who had gone before them, and who had died, as they were dying now for the victory certain to prove hollow or fighting against the defeat never to be accepted. Behind the lines, meanwhile, a great sickness was spreading over the earth. Only a handful of remote Pacific islands would escape it.

This pandemic, of mysterious origin and amazing virulence, had broken out at Camp Devens, thirty miles west of Boston, in mid-September.[1] In the days before jet travel epidemics spread comparatively slowly, from person to person. Inexplicably, the day this new strain of influenza reached Boston it also reached Bombay.[2]

In India, in New England, soon all over the world, cortèges clogged the streets. The sickness spread like a biblical judgment of wrath, as if none but a handful were innocent, none but a handful were safe. In New York City the death toll climbed to 4,500 a week; in Philadelphia it passed 1,000 a day.[3] In nine months this epidemic would claim at least 550,000 American lives.[4]

Processions of black carriages, drawn by high-stepping black horses and guided by coachmen in top hats of black silk, or files of new high-

15

topped black limousines sporting huge nickel-plated lamps passed almost unbroken down the roads approaching city cemeteries. At Boston's Dorchester cemetery the gravediggers, like gravediggers everywhere, fell days, then weeks, behind. Coffin mountains formed at the cemetery gates, and wet leaves in the dazzling hues of a New England fall covered them, briefly shrouding these mostly poor and humble dead in a mantle of gold and crimson glory. When a circus tent was fetched to shield the coffins from the rain it soon filled up and overflowed.[5]

The Spanish influenza hit hardest in the slums. In Harrisburg, Pennsylvania, Maimie Pinzer, arriving at her brother's house on an urgent summons, found a household of six people prostrate from illness and exhaustion, while her sister-in-law Caroline lay dead and unattended in the front bedroom. The stench of putrefaction penetrated the entire house. Maimie, a former prostitute, former drug addict, and with only one eye thanks to venereal disease in childhood, had to open the dead woman's arteries herself. She then washed and dressed the body for burial. A laundry basket served as Caroline's coffin. It was borne to the cemetery in a borrowed grocery truck.[6]

At Camp Devens, meanwhile, Private Fred E. Beal, recently drafted, was still in basic training. Yet there really was no training now. He and his fellow recruits were not spending their days on the rifle range or the obstacle course. They were helping to dispose of the seventy to eighty men who died each day. Beal and several other recruits were assigned to slop the intestines of the dead into steel buckets, take the contents of the buckets to a remote spot, and burn them. That done, they carried the disemboweled corpses away, laid them side by side under canvas until coffins could be made, and tied name tags to the toes. The brisk October wind blowing across the camp ground lifted the edges of the tents, periodically revealing hundreds of stiff, white feet, and set the name tags fluttering like startled moths.[7]

Before it had run its course the Spanish influenza took 20 million lives; as many as the war had claimed in four years of deliberate slaughter. The death toll from influenza in the United States was five times the country's death toll from the war. Yet the rhythms of everyday life spun on unbroken. People buried their dead while little girls in the streets skipped rope and blithely sang,

> I had a little bird,
> And his name was Enza;
> I opened the window,
> And in flew Enza!

In Massachusetts, while the coffin mountains formed and Fred Beal was occupied with his grisly chores, Calvin Coolidge was running for governor. Two ex-Presidents, Taft and Roosevelt, were singing his praises. In Michigan, Henry Ford was running for the Senate against Truman H. Newberry, a former secretary of the navy. Ford, one of the richest men in the world, spent almost nothing on his campaign. Newberry, supported by rich Republicans, was spending a fortune. In New York, Al Smith was running for governor. Like candidates everywhere, he found it hard to locate a hall or school auditorium where he might address the faithful. Nearly every hall and auditorium was shut because of the influenza epidemic. When he did find a venue, Al Smith looked out on a curious sight —a faceless assembly, row upon row of people, their faces hidden under homemade masks fashioned from gauze. Although there was barely a face he could recognize, he, a plain-looking man of medium build, was instantly recognizable. For this campaign Al Smith had adopted a sporty brown derby hat.

As polling day neared, President Wilson issued a fervent and dramatic appeal: the nation could show its approval of his wartime leadership by giving him a Democratic Senate and House. When polling day arrived, on Tuesday, November 5, the people gave him a Senate and House with Republican majorities. Newberry narrowly defeated Ford. Coolidge squeaked to victory in Massachusetts. The influenza epidemic kept the poll low in nearly every state. But sickness or no sickness, Tammany Hall got its voters out. Al Smith won in the teeth of the Republican tide. It was a famous victory. It made Al Smith a potential presidential candidate one day.

II

The epidemic had passed its peak. The coffin mountains dwindled. Traffic began to flow normally again. But at Camp Devens the atmosphere remained gloomy until suddenly, on the Monday following the election, newsboys rushed into the barracks carrying newspapers with huge headlines, and shouting, "Germany surrenders!"[8]

Calvin Coolidge, resting in Maine, at once hurried back to Boston for the victory celebrations scheduled by the outgoing governor for the next day. Coolidge arrived in a city that had already thrown itself into a frenzy of spontaneous revelry.

Among the exulting crowds swirling from the Common into the streets, from the streets back onto the Common, was Sanford Bates. Young, idealistic, and ambitious, Bates stood at the beginning of what he hoped would prove a successful political career. Bates had wanted to be appointed streets commissioner when Andrew J. Peters, whom he had worked to elect, became mayor in 1917. But streets went to someone else and Bates was given penal institutions instead. He worked diligently at it, if without much enthusiasm. But now, in the swiftly gathering darkness at Scollay Square, in the middle of the din erupting around him, Bates found himself thinking about the 400 men imprisoned out in the harbor, on Deer Island. It seemed absurd that prisoners were denied even the opportunity to celebrate their country's victory in war; a witless denial, he thought, of their common humanity.

Bates hurried away. He called a judge noted for his extemporaneous speeches and familiar to many a Deer Island resident as the man who had sent him there. Bates then called a friend who boasted a fine voice and was experienced in leading community singing. Last, he called his wife, a zealous amateur pianist.

Braving the November cold and darkness, this improbable quartet was ferried across the riptides of Shirley Gut in a lifeboat, to be greeted by astonished guards and prisoners. The prison chapel was soon filled. The judge delivered a short patriotic speech. Mrs. Bates pounded the chapel's twenty-five-dollar piano. Under the leadership of Bates's friend several hundred denim-clad prisoners raised their voices in patriotic song. They sang with a fervor that moved Bates deeply. His personal ambitions suddenly seemed trivial. He was to become one of the leading reformers of his generation.[9]

III

The war ended with nearly 2 million American servicemen in Europe. The Royal Navy had carried half the American Expeditionary Force to war. But the British fleet was too occupied these days returning the Commonwealth and imperial forces to their own countries to take Americans home. Every warship that came back from Europe that winter was crammed with soldiers sleeping in passageways and holds—anywhere a hammock might be strung. Nearly sixty cargo ships were hurriedly converted to bring the AEF home. The first of these converted cargo ships was an aging 5,000-ton veteran of the Spanish-American War called the *Buford*.[10] While they kicked their heels for transportation to arrive, the soldiers of the AEF lamented in song:

> We drove the Boche across the Rhine,
> The Kaiser from his throne.

Oh, Lafayette, we've paid the debt,
For Christ's sake, send us home.[11]

Sooner or later, they got what they asked for, and they came back to effect some minor but lasting changes in American mores. It was the AEF that made it acceptable for a man to smoke cigarettes instead of cigars or a pipe; to wear a wristwatch instead of carrying a pocket Ingersoll; to use a safety razor instead of a cutthroat; to have a zipper fly instead of buttons.

Among the thousands of wounded brought back that winter was Sergeant DeWitt Wallace, badly injured in the Meuse-Argonne offensive. He amused himself during a long convalescence by cutting out magazine articles, then editing them so as to retain their sense while reducing them by half their length. In his mind the idea for a new kind of periodical was forming.

Two other young men who got out of the army that winter were also toying with an idea for a new magazine. Briton Hadden and Henry Luce had spent their brief time at Camp Jackson, South Carolina, waiting to go overseas, only to be thwarted by the armistice. They had taken long walks to kill time, thinking out loud about journalism. At Yale, Hadden had been chairman of the *Daily News*, Luce its managing editor.

The war only confirmed, they agreed, what they had both known back at Yale—that most people were hopelessly uninformed. The war itself could be considered the inevitable result of human ignorance on an enormous scale. As they walked along the palmetto-fringed roads, sparking off ideas and ambitions, these two very different young men— Hadden, stocky and dark, voluble and pugnacious, shoulders thrust aggressively forward; Luce, tall and slender, fair and shy—they decided, these two twenty-one-year-olds, that they would launch a publication that would set the world aright.[12] But for the moment they had to go back to Yale to graduate.

In late February 1919 the Cunard liner *Aquitania* rolled westward carrying a black infantry battalion in her lower depths, with white passengers filling the decks above. "Her voyage resounded to bugle calls. Every morning for two hours an officer marched the 900-foot decks to inspect the ship, with fanfares echoing before him. The flourishes began on the upper decks, to the dismay of passengers in first class, and descended until the bugles pealed faintly from the hold, where troops were quartered."[13]

The officer was one of the youngest generals in the army, boyish, athletic, and slim. These early morning inspections, with an immaculate retinue at his heels and four buglers advancing before him, helped sustain morale and discipline among the bored, cramped, often seasick soldiers down below the waterline. And the general himself, in a tight-fitting jacket of his own design, a pair of decidedly nonregulation British officer's "pink" breeches, and gleaming cavalry officer's boots, outshone the other notables aboard, including J. P. Morgan and the new British ambassador to Washington, Lord Reading. Brigadier General William Mitchell of the U.S. Army Air Service, the first American to come under fire in the Great War, was coming home. As the *Aquitania* steamed down Long Island Sound a string of combat aircraft from Mitchell Field swooped low over the liner and roared up into the sky waggling their wings.

But for Private Fred Beal there were no celebrations; not even release. Still untrained, he stayed on at Camp Devens well into the first year of peace. He was helping to process other men out of the army. "Almost every night I could hear the tramp, tramp of feet, first in the distance, then marching by our barracks. And a sorrowful lot of soldiers they were! The French girls weren't as beautiful and free as they'd dreamed. They didn't hang the Kaiser from a sour apple tree. And then there were the rumors that the stay-at-homes had taken over their jobs. All that the boys brought back with them were lice, obscene pictures, and venereal diseases."[14]

Among the men separated from the army at Camp Devens on a sparkling spring day was Robert E. Burns. He collected $300 in back pay and left in high spirits to return to his girl and his job. But the girl had gone to another; so had the job. Burns, formerly a prosperous young accountant, became a hobo. Yet he, too, was to leave a mark on his times.

That same spring, Lieutenant Charles Rumford Walker, a cavalry officer, returned from France with his regiment. He was assigned to Camp Eustis, Virginia, a post crowded like nearly all army camps those days with men "awaiting demobilization and praying earnestly for it day by day, as men pray for pardon."[15] Lieutenant Walker passed the dripping spring days exercising cavalry horses in the mud, wondering what civilian life might hold in a country that had passed through a war.

It seemed to him that steel was at the center of things in a modern industrial nation. His was probably the last generation who saw romance in the huge white fires and great plumes of red smoke; who thrilled to the idea of rivers of molten metal being forged by men into great ships, great railroads, great cities. Steel was at the heart of the life he saw around him. He would learn about steel from the bottom up. Lieutenant Walker resigned his commission in the regular army, moved to a grimy Pennsylvania steel town and bought some secondhand clothes.

A month after the armistice Wilson was aboard a troopship (formerly a German liner) heading for France, adulation, and the conference at

Versailles. Europe acclaimed him as the greatest man on earth, the savior of a shattered civilization. Hopes were pinned on him that no man could ever hope to fulfill, and within the haze of glory that surrounded him there moved a hamstrung President, repudiated at the polls, facing a recalcitrant Congress in the new year. Given the certainty of Republican domination on Capitol Hill for the next two years, it was worse than foolish that there was no important Republican in the delegation that traveled so hopefully aboard the *George Washington* as it steamed eastward through the heaving gray seas of the North Atlantic in winter. He arrived in France on Friday, December 13.

Ten weeks later the President came home bearing the draft of the Covenant of the League of Nations. To score off Henry Cabot Lodge, he chose to land at Boston and endure the nasal, deadpan greetings of the new governor. Wilson had asked Lodge to say nothing about the covenant until it had been presented to Congress. Lodge had respected that request.[16] And now the President, having secured the senator's silence, had put ashore at Lodge's hometown to ride triumphantly to Mechanics' Hall and there give an impassioned speech on the glories of the covenant. Lodge felt betrayed. Yet this hour at least belonged to Wilson. He seems not to have noticed that along his route from dock to hall dozens of Secret Service men crouched on the rooftops, that all windows along the way were kept firmly shut by Boston's police. Assassination was in the air of the country to which he returned.[17]

The President brought back more than a piece of paper: he brought back an obsession with the League. Congress for its part was obsessed with Wilson. In the year ahead neither would show much interest in domestic affairs. On March 4, 1919, the President sailed for France once more, leaving the newly sworn-in sixty-sixth Congress to digest the draft of the covenant.

The delegation left behind at Paris had, meanwhile, toyed with the idea of separating the League from the Treaty of Versailles; patching up a peace, that is, and arranging enforcement later. Wilson promptly put a stop to that. To him, League and treaty were a single thread which alone could stitch up the carnage of the war.

At Paris, Wilson's temperament failed him; so did his health. The President had always possessed a streak of vanity and arrogance. Some of his tastes—vaudeville, football, limericks—were pleasantly plebeian. But his essential nature was solitary and aloof. "No one known to history ever called him 'Woody.' "[18]

Wilson's intellect could be formidable, on certain subjects. Admiration for the President as thinking machine was almost as common among his critics as among his friends. Yet he was also a deeply emotional man. A longtime confidant, Colonel Edward M. House, advised a friend on how to win the President's support. "Never begin by arguing. Discover a common hate, exploit it, get the President warmed up, and then start your business."[19] Wilson's intellectual powers were failing, moreover, from the very outset of the eight months of deliberations at Versailles. John Maynard Keynes, destined to become a major architect of the twentieth century but for the present merely the British Treasury's man at the peace conference, was taken aback. Here was not the philosopher-statesman so feverishly acclaimed in the streets and the press. Instead there was a man of little culture, awkward with strangers and often slow to grasp a complicated issue.* Keynes decided that the President was at heart a Nonconformist minister, "His thought and temperament essentially theological, not intellectual."[20]

It was assumed that on Wilson's first triumphal journey to Paris he would carry detailed plans for turning his celebrated Fourteen Points into a practical treaty of peace. But he arrived empty-handed. There were no plans, only a few, rough, unfinished sketches circulating among the bright young men of the American delegation. Nothing had been thought out in detail. Sermons, prayers, homilies—these the President offered in abundance. But a design that matched the realities of European politics, of that there was not even a hint, because the President and his advisers knew almost nothing of Europe.

Even this gap in their knowledge might not have proved crippling. After all, clever men—and there were some very clever men with Wilson —learn quickly. Lloyd George arrived at Paris in a state of innocence that the President could barely match. Unhappily, Wilson suffered from a handicap that no one anticipated—he was strangely slow-witted in the give-and-take of council meetings. He proved inept in those shifts of emphasis, the slight changes in wording, the timely minor concessions, in the arts, that is, of negotiation. He failed to hold his own against Lloyd George, Clemenceau, and Orlando, even though his was by far the strongest hand. The only negotiating tactic he appeared to know was the last-ditch defense. He tended to dive into it the moment opposition raised its head above the horizon.

The strain on the President was obvious. The nervous twitch that had

---

* Keynes may have been setting unreasonable standards, measuring other men's tastes, interests and abilities against his own, by which almost anyone would seem limited. Keynes was bisexual, a balletomane, a man who married a ballerina, created a theater, drank champagne for breakfast, made himself a millionaire by talking for a few minutes on the telephone with his stockbroker before he got out of bed, the most influential economic thinker since Marx, and a member of that literary and artistic dovecote known as the Bloomsbury group.

developed at his left eye during the last year of the war became a spasm that wrenched the entire left side of his face up and down at the peace conference. He worked himself to the brink of collapse, fell ill, became deeply depressed, and rallied only during tirades against the French and British. On April 3 he was prostrated by what his doctor, Cary Grayson, diagnosed as influenza. In Paris only a few weeks earlier influenza deaths had been running at 100 a day and the American delegation was decimated with sickness for the entire period of the conference. Grayson's diagnosis, therefore, came as no surprise. But in retrospect it appears very possible that the President had actually suffered a slight stroke.[21]

The President rose from his sickbed gripped by paranoia—everyone was spying on him, his furniture was being stolen, the delegation automobiles were being used for immoral purposes. Matters such as these now interested him far more than the fate of Armenia or the amount of German reparations. He devoted a half hour one day to rearranging the couches and tables in his sitting room, he who had previously hardly found time to eat. He scorned his advisers, ignored the other conferees, and sulked in his quarters.[22]

Elsewhere in Paris a draft copy of the treaty found its way into the hands of Herbert Hoover. "I was awakened at four o'clock on the morning of May 7, 1919, by a troubled servant who explained that there was a messenger waiting with a very important document. . . ."[23] It was inevitable that Hoover would be contacted in some way, even though he was not a member of the American peace delegation. His American Relief Administration had men working in nearly every corner of Europe. Many of these men were remarkably able and astute.[24] For objective and timely intelligence on political, social, and economic conditions between the Urals and the Tagus, Hoover's ARA was not simply the best source, but often the only one.

Keynes, critical of nearly every major figure at the peace conference, would later describe Hoover as "The only man who emerged from the ordeal at Paris with an enhanced reputation. This complex personality . . . his eyes steadily fixed on the true and essential facts of the European situation, imported into the Councils of Paris, when he took part in them, precisely that atmosphere of reality, knowledge, magnanimity and disinterestedness which, if they had been found in other quarters, would have given us the Good Peace."[25]

That May morning Hoover sat reading the draft of the treaty in a state of horror. The entire document was permeated "with a spirit of hate and revenge."[26] Depressed and unable to sleep, he left his hotel as dawn broke over the city and walked deep in gloomy thought along the empty, ringing streets. Keynes had also been up all night, sick at heart over the draft treaty, and a third man, the South African prime minister, Jan Smuts, had similarly agonized over it. Keynes went out into the street, troubled in mind and conscience. So did Smuts. By chance the three men came together at a street corner.

The treaty, they agreed, was a disaster. It had to be changed. Over the next few days they, and other men, prevailed on Clemenceau and Lloyd George, its principal authors. But to their astonishment it was the treaty's principal critic, Wilson, who could not be moved.[27] Having once given it his blessing, however reluctantly, he became granitic. The treaty had faults. He acknowledged that. But the League would set everything right. The League was the thing.

The President brought the treaty home for the Senate's inspection. Harsh in spirit, the document he carried forced on the Germans various impossible obligations. In structure and attitude the Treaty of Versailles stood in stark contrast to the Fourteen (enlightened) Points of 1917. This treaty seemed certain to produce another war.* Even its signing on June 28 was stage-managed to accentuate the humiliation of the German delegates. They were herded about as if they were naughty children. Around them, the French strutted and preened.

Wilson scorned every doubt raised in the Senate over the treaty. He held no high opinion of senatorial intelligence. He may have been right. But it was a mistake to show it. He had also managed to alienate many of his natural supporters: the western progressives and eastern liberals, who considered the treaty catastrophically harsh; the Irish-Americans, who considered it pro-British; the Italian-Americans, who considered that Italy had been cheated of her rightful prizes; and the German-Americans, who considered the treaty unspeakable. It was surprising that the treaty stood any chance of passage.

In his prime, and belying his professorial appearance, Wilson had been a marvelous orator. It had been his speeches that sealed his early political successes. With discordant voices rising in the Senate the President played his trump card—he would go to the people. In the days before radio, it meant literally that. On September 3, 1919, he left Washington, over the strenuous protests of his doctor. He was plainly worn out even before he climbed aboard the presidential train.

Yet he gave two, three, four speeches a day. His audiences were large and enthusiastic. Every city acclaimed him. It was another triumphal

* It also produced countries. There were 19 European states in 1914; after the conference at Versailles there were 26.

progress. But when he reached Seattle something strange happened, something that baffled and hurt. Vast crowds cheered his motorcade until it reached one of the poorer parts of town. And then the cheering stopped. The line of shiny limousines headed by the President's Pierce-Arrow rolled along streets that were crowded from storefronts to curb. Yet these masses were eerily silent. Men in work clothes lined the sidewalks, arms folded, staring stonily ahead, as if the President were not there, did not even exist. On their heavy denim shirts were stitched strips of cloth, reading in large letters, RELEASE POLITICAL PRISONERS.

Wilson was stunned. The top hat he had been waving hung motionless at his side. His face went white. He fell back in his seat, shaken. For six blocks there were packed sidewalks, and utter silence.[28]

After Seattle the President's train, the *Mayflower*, turned east for the long run home. The September heat sapped the strength of the President's party. Wilson hardly slept at night; splitting headaches tormented him by day. On September 25 the *Mayflower* pulled into Pueblo, Colorado.

The President needed the support of a Secret Service agent to mount the single step at the entrance to the Pueblo auditorium. When he went onto the platform, however, he was erect and alert. He spoke with his usual fluency even if his voice had lost its earlier resonance and strength. "Germany must never again be allowed . . . ," he said, and stopped as if he had forgotten what came next. He retraced his steps. "A lesson must be taught to Germany . . ." Another blank. He made a third attempt. "The world will not allow Germany . . . ," He swayed slightly and looked dazed, like a man about to faint. Edmund Starling, the Secret Service agent appointed his bodyguard, tensed himself: "I stood close behind him," said Starling years later, "afraid he might collapse at any moment."[29]

But there remained one last measure of strength at the command of Wilson's extraordinary willpower. He remained on his feet. He finished the speech. He closed by recalling an address he had delivered at a military cemetery in France. Then he stopped. For a moment the hall was tense and hushed with expectation. No one seemed sure whether the President had finished. Suddenly the entire audience of 10,000 realized that before them stood the President of the United States, head bowed, sobbing. He turned away into the arms of his weeping wife.[30]

As the *Mayflower* rolled east that night Wilson suffered a massive brain thrombosis. The speaking tour to rally a nation had felled a President. The *Mayflower* raced along hastily cleared tracks for Washington. A few days later the President collapsed in his bathroom.[31]

Rumor had it that the President had gone mad, was dying of syphilis, was already dead. Robert Lansing, the secretary of state, called a Cabinet meeting to discuss the President's condition. Grayson was sent for. He lied to them. The President was suffering from nervous exhaustion and indigestion, he said; nothing worse. Grayson did not tell them that the President was paralyzed at this moment on the second floor of the White House; that he was, in fact, close to death. Grayson, the President's secretary, Joseph P. Tumulty, and Mrs. Wilson—these three guarded the sickroom door. The business of the Executive branch ground on, but without direction, a headless creature acting out of habit. Appointments went unfilled, resignations unacknowledged, ambassadors unreceived, allegations of high-level corruption unheeded.

In mid-October the Volstead Act, providing for enforcement of the Prohibition Amendment, was sent up to the White House. When it came back to the Hill the erratic signature that vetoed the bill was utterly unlike the President's firm, regular penmanship. Angry disputes broke out in the Senate cloakroom. A microscope was sent for. A handwriting expert was brought in. The veto was easily overridden. But that wayward scrawl made plain the seriousness of the President's illness. In the Senate Foreign Relations Committee, debating the Treaty of Versailles, Senator Albert B. Fall of New Mexico beat his fist on the committee table and shouted, "We have petticoat government! Mrs. Wilson is President!" [32]

Wilson had made a bitter enemy of Fall the previous year. While Fall was running for reelection the influenza epidemic had killed his only son and one of his daughters. His campaign faltered while he grieved for his dead children. At that moment Wilson made an emotional attack on Fall, urging that he not be reelected. On polling day Fall won a close victory. Sympathy for the bereaved senator may well have assured his reelection. Fall returned to Washington with loathing for Wilson as a man as well as a president. And the difference between a Democratic and a Republican majority in the Senate was just one seat. Had Fall lost, the Foreign Relations Committee would have been chaired by a Democrat, not by Henry Cabot Lodge.

All that November impeachment talk circulated in Congress. But no resolution was passed concerning the President's condition, not even a resolution of sympathy. In early December, however, Fall introduced a resolution in the Foreign Relations Committee that the President ought to be consulted over relations with Mexico. It was an obvious ploy: there was always trouble with Mexico. But the resolution passed. Fall and Democratic Senator Gilbert Hitchcock of Nebraska were chosen to call on the President. Yet, although they might call, would he receive them?

Fall and Lodge assumed that he would not. Wilson refused to see his

Cabinet members. They had to take their business to Mrs. Wilson, in an antechamber off the room where the President lay. And after the President had refused to see a Senate delegation on urgent business, then an impeachment resolution would—alas!—be inevitable. To the astonishment of the entire committee, word arrived from the White House that the President would be pleased to receive the delegation at once, that very afternoon.

Grayson and Tumulty had arranged a little charade. As luck would have it, the President had just enough strength that day to carry it off. Fall's mission was as contrived as Wilson's show of recovery. But it was not as well rehearsed. When the jerry-built structure of crisis consultations began to fall apart, the two senators sought a hasty departure. Fall went to the bed in which the President lay, never wondering why Wilson's left arm was kept completely out of sight, and murmured sympathetically, "Mr. President, I am praying for you."

Wilson chuckled. "Which way, Senator?"[33]

IV

For the first time in history the mass of Americans had been brought into contact with events abroad. For the first time millions of them had mixed with foreign people, trod foreign soil, entertained foreign ideas. Their leaders for the first time sat at the council tables where world affairs were directed. In the early stages it had been a thrilling experience, as heady as strong wine. But responsibility, hard choices, deep thought—these burdensome novelties soon appeared and spoiled the fun. Nor had most Americans much love for their allies. The English seemed aloof, smug, and devoted to exploiting their imperial possessions. The French seemed greedy, small-minded, and devious. If there was little love for the Allies, there was even less hatred for the Germans once the war ended. Men of the AEF frequently considered the Germans they met more honest, more friendly, and much cleaner in their habits than their ostensible brothers in arms.[34]

The sense of flux that characterized American life at the armistice can hardly be exaggerated. The nineteenth century had suffered a death-blow in the war, but the corpse still twitched; the twentieth century was alive, but still in its cradle. Outriders of the new age had appeared on the eve of the conflict: Freud had lectured at Clark University in 1909; *Poetry* began publication in 1912; the Armory Show, which introduced Americans to Cubism, was held in 1913. Pessimism, disillusionment, and youthful rebellion were all well advanced, only to be interrupted by something more spectacular—the war. When the armistice was declared they revived rather than being created anew. But now they were considered typical of the new age.

For most people, the twentieth century arrived in the shape of things, not ideas. It showed up in objects like the four army airplanes that crossed the continent in the summer of 1919, or the British R-34, a dirigible 650 feet long. In July 1919 it became the first airship to cross the Atlantic. Landing at Mineola, New York, it drew a crowd of 250,000 people gaping in awe. Only a few weeks earlier two British fliers had made a nonstop air crossing of the Atlantic by flying nearly 2,000 miles from Newfoundland to Ireland. Feats such as these seemed to make the world grow smaller, throwing people together whether they wished it or not.

In the new age people began to look different, women especially. The layers of cotton underwear which had swaddled women for generations suddenly gave way to a layer or two of silk. The high-laced, ankle-binding shoe vanished and in its place appeared the low-cut pump. The abolition of the ankle-length skirt in the aftermath of peace marked the sharpest single break in fashion for several hundred years. Skirts rose by six inches virtually overnight. By definition, a skirt had been a long garment. What replaced it was more like a tunic, barely reaching the knee. As skirts went up, long black cotton stockings gave way to silken hose. Into limbo with the long skirt—detested by generations of young women—went the even more hated corset.

Long hair, traditionally venerated as a woman's crowning glory, was shorn.* "Bobbed heads bore pert bright faces which soon would be rouged as only a prostitute's had been before the war."[35] As women's hair was cut shorter, so women's hats became smaller and simpler, little more than cloth helmets. This spelled the end of the huge hat weighed down with ornamental birds and flowers. Gone was the curse of the crowded trolley car, the eight-inch hat pin.

The war had ushered in the simple black dress when mail order catalogs began advertising "Dress for Mourning and General Wear." A new fashion was created. Long after the armistice, city streets were filled with women dressed in black, as if still in mourning years after the fighting had stopped.[36]

---

* The most plausible explanation has it that the dancer Irene Castle accidentally singed her hair, cut the remnants short, and fashioned a bob from what still remained. Surprisingly, it looked attractive; at least it did on her.

2. Striking Episodes

I

Every honorably discharged veteran received a bronze button for his lapel to show that he had served. Wounded veterans were given buttons of silver. No man was sent into civilian life with less than sixty dollars and his fare home. Most men had back pay to collect and were discharged with several hundred dollars. Seventeen states provided bonuses worth ten to thirty dollars for every month of service. But apart from making sure that every soldier and sailor returned to civilian life with some money in his pockets, veterans' affairs may be fairly described as chaotic.

Responsibility for crippled men was parceled out among competing agencies. When this was set right and a Federal Board of Vocational Education was organized to deal with all of the crippled veteran's needs, one high-ranking official gave these instructions on how to deal with applicants: "Be hard-boiled," he said. "Put cotton in your ears and lock the door."[1] Servicemen from various wars were entitled to various benefits. Whether a man received a military pension depended on which war he had served in.[2]

Throughout 1919 every town of any size, every city, every state, was holding parades for its returning veterans.[3] This was pleasant, but as far as most men were concerned it was irrelevant. It hardly compared, for example, with getting a job and finding somewhere to live. The United States proved as unready for peace in 1918 as it had been for war the previous year. The armistice came at the worst possible time, moreover, because employment peaks between April and October. From November through March it steadily falls.

In the immediate aftermath of peace there were a few wholesale transfers of labor from the production of airplanes or nitrates or some other war matériel to factories producing consumer goods. But by the spring of 1919 these transfers had stopped. Instead of taking on two to three thousand new workers at a time, as they had done the year before, even large employers were now taking on only two or three.[4]

The federal government could do less to help than it had done a few months earlier. Every wartime agency that might have aided the transition to peace was ordered to go out of business. Congress rejected every attempt to provide public works employment for veterans. Some men headed for the wartime boom towns, such as Bridgeport, Connecticut, seeking work. Bridgeport's population had doubled between 1915 and Armistice Day, and approached 200,000. What had been a pleasant, cohesive community had been transformed into a seething, restless place. Men slept ten to a room. Vice of every kind flourished. The streets were dangerous after dark. In boom towns the veterans found neither jobs nor hope. Men were discharged higgledy-piggledy, with expediency the only criterion. With money for railroad fare in their pockets the veterans bought tickets—but for Baltimore, not Podunk. Baltimore was near, Podunk far; Baltimore was wet, Podunk dry. Their money gone, discharged soldiers had moved on to Washington, to panhandle up and down Pennsylvania Avenue and demand a bonus from Congress.

Still, even the panhandlers would eventually find their way home. If they found it hard to get a job, it was harder to find a house or flat. Before 1914 there was no housing shortage in most cities and towns. The majority of people rented instead of buying. Competition in building kept construction costs down and kept supply in balance with demand. But for four years residential construction had fallen precipitously. The United States was short of about one million dwellings. There was little homelessness, but there was a lot of overcrowding. Speculators and rapacious landlords squeezed till it hurt.

The housing crisis was most acute in New York City. The state legislature enacted rent control laws as emergency legislation. Rents in the city had barely doubled between the Civil War and 1914. Between 1914 and Armistice Day they doubled, and doubled again. If rent laws could not keep housing costs down, they could at least put an end to the wave of evictions. In the long run, however, they would act as a brake on new construction.

The government emerged from the war as the owner of twelve

wooden cities, built by the U.S. Housing Corporation to provide shelter for war workers. Each city housed 1,500 to 30,000 people. Most of these temporary towns had been built in remote locations for the employees of explosives plants. But to get the government out of the housing market, Congress ordered the U. S. Housing Corporation to wind up all its operations. The wooden towns were dismantled, board by board.[5]

II

All through 1919 and 1920 there were bitter complaints over a condition known as "HCL." Far from being an illness, like TB or the DTs, the condition referred to was the "high cost of living"—what we would call inflation.

The federal government had produced most of it by the massive borrowing with which it financed the war effort. The Federal Reserve began operations in 1914. After a quiet beginning it was awash with government securities. By 1919 the money supply had increased by 75 percent. A rapid increase in purchasing power was considered a good thing at the Treasury because, the reasoning ran, that would raise demand for all goods and services. As demand rose, production would swiftly follow. The only flaw with this reasoning was that it did not work. Shipbuilding went up, while automobile production went down. Cigarette production went up like a rocket, while housing construction fell like a stick. The end result of the Treasury's ventures into economic management—aided by the Federal Reserve—was a virtual doubling in prices between 1914 and 1920. Over the same period output rose by about 2 percent.[6] In real terms per capita income had fallen below the prewar level.[7] By December 1919 the five-dollar-a-day wage introduced by Ford in 1914 was worth $2.40. As inflation spiraled upward it spread fear and restlessness throughout American society.

Inflation stayed high because until the middle of 1920 spending was buoyant. Some war production, such as shipbuilding, was maintained. Demobilized soldiers had money to spend. Cancelled war contracts were settled on generous terms. The Allies were still receiving loans to buy American goods. Wartime savings were spent lavishly either on deferred purchases or because of inflation. The price of food, shelter, and clothing shot up.

But in the spring of 1920 the money began to run out. Savings were gone, loans were cut back, demobilization pay had been spent, but most of all, government spending was vigorously slashed. Its momentum broken, the economy fell back. Unemployment rose sharply. A sense of

gloom quickly spread among workers. They began to look back, as if to
some golden age. "They liked to brag about how much money they'd
made during the war, and how lavishly they'd thrown it around on broads
and booze."[8]

Apprehension had expressed itself during the past year in an unprecedented wave of strikes. There was less labor unrest in the first four
months of 1919 than there had been in the first four months of 1918. But
by the end of April the wartime system of government arbitration had
been wound up. The entire structure of wage and price controls had been
allowed to die out. The Administration clung resolutely to a utopian belief
that everything would take care of itself. Business and labor, they believed,
would resist any effort to direct reconversion. This assumption set the
stage for a trial of strength.

It was not a struggle for which labor was well prepared. The United
States possessed, paradoxically, one of the most industrialized economies
and one of the weakest labor movements. The number of factory workers
had doubled in the twenty years after 1900, from 4.7 million to more than
9 million. A further 3 million people worked in manufacturing as salaried
employees.[9] In virtually every country rapid industrial growth had brought
strong labor organizations in its wake. Not in the United States. Here,
much of the labor force that bore the brunt of industrialization was foreign-born. That gave it a different social history from industrialization
elsewhere.

Nearly all the millions of immigrants arriving since 1890 had gone to
work in the industrial sector. Few went into agriculture or the professions.[10] This allowed industrialization in the United States to forge ahead
at a furious pace. Immigrant workers would do almost any job, no matter
how dirty or dangerous; accept almost any wages, no matter how low;
work cruelly long shifts, and make almost no fuss. This docility obscured
the depth and the extent of the strains of rapid industrialization, strains
that harmed both individuals and society.

Immigrants did not hinder the labor movement simply by undercut-
ting wages. Being what they were—strangers to American ways and beliefs, usually unable to speak English, and therefore shut off from most of
the life around them—they were impossible to organize.

Wages were also kept down by child labor. The 1920 census counted
1.1 million children aged ten to fifteen as being gainfully employed. This
was the bottom line, because the census did not count workers under ten,
of whom there were probably hundreds of thousands. The National Child
Labor Committee, for example, estimated that two-thirds of the workers
in various crops, for example, sugar beets, were children down to the age

of five.[11] The Census Bureau figure was low for another reason. For decades it had surveyed child labor in April, a busy month on farms, where much child labor was concentrated. In 1920 it made the survey in January, the quietest month in agriculture.

Meanwhile, in city tenements there were many thousands of children under ten working every afternoon and most weekends. They gave the finishing touches to artificial flowers or filled thin white cards with buttons, needles, or metal fasteners. It was work that called for nimble fingers and complete submission. Work of this kind paid as much as 20 cents an hour.

Progressives had managed to pass two child labor laws. But in the immediate aftermath of the war, both laws were struck down by the Supreme Court. This was irrelevant, however, to the little street traders, the tiny beet lifters, the sweated tenement house children, because neither law had protected them.

Besides the exploitation of women and children, wages were kept low and union organization slowed by the presence of women in the labor force. After the armistice many of them came under intense pressure to give up their jobs. In Cleveland the male streetcar conductors struck to force the dismissal of female conductors hired as a wartime measure.

There was a widespread and false impression that women had taken large numbers of jobs to release men for fighting and were now keeping the veterans from being rehired. But the vast majority were women who would have been seeking work had the Austrian Crown Prince never visited Sarajevo. They and their families needed the money. The war had only accelerated the entry of women into some occupations traditionally reserved for men. The trend toward greater employment of women had been developing strongly since the turn of the century.

Most of the women employed during the war held on to their jobs or found others. They stayed in employment because they accepted low wages.

Organized labor had put its trust in Wilson and wartime agencies, such as the War Labor Board. But the agencies had been abolished. The President was sickly and distracted. A new, conservative Congress had been elected. The courts were becoming decidedly hostile, stretching the injunction power like so much legal elastic. A judge in Lafayette, Indiana, in December 1919 issued an injunction against a pro-union speech being delivered in that city. A judge in Spokane had already enjoined anyone from membership in the Industrial Workers of the World (IWW).[12]

Even in its torpor the Administration had to take heed of the labor unrest of 1919. It called a National Industrial Conference to meet in September and moderate between management and labor. Eminent citi-

zens were enlisted to represent the public interest and form a bridge between the two contending forces. These public representatives included
such men-in-the-street as John D. Rockefeller, Jr., and the chairman of
the board of United States Steel, Judge Elbert D. Gary. Labor withdrew
from the NIC. It became an agency for promoting company unions.[13]

The War Labor Board had banned yellow-dog contracts, under which
employees promised not to join unions. But soon after the war more than
a million workers were forced to sign them. They became common in
nonunion coalfields, boot and shoe factories, and streetcar companies.
The Supreme Court upheld the legality of the yellow-dog contract. Lower
courts enforced them by injunction.

The determination of big business to roll back labor's wartime gains
made this the golden age of the private detective agency. The classified
telephone directory of every major city offered a choice of from several to
a score of agencies listed variously under "Detective Agency," "Industrial
Engineer," and "Investigator." The larger outfits boasted a national network of branch offices, with hundreds—sometimes thousands—of "operatives."[14] During the war these men were exempted from the draft. Most
operatives were labor spies, diligently filing reports of mind-numbing pet-
tiness—who was smoking in the washroom, who was three minutes late
for work, who left five minutes early, who liked gossiping too much. It was
not elevating work. But as R. J. Coach, operator of Cleveland's biggest
agency, discovered: "There's more money in industry than there ever was
in crime."[15]

Organized labor, frustrated and fractious, its independence compromised by the wartime alliance with Wilson, harried in the courts, libeled
as a Communist conspiracy in the press, knocked about by company
thugs, terrified by the sudden rise in the rate of inflation, fell back grimly
on its weapon of last resort—the strike. No industrialized country had
ever seen anything like the labor struggles that now developed.

III

Seattle in 1919 was largely a frontier town in both spirit and appearance. Hundreds of saloons, missions, and whorehouses filled a huge skid
row.* Filled, that is, the area that had given Wilson the silent treatment.
The streets were crowded most days with loggers in red mackinaws,
stagged overalls, and caulked boots; with hookers offering their services

---

* From the "skid road" of the logging camps, down which cut timber skidded to the
sawmill.

from windows and doorways; with panhandlers, bearded and ragged; with seamen in blue turtleneck sweaters and jeans; with all the motley of a rough-and-tumble port mixed up with the raw energy of a town on the western frontier.

But on Thursday, February 6, 1919, at 10 o'clock in the morning, when this brawling, lusty city ought to have been fully alive, it was wrapped in an unnatural calm. No smoke poured from the chimneys that marked its foundries and factories. In the schools, classrooms were empty, playgrounds deserted. Few people moved in the bright morning along the city's sidewalks, past the stores with their strangely bare shelves, empty of food and other essentials; empty, too, of guns and ammunition. Many large houses in the better parts of town were similarly deserted, their owners have departed in haste.

Armistice Day had found Seattle a bitterly divided city. Two well-respected executives of the American Federation of Labor (AFL) were about to go to jail for having criticized the draft before Congress had even enacted conscription. The IWW's hall had been raided and shut down. All Wobbly gatherings were banned.* Local employers had launched an open shop—that is, union-busting—drive. The local branch of the American Protective League (APL) directed the energies of 2,500 vigilantes and *agents provocateurs.*[16] The Seattle Metal Trades Council, an AFL affiliate, was organizing Soldiers', Sailors', and Workingmen's Councils. Long-shoremen were threatening to refuse to load arms shipments destined for White Russian forces. Rallies were being organized to demonstrate support for the Russian Revolution.

A pro-Soviet rally at a vacant lot on January 12, 1919, attracted several thousand people. A riot broke out when scores of police, supported by APL "Minutemen," charged the meeting. Four days later another demonstration, protesting the behavior of the police and the APL, was held. Nearly 6,000 people gathered. Singing Wobbly songs, they moved off to invest city hall. Mounted police rode hard into the crowd, scattering it.

Anger at confrontations such as this now merged with unrest in the shipyards. Wartime prolabor policies had left them almost completely unionized. But since the armistice, there had been heated disputes between labor and management. To the unions, the wartime system of wage negotiations had lost all authority the day the war ended. Then in mid-January the chairman of the Emergency Fleet Corporation, Charles Piez,

---

* "Wobbly" is said to have originated with a Chinese cook at a logging camp in British Columbia. He liked the IWW men whom he cooked for, and used to defend them with voluble assertions of "I likee Eye Wobbly Wobbly." Stewart Holbrook, "Wobbly Talk," *American Mercury*, January 1926.

threatened to cut steel shipments to the Seattle yards if their owners capitulated to current wage demands.

This information was dispatched by telegram. The Western Union delivery boy misread the intended recipient, the Metal Trades Association, and delivered the telegram to the Metal Trades Council instead.[17] Outraged by what they considered corrupt pressure (Piez was a major shareholder in eastern shipyards), the shipyard unions voted to strike.

The Seattle Central Labor Council received a proposal at its next weekly meeting to support a general strike. Many of the labor council's senior and more conservative leaders were in Chicago that week for a national meeting on Warren Billings and Tom Mooney, whose imprisonment many in the labor movement had for years considered a frame-up. The meeting in Seattle was virtually leaderless. It turned clamorous. Orderly procedure was impossible. Business was halted every few minutes by outbursts of fervent singing accompanied by vigorous handclapping from the large Wobbly contingent. In the middle of this uproar the proposal asking union locals to support a general strike was accepted.

Within three days, building laborers, hotel maids, roofers, iron workers, barbers, carpenters, newsboys, maintenance engineers, leather workers, jewelry workers, electrical workers, and people in a dozen other trades had voted to strike in support of the shipyard unions. Yet, all told, less than half of the city's locals in the end voted to come out. There was also a seriocomic confusion over what the exact purpose of the general strike was to be.

The idea of a total shutdown posed no problem for the Wobblies. They had been preaching the general strike for years. To the rest of organized labor it was a frightening novelty. Most union leaders thought in terms of wages, hours, conditions, not apocalyptic confrontations with capitalism and the state. To the IWW it was obvious what came after the general strike—the revolution, of course. But to Seattle's union locals what came after the general strike was a blank. Still, a General Strike Committee was formed and a strike date set—February 6.

The chief of police prepared to face this emergency by equipping hundreds of APL Minutemen and discharged soldiers with clubs to carry and stars to wear, enrolling them to keep the peace for five dollars a day. The strike committee responded by forming a 300-man strike guard, unarmed, unpaid, and distinguished solely by the piece of white ribbon each man wore. These guards were chosen not for their muscles but for their quick wits and an ability to talk persuasively.

The General Strike Committee made sure the city had light, heat, milk and mail deliveries, fire protection, and laundry services. Cafeterias were set up to feed those unable to eat at home. The strike committee sat

virtually nonstop in its attempts to square the circle. The strike was supposed to bite deep, but hurt no one.

A dodger headed "Russia Did It" circulated through Seattle. It urged
workers to seize the shipyards. This leaflet sent a tremor of alarm through
an already frightened city. It was widely assumed to be the work of the
strike committee. It came, in fact, from a roving radical named Harvey
O'Connor, who was under orders from no one.[18] But when the sun went
down on February 5, "numerous Seattle families sat behind closed doors
that night cleaning rifles, shotguns and pistols. . . ."[19]

And still in their minds was the editorial published several days earlier
in the *Seattle Union Record*, the only successful labor daily ever to establish itself in the United States. In a city of 350,000 the *Union Record*
boasted a paid circulation of 112,000. The editorial on the impending
strike was headed "No One Knows Where." It not only welcomed the
strike—it welcomed the prospect of chaos, bloodshed, and revolution.
This farrago of proletarian tough talk, larded with Leninist catchphrases,
was the product of no pen-wielding laborer but of Anna Louise Strong.

She had arrived in Seattle in 1915 with her father, a minister committed to the social gospel. Miss Strong was one of the few women in the
United States with a Ph.D., which she had earned at the University of
Chicago. She was elected to the Seattle school board. Her love of books
and left-wing causes led to her being hired as features editor on the *Union
Record*. Excited by the imminent strike, she wrote "No One Knows
Where" to express her solidarity with whatever might happen. It was a
public relations disaster. By embracing chaos before it had broken out,
she turned moderate opinion in Seattle solidly against the strike and provided city authorities with a mandate to crush it, if they could.

When February 6 dawned the only vehicles moving on the streets
—such as ambulances and hearses—carried large signs that read:
EXEMPTED BY THE GENERAL STRIKE COMMITTEE. In the
silence an automobile backfired. Crowds came running to see the shooting
they assumed had broken out. Rumors flew in all directions—the mayor,
Ole Hanson, had been assassinated; hundreds of Bolshevik gunmen had
arrived from Chicago; the food supply had been poisoned.

That morning a regiment of state militia had moved quietly into
towns outside Seattle. But that first day belonged to the strikers. They
were awed by what they had wrought. The AFL had opposed the strike in
every way it could. Yet the strikers had brought it off. For the first time a
general strike had paralyzed an American city.

Friday morning the soldiers appeared. Ole Hanson, in his car, over
which was draped an enormous American flag, led a regiment from Fort
Lewis into the city. Throughout the afternoon infantrymen fanned out,

setting up machine guns at the major intersections. A few days earlier Hanson had invited several of the strike committee leaders to lunch, where he pleaded with James Duncan of the electrical workers: "Jim, Jim, give me my lights. I don't care a damn about the streetcars, but I need my lights."[20] Once the soldiers were in the streets, however, Ole Hanson turned bold. He demanded that the strike be called off immediately.

Many of the locals had wanted to strike for only two days. Rather than appear to capitulate to the mayor's ultimatum, they chose to extend the strike until Tuesday. By then it had petered out.

The Seattle general strike was not a labor failure. It was a catastrophe. Ole Hanson, a chubby little grocer turned real estate broker, a man who both looked and acted like Sinclair Lewis's George F. Babbitt, a man widely taken for a clown, elected only because his more intelligent rivals had cancelled one another out in the 1918 election, was suddenly hailed as America's answer to the Communist menace.

His office filled up with sacks of adulatory telegrams. Later in the year Ole Hanson resigned as mayor. Under the tutelage of the Redpath Lecture Bureau the "Savior of Seattle" would tour the country with his thrilling account of victory over Bolshevism. He wrote a book about it. Anticommunism paid. Ole Hanson made nearly $40,000 in his first seven months on the lecture trail.[21]

Meanwhile Wobblies were being rounded up. Anna Louise Strong and the rest of the *Union Record* staff were arrested and charged with sedition. The AFL carried out a purge of its own. The shipyard workers did not win the 10 percent wage increase they had struck for. The Emergency Fleet Corporation cancelled most existing orders. The yards shut down or cut back. Industry shunned the city. Payrolls fell from year to year. Industrial growth in Seattle was dead for more than twenty years.

IV

In the America that emerged from the frontier the third most dangerous occupation was that of policeman. It was deadlier than mining coal.[22] Being a policeman was not only dangerous, it was very poorly paid. Not surprisingly, most policemen had little more than a grade-school education. They cut an unimposing figure. In cities such as Boston they still wore dome-shaped helmets, wing collars, and high-necked frock coats that were gathered at the waist by a big leather belt. They sported mustaches and long wooden nightsticks. They looked, in short, like the Keystone Kops.

During the war big-city police earned half as much as shipyard or skilled factory workers. Station houses were dilapidated, filthy, and crowded. The policeman worked a twelve-hour shift on duty that was frustrating as well as dangerous. When American workers clamored for large pay increases in 1919, the police clamored with them, when not otherwise occupied in breaking strikes.

In Boston the city council voted a $200 raise and felt generous. The most a policeman could earn on the new wage scale was $1,600 a year. The police pressed for a scale up to $2,000. And they turned their recreation society, the Boston Social Club, into a putative union, linked to the AFL.

This action incensed the police commissioner, Edwin U. Curtis. Back in 1884 he had been, at the age of thirty-four, Boston's youngest-ever mayor. He was diligent and honest. He was also unimaginative and irascible. He accepted appointment as police commissioner from Coolidge's predecessor in the statehouse with the air of a man who is doing his fellow citizens a great favor.

To Curtis, the policemen's union was an act of lèse majesté. It was he who had pushed the pay increase through the council. To his mind such ingratitude could only be explained as a Communist plot. The Boston police, overwhelmingly Catholic and of Irish descent, found this suggestion more bewildering than insulting.[23] They were equally puzzled by Curtis's determination to deny them a union when police in thirty-seven other cities were already affiliated with the labor movement. Curtis suspended nineteen members of the Boston Social Club from their jobs for flirting with the AFL.

Having been appointed by a former governor, Curtis was to all intents and purposes accountable to no one; certainly not to the mayor, Andrew J. Peters. The mayor was himself something of an anomaly. An upper-class New England Democrat, Peters was Harvard '85, old stock, and, it seems likely, a man with an eleven-year-old mistress with the beguiling name of Starr Faithfull, playmate it seems to both his children and himself.[24]

Peters had served briefly as assistant secretary of the treasury in the Wilson Administration. Elected mayor in 1917, his single term in office provided a brief interregnum in a century of graft at Boston city hall. Peters possessed a high forehead, dark red hair, bushy eyebrows, and a strangely high-pitched voice. As the crisis at the police department mounted, he busied himself with golf and yachting and appointed a committee to take the problem out of his hands. The committee handed it back a little hotter than they had received it. The Boston Policemen's Union, the committee said, ought to be recognized, provided it had no formal links with the AFL.

Curtis rejected this compromise, held disciplinary hearings on the suspended men, fired them, and dared the police to do their damnedest. Within hours the police voted to strike, by 1,134–2, and called a walkout for the very next day, Tuesday, September 9, at 5:00 P.M., when shifts changed.

On the Monday evening, with the strike less than twenty-four hours away, Coolidge dined with Peters and members of the spurned committee. The governor spurned all talk of compromise. He put his trust in the police commissioner's assurances that peace would be maintained. Peters, who lacked his faith, had already held anxious discussions with the adjutant general of the state militia. The adjutant general decided to order his sole mounted squadron to assemble at the Commonwealth Armory in Boston.

Coolidge was preparing to go to bed when word reached him of strange activity at the armory. There are few more dangerous moves in a democracy than to call out the troops a day too soon. Better a day too late. Coolidge hastened to the armory with Curtis in tow. Passing rapidly under the arch at the entrance, they came face to face with a hundred surprised troopers standing among piles of freshly drawn equipment— belts, swords, rifles, saddles, bridles, spurs. Coolidge shrieked, in his inimitable nasalized tones, "Who told you people to come here?" He and Curtis hurried upstairs to see the adjutant general.

When they descended a few minutes later they saw Peters hurrying up the stairs in a rage. Governor and mayor began to quarrel. "You have no business here," said Coolidge. Peters charged at him, arms flailing. He hit the governor flush on the right eye. Troopers ran forward to restrain him from inflicting further damage. The governor reeled away, a hand clapped over his face.[25]

The next day, Tuesday, Peters made a formal request to Coolidge to call out the state guard. Coolidge again refused. Curtis again insisted that he would keep the peace in Boston. At 5 P.M. the police went on strike.

When evening fell, gamblers turned Boston Common into a dice parlor. A streetcar was stoned and its occupants forced to flee. The peace of several neighborhoods was broken by the sound of shattered glass. In and around Scollay Square, a neighborhood kept lively by a variety of dives catering to all manner of tastes, a large mob formed and a score of stores were calmly, systematically looted. In South Boston several streetcars were overturned.

Businessmen and college students donned armbands and took to the streets to direct traffic. Nearly all the major stores had hired armed guards. They were left alone. Here and there uniformed police, part of the few hundred who had chosen not to strike, made an appearance.

By dawn on Wednesday, Peters had discovered that he possessed emergency powers over all state guard units stationed in the city, powers that neither Coolidge nor Curtis could annul. Peters called out the Boston units.

In late afternoon the guardsmen appeared on the streets, rifles in hand, bayonets fixed. By putting the adjutant general in charge of both the guardsmen and the police who remained on duty, Peters had effectively supplanted Curtis. That night the guardsmen crushed outbreaks of lawlessness: a stone-throwing mob in South Boston was dispersed with rifle fire that left two men dead; a rioting mob in Scollay Square was broken up by mounted troopers and one man died; a scuffle on the Common ended in the fatal shooting of a sailor. In all, six people died in clashes with the militia. But by dawn Thursday, Boston was quiet.

The moment was right, Coolidge decided, to exercise *his* emergency powers and reinstate Curtis. To humiliate Peters still further, Coolidge then called out the entire state guard.[26]

By Thursday evening the city was swarming with guardsmen. They arrived by the thousands throughout the night. Coolidge, not Peters, would in time be credited with restoring order to Boston. Not that it had been quite the hotbed of anarchy the press conjured up. All the damage caused by the strike was settled by the city for $34,000, roughly the cost of a small fire.[27]

On Thursday the police, by voting to call off the strike, acknowledged that they were beaten. On Friday the president of the AFL, Samuel Gompers, sent telegrams to Coolidge and Peters, urging them to mediate between the police and Curtis. Coolidge sent a stiff and lengthy reply that amounted to no. Gompers sent another telegram, this time dwelling on the right of the police to express their grievances. Coolidge sent another dusty answer, which concluded, "There can be no right to strike against the public safety by anybody, anywhere, anytime."

This single utterance capped Coolidge's fame as the man who saved Boston. It carried his reputation into obscure hamlets where news from the great cities rarely penetrated.

To a man, the policemen who had struck were fired. A new force was recruited made up mainly of ex-servicemen. In the fall of 1919 they patrolled the streets of Boston clad in their old army greatcoats and breeches, with silver badges and holstered revolvers, and new-style flat blue police caps.[28]

V

In late June 1919, Charles Rumford Walker, ex–U. S. Army, arrived in Bouton, a mill town outside Pittsburgh. Dressed in his ill-fitting, drab, secondhand clothes, he went to work at the lowest job he could find, cleanup man in the pit of an open-hearth furnace. He exulted in his new life.

The romance of steel was no myth. It was built on men who were strong, brave, and agile. The huge dark furnaces, the showers of brilliant sparks, the thudding rivers of incandescent molten steel—here was a setting for male friendship as exciting and vivid as being in a front-line regiment at war. And like the regiment, the mill was a young man's world. In the pit, on the floor, most men were in their twenties; there was no one over thirty-five. In this place of sweat and flames men literally washed each other's backs. Everything here seemed larger than life. It offered scenes so potent that a New England intellectual, Mary Heaton Vorse, wrote in that same year, 1919, "I would rather see steel poured than hear a great orchestra."[29]

But the *tableau vivant* of steel rested on a regimen that was a relic of that orgy of work generally known as the nineteenth century. Steel production was based on the twelve-hour day and the seven-day week. And for those who like Walker did not work the twelve-hour day, it meant a ten-hour day for two weeks, followed by two weeks of fourteen-hour days. When a man changed from one shift to the other he worked "the long turn"—that is, twenty-four hours straight. The long turn was unique to American mills.[30]

Nor did all this work pay very well. Three-fourths of the men at US Steel earned less than the government's standard for minimal health and comfort. "The Corporation with a Soul" was how US Steel termed itself in advertising that pointed to the millions it had spent on welfare programs for its workers, on safety, on health clinics.[31] But in most steel mills safety measures consisted of a Slavic word, *Tchekai*—watch out! Even the Americans used it. "It's a word that is ringing in your ears all night," Charles Walker discovered. "Watch out for the crane that is taking a load of hot metal over your head . . . watch out for the load of hot cinder coming down . . . for the trainload of hot ingots that passes your shoulder."[32] There was no special clothing, no special safety instruction, only natural agility and a shouted *Tchekai!* And on the long turn men lost their alertness and, with it, their lives. Mary Heaton Vorse, touring the steel mills that winter, heard the stories: of the men who had become part of towering skyscrapers; of the men who had become part of iron rails; of the men who had become part of great bridges.

Steelworkers stoically endured. Most were immigrants, glad to have a job. US Steel, moreover, had proved the industry leader in more than output and prices. On its formation in 1892, the corporation with a soul set out to create a tractable work force by destroying its organizations. US Steel would order a lockout at the drop of a hammer. It employed a corps of informers any police state might envy. It armed itself with several thousand private detectives who carried guns and clubs. By 1897 the corporation had won. More than twenty men had been killed in the struggle, but US Steel had an open shop, the twelve-hour day and no collective bargaining.

That was still the way it was in 1919. According to Judge Gary, it would be that way forever. The gospel known as Garyism ran, "We do not deal with labor unions."[33] And that was the doctrine of the steel industry.

Yet, in the steel towns, where the soot fell steadily and workers' wives deliberately kept bright white curtains in their windows as a mark of defiance,[34] one man was trying to do what nearly all union leaders knew to be impossible. William Zebulon Foster was organizing the steel workers. Tall and thin, with a narrow, intelligent face and a high forehead, Foster was the product of some of the worst slums of the nineteenth century. At the age of ten the orphaned Foster left home to roam the country. He traveled from one dirty, exhausting, badly paid job to another, reading voraciously and developing a deep love of classical music. A vegetarian, a teetotaler, a hobo when work was scarce, Foster had become "a restless, self-educated, rebellious worker, a type that radicals dreamed about but rarely were."[35]

In 1918 he had organized 200,000 packinghouse workers in Chicago with the tepid blessing of the AFL, which distrusted his radicalism. On the basis of his Chicago success he moved, with AFL support, into the steel towns.[36]

To organize a strike under the noses of so many informers and hired thugs, and with his ostensible allies ready to abandon him given half an excuse, Foster needed courage, skill, patience, guile, energy, and luck. He had several assistants, none remotely as competent as Foster himself. They were undeniably brave, though. One, a woman named Fanny Sellins, on loan from the United Mine Workers (UMW), was murdered by company guards in August 1919.[37]

Foster was no theoretician. He was not much of an orator. He only knew how to build a local, how to move from there to creating a system of locals, and how to bring them out on strike. Most of his organizing had to be done in secret, or at least in shadows.[38] In the steel towns scores of social clubs with innocuous-sounding names suddenly came into existence.* The steel strike would, in fact, show that it was not always neces-

---

* In later years, after Foster joined the Communist party, he would become the chief advocate of "boring from within."

sary to have a union to have a strike, that workers could strike to have a union. On September 22, 1919, the impossible happened. More than 350,000 steel workers struck.[39]

There had never been a strike like it—spread across ten states, involving twenty nationalities, bringing to a halt fifty towns and cities. This was like fifty strikes rather than one. Yet steel workers acted in unison over an area several hundred miles wide and a thousand miles long. Here was the first modern strike involving an entire industry. It surmounted language barriers, it surmounted distance, it surmounted fear. In some towns not a single strike meeting was held. Yet the men came out and stayed out.

There also were places where the lack of leadership kept men at work. In Bouton, Walker found, there were no organizers, no meetings. The stories around the steel mill said that the organizers were taken off the train before they reached town. The Bouton newspapers carried no news of the strike. Throughout the area all public meetings were banned.[40] In Duquesne, the mayor, James S. Crawford, bragged, "Jesus Christ himself couldn't hold a meeting in Duquesne."[41]

The Pennsylvania state constabulary joined the 6,000 coal and iron police (private detectives hired by the steel companies and given police powers by the state) in terrorizing steel towns. In Braddock, mounted state troopers cleared the streets with cavalry charges which sent the unwary fleeing for shelter. Even small gatherings were impossible. In their zeal, the troopers even charged and dispersed a funeral procession.[42] Similar events were reported throughout the steel region, although authorities in Ohio and West Virginia acted with far more restraint than those in Pennsylvania.

Two-thirds of steel workers were foreign-born. The mainly American-born supervisors and office workers refused to join the strike. It became overwhelmingly a strike of immigrants. Posters in the steel towns showed an agitated Uncle Sam making a passionate plea:

> Go back to work!
> Ritornate al lavoro!
> Wracajcie do pracy!
> Griz kite prie darbo!
> Idite natragna posao!
> Chodte nazad do roboty!
> Menjenek vissza a munkaba![43]

Newspapers said almost nothing about the strike, except to report almost daily that it was over.[44] September gave way to October, October to November, and every week the strike was virtually ignored. The silence began to wear on strikers' nerves. They felt isolated from one another, ignored by the world at large. And winter was rapidly approaching. Cold and hunger began to take their toll. There were defections. Yet the strike still held.

Then, at the beginning of November, the Amalgamated Association of Steel, Iron and Tin Workers, an AFL craft union, went back to work. In effect, the thin top layer of skilled workers abandoned the unskilled to their fate. And the steel mills were beginning to fill up with black strike-breakers, herded through the gates by armed state constabulary and the coal and iron police.[45]

November passed. So did December. Tent cities housing evicted strikers flapped disconsolately in the snow. Hunger, disease, and despair stalked these frozen camps, where the most common sound borne on the frigid wind was that of babies crying.[46] In January, after 109 days, the strike was called off.

It had cost more than a dozen lives. "The number of wounded was not known. People nursed their wounds in silence."[47] More than $112 million in wages had been lost. The strikers won nothing.

VI

During the war, coal miners had struck a rough bargain with the U.S. Fuel Administration: a no-strike pledge in return for inflation-beating wage increases. In 1919, wage agreements in both the anthracite (hard coal) and bituminous (soft coal) fields were drawing to a close. The miners asserted their freedom to bargain as they wished. The Administration insisted that although the shooting had stopped, a state of war was still formally in effect and the miners were therefore tied to their agreement. The miners, meeting in convention in September, angrily passed resolutions calling for a national labor party and for nationalizing the mines.

Under their acting president, the forty-year-old John L. Lewis, they prepared to strike. They sought a 60 percent increase in base pay, a six-hour day at the coal face (some miners spent up to two hours to reach it), and a five-day week. Negotiations with the coal operators broke down.* A strike was called for November 1.

On October 31 the Administration secured an injunction under the wartime Lever Act. A shock wave passed through organized labor. The AFL had supported passage of the Lever Act only after Wilson had promised that it would never be used to hinder legitimate union activities. The AFL had opposed the coal strike. Feeling betrayed, it supported the strike.

Attorney General A. Mitchell Palmer defended the injunction. The

---

* "Coal operators" refers not only to owners of mines but to coal railroads as well.

strike, he said, was not a strike. It was a Bolshevik plot to bring down the
government. Lewis and the United Mine Workers considered the injunction too contemptible to recognize with a legal challenge. A brief notice
was issued that the strike had been banned by law.

On November 1 some 450,000 miners stayed at home. The Administration was forced to negotiate, but secretly. After allowing his miners to
rest at home for ten days, Lewis ordered them to go back to work. Most
did so, but 50,000 stubbornly refused. Lewis had won an agreement that
provided a 31 percent increase in base pay. This gave miners a minimum
of $7.50 a day, the highest basic wage in industry. On the strength of this
contract he became president of the UMW.

This put Lewis second only to Gompers in the labor hierarchy. He
was one of the best orators the country could boast. He led the only union
to have organized a major industry, an industry second to none in importance. Coal was America's chief energy source by a large margin.

Most of the coal was bituminous, and from the UMW's point of view
it was *too* easy to get out of the ground. Bituminous mines had spread
rapidly during the war. They were scattered from northern Pennsylvania
into Alabama, and as far west as Colorado, unlike anthracite mines, which
were concentrated in half a dozen Pennsylvania counties. And non-
unionized bituminous mines had turned out six million tons of coal during
the brief strike, making it less effective than it could have been. Soon after
the strike settlement came a strong organizing drive in the heart of the
soft-coal fields, southern West Virginia. It was an epic struggle.

In places such as Logan County the coal owner owned far more than
the mine. One miner protested, "We work in *his* mine. We live in *his*
house. Our children go to *his* school. On Sunday we're preached at by *his*
preacher. When we die we're buried in *his* cemetery."[48] In Logan County
the sheriff and his deputies received a retainer of $3,000 a month from the
coal companies for "police protection."[49] Evidently even this was inadequate. Throughout the coal fields were hundreds of hard-faced men in
black suits and hats and carrying revolvers, more private detectives hired
to smash the union.

Strangers arriving in town could expect to be followed. Every train
was met by armed deputies. Anyone without a good and acceptable reason
for his or her visit was persuaded to stay aboard. Mistakes sometimes
occurred. When J. L. Heizer, grand chancellor of the Knights of Pythias,
arrived in the town of Logan he was allowed off the train to carry out his
mission, that of inducting new members into the order. But the sheriff
mistook the induction ceremony for a union meeting, pistol-whipped Mr.
Heizer, shot up the Jefferson Hotel where the ceremony took place, and
ran the grand chancellor out of town.[50]

The deputy sheriffs were eager to discourage what they termed "bunchin'." This dreadful practice occurred whenever a group of men got together and started talking to one another. Bunchin' could lead to union talk. Discouragement often required the vigorous application of blackjack and pistol butt. But the principle weapon of discouragement was a piece of paper, a typewritten notice that appeared in company stores, at mine gates, and on telephone poles. The notice informed all who might be concerned that joining a union meant eviction within twenty-four hours.

Through such practices the UMW had been virtually shut out of southern West Virginia. Then in 1920 the coal operators began cutting wages. Men became too angry to care any longer about beatings and shootings and evictions. As violence flared, the old feud between Hatfields and McCoys revived, with members of each family scattered liberally among both strikebreakers and miners.

In May the sheriff of Matewan in Mingo County showed his sympathy for the miners and tried to stop the wholesale evictions.[51] An attempt was made to arrest him. The mayor hurried across the town square to help defend him. Guns were drawn by the sheriff, the mayor, a group of miners, and a posse of Baldwin-Felts detectives who were intent on making the arrest. Sheriff Hatfield dropped the two Felts brothers leading the posse. For a minute the square rang with the sound of gunfire. When the firing stopped as abruptly as it had begun and the smoke cleared, seven detectives and three miners lay on the ground dead or dying.[52]

Sheriff Hatfield was summoned to appear in court. As he mounted the steps unarmed and accompanied by his wife, Baldwin-Felts gunmen, hidden behind the courthouse pillars, shot him dead. By 1921 a guerrilla war was raging across southern West Virginia. Up to 60 people had been killed, hundreds wounded, and 10,000 evicted.[53]

When summer arrived, thousands of miners in the Kanewha Valley rallied to the cries of the embattled communities of Mingo and Logan counties. Dressed in blue overalls, with red bandannas tied around their necks, they marched south, cutting telegraph and telephone lines as they went. The governor mobilized the state police to stop them. The coal operators organized a four-airplane air force that bombed and strafed the two-mile column.

The miners fought back with rifles, submachine guns and homemade grenades and "engaged in heavy fighting with deputies and volunteers at five different points. The miners' army was increased by new arrivals, including 500 on a commandeered train."[54] Now 7,000-strong, they punched a hole in the cordon of private detectives, state police, and American Legionnaires.

Only the hurried arrival of more than 2,000 federal soldiers, spearheaded by Billy Mitchell and his 88th Light Bomber Squadron, forced the miners' army to halt.[55] The alternative was annihilation. The battle had raged for a week. Scores had died, hundreds had been wounded by gunfire and shrapnel.[56] On the hills around the halted column was strung a tent city holding thousands of evicted miners' families.

The miners' revolt had been crushed. The demand for coal was falling dramatically. Non-union fields undercut those that were unionized. Wage cuts and unemployment eroded the miners' determination. Lewis stopped the organizing drive before it failed.[57]

The coal operators now delivered the coup de grace: an injunction. It bore the names of 316 complainants, nearly every non-union coal company in West Virginia. The injunction restrained the miners in every conceivable way. They were even barred "from further maintaining the tent colonies of Mingo County or in the vicinity of the mines of the plaintiffs."[58]

The next year, 1922, brought another murderous clash, but this time in the soft-coal fields of that area nicknamed "Egypt," where southern Illinois meets Missouri and Kentucky. The climate here is southern rather than northern. In temperament, so are the people. During the Civil War only the presence of tens of thousands of Union troops kept Lincoln's native region from joining the Confederacy. In this area, the feud seemed as intrinsic as in West Virginia.[59]

In the summer of 1922 a strike by Illinois's bituminous miners shut down nearly every soft-coal mine in the area, because this was one of the few highly unionized bituminous fields. A strip mine owned and run by W. J. Lester in Herrin stayed open under the guns of private detectives and worked by strikebreakers brought in from other areas. Other coal operators did the same thing. But W. J. Lester tried to ship his "scab" coal out. This threatened the success of the strike.

Hundreds of miners converged on Herrin in response to a call from the UMW local. They marched into town like a relieving military column. They were greeted like a liberating army. The next morning they marched out to the Lester strip mine to back up the local men. The two-story company headquarters was invested from all sides. On the second-story porch the mine supervisor and his foreman looked down on the besieging miners. Armed strikebreakers and private detectives waited behind an earth barricade scooped up with a steam shovel. A five-man union committee approached the company headquarters under a white flag. A shot rang out. One of the committee men fell dead.[60]

The miners pulled out their guns. The men behind the earth barricade fired back. Throughout the day each side sniped at the other. The siege continued throughout the night. When the next day dawned the miners had crept to within forty yards of the barricade and were preparing to storm it.

Rather than be massacred, the forty-five strikebreakers and twenty-five armed guards raised a white flag. Promised fair treatment, they threw down their arms and surrendered—too late. The miners' bloodlust was up. A truckload of detectives coming to the rescue had already been ambushed and three men shot dead. Now the supervisor, a one-legged man named McDowell, was led into the woods and murdered.

As the miners marched their prisoners toward town they paused at the cemetery. Their captives were told to run for their lives or be shot where they stood. They fled in terror into the surrounding woods. Armed miners crashed through the underbrush behind them, killing anyone who stumbled or lost his way. As evening drew on, six survivors were recaptured and taken back to the cemetery. There, in cold blood, they were shot dead. In all, the strikers that day murdered twenty-two men.[61]

"Egypt" proved its union solidarity. A local jury set the killers free and blamed the deaths on the coal operators. The UMW had the final word on the Lester strip mine. It bought out W. J. Lester.

VII

No one knows how many workers struck in 1919, or how many strikes there were. Most estimates are in the region of 4 million strikers and 3,000 strikes. At all events, it was the most strikebound year in American history. It left a heritage of fury that was to torment organized labor throughout the Twenties.

One state, Kansas, attempted to legislate its way out of such bitter, often fatal, disputes. In 1920 it passed a labor law that made all strikes illegal. A labor court was created with absolute jurisdiction over all labor questions. The court was to set "fair" wages and hours. Its decisions were supported by stiff penalties. Most of the decisions it made were common sense garbed in the robes of judicial wisdom.[62] But in 1923 the Supreme Court nullified an order to raise the wages of packinghouse workers. The Kansas Industrial Court might issue decrees; it could not enforce them.

Aside from this novel experiment business and labor were allowed to have at one another. Despite the failure of nearly all the major strikes, union membership rose to 5 million in 1921. Thereafter, the figure fell steadily. Union members grew tired of losing strikes. The unions also faltered because business launched a strong counterattack.

The National Association of Manufacturers, the U. S. Chamber of

Commerce, the American Bankers Association and the National Grange led a powerful public agitation on behalf of what they termed "the American Plan." It was really an attack on the union shop.

But what took most of the steam out of the labor movement was the recession. When government spending dropped by 25 percent in 1920 and foreign countries ran out of dollars to pay for American imports, the economy curled up its toes.

Hundreds of thousands of men were thrown out of work each month. Depression seemed to be in the air.[63] Business profits fell from 1919's $8 billion to barely $1 billion in 1920. Bankruptcies tripled in a year. Wages were cut across a broad front, dropping 10–20 percent in most industries; cuts of 30–40 percent were not unknown.[64] Prices fell, but not as sharply as wages.[65] Wage cuts and layoffs put teeth into the American Plan.

Millions of men, possibly as much as a tenth of the work force, were jobless. Yet in the *New York Times Index* for 1920 you will find no entry for "Unemployment," only a short reference to unemployment insurance. Before this time unemployment—the specter that haunts the twentieth century—was not considered a major social problem. In fact, it was hardly given a moment's thought.

Joblessness was regarded by the Progressive much as it had been regarded by the Puritan—as a manifestation of shiftlessness or vicious habits, such as drugs or drink. Far more important to the enlightened mind of the High Victorian was the brutal exploitation of those who had jobs. Besides, the occasional recession purged the economy of its dross: the badly run firm, the unproductive workman, the stock market speculator.

Yet these men, now trudging the city streets looking haggard and threadbare, crowding the sidewalks outside employment agencies, gathering in sordid, evil-smelling shanty towns—they were not dross. They were veterans, many of them, the remnants of the adored AEF.[66] The crust of traditional ideas began to fall apart; a new awareness began to break through.

On Boston Common, in the fall of 1920, a remarkable sale was held for the benefit of local businessmen. Mr. Zero held a "slave" auction. A successful businessman in his own right, Urbain Ledoux had once said modestly when asked to talk about himself, "I am nothing." He gave up comfort and business to live among the poor and unemployed. And on the windswept Common, in the swirling, falling leaves, he mounted a soapbox and offered wage slaves, stripped to the waist, to the highest bidder. Mr. Zero was shaming a nation.[67]

3. The Red and the Black

I

Following the declaration of war in April 1917, Congress had promptly passed the Espionage Act. Hastily drawn, it was a legal blunderbuss. In 1918, after a year's pause for reflection, the act was amended and made worse. Virtually anything that could be construed as interfering with the war effort or offering a crumb of comfort to the Germans was a criminal offense. Words, naked, unsupported by action, sufficed for conviction. Anyone so foolhardy as to make an unflattering observation on American military uniforms, for example, risked going to jail.

Mrs. Rose Pastor Stokes, a noted feminist and Socialist, wrote in the *Kansas City Star*, "I am for the people and the government is for the profiteers." For this dangerous utterance she received a ten-year sentence.[1] Mrs. Kate Richards O'Hare also received a ten-year sentence for advising women not to bear sons, because the government would one day consider them cannon fodder. Victor Berger, a noted right-wing Socialist, was under indictment when the war ended for his *Milwaukee Leader* editorials, which suggested that combat drove some men mad, that there were young men who did not want to be drafted, that the Bible sanctioned pacifism, and that the United States had entered the war to protect its investment in Allied loans.

Under indictment, Berger ran for election to Congress from Wisconsin's Fifth District and won. The next month he won a twenty-year prison sentence from Judge Kenesaw Mountain Landis. He appealed his convic-

51

tion. When the Sixty-sixth Congress convened in March 1919, Berger proposed to take his seat. The House proposed to take it away from him.

It was not socialism that the members objected to. Three Socialists had already served in the House. An espionage conviction, no matter how footling the cited offense, was considered tantamount to proof of treason (except in the Fifth District of Wisconsin). A new election was called for December 1919. Berger won again, by a larger margin. And although the war was over, Espionage Act prosecutions ground steadily on.

It was against this background that in 1919–20, thirty-two states passed criminal syndicalism laws. Four states that had abolished the death penalty (Arizona, Missouri, Oregon, and Washington) restored it. The loyalty of schoolteachers was screened by local vigilance committees. Hundreds of teachers appear to have lost their jobs for reading the wrong books, having the wrong friends, holding the wrong opinions, or joining the wrong groups.

A committee of the New York State legislature, chaired by Clayton R. Lusk, an upstate Republican, led the grass roots attack on radicals. His committee raided the unaccredited Soviet embassy, the IWW headquarters in New York City, and the Rand School of Social Research. These raids were illegal from start to finish.[2] That made no difference. In 1920, over governor Smith's veto, the legislature passed a clutch of statutes known as the Lusk Laws. These imposed a loyalty oath on teachers, made the Socialist party illegal and set up a state bureau of investigation. This last measure proved Lusk's undoing. The hero was a crook. He hired investigators only after they agreed to split their salaries with him. The hero went to jail.

The New York legislature had meanwhile held hearings on five Socialist members, decided that they were "plotting to overthrow our system of government by force," and expelled them.

State criminal syndicalism statutes were more than empty gestures. In Chicago, 1920 saw the prosecution of a score of defendants in a single trial on charges of Bolshevism. An undercover agent from the Justice Department claimed that there was a special Communist party yell for important occasions that went, "Bolshevik, Bolshevik, Bolshevik, bang!" He appeared on the stand wrapped in a red banner. He swore that one of the defendants had an American flag covering his toilet floor.[3] All the accused were convicted.[4]

In Connecticut a clothing salesman named Joseph Yenowsky attempted to discourage a persistent bond salesman by making critical remarks about capitalism and John D. Rockefeller. To Yenowsky's astonishment, the bond salesman went for a policeman. Connecticut had what amounted to the shortest sedition law ever, and probably the broadest. In its entirety it read: "No person shall in public, or before any assemblance of 10 or more persons, advocate in any language any measure or doctrine, proposal or propaganda intended to affect injuriously the Government of the United States or the State of Connecticut." Yenowsky received a six-month jail sentence.[5]

An aroused citizenry was inclined to take matters into its own hands. In Hammond, Indiana, in February 1919, Frank Petroni, a naturalized citizen, was tried for murdering Frank Petrich, an alien. The defense was that Petrich had said, "To hell with the United States." The jury, after solemn deliberations that lasted two minutes, set Petroni free.[6]

On May Day that same year Socialist red-flag parades were broken up in a dozen cities by outraged mobs. Three people were killed, more than a hundred injured. In New York the offices of the Socialist *Daily Call* were ransacked by uniformed servicemen to ecstatic applause from a crowd in the street. In all these riots the people arrested, and later tried, were Socialists. Their attackers were left alone.[7]

It was also in May that a spectator refused to rise for the national anthem at a Victory Loan rally in Washington. As the strains of "The Star Spangled Banner" faded, a uniformed sailor ended his salute, drew a revolver, and fired three shots into the back of the lone seated figure. The man fell over, critically wounded. The stadium crowd broke into ecstatic applause.[8]

This spontaneous identification with wanton violence occurred because many Americans believed the country was under violent attack. Congress, having done almost nothing to ease the problems of demobilization, blamed all the current ills on Bolshevism. The war had ended with the country still at a fever pitch of emotion. The press, rarely noted for sobriety in the struggle to be heard, peddled sensationalism rather than news. Business tarred nearly every strike as an attempt at revolution. Yet what made the red-baiting nonsense credible to ordinary Americans was a handful of anarchist bombers who, in the spring of 1919, went into action.

Ole Hanson's office had been awash with congratulatory mail ever since the general strike. On April 28 a small parcel arrived, evidently from another of Ole's countless admirers. Dozens of small gifts, from pies to golf clubs, had already accumulated. The package was set aside until the busy mayor could get around to it. After a while the package began leaking a substance that stripped the varnish from the tabletop. The Savior of Seattle had been sent a crude homemade bomb with an acid-activated fuse.

On the next day, Thomas W. Hardwick received a similar package at

his home in Atlanta. Until a few weeks earlier Hardwick had been Georgia's senior senator, and chairman of the Senate Immigration Committee.
Advancing years had induced him not to run for reelection. When the
Sixty-fifth Congress ended, Hardwick went home for good. The Hardwick's black maid opened the package. It exploded and blew off both her
hands. Mrs. Hardwick, standing beside her, also suffered extensive injuries.

On the following day, April 30, a New York postal clerk named
Charles Kaplan read the news from Atlanta as he rocked home on the
subway after working until past midnight. Kaplan only a few hours earlier
had put aside sixteen packages, all in Gimbels' wrapping paper and marked
"Sample," for insufficient postage. Not that the intended recipients—people such as J. P. Morgan and John D. Rockefeller—were going to be hard-
pressed to afford seven cents. Kaplan got off at the next station, changed
trains, and returned to work. The packages were gingerly opened. Every
one contained a bomb.[9] Half a dozen similar packages already in the mails
were intercepted before delivery.

The Administration came under intense pressure from the public,
the press and Congress, but the recently appointed attorney general,
A. Mitchell Palmer, refused to be panicked. Palmer was a genuine Wilsonian Progressive. His Quaker beliefs made him refuse appointment as
secretary of war. He had proved to be a zealous and popular alien property
custodian. It had been a rapid rise since his election to Congress from
Pennsylvania in 1908. Palmer was able, incorruptible, and hard-working.
He had consistently favored organized labor, votes for women, and the
abolition of child labor.

One of his first actions as attorney general was to secure presidential
clemency for nearly half of the 239 people still in prison under Espionage
Act convictions. He resisted efforts to force his department to use its wide
powers of investigation and arrest to round up aliens and radicals. He
dropped scores of pending Espionage Act prosecutions. Palmer stood firm
against the clamor.[10]

On the night of June 2, explosions shattered the sleep of various
cities. In New York a watchman was killed by a bomb left outside a judge's
house. A Philadelphia church was blown up. In Pittsburgh bombs went
off at the homes of a federal judge and a chief inspector with the U. S.
Immigration Bureau. In Boston the home of yet another judge was virtually flattened by dynamite. The house of a Massachusetts assemblyman
who had sponsored antianarchy legislation was ripped apart by a bomb
elsewhere in the city.

In Washington that same evening the attorney general and his wife were preparing for bed. The time was eleven-fifteen. Palmer was startled by a loud noise from downstairs. It sounded as though something had been thrown against his front door. He stepped onto the landing and listened intently. A huge explosion rocked the house. Broken glass showered down on Palmer's head. A mighty elk's head that brooded in antlered majesty over the landing fell off the wall and came to rest at his feet.

Living across the street were the assistant secretary of the navy, Franklin D. Roosevelt, and his wife, Eleanor. The explosion sent their cook into hysterics. She ran through the house screaming, "The world is coming to an end!"[11] While Eleanor remained behind to calm the cook, Franklin went to help the Palmers.[12]

The two men surveyed the shattered Palmer porch from the lawn. In the darkness they stumbled over the gory portions of what had once been a (clumsy) human being. Here and there were shreds of a pin-striped suit and a polka-dot bow tie. Spiked on the bushes and tree branches were copies of a pamphlet titled "Plain Words" and signed "The Anarchist Fighters." The pamphlet called on the proletariat to rise up and overthrow the government.

Following the maladroit bombing of his home Palmer secured a large congressional appropriation to finance an antiradical campaign.

II

All through the Twenties and after there sounded a lament: "Whatever happened to progressivism?" And the implication was that progressivism was dead—too young, its achievements cruelly incomplete.

The very meaning of the word had changed. Under Teddy Roosevelt it had meant "Down with the Trusts," "Government of the People, directly by the People," and "Social Welfare." But following the war no one could get very excited over the trusts; "trustbuster" had gone the way of "free soiler." No one any longer became passionate over reform, referendum, and recall. Hardly anyone except settlement house workers had any idea what "social welfare" referred to.[13] Yet the change reflected success rather than failure.

The war had seen the fulfillment of many Progressive aims. Government regulation of agriculture, industry, and railroads was now a reality. Collective bargaining and the eight-hour day had been forced on much of business by wartime agencies. Health insurance had made rapid strides. There had been dramatic improvements in public health. Under the stimulus of wartime patriotism Americanization had accelerated in the immigrant communities. Progressive campaigns against alcohol and prostitution had come to fruition with the closing of hundreds of red-light districts to protect servicemen from VD and the enactment of prohibition to fight the war sober. Successes such as these took the urgency out of the Progressive movement.

What arose in its place following the war was a more sophisticated interest in social and economic issues, such as the developing concern with unemployment. Farmers and labor officials began to talk the language of tax reform, lines of credit, railroad legislation, and energy policy. There was less crusading, more organizing. Evangelism was for the Salvation Army.[14]

But the new age did not arrive full-blown. It arrived piecemeal, and like a jigsaw puzzle as it tumbles from the box, the pieces did not fall out in logical order. The harshness of industrialization was often aggravated by confusion. And while progressivism might be dead, there were many who still hungered for justice.

In 1919 there was life all along the Left. The American Labor party came into existence in New York. In Chicago a Labor party based mainly on the AFL was launched. In St. Louis a Committee of 48, composed mainly of aging, prewar Progressives, tried to create a new party. Their efforts bore fruit the next year in Chicago when the Farmer-Labor party was formed.

The chief party on the Left remained, as it had been since its founding in 1908, the Socialist party. The American Left on the eve of the war had been, like Gaul, divided into three parts: the Socialist party, the IWW, and the Socialist Labor party. The SLP was composed mainly of German-speaking immigrants. The war saw its immediate and irreversible collapse.

The high tide of socialism coincided with the high tide of progressivism, in the election of 1912. That year Eugene Debs ran as the Socialists' presidential candidate and won nearly 1 million votes. More than a thousand Socialists won office in state and local government. Cities from Berkeley to Schenectady were taken over by Socialist administrations. That same year saw the IWW's high-water mark, when it came east and led 25,000 striking textile workers to victory in a bloody two-month struggle at Lawrence, Massachusetts.

After 1912 the Socialist party went into decline. Wilson won over many left-wing intellectuals. His agricultural policies won over many farmers who had drifted from populism into socialism. The hundreds of idealistic Socialist officeholders discovered that to get things done meant learning to compromise. As the faith became diluted, they took up middle-class pursuits such as golfing and money.

Debs remained pure. His politics were untainted by practical considerations. Quarrels inside the party would drive him to bed for days on end, nursing splitting headaches. Around this tall, gaunt man hung an aura of suffering and loneliness that inspired intense personal loyalty that had little to do with political opinions.[15]

The Socialist party was, from the outset, an uneasy alliance. When the war broke out it proved impossible to keep its right and left wings in harness. Much of the Left broke away. The right wing, led by Berger, stayed on. So did the centrists, who looked to Debs for leadership.[16] Whatever its internal divisions, those outside it persisted in seeing the Socialist party whole, and when Socialist leaders were rounded up on Espionage Act indictments they were rounded up wholesale.

Socialists such as Debs and Berger were antiwar, but not pro-German. This distinction eluded most Americans to whom the least whisper of opposition was the same as cheering for the enemy. The gist of the indictment against Debs was that his speeches undermined faith in the draft. The result of his trial at Canton, Ohio, was certain before it began.* Debs had the last word. Sentenced to ten years in prison, he addressed the judge: "Your Honor, years ago I recognized my kinship with all living beings, and I made up my mind that I was not one whit better than the meanest on earth. I said then, and I say now, that while there is a lower class I am in it, while there is a criminal element I am of it, and while there is a soul in prison I am not free."[17] Armistice Day had found Debs in Atlanta penitentiary, where even violent prisoners regarded him as a saint.

The jailing of Eugene Debs troubled many people who were far from being Socialists, and it was impossible to portray him as a Marxist. John Brown was more important to him than any European theorist. Debs had applauded the Russian Revolution as a step toward freedom for the Russians. Thereafter he never failed to recognize Soviet tyranny for what it was and condemned it without reservation. Palmer twice asked Wilson to set Debs free. Wilson twice refused.[18]

With many of its ablest leaders in jail and large numbers of native American members dropping out, the Socialist party fell under the domination of its foreign-language federations. As the remaining native American members fought a rearguard action against the federations, and right

---

* Not until early 1919 did any of the Espionage Act cases reach the Supreme Court, and it was one of these that gave rise to Oliver Wendell Holmes's doctrine of "a clear and present danger." *Schenck v United States* 249 US 47 (1919). Legal scholars have generally agreed that had this doctrine been formulated earlier many Espionage Act convictions, such as Debs's, would have been impossible.

wing slugged it out with left, the entire party in 1919 teetered on the brink
of collapse. A left-wing rump, led by Benjamin Gitlow, Louis Fraina,
Charles Ruthenberg, and John Reed, attempted a coup that would have
led to a Leninist revolutionary party.[19] The national executive committee
resisted fiercely, expelled left-wing branches, and suspended most of the
foreign-language groups.

When the annual Socialist convention opened at Chicago in August
1919 the left-wingers were literally stopped at the door and kept out in a
free-for-all of boots and fists. The Left departed with black eyes and bloody
noses, split over doctrinal differences, and elsewhere in the city gave birth
not to one but two Communist parties—the Communist party and the
Communist Labor party.[20]

First the rash of anarchist bombs, then two Communist parties. And
there was the infamous "Decree of the Socialization of Women." Paragraph 6, for example, read: "All women according to this Decree are
exempted from private ownership and are proclaimed the property of the
whole nation." Paragraph 9 went into details: "Men citizens have the right
to use one woman not oftener than three times a week for three hours."
The decree was as phony as the Donation of Constantine or the Protocols
of the Elders of Zion. But Bolshevism and sexual titillation made enthrall-
ing reading.[21]

The atrocity stories and forged documents had an unintended effect
on young liberals such as Granville Hicks, who entered Harvard in the fall
of 1919. "We were bound to look with some sympathy on Soviet Russia, if
only because the defenders of the status quo were so frightened by it and
told such outrageous lies about it."[22]

Lincoln Steffens, returning from the Soviet Union at about this time,
stopped by the studio of sculptor Jo Davidson. He found Bernard Baruch
sitting for a portrait bust. Steffens, famous as one of the great muckraking
journalists of the Progressive heyday, was greeted by Baruch in his lordly
way. "So you've been over in Russia?" Steffens replied with studied ca-
sualness, "Yes, I've been over into the future, and it works."[23] This remark
swiftly passed into legend.* Among American Communists it became, for
the next generation, an article of faith.

---

* Steffens had gone to Russia with William Bullitt on a mission for Wilson during the
Versailles Peace Conference. Steffens, said William Allen White, returned "bug-eyed with
wonder." He bored everyone he met back in Paris with an exhaustive account of the marvels
he had seen. "One of Steff's favorite phrases in that stirring tale was, 'I have seen the future,
and it works!' It was an impressive sentence. I had heard him spring it several times, and I
liked it. But it was beginning to pall. . . ." The Autobiography of William Allen White (New
York, 1946), pp. 562–63.

III

With his emergency appropriation of $500,000, Attorney General Palmer created a new intelligence body within the Justice Department's Bureau of Investigation. Palmer's creation was called the General Intelligence Division. It was to work exclusively on domestic radicalism. To head the GID, Palmer chose the twenty-four-year-old J. Edgar Hoover, who had entered government service as a file clerk at the Library of Congress. In his new job Hoover rapidly built up a file of 250,000 cards, neatly cross-indexed, and headed *Radicalism*.

In his war on subversion Palmer surrounded himself with assistants whose belief in revolutionary conspiracies was never deterred by a lack of hard evidence. They proved omnivorous readers for turgid, hysterical pamphlets such as "Plain Words," and believed every word they read.

Palmer, having hastened from the baggage train of the Red Scare into the vanguard, was nursing hopes that he might ride it all the way to the Democratic nomination in 1920. To show that he and the GID were ready to meet subversion head on, Palmer announced the date set for the Communist uprising. It was July 4, 1919.

On June 29 a conference was held to brief the police chiefs of all the major cities. On July 4 police contingents were massed out of sight in armories and auditoriums. State militia were put on alert.

There was only one notable instance of violence that day. In Toledo, Jack Dempsey fought Jess Willard for the world heavyweight crown.

Nothing dismayed, the Justice Department turned its attention to rooting out the radicals. The tactic it adopted was that favored by the average American—deportation. Nearly all anarchists, whether of the philosophical, pacifist variety, or given to violence, were either Russian or Italian by birth. Most Communists and Syndicalists were Slavs or from southern Europe. On the face of it, therefore, most radicals were vulnerable to deportation proceedings.

Deportations had been tried against radicals on a fairly small scale. During the buildup to the Seattle general strike the Justice Department had rounded up foreign-born IWW members. When the strike began, 36 of those arrested were hurriedly shipped east aboard a train dubbed "The Red Special." But of the 200 men rounded up in this early drive only about 30 were eventually deported. Many were paroled by the courts. Others were freed on writs of habeas corpus.[24]

Despite the safeguards, deportation proceedings tended to be harsh, characterized by mass arrests, excessive bail, and lengthy confinement incommunicado. That was the way the Immigration Bureau had handled deportation for the past twenty years, since a Supreme Court ruling that deportation was not punishment for a crime but merely an administrative procedure.

Congress had amended the deportation laws in 1918 to exclude radicals from entry into the United States. The secretary of labor, William B. Wilson, thereupon ruled that membership in a radical organization, such as the Communist party, was grounds for deportation. This ruling provided an unprecedented opportunity for Palmer and his aides. The General Intelligence Division, with not a shred of authority to do so, promptly threw itself into the deportation business.[25]

The evening of November 7, 1919, Justice Department agents, acting with the assistance of local police, raided dozens of meetings in cities all over the country. In New York alone more than 600 aliens were arrested. The focus of the New York raids was the Russian People's House, busy that night with such revolutionary activities as English classes, music practice, and games of chess. The raiders virtually demolished the interior of the building, ripping out the stairs in their search for evidence, stairs down which the people on the upper floors had been driven with clubs. The occupants of the Russian People's House stumbled into waiting police vans with their heads swathed in blood-stained strips of cloth.[26] The assistant secretary of labor observed drily: "There were marked indications that the raid was intended to be terrifying."[27]

Seven tons of "anarchistic" literature were taken in this one raid alone. Yet the legislation which authorized the arrest of aliens stated categorically that no home or meeting hall could be searched, no papers or property could be seized. Such actions called for a search warrant, and such a warrant could be issued only in a criminal, not an administrative, procedure. Under Palmer the law, in the name of the law, was destroyed. More than 400 aliens were brought in that night. Fewer than 50 were eventually deported. The rest, after being frightened and threatened, were set free.

December brought another massive raid. Some 43 anarchists, 184 members of the Union of Russian Workers, and a sprinkling of vagrants and petty criminals were rounded up and hurried to the New York waterfront. There was no time to locate a lawyer, bid good-bye to friends, make arrangements for the welfare of wives and children. It was more like a kidnapping than the action of responsible officials. The 249 deportees were bundled aboard the *Buford*, along with a platoon of armed infantrymen.

The secretary of labor had ordered that no one with wife or children in the United States could be deported—families were not to be broken up. Where no crime had been committed, it was unconscionable that innocent women and children be made to suffer. Officials in the Immigration Bureau and the Justice Department never found a way around this order. They simply ignored it. As the *Buford* raised steam, there were pathetic scenes as weeping women and children rushed onto Ellis Island and hurled themselves at the ferry gates in despair—an event described in newspaper headlines the following day as REDS STORM FERRY GATES TO FREE PALS.[28]

The *Buford* set sail dubbed "the Soviet Ark," but she landed at Hargo in Finland. Lacking diplomatic relations with the Soviet regime, it was impossible to arrange for the *Buford* to enter a Soviet port. Back in the United States that Christmas Eve the Justice Department asked the Immigration Bureau for 3,000 warrants.

The solicitor of the Labor Department, used as he was—or had become—to signing large batches of warrants, balked at this. A few hundred warrants were granted, and the remaining thousands of affidavits set aside. The Justice Department was planning massive raids on the evening of January 2. Without warrants its agents had no powers of arrest. Undeterred, they took nearly 2,000 people into custody on January 2, demonstrating that even warrants could be dispensed with.

The meetings Palmer's men raided that night were as legal as could be. Arrests were made in pool parlors, foreign language clubs, restaurants, and meeting halls.[29] A bakery at Lynn, Massachusetts, was raided on a tip that foreigners were meeting there in the middle of the night. A midnight swoop netted 39 bakers who tried to explain in several languages that they were meeting to set up a cooperative bakery.[30]

Beatings were the usual accompaniment to arrest. What most agitated those who were seized was less the beatings than the conditions of their confinement. The 800 arrested in Detroit were held incommunicado for up to ten days. They slept on the bare stone floor of the federal building, shared a single toilet and a single water fountain. The Justice Department agent-in-charge, Arthur L. Burley, announced triumphantly to newspapermen: "We didn't leave them a scrap of paper with which to do business."[31]

More than 400 of those seized in New England were taken to Deer Island. En route, they were marched through the streets of Boston in chains, under armed guard, to the jeers and taunts of an irate crowd. Prison officials were staggered. No one had alerted them to be prepared for this influx. The new arrivals were crammed into parts of the prison so decayed they had been virtually abandoned; areas where there was no heat, little light, only one working toilet. One man went mad, another committed suicide. Two died of pneumonia.[32]

The arrests went on, warrants or no warrants, at a rate of 200 a week. But in March, Secretary Wilson fell ill. Louis F. Post, the assistant secretary, became acting secretary of labor. Post was seventy-one, but a vigorous and quick-witted seventy-one. With his round, wire-frame spectacles, tousled hair, graying goatee, and pugnacious personality he bore a striking resemblance to Leon Trotsky. Post had been a Populist and Henry George "single-taxer" almost from youth. He was a living link in the Wilson Administration with the Democratic party's agrarian, western past. For the past six months he had watched the collapse of orderly administrative procedures into a witless orgy of arbitrary arrest and vicious maltreatment. His sense of justice and his sense of order alike had been outraged. Post brought what he termed "the deportations delirium" to a halt.

The Justice Department had accumulated 2,000 signed warrants. With these it planned to celebrate Easter, 1920. Post cancelled nearly all these precious warrants. Hundreds of people were in custody ostensibly on the authority of the Department of Labor. He ordered them released on low bail or on their own recognizance if the bail was still too high for their means.

Impeachment proceedings were begun in the House to remove him from office. Post made an appearance before his congressional critics. He proceeded to demonstrate that he knew vastly more about the subject of deportation than anyone in Congress, in the Justice Department, or newspaper offices. The Christian devoured the lions.

Post had also shattered Palmer's fondest hopes. The mass arrests, so popular with press and public, came to a screeching halt at the worst possible time—the beginning of the primary season. The attorney general staked all on another bold prediction: the Red revolution would break out on May Day. When May 1 came, nothing happened. Palmer's political prospects dissolved to the sound of mocking laughter.

IV

Still tracking down "Plain Words," the Bureau of Investigation received a tip at the end of February 1920: the pamphlet found on the Attorney General's lawn had been printed at Canzani's Printing Shop in Brooklyn. Federal agents staked out Canzani's. On March 7 they made a midnight raid. They arrested the owner, Robert Elia, and his typesetter, Andrea Salsedo. The latter turned out to be a former assistant to Luigi Galleani, the most important anarchist in the United States until his deportation in May 1919. Galleani, as editor of *Cronaca Sovversiva*, was a passionate and charismatic figure, virtually worshiped by men who normally despised idolatry. Under arrest, Elia and Salsedo were held incommunicado for two months.

Their fellow anarchists became increasingly anxious for them. Each Sunday afternoon the Italian anarchists of Boston, for example, would meet at the Italian Naturalization Club in a rundown hall overlooking the docks. On April 25 the discussion was concerned almost entirely with Elia and Salsedo. For the past five weeks the Boston anarchists had been raising money to help them and sending it to New York. But from New York they heard nothing, good or bad. Someone would have to go and make inquiries. The man they chose ought to have no steady job or family to consider; they chose a man named Bartolomeo Vanzetti.

He made the trip to New York, learned nothing definite about the two arrested men, but returned with a warning, which he passed on at the next meeting on May 2. Federal agents were preparing a fresh wave of raids in New England, he told them. The man who had given Vanzetti this warning, Luigi Quintilliani, was organizing the defense of Palmer-raid victims; he seemed in a position to know what to expect. He urged the Boston anarchists to get rid of their literature, those fiery pamphlets that federal prosecutors loved to put into juries' hands, those angry words that were taken for subversive deeds.

A rally would be organized to publicize the plight of Elia and Salsedo and a defense fund set up. In the meantime, Vanzetti and two other anarchists, Nicola Sacco and Ricardo Orciani, would try to collect that dangerous literature. Someone remembered that an anarchist turned bootlegger, by the name of Mike Boda, had an old car. Perhaps he would let them borrow it?

In the early hours of May 3, Salsedo, plummeted from a fourteenth story window at the Justice Department Building in New York. Did he jump or was he pushed? The most likely explanation is suicide as a result of judicial terror. Yet even Louis Post called it "homicide."[33] Salsedo's death was one of the most sensational episodes of the Red Scare and helped drive the nails into its coffin.

But its effects were to reverberate far into the future because on the evening of May 5, Sacco, Vanzetti, and Orciani went with Mike Boda to the shed in Bridgewater, Massachusetts, where Boda's dilapidated Overland had been dragged for repairs. The shed was under police surveillance. The Bridgewater chief of police, Michael Stewart, had participated in the Palmer raids. Anarchism fired his imagination now. He saw the black hand of anarchy in nearly every major crime, such as the big payroll robbery at South Braintree, fifteen miles from Bridgewater, back on April 15. Two men had been shot dead and $15,000 stolen. There was no proof of it, but Chief Stewart was sure that this was the work of anarchists. He knowingly observed, "The men who did this job knew no God."[34] It was his pursuit of anarchists that led him to put a watch on the ramshackle shed. Boda shared a house with an Italian anarchist named Ferruchio Coacci, who had just been deported. Perhaps Boda, too, was worth keeping an eye on.

By the time word reached Chief Stewart that three men had come to look at the Overland they had already left the scene, sensing a trap. Orciani roared away on his motorcycle. Sacco and Vanzetti boarded a trolley car. The police farther down the line were alerted by telephone. At Brockton police boarded the car and arrested Sacco and Vanzetti.

At the police station they denied they were anarchists. They lied about their movements that evening. They were evasive about their beliefs and activities in general. Both men had actually been involved in major strikes. Sacco was a skilled shoe trimmer. He played a leading role in a long shoe workers' strike in 1918. Two years before that, Vanzetti had engineered the first strike to shut down the New England rope mills. A vicious and bloody struggle won considerably higher wages for cordage workers. But Vanzetti left the cordage mills to become an itinerant fish peddler.[35]

Both men, police investigation revealed, had evaded registering for the draft. All men aged twenty-one to forty-five were required to register even though many—aliens, men with families, cripples—could not be drafted. Registration was enough to make anarchists suspicious. Sacco and Vanzetti had gone to Mexico rather than comply.

Searched, they proved to be armed. For men who professed to be pacifists this hardly showed a pacific state of mind, but Sacco worked on occasion as a factory night watchman, and most night watchmen carried guns. The real reason, however, was probably even simpler: this was a turbulent and dangerous time for radicals. When danger threatens, half the men in America are likely to arm themselves. To this extent, Sacco and Vanzetti were Americanized. Louis Post was unimpressed when Justice Department agents reported the arrest of aliens carrying pistols and revolvers: "Possession of them signified nothing lawless."[36]

Sacco was through with such anxieties. Anarchists were persecuted, immigrants despised. He was going back to Italy. It had taken ten years of hard work and diligent savings, but he had accumulated nearly $1,500— no fortune, yet enough to start a new life. On April 15 he had taken two copies of a photograph of himself, his wife, and his son to the Italian consulate in Boston and applied for a passport. He expected to be aboard ship by the middle of May, sailing for Italy.

In the middle of May he was still in the Brockton police station, and Chief Stewart was convinced that here were two men guilty of robbery and murder. He had also concluded by some kind of divination—there was not a shred of evidence for it—that whoever committed the South Braintree crime had attempted a payroll robbery in his own bailiwick, Bridgewater, back in December 1919. There was no logical connection between December's amateurish, almost farcical robbery, a holdup that was bound to fail, and the highly professional and successful heist in April. But Chief Stewart guessed there was a connection, and having made his guess was sticking to it.

The interrogation of Sacco and Vanzetti ground on. "No precautions whatever were taken to guard against mistaken identification. . . . There was no lineup. Witnesses were taken to the jail or police station to view Sacco and Vanzetti, as if they were animals in a zoo."[37] Orciani was released: time cards at the foundry where he worked gave him a perfect alibi for December 24, 1919, and April 15, 1920. Boda had to be released as the fourth potential member of Chief Stewart's gang of anarchist stickup artists because he was barely five feet tall. No one had mentioned a midget bandit or was likely to forget one. Eventually Sacco was also released. There was absolutely nothing but Chief Stewart's guesswork to link him to either robbery. Vanzetti, however, had a mustache and so had one of the Bridgewater desperadoes.

Vanzetti's mustache was full and flowing, a walrus type of remarkable size. The object identified by the Bridgewater witnesses was small and closely cropped. In the course of various hearings and trials the identification of Vanzetti by his mustache would grow stronger and stronger. Early tentative remarks eventually grew into a welter of elaborate detail, then total recall.

Vanzetti's trial opened in Plymouth, Massachusetts, before Judge Webster Thayer. "He was about five feet two inches tall, with the edgy vanity of many short men . . . a high forehead, a sudden little hawk nose bridged by a pince-nez, thin gray hair and mustache, dark-circled eyes,"[38] and a thin, hard mouth. With vanity went a petulant nature. No scholar, he had read law in an office in Worcester, Massachusetts. The name was patrician, but the bearer was not. Thayer was the Worcester butcher's son. He practiced law in his pedestrian way in his pedestrian home-town, joined the Odd Fellows, dabbled in local politics, until in 1917 his old Dartmouth classmate, Governor Samuel McCall, put him on the bench. There he passed the next three years with neither distinction nor disgrace. In August 1920 the trial of Bartolomeo Vanzetti began in his court.

Vanzetti's defense rested on his alibi witnesses. There was one day each year when Italians made a ritual meal of eels. That day was Christmas Eve. On the morning of December 24, 1919, Vanzetti the fish peddler was delivering eels door-to-door in Plymouth, twenty-five miles from Bridgewater. There were sixteen people, all of good repute, who swore to it. But their English was shaky, and they swore, as they testified, in Italian. The Anglo-Saxon jury was not much impressed.

Vanzetti's alibi also lacked its chief witness—Vanzetti himself. To put him on the stand would have exposed him to questions about his anarchism and the flight to Mexico. Vanzetti was an orator of some fame among his friends. Once on the stand, his lawyers feared, he would turn it into a soapbox. They advised him to remain mute. Vanzetti, convinced that sixteen people would have to be believed, complied.

Convicted of attempted robbery, he received from Judge Thayer a twelve-to-fifteen-year sentence, double the usual penalty for armed robbery by a first offender. And Vanzetti faced another trial: he and Sacco were to be tried for the South Braintree holdup after all.

The senior police officer directing the investigation of the South Braintree crime was removed from the case by the district attorney, apparently because of his growing conviction that neither Sacco nor Vanzetti had been involved.[39] The investigation was turned over to Stewart.

Despite his imposing title of chief of police, Stewart was no more than a rural constable. He was the entire full-time police force of Bridgewater. His burdens were shared with a part-time assistant. He could boast no experience in dealing with serious crime, was virtually untrained in investigation, and as far as is known had never solved anything. In towns like Bridgewater and South Braintree the state police took charge of investigations into major crimes; the Stewarts were occupied with keeping an eye on the town drunk, the peeping Tom, the adolescent rowdies. In this instance a state police captain with twenty-three years' experience and more than a hundred capital cases behind him was summarily removed and his assignment given to Chief Stewart.

Following his conviction, Vanzetti had lost faith in his lawyers. A defense committee composed mainly of his anarchist friends was prevailed upon by Elizabeth Gurley Flynn and her lover, Carlo Tresca, the successor to Galleani, to accept a lawyer from the west, Fred H. Moore.

A decade earlier Moore had been a railroad lawyer in Seattle. He moved south and became a corporation attorney in Los Angeles. Conventional success soon bored him. He began to let his hair grow long. He affected the broad-brimmed black felt hat of the prewar bohemian. When a Wobbly he had once met called him from the San Diego jail one day, Moore picked up his expansive hat, tucked a loaded revolver into his belt, told his partner he would be back in a day or two, left the office, and never returned.

In 1912 he went east to help the Lawrence strikers. It was there that Flynn and Tresca came to know him. Over the next few years he was involved in various IWW struggles. But his unreliability—long, unexplained absences, a habit of missing filing deadlines in difficult cases—led the IWW to dispense with his services at the end of 1919. His career as a radical lawyer seemed over. Then in the fall of 1920 came the summons from Tresca and Flynn.

Moore arrived in Boston wearing a sombrero. He was nearly forty—a dangerous age. Moore seized on the Sacco and Vanzetti case as a starving man falls on food.

Vanzetti was not taken with Moore, and Sacco disliked him from the moment they met. Away from the courtroom Moore spent his nights in a narrow four-story house on the déclassé fringe of Beacon Hill, talking, singing, drinking, seducing college girls attracted to the cause. Yet he wasted no time in bringing the AFL and the ACLU into the defense effort. He also brought in two highly competent local attorneys, Jeremiah and Thomas McAnarney, who took the case only after interviewing Sacco and Vanzetti and deciding that the two men were innocent.

The McAnarneys approached the case as a case; Moore approached the case as a cause. He was out for glory. In an earlier trial of two Italian anarchists, he had conducted an exhaustive investigation that undercut the prosecution case; organized a strong defense based on forensic evidence and unimpeachable witnesses; hired respected, conventional local attorneys whom a local jury would trust; and sat quietly in the courtroom as the proceedings moved steadily toward acquittal. That was what the Sacco and Vanzetti defense committee thought it was being offered. But Moore could no longer be bothered with the dull, plodding work of pretrial investigation and pretrial preparation. He would rather try the case in the streets and in the newspapers. Moore wanted to save his clients. He also wanted to exalt himself.

The trial opened in 1921 before Judge Thayer. This was no coincidence but the result of an arrangement. Trials were rotated from court to court, judge to judge. But Thayer asked the chief justice of the Commonwealth to be given the trial of Sacco and Vanzetti, and for some reason the usual procedure was set aside.

When the trial opened, Moore did everything he could to draw attention to himself short of doing handstands on the defense counsels' table. He kicked off his shoes, sprawled ostentatiously in his chair, unknotted his tie, undid his vest, and found various other ways to outrage petit bourgeois sensibilities. The McAnarneys were astonished. Moore, for no reason they could imagine, was deliberately antagonizing the judge and jury, and two men's lives were at stake. They tried in a state approaching desperation to remove Moore from the defense. They offered to drop out of the case if he would drop with them. Nothing could detach Moore from his great opportunity.

Moore's behavior shocked the defense committee, created mainly by a printer named Aldino Felicani. Tall, thin, melancholy, Felicani was another who affected the bohemian style of broad-brimmed hats, red shirts, and flowing black ties. The gentle, soft-spoken Felicani came from a family of radicals. In Italy he had shared a jail cell with another young radical named Benito Mussolini. In 1911, Felicani fled to the United States to avoid another long spell in jail. He found work as a typesetter in Boston, joined the anarchist circle at the Italian Naturalization Club, and so met Vanzetti. The two men rapidly became close friends.

With the help of the Boston Italian community and a sprinkling of New England blue bloods, Felicani had brought the Sacco-Vanzetti Defense Committee into existence. And several upper-class liberals were early drawn into the struggle, notably Elizabeth Glendower Evans and Gardner Jackson. Mrs. Evans was a middle-aged matron of impeccable lineage and a million-dollar fortune. She began tutoring Vanzetti in English in his jail cell.

Gardner Jackson was a rich young man from Colorado who had been educated at Amherst and Columbia. In 1920 he began a career in journalism by starting as a cub reporter on the Boston Globe. One morning at breakfast, in 1921, his wife told him that she had been reading various accounts of the trial at Dedham of two Italian anarchists. The stories troubled her. She had a feeling, she said, that the trial was unfair.

Jackson went to see the Globe's reporter at the Dedham courtroom, an elderly, much-admired journalist named Frank Sibley. He told Jackson, "Your wife's perceptive. It's an outrage that's being perpetrated here." It was less a trial, he concluded, than a frame-up.[40] Deeply upset by this, Jackson went to see Felicani. In time, he would give up all his energies and a considerable part of his life to the struggle to save Sacco and Vanzetti.

The trial itself contained so many peculiarities that a frame-up seemed as logical an explanation as any. Many remain convinced to this day that that was what it was. Yet Sacco and Vanzetti were more the victims of bad luck, prejudice, and lapses in trial technique than anything else. Evidence that would not have been accepted in most other criminal trials was accepted in this one or not properly scrutinized by the defense. Moore's trial tactics horrified conventional lawyers. Clarence Darrow might have got away with them. Moore was no Darrow. Whatever his faults, however, Moore can hardly be accused of conscious involvement in an attempt to frame Sacco and Vanzetti.

Only one witness, a railroad crossing keeper, placed Vanzetti at the South Braintree payroll robbery. But in the immediate aftermath of the murders the witness told four people, including a newspaper reporter and a close friend, that he had been so transfixed with fear that he could not remember what any of the men in the bandits' car looked like. As the investigation wound its bizarre way, the crossing keeper began to remember things—he particularly recalled a man with a dark complexion and a large mustache who drove the car.

All the other witnesses—a dozen altogether—agreed that the driver was fair, young, and emaciated. So Vanzetti was moved by the prosecution into the front passenger's seat. But then came a third man whom the prosecution placed firmly in the car even though no one could offer a very clear description of him. He was placed, by general agreement, in the back seat. Finally came the three gunmen, hurrying toward the car after the guards had been shot and the shoe factory payroll seized. All three jumped into the car and it sped away. All the witnesses, including the crossing keeper, agreed on the number of bandits involved in the crime —five. And that left no room in the car for Vanzetti.[41]

The eyewitnesses who placed Sacco at the scene of the crime contradicted one another completely on what he was wearing and the time they had seen him. Several later recanted their testimony. One had a criminal record and was vulnerable to prosecution pressure. Another had a conviction for fraud. A third was known throughout the factory where he worked as a compulsive liar. On the defense side, a bank official, an advertising agent, a clerk at the Italian consulate, and a highway surveyor all swore that between 1:00 P.M. and 4:00 P.M. on April 15 they had seen Sacco in Boston, more than twenty miles from the crime. These four were unimpeachable alibi witnesses; all were non-Italians; all held positions of responsibility.

There was no physical evidence to link Vanzetti with the crime, only the shaky testimony of the crossing keeper.[42] But there was a possible physical connection between Sacco and one of the dead payroll guards— a bullet fired from a .32 pistol. Sacco asked for a test-firing to be made with his pistol for ballistics examination. This test took place thirteen months after his arrest and the confiscation of his gun. The prosecution had opened by saying that it would not try to claim that any of the six bullets recovered at South Braintree had been fired by any particular weapon. Suddenly strange things began to happen to the testimony of the prosecution's ballistics experts. Even stranger things happened to the fatal bullet. There is at least a prima facie case that the genuine bullet was switched for the bullet test-fired through Sacco's pistol, because the identifying marks on the bullet in question do not appear to match those on the other bullets.[43]

An attempt was made to show that Vanzetti's .38 caliber Harrison and Richardson revolver was taken from one of the two dead guards, who was known to carry an H&R revolver. But according to the gunsmith who repaired this weapon it had been of .32 caliber.

It was a long case, but not a strong case. Sacco and Vanzetti, supposedly two members of a gang that had just pulled off a big payroll robbery, had been arrested while trying to borrow a broken-down car from a fellow anarchist; had almost no money on them and rode around on streetcars; and stood on street corners in shabby clothes to make speeches in defense of the Palmer-raid victims. These men, with thousands of dollars presumably due them as their share of the loot, were out in public, drawing attention to themselves, begging for nickels and dimes.

Even so, they were convicted. A determined prosecution prevailed over a fragmented defense. Vanzetti gave windy speeches on the evils of capitalism. The lies told at Brockton police station, the draft-dodging journey to Mexico, Vanzetti's conviction for the Bridgewater fiasco, and their guns—especially those guns—conjured up an impression of the defendants that while true enough in its details was false in effect. The prosecution mocked their claims of pacifism, and Vanzetti's speeches opened opportunities for fervent patriotic speeches in rejoinder, an opportunity the judge could not himself resist. And what dangerous men these two anarchists were! Six times each day—in the morning, the evening, and at lunchtime—they were marched through the streets of Dedham, from jailhouse to courthouse and back again, handcuffed and surrounded by heavily armed guards. What jury could fail to be impressed?

IV

The fears anarchists inspired were exaggerated. For every anarchist willing to shed blood there were a dozen or more who detested government because it embraced force and violence. But five days after the indictment of Sacco and Vanzetti, on September 16, 1920, a horse drawing a cart plodded to a halt at the corner of Broad and Wall streets, the hub of American capitalism. At this corner the United States Sub-Treasury, the United States Assay Office, the New York Stock Exchange, and J. P. Morgan and Co. faced one another across streets where light penetrates only briefly each day. As they became crowded and lively with workers caught up in the morning rush hour, the entire cart seemed to blow up in the face of the House of Morgan.[44]

The explosion boomed, and its force was magnified, along these concrete canyons. Thirty-four people died, more than 200 were injured. The blast was so intense that people at open windows six stories above the explosion were burned.[45] The dead and crippled of this blast were not the caricature plutocrats who featured in pamphlets like "Plain Words" but ordinary people, such as clerks, runners, and typists.

4. Return of the Nativist

I

At dusk on Thanksgiving Day, 1915, a dozen men, most of them long past youth, puffed laboriously up Stone Mountain, the famous outcropping of rock outside Atlanta. They busied themselves with some crude work of construction. When night closed in, a large wooden cross, wrapped in straw and oil-soaked rags, flared into an orange spire of flame on the darkened mountainside. The Ku Klux Klan had been reborn.

On December 4 the state courts issued a charter for a new fraternal order to be known as "The Invisible Empire, Knights of the Ku Klux Klan, Inc." Its Imperial Wizard, the man who had organized the cross-burning, was William J. Simmons. He was then thirty-five years old, tall and thin, with red hair, and a large nose on which sat a pince-nez. For a time Simmons had been a circuit-riding Methodist minister. When he failed to secure a church of his own he became a hard-drinking membership sales-man for a fraternal order called the Woodmen of the World.[1] Simmons had some military experience, and he styled himself colonel. But during his service in the Spanish-American War the highest rank he had attained was that of private.

Simmons belonged to seven fraternal orders. The revived Klan was only one more, but with the added charm that Simmons could run it.[2] After America's entry into World War I, Simmons moved the Klan into the vigilante business. It became a secret organization. Translated to higher spheres than mere good fellowship, the new Klan evolved a militantly moralistic patriotism. It harried the idler, the slacker, the draft dodger, the prostitute who solicited servicemen, and "the laborer who is infected with the I.W.W. spirit."[3] The Simmons Klan adopted some of the ritual, paraphernalia, and terminology of the old Klan of Reconstruction. The colonel, however, had an inventive mind of his own. He built up an edifice of mummery and mumbo jumbo that dwarfed his predecessors'. The release of D. W. Griffith's *Birth of a Nation* in the summer of 1915 had given him a fair wind at the start. To southerners, the old Klan appeared as noble and idealistic as King Arthur's knights.[4] Despite Simmons's inventiveness, good luck, and the opportunities provided by the war, the Klan in 1920 had only 2,000 members.[5] It appeared permanently stranded on this plateau. The Imperial Wizard was proving to be an inept organizer and an appalling judge of men. His assistants almost ruined his creation by looting the treasury, then hastening to distant parts before the colonel sobered up.

The Klan was so hapless these days it could not even capitalize on the Red Scare. In the middle of these doldrums Simmons met two expert hucksters, Edward Young Clarke and Elizabeth Tyler. They were as wayward as the Colonel,* but a lot better organized.

Clarke was an unprepossessing man. Yet he was an accomplished fund-raiser. The war-loan drives were the school of modern promotion techniques, and afterward, "Promotion itself, on a percentage basis and for any cause, became a trade."[6] Mrs. Tyler was chubby, fair-haired, and vivacious. She was a survivor. She had to be. Married at fourteen, she was a widow with a child to support at fifteen. She and Clarke ran the Southern Publicity Association. They offered their services to Simmons: they would find Klansmen for him for a fee.

The SPA was to retain $8 of the $10 initiation fee (the klecktoken). With this incentive to inspire them, Clarke and Mrs. Tyler hired 1,100 membership salesmen (kleagles), "with instructions to play upon whatever prejudices were most acute in the particular area the Kleagles were working."[7] The kleagles were not without an incentive of their own—they could keep $4 of the klecktoken for themselves. By October 1921 they had enrolled 1 million new Klansmen. They were particularly successful in the fast-urbanizing cities of the South. In Alabama, Birmingham's Robert E. Lee Klan No. 1 boasted 10,000 members.[8]

In Texas, the kleagles played on hatred of Mexicans; in California, on hatred of the Japanese; in New York, on anti-Semitism and xenophobic

---

* In October 1919, Clarke and Mrs. Tyler had been arrested half-naked and evidently drunk. They were fined for disorderly conduct.

hatred of immigrants; in New England, on the traditional contempt for French-Canadians; in the Deep South, on anti-Catholicism and racial prejudice. The local Klan would usually form links with the dominant political party; in the South that meant with the Democrats, elsewhere with the Republicans. The Klan was in spirit a small-town phenomenon. Yet in some ways it flourished most strongly in newer cities, those which had been small towns only a generation before. It even gained a strong footing in the industrialized Northeast. In May 1923, for example, an estimated 10,000 New Jersey Klansmen held a klavern in New Brunswick, almost within sight of Manhattan. They burned a sixty-two-foot cross to mark the occasion.[9]

In the words of Simmons's successor as Imperial Wizard, the Klans "were mostly composed of poor people."[10] For many, the Klan was still a fraternal organization, the only one they ever joined. The regalia, rituals, and camaraderie attracted more people than the chance of flogging somebody. Klan parades were a release from the dreariness of small-town life before radio helped occupy the evenings. The Klan, like radio, appealed to people whose imaginative needs were limited but unsatisfied. And there were the Klan picnics, boat trips, debating contests, spelling bees, and sightseeing tours. The large numbers of Pennsylvania Dutch (a corruption of Deutsch) who joined the Klan held sauerkraut dinners and goat roasts.[11] A typical Klan ceremony involved entire families, drawn by fireworks, bands, a barbeque, hymn-singing, and setting fire to a forty-foot cross.

The ordinary Klansman wore a robe and a hood of white cotton; Klan officers—of whom there were many—dressed in satin robes of brilliant colors, lavishly embroidered with silk. And what a sensation they caused on a Friday night in some drab little town when they paraded holding blazing torches. A Klan parade passed by in utter silence, a silence so complete, some claimed, that you could almost hear the breathing of the crowd.[12]

What a release this was from the inferiority complex of these grade-school graduates, struggling for a crust in a severe economic recession, forced by an industrialized, urbanized world into daily awareness of their position at the bottom of society. They fastened like the shipwrecked to the one positive attribute they possessed—their old-stock Americanism. In their daft way they believed that this single virtue qualified them to be guardians of society. Don the flowing robes, converse in the cryptic speech of the Klansman, parade past a crowd awed into silence, and for a while the burning sense of inferiority was gone. A nobody in the world became a somebody in the Klan.[13]

They had grown up in a society that proclaimed the equality of men and the equality of opportunity. There may have been some truth to such beliefs out on the frontier. It certainly was not true here and now. The tensions produced by inferiority and impotence were for many Klansmen released in their masquerades. But there were others in whom these tensions exploded, where release demanded tarring and feathering, flogging and lynching.

And here violence merged with a crusading passion: to restore the status quo of about 1890—"the separation of church and state, the primacy of Fundamental Protestantism, white supremacy, a capitalist economic system, dominance of the native-born whites in American society. . . . It encompassed efforts to preserve premarital chastity, marital fidelity, and respect for parental authority; to compel obedience to state and national prohibition laws; to fight the postwar crime wave; and to rid state and local government of dishonest politicians."[14] In their struggle to resist the modern world, Klansmen discovered that "liberals were a worse menace than foreigners."[15]

In cities where the Klan was strong—for example, Detroit, Milwaukee, Pittsburgh, Dayton, Indianapolis, Denver, and Chicago[16]—were millions of newly urbanized people. The Klan encouraged an illusory hope of imposing rural values on this dangerous but exciting environment. Here the Klan took up the cause of law and order and rarely strayed into violence. But in a state like Oklahoma, a territory until 1907, the frontier was still close.

In Oklahoma the Klan carried on from the town-tamers, cleaning out the whores, the bootleggers, the gamblers, the procurers, the men who pestered respectable women, the men who scoffed at the law. Oklahoma City boasted a Klan "whipping squad" of eighteen picked floggers. Shawnee had no fewer than five whipping squads. In a single year the Oklahoma Klan was held responsible for 2,500 floggings.[17] And in Marlow a black man was accused of "breaking a custom of many years' standing" that blacks got out of town by sundown. He was lynched. So was the white hotel proprietor who employed him as a porter.[18]

Over much of the Southwest a reign of terror descended. A Houston lawyer was whipped and tarred and feathered for accepting the "wrong" kind of clients, such as blacks and recidivists. Similar punishment was inflicted on a woman accused of bigamy, a doctor suspected of performing abortions, and a price-gouging storekeeper. A Louisiana wife-beater was stripped naked, tarred and feathered. A dishwasher suspected of burglary was whipped until he confessed. A notorious philanderer was kidnapped and flogged senseless. There were literally thousands of such episodes in 1921–23.

The Klan called these forays "night-riding." They invariably ended with someone being flogged, tarred and feathered, lynched, castrated, or branded. In virtually every case the police stood aside.

People fought back, especially north of the Mason-Dixon line. The Catholic immigrant workers in the Pennsylvania coal and steel towns broke up Klan parades with brickbats, fists, and gunfire. Shortly after the Herrin massacre the Klan moved into "Egypt" and closed the brothels and speakeasies. Anti-Klan townspeople resisted with force. Shoot-outs in the Herrin streets left as many as six men dead in a single day. More than $5 million in bail bonds was outstanding at a time when the entire town could have been bought up for less.[19] On the streets, virtually every man carried a gun. When the Klan organized in Perth Amboy, New Jersey, in 1923, so did local Catholics and Jews. "A mob, six-thousand strong, closed in on the Klan meeting place, overwhelmed the entire police force and fire department, and fell upon some five hundred Ku Kluxers, kicking, stoning and beating them as they fled."[20]

One episode of Klan violence horrified the entire country. In Mer Rouge, Louisiana, there were two outspoken foes of the Klan named Filmore Watt Daniels and Thomas F. Richards. In the summer of 1922 they were seized by hooded men as they returned from a picnic. Two months later their bodies, mutilated and showing the signs of unspeakable torture, were recovered from a nearby lake. Meanwhile, two elderly men, including Daniels's father, had been kidnapped and flogged.[21] The governor of Louisiana, John M. Parker, put Moorehouse Parish under martial law while an investigation was carried out. Witnesses proved too terrified to speak. A trial was held, featuring eighteen defendants. All eighteen were acquitted.[22]

Despite such atrocities, the vast majority of Klansmen were convinced that they were God-fearing, Christian men. North and South, most Klansmen were Baptists and fundamentalists. Every local klavern had a chaplain (the kludd). Each klavern meeting opened and closed with prayer. The semiofficial anthem was "The Old Rugged Cross," and another favorite was transformed into "Onward Valiant Klansmen."

The most vivid assertion of the Klansman's faith came in the church visitation. An entire klavern, numbering up to 200 men, would enter a church without warning, march gravely down the aisle in full regalia, and stop the service to give the minister an envelope stuffed with money. They would depart as swiftly and as silently as they had arrived. When brought off successfully, the church visitation "had much of the dramatic quality of a hold-up in broad daylight."[23]

The Klan thrived on anti-Catholicism. Hostility went beyond historical and theological antipathies. Klansmen were convinced that Catholics were invariably disloyal to the United States, that their real allegiance was to the Pope. Suspicion of Catholics was no Klan monopoly. Most Protestants probably shared it. But the Klan's anti-Catholicism revolved around paranoid fantasies.

There was, for example, a rumor that went back to the Know-Nothings of the 1850s, according to which the birth of a Catholic baby was celebrated by burying a gun and fifty rounds of ammunition beneath the local Catholic Church. When the time was ripe and all the little Catholics had grown up and learned how to shoot straight, the guns would be dug up. Catholic revolutionaries would seize power and give the United States to the Pope.[24]

Robert Coughlan, a Catholic teenager growing up in Kokomo, Indiana, took an interest in the Klan propaganda circulating around town. "The Borgias were an endless mine of material, and their exploits came to be as familiar to readers of the Klan press as the lives of soap opera characters are to modern housewives. Constant readers must have begun to think of them as The Typical Catholic Family of the Renaissance."[25] Half of Kokomo seemed convinced that at any moment the Pope would arrive to claim the United States. And then it happened. Word suddenly spread that "the Pope was finally pulling into town on the south-bound from Chicago to take over. A mob formed and stoned the train."[26]

The discovery that the Klan had been revived shocked millions of people. Nearly everyone assumed that it had been dead for half a century. In September 1921 the *New York World*, the most important liberal newspaper of the twenties, began running a series of critical articles on the new Klan. Although these stories appalled millions, they were a publicity windfall. Hundreds of thousands of people, far from being alarmed, were thrilled and captivated by the thought of an organization dedicated to preserving the old virtues at almost any cost. "Some zealots even mailed their applications for membership to Atlanta on sample forms printed in the newspaper to illustrate the *World*'s articles."[27] Kleagles no longer had to beat the rural byways for recruits: applications poured in at the rate of 5,000 a day.

The next month the House Rules Committee held hearings on the Klan. Simmons was summoned. It was as if he had prepared himself for this moment for years. Relaxed, loquacious, sincere, he more than held his own under intense questioning.[28] Disarmed by the colonel, Congress decided to do nothing about the Klan. He had turned the hearings into a recruiting stand and more free publicity.

For Simmons, that was the summit of his Imperial Wizardry. A year later a palace revolt led by a dentist from Dallas, Hiram W. Evans, deposed him. The colonel was bought out for $146,500 in cash and some valuable property.[29] Clarke was ousted in March 1923 and his influence destroyed by a White Slave Act conviction. Mrs. Tyler remarried and left the Klan to its own devices under new management. Evans became Imperial Wizard. Every Klansman was forced to swear a new oath of allegiance, pledging himself to the plump, bespectacled person of Hiram W. Evans.

Under the new regime no one would become rich on klecktokens; all officials were put on salary. They were forced to lead blameless private lives. Lynching and flogging stopped. Cleaned up, the Klan, its membership reaching 4 million, moved on to other business. It prepared to move into the political mainstream where it might play a decisive role in American life.

II

A Klansman was xenophobic, if nothing else. He justified his hostility to foreigners on the grounds that the pioneers who had built America had done it for their direct descendants. But by 1920 there were 105 million people in the United States, a large proportion of whom had (to pioneer ears) strange-sounding names. There were 14 million who were foreign-born. The old-stock Americans were deeply troubled by figures such as this. Even a French visitor was led to wonder, "Is it possible to contemplate a United States that is neither Protestant nor Anglo-Saxon?"[30]

Before 1890 some 80 percent of immigrants came from northern Europe, of the same stock as the pioneers. They brought with them most of the social, political, and religious values the country had been built on. Like the pioneers before them, they headed west. The immigrants who arrived after 1890 were mainly drawn from southern and eastern Europe. They were Catholics and Jews. They had little experience of democratic institutions. They crowded into the cities of the East. Their numbers rose sharply from year to year.

By World War I immigration was running close to 1 million a year, and 80 percent was the "new" immigration. It was the post-1890 influx which accounted for the astonishingly rapid urbanization of postfrontier America. As it made the cities grow, so it transformed them. There were eastern and midwestern cities where up to three-fourths of the population in 1920 was foreign-born. Cleveland, for example, supported newspapers in twenty-one languages other than English.

The new immigration was composed mainly of men aged twenty to forty-five, men like Sacco and Vanzetti, both of whom arrived before they were twenty-one. Young working-class men were harder to assimilate and more restless than men with families.* Yet they were also more adaptable, willing to work at almost anything, and better able, if they were ambitious, to work their way up from poverty than a man with three or four dependents.

Little more than half the population in 1920 was white and born of American-born parents. Even though aliens were exempt from the draft, 20 percent of the wartime army had been foreign-born. WASPs did not carry figures such as these on slips of paper in their pockets. What they carried was a sense of being cornered within their own country. And when figures were produced, they were seized on with avidity. Almost everyone seemed to know that the entire new immigration had done badly on the Alpha intelligence test taken by all potential servicemen, scoring far below native-born whites, Canadians, and immigrants from northwestern Europe. The old stock did not have much to boast about—a mental age, on average, of fourteen. But the new immigrants scored two years below this, and blacks lower still. These figures, produced by an almost laughably crude test, set the prejudices of the age in the concrete of pseudoscience.[31]

Even reputable scholars were convinced that from the melting pot would come only base metal.[32] Two noted psychologists, William C. McDougall and Carl C. Brigham, in *A Study of American Intelligence* (Princeton, 1923), asserted flatly: "The intellectual superiority of our Nordic group over the Alpine, Mediterranean and negro groups has been demonstrated." Biologists such as Henry Fairfield Osborne, president of the American Museum of Natural History, agreed. The *New York Times* expressed, as tastefully as it could, fears that the United States was being "mongrelized."[33]

Everyone knew that besides being dim the new immigrants brought with them a variety of dangerous ideas, such as socialism and anarchism; were only one generation removed from serfdom; were therefore deficient in the quick wits, the self-reliance, the energy and mechanical aptitude of the native-born. There were also much higher rates of pauperism and insanity among the newcomers. The figures, once again, proved it. But what they really showed were the inevitable consequences of poverty. Most immigrants arrived poor. Most stayed poor. And in the struggle to adjust to a strange, impersonal culture, to master a difficult language, there were bound to be many who failed and whose characters disintegrated under the strain.

The immigrant had to look for a job when he arrived: the law pre-

* An estimated 50 percent of Wobblies were immigrants: Robert W. Bruère, "The Industrial Workers of the World," *Harper's*, July 1918.

vented him from finding a job in advance. He stood a good chance of being fleeced before he ever set sail by being sold a false passport or a ticket that was no good. There were other snares along the way. It was not unusual for someone to set off with several hundred dollars, painfully saved over a period of years, and to arrive at Ellis Island with little more than loose change. So the immigrant set out to find a job without delay. If he went to an employment agency, there was an excellent chance of being fleeced all over again. Young women and girls were easily lured by promises of work as servants and maids, only to be broken into white slavery by gangs of tough young rapists. Kidnapped, starved, raped day after day until they no longer cared what happened to them, they were then farmed out to brothels, broken in spirit.[34]

The immigrant who turned to the courts for protection was lucky to escape the ambulance-chasing lawyer, the crooked lower court justice, the rapacious court constable. Immigrant workers were commonly cheated in workmen's compensation cases. In some towns they could expect to be arrested on specious charges and heavily fined. The fine was divided between the judge and the arresting officer.[35] And the Little Italys, the Lower East Side, the Back of the Yards, the Chinatowns, the little Tokyos provided no refuge from the unscrupulous. The foreign-language press, so important in providing a sense of identity and cohesion, survived on advertisements that promoted quack doctors and bogus remedies.[36]

Immigrants were under strong pressure to assimilate, and the Sixty-sixth Congress passed an Americanization Act. Peace had left the American Protective League's 250,000 members with nothing much to do. As an auxiliary of the Justice Department the wartime APL provided an army of informers and vigilantes, ever alert to signs of defeatism, disaffection, and draft-dodging. And there was the American Legion, organized in France in February 1919, relaunched on American soil at St. Louis a few months later. The Legion was pledged to work for "100 percent Americanism."

The Legion and the APL, in conjunction with Chambers of Commerce and the YMCA, began to conduct English classes for immigrants with money provided by the Americanization Act. Americanism, of an uncritical, hyperpatriotic variety, was forced down foreign throats along with instruction on word order and how the gerund is formed. Two states passed legislation to support the Americanization drive by requiring all illiterate or non-English-speaking aliens to attend special schools.

If Americanization advanced rapidly, programs such as these had little to do with it. The army had naturalized more than a million aliens in very short order. Forced into close contact with Americans, they soon learned to speak English and absorbed many American values and ways.

Millions more went to work in shipyards and munitions plants, "where it was best for them to speak English and show as few evidences of their foreign origin as possible, particularly if they came from Central Europe. . . ."[37] One indication of this kind of success was the hundreds of foreign-language newspapers that folded in 1919–20.

Americanization had previously been left to social reformers, who approached it as an extension of their commitment to help the disadvantaged. But aliens were now being visited by local Americanization committees to ask when were they going to apply for citizenship, and, were they learning English? On occasion feelings ran high and a demonstration of loyalty was called for, such as kissing the flag under threat of a beating.

Some immigrant leaders began to resist, telling the Americanizers what they could do with their unsolicited and parochial opinions. There were immigrant communities that became more, not less, chauvinistic. They boldly flaunted their native costumes, food, dress, and speech. The Americanization drive at this juncture turned ugly. It merged with the deportations delirium and the Red Scare.

The hatred of all things foreign reached a pitch of viciousness hard at this distance to credit. But in the coalfields of "Egypt," on the night of August 5, 1920, and all the next day "hundreds of people laden with clothing and household goods filled the roads leading out of West Frankfort. . . . Back in town their homes were burning. Mobs bent on driving out every foreigner surged through the streets. . . . The Italian population was the chief objective."[38] Italians were dragged from their homes, beaten with fists and clubs, stoned and kicked, while their homes were set on fire. The mob raged for three days. Two children were missing and were later found dead. A rumor went around that the Italians had kidnapped them for some sinister, foreign purpose.

When the Red Scare died down coercive Americanization lost its momentum. The superpatriots had already begun shifting their energies to immigration control. By 1921 it was becoming a national crusade. The recession caused the AFL to lobby vigorously for a two-year ban on all immigration.[39] In Congress, every Progressive in the Senate and all but one in the House was pressing for a sharp cutback. The lone exception was Fiorello La Guardia, who represented an urban constituency made up largely of recent immigrants; people, that is, with relatives still to bring over.[40] There were a few businessmen who resisted immigration restriction—those who employed a lot of unskilled, low-wage labor. These exceptions aside, the vast majority of Americans, liberal or conservative, Democratic or Republican, were strongly in favor of immigration restriction.

Unlimited immigration had to end. Even with the best will in the world the United States could not indefinitely absorb up to a million people a year; and 1 million would certainly have led in time to 2 million or more. What was wrong was not restriction as such, but the principles on which restriction was based.

Before 1882, when the Chinese Exclusion Act was passed, almost anyone could enter the United States. Just as it was easy to come in, so was it easy to become a citizen. But by 1914 Congress had passed 11 immigration statutes, excluding an ever-wider range of potential immigrants. In 1917 Congress imposed a literacy test, in a language of the immigrant's choice. Like most of the other curbs, this set a higher standard instead of cutting immigrant numbers outright. Had, say, 10 million healthy, literate, law-abiding foreigners presented themselves at Ellis Island on a Tuesday morning, all 10 million would have had to be allowed in. It was the war that cut the flow.

By 1920 the influx was approaching prewar levels once more. The price of passage and landing fees, the literacy test, and other requirements meant that almost all present immigrants were drawn from the skilled, respectable part of the working class. Yet the projection for fiscal year 1921–22 was for 1 million immigrants. Congress passed a new immigration statute, imposing for the first time an annual quota. In almost his last act as President, Wilson vetoed the bill.

The new Administration was in turn presented with the bill in the guise of emergency legislation. The quota was set at 350,000 places. These were parceled out on the basis of 3 percent of each foreign nation's representation on the 1910 census. If the census had reported 150,000 Danes among the foreign-born, then the Danish quota would be 4,500 a year. The 1921 Immigration Act's national origins system of quota places set the pattern for half a century of immigration laws. For the present, it kept out 2 million people waiting to enter the United States. Most of these 2 million were Greeks, Italians, Jews, and Slavs.[41]

Something approaching panic gripped European ports. The last day of each month soon found up to a dozen ships crammed with immigrants waiting at the entrance to New York harbor. At a few minutes to midnight the ships would get under way, racing to cross the line at the beginning of the month and so unload their cargoes within that month's quota. These races down a narrow shipping channel brought huge ships within feet of one another, terrified the passengers, and made an ass of the law. Captains who made a slight miscalculation would pass Ambrose Light a minute or half a minute too soon. Their entire cargo of immigrants would then be declared ineligible for entry, because that month's quota was full.[42]

Ellis Island was not a pleasant place at the best of times. It was designed to handle 1,700 immigrants a day. On the first of the month as many as 15,000 were now arriving together.[43] Chaos raged while medical inspections, usually rudimentary, but at times humiliating, were carried out. There was a way to avoid the chaos and the risk of humiliation, however—travel first class. As one first-class passenger discovered, the inspection "consists in a doctor strolling through the saloon whilst you are eating your breakfast and looking at the back of your neck to be quite sure that you have not got smallpox."[44] Immigration restriction was not only a matter of race; it was also a question of class.

III

When Reconstruction gave way in the 1870s to the reassertion of white domination in the South, blacks began moving out in impressive numbers. Many moved west, to the frontier. The war speeded up black migration and altered its principal direction. Blacks who left after 1914 almost always headed north. The earlier migration had been from the border states. The wartime migration, as if impelled by a greater force, drew blacks out of the Deep South in hundreds of thousands.

They found well-established black neighborhoods in many northern cities. In New York there was a black population of 100,000 scattered throughout the five boroughs. There were black streets in Chicago and Philadelphia and Boston. But there was not yet a black community anywhere, and nothing that could be termed a black ghetto. It took the wartime migration to link up black neighborhoods and produce Harlem and the South Side of Chicago.

The black migrants wanted jobs and education, and freedom from lynching and virtual slavery. Wartime compulsory work laws were being enforced in southern states in what amounted to peonage.[45] Little wonder that half a million blacks went north between 1916 and 1920. They were zealously encouraged by the black press. The *Chicago Defender* circulated far into the South. Every issued urged them to come north, on occasion resorting to verse as in "They're Leaving Memphis in Droves":

> Some are coming on the passenger,
> Some are coming on the freight,
> Others will be found walking,
> For none have time to wait.[46]

The black communities that developed in the harsh, anonymous and stimulating cities produced a new generation of black leaders, notably

Marcus Garvey, the first to win a mass following. A short, chubby Jamaican, Garvey arrived in the United States in 1916 at the age of twenty-eight to raise money for his creation, the Universal Negro Improvement Association. In his home island, the UNIA provoked yawning indifference. Yet Garvey dreamed of creating a Jamaican version of the Tuskegee Institute.

By 1919, however, Garvey's UNIA was generating more interest in black neighborhoods here than it had ever sparked in Jamaica. Garvey made a whirlwind tour that year, speaking in thirty-eight states and raising UNIA membership from two or three thousand to approximately a quarter of a million. When the little fat man boomed, "Up! Up, you mighty race!" a thrill ran down the spines of his poor and humble listeners.

Less Messianic leaders were meanwhile struggling with the prosaic difficulties of a people rapidly translated from rural poverty to crowded city streets. Blacks had proved virtually impossible to organize. What political loyalties they had, they gave to the Republican party. Blacks were assumed to be irredeemably passive and conformist.

As they flooded into the cities the Urban League endeavored to find jobs for them and to educate them out of rural, southern habits. It was perfectly acceptable to sit on the front porch of a shanty beside a red clay Georgia road, for example, talking and eating watermelon and flinging the rind out beyond the porch where the pigs would soon gobble it up. But to sit on a porch on the South Side and do the same thing created trouble with the neighbors.

That was the last thing most black people needed. Racial tensions were already at a dangerous pitch. All through the summer of 1919 racial tension boiled up in northern cities with their new, desperately overcrowded black communities. When such anger rose up, the frontier resort to lynch law was never far away. Since 1890 this lingering emotional involvement with the pioneer past had taken 3,000 lives, male and female, white and black.[47] In 1919 at least one lynching was advertised. The *Jackson Daily News* (Miss.) reported the arrest of a suspected black rapist and announced: "The officers have agreed to turn him over to the people of the city at four o'clock this afternoon, when it is expected he will be burned."[48]

The first riot came in May when a scuffle broke out between a black man and a group of white youths at a fairground in Charleston, South Carolina. White sailors rampaged through the streets, broke into shooting galleries at the fair to arm themselves, and used their looted rifles on fleeing blacks. Two were killed and seventeen wounded.

The next month, in Longview, Texas, a black man named Lemuel Walters was discovered to be having an affair with a married woman who happened to be white. In the South, it was rape when a black man had sexual relations with a white woman, even if she consented, even if she seduced him. Walters's naked body was found near the railroad tracks outside town.

A local black high school teacher, S. L. Jones, sent an account of his investigation of the killing to the *Chicago Defender*. Jones was beaten up on the street and told to get out of Longview or die. His friends armed themselves and prepared to defend Jones's home. A party of white men stormed the house late one night. A volley of gunfire left four of the raiders dead on the lawn.

In the early hours of the morning, a white mob said to be a thousand strong broke into the hardware store downtown and stripped it of dozens of rifles, shotguns, and revolvers. Boxes of ammunition were broken up, and men filled their pockets with bullets and shells. But Jones and his defenders had already fled. His house and five others owned by "uppity" (middle-class) blacks were burned down. An elderly black man related to one of Jones's defenders was brutally murdered in cold blood. Only when Texas Rangers moved in was order restored to Longview.[49]

On July 20 an altercation between whites and blacks on Pennsylvania Avenue brought the riots to the seat of government. Soldiers, sailors, and Marines raided restaurants and trolley cars to drag helpless blacks into the streets where they were mercilessly beaten and kicked. Six people died, more than 100 were injured. Order was restored by federal troops and a torrential summer storm.

Horrifying as these riots were, the worst was yet to come. In Chicago, emotions mounted steadily as the thermometer rose into the nineties. By late July, 25 percent of Chicago's work force was either on strike or threatening to strike. The city had the most unionized working class in the country. But blacks were strongly antiunion. And why not? The unions were almost solidly antiblack. There were sporadic labor clashes in the stockyards that summer, "all racially inspired."[50]

Blacks were not exactly newcomers to Chicago. The city's first permanent resident was black. Jean Baptiste Point de Saible had come from San Dominica and built a trading post at the mouth of the Chicago River in 1779. The trading post had flourished. But ever since Jean Baptiste moved into the neighborhood, blacks had trouble finding somewhere to live.

Before the war there had been nearly 50,000 blacks in Chicago. By the summer of 1919 that figure had virtually tripled.[51] As blacks arrived they squeezed into already overcrowded poor white neighborhoods. Since mid-1917 there had been a bombing a month of houses that blacks had moved into, or of the homes of white realtors who dealt with black clients.

In June 1919 the clashes turned deadly. In separate incidents two black youths were murdered, without provocation, by gangs of young white toughs. At parks, playgrounds, and beaches blacks were knocked about or threatened with violence. On two occasions hundreds of extra police had been summoned at the double to defuse potential race riots.

As July wore on, there was little respite from the heat. Ten blocks south of Grant Park, hemmed in by the railway tracks skirting the lake shore, was a dreary stretch of sand cooled by lake breezes. A tacit understanding had evolved in recent years that whites would keep to the southern end of the beach and blacks to the northern end at 27th Street. At 4:00 P.M. on Sunday, July 27, several black youths entered the water from the northern part of the beach. A hundred feet out from the shore they drifted southward on a crude raft they had lashed together. As they entered the white section a man began throwing rocks at them. One of the youths, seventeen-year-old Eugene Williams, suddenly sank from sight.[52]

While he was drowning, a scuffle broke out onshore between whites and blacks. It was a replay of the larger scenario: too many people, not enough room. Women and children cowered in the sand while a hail of rocks, tin cans, and bottles, hurled in anger, fell around them. Several blacks had also cornered a white man, accusing him of knocking Eugene Williams into the water with a stone. The solitary policeman on the beach refused to make an arrest.

Rumor swept along the beach and into surrounding streets: a white boy had been stoned by blacks and drowned; a white policeman was keeping rescuers back at gunpoint while a black youth was drowning; whites and blacks were clubbing one another to death and the beach was red with blood. In truth, swimmers of both races were diving valiantly for more than an hour in an attempt to find the boy.

But on the beach passions still ran high. And then a white man accused a black man of assaulting him. A policeman was summoned and made an arrest. The black crowd vented its anger by mobbing the policeman and setting his captive free. Whites fell with fury on the black crowd. The riot had begun.

Police from the neighborhood were arriving on the beach in twos and threes. Fights were breaking out all over the five-block stretch of sand. A black man named James Crawford pulled out a revolver and fired into a squad of policemen running toward him. A black policeman returned fire, killing Crawford with a single shot. As darkness fell, gangs of whites began moving into black neighborhoods all over the South Side. Violence flared throughout the night.

On Monday, white mobs charged trolley cars bringing black workers home. Blacks retaliated by murdering whites. Monday night, carloads of whites raced through South Side streets blasting away with rifles and shot-guns.

Tuesday morning the trolley cars stayed in their sheds. People who had to walk to work virtually took their lives in their hands. The violence spread into the Loop, Chicago's downtown business district. Servicemen in uniform dragged blacks from restaurants, hotels, and railroad stations, beat them unconscious or shot them out of hand before rifling their pock-ets, stripping rings from unresisting fingers, and tearing watches from wrists. That night dozens of black homes were vandalized and some were set on fire.

On Wednesday the police were desperate for rest. For days neither the mayor, William Thompson, nor the governor, Frank Lowden, would take responsibility for calling out the National Guard. With the police at the end of their string, Thompson had no choice. The guardsmen ap-peared on the street shortly before midnight. As they took up positions rain began to fall—heavy, steady, chilling. It broke the oppressive heat and drove people indoors.

Thursday dawned on a city that was sopping wet and suddenly peace-ful. On Saturday fire swept through the Back of the Yards, gutting a neighborhood occupied mainly by Polish and Lithuanian families. Forty-nine homes burned down.

The riot had taken 38 lives (23 black, 15 white), injured 537 people, and made a further 1,000 homeless and destitute. Eugene Williams's body was recovered from Lake Michigan. The coroner found no marks to show that the youth had been struck by anything. He had simply drowned.

The Chicago riot was not the end or even the beginning of the end. In August, race riots erupted in Knoxville, Tennessee, and Caldwell, Georgia.[53] In September there was a dramatic racial clash in Omaha. As in Chicago, there had been racial friction in the packing plants all sum-mer. The press carried sensationalized accounts of blacks molesting white women. Inevitably, when a black man was arrested and charged with rape, a mob converged on the jail.

The mayor, Edward P. Smith, mounted the courthouse steps to plead with the lynchers. To taunts of "nigger-lover," Smith was seized. A rope was put around his neck and an attempt made to hang him from a trolley pole. Before Smith expired, the police fought their way through the crowd and cut the rope. The courthouse, which contained the jail, was set on fire. The accused rapist was dragged out, shot, hanged from a lamppost, and his body burned. The mob proceeded to rampage through the city. Four people were killed. Once again it took heavy rain and troops to restore order.[54]

In October, friction between black tenants and white landowners in southern Arkansas produced a rural tragedy that matched urban blood-shed. Black tenants crowded into a church at Hoop Spur in Phillips County to organize a farmers' union. A shooting affray broke out that left a white deputy sheriff wounded and his white companion dead. Rumors swept the state that a black uprising was under way. The governor wired Washington for federal troops. Three hundred special deputies were hastily sworn in.

For a week posses thrashed about in the canebreaks searching for armed blacks. Any black man acting suspiciously risked being shot on sight. The only blacks who were allowed out of doors were those carrying a letter from a white employer vouching for their loyalty. Five whites and at least twenty-five blacks were killed in this landlord versus tenant war. Nearly 100 blacks were sent to prison.[55]

Lynch mobs were no southern monopoly. In Duluth, in June 1920, a mob stormed the jail and murdered three black prisoners.[56] And one of the worst riots of the era occurred in 1921 after the superheated atmosphere of the first year of peace had passed into history. In Tulsa, on the night of June 1–2, a white mob raged through the black quarter, killing at will, setting homes and businesses on fire. A black youth had entered an elevator, stumbled against the girl who was operating it, and accidentally stepped on her toes. The girl screamed; the youth ran. A rumor quickly spread that a black man had raped a white girl in an elevator. It was a rumor that cost thirty lives.[57]

Behind the riots was a desire to put blacks in their place—the place they had occupied before the war. The New York Times spelled it out in an editorial on the Washington race riot: "The majority of Negroes in Washington before the great war, were well-behaved . . . most of them admitted the superiority of the white race and troubles between the two races were unheard of."[58]

But the message of the riots was plain: there was no going back. When racial violence broke out, blacks no longer allowed themselves to be slaughtered. In Longview, in Chicago, in Arkansas, they had armed themselves and fought back.

There was another change as well. In the summer of 1923 a black man named Walter Lee was arrested in Savannah, Georgia, and accused of raping a white woman. A mob formed and tried to rush the jail.

The sheriff, his deputies, and the mayor held fast under a shower of bricks and a volley of gunfire. One man was killed, several badly wounded. The militia were summoned. Martial law was declared. Scores of rioters were arrested. But Walter Lee remained unmolested in jail.[59]

5. Pioneers! O Pioneers!

I

Walt Whitman's pioneers, with their "diet hard and the blanket on the ground," cast long shadows deep into the twentieth century.* Frederick Jackson Turner, who had delivered the funeral oration over the frontier, was still alive, still writing, in the 1920s. Alive, too, were semilegendary characters of the Old West, such as Wyatt Earp, Bat Masterson, and Annie Oakley.

Adjustment to the social problems created by industrialization came slowly, because there had for so long been an alternative to it for working people—the frontier. Approaches to that adjustment were halfhearted until after the free land was gone. Out West, life retained a vigorous, spacious character that came as a shock to the foreign visitor of the Twenties.[1] That character lived on to a large extent where one might least expect it: at the very bottom of the working class, among the million men who lived a migratory, homeless existence—the hobos.†

They were not bums or tramps. As one of them (who later became a sociologist) expressed it: "They are, as it were, belated frontiersmen."[2] When the frontier moved westward, these migratory workers moved in

---

* Do the feasters gluttonous feast?
Do the corpulent sleepers sleep? have they lock'd and bolted doors?
Still be ours the diet hard and the blanket on the ground,
Pioneers! O Pioneers!
† From "hoe-boy," a farm laborer.

89

behind it, to build the roads, lay railroad track, provide seasonal labor, cut timber, work the riverboats, mine coal and precious metals, and put up the telegraph lines. But the frontier had faded away. Permanent settlers had taken possession of the now-tamed wilderness.

Stranded between two worlds, the hobos created communities of their own—the hobo jungle and the hobohemia. There were thousands of jungles; most were temporary, but some lasted for decades. Carved out in the woods near a railroad junction, the jungles were far from being what their name suggested. They were neat and unobtrusive. The hobo in the jungle kept his clothes well washed and in good repair. He was adept at campfire cookery. He delighted in the easy, democratic manners of his companions. Most jungles raised no color bar. They harked back to the honesty, cleanliness, frugality, and friendship of the cow camps on the open range, where utensils and furnishings were left for use by all and in the ownership of none. In the jungles, as in the cow camps, nothing was more shameful than wastefulness or stealing.

To the hobo, life in the jungle was warm, whereas the city was cold and harsh. Men who had known this life when young remembered it fondly, even if they broke away from it later. Typical was the reminiscence that ran, "Nothing appeals to my imagination any stronger than an evening in the 'jungle' after a good supper, to lean back and smoke and tell stories of adventure, and be free, out in the open spaces."[3]

The hobo preferred to pay his way through life by hard and honest toil. But when times were hard and jobs scarce, some were reduced to panhandling. Still, the man who was careful might live on a dollar a day in the city. And "If he is not too fastidious he can live for sixty cents, including a bed every night."[4]

His transportation was provided by the railroads. With money he could "ride the cushions." As a rule he would "ride the rods" (underneath a railroad car) or climb into an empty boxcar. He might, if he was in a hurry, take a passenger instead of a freight and "ride the blinds"—the narrow space between the engine and the first car. There he would straddle the coupling equipment and hold fast to it. It was a dangerous and sooty place to be.

There were dangers enough in the hobo life. There were those such as Carl Panzram, for example, who were both hobos and criminals. Self-educated and possessing great strength, Panzram's preferred reading was Nietzsche and Schopenhauer. His considered opinion on life was that most people were better off dead. Panzram typified the worst of the rootless men, drifting from town to town, burglary to burglary, anal rape to anal rape, and murder to murder.[5]

The law, too, posed dangers. Martin Tabert, an eighteen-year-old farm boy, was typical of thousands when he ran away from his family in South Dakota to take up the hobo life in 1921 on a quest for work and adventure. In December he was arrested in Florida on a vagrancy charge —a hazard that every 'bo faced. Convicted, Martin Tabert was unable to pay his $25 fine. He was bound over to work it off as a convict laborer in a lumber camp. This, too, was not unusual. But in January 1922 he died from the effects of a merciless flogging from a company supervisor. His death was reported as a case of malaria.[6] Vagrancy charges, convict labor, police brutality, the rootless psychopath—all were elements of the hobo life.

When winter set in, hobo jungles became cold and wet, construction crews were laid off, logging camps were buried in snow and ice, the fields were bare of crops and men. The hobos rode the rods and the blinds and the freight cars back to the cities. There they waited out the weather in the hobohemias that merged with the skid rows. Chicago had the largest hobohemia with a winter population of 75,000.

In hobohemia the saloon defied Prohibition. There would be a saloon or two on every block, mixed in with the cheap dives, missions, flophouses, pawnshops, barber colleges, secondhand clothing stores and employment agencies. There was also, among the predictable business establishments for the poor, something else: the radical bookshop. Among these poor, straddling for a generation the ground between the frontier and the industrial society, a home-grown radical movement briefly flourished. This was the age of the Wobblies.

II

Social and economic conditions in the logging camps, on the vast ranches, or down in the western mines were volatile and raw. There was no middle class, only employers and workers, frequently divided still further by differences of language, ethnic background, and moral values. Yet they were yoked together by mutual need in conditions that verged on the claustrophobic. The rule in these communities was usually autocratic, while the spirit of the men who worked there was democratic. Such powerful antagonisms often exploded into violence. In the logging camps especially, conditions had not changed much since frontier times:

> The typical logging camp lay at the end of a railroad spur or dirt-road leading down through desolate cut-over lands to a small town in a valley. In Idaho or Montana, the camp might not even boast a road or a railroad connecting it to civilization, but rely instead upon a wild mountain river down which the logs

were floated and up which the camp's supplies came. A half dozen or more rough shacks served as bunkhouses for the working crews. Outside the huddled ring of shacks stood the foreman's office, the camp store, the "cookie's" shack with its garbage piles and its swarms of flies, and the latrines. About two dozen men, oftentimes more, slept in each bunkhouse in fetid congestion. . . . Loggers worked in all kinds of weather and frequently returned to camp in wet and muddy clothes. Most camps had no facilities for bathing or for drying clothes, and the men ate the leaden supper of cheap starches and greases while sitting in their wet clothes. After supper the men would gather in the yard in sullen groups to wait for darkness to drift up from the valley below before they squeezed into the crowded bunkhouse.[7]

The bunkhouse probably had no windows. The air inside would be thick and heavy with the smell of pipe smoke, sweat, tobacco juice, and drying clothes. No wonder that when the talk got around to politics it usually ran in a radical vein. Similar conditions, similar talk, could be found in other places worked by migratory labor.

These uneducated men would read and argue over some of the most formidable political and philosophical works of the modern world. They were mostly men in their thirties and forties, men who had never known the security and warmth of happy, stable homes, men who had known little of the love given by a woman or child. The only home that many of them knew was not the fetid bunkhouse owned by the hated company, but the IWW hall. The only family that such men recognized were fellow Wobblies. The only leader they acknowledged was Big Bill Haywood.[8]

He had been born on the frontier: Salt Lake City, 1869. William D. Haywood grew up in western mining towns where massacres, lynchings, and "shooting scrapes" were everyday events, yet where a thirst for culture made the arrival of the Lightning Calculator, who performed prodigies of mental arithmetic, an occasion to be celebrated. Rough young miners a century ago carried well-thumbed volumes of Voltaire, Darwin, Burns, or Milton in their packs. Bill Haywood's own great love was Shakespeare.

Even as an adolescent he was massive. But zest for the rough-and-tumble games of boyhood had cost him an eye while whittling a slingshot. Barely in his teens, the strapping Haywood left home to prospect for gold and silver. He punched cows and tried homesteading. In an abandoned army fort he was midwife at his daughter's birth, hurriedly reading "the doctor book" as he worked. When he claimed his 160-acre homestead he built his own house, barn, and outbuildings, put up his own fences, dug his own ditches. To earn some ready cash he went back to the mines for a few months each year. Then the homestead he had built up with government sanction was taken away without compensation when the area was given back to the Indians.

Haywood became a teamster for a time, but once again went back into the mines. Only now when the talk after work turned radical did Haywood begin to organize the men to give weight to their protests.[9] In 1893 the Western Federation of Miners, with Haywood as secretary-treasurer, came into existence in the wake of several bitter strikes and lockouts.[10]

Over the next twelve years his integrity, ability, and energy made Bill Haywood one of the most important labor leaders in the United States. Six feet, three inches tall, with wide shoulders and massive arms, unruly black hair, and one glittering black eye, Haywood had tremendous presence. There was also a rough-hewn simplicity and directness in his manner that won people to him heart and soul. Haywood was one of the most thrilling orators ever to come out of the West. But so long as the WMF was concerned by definition only with the grievances of miners, Haywood's abilities were contained within a narrow channel.

In 1905 he broke fresh ground. The aim was nothing less than the organization of the entire working class within a single union. Its ultimate goal was nothing less than the capture of power through a workers' takeover of industry. At a secret conference in Chicago, attended by delegates of a score of labor organizations, the Industrial Workers of the World came into existence.[11] Haywood chaired the conference. In time he became chairman of the IWW.

The IWW came into the world with a roar. The preamble to its constitution began: "The working class and the employing class have nothing in common. There can be no peace so long as hunger and want are found among millions of working people and the few, who make up the employing class, have all the good things in life. Between these two classes a struggle must go on until the workers of the world organize as a class, take possession of the earth and the machinery of production, and abolish the wage system."

To themselves, said Ralph Chaplin, Wobbly poet, artist, and author of "Solidarity Forever," they were, "in our own estimation at least, the world's only simon-pure rebels—the revolutionary proletariat."[12] The AFL was mocked as "the American Separation of Labor." Machinery was sometimes sabotaged, euphemistically termed "striking on the job." An all-out IWW strike was like a revolution in miniature. "Organizers moved in on spontaneous outbursts of mass rebellion, gave them leadership to the extent of fiery and thrilling oratory, spurning negotiations and compromises, and personally led wild, bloody clashes with the police."[13]

Because anarchism was generally believed to be an infection brought in by immigrants, most people became convinced that the IWW was a variant of communism, financed by Bolshevik gold. Yet this was not the anarchocommunism which looked to the creation of a revolutionary party which would seize power in the name of the dictatorship of the proletariat. This was the proletariat being urged to organize a general strike, then seize the factories and farms for themselves. There was, moreover, a strong streak of agrarian contempt for all "nonproducers" that was typical of the old frontier.[14]

Wherever they went—and they went almost everywhere—the Wobblies left their mark, usually an IWW sticker. "It was said that every boxcar in the country carried at least one good reason for joining the IWW," said Chaplin, who had designed most of the stickers himself.[15] These "silent agitators" appeared for more than twenty years on factory gates, bunkhouse walls, pick handles, shovels, lampposts, billboards, jail cells, and skid-row flophouses.

At some time most transient workers joined the IWW, but dedicated Wobblies were a minority. During harvest time IWW "organizers" rode the freight trains to conduct "boxcar recruiting." This consisted of throwing off anyone without the red IWW membership card. Many a hobo paid his dollar in the spirit of the man who takes out insurance.

Although the IWW frightened a large part of the middle class, it was doomed from the start. It was trying to ride two horses at once. It wanted to be both a mass union and a revolutionary party. It never became either. And two events in 1917 marked its inevitable demise—America's entry into the war and the outbreak of the Russian Revolution.

The IWW denounced the war as another bourgeois crime against ordinary working people throughout the world. Yet after April 1917 it called only three strikes (compared with 2,000 sanctioned by the "'patriotic" AFL). The IWW was vulnerable: many of its members were foreigners with strange accents and strange-sounding names, and they were concentrated in industries vital to the war effort—metal mines, lumber, and agriculture. There were countless acts of violence against them. In Tulsa on November 9, 1917, nearly a score of Wobblies were publicly tortured "in the name of the women and children of Belgium."[16]

Haywood, Chaplin, and thirty-eight other IWW officials were arrested in a raid on the Chicago headquarters in the spring of 1918. They were charged with "10,000 specific crimes," chiefly in speaking and writing against the war. Convicted, they received from federal Judge Kenesaw Mountain Landis sentences ranging from four to twenty years. Prosecutions of this type during and after the war, in federal and state courts, sent nearly 3,000 IWW members to prison, nearly always on the basis of fiery utterances, hardly ever on proof of a violent act.

In the Pacific Northwest the return of peace saw the lumber companies trying to roll back the wartime gains of loggers and sawmill workers. Not that these gains amounted to much. Lumber prices had risen as much as 1000 percent in only two years, while wages went up by 10 cents an hour. The IWW in the summer of 1917 had organized a strike in the woods that paralyzed the logging camps. Government and the lumber companies called it treason. Thousands of strikers were jailed. The War Department organized its own union, the Loyal Legion of Loggers and Lumbermen (the 4–Ls). This was a union with a difference. Every member took an oath which pledged, "I will stamp out any sedition or acts of hostility against the United States which may come within my knowledge." [17]

After the war the 4–Ls stayed in business. The IWW denounced it as a sellout to the ruling class. Yet the 4–Ls had introduced the eight-hour day into the woods and it was cleaning up the worst conditions in the logging camps.

The 1917 strike left a heritage of bitter hostility throughout the tall timberlands. In early 1918 the Wobblies had opened a hall in Centralia, Washington, for the first time. Centralia was a typical timber town with an economy based almost entirely on its sawmills and a population of 20,000. The IWW hall was also typical of its kind: more than a union hall, it was club, mess hall, dormitory, and mail drop. Young men in rough work clothes could be found each evening brewing a mulligan stew, arguing over economics or theology, reading Socialist or IWW newspapers, singing their way through the famous IWW *Songbook* around a battered piano, and hawking into the bronze spittoons.

Shortly after the hall in Centralia opened, a Red Cross parade was routed past it. Some of the marchers broke away and smashed the doors and windows. Wobblies were beaten up, their poor furniture was dragged outside, their literature was made into a bonfire in the street. A local glove manufacturer stole the phonograph; the chairman of the local Chamber of Commerce took the desk. The bleeding Wobblies were dragged into a truck, driven out of town, beaten up again, and warned against coming back. The sole Wobbly sympathizer left in Centralia was a blind newspaper seller named Tom Lassiter. He, too, was beaten up in due course, kidnaped, taken out of town, and thrown into a ditch. [18]

For more than a year the IWW stayed clear of Centralia until in September 1919 the Wobblies opened a new hall. Since the Seattle general strike a reinvigorated IWW was asserting itself throughout the Pacific Northwest. Reopening the Centralia hall was a challenge.

In October came the response. A group of local businessmen and

American legionnaires formed the Centralia Protective Association. The Legion had for some time been planning a parade for the Armistice Day celebrations. Rumor went around town that the planned festivities featured yet another raid on the IWW hall.

The Wobblies sought police protection and were promised nothing. A local lawyer, Elmer Smith, advised them that they had the same right as anyone else to defend themselves and their property. The IWW men armed themselves, but they also printed and distributed a leaflet which begged the people of Centralia to leave them alone. They warned that any attack on their hall would be strongly resisted.

The parade plans called for a march past the IWW hall not once, but twice. As the parade was passing the hall for the second time the Centralia platoon of the American Legion halted, ostensibly to dress ranks. But some men broke away. They ran toward the IWW hall. When they reached the door they were met by a hail of gunfire. Three legionnaires fell dead, a dozen others were wounded.

The hall was sacked; the IWW men were rounded up. Only one, Wesley Everest, had escaped. He fled toward the Skookumchuck River. A posse tracked him down as he tried to ford it and was forced back by the current. Everest stood in the river up to his waist. A young Legionnaire and local football hero, Dale Hubbard, plunged through the water to seize him. When Hubbard refused to go back, Everest shot him with his last bullet. Hubbard fell dead in the water.

Everest was overpowered and taken back to Centralia with all his teeth knocked out. That night, the lights went out all over town. A mob broke into the prison. According to IWW lore, Wesley Everest was dragged outside shouting, "Tell the boys I died for my class!"[19]

On a rapid ride down to the Chehalis River, Everest was castrated with a hunting knife. He begged his captors to shoot him and end his agonies. At the river he was hanged by a short rope from the railroad bridge, hauled up while still conscious, and hanged again with another, longer rope. Pulled up once more, he was hanged once more. Dead at last, his body was illuminated by car headlights. It still provided sport: the lynch mob emptied their guns into Everest's corpse. This shredded, sodden body with a neck that was a foot long was later cut down and dumped in the Centralia jail for the edification of Everest's fellow IWW members.[20]

The Centralia massacre set off raids on Wobblies in other cities—Tacoma, Seattle, Spokane, Oakland. In Los Angeles, the IWW headquarters was sacked and the people found there, men and women alike, forced to choose between running a gamut of club-wielding vigilantes or jumping from the second-story window. "Several preferred to jump."[21]

The county coroner's report on Wesley Everest turned in a verdict of suicide. After breaking out of jail, the report concluded, the deceased had hanged himself, but drew a revolver before expiring and shot himself several times. Then, with his ebbing strength, he unsheathed a knife, reached up, and cut the rope. Falling into the river, he drowned.[22]

Ten IWW members and Elmer Smith were tried for the Centralia killings. Throughout their trial, at Montesano, state militia camped on the courthouse lawn. The defendants were charged with first-degree murder. The trial turned not so much on the blatant, occasionally laughable, attempts to intimidate the jury, but on the judge's rulings as to what evidence might be admitted, which witnesses might be heard. When the first judge made several rulings that made a sound legal defense possible, the governor swiftly replaced him. There was no proof that any of the defendants had fired even one shot in the hail of bullets that greeted the legionnaires. Elmer Smith was acquitted on a directed verdict. Two other defendants were acquitted by the jury. A fourth had gone insane. The remaining seven were found guilty of second-degree murder and received sentences ranging from twenty-five to forty years.

After the trial dozens of affidavits were collected, including several from legionnaires, which swore that the shooting had started only after the IWW hall was rushed. Half the Montesano jury admitted they had felt coerced into handing down guilty verdicts. But the seven men remained in prison a long time, where they found many other IWW men to keep them company.

The Wobblies were the most colorful element in the large American prison population of the Twenties. They had the strongest discipline and they turned their ample leisure time to serious reading. They never applied for parole. They looked upon the hardest, dirtiest jobs in prison as theirs by right. They would have refused easy jobs if offered them. To some hardened criminals the IWW men gave even the toughest prisons, such as San Quentin, the only example of nobility they were ever likely to witness.[23]

But in the world outside the walls, the IWW had lost much of its old militancy. Violence, trials, prisons, leading to more violence, trials, prisons, did nothing to bring about the One Big Union of the working class. The IWW leadership turned its attention to "education" and "research." For a time its resident genius was an engineer named Howard Scott.

Chaplin, released on bail from Leavenworth while his appeal was being heard, met Scott toward the end of 1919. Tall and talkative, Scott poured out figures like an adding machine in the hands of a feverish bookkeeper. He urged the IWW to create a Bureau of Industrial Research to survey the nation's industrial plant. After all, how would they be able to run this plant when they took power if they knew almost nothing about it? "His tall body spread on an untidy sofa, smoking innumerable cigarettes, Scott proceeded to marshal impressive arguments to prove that social revolution was a job for the engineer as well as the proletariat," said Chaplin. "But I resented the Bohemian atmosphere in which Scott seemed to thrive. All the time he was discoursing so plausibly about teardrop automobiles, flying wing airplanes and technological unemployment, I was looking at the other side of the studio where an appalling phallic watercolor painting was displayed among blueprints and graphs on a big easel."[24]

Scott's involvement with the IWW lasted only a year, but his influence was pervasive. Through the adoption of his ideas these belated frontiersmen tried to come to terms with the impersonal modern forces of mechanization and standardization. All through the Twenties IWW halls and newspapers resounded to arguments over the partnership of technicians and workers. And in time, Scott, jokingly termed "Great Scott" behind his back, would one day make a brief but spectacular reappearance on the national scene.

Meanwhile, Bill Haywood, out on bail from Leavenworth, was fleeing to the Soviet Union aboard *Oscar II*, Henry Ford's ill-fated "peace ship" of 1916.[25] Chaplin had been offered the same opportunity to flee but turned it down. When the Supreme Court rejected his appeal, he went back to Leavenworth.

Haywood lived on in Moscow, gnawed at by the thought that he had betrayed his friends and his ideals, skeptical of the American Communists with whom he had taken up, in despair over the treatment of ordinary people in the workers' paradise. It was a sorry thing for a man who had grown up on the free and open frontier to end his days living on the crumbs that fell from Stalin's table.

III

There was one place where the frontier in all its roughness and vitality lived on far into the Twenties. When the war ended, there was a widespread belief that the United States was fast running out of oil. The Bureau of Mines reported that half the country's oil reserves were exhausted. As the reserves ran dry, imports began for the first time to flow in. Dire warnings were sounded that industrial collapse was inevitable. By the 1970s, ran the conventional wisdom, the world would have run out of oil.[26]

Oil prices soared. In Texas, $7 million was said to have been refused for a 160-acre lease. Oil wildcatters were roaming the countryside, their pockets stuffed with blank lease forms. Plots as small as 1/100 of an acre were diligently drilled. Royalty shares as small as 1/800 of an acre were carved out.[27] It did not take much to get into the oil game. And the results really could be beyond the dreams of avarice.

At the end of July 1918 a group of wildcatters had brought in the Burkburnett Pool on the Red River, northeast of Houston, then little more than a nondescript cow town. Burkburnett was one of the biggest oil bonanzas in history. "It became impossible to walk down the streets of any important American city without encountering a store window with the immemorial sign of the dealer in wildcat oil stocks—a miniature wooden derrick and rig, operated by an unseen electric motor, pumping some black fluid into a little tank."[28]

Oil stock promoters were usually flamboyant, plausible, and unscrupulous. They drew the suckers from far and wide. On one occasion when postal inspectors raided a promoter's office they found it so full of mail sacks they could hardly open the door. "The letters had not been answered, but the checks had been removed."[29]

All across the Southwest, tenant farmers were abandoning the land and their families to look for oil. Returning veterans swarmed into the oil fields to work as roustabouts. Many headed for Burkburnett. They knew nothing about the work. The put up tents and shanties and waited for opportunity to come their way. Winter arrived first. They froze in their hovels. Eight people, mainly women and children, were found frozen to death in Burkburnett in the winter of 1919–20.

The hunt for oil spread from Texas and Oklahoma into the surrounding states—Arkansas, Louisiana, New Mexico, Kansas. Oil had been drilled for in Arkansas back in 1917 without much success. Then in 1920 the El Dorado field in Union County was brought in and soon supported 100 wells. Here was an area thick with timber, with virtually nothing that could be called a road. The summer heat was exhausting, the winter rains heavy and prolonged. But by the spring of 1921 El Dorado had 500 wells, many of them flowing wild.

The next year brought an even bigger strike in southern Arkansas when, in April, a gas well blew up, leaving a crater 50 feet deep and 450 feet across. It could be smelled a mile away. It was filled to the brim with blue-black oil. The nearby hamlet of Smackover boasted a population of 150. Two years later the population topped 20,000 and the postmaster sent a telegram to Washington in protest: "Office out of my control; letters arriving 5000 to 7000 a day; parcel post by the ton; accept my resignation."[30]

Smackover and its neighbors, Louann, El Dorado, and Griffin, were struggling with unpaved roads that for half the year were no more than knee-deep mud. One mudhole alone was reputed to have swallowed up to sixteen mules in a single day. There were malarial swamps, wild razorbacks, and "The Largest Oil Well in America," according to a sign on one of the washed-out roads. It took three days to cap that huge well, during which time it shot a stream of oil six inches thick 200 feet into the air.

"The shacks of Louann came in sight," a visitor wrote. "Eager faces were flattened against the glass. . . . Louann's business street was lighted with natural gas, hollow iron poles stuck into the ground connected in primitive fashion with the surface gas line which is laid entirely through the field, with a torch on top. The ghostly flickering revealed Louann's freshly painted welcome to the world: 'Eventually, Why Not Now? Louann—The Town of No Regrets!' Shouts of derisive laughter swept the dimly lighted car."[31]

Across the Southwest an estimated 250,000 men were moving across the landscape in search of oil. They drilled 20,000 wells a year, more than 90 percent of which produced only air and water. But those few men who made a big strike became legendary figures all over the oil fields. The legends were, invariably, about the men who had refused to give up, men like Blake Smith, who had a hunch about an impoverished village 100 miles south of Dallas, a place called Mexia.

Blake Smith drilled ten dry holes on the strength of his hunch. Broke and exhausted, he went one morning to say farewell to his career in the oil game by looking at his most recent dry hole. Just as he said good-bye, gas bubbled up from the hole. He scraped a few hundred dollars together and drilled deeper. He found nothing, not even more gas. But he found Colonel A. E. Humphreys, "the King of the Wildcatters," and formed a partnership.

The colonel soon departed the insalubrious air of Mexia for the cooler climate of the Gulf, at Galveston. Each day a telegram from Smith arrived at the Western Union office. If the news was bad, a white flag was hoisted from the roof so the colonel might see it from the beach. Each evening the colonel wired to Mexia: "Drill deeper." He too had a hunch. On November 19, 1920, after drilling as deep as anyone had ever tried to go, a new flag appeared above the Galveston Western Union office, this time bright red.

Mexia was one of the biggest fields ever brought in. In four months the population rose from 3,000 to 25,000. "Boys peddled water in the streets at five cents a glass. A cot in a hallway cost $2.50 a night."[32] Towns like this were as rough and dangerous as any on the old frontier. Mexia had so many robberies and murders it had to be placed under martial law.

Burkburnett spawned Bradley's Corners, which claimed to be "the wicked-est town that ever existed." Social life revolved around the Bucket of Blood Dance Hall. Shootings in Mexia were too commonplace to excite much interest.[33]

Meanwhile, up in Wyoming, there was a roustabout named Robert S. Lynd, who would one day become one of the most famous sociologists of the twentieth century. He was working in the Elk Basin field for $4.00 a day. He put in a seven-day week, lived in a community of tar-paper shacks, relied on cistern water that tasted so foul it had to be brewed as tea before it was (just) drinkable. Women and baths were equally rare. Yet, despite the harshness of this life, Lynd enjoyed the company of his fellow roust-abouts. "Their easy raillery bespoke an open air life free from the grosser fatigues of the machine operator."[34] Elk Basin, three miles long and a mile wide, was "literally a hole in the ground, gouged out of the naked clay and sandstone. No water, no trees, no grass—not a living, growing thing in sight save the straggling sage brush." And thrust upon this bleakness were the derricks, a cluster of clapboard bunkhouses and bungalows, dozens of tar-paper shacks, and the snaking pipelines that led out to a modern, industrialized world that had suddenly developed an insatiable thirst for oil.

IV

The people who came to prominence and power in the Twenties were mainly people who had grown up in the predominantly agricultural world that was just this side of the frontier. A strong current of nostalgia ran throughout the entire decade. "As I look back on it," one man recalled, "I constantly think how clean it was. There was little about it that was artificial. It was all close to nature and in accordance with the ways of nature. The streams ran clear. The roads, the woods, the fields, the people —all was clean."[35] It was plainly a moral reference as well as a physical one. Such elegiacal memories were common to millions of urban dwell-ers.

They regarded their pioneer ancestors with something like awe, per-haps because the spirit seemed oddly cramped at times in the new age that was opening up. In 1900 the idea that people could be sent to jail on account of their opinions, for example, would have been thought ob-viously absurd; no intelligent person would have taken it seriously.[36]

To foreign visitors who had known the United States before the war, the *real* America and the *real* American seemed to be vanishing. What they recalled was an Anglo-Saxon country with something of the air of

Colonial times still to be found.[37] Arthur Conan Doyle, returning in 1922 after an absence of fifteen years, was surprised and saddened. "The older generation was hirsute, angular, full of whimsical character and humorous exaggeration; as different as possible from their quiet, efficient successors. There was something we used to think typically American in the intense individuality of the men of the last century."[38]

Nostalgia was expressed in various ways. There were outbursts of resentment at the change from rural to urban life, such as the Klan both expressed and exploited. There was also an upsurge of interest in the ballads of the old frontier. Parties would be spun out for hours to pianoside renditions of "The Cowboy's Lament," "Frankie and Johnny," "Oh, Susannah!" and other favorites gleaned from one of the big best-sellers of the Twenties, a collection entitled *Songs My Mother Never Taught Me*.

The hazy glow of nostalgia obscured the less pleasant features of the old life. What was forgotten was the cost to families of all that rugged individualism, of a country rapidly pushing westward, rapidly industrializing, rapidly urbanizing, and taking in millions of immigrants. Life was turbulent and harsh. Drunkenness had been a common sight in nearly every city and town. Drug addiction, often linked to patent medicines laced wth narcotics, was widespread. So too was venereal disease: 10 percent of the men inducted into the wartime army had syphilis.[39] As family life crumbled, the number of children and young women reduced by poverty and brutality to lives of prostitution was enormous.

It was the effort to save family life that inspired a wide range of reform movements at the turn of the century. The result, in time, was the Harrison Narcotics Act, the Mann White Slave Act, and the Prohibition amendment. Protection of the family had become more important in the modern world than the individual's right to do as he pleased.

Still, the earlier generation did have something that people needed and missed: a sense of belonging to a coherent society. In morality, there was puritanism; in culture, the Anglo-Saxon literary heritage; in politics, belief in progress. On this trinity the Late Victorian age had gone about its business. It was a trinity that had seemed as fixed as the stars in the night sky.[40] Yet now when an American raised his eyes in search of a bright, invariable point he was likely to find himself staring into a cold and yawning blackness.

6. The Right Time

I

By February 1920 President Wilson was lucid most of the time. One of his first actions on recovering was to fire Robert Lansing. The President spoke and acted as if this were the first he had heard of the Cabinet meetings Lansing had called to discuss government business. And that raised doubts about the torrent of reassuring bulletins that had poured from the White House for three months. To many people in the capital there could hardly be a better time for Cabinet meetings than during a presidential illness.[1] The sacking of Lansing revived the stories that the President had lost his mind. Nor was this speculation stilled when the urbane and respected Lansing was replaced as secretary of state by an obscure lawyer on the Shipping Board named Bainbridge Colby.

Wilson was far from insane. More prosaically, he was a crotchety, embittered invalid. The world, as he saw it, had treated him badly. Even Grayson and Tumulty had served him ill. At times he thought out loud about resignation; at other times he yearned for a third term.[2] But all his thoughts kept coming back to the League and the detested Henry Cabot Lodge.

Back in 1916 the senator had been an eager advocate of Theodore Roosevelt's proposed "League to Enforce Peace." By the time of the armistice he had acquired serious doubts. He took his doubts to the bedside of the dying TR.[3] To Lodge, the League was now a matter of conscience. But as the quarrel with Wilson grew, it brought out the worst in both men.

By 1920 Lodge's objections were tainted with spite and malice. He was no isolationist. His main fear was that entering the League would curb America's freedom of action. He was, if one word could describe him, an imperialist.

His motives had become hopelessly tangled. He had concluded during the Mexican crisis of 1914 that Wilson's principal characteristics were vanity and vacillation, and nothing since then had altered his opinion. He felt betrayed by Wilson, as noted earlier. Yet he was alive to the need for some kind of international peacekeeping arrangement in which the United States played a full part. A league—perhaps; a *Wilson* league— no.[4]

He knew that there was a majority for the treaty in both Senate and nation. Had he flatly opposed it he could never have carried the Senate Foreign Relations Committee with him. His strategy was to encrust the treaty with impossible reservations—impossible, that is, for Wilson to accept.

Lodge was not alone in his misgivings. What America received from Versailles, said one of the journalists there, "was only the facts and not the truth."[5] The Allies had insisted that Germany and Austria accept sole guilt for the war. It was on this basis that Germany was required to make reparations: sole guilt made reparations moral. Otherwise they would have been no more than a venal, vengeful looting of threadbare Germans. The French dominated the Reparations Commission, which had set the figure at $32 billion plus interest. This completely unrealistic figure was a compromise. The French wanted at least $50 billion plus interest. The Germans had signed the treaty, but in their hearts and minds they repudiated the war guilt clause and with it all moral claim to reparations.

By 1920 awareness of this was growing rapidly. Among informed people there was open apprehension that the treaty would create in Germany a lust for revenge that would poison that country's political life for a generation and make another war inevitable. It was noteworthy that among the Senate Irreconcilables who aligned themselves with Lodge were Progressive stalwarts such as William Borah, James A. Reed, Hiram Johnson, George W. Norris, and Robert La Follette. Isolationism no doubt turned them against the treaty, but so did a conviction that it secured neither justice nor peace.[6]

About four-fifths of the Senate was prepared to vote for ratification in some form. There were forty-three Democrats and one Republican who would vote for the treaty; there were ten to fifteen "mild reservationists," mainly Republicans; a further twenty Republican "strong reservationists"; and finally the Irreconcilables, twelve Republicans and three Democrats in all.[7]

The treaty was presented for ratification in November 1919 while Wilson was prostrated and the Administration with him. The forty-three Democratic loyalists were instructed, however, to vote against the treaty when it appeared on the Senate floor tricked out in the Lodge amendments. It promptly went down to defeat.

It was a victory that brought Lodge little joy. He had hoped that the League would be accepted by a two-thirds vote *with* reservations festooned all over it. It would be for Wilson then to take on himself the onus of being the man who did the League—his own child—to public death, a sacrifice to his vanity and obstinacy. In seeming triumph Lodge stood dismayed. It was he who would now stand at the bar of history (that subject on which he prided himself and in which he held a Ph.D.) as the man who had wrecked the hopes of lasting peace.[8]

In March 1920, with Wilson able to provide personal direction of the fight, the treaty was presented for ratification once again. The President had lost none of his adamantine determination to have his own way down to the last comma and period: like Moses with the tablets of stone, it was to be what he had given them or nothing. Wilson did not care for an instant that Lodge's reservations were little more than platitudes and tautologies. They gave out a tub-thumping, chauvinistic sound that made them popular; it was music that Wilson himself had often made. Yet they suffered that one fatal defect—they were the work of the hated Lodge.

The loyalists were once more instructed to scuttle their ship rather than see it boarded by a dyspeptic little man with a white beard and an arrogant manner. This time not all the loyalists obeyed. The vote for the treaty, with its reservations, was 49–35; a substantial majority, but not two-thirds.[9] Had only seven more Democratic senators mutinied, the United States would have entered the League of Nations.

II

The death of Theodore Roosevelt in January 1919 made the Republican nomination stakes an open field crowded with dark horses chasing an obvious heir-apparent—General Leonard Wood. After a lifetime of seeing his achievements (for example, command of the Rough Riders, creation of the Plattsburg camps) credited to his mentor, TR, he would at last receive his reward.

Wood was a remarkable figure in his own right who had entered the army, not through West Point, but via Harvard Medical School. Out in the Arizona desert during the Geronimo campaign, Lieutenant Dr. Wood showed so much courage and zest for the fight that he won the Medal of Honor. He had presence and integrity. He also had Roosevelt's campaign

manager, John T. King. But on the run-up to the convention he dismissed
King and entrusted his fate to rich, conservative political amateurs who
were wild about Wood but ignorant about nomination politics. His mentor
now was Colonel W. Cooper Procter, the Cincinnati soap magnate. What
he had done for Lifebuoy, Procter hoped to do for Wood.

There was a comparatively new road to the nomination through the
presidential preference primary. This measure, long favored by Progressives, had by 1920 been enacted in twenty states. With the aid of Procter's
fortune, Wood traveled this road, only to be tripped up by Senator Hiram
D. Johnson of California before he reached the end of it.

Johnson was an irascible, silver-haired Progressive. People who supported Johnson the idealist often found it impossible to get along with
Johnson the man. During the war he had stood unflinchingly for free
speech and everything else in the Bill of Rights. He loathed Wall Street,
Europe, railroads, and Orientals. He was laughably vain. When elected
governor of California he had put thirty-seven newspaper editors on the
state payroll to flatter him at public expense.[10] He spoke as a rule through
clenched teeth, lending an incongruously ferocious facade to his cherubic
features. Johnson's face was pink, and when he rose to speak he looked
like a bad-tempered baby.

When he arrived at the Republican convention, however, he carried
a large scalp in his hands, that of California's adopted son, Herbert Hoover. Johnson had trounced him in the primaries. He had also beaten
Wood four times. The general had won more primaries, but the senator
had won the most votes.

More damaging still to Wood was the revelation that he had spent
$1.5 million on his campaign, a third of which came from Procter. Wood's
campaign expenses were bitingly criticized by Republican Progressives,
notably Senator William D. Borah of Idaho. He remarked that while $1.5
million was too much for the nomination, that was too little for the presidency, assuming it was for sale.[11]

The strongest opponent Wood faced was Governor Frank O. Lowden
of Illinois, an unusually competent man of decidedly liberal views. Yet he
suffered two serious handicaps—he was rich, and he was married to a
Pullman heiress. Multimillionaires were death at the polls, including railroad tycoons. Lowden was burdened, moreover, with a serious cast of
mind that made him a dull campaigner: the easy platitude died on his lips,
the shabby compromise fell apart in his hands. On the first ballot, Wood
gained 287½ votes, Lowden 211, and Johnson 133. In fourth place was
Warren G. Harding of Ohio with 65½.

Wood was not, despite Procter's lavish spending, a man who could be bought. There were persistent stories among knowledgeable men that the nomination might have been his twice over had he accepted the help offered by a crooked Oklahoma oil millionaire named Jake Hamon, or of the Pennsylvania boss Senator Boise Penrose. And, the stories concluded, Wood flatly refused to deal with either man.

Ballot after ballot produced deadlock after deadlock. Lowden and Wood took a taxi ride around the city, safe from prying newsmen. They talked for more than an hour. Yet neither could bring himself to accept second place to the other. Both were men of forceful character, and the country had endured eight years of forceful leadership. The Republicans at least were in no mood for more of the same.

Nor was Hiram Johnson anyone's logical alternative to the impasse between Lowden and Wood. Johnson was a proven Progressive; he was also a proven Irreconcilable. He had spent his entire political career taking a firm stand on anything and everything. That had left him with scores of powerful enemies. Of the four leading contenders, Harding alone had antagonized no one.

The mere fact that he came from Ohio ("Mother of Presidents"), a state that had produced six of the last ten presidents, made him a serious contender, and while he was almost no one's first choice, he was nearly every delegate's third or fourth. His true strength was therefore greater than the first few ballots suggested. From the third ballot he began to move steadily up.

Harding was not the obscure figure modern political mythology presents. He had nominated Taft at the 1912 convention. In 1914 he became one of the first men elected directly to the Senate. He was the keynote speaker at the convention of 1916. In 1919 he was being widely touted in the press as a potential nominee in 1920.[12] His candidacy was not, as most accounts suggest, due to Mrs. Harding's playing Lady Macbeth to her husband's faint-hearted ambition.[13] Harding ran for the presidency to secure his political base in Ohio, where the Republican party was badly split. As a candidate for the nomination he could put himself far above mere local squabbles. When, during the Lowden-Wood deadlock, his vote began to mount steadily from ballot to ballot, Florence Kling Harding became anxious. "I cannot see why anyone should want to be President," she told a reporter. "I can see but one word written over the head of my husband if he is elected, and that word is 'Tragedy.'"[14]

Harding spent almost nothing on his campaign. He was so short of money that he could not mount a decent challenge to Wood in his own state of Ohio. So, said Samuel Hopkins Adams, "Harding took a train for Chicago reluctantly and without hope."[15]

But back in February, Harding's campaign manager, Harry Micajah Daugherty, had taken a different view, in a moment of asperity. He was about to check out of the Waldorf-Astoria, long the hostelry of visiting provincials, when he was impeded by two determined reporters. One of them taunted the uncooperative Daugherty that because Harding could not hope to win the nomination as the convention's first choice, Daugherty must be expecting victory by manipulation, say in a smoke-filled room at two in the morning. Daugherty, a man easily irritated, was hurrying to catch an elevator. He retorted sarcastically, "Make that two eleven."[16] The story that appeared in print next day did not feature Daugherty being pestered while he wrestled with his luggage. Instead, he was reported as complacently observing, "I don't expect Senator Harding to be nominated on the first, second or third ballot. But I think we can well afford to take chances that about eleven minutes after two o'clock on Friday morning at the convention, when fifteen or twenty men, somewhat weary, are sitting around a table, some one of them will say, 'Who will we nominate?' At that decisive time the friends of Senator Harding can suggest him and afford to abide by the result."[17] Of such humble materials are political legends made.

In the early hours of Friday morning a meeting of sorts *was* held at the Blackstone Hotel, in the rooms of Colonel George M. Harvey, a putative Democrat. As publisher of *Harper's* and *North American Review*, he had been among the earliest and most influential supporters of Woodrow Wilson for the presidency. But the Democratic cause was doomed in 1920. Harvey, who loved to feel that he was at the center of events, loved to intrigue, loved to be talked about, appeared at the Republican convention.

He wore large, horn-rimmed glasses in an effort to appear wise. His vanity made it impossible for him to think clearly for long or act consistently. Tall, he carried himself with a bearing he considered suitable to that of a great personage and dressed with impeccable severity. When the Republican leadership began seeking ways to break the Lowden-Wood deadlock, Harvey was drawn into their deliberations as if he were one of them. And if Wilson were right, he was. Wilson had long since seen through Harvey, dismissing him as "an errand boy of Wall Street."[18]

The meeting at the Blackstone was desultory and broke up inconclusively. There is a story that Harding was summoned; that Harvey asked him to think if there was anything to disqualify him from the presidency; that Harding retired to an adjoining room and emerged ten minutes later to swear that his conscience was clear. The trouble with this story is that its sole source is George M. Harvey. But, the legend goes on, this cabal of

Republican senators, wreathed in cigar smoke in Suite 404, had decided to force Harding's nomination on the convention.[19]

If so, they had a bizarre way of doing it. Of the sixteen senators present at this meeting, thirteen of them voted on the next ballot for Lowden, Wood, or Johnson. And they did the same thing on the one after that. In fact, some of the conspiratorial sixteen never voted for Harding at all.[20] Harding's real asset was Daugherty, who had worked for McKinley, had led the Taft forces on the floor of the 1912 convention, and had labored at the 1916 convention for Charles Evans Hughes. Daugherty was experienced, determined, and tireless. Patiently and systematically he weaned delegates away from Lowden and Wood. And Harding had presented himself from the outset as the compromise candidate. That was how he won the nomination.[21]

With Harding's victory secured, the Republican leaders agreed on Senator Irvine L. Lenroot of Wisconsin, a moderate Progressive, to run as Vice-President and balance Harding's moderate conservatism. "After Lenroot's nomination and several seconds had been given, a small, haggard-looking man named Wallace McCamant stood on a chair in the Oregon section, crying for recognition. Frank Willis, who was then presiding, apparently thought it was another request to second Lenroot and recognized the Oregonian."[22] Instead, McCamant nominated Calvin Coolidge.

There followed an emotional outburst that swept the nomination into Coolidge's lap. Delegates had spent five days being told how to vote. Here at last was a chance to speak for themselves. Lenroot, who had no known political enemies, was trampled in the stampede and never heard from again.

III

Every four years William Jennings Bryan would make another hopeless bid for the Democratic nomination. In 1920 he ran on the strength, if that is the word, of winning a single primary, that of his home state, Nebraska. He had become an object of ridicule within his own party, his hopes mocked in doggerel:

> The tumult and the shouting dies,
> The bosses and the gangs depart;
> And now the thrice-strung sacrifice
> Is ready for another start.

Yet this was so plainly Bryan's last hurrah that the Democratic convention, when it opened at San Francisco, gave him a tumultuous ovation that was really a farewell.

Equally hopeless was Palmer's ambition. Party leaders favored him; voters did not. An attempt to redeem Palmer's lackluster showing in the primaries by predicting red revolution on May Day 1920 only made him seem ridiculous when the day passed quietly.

By far the strongest potential contender was William Gibbs McAdoo, Wilson's son-in-law. He possessed strong appeal among Democratic voters.[23] His marriage to Wilson's daughter Eleanor led to gibes about "the Crown Prince" and "the Heir Apparent." Still, he was generally considered the ablest man in his party. He had been an eminent lawyer, secretary of the treasury, chairman of the Federal Reserve Board, and wartime director general of railroads.* He was a star performer before congressional committees.

With his hair parted in the middle, his old-fashioned high collars and his imposing height, McAdoo was a well-known figure, easily recognized. His manner was self-confident and forceful. He was praised by Walter Lippmann as "a statesman grafted on a promoter."[24] His convictions were usually Progressive. Yet he also demonstrated a vulgarian's avidity for money and for seeing his name in print.

Among the wing of the party that was both Progressive and prohibitionist—a wing strong in the border states and Southwest—loyalty to McAdoo was fanatical. He made much of his small-town Georgia origins. He proclaimed his detestation of Wall Street, unembarrassed by a career as a corporation lawyer. He proclaimed his loathing of cities, even though he had lived in New York for thirty years. And he was bone-dry. Eastern liberals and conservative party leaders alike considered him a strange fish and treated him with profound distrust. On the eve of the convention, McAdoo announced his noncandidacy.

His position was impossible. Wilson clearly yearned for the nomination. Equally clearly, he was not going to get it. But McAdoo did not want his wife, Mrs. Wilson, the President, or the President's close friends in the party, to hold him responsible for Wilson's inevitable rebuff. McAdoo enjoyed fame for his decisiveness. One story had it that as secretary of the treasury he had made up to six important decisions while de-

---

* Admired, his industry was also mocked on occasion:

> The Who, pre-eminently Who,
> Is William Gibbs, the McAdoo,
> A man of high Intrinsic Worth
> The Greatest Son-in-Law on Earth.
> With all the burdens thence accruing,
> He's always up and McAdooing;
> From Sun to Star and Star to Sun
> His work is never McAdone.

scending in an elevator. Now he stood aside, hoping desperately to be drafted.

Wilson's position was much the same. He longed to be nominated, but dare not ask for it. The taboo against a third term was too strong to be challenged squarely. Wilson's hopes of seeing the nomination thrust on him were shattered on the first ballot. McAdoo won 266 votes, Palmer 256, and Governor James M. Cox of Ohio 134. Behind these three trailed twenty other hopefuls, including Wilson.

Cox was a self-made newspaper publisher, mildly liberal, mildly wet, mildly able. He was bluff and kindly in manner, with few ideas but a generous heart. He was for the League because it sounded like a good thing, like widows' pensions and higher pay for schoolteachers. But he was chary of ideas, and when Ohio State University began to show a strong interest in them, it soon heard from the governor.[25]

Cox, of medium height, cut an instantly forgettable figure, with a round innocuous face and a feeble "like me" grin. The most striking thing about him was his wealth. The governor was worth at least $2 million; by today's standards, a multimillionaire. The string of small-town newspapers that provided the ostensible basis of this fortune hardly seemed productive enough to rear so great a money machine. Cox made a few halfhearted and unconvincing attempts to explain how he had become so rich so quickly. Across much of Ohio he had the reputation of a crook.[26] The biggest handicap he faced as a presidential nominee was that he had been divorced. Nor did he commend himself to liberals in his party by pushing through his pet legislative project of 1919—an absolute ban on teaching German in the public schools of Ohio.

On the fourth day of balloting and on the forty-fourth ballot the nomination went to Cox. McAdoo had ruined his chances by running and not running at the same time. Cox chose the thirty-eight-year-old Franklin D. Roosevelt of New York as his running mate. Roosevelt was the true darling of the convention—athletic, energetic, democratic, yet carrying one of the must lustrous names in American politics.

When word of Cox's nomination reached the White House, Wilson flew into a vitriolic rage. Keynes's Nonconformist minister sprayed obscene denunciations in every direction: at his party, at Cox, at the American people, at the world, at his enemies, at his friends.[27]

IV

No one had ever had to encourage Harding to go into politics. He was an ardent and active Republican long before he could vote. He bought and edited the *Marion Star* (Ohio) at a time when every small-town newspaper was a party newspaper.

In the course of his rapid political ascent he developed a liking for what he termed "bloviating" out on the hustings. But what could thrill a crowd of farmers at a picnic or state fair tended to fall flat on the Senate floor. His oratory was immovably set in the nineteenth-century style, with an emphasis on outflung arms, an abundance of patriotic clichés, and the fervent ejaculation, "Oh, Senators!"

His friends in the Senate were the second-raters rather than the leading lights of the Republican party. If he did not work very hard, neither did most other senators. Provided they were regular on a handful of issues, no one minded greatly if they amused themselves with cards, or horses, or golf, or women. Their correspondence was usually light; their constituents made comparatively few demands. Not one senator in ten treated his office as a full-time job.

Harding's chief ambition was to be liked. He suffered, as one reporter observed in 1920, "from that vertebral weakness which is the one material infirmity in his character."[28] Yet on the rare occasions when he chose to make a stand he proved impossible to shift. And on matters where his party was committed one way and his conscience was committed another, the senator refrained from voting. Nor would he fall in with everything that was done in the name of patriotism, as most politicians of both parties had done during the war. He was extremely critical of the high-pressure selling of Liberty bonds, calling it "hysterical and unseemly."[29] It was true that he showed little initiative in the Senate.[30] That may have had something to do with the fact that the Senate was firmly under Democratic control up to March 1919.

Besides, initiative could find other outlets. When Hoover was food administrator during the war he worked from dawn to midnight. Much of his time was taken up by congressmen trying to wheedle favors or put their friends on the government payroll. One morning a senator Hoover had never met arrived unannounced. He was quickly ushered in. "I haven't come to get anything," the visitor declared, as if sensing Hoover's apprehension. "I just want you to know that if you wish the help of a friend, telephone me what you want. I am here to serve and to help." With that, Harding said good-bye to the astonished, and deeply impressed, Hoover.[31]

What resolution Harding possessed was frequently attributed to his wife. Florence Kling DeWolfe was plain, had a sharp tongue, and was five years older than Harding. But, as her maiden name suggested, she had the tenacity of a limpet. She had made an appallingly bad start by marrying an alcoholic ne'er-do-well named DeWolfe when she was only nine-teen. Divorce rectified that, although it left her with a son to bring up on her own. At thirty it was she, not one of Marion's belles, who snared the handsome, fast-rising Warren G. Harding, who was going places with the *Star*. Flossie, as she was then known, was determined and ambitious. She had defied her father to marry the wretched Peter DeWolfe. She defied him again to marry Harding, whom rumor credited with Negro blood.

Flossie found the *Star* office far more interesting than the nursery. She stopped by one day to do an errand, she liked to recall, "and remained 14 years." She and Harding together turned the *Star* into a very successful business. She was eager for him to make his mark in politics as well. Yet once Harding reached the Senate, her ambitions were satisfied. When his friends urged him to run for the presidency, Flossie urged him to stay where he was. Life in the Senate was congenial. Life in the White House was likely to prove a bed of nails.[32]

The other candidate for brace to Harding's spine was Daugherty, a paunchy, jowly, grizzled, small-town, small-time lawyer. He looked like what he was—a political fixer. But to Daugherty, Harding looked like what he was not—a president. It became Daugherty's ambition in life to make Harding into what he only appeared to be. That at least was the way Daugherty always told the story.

So Daugherty courted Harding. That was the nature of their relation-ship at the start. That was the way it remained. Daugherty had a habit of exaggerating his own importance in furthering Harding's rise. He was brutally reminded of his place in 1918, however, when he unwisely at-tempted to drag Harding into a vendetta against Daugherty's enemies in the Ohio Republican party. The senator sent for his reputed string-puller. He pointed out that Daugherty's methods had never raised Daugherty beyond the state legislature, although he had larger aspirations. Harding's methods on the other hand had put Harding in the Senate. Harding was the success in politics, Daugherty the also-ran. The senator did not feel that he would be risking much if he decided to dispense with Daugherty's services. Called to heel like a dog, Daugherty thereafter trotted obediently behind.[33]

No one ran Harding but Harding. His 1920 election campaign was entirely in character. He was one of the very few men who has ever loved to stand for two or three hours shaking hands with a huge train of strang-ers as they filed past, exchanging small talk. When his secretary, George B. Christian, objected that he was wearing himself out in this fashion, Harding replied simply, "It is the most pleasant thing I do."[34] So Harding stood on the front porch of his Marion home, the crowds came to shake his hand, "and the flagpole that stood on McKinley's lawn was transferred to Harding's."[35] But the demand for a campaign tour became overwhelming. In McKinley's day the railroads had carried hundreds of thousands of Republicans to Ohio for nothing. These days, pilgrims paid their way.

The style of the campaign was entirely Harding's. He believed deeply in conciliation, strove to avoid wounding anyone's feelings, invited Bryan to lunch, and spoke courteously of Cox. He worried aloud over Wilson's health, and publicly praised Wilson's intelligence. When it was suggested that he exploit the powerful anti-Wilson mood that had built up in the country, Harding was disgusted. "I guess you have nominated the wrong candidate, if this is the plan. I will never go to the White House over the broken body of Woodrow Wilson."[36] His speeches were platitudinous, and he was severely criticized by people who considered themselves more intelligent than he for saying that the country needed "not nostrums but normalcy." But he gave a definition that was entirely reasonable. "By 'normalcy' I don't mean the old order but a regular steady order of things. I mean normal procedure, the natural way, without excess. I don't believe the old order can or should come back, but we must have normal order or, as I have said, 'normalcy.' "[37]

The central issue in the 1920 election was the League. Harding sought refuge in obscurity and evasion. As a senator he had twice voted for the treaty, with reservations. Even after coming out flatly against the League at Des Moines on October 7 he could not leave it alone. He began advocating something that was very much like a League without actually being a League: he wanted, he said, "an association of nations." This association would be charged with safeguarding world peace. Of course, it could not interfere with America's freedom of action. Cox, meanwhile, was campaigning for the League, the whole League, and nothing but the League.

Neither candidate wanted to make an issue of Prohibition. Harding had voted for the Eighteenth Amendment and the Volstead Act, which enforced it. But his personal acquaintance with the bottle did not encourage close scrutiny during an election. Cox was similarly placed. He only pledged to uphold the law, not believe in it.

Race entered the campaign by a side door. The rumor that Harding had black blood had dogged him in every election he had fought. It was a story that had attached to the Hardings for three generations. And while it was possible, there was not a shred of evidence to support it. In 1920, however, Professor William Estabrook Chancellor of the College of Wooster, Ohio, worked up several genealogies that purported to substantiate this rumor. He published two leaflets, one headed, "Harding's Family Tree," the other, "To the Men and Women of America," which asserted, "Warren Gamaliel Harding is not a white man."

An attempt was made to interest the Democratic National Committee in distributing Chancellor's leaflets by an approach to Tumulty. He soon showed his visitor to the door. "Suppose Senator Harding is elected," Tumulty said. "What a terrible thing it would be if it came out that we had a President alleged to be part Negro!"[38] Someone, certainly not Chancellor, a poorly paid college professor, nevertheless spent up to $20,000 to print and distribute the leaflets.

Unhappily for Chancellor, he had attached the college's name to his efforts. Reporters crowded into Wooster. The errant professor was summoned to face the college's board of trustees. He appeared, flustered and excitable, and tried to deny his authorship. It might have worked, until he moved from denial into a rambling account of extraordinary black conspiracies against him, dating from his term as superintendent of schools in the District of Columbia. Harding's candidacy, the professor confided, was the centerpiece of a gigantic plot by blacks to take over the United States. The reporters present became embarrassed.[39] The trustees fired Chancellor for using the college's name without authorization.

The Chancellor press conference was the biggest story of the entire election campaign. Yet nearly every newspaper in the country suppressed it. Republicans who had not heard the rumor—and that meant most Republicans outside Ohio—were bemused to find in their mail elaborate genealogies that traced the Harding line back to one Stephen Harding, a Massachusetts Puritan of the late seventeenth century.

On election day the outcome was never in doubt. The most interesting feature in the day's events was that women voted in a presidential election for the first time. Taking democracy to mean majority rule, the United States was at last a democratic country—the twenty-second to become so.

Harding won a victory that was unprecedented in American history, burying Cox by a 2–1 margin. To Democrats and liberals it was a stunning defeat. Then, and later, the usual explanation was that the people were venting their anger against Wilson and the war. But a Republican victory was virtually inevitable the moment the Republicans became united. It was their internal divisions since 1910 that had made possible Wilson's election and reelection. The Republicans were the majority party by a very large margin. And there were some serious grievances on voters' minds, such as high inflation followed by deep recession. The "repudiation of Wilson" and "repudiation of the war" theories were persistent, but very much overdone.

The real cause of Harding's landslide victory was Harding's campaign. "Appearing humble and non-disputatious, he said the right things and appealed to the right instincts."[40] A Republican party that had been split

into violently antagonistic factions for a decade, a party that was divided
and confused throughout its nominating convention, a party with a nominee widely touted as a mediocrity under the thumb of unscrupulous
bosses and corrupt oil men—this was hardly the scenario for a landslide
victory at the polls. Harding made his success certain by pulling his party
together. Men who would never again be found supporting the same
presidential candidate—men as diverse as Lodge and La Follette, Penrose
and Hoover—Progressives and conservatives alike, were brought together
by Harding and campaigned for him.

Since the idea had first occurred to him around 1916 he had overcome some formidable obstacles: the absence of rich patrons, his own
limited intellectual abilities, the anxieties of his wife, the strain of leading
a double life, a weak heart, and an innate distaste for conflict. That he
arrived at the White House was a tribute to both remarkable luck and
astute political skill.

At times the prospect of victory troubled him. He had never been
gripped with an all-consuming desire to be President. He would never
have put himself forward as a candidate had he not feared for his seat in
the Senate. He had confided to a friend in 1919, "The only thing I really
worry about is that I might be nominated and elected."[41] And he was a
genuinely humble man. But too much ought not to be made of his protestations of unfitness for the White House. He had said virtually the same
things about himself when he was in the Senate. Harding was continually
belittling his abilities, always listened courteously to other people's opinions, unfailingly tried hard to please.

As his inauguration neared he would go for midnight walks in the
company of newspapermen. To an extent unique among presidents,
Harding felt at ease with reporters. Striding up and down the tree-shaded,
darkened streets of Washington in the frosty air of winter, Harding would
unburden his mind, musing out loud on the kind of presidency he wanted
to provide. "I can't hope to be the best President this country's ever had,"
he admitted one night. "But if I can, I'd like to be the best-loved."[42]

7. Uncle Warren Sees It Through

I

Most accounts of the Twenties at some point draw attention to the finding of the 1920 census that the United States had gone from being a predominantly agricultural nation to being predominantly urban. For the first time, said the Census Bureau, a majority of the population lived in communities of 2,500 people or more. As far as it went, the figure was true; what it was meant to suggest was not. Then, as now, a community of 2,500 was really only a large village.* And as such communities acquired newcomers, one contemporary protested, "people who were 'rural' may become 'urban' without the trouble of leaving their homes."[1]

To a very considerable extent, the United States in 1920 was still an agricultural nation. Farming was by far its biggest business, with an investment value greater than that of manufacturing, all the utilities, and all the railroads combined. Nearly 400 million acres were under cultivation. A third of the population relied on farming for its livelihood. As for the fast-growing cities, their streets were thronged with people straight off the farm, liberated from its hardships but formed by its ways.

* One of the most influential village studies of modern times was under way in 1920–21, involving 140 communities. Its working definition of a village was a place with 250–2,500 inhabitants. Edmund deS. Brunner et al., *American Agricultural Villages* (New York, 1927).

Left behind them were 7 million farming families, many still living in conditions close to those of pioneer days—"and the habits of life learned then are still strongly manifest in the attitudes of the farm population," noted one observer.[2] Not one house in ten enjoyed running water; only one in fourteen had gas or electricity.[3]

Farmers reminisced now about the years just before the war, agriculture's "golden age." They had not seen a lot of cash in those days, but the prices of farm products remained stable and what they needed, they could buy. The war destroyed price stability. For a time, that did not matter, because the war also spread money all over the land. Modern industry paraded its wares before them—gasoline tractors, milking machines, electrical millers, and a score of other machines that would make farming cleaner, safer, more productive. The farmers bought in and out of season the way most people buy only at Christmas. Not only did they splurge on machinery, they bought land as well. The size of the average farm, declining for decades, went up.[4]

By the armistice, farmers were diverting themselves with speculation in purebred livestock, such as Rag-Apple the Great, a Holstein-Friesian bull who fetched $125,000.[5] Farmers were so dazzled by riches that they were actually dabbling in the stock market. But the chief object of rural speculation was land. Iowa farmland that sold for $82 an acre back in the golden age was selling in 1919 for $400.[6] They bought on cash; they bought on credit. No one wanted to be left out. Something like euphoria swept across the rural hinterland because farm income had doubled in six years. Output had gone up by a far less impressive 10 percent. It was prosperity balanced on a wire.

The Administration helped to keep it aloft by supporting wheat prices for eighteen months after the armistice. The American Relief Administration fed the farmers' surpluses to the world's starving. But in May 1920 the government stopped its support operations. The wheat price fell like a brick. Farmers fell with it. All that machinery, all that extra land, the stocks and bonds, the prize livestock—it all depended on credit. The farm of 1920 carried twice the mortgage debt of the prewar farm. American farmers had absorbed virtually all the credit the old system created. Suddenly, they were desperate for more. They demanded that the Federal Reserve allow banks to accept agricultural paper. But the Fed was at last committed to damping down the inflation it had done so much to encourage.[7] Part of the folklore of rural America for the next fifty years was that the Treasury and Federal Reserve had spent the 1920–21 recession trying to beggar the farmer by a brutal policy of deflation.[8]

The farmer also hated the railroad and the elevator company, convinced that they had one hand around his throat and the other in his pocket. Yet agriculture was vulnerable at so many points that to dwell on one or two explained nothing. Changes in diet meant that the average American of 1920 ate seventy-five pounds of food less than his predecessor a decade before. The impoverishment of Europe meant the loss of export markets. The development of synthetic fibers meant a drop in demand for traditional fibers. Cotton sacks gave way to paper bags. Prohibition abolished nearly half the market for barley and much of the market for grapes. And the 1920 harvest brought the farmer the last thing he wanted—bumper crops.

Agriculture was not yet a government dependency; nor was it as free and independent as it had been when a family would be given a quarter-section of 160 acres and left to get on with it. At these crossroads something important was happening. The world inside the farmer's head was being rearranged. With his back to the wall, he no longer looked to himself —he looked to the government. Out on the western plains there had been various movements of protest when the frontier gave way to the modern world—populism, the free coinage of silver, the single tax. And the last in this line came during the war, in North Dakota, where A. C. Townley, a Socialist, was trying to get rich quickly and A. E. Brown, another Socialist, was trying to carve out a career in politics. They created an organization they called the Non-Partisan League and enlisted Fred B. Wood as a founder member because he was a genuine farmer and had sufficiently good credit to buy a car.[9]

The NPL was based squarely on the farmer's deepest grievances against grain dealers, speculators, bankers, and tax collectors. From the Socialist party it adopted the principle of a dues-paying membership, and its approach to recruiting was the one later adopted by the Klan. A dozen farmers in each county were appointed organizers, given a territory to work, and authorized to keep a large share of the initiation fee of each new member they found.

Farmer-organizers fanned out across North Dakota in their Model Ts. In their first year they signed up 50,000 members. The state Republican party was captured. An NPL governor was elected in 1918. The movement spread rapidly into surrounding states, becoming a major political force in South Dakota, Minnesota, and northern Wisconsin. Mismanagement by NPL politicians and the autocratic structure of the NPL itself, which Townley ruled like a tin-pot tyrant, had by 1921 frittered away many of its early gains. It was also undermined by success, notably the introduction of state-owned and operated grain mills and elevators and the adoption of crop insurance. What finally brought the NPL down was something typically agrarian—the postdated check. Farmers, always short of cash, had for years been paying their way with postdated checks. The NPL's 1921 membership dues were in checks dated for after the 1920 harvest. When farm prices collapsed, the NPL went bust overnight. In 1921, farm journals began carrying simplified guides to bankruptcy.

In the South, where cotton prices had fallen from 40 cents a pound in 1920 to 10 cents a pound in 1921, farmers were trying to keep their cotton off the market, while bankers who held their notes were trying to force them to sell before the price dropped even farther. "Night riders" began to burn down cotton gins. More than 25,000 bales were reported destroyed. In Kentucky, tobacco farmers were terrorized into keeping their crops from going to market.[10]

In a year American farmers had suffered a net loss estimated at $6 billion. Some literally walked away from the wreckage, leaving the banks to do as they wished with the derelict barns, the unseeded land. The others hung on, knowing that for the incoming Administration the farm crisis would have to be the first order of business.

II

In its final days the Wilson Administration was like a rabbit transfixed by the headlights of a car as the future hurtled toward it. Four Cabinet members were replaced in eighteen months, to make way for three conservative mediocrities and the disastrous Palmer. The farm crisis was a watershed in the country's life, a social and economic collapse that would sap the United States for the next twenty years. Wilson preferred to ignore it. Farmers had fallen into a state of permanent dependency, but neither they nor the government was prepared to face this unpalatable fact squarely. In Congress, an attempt was made to revive the War Finance Corporation and direct it to provide credit for agricultural exports. Wilson vetoed the bill. Congress overrode his veto.

The new Administration, seeking a quick fix for the farmers, listened to the cries of "Tariff! Tariff!" that every breeze seemed to carry from Capitol Hill. Congress was called into emergency session. An emergency tariff act was passed to replace the moderate Underwood-Simmons tariff of 1913. Then Congress and the White House settled down to the business of writing a new omnibus tariff bill with walls so high that the most nervous protectionist could sleep soundly at night. In one year both exports and imports had fallen by 40 percent. No matter. The walls were going up.

There was a touching, immolatory faith in high tariffs. The main thing, all sensible people agreed, was to save the farmer. Their faith blinded them to the fact that the emergency tariff of 1921 was going to do nothing to aid the farmer, because agricultural imports never amounted to much, even at the worst of times. On the other hand, higher tariffs were almost certain to destroy a large part of the agricultural export market. But faith is powerful and faith prevailed. The farmers and their friends wanted the new permanent tariff bill offered by Representative Joseph W. Fordney of Michigan and Senator Porter J. McCumber of North Dakota, and they got it.

The United States had become the world's largest creditor nation and one of its biggest exporters. Yet, the old protectionist outlook was as lively as ever. "In the long run, the most serious defect of the Fordney-McCumber Tariff was not its high rates . . . but its total failure to recognize the changed economic role of the United States in the postwar world." [11] It attempted to enjoy things both ways: to reap the advantages of a strong economy (providing credit) and a weak economy (taking refuge in protectionist tariffs) at the same time. As is often the case with selfishness, this was not very bright.

Harding's approach to the tariff question was to accept the dogmas of protectionism, while deploring the rigidity and harshness of the system in practice. It was obvious, moreover, that Congress was going to pass a high tariff bill no matter how Harding felt about it. He devoted his efforts to making the scales flexible and won the power to alter rates by as much as 50 percent.

The tariff on agricultural products was doubled in most cases. The list of tariff-free items was sharply reduced. Fossils, horsehair, divi-divi, lava, junk, leeches, bristles, pulu, and spunk, however, could still be imported in unlimited quantities, free of duty. And what was the gain to the farmer of such vigilance against foreign products? For each dollar that protection gained him by keeping out agricultural imports, he had to spend an extra $3.50 on other things that he needed to buy. [12]

Another quick fix was sought in farming cooperatives. [13] These often fell foul of the Clayton Anti-Trust Act. But in 1922, cooperatives were given permanent exemption from prosecution. So far most had been limited to bakeries and grocery stores. Now they spread rapidly throughout rural America under the name of the "Sapiro Plan," after Aaron Sapiro, no farmer, but an astute and energetic lawyer. Sapiro's goal was to enroll at least 50 percent of the producers of a given commodity and then make them agree to hold their products off the market until prices had risen to an acceptable level. This technique was called "orderly marketing." It depended on an autocratic and bureaucratic organization. It appealed tremendously to farmers. It appeared to offer protection from that Hobbesian war of all-against-all into which they had fallen. Yet, in time, the Sapiro Plan too proved to be only another mirage. It called for a degree of self-discipline and mutual coooperation—and trust—that was never a realistic possibility among millions of people spread all over a continent.

Farmers were never short of their own organizations. But the National Grange and the Farmers' Union had seemed a trifle outmoded when the vast uncertainties of the postwar world began to oppress farmers' minds. In February 1919 an organization drive had been launched for a new, more vigorous, modern—that is, militant—body. In March 1920 the American Farm Bureau Federation met to celebrate its arrival as a force in American life. There were more than 1 million AFBF members—twice as many as in the Grange. Born in changed circumstances, the AFBF had a new style. It became the strongest lobby in Washington. Over the next generation it would forge a very close alliance with government, whether government liked it or not.

By 1921, Farm Bureau lobbyists were meeting regularly with more than twenty western and southern senators. These meetings were strictly nonpartisan, suggesting that, like war, farming was above party lines. The result of these discussions was the emergence of the farm bloc, embracing both Senate and House and a dozen key officials in the Department of Agriculture.[14] The farm bloc would dominate agricultural policy for the next fifty years.

A joint congressional committee opened hearings in June 1921, at the farm bloc's prompting, to probe the farm crisis. To farmers, their distress could be explained only in terms of conspiracies. One popular theory, for example, was that the meat packers were callously exploiting their monopoly position to wring every last nickel out of the farmer's work-gnarled hands. After decades of agitation the Packers and Stockyards Act of 1921 put all the packers' operations under federal supervision. A Farmers' Loan Act transformed short-term debts into long-term debts. A Grain Futures Act put penalties on grain speculation. The Federal Highways Act of 1921 was one more response to farmers' demands to help them move their perishable products swiftly to market and reduce their reliance on the railroads. Although called a highways act, its administration was entrusted to the Department of Agriculture. It was destined to leave the United States with a magnificent network of national highways. But this legislation, like the rest, did nothing to raise farm income.[15] Every attempt to legislate the farmer back into his golden age failed, as it was bound to fail. And the weather could not have been worse—that is, better. In 1921, 1922, and 1923 the weather was ideal for growing things. There were bumper crops year after year.

But the bankrupt farmers and their families were no longer there for the harvest.[16] The red lead paint peeled from the deserted barns, sagging fences bore stark foreclosure signs, and the black Model Ts chugged off toward the city, overloaded with people and their poor possessions, like refugees in flight from the ravages of war.

III

"From Wilson," writes Harding's biographer, Robert K. Murray, "he received a disintegrating Presidency, a confused and rebellious Congress, a foreign policy in chaos, a domestic economy in shambles, a society sundered with hatreds and turmoil."[17] His Cabinet choices were to set the tone of his Administration. The Harding Cabinet was, on one side, one of the best of the modern era; on the other side, it was one of the worst. Even the *New Republic* applauded his choice of Charles Evans Hughes as secretary of state and Herbert Hoover as secretary of commerce. But it warned, "Men like Mr. H. M. Daugherty and Senator A. B. Fall are unspeakably bad appointments."[18]

Similarly with the second echelon of the Administration. Harvey's efforts on behalf of Harding at Chicago put him in a position to demand, and receive, the ambassadorship to the Court of St. James. Harvey was an alcoholic. At official banquets he had a bad habit of making a fool of himself. He was uniquely unfitted to be ambassador to any country except a very dry one. On the other hand, Myron T. Herrick, a friend of Harding's from Ohio, went to Paris, where he proved a distinguished and respected ambassador. Herrick had been offered a Cabinet place, but refused to sit down at the same table as Daugherty. He warned Harding, "Daugherty will wreck your administration."[19] But to Harding, loyalty was the supreme political virtue. If Daugherty wanted Justice, then Justice he would have.[20]

Installed in the White House, with his Cabinet running their departments much as they wished, Harding began to work with suicidal zeal on the nation's business. Two months after taking office a weeping Harding was at a Hoboken pier to welcome the arrival of 5,200 coffins containing dead American soldiers.[21] Shortly after, on July 2, he signed a congressional resolution that formally ended America's declaration of war. Hughes speedily secured separate peace treaties with Germany and Austria. He reserved to the United States all the prerogatives granted the victorious Allies under the Treaty of Versailles. He assumed none of the responsibilities.

Rejection of the war fired a deeply felt antimilitarism in which even military men, such as General Pershing and the former army chief of staff, Major General Tasker H. Bliss, joined.[22] The mood in Congress was so strong that it cut the army to 150,000 men—less than a third the size the War Department recommended. The navy was cut down on much the same scale.

Against this background, Hughes invited nine nations to a conference on naval disarmament. The delegations came together in Washington on November 11, 1921. That day was spent in a quasi-religious ceremony. The delegates assembled and traveled with great solemnity to Arlington Cemetery for the burial of an unknown soldier killed in the war. It was a ritual Roman in its combination of melodramatic effects brought off in a somber spirit.

This ceremony provided the setting for the conference, which opened the following day. William Allen White, the most admired American journalist of the age, was no stranger to great events. Yet he would recall, many years later, at the end of a long and colorful life, that, "Of all the human conclaves I have ever witnessed the gathering of the Disarmament Conference in Washington furnished the most intensely dramatic moment I have ever witnessed."[23] Here was one of the most glittering assemblies of the century, and one elevated by a noble purpose, unlike the conference at Versailles.

Hughes seized the moment. Instead of opening with the anodyne observations everyone expected, he was asking the assembled world leaders and their admirals to write off 2 million tons of battleships either at sea or currently under construction. He took them completely by surprise. They hardly had time to take in what he was saying before Hughes was naming the very ships to be sunk or scrapped. Never has an assembly of powerful, hardheaded men been so lost for words.[24] When the response came, it burst forth in cheers and thunderous applause. Men wept, waved their hats, stamped their feet, and bellowed themselves hoarse. Hughes, in his bold stroke, had even renounced the stated American commitment to building the largest navy in the world.* It was a gesture so bold, so generous that no one present could fail to be affected. The emotional outburst that closed the day's proceedings lasted ten minutes.

Yet beneath the euphoria, which was rapidly transmitted from the conference hall to all parts of the world, lay more than a little *realpolitik*. Harding and Hughes had found an instrument for breaking the Anglo-Japanese Naval Treaty which had for twenty years bedeviled American strategic planning in the Pacific. When passions cooled, it was evident

---

* The United States took second place to Britain by 30,000 tons, a fact obscured by the 5 : 5 : 3 : 1.75 : 1.75 ratio of the eventual Five-Power Naval Treaty.

that the Washington Conference was, among other things, a conclave of the white naval powers to contain the Imperial Japanese Navy. Hughes hoped to extend the agreed ratio of capital ship tonnage (5 US : 5 UK : 3 Japan : 1.75 France : 1.75 Italy) to cruisers, destroyers and submarines. This was not to be.

The Washington Conference stood in sharp contrast to the isolationist spirit of the age. But this mood, although strong, was never predominant among thoughtful people. The distinguished, and, in time, very influential Foreign Policy Association came into existence in 1921 and its publication, *Foreign Affairs*, began to appear shortly after the Washington Conference broke up.

The predictions that the Treaty of Versailles would produce dangerous instability in Germany were already coming true. A putative Communist revolt had been bloodily suppressed. The German economy stood no chance of recovery so long as it was treated like a bone to be fought over by dogs. In 1922 the French marched into the Ruhr in a vain attempt to dig coal with bayonets. In 1923 the number of marks to the dollar went from 8,700 to nearly 7 billion at the official rate of exchange. Those who wanted to drive a harder bargain could do better than this.

Relations with the wartime Allies were poisoned by the issue of war loans. To most Americans it was not so much a question of money as morality. Honest people paid their debts. The British, who had loaned heavily to others before becoming dependent on American loans, proposed a general debt cancellation. This idea was dismissed as a polite way of welching. And Anglo-French protestations against sordid money-grubbing by "Uncle Shylock" seemed less than lofty when it was recalled that the British had charged nearly $100 for every American soldier carried to Europe on a British ship; that in France the AEF had to pay cash on the spot for every item the French provided, from cabbages to shells. The United States had been obliged to pay the highest wartime prices for raw materials that came from the British Empire. The Allies, in short, had seized every opportunity that came their way to make an extra dollar. There was never a suggestion then that all resources ought to be pooled. That came later, when payment on the loans was claimed. Harding, like his predecessor and like his successors, expected the debts to be paid.

Approximately $10 billion was outstanding. In 1922 a Debt Funding Agreement set a twenty-five-year limit, at 4¼ percent interest. But in 1923 Harding eased these terms for the British, to sixty-two years and interest of 3–3½ percent. This agreement set the pattern for all the other debt settlements. Yet any debt agreement was certain to become enmeshed with the issue of German reparations. The Allies expected reparations to pay off their war debts. They clung to that expectation as children cling to toys.

For the present, however, the British debt agreement was a public triumph. It made Harding far more popular than Congress and thereby added to the strain on relations between them, for the longer Harding was in the White House, the more critical he became of Capitol Hill. By 1923 he held Congress in the same lofty disesteem that Wilson had so often demonstrated. And he was by now pursuing a foreign policy that went against the isolationist grain, trying to get the United States onto the World Court, provided, he blandly remarked, that it was "a world court and not a League court."[25] He had actively involved the United States in the League's humanitarian, social, and economic programs, even though it was impolitic to praise the League out loud.

Harding's approach to the Soviet Union was to continue the Wilsonian policy of nonrecognition, but he "gladly recommended" a $20 million appropriation for Russian famine relief. He doubted the wisdom of nonrecognition. But Hughes and the rest of the Cabinet were strongly for it. He was not going to fight all of them over the issue.[26] His opposition to communism was deeply felt. He couched it "not in righteous anger—or in fear—but in regret."[27]

When Harding took office, there were American military units in Haiti, Cuba, and the Dominican Republic, dispatched by Wilson to protect American property and pro-American regimes. These occupation forces tarnished America's reputation, at the same time crushing any chance for responsible government to evolve in those countries. Harding's policy could not have been simpler: to get the troops out.

The military occupation of Haiti was based on cold-blooded slaughter. Nearly 3,000 people—most of them unarmed—had been killed, as against the loss of one American officer and twelve enlisted men.[28] The guerrilla war in Haiti was fought in virtual secrecy. When questions were raised, the answer was that the United States was pacifying the island. "Pacification," reported James Weldon Johnson, a former United States Consul, "means merely the hunting of ragged Haitians in the hills with machine guns."[29] This secret war had created hundreds of jobs for "deserving Democrats." They lived in the grand colonial style with large cars, large houses, and a coterie of cheap servants to attend on them. The cost of the military occupation and the white colonial rulers was borne entirely by the Haitian government. That government in turn was inclined to butter its bread as lavishly as it could at the expense of a pitifully impoverished people.

Haiti defeated Harding. He simply could not find a way to bring about an orderly, noncontroversial withdrawal. But he managed to bring American forces out of Cuba and the Dominican Republic. He also brought home the occupation force left in Germany, in January 1923.

IV

The appointment of Hoover as Secretary of Commerce was strongly resisted by the conservative elders of the Republican party. The man was altogether too much of a Progressive for their liking. Harding however was adamant.[30] Hoover's appointment was almost as popular as Hughes's.

Everyone had heard of Hoover. Few knew anything about him. An inordinately shy man, Hoover was served by a corps of able assistants who labored to publicize his achievements without revealing much about "the Chief." Hoover did not have a striking appearance, did not say clever things, did not make big gestures, did not adopt memorable poses. Yet Harding promptly came under his spell, writing to a friend in Ohio, "Hoover is the smartest 'gink' I know."[31]

Hoover's rise to prominence had been a dazzling ascent that took him from anonymity to worldwide fame in less than five years. He would have been an obscure, highly paid mining engineer for the rest of his life had he stuck to his last. He was not the world's greatest engineer by any means. But he was both an accomplished engineer and a very astute businessman, and this combination of talents had made him a millionaire several times over by the age of forty. His achievement in getting thousands of war-stranded Americans safely home from Europe when the war broke out in 1914 brought him widespread notice. His organization the next year of Belgian relief, triumphing over the opposition of both the Germans and Allies, was one of the most effective humanitarian operations in modern history. His reputation for probity and efficiency was unassailable. The only major wartime agency spared congressional investigation was the Food Administration, although it had collected and distributed foodstuffs worth $7 billion.

In the summer of 1921 the harvest in the Ukraine and the Volga valley failed. Maxim Gorki made an appeal to Hoover to save the Russian people from famine. Hoover accepted, but laid down certain conditions —control of distribution by the American Relief Administration, equal shares regardless of "class origin," full freedom of travel for ARA officials, and the release of American prisoners being held in Soviet prisons, usually for political reasons. The Russians accepted Hoover's conditions.

With the ardent support of Hughes and Harding, Hoover set about convincing the reactionaries in the Cabinet and the State Department that for once political differences had to be set aside. Harding won a grudging $20 million contribution from Congress. The War Department handed over tons of surplus medical supplies. And Hoover raised an additional $70 million from private contributions. When at a public fund-raising a woman rose and protested that in effect he was saving the Bolshevik regime, Hoover lost his temper and banged on a table in rage. "Twenty million people are starving. Whatever their politics, they shall be fed!" [32]

Nearly a million tons of food were shipped to the Soviet Union. Famine relief was only the first step in rehabilitation. ARA workers restored telegraph lines, hospitals, nurseries, and schools. Teams of health workers roved far and wide to inoculate millions of Russians against typhoid, smallpox, cholera, and typhus. To Hoover, a program of this kind was both humanitarian and patriotic. [33]

In his rapid ascent, Hoover's energies seemed boundless, and in the Cabinet he was known as "Secretary of Commerce and Under Secretary of Everything Else." He turned his department from being one of the newest and least important into one inferior only to State, Treasury, and War. He, too, labored against the isolationist grain, committing his department to carving out a larger place for the United States in world trade. He waged protracted war against British and European cartels and monopolies. Yet he stubbornly adhered to the patriotic view of high tariffs—right when the United States raised them, wrong when other people did the same. [34] His fellow Cabinet members were not always enchanted with Hoover's zeal for taking everything as his rightful province. The secretary of agriculture, Henry C. Wallace, was particularly outspoken in his resistance to Hoover's theory that farming was a business and therefore really belonged to the Commerce Department.

Hoover's energetic departmental imperialism was an expression of his progressivism. That historic movement had revolved around two points—greater democracy, and greater efficiency. Both of these ideas affected Hoover deeply, but the second was probably the stronger. It was this which led him into a two-year struggle to end the twelve-hour day at US Steel.

Those twelve hours came on top of the time it took to get to work, the time it took to go home, half an hour for breakfast and the morning toilet, half an hour for a meal at work. Steel jobs were nearly always exhausting. Eight hours of sleep were essential for most men. That left a man with two hours a day for his home life, for self-improvement, for recreation, and whatever else he needed or wanted to do. Steel workers literally had no time for a secure family life or good health.

In every other Western steel industry the eight-hour day and the six-day week were standard. But US Steel was absolutely committed to the seven-day week and the twelve-hour day. It was not a matter of economic necessity. The corporation held nearly $1 billion in cash reserves and undistributed profits. In most years its after-tax income was well above $100 million. To introduce an eight-hour day and keep workers' earnings at current (low) levels would cost less than $25 million a year.[35]

Hoover, who loathed inefficiency and inhumanity, found it easy to enlist Harding's support. Carnegie himself had said that the twelve-hour day would have to go.[36] Harding publicly appealed to Gary to relent. The answer was still no. Hoover refused to give up. The struggle went on, out of sight, to wear down US Steel's resistance.[37]

V

Hoover was the price the Old Guard had paid to secure the appointment of Andrew Mellon as secretary of the treasury. Harding wanted Hoover; the Old Guard wanted Mellon. He would not take one, he told them, without the other.

This was a time when folk memories were still sharp of the nineteenth-century financial titans, such as Jay Gould, who could hold the government to ransom one day and bail it out the next. A handful of very rich men were believed to prop up the world economic order, much like the elephants were once believed to hold up a flat earth. Mellon was one of this handful. He was therefore held in awe by millions. As the president and principal stockholder in the aluminum monopoly, Alcoa, he was the third richest man in the country, after Ford and Rockefeller.

Mellon was sixty-six in 1921, an age when most men are thinking of retirement. Yet he traveled humbly to Marion and sat meekly in Harding's house, waiting until the President-elect was informed that the legendary Andrew Mellon had called. He was a wisp of a man, below average height, usually dressed in a black suit and a straggly bow tie, with a cheroot hanging from the corner of a thin-lipped mouth. He invariably looked sad. Behind the cold blue eyes was an alert intelligence. And Mellon, despite the improbability suggested by his appearance, was an authority on art. Strongly conventional taste plus a large fortune had combined to produce the finest collection of old masters in the United States. Unlike most of the important collectors who came after him, Mellon had carried off many of his biggest prizes at fire-sale prices.

He was barely installed in Washington before he was being damned by some as the worst possible choice and hailed by others as "the greatest

Secretary of the Treasury since Hamilton."* His admirers usually knew little about the Treasury and even less about Hamilton. Mellon devoted most of his energies to cutting taxes. Income tax was an onerous novelty, only eight years old when Mellon took office. When he failed to get the cuts he wanted, he found other ways to his goal—tax credits, refunds, abatements.

He came into office at a time when the economy was in a deep slump. Unemployment was high and rising. Investment had fallen far below the rate of inflation. The Federal Reserve had raised the rediscount rate to 7 percent, at that time a draconian level. Agriculture was reeling as prices and markets collapsed. Foreign trade had fallen 40 percent in a year. Bankruptcies had tripled.

The traditional response of the federal government to a recession or depression was to ignore it, much as it ignored thunderstorms and for the same reason—there was nothing it could do about them. Harding, however, saw beyond the figures to the human distress they represented. He was constitutionally incapable of sitting still while other people were hurting. He broke with precedent and called a President's Conference on Unemployment to be chaired by Hoover. The conference reported to him that 4.3 million people, roughly 15 percent of the work force, were unemployed. This was the minimum figure.[38] The Administration pressed for the large increases in public works spending that the conference recommended.[39] Old ways could not be changed overnight. This proposal verged on radicalism. The traditional wisdom held that public works ought to be expanded only in good times and cut back in bad.

Despite strong pressure on him to do so, Harding refused to make special provision for veterans. Congress passed a bonus act that would have given every veteran $50 for each month of wartime service. The usual justification was that the veterans had made a serious economic sacrifice. But most were young and without dependents; too young, as a rule, to have risen far in their careers. And although the men who stayed at home made more money, wartime inflation made sure that it did not go very far. Very few men suffered in their careers because of military service; many gained from it. Harding viewed the bonus bill, moreover, as special-interest legislation. To the relief of the Treasury, he vetoed it.

The country had borrowed heavily during the war. National debt had risen from $1.2 billion in 1914 to $24 billion in 1921. Debt interest alone came to $1 billion a year, more than the annual expenditure of prewar

---

* How quickly they forget. McAdoo had also been hailed in his time as "the greatest Secretary of the Treasury since Hamilton."

government. Even after cutting back severely, the cost of government in the early Twenties could not be reduced much below $4 billion—roughly six times the level of a decade before. The wartime excess profits tax was kept in effect for three years after the armistice simply because the Treasury needed the billion dollars a year it provided.

There was much heartfelt grumbling over the "crushing burden of taxation" these days. For a single person, income tax started at $1,000 a year; for a married couple at $2,000 a year. But not one person in 500 actually paid income taxes. And of those who did, the top 2 percent paid 75 percent of the total. The rich bore nearly the entire tax load.[40] While they could well afford it, they resented it deeply. They looked to Mellon for relief. They did not look in vain.

The excess profits tax was abolished, income taxes were cut, and the Bureau of the Budget was created to bring federal spending under tighter control. The bureau was entrusted to Charles Dawes, the Chicago banker whose idea it had been.* Harding had first offered Dawes the Treasury Department. He had refused it on the grounds that the Treasury Department could never control government spending. What was needed, his argument ran, was a budget for the entire Executive branch, entrusted to a budget director with so much authority that he could defy the Cabinet if the need arose—something no Cabinet member could do. Harding agreed with him, secured the necessary legislation, and installed Dawes to run the bureau.

In 1922 the economy rebounded spectacularly, regaining the level of output reached in 1918.[41] The Federal Reserve slashed interest rates by 50 percent. Investment recovered, and by 1923 there was a labor shortage. After two years of cuts, wages began rising sharply toward wartime levels.

With recovery, however, came a revival of labor unrest. Harding found himself embroiled in a bitter dispute, the railroad strike of 1922. To his dismay he found that patience, tact, and moderation this time got him nowhere. As frustration built up over the resulting impasse, he began to show signs of strain. He slept badly, lost his wonted joviality, agonized for hours over whether to intervene, and allowed himself to rely in the end on his wildly antilabor attorney general. It was a mistake that was to cost

---

* Dawes was a small-born Renaissance man. A competent pianist and flautist, he had written a short piece for violin that was played by many famous fiddlers of the day, "Melody in A Major." It reappeared as a popular song in the 1950s, "It's All in the Game." Dawes was also a successful lawyer, a self-made millionaire, a major general during the war, when he was on Pershing's staff, a founder of hostels for homeless men, and president of Chicago's biggest bank. In time, he also became in turn Vice-President, ambassador to Great Britain, and the first director of the Reconstruction Finance Corporation.

Harding something he cared about profoundly—his reputation for fairness.

VI

For a century the railroads had been looked on as a marvel. They possessed a mythical and poetic character, a part of every boy's store of happy memories and an essential element in American history. The railroads had tamed the West as surely as the rifle and the plow. The frontier had been just beyond where the railroad tracks ended.

"Everyone at some time has stood at the railroad crossing in the country and watched the passing of the 'Limited,' " recalled Charles Pierce Burton in 1923.[42] From youth, Americans had grown up with deeply romantic feelings about railroads. They were more than a mere form of transportation, but by the 1920s their best days were plainly behind them.

Expenditure on roadbuilding outstripped new railroad investment by 4–1; that gap was widening each year. Construction of new track had barely kept pace with population growth since 1890, and was now falling behind it. There were more than 2,000 railroads, 90 percent of which were small lines feeding into the 200 Class I systems. Many of the railroads were virtually broke.

In 1919 the railroad brotherhoods, impressed with the orderly operation of the lines under government supervision during the war, began to urge railroad nationalization. Instead, Congress in 1920 passed the Esch-Cummins Transportation Act, which aimed at consolidation of the smaller lines. The bill allowed the ICC to set a "fair rate" of return on railroad investment. The ICC set this at 5¾ percent, which allowed some lines to raise their rates by up to 40 percent. The ICC also had the power to "recapture" net earnings above the limit it had set. The Esch-Cummins Act created a Railway Labor Board to settle wage disputes and assume responsibility for the health and safety of railroad workers. The powers given the ICC and the RLB overnight turned the railroads from the least-regulated big business into the most-regulated, and the RLB was the government's great white hope of labor peace.

While Esch-Cummins was still being debated in April 1920, the railroad workers had struck. Palmer had struck back, using the wartime Lever Act. Not content to rely on injunctions, he had attempted to whip up public hostility to the strikers, accusing them of fomenting subversion even when his own agents were reporting back that the sole issue in the strike was wages.[43] When the RLB came into existence a few weeks later, it wooed the railroad workers by granting them large increases.

Yet the railroads were caught up in the recession along with everyone else. In 1921 the wage agreement was abrogated and wages dropped by 12 percent. In 1922 the railroads proposed to cut wages still further. But the railroad brotherhoods were the most powerful element in organized labor. Between them, they accounted for more than 1.5 million members. The Brotherhood of Locomotive Engineers and Firemen formed the aristocracy of American labor: highly organized, well paid, holding jobs that were secure against strike-breakers, yellow-dog contracts, and the open shop. There were also half a million railroad shopmen who made and maintained locomotives, built and repaired the tracks, and enjoyed low wages and little security. They were vulnerable and militant. In July 1922 when wage talks broke down the shopmen struck.[44]

Harding urged mediation. Agreement was nearly reached, but the railroads refused to give a promise not to victimize strikers. The shopmen stayed out. The Labor Department in the Twenties did little more than collect and distribute statistics. By default, the government agency most involved in the strike was Daugherty's Justice Department.

The attorney general was convinced that he was dealing with "Red Borers" acting on instructions from Moscow to force the government to take control of the railroads. This would lay the foundation for socialism, and that of course was the next thing to communism. The violent clashes that the strike sparked off were therefore tantamount to civil war. This was the way he presented the issue to Harding, and advised him that RLB decisions were absolutely binding, which made the strike illegal no matter what the merits of the strikers' case. Either Daugherty was lying on purpose or he did not understand the law. The RLB had no binding powers.

With the President's approval Daugherty traveled to Chicago, where the shopmen's brotherhood had its headquarters, to seek an injunction from federal Judge James H. Wilkerson. It was a decree without precedent. The Wilkerson injunction barred strikers from doing anything to impede the railways, right down to "jeers, taunts and entreaties." The strikers were barred from gathering within the vicinity of the yards, the terminals, and the tracks. They could not publicize their strike, could not ask others to support it, give an interview to explain their position, write a letter to a newspaper, or send a telegram to a railroad official. They could not picket, meet to consider strike tactics, or put up a poster. All that they could do, under the Wilkerson injunction, was sit at home and wait.[45]

Hoover was incensed by this decree. It went far beyond anything Harding had countenanced. To the country and to much of the Cabinet the Wilkerson injunction was so unfair that it bordered on the malicious. Daugherty was roundly denounced by Hoover before the President and the Cabinet, and Harding, aware at last that he had been misled, joined in the attack on the attorney general.[46] He demanded that the noose the injunction fastened around the shopmen's necks be loosened.

The injunction, however, had broken the nerve of the strike leaders. After two months, and with nothing to show for their stoppage, the strikers went back.

The other major strike of 1922 came in the coal mines. Lewis brought out 600,000 miners in April in a protest against wage cuts. It was in the third month of this strike that the Herrin massacre occurred. At the end of August, Lewis won an agreement to maintain wages. This was a victory won at a heavy cost. The UMW was almost bankrupt. And the UMW had gone back to work before the nonunion miners had won recognition, callously abandoning them and creating a heritage of bitterness between union and nonunion miners that would last for decades.

Daugherty's blind and unrelenting hatred of organized labor had given the Harding Administration an undeserved reputation for a reactionary labor policy. But more damaging yet was the reputation that Daugherty and his friends were to fasten on it for corruption. In this, however, Harding was himself to prove his own worst enemy.

VII

Virtually no provision had been made to receive the tens of thousands of men who returned from the war totally disabled by wounds or suffering serious mental illness. Congress tardily created a division of rehabilitation within the Federal Board of Vocational Education. After eighteen months in which more than 100,000 men established their eligibility for assistance, the board had trained and placed 217. Applications for help gathered dust for up to a year.[47] Limbless men were trying to live by peddling shoe polish and pencils on streetcorners; the mentally ill were being forced into institutions for the criminally insane for want of anywhere else that would take them.

Harding was depressed by this situation. One of the first actions of the new administration was the creation of the Veterans Bureau. When he looked for someone to reorganize the shambles of veterans' affairs, he thought of Charlie Forbes. And why not? "Everybody who made contact with the breezy, joke-cracking, hustling, red-headed Forbes was impressed by him. He was of a familiar American type, the go-getter."[48]

Harding had met Forbes back in 1915, at Pearl Harbor, where Forbes was in charge of construction at the naval base and the senator was passing through on a leisurely tour of inspection. They became poker-playing pals. Forbes was a colorful figure with a checkered military career: a one-time army deserter, he finished the Great War as a lieutenant colonel and Medal of Honor winner. Over Daugherty's objections, Harding installed Forbes as head of the Veterans Bureau.

By 1923 the bureau was one of the biggest spending agencies in the government. Its director was to be seen these days in all the smartest, most expensive hotels up and down the eastern seaboard, entertaining like a drunken millionaire sailor. In running his half-billion-dollar-a-year department, Forbes appeared to have developed a strange obsession with cleanliness. He had bought enough floor wax and floor cleaner to last the veterans' hospitals a hundred years. His zeal for hygiene was so strong that he was willing to pay 98 cents a gallon for cleaners that were normally sold for a nickel. At the same time he was disposing of $1.37 sheets (100,000 of them) for 26 cents a pair.[49]

Rumors began reaching the White House that some of this surplus was not, strictly speaking, surplus. Doubts were also being raised over the location and cost of new veterans' hospitals.

One story current at the time was that the President of the United States had been surprised by a visitor in the Red Room with his hands around Forbes's well-fed throat and shouting, "You yellow rat! You double-crossing bastard!"[50] At all events, Forbes saw fit to hasten to Europe. From there he cabled back his resignation to his old poker pal.

Shortly after this, Forbes's chief assistant at the Veterans Bureau, Charles F. Cramer, was notified that the Senate had decided to investigate the bureau. Cramer saw his wife off to New York on a pretended errand of importance. Returning home to the house at 2134 Wyoming Avenue that he had bought from the Hardings, he went to the bathroom and stood before the mirror. Cramer raised a heavy .45 pistol to his right temple and squeezed the trigger. This event alarmed a number of people, notably Daugherty's close friend Jess Smith.

Mr. Smith went to Washington mainly to keep his idol company. Tall, flabby, pigeon-toed, with a diabetic's jowliness and a pair of wet brown eyes that viewed the world apprehensively from behind shell-rimmed glasses, Jess Smith adored Harry Daugherty. He, in turn, was Daugherty's protection against loneliness. Mrs. Daugherty was an invalid, left behind in Columbus. The two men shared a house in Washington, on H Street, before they moved into an apartment in the Wardman Park Hotel. At the Justice Department there was even a little office for the attorney general's friend.

But most of the time Jess did business elsewhere, at a house on K Street rented by two other acquaintances of Daugherty's from Ohio. This house was a combination card parlor, speakeasy, house of assignation, and bribery exchange. Pardons and appointments were bought and sold, as were liquor withdrawal permits, introductions to the right people, immunity from prosecution, and government surplus that was not altogether unwanted. Jess Smith could be seen on the corner greeting the many visitors who came by each day with "Whaddya know?" and humming a line from that hit of the early Twenties, "My God, how the money rolls in!"[51]

Behind the jolly man was a sensitive nature. That joviality depended on a couple of large drinks from time to time. But one too many would set Jess Smith blubbering. And in the spring of 1923 the worst thing he could imagine happened to him: he was banished from the Daugherty presence. Word of the odd goings-on down at K Street had reached the President's ear. Harding brusquely told Daugherty, "Get him out of Washington."[52]

Jess went back to Ohio for a while. But he soon came back, looking haggard and frightened. Daugherty moved into the White House and asked his secretary, Warren F. Martin, to stay with Smith at the Wardman Park apartment. On May 30, at half past six in the morning, Martin heard a loud crash. He found Jess Smith sprawled on the bedroom floor, still in his pajamas. His head was in a waste basket. A smoking pistol was in one outflung hand.[53]

Behind an outward show of calm, consternation prevailed in the White House. And a third scandal appeared to be in the brewing. A Senate investigating committee was laboriously working its way through forty filing cabinets stuffed with documents relating to oil leases in California and Wyoming.

Harding became distracted and despondent. If there was one man in the Senate he trusted, that man was Albert B. Fall. Certainly Fall cut an impressive figure.[54] "He was a go-getter, a bit of a bluff in his quiet way, with a touch of the Bad Man from the Border, dressing the role in a broadbrimmed hat and flowing tie, and playing it with a slow drawl from beside the cigar which he habitually held in his teeth. . . ."[55] His bright-blue eyes had the piercing gaze of the man who spends his life out-of-doors in country that has distant horizons. He was blessed with a reputation for physical courage and the bronzed look of the frontiersman. At eleven Fall had gone to work in a Tennessee cotton mill. In manhood he spent three years as a United States marshal in Texas and on one occasion had disarmed the fastest of the gunfighters, John Wesley Hardin, in an El Paso saloon.[56] He bore himself with the erectness of a man who has spent many hours in the saddle. For a time he was a prospector and mine supervisor in Mexico. During the Spanish-American War he rode with the Rough

Riders. Self-educated and ambitious, he eventually became a lawyer. When New Mexico became a state in 1912, Fall went to the Senate.

He immediately made an impression in the capital, with his big black Stetson, his flowing black cape, and his huge handlebar mustache. His knowledge of Mexico won him a place on the Foreign Relations Committee. And he got on well with the man seated at the desk next to his on the Senate floor, Warren G. Harding, whom he introduced to the Senate's ways. Their temperaments were utterly different, as were their politics— Harding the Stalwart, Fall the Bull Moose Progressive. Yet they became close friends. Liberals objected to Fall's appointment to the Cabinet, but in most of the press it was a popular choice.* Fall was a westerner, from the area where most of the Interior Department's responsibilities lay. He was also an authority on oil. He was respected by his colleagues. News of his appointment was brought to him on the Senate floor. He immediately resigned his seat and was at once unanimously confirmed by a cheering Senate.[57] He was the only Cabinet member ever confirmed without a Senate hearing.

Fall was barely installed in office before he took up the question of the official oil reserves. During the Taft Administration conservationists had succeeded in having two large oil deposits in California set aside to be exploited by the navy should it ever face a shortage. In 1915 Wilson set aside a third deposit, popularly known as Teapot Dome after an oddly shaped geological feature in the part of Wyoming where it was located. Officially this pool was known as Naval Oil Reserve Number Three. Conservationists expected that as much as a century might pass before these three large, unspoiled areas were torn up for wells, roads, and storage tanks. Success had come their way because they had linked conservation with national defense. Yet even this proved a frail reed. Robert K. Lane, Wilson's secretary of the interior, attempted to lease the reserves to private operators at the end of the war. When Wilson learned of this, Lane was fired.

Fall took office with a long record of hostility to conservation. The same was true of the new secretary of the navy, Edward F. Denby. A month after taking office, Denby transferred control of the three naval oil reserves to Fall's department.

* Both Mark Sullivan and Samuel Hopkins Adams, two of the most knowledgeable journalists of the era, found Fall impressive. But William Allen White met Fall only once and took an instant dislike to him: ". . . tall, gaunt, unkempt, an ill-visaged face that showed a disheveled spirit behind restless eyes. He looked like the patent medicine vendor of my childhood days who used to stand, with long hair falling upon a long coat under a white hat, with military goatee and mustache, at the back of a wagon selling Wizard Oil." *Autobiography of William Allen White,* pp. 619–620.

Conservationists were outraged. What aroused the wrath, however, of the country's leading conservationist, Gifford Pinchot, former chief forester of the United States, was Fall's evident intention of taking over the Forest Service as well as the oil reserves. Oil was one thing, but trees were sacred. A national campaign was launched to "save" the Forest Service. Its chief tactic was to discredit Fall.

The campaign's day-to-day manager was one of Pinchot's former aides, Harry K. Slattery. Since leaving Pinchot, he had been an assistant to Robert K. Lane, a Washington lawyer and now a lobbyist for various Progressive causes. Slattery knew the right people to see, knew how to read government documents, knew how to generate support on Capitol Hill. And Slattery, who set out to save the trees, found himself reading up on oil.

In April 1922 the Interior Department began leasing the reserves. Number Three, in Wyoming, had been turned over to Harry F. Sinclair in return for a 17 percent royalty on the value of all the oil extracted. Number One, at Elk Hills, California, had been leased to Fall's old prospecting partner, Edward L. Doheny. Navy officers objected to the leasing policy. But the Interior Department maintained that the oil was draining into surrounding oilfields through geological faults. Elk Hills alone, the department said, had already lost more than 20 million barrels. Not only would this loss be brought to a halt, but the navy would receive something valuable in return: oil at Pearl Harbor. That would transform it into the chief base of the Pacific Fleet. Doheny was to build and fill a dozen huge storage tanks and construct a complex of docks, wharves, roads, and railroad lines to keep the fleet fully supplied in peace and war.[58]

Slattery prevailed on Robert La Follette of Wisconsin to introduce a Senate resolution calling for an investigation of the oil leases. The resolution passed 58–0, and was entrusted to the Committee on Public Lands and Surveys. Fall dumped masses of documents on the committee, possibly hoping to bury it. But a fellow westerner, Senator Thomas A. Walsh of Montana, whom Fall had taken into his home after the death of Walsh's wife, began working his way through the forty filing cabinets of material with the stolid determination of a beaver.

As the rumors gathered around Fall's black-caped figure, Harding began to lose faith in him. And Fall, tired and impatient of criticism, chose the second anniversary of his appointment to resign. He returned to his sprawling Three Rivers Ranch in New Mexico. A few months later, in August 1923, two geologists were also traveling west, sent by the Committee on Public Lands to report back on Teapot Dome. The oil there was now said to be trapped in a "saddle." If that were true, it could not drain out.

VIII

The Hardings had literally let life and light into the White House. For eighteen months the mansion had been dark and hushed, a place of sickness and anger. When Mrs. Harding came downstairs on the first day of the new Administration she found the servants drawing the window shades. She asked why they were doing that. Because the people outside would crowd up to the windows and look in, came the reply. She ordered the shades raised. "Let 'em look if they want to. It's their White House."

To fashionable Washington this was just what might be expected from such obvious provincials as the Hardings. It troubled Harding that as President he was served before his wife at meals.[59] He chewed tobacco, a habit for which American men had been notorious since Colonial days. But smart people did not chew, and Mrs. Harding, whom he in his lowbrow way called "Duchess," struggled to keep him looking presidential by taking his tobacco away. The President, however, continued to chew surreptitiously, hiding his plugs in obscure corners of the White House. He was the most natural, the least pompous of men, and his geniality led to his being known as "Uncle Warren."[60]

No president could have worked harder. The working day ran from 7:00 A.M. until midnight. Everyone who met Harding saw that he was pushing himself too hard.[61] Even a routine letter to the White House was likely to bring a labored reply from the President himself, instead of a routine acknowledgement from an aide. He was driven to despair within the cage of his intellectual limitations. He wanted so much to make the right decision. But the details of legislation, the intricacy of economic problems, the stubbornness of both sides in labor disputes, matters such as these soon brought him to the boundaries of his mental powers and demonstrated the limitations of mere goodwill. He suffered acutely, fell into long periods of deep depression, and began to complain to casual visitors about the burdens of office. He worried over his wife's poor health and when kidney failure nearly killed her in the fall of 1922, he was virtually paralyzed with anxiety.

The Duchess was as dedicated in her own way as the President. Seriously ill for much of her time in the White House, she cheerfully met all the social duties that devolved upon a First Lady, and gave herself an additional task. Each month she would visit the disabled veterans at Walter Reed Hospital, taking huge masses of flowers from the White House grounds, and there she would spend an hour or two talking in a motherly way to lonely, crippled men.

Harding was a typical American of the Twenties in that he was sincerely and publicly dry, while remaining privately and regularly wet. He promised to enforce the law. But he resisted attempts to enforce it on himself. Twice a week he dined early so that he could relax for a few hours playing poker. The Harding Poker Cabinet included Daugherty, Smith, Forbes, Fall, and, on occasion, Harry Sinclair, George Harvey, and Charles G. Dawes. Even Mellon and Henry C. Wallace were known to sit in. The Duchess moved among the cigar-smoking, bantering card players, dispensing drinks.[62] This was the atmosphere that Harding liked best. It was the leisure of the small-town pol, an environment in which the supreme political virtue was loyalty, not some abstract ethical ideal or a set of intellectual convictions, but loyalty freely given between one man and another.

Loyalty was the glue that kept the party system—and with it, government—together. Without loyalty there could be no politics. So as the whispers were brought to him about Daugherty-this and Daugherty-that, Harding grew troubled, but stood by his friend. Ironically, Harding, whose reputation was to be destroyed by some of his appointees and their hangers-on, was by 1923 thoroughly disenchanted with the whole patronage system that was bound up with political loyalties. He had come to believe deeply in appointment strictly on merit. He was antagonizing his own party, but winning the praise of the Civil Service Reform League by putting merit before patronage.

Criticism of what in time became enshrined in political mythology as "the Ohio Gang" was vastly overdrawn. Harding picked people he knew for many appointments. These inevitably included a large proportion of Ohioans, much as Truman was surrounded by Missourians, Kennedy by New Englanders, and Carter by Georgians. Some of his Ohio choices were laudable. When he placed William Howard Taft on the Supreme Court as Chief Justice no one said, "Not another hack from Ohio!" It was an appointment all the best people applauded.

What was causing Harding so much anxiety in 1923 was less the people he had brought from Ohio than *their* hangers-on, who flocked to Washington from their home state in search of easy pickings secured by old friendships. Nearly every nineteenth-century President had been pestered in this way. Harding's worries were evident to only a few. For the most part, he basked in public adulation. He enjoyed the most favorable press any President has ever had. It was not simply that most publishers were Republicans, which they were, but journalists liked and trusted him. He answered their questions without pomposity or evasion. Harding opened up the presidency to press inspection. And to one reporter of international reputation, the highly educated, much-admired Mark Sullivan, Harding was not what he seemed. Sullivan, like most political reporters, was accustomed to looking at politicians objectively. To him, the real Harding was a more complicated man, a deeper, more interesting man, than the smooth, polite, generous surface suggested.[63]

As presidents invariably do, he found himself at loggerheads with Congress as his Administration wore on. The theory that an ex-senator would enjoy a uniquely harmonious relationship with Capitol Hill proved unfounded. Nor did it seem to matter that his party held a majority in both houses of Congress.

In the election of 1922 those majorities fell sharply, from 24 to 10 in the Senate; from 166 to 20 in the House. The election was also a portent: every big (150,000+) city turned solidly Democratic in its congressional representation for the first time.[64]

But Harding's popularity was not in doubt. In March 1923 he announced through Daugherty that he intended to run for reelection. This early declaration was intended to answer rumors that his health was failing. Its effect was lost when he hurriedly left for a month's vacation in the South.

Harding's Administration had proved to be neither prolabor nor probusiness. His belief in reconciliation was too strong for him to play the partisan. His concern for the poor led him to urge on several occasions the creation of a Department of Welfare, a suggestion which horrified much of the Republican party, and provided another instance where the Republican majority in Congress devoted itself to frustrating a Republican president.

Harding's generous impulses therefore had to find expression in other channels. Under Wilson the radical periodical *The Masses* was deprived of its second-class mail permit. It changed its name to *The Liberator*. It was still obliged to use the much more expensive third-class mails. Under Harding's postmaster general, Will Hays, *The Liberator* not only received a second-class permit but a refund of $11,277 on the difference it had paid in using the third-class mails.[65]

Harding took an interest in the fate of Eugene Debs. He asked Daugherty to interview him and make a report. Debs traveled from Atlanta on his own and returned to prison on his own. Daugherty, who fancied himself a shrewd judge of men, reported that Debs was an unprincipled scoundrel.[66] Harding made his own decision and extended executive clemency to Debs on Christmas Eve, 1921, and invited him to visit the White House.

Agitation over the political prisoners virtually disappeared after Debs's release. Yet Harding remained interested in these men. One bright spring day in 1923, Ralph Chaplin, who had returned to Leavenworth after losing his appeal, was pruning the prison's rose bushes when he was sent for. An ornate document had arrived for him from Washington. It began with a baroque flourish and continued in the same vein: "Now therefore I, Warren G. Harding, President of the United States of America, on consideration of the foregoing premises and other good and sufficient reasons to me thereunto do hereby commute the sentence of Ralph Chaplin to the time already served, upon condition that he will be law-abiding and loyal to the Government of the United States. . . ."[67] Of the 200 Federal political prisoners when Harding took office, he had freed nearly all by the summer of 1923.

By this time the President had become very overweight—240 pounds. He had suffered from hypertension for twenty years. The punishing work schedule had led to severe chest pains and bouts of faintness. He had a history of nervous disorders, which he had treated by periodic visits to the Seventh Day Adventist Sanitarium at Battle Creek, Michigan, run by Dr. J. P. Kellogg, the cornflake king. A noted heart specialist who met the President in 1922 confidently expected Harding to be dead within six months.[68] It was obvious that he needed rest. His doctors gave their approval to a proposed leisurely tour of Alaska.

Harding's idea of rest meant taking his poker-playing friends along. The list of fellow travelers grew and grew. Important Republican leaders insisted on turning the trip into a minicampaign, to reverse the losses of 1922. When his doctors saw the final itinerary, they urged Harding to cancel the journey.

Worried over scandals in the making,[69] Harding sought oblivion while he traveled by playing bridge for hours on end as the presidential train, the *Superb*, raced from town to town. He made as many as five speeches a day, met dozens of people at every stop, and tried to keep up with the inevitable paperwork of executive power. When the train reached San Francisco at the end of July 1923, Harding collapsed.

A bulletin was issued announcing that he was suffering from food poisoning traced to tainted crab meat. But he had eaten no crab. On August 2 he won a famous victory over one of his most stubborn opponents: Judge Gary announced the end of the twelve-hour day at US Steel. Harding however was unable to savor his triumph. That same day, while being read to by his wife in the Palace Hotel at San Francisco, he died.

On the other side of the continent Calvin Coolidge was at his father's Vermont home that afternoon performing tree surgery on a sick maple. The message that was flashed 3,000 miles in minutes had to be delivered by hand up a darkened, winding country road. The Coolidges usually retired early, at around 9:30 P.M. Shortly before midnight, Coolidge later wrote, "I was awakened by my father coming up the stairs calling my name. I noticed that his voice trembled."[70]

The President had died from a cerebral hemorrhage or a coronary thrombosis.[71] But Mrs. Harding refused to permit an autopsy, and the doctors who signed the death certificate entered the cause of death as apoplexy.

Harding's casket was placed at the level of the windows on the *Superb*, speeding eastward along hurriedly cleared tracks. Millions of people waited patiently for him. When the *Superb* passed through Honey Creek, Iowa, at 4:00 A.M. on August 6, "A blurred, agonizing glimpse into the dimly lighted observation car heaped to the ceiling with wreaths and flowers was all that Honey Creek got—and for this her 76 inhabitants had shivered on the dreary station platform for hours."[72] Yet, to them, it was worth it. The fractious, bitterly divided country Harding had inherited had been bound up. The economic recession had given way to an economic boom. Most of all, Harding's spirit of moderation and tolerance had made itself felt.

In Chicago more than a million people lined the tracks. In Ohio, millions more waited all day and night, softly singing hymns. Even out in the countryside, miles from any habitation, there were people standing bareheaded and silent as the *Superb* went by.[73]

Harding had died in the love he desired.

PART II

THE HIGH TIDE
OF THE TWENTIES

8. Modern Is as Modern Does

I

The crisis of belief that colored the entire life of the Twenties had been in the making for decades. The war was wrongly blamed for blowing up a 2,000-year-old moral order which had really been steadily undermined by nineteenth-century scientists and intellectuals.

Large numbers of educated people were now ready to accept what only a handful of advanced thinkers had formerly countenanced—that all belief is rooted in a desire to believe, not in nature; that all ethical systems are based on custom and imagination, not on divine sanction.[1] Man turned out to be the measure of all things after all. Following the slaughter on the Western Front that was a thought to chill the blood.

The Jazz Age could with equal justice be termed the Age of Dismay, which may be why it partied so vigorously. Nearly all the major writers of the time were pessimistic and alienated. There was a general conviction that another war, even bloodier than the last, was inevitable.

When they looked at their own society, American intellectuals reacted like silent-movie heroines discovering Frankenstein's monster: they threw up their hands in astonishment and horror. A symposium called *Civilization in the United States*, representing the cerebrations of more than thirty thinkers, decided that "The most moving and pathetic fact in the social life of America today is emotional and aesthetic starvation."[2] A descendant of the Adams family, which had illuminated the cultural life of Boston for more than a century, was so pessimistic about the state of mind of his own country that he facetiously suggested, "Europe might supply us with ideas in exchange for dollars."[3]

American life was still largely dominated by small towns and frontier values, a life in which artistic and intellectual interests seemed less important than social and personal ones.[4] There were more than 30 million people enrolled in some 800 fraternal organizations. "Half the adult population now owns a fez, a scimitar, a secret code, two feet of plume, a cutlass, or a pair of Anatolian breeches," reported Charles Merz.[5] And the emotional attachment people were supposed to feel for their hometowns was limitless, for example:

> And when my travels all are o'er, Spokane,
> And when I stand on Jordan's shore, Spokane,
> When heaven lies across the way,
> Its streets of gold, its banners gay,
> I'll bet I rub my eyes and say,
> "Spokane!"[6]

Adrift in a universe that was morally neutral, part of a society that seemed absurd, large numbers of people inevitably turned inward.[7] "Common values and common beliefs were replaced by separate and conflicting loyalties."[8] Above all, Americans discovered Freud.

There were more than 200 books and articles on Freud and his theories published in the United States before 1920, but most of them were of interest only to doctors and to psychologists. It was in the Twenties that Freud became famous. The young celebrated him because he stood as a complete break with the past. Freudianism rejected two of the most important elements in traditional Protestantism: its absolute moral judgments and its asceticism. And there was a new word for all the world's ills —repression. America's entire history was portrayed as three centuries of puritanical repression, thwarting all that was healthy, spontaneous, life-affirming, and gracious.[9]

Dream analysis was Freud's "royal road to the unconscious," and few works had a greater impact on the period than *The Interpretation of Dreams*.[10] Psychoanalysis was looked on as a kind of miracle cure. Once properly applied, the patient was released from his torments instantly and forever.

Just as mechanistic was behaviorism, the creation of Dr. John B. Watson. He did not create it from whole cloth. Watson borrowed freely from other researchers.[11] He then took a step from which they had shrunk. Watson transferred the techniques and assumptions of animal psychology to human psychology, as if there were no important differences between the two. He denounced other psychologists, who were trying to unravel instinct, the mind, emotions, and the like, as dabblers in spiritualism. Boldness made him famous. It also got him fired from Johns Hopkins.

This freed Watson to make a small fortune in the advertising business and to propagate his ideas more energetically than ever.[12] Man is a machine, he insisted, and he challenged his critics: "Give me a dozen healthy infants, well-formed, and my own specified environment to bring them up in, and I'll guarantee to take any one at random and train him to be any type of specialist I might select—doctor, lawyer, artist, merchant-chief and, yes, even beggar-man and thief, regardless of his talents, penchants, tendencies, abilities, vocations, and the race of his ancestors."[13] By the careful, systematic control of the mental and physical stimuli to which a child was exposed, Watson was confident that he could make a personality to order as a tailor makes a suit. Far from horrifying people, Watson's theories fascinated them. In its 1925 edition, his *Behaviorism* was hailed by one influential critic as "Perhaps the most important book ever written."[14]

Watson's influence cannot be overestimated. His theories informed the fashionable literature on child-rearing for more than twenty years. Firmness was the main thing. Children were to be fed by the clock, they were to learn from birth that crying for attention would not work, there was to be no self-indulgence, no sentimentality, and no arguing back. This regimen was enshrined in the most widely read government publication (excepting possibly the 1040) of all time, "Infant and Child Care." This was the faith that prevailed pre-Spock.

The third great guru of the Twenties was a pharmacist from Nancy, Emile Coué. He traveled to the United States in 1923, to be received like a conqueror, although he was short, elderly, and had sharp, unattractive features.[15] He dressed soberly in black and wore a beard and he had, in effect, reinvented the rosary. The devotee was supposed to put twenty knots into a piece of string, then, using the knots to keep count, was to intone twenty times, "Every day, in every respect, I am getting better and better." This exercise of the will upon the subconscious was to be performed each morning and night.[16]

Coué disclaimed that he was a healer, and much of Couéism was no more than positive thinking. But his theory that conscious autosuggestion could determine the sex of a child after conception was never proved. The failures seem likely to have equaled the successes.

It was an age when cults prospered. When belief fails, people do not simply cease to believe something. Instead, they are likely to believe anything. Ouija boards proliferated, there was a sudden interest in yoga, and before the Twenties were out the growing cult of the body spread nudist colonies to most of the warmer states.

Among the avant-garde there was also a fascination with death. Suicide became a fashionable topic of conversation, and the most admired exit was the motiveless suicide—a pure gesture of contempt for life.[17] An artist named Hans Stengel, in 1928, even threw a suicide party on the way out. "If you ask me," said his girlfriend, trying to explain why a healthy young man would take his own life, "he killed himself just to see what it was like to be dead."[18]

The living could escape to what remained of America's bohemias. Greenwich Village was still a place where one could see people walking along the street in their pajamas, where parties went on all night, where there were earnest, open discussions of "free love"—that is, casual, recreational sex. It was free love that gave the Village its greatest allure and brought coachloads of sightseers on tours of this new Sodom.

"Tea rooms" flourished here, places where free-verse poets read their works by candlelight.* Around 1920, embodying both free love and free verse, "Edna St. Vincent Millay *was* the Village."[19] And the religion of the Village was Freudianism. In 1922 when Joseph Freeman introduced himself to Floyd Dell,† one of the Village's leading lights, Dell was advising him only a few minutes later, "Have yourself psychoanalyzed. It's the only thing to do. Everybody is being psyched these days."[20]

If Greenwich Village wouldn't do, there was always Paris, to which hundreds had fled by 1920. There was an even greater exodus after 1925, when the pioneers had done their work of publicizing and making glamorous the Left Bank, the Rotonde, and the rue de Fleurus. When Matthew Josephson, one of the pioneers, returned to Paris in 1927, "There were certain quarters where one heard nothing but English, spoken with an American accent. . . ."[21]

One way and another, millions took flight. Disgusted with what they were or with what their country had become, they sought escape in bohemia, in sex, in psychoanalysis, in yoga, in Couéism, in death, in art, in nudism, in spiritualism. It was an obsession with self which we now take for granted as being typically modern.

---

* The tea rooms made candles chic. Fashionable restaurants began to put them on their tables, after an absence of twenty-five years or more. In time they even reappeared in the home.

† Dell, the author of *Moon-Calf* and other works on the struggles of an artistic, sensitive young man born into a philistine society, was an important figure in his time. He represented much that other young men wanted to be—published, famous, and a busy champion of free love and contraception. Before the decade was out he was happily married and a doting father. He was to become a Village unperson.

II

In our age, there is nothing more modern than youth. The war had a lot to do with that. The destruction of an entire generation of young men in half a dozen countries put a premium on youth that spilled over into the United States despite its comparatively light losses. The very fact that two million young men had been to the war invested them with an exposure to death that made their elders respect them, reversing the roles.[22] The obsession with youth may have also been a counterpoint to a fundamental social fact—since the turn of the century the average age had been rising steadily. During the Civil War, half the population was under twenty-one and only one-tenth was over forty-five.[23] There was now, comparatively, far less youth about.

For those with adolescent sons and daughters it was, by all accounts, a trying time. "Babbit had heard stories of 'goings-on' at young parties," reports Sinclair Lewis, "of girls 'parking' their corsets in the dressing room, of 'cuddling' and 'petting' and a presumable increase in what was known as Immorality." And Babbitt knew there was nothing he could do about it.

When adults wrung their hands over the young, what they chiefly deplored was the evidence of moral collapse. For that, they blamed the girls who dressed in provocative clothing, smoked cigarettes, swore as fluently as sailors, kissed promiscuously, and allowed boys to fondle their breasts.[24] The name for these girls was flappers.*

During the war young women had been encouraged to be assertive in public for the first time. They handed out flags and badges, collected money for war charities, sold bonds, and "a policy of 'being good to boys in uniform' readily expanded into a policy of being good to all boys."[25]

Among college students, who were somewhat older than flappers, there were sheiks and shebas. The expression derived from a cartoonist and satirist named John Held, who began by drawing what he saw, but in time college students began looking to Held's cartoons for guidance on language, dress and behavior. Before long they were pretending to be what they were.

Sheiks wore Fair Isle sweaters and Argyle sox, checked plus-eights or bell-bottomed flannels. They went hatless and put Slikum on their hair.†

---

* The dictionary definition of a flapper was a fledgling attempting to fly before it had grown the necessary feathers. It became current in England during the war to describe free and easy young women. H. L. Mencken introduced the same expression for the same purpose into the United States.

† In later life one of these sheiks tried to describe it. "Slikum," he recalled, "was a mystery fluid the color of Benedictine. If applied when the hair was wet it gave the effect of spar varnish. A tornado could not have ruffled a hair." Francis Russell, *The Great Interlude* (New York, 1962), p. 118.

A sheik with a few shekels to spend would drive a topless Model T, from which the windshield had been removed, and would swathe himself in a raccoon-skin coat that reached to his ankles. Shebas wore close-cropped shingled hair, short skirts or short sheath dresses; even their coats reached only to the knees, and when they sat down they did not, to the horror of their mothers, keep their knees together. They taped down their breasts and rolled down the tops of their stockings. The sheik carried a hip flask, his sheba a cigarette holder, and the ritual around which their lives revolved was the Big Game on Saturday afternoon.

Their parents simply could not figure them out. Even someone as sympathetic to youth as the poet Vachel Lindsay, in a poem of 1925 called "These Are the Young," termed them "a separate race, speaking an alien tongue." While they were freely criticized and diligently worried over, they had their defenders who pointed to their openness, their energy, and their sincerity.[26]

The worm in the bud, however, the source of so much parental anxiety (and adult envy), was sex, not sincerity.

III

There is nothing that characterizes twentieth-century life more thoroughly than our preoccupation with sex. In times of peace as well as war, whether other social change speeds up or slows down, in good times and bad, regardless of the decay or health of the culture, it alone flourishes in thought, word, and deed. Sex has come to occupy the place in modern life that religion occupied in the Middle Ages.

In the Twenties sexual desire was still referred to in polite circles as "the mating instinct." That it was natural, the Victorians had reasoned, did not mean that one had to approve of it. Nature appeared to have botched the job by not finding a more elevated method of reproduction. Then came Freud. Nineteenth-century psychology had attributed neurosis to uncongenial environments and mental traumas caused by unwelcome events, such as the death of a parent or child. Freud added a third source: suppressed desires. The most potent of these nearly always involved sex. The British writer Havelock Ellis probably did far more than Freud to encourage a less rigid, more levelheaded approach to sexual relationships. Psychoanalysis, however, attached itself to the fast-rising star of science, whose light appears to have dazzled every Western population into submission. Sexual freedom appeared to be scientific, more or less.

It became possible in the Twenties for the first time to carry out systematic surveys of sexual behavior. By later standards, they cannot be considered very reliable. But the general outlines are likely to be accurate, and these suggest that sex in the Twenties was of a highly conventional kind, with little fellatio, cunnilingus, or sodomy, and little experimentation with positions.[27] Even the young intellectuals committed to freedom and novelty had to learn by painful steps, and slowly. In 1919 Edmund Wilson, then twenty-four, visited a Greenwich Village drugstore—after waiting until there were no women customers inside—and bought his first condom. He was visibly nervous. To reassure him that the product was sound the clerk blew it up like a balloon.[28]

"By 1926 the universal pre-occupation with sex had become a nuisance," said Scott Fitzgerald, one of Wilson's classmates at Princeton.[29] Fitzgerald was wrong. *He* may have wearied of the subject, but few others did so while still young and healthy. To the educated, one of the reasons why Margaret Mead's *Coming of Age in Samoa*, published in 1928, was a masterpiece was its portrayal of a society that enjoyed recreational sex without guilt or pretense.[30]

There can be no doubting the reality of the sex revolution of the Twenties; it was not a matter simply of greater openness. Sexual freedom was essential to the repudiation of the Victorian/Puritan past. One of the leading gynecologists, in practice since 1890, said of his unmarried patients at the end of the decade, "Sexual experience in some form has been known by 100 per cent."[31] This was something that was not true a generation earlier.[32] Among women college graduates there appears to have been widespread lesbianism, and more than half in one survey of 2,200 women admitted that they regularly masturbated.[33]

Serious works on sex were likely to take as their central theme the sexual needs and rights of women, pleading again and again that men had to show more consideration and take their time.[34] There were also the women pioneers, such as Mrs. Grace Burnham, an attractive widow in her thirties, who decided to have a child in the eugenic way. She chose a young man of good character, in excellent health, possessed of keen intelligence, and coming from an upper-middle-class family. She made her wishes known, found him receptive, and after her pregnancy was well established she and he bid one another a friendly good-bye. The baby proved to be a girl and was named Vera (for truth). Mrs. Burnham was not the least nonplussed about revealing what she had done.[35]

And there was Edna St. Vincent Millay confounding male pride even as she excited the admiration of women, declaring openly that a former sexual liaison was ". . . insufficient reason / For conversation when we meet again." Or reflecting,

What lips my lips have kissed, and where, and why
I have forgotten, and what arms have lain
Under my head till morning . . .

The sexual revolution coincided with, and spurred along, a spectacular decline in prostitution. On the eve of the war there were hundreds of thousands of active, full-time prostitutes; perhaps as many as half a million.[36] Nearly every major city had its red-light district, as had hundreds of small towns. Usually close to downtown, they were openly acknowledged. Some were recognized by local ordinance. Crowded with saloons and whorehouses, every night was party night. A walk up an alley could take you to a crap game, a prostitute, or a mugging. There was a frontier atmosphere of licentiousness and violence. Prostitution was an offense in only half a dozen states. Pimps advertised their girls in the local newspaper; whorehouses printed and distributed lavish brochures.

The Progressives, however, were mounting a strong counterattack. Panic over white slavery led to the passage in 1910 of the Mann Act, which made it a federal offense to transport a woman across state lines for an immoral purpose. The newspapers began to run antivice campaigns. Good Government candidates (Goo-Goos) were swept into city hall. And the military closed down the remaining red-light districts during the war to protect 4 million mothers' sons from VD.[37]

The antivice movement was more dramatic and more effective than the fifty-year struggle to abolish the saloon. But it could not hope to abolish prostitution. Thousands of brothels went out of business and there was far less streetwalking and open solicitation. At the same time, a new type of prostitute appeared—the call girl, with her own apartment, her own telephone, and often without a pimp. Nightclubs also proliferated. Usually attributed to Prohibition, the nightclub boom owed more than a little to the repression of open prostitution. Forced off the streets, deprived of the saloon's back room, ejected from the old-fashioned brothel, the trade flourished in many of the new nightclubs where the girls were known as "hostesses."[38]

Prostitution was also dispersed into lower-class neighborhoods and slums, such as Harlem and the South Side. Among the reasons for the spectacular decline in white prostitution were the new immigration laws, which deprived the trade of poor and friendless girls in a country where they hardly knew the language and work was hard to find. But at the same time tens of thousands of young black women were moving north. By 1930, black hookers far outnumbered white in Chicago[39] and New York.[40]

At the other end of the scale were the Lorelei Lees, celebrated in *Gentlemen Prefer Blondes*, a best-seller that was a clever, unaffected tribute to successful prostitution.* It was so clever, in fact, that it had no trouble with censorship. Edmund Wilson judged it the best novel of 1926.[41] Anita Loos, the pixylike author of *Gentlemen Prefer Blondes*, was snowed under with admiring letters from prim housewives, YMCA secretaries, and women's club officers, nearly all of whom had missed the point. They found Lorelei Lee sweetly virginal and gently corrected the wayward, chorus-girl grammar in which the book was written.[42]

Authority did not give in to the new wave of sexual freedom without a struggle. At Miss Millay's alma mater, Vassar, the dress regulations were carefully rewritten in 1925 to ensure that the young ladies did not bare their knees.[43] The State Department denied entry to persons cited as corespondents in divorce cases based on adultery, considering them guilty of "moral turpitude."[44] When the April 1926 edition of *American Mercury* appeared it contained an article called "Hatrack," about a very thin, small-town prostitute. Hatrack asked every customer if he was Catholic or Protestant. "If he was a Protestant she took him into the Catholic cemetery; if he was a Catholic she took him into the Masonic cemetery." This reminiscence of copulation among the tombstones was denounced from a thousand small-town pulpits, and immediately banned in Boston. It took a federal court order and thousands of dollars in legal fees to get the offending edition distributed by mail.

Throughout the period there were lively struggles over the censorship of plays and books. A dozen theaters were padlocked in New York, some for up to a year. The post office maintained an index of forbidden books that ran to more than 500 titles.

Yet the struggle to maintain at least the forms of the old morality was doomed to failure. It was a morality of small, stable communities. And here was a society coming increasingly under the sway of big cities. Vast and anonymous, they tolerated or ignored unconventional behavior. The village atheists, the small-town radicals, the revolutionary orators did not have to create their own quarter in the city to feel safe anymore. "The bohemian life becomes increasingly characteristic of the city at large."[45]

As it does so, it forms the ideal setting for the Don Juan, the rootless, predatory, handsome man. At least one, Ward Smith, kept a diary of a sexual career between the wars.[46] He was in Los Angeles when the town

---

* There was a real-life Lorelei Lee. Her name was Peggy Hopkins Joyce. She had been a Ziegfeld girl between marriages, earning $700 a week for revealing her astonishingly beautiful legs. Although she was mistress and wife to various millionaires, her talent seems to have been more for shopping than sex. She took her third husband, Stanley Joyce, on a one-week tour of Manhattan's shops that cost him $1 million (about $4 million in current prices). When she divorced him she received $2 million. Her life was lived largely on the front pages of the tabloids. *Time* called her "the most famous woman in the United States."

filled up with girls hoping to break into movies. Advertising as a talent scout, he seduced as many as six girls in a day. In New York, attaching himself to a millionaire rake, Cornelius Vanderbilt, he had sex with hundreds of good-time girls who liked going to rich people's parties. In Florida during the land boom, Ward Smith was there for more of the same. Casanova never did so well. It was a life that could only have been lived in the modern world. Ward Smith was not rich, powerful, or famous, yet he made love to more than a thousand women. The secret of his success was modern life, and mainly modern cities, filling up with lonely, bored, unattached young women. The reader may (or not) be pleased to know that Ward Smith considered his life a failure.

Sex had not yet become as available as tap water for everyone, or even for the majority. But the sexual liberty of the Twenties is nothing less than amazing when compared with the sexual repression only a decade or so earlier. And the decline in commercial vice was one of the best things that had happened to American society in modern times. It meant, among other things, that although industrial wages were still too low by most standards, they were now high enough (just) to keep tens of thousands of working-class girls from selling themselves for sex. A generation earlier a teenager who wanted to lose his virginity would have gone to the local whorehouse. These days he was far more likely to try to seduce his high school sweetheart.[47]

It was a world removed from the nineteenth-century ideal of the one-love-in-a-lifetime. A great love had been considered heroic and triumphant, worth anything that a man or woman could give. "Love is best," said the Victorians. It was better, far, than fame or wealth or power. But the new generation, wrote Joseph Wood Krutch in one of the intellectual landmarks of the Twenties, *The Modern Temper*, "though it is more completely absorbed in the pursuit of love than in anything else, has lost the sense of any ultimate importance in the experience which preoccupies it."[48]

The new sexual freedom rolled forward as implacably as a tank division advancing across an agricultural plain, its weight and speed flattening everything in its path. Café arguments for or against were irrelevant. All the forces of modern life were behind it—the growing economic and intellectual independence of women, the craving for excitement in a world becoming dull and standardized, the energy and loneliness of life in cities, the development of birth control, the sanction of science, the collapse of the old moral order, the rejection of puritanism.

Perhaps more important still was another of the formative influences of our century, democratization. Politically, democratization has meant change spreading from the top down. But in cultural and social matters it has usually meant the infiltration upward of lower-class interests, manners, and speech, so that even highly educated people now freely employ gutter langauge. They are no longer expected to put their ribald observations into Latin, or at least French. The music, the dress, the language, but above all the easy-going love 'em and leave 'em sexuality traditionally allowed the lowest classes, have become the property of everyone.

IV

Before the First World War women were arrested for smoking cigarettes in public, for using profanity, for appearing on public beaches without stockings, for driving automobiles without a man beside them, for wearing outlandish attire (for example, shorts, slacks, men's hats), and for not wearing their corsets. Women accused of such offenses against public order and common decency were summoned before the courts, not only of small towns, but of big cities such as Chicago.[49]

In less than a decade these prosecutions stopped, simply because they seemed as absurd as they were futile. Outwardly at least the position of women had been transformed. Population changes for the first time in history began working in their favor. Historically, the death rate for women had been higher than the death rate for men. In a generation, that had been completely reversed.[50] Women now made up 20 percent of the work force, and without their labor the economy would collapse. When the Nineteenth Amendment was put to the states in June 1919, proposing that women be allowed to vote, it took little more than a year for it to be ratified and become part of the Constitution.*

This was a victory for which American feminists had labored for more than thirty years. But in the hour of triumph they were finally free to fall out and promptly did so. Under the prompting of the sixty-five-year-old Carrie Chapman Catt, the country's greatest feminist, the National Woman Suffrage Association went out of business, and then set up the League of Women Voters to encourage women to use what had taken so long to win.

To other feminists this was not enough. In 1923, after years of bitter disagreement, they created the National Woman's Party, headed by Alice Paul, who had risen to prominence through her involvement with the English suffragettes. The NWP had a single aim: the Equal Rights Amend-

---

* It was not only an idea whose time had come; it was really overdue. Some twenty-one nations had women suffrage before the United States.

ment. The NWP was composed mainly of middle-class women who were college-educated and living in comfortable homes. Their dedication was equaled by their naïvety. Absolute equality would have stripped from working-class women the small measure of protection that had been so arduously won. The death and injury rates for women were almost double those for men in the same working-class occupations. Protection against excessive fatigue, lifting heavy loads, exposure to constant noise, high heat, and the twelve-hour shift was absolutely essential to the health of working women.[51] The Equal Rights Amendment was a threat, moreover, to mothers' pensions and maternity insurance. Women social workers and others who knew the conditions under which most women had to work fought the ERA to a standstill.[52] In effect, in the 1920s it never got beyond the women's movement. The same was true of the demand made by feminists that wages be paid to housewives.[53]

Feminism itself was rapidly losing its appeal. Having won the vote, most women did not bother to use it. They, too, turned away from public affairs to private concerns. The enlightened woman devoted her energies to her job, if she had one, and her love life (ditto). And if there was a choice to be made between one and the other, most gave up the struggle and settled for the man instead of the job.[54] Feminism had even become a term of opprobrium among young women, conjuring up images of aggressive man-hating frumps in nondescript tweeds.[55]

Here was a different generation. The young women who had gone to college before the war had been cast in a defiant, independent mold. The college woman of 1910 was likely to dedicate herself to a career.* Her counterpart of 1925 could almost always be expected to dedicate herself to marriage and children.[56] Where women did remain defiant they pitted themselves against social conventions, instead of social conditions.

They took up smoking and drinking. They dressed in next to nothing. They bore almost the entire burden of the new sexual frontier. Adventuring from bed to bed involved comparatively few risks for men, and it was actively encouraged by traditional masculine envy of the Don Juan. Women ran the risk of pregnancy, possibly leading to a dangerous abortion. They risked, too, another masculine tradition—contempt for the woman who offers herself too freely. Even in Greenwich Village, women who were known to be promiscuous were scorned.[57]

The vast majority of women, however, took no part in these struggles. The right to vote, the fate of the Equal Rights Amendment, sexual equal-

---

* The top women's colleges before 1914 concentrated on the teaching of science, notably chemistry and physics. The result was that 10 percent of the country's doctors were women. By 1925 that figure had fallen by half.

ity with men, marriage versus career troubled them hardly at all. What they were interested in was not feminism but femininity. It was the Twenties that put a beauty parlor in nearly every small town, saw cosmetics grow from a minor business into one with a turnover worth $500 million a year, and created a whole new career for young women, that of the beautician. And while this interest in looking beautiful may have had something to do with self-confidence and self-respect, it also had a lot to do with finding the right man.[58]

V

By the late Twenties nearly all the young single women who were seen by the gynecologist referred to a few pages back confidently expected to be married. They had good reason to be so positive about it. Since 1890 the marriage rate had risen sharply. In frontier times half the male adult population never married. Now the figure was down to one-third and dropping steadily.[59] Marriage and ordinary family life had become the norm. It literally represented the settling down of American men after the frontier passed into history.

As marriage increased, however, so did divorce. In 1890 there had been one divorce for every seventeen marriages; by the late Twenties there was one for every six.[60] Since the rise of Christianity marriage had meant indissolubility and monogamy. It was a union sacred and divine. It was one subject on which Catholics and Protestants took almost exactly the same view. In the past fifty'years, however, people had found ways around marriage as a lifetime commitment through civil ceremonies and ever-easier divorce laws. What had come into existence was serial monogamy (one woman at a time); commitment hedged with reservations; and rejection of marriage as something sacred and divine.*

Divorce was particularly likely among couples without children.[61] Such unions constituted 16 percent of marriages, but produced nearly three-fourths of all divorces.[62] Serious journals agonized over the divorce problem.[63] Yet Nevada turned it into the state's cottage industry, and when other states tried to steal business by lowering their residence requirements, Nevada undercut them in turn, repeatedly, until its requirement reached forty-two days.[64]

---

* There was a popular piece of mocking verse:
> Still the Census taker tarried
> With a poised and ready pen;
> "One more question, Are you married?"
> Came the answer, "Now and then."

At the same time, novels, plays, and works of social criticism steadily derided marriage as an outmoded institution, something the modern world could well do without.[65] There were confident predictions that marriage would die out before the end of the century. Judge Ben Lindsey of Denver held out an alternative arrangement—the companionate marriage, as he termed it.[66] It was what we call living together, until the depth of the commitment involved became clear and the two parties to it had proved to their own satisfaction that they could and would get along. At that point a marriage service could be arranged and the couple could proceed to have children. Companionate marriage created a great stir at the time, and was thereafter almost completely forgotten.

Critics and reformers notwithstanding, there was instead a rallying to the old institution. A college course in marriage was begun at the University of North Carolina. The example spread to other colleges and down into the high schools. The old moral order which had sustained the ideal of marriage as a lifetime union may have collapsed, but the ideal somehow remained, free-floating, harder than ever to realize, yet almost magical in its appeal, for the more that people turned inward, the less they liked what they found.

VI

Thriving abortion clinics operated all over New York. They had become by the Twenties a rich source of payoff money for hundreds of policemen and politicians. When, as sometimes happened, a doctor was arrested for performing an illegal abortion it meant that he had forgotten or refused to pay up.[67] In the country as a whole, it was estimated that up to 1 million women a year were criminally aborted. There was abortion by knitting needle, coat hanger, and buttonhook. Desperate women swallowed poisonous concoctions in an attempt to induce a miscarriage. Criminal abortion killed as many as 50,000 women a year.[68] Yet it was absolutely against the law to disseminate·birth control information or devices, under Section 211 of the United States Penal Code.

Before 1873 anyone could print or mail anything. There was no legal barrier of any kind to the distribution of pornography or anything else to do with sex. Section 211 was written into the Penal Code to satisfy one man, Anthony Comstock. It prohibited "mailing, transporting or importing anything lewd, lascivious or obscene," which was so vague it could sometimes be evaded. But it specifically barred "anything preventing conception." Comstock, a towering figure in his time, a lifelong crusader for the old moral order, was well pleased. With the enactment of Section 211, state after state followed suit and went into the antipornography business, and birth control information was considered pornography. The American Medical Association did its part, too, instructing doctors only to give birth control information in the cause of preventing disease. It was only in the struggle to check venereal disease, which by World War I had reached epidemic proportions, that condoms became legally available.

Meanwhile, growing up in Cornell, New York, was a gray-eyed, auburn-haired girl who was very pretty and very thoughtful. Her name was Margaret McKee and she reflected later with some bitterness, "Mother bore eleven children; she died at forty-eight. My father died at eighty."[69] As she grew up, she noticed that the poor had many children, the rich few. To her, it was cause and effect, a long life or an early death, happiness or sorrow.

Coming as she did from a poor family, there was no chance for her to become a doctor, which she longed to be. She entered medicine through nursing instead. She met and married a young architect, William Sanger. They moved to Hastings-on-Hudson, a charming, new upper-middle-class suburb, and there they raised three happy children, played croquet, and were very, very bored. After nine years of mounting ennui, they abandoned their dream house and ran away to Greenwich Village; to the company of John Reed, Emma Goldman, Eugene Debs, and Mabel Dodge. They arrived when the Village was at its bohemian peak, on the eve of the war. Sanger fell in with a circle of avant-garde painters, his wife with the feminists and direct actionists. And she returned to nursing, in the slums. She had to confront what she had known too well in childhood all over again.

The moment when she saw her true life's work spread out before her, almost in a vision, came in the early morning hours after a poor woman, bearing a child she did not want, died in childbirth. The infant was stillborn. As dawn broke coldly over the Lower East Side, Margaret Sanger looked over the tenement rooftops in a kind of revery. "I knew a new day had come for me and a new world as well. . . . There was only one thing to be done: Awaken the womanhood of America to free the womanhood of the world! I released from my almost paralyzed hand the nursing bag which unconsciously I had clutched, threw it across the room, tore the uniform from my body, and renounced all palliative work forever."[70]

She plunged into six months of intensive research, only to discover "there was no practical medical information on contraception available in the United States."[71] At which point one of her left-wing friends, Bill Haywood, advised her to go to France, where (to the despair of its generals) families were small, whether rich or poor.

Such, at least, is the way Margaret Sanger told the story—the revelation, the symbolic casting aside of her former life, the bottomless depths of ignorance she had to overcome. There was, in fact, an extensive literature on contraception in every large library, in the works on medicine. But it was necessary for her to create a legend of herself for the work she had taken on. And a European trip was essential, if only because the birth control struggle was more advanced there.

She speeded her departure, however, by first writing a pamphlet on contraception and trying to distribute it. A federal indictment was brought against her. She fled to Montreal, and then to England aboard a ship loaded with munitions for the war which had recently broken out. Under the Comstock Act she could be fined up to $5,000 and spend five years in prison.

It was in England that she found her true métier. She met and fell in love with the great sage of sex without guilt, Havelock Ellis. He guided her reading and advised her on tactics. In New York she had turned her prodigious energies over the entire spectrum of radical interests, agitating against marriage, capitalism, religion, bourgeois hypocrisy, conventional politics. Ellis convinced her to devote herself entirely to birth control, a phrase which she had coined. Each day Ellis took her to the British Museum to introduce her to the volumes she needed to read. Among them was George Drysdale's *Elements of Social Science*. Drysdale envisaged the world running out of love before it ran out of food, and a world short of love would be as desperate and brutal as one where food was scarce. Artificial contraception was the only hope of increasing the amount of love in the world. "Drysdale was thus probably the first modern thinker to perceive the possibilities of applying the achievements of science to the enhancement of romantic love."[72] Until now, feminists had usually tried to free women *from* sex. Margaret Sanger left the British Museum to free women *for* it.

In her absence William Sanger had taken up the struggle by distributing his wife's pamphlet, "Family Limitation." He was arrested in his studio by none other than the elderly Anthony Comstock. He chose to go to prison rather than pay a fine. Margaret Sanger hurried home in September 1915, knowing that her marriage was already doomed, but determined to save her husband from prison.

His sentence was set aside and the indictment which had prompted her flight to Europe was dropped, to her disappointment. For she was now eager to wear a martyr's crown.[73] Free instead to do as she pleased, she opened a birth control clinic in the Brownsville section of Brooklyn. She covered the neighborhood with a leaflet, printed in English, Yiddish, and

Italian. She offered a contraception counseling service for a 10-cent registration fee. She expected to be arrested. She was. Both she and her sister, Mrs. Ethel Byrne, were convicted of breaking the New York State version of the Comstock Act and went to prison for thirty days. On her release from prison Margaret Sanger and Frederick Blossom began publishing *Birth Control Review*.

By the armistice there were rivals in the field, chiefly the National Birth Control League organized by Mary Ware Dennett. The NBCL devoted itself to lobbying for changes in the law. Mrs. Sanger continued opening birth control clinics. This was the direct action approach of her Greenwich Village years. Yet, as she became an important figure in her own right and as she fell into heated quarrels with other workers for birth control, she left her radical friends behind and set about creating her own empire.

In 1921 she organized the first American Birth Control Conference, out of which came the American Birth Control League—president, Margaret Sanger. The proceedings were thrown into confusion when the newly installed president stood up to speak on "Birth Control: Is it Moral?" at a meeting in Town Hall on the last day of the conference. The New York police burst through the doors and raced down the aisles. Charging onto the platform, they dragged the speakers out into the street, as the audience stood defiantly singing "My Country 'Tis of Thee." The drama continued outside the hall. Mrs. Sanger strode, head held high, up Eighth Avenue to the 47th Street police station, followed by a crocodile of slower-moving policemen, hundreds of supporters, and a crowd of curiosity-seekers. Police reserves had to be summoned to control the crowds that surrounded the police station.[74] The raid had been at the urging of the Roman Catholic archbishop of New York, Patrick J. Hayes. When this became known there were cries of outrage the length and breadth of the country. It was the best send-off the ABCL could have asked for.

A year later she remarried. Her second husband was an elderly millionaire, J. Noah H. Slee, the creator of Three-in-One Oil. She kept the marriage secret for two years, kept her own (now famous) name, and had a separate residence. The adoring Slee agreed to all her demands for independence combined with security. He also became the principal supporter of the ABCL, raining money into its accounts.[75]

By 1926 the ABCL had nearly 40,000 members; mostly college-educated, married, about thirty, with one or two children. The ABCL sponsored lecture tours, conferences, and clinics. Meanwhile, Margaret Sanger traveled the world, lobbying for birth control. Her hosts were frequently surprised to discover that she was petite, with a delicate face, a mass of beautiful hair, and a quiet, reserved manner. She dressed in a very conservative, modishly feminine way. And her charm was irresistible. She was not the least like the feminist harridan they expected.[76]

She was jealous of her eminence, however. When she found that the people left to run the ABCL during her long absences were running things according to their ideas, not hers, she resigned as president and Slee cut off the flow of money. But by the late 1920s the success of her mission was no longer in doubt. What had begun as a radical cause a decade earlier had become fashionable. What had begun in Greenwich Village had become the vogue among Republican matrons in Scarsdale. Ironically, the proposed liberation of the working class had done more for middle-class women.

Margaret Sanger had begun by arguing for birth control as the greatest of all social reforms. It was to eradicate poverty and, with it, all the crime, the squalor, the misery, and the disease that poverty gave rise to. Birth control was going to save the lower class—most of the human race. And as they rose, the thin upper-class stratum that ran the world would lose its hold on wealth and power.

By the late Twenties, however, the "philosophy" of birth control (philosophy was the word she preferred) had shifted its ground. Birth control had become part of the eugenics movement. It was now supposed to keep the "unfit" from reproducing themselves. It would even slow down the growth of that modern tyranny, the welfare state. Margaret Sanger was, in truth, a transitional figure—half-modern, half-Victorian.

When she came to write *Happiness in Marriage* in 1927 she deplored masturbation (it caused impotence[77]), sex before marriage, and infidelity. Her strictures on diet, manners, and grooming were in the best self-improving bourgeois style. Her descriptions of sexual fulfillment were bathed in the glow of high romanticism. There were dozens of little homilies, along the lines of "Win and woo each time anew." But there were also straightforward descriptions of the sexual organs, and sexual abstinence was dismissed as unnecessary and unnatural. Her emphasis on sex as a pleasure came as a revelation to an entire generation of women, and birth control put that pleasure within the reach of all.

The war had introduced hundreds of thousands of young men to prophylactics. One reporter surveying birth control in Baltimore found that the demand for condoms kept more than 200 salesmen in full-time employment in the mid-Twenties.[78] Vasectomy was being touted as rejuvenation: "if the energy of the testes is deflected from the manufacture of spermatazoa then there remains energy to produce hormones in magnificent quantity."[79] Among older men the results were said to be almost miraculous.

Margaret Sanger was wrong about the poor. She had thought that what was lacking was knowledge of contraception and a cheap, reliable contraceptive device. What was really lacking was a middle-class outlook on life in general and sex in particular. The poor were not used to planning their future. They had jobs, for example, not careers. And for a working-class woman, the only role for which she was prepared was that of wife and mother. Finally, working-class men were rarely prepared to work out in advance the careful management of sexual intercourse that effective birth control required.

Among the middle class, however, it was an overwhelming success. One survey of college-educated couples in the late Twenties showed that 90 percent practiced contraception.[80] Another survey had a similar result.[81] There were, moreover, nearly thirty birth control clinics operating in the United States and more opened every year. There were still raids, harassment, and resistance to be faced. But with the clinics a thriving reality, Margaret Sanger devoted her energies increasingly to lobbying for changes in the law, and lobbying for the support of American doctors. These alone would make her success permanent, and in time she would see them realized.

The Twenties are usually dismissed as a decade when reform was dead. The career—and triumph—of Margaret Sanger tell a different story. Sex could no longer be forced on women as a duty. They had to be persuaded, their consent had to be won. "Whether or not birth control is eugenic, hygienic and economic," wrote Walter Lippmann, "it is the most revolutionary practice in the history of sexual morals."[82] He was right.

9. Damp Yankees

Prohibition grew out of the saloon, and the saloon grew out of the frontier. Building the cities and the factories, putting down roads and railroad track, and hacking away at the wilderness created an enormous thirst. Half the men were unmarried, amusements were few, and life was fairly short anyway. So why not get drunk every payday? Why not blot out the nagging ache of overworked muscles? Why not fill the emotional blank spots with boozy camaraderie?

Saloons matched the pace of urbanization and industrialization every step of the way. Where barrels could be made and a crude clapboard structure put up, there would be a saloon. In the growing towns and cities there would be some blocks where there were more saloons than anything else. There were, in fact, far too many. Supply began to outrun demand, even though the demand was huge and steadily rising. As the saloons competed for business, they became less and less careful about how they did it. They began to provide prostitutes and drugs. Minors were served without hesitation, if they had ten cents or a quarter to spend. There were tables for gambling.

Saloons offered a free lunch—one that was very salty or very dry. And even then, "bouncers threw out any man who ate more than his money's worth of drink."[1] Saloons went their own way, buying off police and politicians when necessary and struggling manfully against woman suffrage. All the while, however, as communities became more settled, resistance to the saloon was growing.

Alcohol itself was under attack. At the turn of the century studies began to appear that demonstrated that even moderate drinking could be harmful to the liver and kidneys, that it was a depressant rather than a stimulant, and was likely to ruin an otherwise healthy stomach. When it did not actively cause a disease, it lowered the resistance to other diseases. The pregnant woman who drank stood a good chance of producing a child with some appalling congenital defect. The scientific case against the saloon won over millions who had never been persuaded by clergymen or women's groups.[2]

Alcohol had for centuries been prescribed as a treatment for colds, as an aid to digestion, as a nerve tonic. But by World War I large numbers of doctors had become teetotalers, and they stopped writing such prescriptions. Hospitals refused to carry it. Pharmacists refused to dispense it. Alcohol, they intoned, was poison.

The cutting edge of the attack on the demon rum, however, was the Anti-Saloon League. It derived most of its support from the evangelical Protestant churches. Episcopalians and Lutherans barely deigned to acknowledge the ASL's existence. Jews and Catholics wanted temperance, not Prohibition. But Baptists, Methodists, and other evangelicals considered any attack on the ASL as an attack on themselves.[3]

The course of events was typified by the experience of Washington State. The railroad came over the mountains and through the forests in the 1880s. Where the railroad went, the saloon quickly followed. By 1903 there were thousands of miles of railroad track, thousands of saloons— and a flourishing arm of the Anti-Saloon League.[4] The arrival of the ASL "Flying Squad" in a town to back up the Prohibition crusade of the local churches was an event, with torchlight parades, brass bands, speakers, singers, and fireworks.

Based on the neighborhood Protestant church, the ASL became ubiquitous and powerful. The man who ran the ASL, Wayne B. Wheeler, was short and thin and appeared utterly insignificant. With his small mustache and thinning hair, he looked remarkably like the cartoonist's impression of John Q. Public. He was, however, the most effective lobbyist in American history. He was an unyielding, single-minded crusader, gifted with energy and intelligence. Wheeler was, at bottom, a brilliant opportunist, easily in the Lenin class.

The ASL did not have the field to itself. It had allies in the Women's Christian Temperance Union, which numbered hundreds of thousands of members. There was also a Prohibition party, founded in 1869. It had begun as a party lobbying for business regulation, public education, votes for women, and liberal immigration policies, as well as Prohibition. By 1914 it was interested only in Prohibition.[5] Prohibition had been taken up by both the Populists and the Progressives, the principal reform movements in American politics at the turn of the century. There were important dry Republican Progressives, such as Borah, and important dry Democratic Progressives such as McAdoo.[6].

In the cities, the Goo-Goos considered the removal of the saloon one of the essentials of municipal reform. It was in the saloons that votes were bought for drinks on polling day. It was in the saloon that the worst type of ward boss held court. Social workers and the people who ran the settlement houses wanted to banish the saloon, mopping up as it did the little money that trickled into the slums.

Health officials traced venereal disease into the back rooms of 10,000 saloons. The man who was liquored up was more likely to sleep with prostitutes than the man who was sober, and before penicillin the syphilitic who drank was harder to cure than the one who was dry.

It would be wrong to suggest, however, that progressivism as such wanted to abolish the saloon. The old-stock, middle-class Progressives certainly did. But those who worked with immigrants and urban labor organizations did not. They considered Prohibition oppressive and unworkable. Only the railroad brotherhoods, composed of the old Protestant stock, provided labor support for Prohibition. There was a similar split in the Socialist party—leadership dry, rank and file wet.

Contrary to the usual impression, Prohibition did not arrive like a thief in the night, taking an unprepared country by surprise. There were five completely dry states by 1908, and twenty-three by 1914. That did not necessarily mean that liquor was not to be had in these states. For example, in Oklahoma, dry since statehood, liquor flowed as freely as the oil.[7] Some states only enforced Prohibition against spirits, tolerating wine and beer.[8]

When the United States entered the war, Prohibition became patriotic. Most breweries had German names attached to them. Congress prohibited the sale of intoxicating beverages to men in uniform. Five more states went dry. But the war only speeded up events. In the elections of 1916, Prohibition was the principal issue in nearly every state poll, and the prohibitionists won. "It seems clear that the American people wanted prohibition and were bound to try it," said Herbert Asbury.[9] National Prohibition, however, could be accomplished only by amending the Constitution. Congress had no direct authority to regulate or prohibit the consumption of anything.

The ASL just happened to have a proposed amendment handy. In December 1917 Congress submitted this to the states. The Eighteenth Amendment proposed to ban the sale, manufacture, and transportation of "intoxicating liquor." It did not outlaw buying it or drinking it. The ASL had wisely stopped short of total Prohibition. The amendment was not to come into effect, moreover, for one year after ratification, which would allow the liquor trade to wind up its affairs and drinkers to fill up their cellars. On January 16, 1919, Nebraska became the thirty-sixth state to ratify the Eighteenth Amendment.

With Prohibition written into the Constitution there remained the problem of enforcement. The ASL just happened to have a draft enforcement statute handy. It was passed in September 1919 and was generally known as the Volstead Act.* It ought with greater justice to have been called the Wheeler Act.

The Volstead Act allowed the manufacture, under permit, of industrial alcohol; its denaturing to render it unfit for consumption; and its withdrawal by businesses, such as paint companies, which needed it. Existing stocks of beverage alcohol could be withdrawn for use in religious services, for medicinal purposes, or for conversion into vinegar. Wheeler defined an intoxicating beverage as one containing 0.5 percent alcohol. But it was no crime to buy a drink, or an entire case if you wished. The crime was to sell it.

When the Volstead Act was presented for Wilson's signature, in October 1919, he vetoed it. The act was easily and swiftly passed over his veto. The Eighteenth Amendment would come into force on January 16, 1920.

Events did not augur well for its future. In Christmas week, 1919, more than seventy people were killed and dozens more blinded in the Connecticut Valley after drinking wood alcohol. The good stuff had vanished into cellars and warehouses. Yet people were prepared to risk death and blindness for the sake of a drink.[10]

On the night of January 15–16, there were midnight services in thousands of Protestant churches. When the law came into effect, bells pealed in the darkness, as if a great victory had been won.

II

Harding had been badgered by Wheeler for years, and Wheeler's only failure with him was that he could never get Harding to take the pledge.

---

* Andrew J. Volstead was personally dry but hardly the fanatic that the statute named after him implies. An obscure, conscientious representative from Minnesota, he rose on the basis of seniority to the chairmanship of the House Judiciary Committee. It had been his duty to report the Eighteenth Amendment out of committee and when it was passed to husband the enforcement statute it called for through the House. Volstead never signed the pledge, never had much contact with the Anti-Saloon League, and in 1916 had narrowly held onto his seat against a Prohibition party candidate. In 1922 he lost it to an opponent who accused Volstead of being an atheist.

They were both from Ohio, and Wheeler had long been the terror of that state's politicians. When Harding went to the White House, Wheeler's influence in national affairs already great, doubled overnight. He installed one of his protégés, Roy Asa Haynes, as Federal Prohibition Commissioner. The Prohibition Bureau was forced on the Treasury Department, which did not want it, instead of the Justice Department, which specialized in law enforcement. Wheeler appears to have feared that the Justice Department would have tried to run the Prohibition Bureau, instead of letting him do it by remote control.[11]

A new assistant attorney generalship was created, to oversee Prohibition prosecutions. Harding appointed a woman lawyer from Los Angeles, Mrs. Mabel Walker Willebrandt. Her zeal matched Wheeler's own.* At the local level, however, many prohibition agents had been given their jobs as a reward for loyal service to a ward boss or party county chairman. What they were given was more than a job (which paid only about $2,000 a year). They had been given a chance to get rich.[12]

There was, for example, Edward Donegan. In 1919 he had eked out a spartan existence by collecting driftwood from the Gowanus Canal in Brooklyn. In 1920, Prohibition agent Donegan banked $1,653,797.25 in only four months. Donegan had cornered the market on withdrawal permits for the entire state of New York.[13] The head of the New York City Prohibition Squad on which Donegan served, Dan Chapin, in time wearied of seeing his $2,000-a-year men arrive in chauffeured limousines. He called a meeting around a huge table in the federal building and ordered his men, "Put your hands on the table. Both of 'em!" When all had obeyed, he informed them, "Every son of a bitch wearing a diamond ring is fired." Half the squad left the room.[14] In its first four years the Prohibition Bureau fired nearly 1,000 agents, attorneys, and clerical workers "for cause." So long as it remained outside the civil service (another concession to Wheeler) it was not likely to improve much.

Some agents, in fact, were enthusiastic and honest. Two became national celebrities, Izzy Einstein and his partner, Moe Smith. Izzy was a short, moon-faced, middle-aged postal clerk when he applied to become a Prohibition agent. Chapin turned him down, telling him that he did not look remotely like a detective. And what, asked Izzy, was a better disguise than that?[15] Moe Smith, with whom he teamed up, was a little taller and even fatter than the rotund senior partner.

Izzy went about his business without ever carrying a gun, and seemed

---

* Strangely enough, Mrs. Willebrandt might have passed for Al Capone's sister. Nose, chin, shape of face, dark hair, the fleshy but determined mouth—all were identical. The only difference was her blue eyes.

able to get in anywhere. He had more disguises than Lon Chaney. Often he simply equipped himself with a humble prop. Who would have expected a Prohibition agent to come into a speakeasy carrying a pitcher of milk or hopping in on a crutch? On one occasion he went from saloon to saloon on an ice wagon. On another day he used a coal wagon and in an hour arrested sixteen saloon keepers who had been fooled by his squat, coal-black appearance. Speakeasies began to put up his picture over the bar, framed in black crepe. Underneath was a sign reading: LOOK OUT FOR THIS MAN! [16]

In the end, Izzy and Moe paid for their zealousness. Between them, they made nearly 3,000 arrests, putting to shame every other Prohibition agent. During one of the periodic reorganizations of the Prohibition Bureau they were organized out of their jobs. To other agents, less resourceful but equally dedicated, it seemed unfair that these two were receiving all the praise and publicity in what was really a thankless cause.

And what were these other agents doing? For one thing, they opened a speakeasy on East 44th Street to trap bootleggers. Meanwhile, they sold drinks to thousands. They were also energetically padlocking. It required only a court order, a padlock, and a few feet of chain to close a saloon for a year. Between 1921 and 1927 thousands of saloons and restaurants were closed in this way. The height of the padlocking crusade came when Prohibition agents padlocked a tree. [17]

Six miles from Dyersville, California, moonshiners had hidden a fifty-gallon still in the cavity of a redwood tree that was twenty-four feet in diameter. The entrance was hidden by a piece of canvas that had been painted to resemble bark. Acting on a tip-off, a squad of agents raided the tree, seized the still, strung a length of chain around the tree, joined it with a padlock, and tacked a sign to the canvas reading: "Closed for One Year for Violation of the National Prohibition Act." [18]

As the number of padlocked premises climbed into the thousands it became harder and harder to keep checking up on them, to make sure they remained closed. Prohibition agents were thin on the ground. In the Pacific Northwest, comprising Washington, Oregon, and Alaska, there were never more than twenty agents, and to cover this vast area they had no automobiles, no airplanes, no boats. [19]

Underpaid and undermanned, with little training and little public support, agents tended to rely on the fast draw, the pistol-whipping, or just plain fists. Nor were these activities necessarily screened from public view. Senator Frank L. Greene of Vermont was only one of scores of victims. Walking down Pennsylvania Avenue with his wife one winter's day in 1924 he passed an alley where a Prohibition agent had set a trap for a bootlegger. When the trap was sprung, the bootlegger resisted and the agent opened fire. The senator fell to the ground with a bullet in his head.[20]

Congress persistently starved the Prohibition Bureau of money. The states were even more niggardly. Total state appropriations to enforce their "baby Volstead Acts" amount to $698,855 in 1925.[21] Some states never ratified the Eighteenth Amendment. Maryland refused to enact a prohibition enforcement statute and four states which had enacted baby Volstead Acts by 1927 had repealed them (New York, Nevada, Montana, and Wisconsin). In still other states enforcement was reduced, in effect, to a local option.

Prosecution was fitful, judges indifferent.[22] Juries proved reluctant to convict in Prohibition cases.* Only in the federal courts was there a serious attempt to crack down on bootleggers. But in time U.S. attorneys began to settle the vast majority of Prohibition cases for guilty pleas and nominal fines, simply to keep the federal judiciary from getting clogged up.

"What the law enforcement bodies of the large cities wanted was not enforcement but a safe sort of regulation of the liquor-selling traffic," said one New York editor.[23] They did not believe for a moment that drinking was wrong. They wanted a quiet life—surreptitious drinking, decent liquor, no violence, no raids, no hijackings—nothing, in short, that would create public alarm. The police in any town or city could have shut down every speakeasy and kept it shut had they wanted to do so.

Philadelphia alone among major cities launched a sustained campaign. It hired a town-tamer, Brigadier General Smedley D. Butler, USMC, who had twice won the Medal of Honor. Butler was a short, wiry man with an enormous Roman nose and a peppery manner. He dressed in a trim blue and gold uniform and wrapped himself in a flowing blue cape lined with red silk. He wanted the bad men to know he was in town. Butler would descend on places of vice in person, in an enormous Packard limousine, its siren blazing, and accompanied by his wife.[24] From January 1923 to December 1924, on special leave from the Marines, he led the life of a comic-book crime-fighter, such as Batman or the Green Hornet.

On one occasion he shut down every speakeasy in the city for forty-eight hours to prove it could be done. Another week he led a city-wide raid that netted more than 1,100 saloon-keepers, gamblers, bookies, and hookers. One night, armed with a service revolver, he flushed seven gang-

---

* One entire San Francisco jury was itself put on trial for drinking up the evidence in a case before it.

sters from their hiding place in the Tenderloin.[25] He fired police lieuten-
ants and sergeants whom he suspected of corruption. His methods were
high-handed, at times illegal. Magistrates who wanted to see him succeed
were at times forced to curb his exuberance.

In the end he was ruined by success. The saloon-keepers, madams,
and gamblers could deliver both money and votes, but only when allowed
to operate. Butler had been brought in to make a show of enforcement, to
whitewash the local machine. For a generation Philadelphia had been as
corrupt and dangerous as any city in America. With the death in 1921 of
Boies Penrose, who had built and run the machine, new men took over
and wanted to pretend they were a different breed. Their ouster of Butler
proved they were not. When he began to go after the rich and powerful
crooks, as well as the foot soldiers of vice, the mayor, Freeland D. Ken-
drick, let the Marines regain the services of their most colorful general.[26]

III

Bill McCoy was a tall, robust boat-builder in Jacksonville, Florida,
nearly forty in 1920 when, on a day in spring, a new car drove up to his
boatyard and a man wearing a checked suit, a bowtie and a dazzling
diamond stickpin got out. He had come to make McCoy a proposition he
could not refuse—$100 a day to sail a schooner from Nassau to Atlantic
City. Oh, yes, he added as an afterthought, the schooner would be carrying several hundred cases of rye whisky.

McCoy took a look at the schooner. He turned down the offer. The
idea, however, appealed. He sold his business and bought a schooner of
his own, one that would sail well with 3,000 cases of liquor in her hold.[27]
At first he ran trips from the Bahamas into remote southern inlets, carrying genuine Scotch whisky bought cheap in Nassau. His contacts began
telling him that this stuff was too good for the impoverished South; just
think how much it would bring in New York. After all, what he was selling
was "the real McCoy"—Prohibition's chief contribution to the language.

So began Rum Row, the line of ships that stood off from New York
harbor, for where McCoy went others soon followed. He also opened
another Rum Row off Boston, bringing liquor down from St. Pierre and
Miquelon.[28] Of all the liquor smuggled into the United States about one-
third came in by sea; the remaining two-thirds was smuggled across the
border from Canada.[29]

Large vessels, loaded with up to 25,000 cases of liquor, would wait
outside the three-mile limit. Small, fast boats would race out from the
shore, make their purchases, then dash at top speed for shelter. Some of

the supply vessels carried a supply of bottles, seals, labels, and a huge tank filled with alcohol. When the contact boats arrived they ordered Scotch or rye, bourbon or gin. They could even name the brand they wanted. Bottles were filled, the necessary seals and labels affixed, and the assembled cases dunked in the sea so salt water stains would show that it was "right off the boat." [30]

Ashore were the bootleggers, rapidly learning their new trade. In the Pacific Northwest a former police lieutenant, Roy Olmstead, built up one of the most effective bootlegging enterprises of the period, based on a small Rum Row, fast boats, unadulterated goods, and low prices. Nor did Olmstead fritter away the money he made on fast women and slow horses. Instead, he built Seattle's first radio station. [31] The Seattle bootleggers, in fact, were open about what they were up to. In 1922 they held a convention at a Seattle hotel, "where without undue hilarity and under Roberts' Rules of Order, they adopted resolutions setting forth 'fair prices' for liquor and establishing a code of ethics 'to keep liquor runners within the limits of approved business methods.' " [32]

At the other extreme was Larry Fay, in the early Twenties New York's biggest bootlegger. In 1919 he was an obscure thirty-year-old taxi driver with a string of minor convictions going back to childhood. One afternoon at Belmont Park he whimsically bet on a 100–1 shot and the horse romped home first. Fay picked up enough money to become his own boss, running several cabs. In 1920 he began using them to ferry booze down from Canada over back roads that appeared on few maps. With the money that began flowing in he opened an expensive nightclub in 1921, the first of half a dozen that he would eventually own. He was meanwhile running a shakedown racket that extorted a small fortune from New York's milkmen. [33]

The biggest bootlegger in the Midwest ran a different kind of operation. George Remus of Cincinnati and Chicago handled nothing but medicinal whiskey. He made more than $5 million by legally buying up distilleries and whatever he could find in their warehouses. Paying off literally dozens of lawmen and Prohibition agents, he removed and sold millions of gallons of whiskey and brandy, supposedly being held under bond for medicinal use. He refilled the barrels left in the warehouses with plain health-giving water. [34]

For thousands of young men living in the poorer parts of the cities, bootlegging was the only independent business that had any appeal. It enjoyed the glamor of danger and the glamor of money. [35] But the average bootlegger was really far from rich. "Often his fine must be paid by someone higher up," wrote a Prohibition agent who had arrested hundreds, "or, if the sentence be a fine or imprisonment, he must serve his time. His wife is not well dressed; his children are ragged and dirty; his mash adorns his living room; his car, though old, is mortgaged; his grocer insists that he pay cash; when the Internal Revenue agent attempts to collect his income tax, he finds the poor man penniless."[36] Bootlegging, in short, was like a banana republic—a handful of millionaires at the top, vast numbers of miserable wretches at the bottom, and virtually no middle class.

It was not generally realized at the time, but whiskey, brandy, and rum continued to be distilled legally after prohibition came into effect. The distilleries worked on a reduced but sizable scale, ostensibly to replenish the stocks in the bonded warehouses. Dozens of wineries were still in operation, presumably making sacramental wine. There were even breweries (renamed "cereal beverage plants") legally turning out 200 million gallons of beer a year.[37] The alcohol was drawn off, rendering it into near beer.*

Nor was American ingenuity lacking. Every region had its specialties based on local raw materials. In southern Florida all that anyone had to do was take a coconut, bore a hole in it, leave the milk inside, add a tablespoon of brown sugar, and seal. Three weeks later they had a pungent, potent, treacly concoction called "cocowhisky."[38]

The fabled beverage of the period, bathtub gin, was not made in bathtubs but in gallon jugs, filled with one-third grain alcohol (bought from your friendly neighborhood 'legger) or nearly two-thirds distilled water, from the drugstore. Then came several fluid ounces of juniper extract, plus a little glycerine. "But with the glycerine you had to be careful. Glycerine is a smoothing agent, and it must also be remembered," cautioned one authority, "that what goes down smoothly can sometimes come up quickly also."[39]

Even the most reputable people were proud to flout Prohibition. On November 22, 1926, *Time* published a formula for making gin that was more or less drinkable. Alice Roosevelt Longworth, wife of the Speaker of the House of Representatives, modestly acknowledged: "We had a small still. . . ."[40] In countless middle-class homes guests were offered applejack, something that had almost gone the way of the log cabin.[41] The most brazen example of respectable defiance occurred when Fiorello La Guardia held a press conference in the summer of 1926 to demonstrate how to make decent beer in safety and with an alcoholic strength of 4 percent. He mixed two parts of malt tonic (heretofore of interest only to anemics

---

* Of course, once the near beer reached the cellars of a speakeasy it could then be "needled" with an injection of grain alcohol and its former state restored. "Needled beer" was a commonplace of Twenties drinking.

and easy to obtain at almost any drugstore) to one part near beer. A brewmaster was standing by to sample the mixture. He pronounced it delicious.[42]

IV

During the Twenties there were places where Prohibition did not even exist. In Harlem, in Boston, in San Francisco, throughout Rhode Island, the Volstead Act was a joke and the Eighteenth Admendment had been repealed. In San Francisco, the diner who wanted a bottle of wine with his meal simply ordered it. Anyone who wanted a drink could walk in off the street into any of a hundred North Beach bars and demand it. The wine was good, the liquor genuine, and the prices reasonable. There was no fuss, no peephole, no "Joe sent me."[43]

It was a little different in New York: furtiveness at the center, freedom at the periphery. On the Bowery there was a saloon—not a speakeasy—on virtually every block. A customer need only walk through the doors and give his order at the top of his lungs, if he wanted to be bold about it. From time to time, one visitor reported, "Reeling helpless drunks come out at the little swinging doors and collide with indifferent policemen."[44] The saloons had changed in one respect, however: they were no longer thronged with prostitutes.

Elsewhere, the saloon had gone, and the speakeasy had arrived. Prohibition had also killed off the old-fashioned cabarets, those ornate establishments that had offered excellent food and long wine lists, platoons of waiters, sedate orchestras, large dance floors, and huge pillared rooms. The name lived on, appropriated by the speakeasy or nightclub, with its tiny tables, mediocre food, hard liquor instead of wine, entertainment that was loud, if nothing else, and a dance floor not much bigger than one of the tables.

Nightclubs had pretensions to exclusiveness. The more exclusive they pretended to be, the more clamorous the howls for admission, and the freer the spending once entry was gained. The most famous of these establishments in its time was the Club El Fey on West 40th Street, owned by Larry Fay, presided over by Mary Louise Cecilia Guinan, known to the entire nation as "Texas." The raucous and overweight Miss Guinan had been a movie star for a while, playing a cowgirl, twirling a lariat, and beating bad men in black hats to the draw. But at forty she found a new role, dispenser of good cheer and sophistication.* Her cry of "Hello, suck-

---

* Tex Guinan herself happened to be resolutely dry.

ers!" to the customers crowding into the Club El Fey was the best-known greeting of the decade. Only she was not joking. Heavily watered Scotch cost $1.50 a drink. "Champagne," consisting of carbonated cider lightly laced with alcohol, cost $25.00 a bottle. There was also a $3.00 cover charge (another innovation of Prohibition). Tex Guinan's frequent brushes with the law added to her fame and she briefly starred in a Broadway musical called *Padlocks of 1927*.

Speakeasies were, oddly, one more forward step for women's rights. Saloons had barred women customers; speakeasies welcomed them. There was, in fact, an easy, democratic air to these places: all of the customers, men and women alike, were breaking the law together. That they were owned by gangsters seemed to trouble no one. Nor did the presence of B-girls and drunk-rollers, or the outbreak of shootings and stabbings when the gangsters started making war on each other. There was overcharging on a prodigious scale. Yet nothing seemed to keep the customers from coming back for more. For various reasons, a great many Americans evidently enjoyed Prohibition, so long as they could buy a drink.

It had, however, put Broadway into a decline from which it would only go from bad to worse. Before 1920 Broadway and its surrounding streets made up an area of elegant hotels, fine restaurants, some of the world's most elegant theaters, atmospheric bars, and stylish cabarets. In many of these establishments the difference between profit and loss turned on the wine and spirits they sold. Prohibition meant they could not even sell beer. Dozens of the country's best restaurants and hotels closed literally overnight. Others succumbed each month. By 1927 "virtually everything that had made Broadway famous was gone, and the amusement area had been turned into a raucous jungle of chop-suey restaurants, hot-dog and hamburger shops, garish night clubs, radio stores equipped with blaring loud-speakers, cheap haberdasheries, fruit-juice stands, dime museums, candy and drug stores, speakeasies, gaudy movie houses, flea circuses, penny arcades, and lunch counters which advertised EATS!"[45]

The people who resented Prohibition most were probably the working class, considering it class legislation, which to a large degree it was. The upper classes had supported Prohibition in order to save the workers by denying them drink. They never intended it to apply to themselves. After all, wine, cognac, whiskey, and champagne were essential to a pleasant social life. They deprived working men of the saloon, heedless to its importance in providing useful services. The saloon had been more than a den of iniquity. It was labor exchange, union hall, a place for wedding receptions and neighborhood dances.

The working class was not simply deprived of the saloon but of hard liquor, which became very expensive. Only the affluent could afford to drink regularly without risking blindness or death. People on average and below average incomes had a strong incentive to stick to needled beer. Arrests for drunkenness became rare. Articles on alcoholism almost disappeared from medical literature. Deaths from alcohol-related illnesses fell dramatically.[46] Workers turned to other, safer amusements than drinking—radio, movies, automobiles. The saloon's days may have been numbered even without Prohibition.[47] Nevertheless, the working class never accepted it, and actively resented it. That has to be taken into account on any balance sheet of Prohibition.

Ironically, as the average consumption of alcohol dropped (by one-third or more[48]), resistance to the Eighteenth Amendment and the Volstead Act grew steadily stronger. The triumph that was supposed to be set in the concrete of the Constitution was falling apart. As it did so, the prohibitionists demanded ever more stringent measures, complaining bitterly that Prohibition was not a failure, it had simply not been tried. Wheeler agitated for stronger denaturants to be added to industrial alcohol to turn it into a poison. If people wanted to commit suicide for the sake of a drink, let them. He remained single-minded to the end, under greater pressure after Prohibition than he had ever been in the days of the saloon. In 1927 he died, aged fifty-six, worn out from his self-appointed struggle to save the nation from booze.

10. The Great Stone Face

I

Minutes after Coolidge was awakened by his father on the night Harding died, a telegram arrived from Daugherty, urging the Vice-President to take the oath as President without delay. Coolidge would not trust Daugherty's word alone. He called Charles Evans Hughes, who told him, "It should be taken before a notary." Coolidge said, "Father is a notary."[1] Colonel John Coolidge, old but erect, with a magnificent white mustache and the lean, bronzed look of a man who had spent his life out-of-doors, calmly changed into his black Sunday suit. At 2:45 A.M. father swore in son as President, in a tiny, plain room lighted by kerosene lamps.[2] It was the most romantic presidential inauguration, for the least romantic of presidents. *

There had rarely been a more provincial occupant of the White House. He had been abroad once, to Montreal, for a week, on his honeymoon in 1905. Yet he brought back to the White House some of the formality and calm that Harding had banished. He strolled the corridors with evident proprietorial satisfaction. In the evening, the Coolidges would dress for dinner in the state dining room, instead of eating casually upstairs.

---

* Alas, it was void. Daugherty later discovered that the law said that the oath had to be administered by a *federal* judge or notary. The colonel held a state appointment. The ceremony was repeated several weeks later, in near-secrecy, in the White House, with federal district judge A. A. Hoehling administering the oath.

As Vice-President he had had to serve as official diner-out of the Administration. "Every night from November to May he must sally forth in his glad raiment and eat for his party and his chief," ran one account of his vice-presidential days.[3] So Coolidge had gone, faithful to his duty. But he was bored by the small talk and snobbery and refused to pretend an interest he did not feel. Thus was born the most enduring Coolidge myth, the legend of Calvin the Silent. At these dinners, "He clowned a little for his own delight, played the dumb man, impersonated the yokel, and probably despised his tormentors in his heart."[4] With people he liked, Coolidge's favorite recreation was conversation, what he in his plain way called "gab."[5]

His relations with Congress were not improved, however, by inviting a dozen or so congressmen to breakfast at the White House and then munching silently with them through waffles, eggs, and bacon, while they tried to fathom what he was up to. Such breakfasts were part of the presidential ritual. Very well, he would observe the ritual. But he would not pretend. When invited, they always accepted, but they never caught on.

Relations with his Cabinet were much easier. He met with them regularly, made no attempt to dominate them, and listened with interest to what they had to say. Taking his role to be that of a coordinator of policy, and not an inventor of brave new initiatives, he allowed them the widest freedom in running their departments. And during the eighteen months that he filled Harding's shoes, he retained Harding's Cabinet and strove to achieve Harding's policies. Not until he had been elected in his own right would the Coolidge presidency really begin.

The Cabinet member with whom he worked most closely was Mellon. They liked one another at once. Coolidge in his matter-of-fact way was not the least impressed with Mellon's stupendous wealth. Mellon was gratified, for his part, that the new President had social and economic ideas identical to his own. Both men considered the rich the creators of the country's prosperity. By making them secure in their riches, prosperity would be secure. Hardly a sophisticated view of a modern economy. But they did not yet realize that it *was* a modern economy. Very few people did, including most of the critics of the Administration.[6] Mellon, moreover, was no cartoon reactionary. Walter Lippmann after meeting him declared, "Once you have seen Mr. Mellon it is easy to think of him as a great man."[7] Mellon wanted unearned income to be taxed at a higher rate than the earned variety. He also tried repeatedly to put income tax on tax-exempt municipal bonds, without success.

The principal object of the Coolidge-Mellon economic policy was to reduce the national debt, which was steadily brought down by $1 billion a year during most of the Twenties. Every new demand on the government's resources was seen as an assault on the nation's virtue. That, however, did not discourage the growing demand for a veterans' bonus.

Since 1919 the American Legion had been lobbying for what it euphemistically termed adjusted service certificates. The aim was to pay ex-servicemen $1 for every day of wartime service within the United States and $1.25 for every day served overseas. The argument for this bonus was retroactive justice; the argument against it was that the country could not afford it. The Treasury put the cost at $3 billion or so. That was approximately what it cost to run the entire government in 1924. The Adjusted Compensation Bill was nevertheless passed five times by the House and three times by the Senate. Harding had vetoed it. Coolidge was sure to do the same.

The American Legion redrafted the bill. When it surfaced again in 1924, it no longer called for a tax-financed bonus. Instead, a twenty-year endowment fund, requiring little initial capital, was to be created. After twenty years, thanks to the marvel of compound interest, there would be enough money in the fund to pay every veteran of World War I a bonus of $1,000 in 1945. Congress passed the bill. Coolidge vetoed it, immune to the charm of its facelift. This time Congress overrode the veto.

Coolidge found himself embroiled in an even more contentious fight with the farmers. In the late fall of 1921 George Peek, president of the Moline Plow Company, had made an appointment to see the secretary of agriculture, Henry C. Wallace. When he was shown into Wallace's office he walked up to the secretary's desk and put a pamphlet on it.[8] The pamphlet had been written by Peek and his friend Hugh Johnson. It looked innocuous, but it was destined to keep Washington in turmoil for a decade.

Before 1919 Peek had been a vice-president of the firm his grandfather founded, John Deere and Company. Seeking a challenge, he went over to the much smaller Moline Plow Company. Thanks to the farm crisis of 1920 he soon found himself working eighteen hours a day to keep the company in business.[9] By late 1921 he and Johnson, with whom he had served on the War Industries Board, had hit on what they thought was the solution and coined a slogan for it—"Equality for Agriculture." Over much of the Midwest this phrase became the American equivalent of "Peace-Land-Bread."

Industry, they reasoned, had for years been dumping its surplus production abroad to keep prices high at home. The farmer ought to be allowed to do the same. That was what they meant by equality for agriculture. They printed 3,000 copies of a pamphlet explaining their idea, and that was what Peek had put on Wallace's desk. They distributed their pamphlet at farmers' conferences, and by 1923 they had won Wallace over to their ideas. Nothing else appeared to be helping. The Department of Agriculture began to draft a bill based on the "Equality for Agriculture" pamphlet.

The chairmen of the Senate and House agriculture committees, Charles L. McNary and Gilbert N. Haugen, introduced the bill in Congress in January 1924 against the opposition of the White House. It did not require much knowledge of farming to spot the flaw in the McNary-Haugen Act. By raising farm prices it would stimulate increased production, which, in turn, would require still more subsidized dumping, and so on, over and over again. At the same time, a tax was to be levied on every bale of cotton, side of beef, bushel of wheat, etcetera, brought to market in the United States. This "equalization fee" was to go into a fund that would cover the cost of the dumping operation. Simply setting aside American surpluses, ran the argument, would be enough to raise domestic prices and enable the farmers to pay the equalization fee.

McNary-Haugenism amounted, protested the Administration, to government-sanctioned price-fixing. Although offered as an emergency measure, it would mark a fundamental change in American life, nothing less. It had a meaning that went far beyond the farmyard and the silo. McNary-Haugenism was to be the chief ideological battle of the Twenties. It was, at bottom, a struggle to redefine the role of American government. It was also a redefinition of the American character. Until now, who had come closer to the traditional American ideal than the sturdy, independent farmer? Finally, it was part of the fight over America's new place in the world.

The cotton South joined with the industrial East to vote down McNary-Haugenism in June 1924. No one believed that it was dead. Across nearly twenty farming states *Wallace's Farmer* was turning McNary-Haugenism into a crusade.

When Coolidge turned his attention to foreign affairs, he, like most of his countrymen, was guided by nineteenth-century ideas instead of the changed realities of world politics. The ideal to which he paid obeisance was noninvolvement with Europe; the reality was that the United States had economic and security interests in Europe. Refusal to face this fact squarely was to bedevil such matters as the League, the war debts, and disarmament for more than a decade.[10]

The most pressing issue was the debts. In 1922 Harding had made Hoover chairman of the World War Foreign Debt Commission. Of the $11 billion outstanding in principal and accrued interest, some $3.5 billion represented postarmistice loans for relief and rehabilitation. Hoover wanted to write off the prearmistice debts of $7.5 billion as part of the

American contribution to the war effort. Hoover knew, however, that Congress would never agree to this,[11] nor was it likely that Coolidge would do so.*

The money loaned the Allies had been at 5 percent interest, a fair rate at the time for an international loan. The government had to raise the money before it could borrow it, and did so on domestic money markets at 4½ percent. The agreement Hoover reached and Coolidge accepted was to stretch repayment over sixty-two years and to reduce interest payments to an average of 3 percent. By this step the United States wrote off more than a billion dollars of debts.

On the related question of German reparations, the United States took a more reasonable attitude than the other Allies. It sought only to cover the costs of the American occupation forces there. And when in 1924 Germany defaulted on reparations payments, the United States took the initiative in working out a compromise. A committee under Charles G. Dawes imposed a one-year moratorium, cut annual payments by 80 percent, and secured a $2.5 billion loan from American banks to help revive German industry. For the moment, it eased a very ugly situation. It provided a figleaf for French withdrawal from the Ruhr and mollified French public opinion, which would accept almost any charade before it would admit that reparations on the scale fixed at Versailles were the stuff that pipe dreams are made of.

The Dawes Plan was a sane idea that had lunatic results. The reparations that Germany made to her wartime foes amounted to $2.5 billion. And the amount the United States collected on the war debts amounted to $2.5 billion. America discovered, tardily and reluctantly, that it was carrying the entire debt-and-reparations structure, paying itself with its own money.

Such was the nature of foreign policy, tricked out in mummers' rags, sustained by "let's pretend." Serious journals were meanwhile filled with articles on the inevitability of another war in Europe and the absolute certainty of eventual war with Japan.[12]

On the borderline between domestic and foreign policy stood immigration. The 1921 legislation had set the quota at 356,000. The 1924 Immigration Act reduced it still further, to 150,000, and the United States unilaterally abrogated the 1907 "gentleman's agreement" under which Japan had severely limited emigration to American shores. Coolidge protested, but Congress had its way. The Japanese were excluded, as the Chinese had been. And as the Chinese had done, they smuggled them-

---

* The remark so often put in Coolidge's mouth, "They hired the money, didn't they?" is an invention.

selves in. Under the new act immigrants from the British Isles and north-west Europe were more favored than ever, and those from elsewhere more excluded than ever. But there were many thousands who defied the immigration barriers. So many seamen jumped ship in American ports (35,000 in 1924[13]) it seems remarkable that their vessels were able to sail home. And despite the ever more stringent controls, some 4 million people emigrated legally to the United States in the 1920s.[14]

On immigration, as on almost everything else, Coolidge was content to walk in Harding's footsteps. There seemed every likelihood as well that in doing so he was helping to ensure his own election in 1924. There was one part of Harding's legacy, however, that still might jeopardize that prospect, and that was Teapot Dome.

Nearly three months after Harding died the two geologists who had spent the summer studying Naval Oil Reserve Number Three reported back to the Senate Committee on Public Lands. The oil, they said, *was* leaking into nearby oil deposits that were not part of the reserve.[15] Republicans were relieved, Democrats disappointed, by this news. As far as Teapot Dome was concerned, the affair seemed over before it began. Except, that is, to one man, Senator Walsh.

He remained convinced that there was something dubious about the leases Fall had signed with Doheny and Sinclair. He continued to dig into the backgrounds of all three men. Coolidge, meanwhile, had sent for Harry Slattery to tell him what all the fuss was about.[16]

It was Fall's bad luck to have Walsh on his trail. There was no more devoted senator, nor a more intelligent one. Walsh, with his flourishing black handlebar mustache, his penetrating blue eyes and level gaze, had grown up in half a dozen frontier hamlets. He was a man who liked plain living, direct expression, and working sixteen hours a day. Yet had it not been for Teapot Dome, no one would remember him now. As he plugged away, stories began to reach him that it might be worth his while to go into the affairs of Fall the rancher. And he discovered a strange coincidence. The prize livestock that graced Fall's Three Rivers ranch had come from a New Jersey stock farm owned by Harry Sinclair. The obvious question was, Had Fall paid for them?

This line of inquiry drew from Fall a tortuous financial statement which mentioned a $100,000 loan from Edward (Ned) McLean, owner of the *Cincinnati Enquirer*, the *Washington Post* and the Hope diamond. Despite his possessions, McLean was taken seriously by few. His fortune had been inherited from his grandfather, and he had married the daughter of a prospector who had gone from rags to millions on the basis of a silver strike. McLean was generally considered so impulsive and so dim that he might well have loaned Fall $100,000 on a whim and without asking a favor in return. Yet he proved coy about appearing before Walsh's subcommittee. And why was he cowering in Palm Beach, bombarding his friends with coded telegrams every night? Walsh went to Palm Beach and wrung from the terrified McLean an admission that he had lied.

Fall *had* asked for a loan, but then returned McLean's checks, saying he had found another source, presumably one who would make the loan in cash—a less traceable commodity than checks. Fall had lied, and McLean had tried to support him in that lie. Fall was now forced to admit the true source of the money—Doheny. At which point 100 million people jumped to the same conclusion.

Doheny readily admitted making the loan to Fall; they had been friends for thirty years. A multimillionaire now, Doheny had been poor most of his life, living on beef jerky and spring water, sleeping on the ground, prospecting first for silver and gold, later for oil. He had no formal education, yet the solitary life in the desert, where men were forced to rise above hardship and disappointment, had made him thoughtful. Those who could not rise went mad or turned to drink, got into shooting scrapes or took drugs. Doheny, however, applied himself to intellectual pursuits, to fundamental questions of morality, of social organization, of political systems. Despite his sudden riches, he still lived modestly and cultivated the acquaintance of scholars. He shunned the abrasive new-rich types such as Sinclair, with whom his only connection came about by accident, through the involvement of both men with Albert Fall.[17]

Had Fall told the truth from the start—that he had borrowed the money from his old friend Doheny with whom he had shared a blanket on the ground; who had struck it rich while he, Fall, had not—that might well have been the end of Teapot Dome. But Congressional Democrats bore down hard on Doheny, refusing to accept his explanation that the sole basis of the loan had been friendship.

Doheny cared nothing about his own reputation, but he bridled at what he considered injustice.[18] So he retaliated by naming four of Wilson's ex-Cabinet members whom he had hired as lawyers and said the most damning thing he could say: "I hired them for their influence." He suggested, as he did so, that there was hardly a Democrat in Washington who could not be bought. There was, in fact, nothing wrong on either side of these transactions. The business he had hired these men for was plain, dull, legal business which they were free to accept in good conscience. The illusion of wrongdoing, however, was more vivid than prosaic reality.

Doheny's lease had been signed seven months before his loan to Fall. The California oil reserves, just like Teapot Dome, were leaking into other oil fields. The Pearl Harbor facilities were needed. And Doheny's company was qualified to do everything the contract called for.* Through agencies under its direction (the Bureau of Mines, the General Land Office, the Geological Survey, and so forth) the Interior Department knew more about oil conservation than the navy was ever likely to know. But Doheny's Elk Hills lease had been granted without competitive bidding. That alone made it questionable.

Even though the contract was under attack and likely to be invalidated in the courts, Doheny pressed ahead with the oil storage complex at Pearl Harbor. His lease called for delivering 75 million barrels of oil to the navy. Every barrel was delivered.[19] The federal courts did in time cancel the Elk Hills and Teapot Dome leases. Fall and Doheny were tried for conspiracy to defraud the government and were acquitted. Sinclair, who had also made large loans to Fall, was tried for conspiracy. He, too, was acquitted.

Long before this, Coolidge had taken Teapot Dome out of Walsh's hands. Following Doheny's appearance before the Public Lands Committee, Coolidge had appointed two special counsels to pursue the matter through the courts, Owen J. Roberts and Atlee Pomerene. Coolidge could not hope to turn Teapot Dome into a Republican asset, but he deftly defused it as an issue at the polls.

Chance had also relieved him of another potential cross, Harry Micajah Daugherty. A Senate inquiry into the attorney general's activities unearthed several curious items, such as a gift for thriftiness that enabled him, a poor man when he took office, he repeatedly claimed, to save $75,000 out of a salary of $12,000 a year. Out of this same salary he had also bought many thousands of dollars' worth of blue chip stocks.[20] When Daugherty refused to cooperate in the inquiry by allowing the senators to examine Justice Department files, Coolidge was provided with a perfect opportunity to ask for Daugherty's resignation. Without an eye for an opportunity Coolidge would never have reached the White House.

II

Under Hiram Evans's leadership the Ku Klux Klan was moving away from violence and into conventional politics. As it did so, membership rose strongly in nearly every state. In 1924 the Klan had as many as 4 million members plus several hundred thousand followers in its newly created women's auxiliary.[21]

---

* These facilities in time proved their worth. Without them the navy would have had to fight the war with Japan from its bases on the West Coast. It was this oil that allowed the navy to take the offensive only six months after Pearl Harbor was attacked.

With the rise in membership went greater political strength. The Indiana Klan in 1922 unseated a Jewish representative and elected a senator, Samuel L. Ralston. Oklahoma that same year elected John C. Walton governor, and although Walton was in public a liberal Democrat he was in secret "Klansman at Large," a title created especially for him.[22] In the neighboring state of Texas the Klan put Earl B. Mayfield into the United States senate in 1922.

In three years the Klan was instrumental in the election of at least six governors, three senators, and hundreds of state legislators, sheriffs, judges, mayors, prosecutors, and police commissioners.[23] It virtually ran the state of Indiana. And on the eve of the Democratic convention in 1924, it had been forged into one of the largest and most cohesive elements in the Democratic party. It had also become a powerful force within the Republican party.

While it was becoming strong, however, it was also courting disaster. The Klan was opposed by nearly half the population: the 20 million foreign-born, the 16 million Catholics, the 10 million blacks, the 4 million Jews—in all, 50 million people, most of them old enough to vote.

III

When the Democratic convention opened, it was in the right setting for a knock 'em down, drag 'em out fight: Madison Square Garden. And to this vast arena came McAdoo, as if in a Roman triumph. He progressed leisurely across the country from California. Wherever he stopped, there were speeches, fireworks, bands, and parades. In the primaries he was opposed chiefly by Senator Oscar Underwood of Alabama. With the Klan's eager support—which McAdoo had never solicited—the dry McAdoo easily defeated the wet Underwood. When he arrived at the Garden he arrived as a conqueror, preceded from the Pennsylvania Station by two brass bands and trailed by thousands of adoring women.

Underwood was still able to cripple McAdoo, however. When the roll of the states was called, Alabama's name led all the rest. The chairman of its delegation, Forney Johnson, put in the knife that Underwood had sharpened. He mentioned the unmentionable—the presence of the Klan among the delegations. The convention was thrown into uproar. Half the delegates leaped out of their chairs and began to parade up and down the aisles, shouting at the seated McAdoo supporters, "Up, get up, you kleagles!" Fistfights broke out on the floor. It went on for more than an hour, while the convention chairman, Senator Walsh, gaveled helplessly against the din.[24]

A resolution was offered to condemn the Klan explicitly. Bryan countered with a resolution to condemn violence, without naming those who were guilty of it.[25] The resolution to condemn the Klan by name failed by less than a single vote, 543-3/20 to 542-7/20. By the time the vote was taken the Democratic party had been split into two irreconcilable camps of nearly equal strength.

When McAdoo's name was finally put in nomination, an hour-long demonstration erupted, led by four women in white Grecian costume, à la Isadora Duncan, who energetically blew silver cornets.[26] The faithful chanted, "Mac! Mac! Mac-a-Doo!" Alas for him he had been named by Doheny as one of the four ex-Cabinet members Doheny had hired at a fee of $100,000. So from the packed, pro-Smith galleries came a counter-point chant of "Oil! Oil! Oil! Oil!"

The greatest personal triumph of the convention came when Franklin Roosevelt pulled himself erect in his leg braces, twenty pounds of steel that supported his polio-ruined legs, and put Al Smith in nomination. With some trepidation (fearing that a rough-and-tumble convention was unlikely to appreciate lyric poetry) he quoted Wordsworth:[27] "This is the happy Warrior; this is he / That every man in arms should wish to be." Roosevelt's nominating speech set off the loudest eruption at an astonishingly noisy convention.

The Garden was already crammed far beyond its 14,000-capacity. Yet in from the streets marched an entire procession, with brass bands, enormous banners, and a contingent of scruffy newsboys. The noise was overwhelming, as battery-operated fire sirens shrieked, bands played, terrified women screamed, and delegates booed or cheered according to their preference. The thick brick walls of the Garden trembled from the uproar. In the midst of it all, standing on a chair in the Kentucky delegation, stood D. W. Griffith, surveying the spectacle with a connoisseur's eye.[28]

McAdoo made the running for 90 ballots, with a bloc of nearly 500 votes rallying loyally to him every time. Smith remained firmly in second place with a consistent 350. Only the two-thirds rule kept McAdoo from the nomination. He and Smith could block one another indefinitely. For a time it seemed they would do just that. This was part of the bitterness left over from the resolution to condemn the Klan. But more important still was Prohibition. The drys clung to McAdoo, the wets to Al Smith. McAdoo was not a Klansman, and never spoke in defense of the Klan, as Smith's supporters knew. But they also knew that he believed in enforcing Prohibition. McAdoo's supporters knew that Smith was not going to ask the Pope's guidance in running the country. But they also knew that he was against Prohibition enforcement. So ballot after ballot was cast, day after day, in a place that was very hot and very humid, from which everyone would normally be trying to escape.

When the 100th ballot approached, Cox, the titular head of the party, traveled to New York from Ohio. He called the Ohio delegation together and suggested a compromise candidate, John W. Davis, nominally from West Virginia, but in truth from Wall Street. The liberal press had touted his candidacy long before the convention.[29] He was intelligent, honest, competent, modest, and courtly. Appointed by Wilson to be solicitor general, he had made an estimable record. From there Wilson sent him to be ambassador to Great Britain. He succeeded so well that the Royal Navy escorted him out to sea when he returned to the United States to make way for George Harvey.

Davis had been nominated by a handful of admirers and had crept up steadily until third place was his on ballot after ballot. With Cox's unsolicited help his support grew spectacularly. On the 101st ballot McAdoo's supporters were released from their pledges and stampeded into Davis's column. On the 103rd ballot he picked up 844 votes and the nomination.

Had the convention been left to its own devices it would have chosen Walsh to run with Davis. He used his position as convention chairman to make sure this honor was not thrust upon him.[30] Davis made a personal plea to Walsh to change his mind, to no avail. A conference of party leaders then chose the Governor of Nebraska, Charles W. Bryan, brother to the Great Commoner, and presented him to Davis as the ideal compromise candidate—a westerner, a Progressive, and a dry.

IV

Progressives of both major parties squirmed when they contemplated the choice before them in November, but they were not without hope. A Conference for Progressive Political Action had been formed in 1922. The CPPA was a coalition of dissatisfied unions and angry farmers. In the fall elections that year it unseated dozens of right-wing politicians, while more than 100 candidates it endorsed were elected. The momentum of that success sped the Progressives toward 1924 with a determination to run their own candidate for the presidency if the Democratic party failed them, as it did.

They had already chosen their candidate—Robert La Follette. Nothing would induce him to form a third party. The time was not ripe, he insisted. So when the Progressive convention opened in Cleveland—three weeks after the Republicans had gathered there to nominate Coolidge—its sole order of business was to anoint La Follette and his running mate, Senator Burton K. Wheeler of Montana. It was not the send-off for a new party. Two candidates only campaigned in its name.

"There were no corrupt bosses, no professional ward politicians, only simple people, serious and rather boring," reported one visitor to the convention. "The atmosphere resembled a revival meeting, but it lacked magnetism . . . for La Follette was old and weary, and crammed with statistics."[31] There were gray-bearded old Populists, long-haired young radicals, middle-aged Socialists, and many middle-ranking union officials.[32] The sixty-nine-year-old La Follette was praised extravagantly, but was not there to hear it.

This son of the Middle Border had been born in a log cabin in 1855. He hated cities, banks, industrialization, big business, and most of the other characteristics of twentieth-century life. Among the intellectual pedestrians of the Senate, he stood out as a man of wide learning. His arrogance and vanity were betrayed by the high sweep of his gray pompadour and the exaggerated tilt of his head. Those who loved money did not love La Follette. Those who cared for moral questions considered him a saint. His enemies denounced him as a man too emotional to be trusted, and his oratory was passionate and ornate. Yet he had never betrayed a trust, broken a promise, or tried to line his pockets. He was a feminist, a conservationist, an isolationist, a reformer of the civil service, a champion of civil liberties, an advocate of progressive taxation and the regulation of business. His deeply emotional nature made him an implacable foe and a difficult friend.

The Progressive party platform was of a piece with its candidate. In its concerns and remedies it harked back to the populism of the 1890s, or as one description put it, it was "nostalgic."[33] And La Follette, once "the Little Giant of the West," was too tired to breath new life into it. He was a symbol, not a force.

His support depended heavily on the railroad brotherhoods, and the AFL broke with long-standing policy to endorse (tepidly and with conditions) La Follette's candidacy. Little money came in from the unions, however, and by election day the AFL had virtually washed its hands of the Progressive party.

V

The Republican campaign slogan in 1924 was coined by George Harvey: "Coolidge or Chaos." It was hardly the slogan of a party on the defensive. But the Democrats were too disorganized, too bitterly divided, to put them there. Davis ran a diffident campaign, one that added to his reputation as a gentleman while adding nothing to his attraction at the polls. Coolidge was even more diffident, in a way. He stayed in Washington and allowed the very energetic and voluble Charles G. Dawes, his running mate, to do the campaigning for both of them.

The chief issue in the election was Mellon's proposed tax bill which would reduce the surtaxes on incomes over $10,000. Democrats and Progressives denounced this as pandering to the rich.[34] They failed completely in their attempts to make Teapot Dome an election issue. The voters remained unconvinced that there was serious corruption in the higher ranks of the Republican party. Even Gifford Pinchot gave his support to Coolidge.[35]

The Socialist party was so demoralized that it failed for the first time in thirty years to run a candidate of its own. It supported La Follette instead.

On election day La Follette won nearly 5 million votes. Labor proved a disappointment, and the farmers proved an even more fickle crowd. The 1924 harvest was the smallest for several years, and farm prices rose sharply that fall. The Progressive movement had been based to a large extent on the embittered farmer. Wheat at $1.50 a bushel changed him overnight into a dutiful Democrat or Republican. La Follette's vote was a city vote. Only in Wisconsin and North Dakota did many farmers vote for him.

Generally, 1924 was "the year of the great indifference."[36] Barely half the qualified voters cast ballots. Coolidge polled 15.7 million votes to Davis's 8.4 million. Coolidge credited his overwhelming victory to "Divine Providence."[37]

For the Klan, the elections were a mixture of success and failure. The Klan's forays into the political mainstream stirred conventional politicians and political groups to fight back. All across the country elections for mayor, governor or senator were drawn along pro-Klan and anti-Klan lines. Most of the Klan-backed candidates lost. Yet in Montana the Klan came close to unseating Walsh, and in Kansas, Colorado, Oklahoma, Indiana, Iowa, and Kentucky, the Klan's candidates won Senate seats and governors' chairs. The rise in hog and wheat prices, however, dashed many a Klan politician's hopes. The farm crisis had pushed many an angry farmer into the Klan. The resurgence (cruelly brief) of farm prosperity dragged him out.

There was one state where the future looked secure, and that was Indiana. On the street corners of every Indiana city newsboys were hawking *The Fiery Cross*.[38] There were 400,000 Klansmen in the state. Most of its politicians were overawed by David C. Stephenson, the head of the Indiana Klan, who boasted with considerable accuracy, "I am the law in Indiana."[39] In the November election Stephenson patched up his running quarrel with Hiram Evans,* and the Klan put Ed Jackson into the governor's mansion. The Indiana Klan, brimming with confidence, expected to put Stephenson in the Senate in 1926.

The way his ambitions tended was suggested by the bust of Napoleon that Stephenson, a chubby man in his early thirties, kept on his desk, not far from his fake "direct line" to the White House.[40] From his various enterprises, which included a coal and gravel business as well as selling Klan memberships, Stephenson had amassed a fortune estimated at $3 million.[41] He had yachts, bodyguards, hotel suites in several cities, a suburban mansion, and a variety of mistresses. A compulsive womanizer, the twice-married, twice-divorced Stephenson attempted to seduce a plain, fat office supervisor in the Indiana statehouse, twenty-eight-year-old Madge Oberholzer. When she refused to go with him to Chicago, he and his bodyguards kidnaped her.

On the train to Chicago he raped her, biting her all over her body, drawing blood in a score of places. While briefly unguarded, Madge Oberholzer poisoned herself with a lavatory cleanser. She suffered a lingering death, providing ample time for her to tell the police what had happened.[42]

Stephenson discovered that he was less the law than he imagined. A jury convicted him of second-degree murder. He was sentenced to life imprisonment. Stephenson confidently waited for Jackson to pardon him, unaware he had fallen so low that anyone who raised a hand to help him would have been dragged down with him. When that fact dawned on him, Stephenson had his revenge. He talked and talked and talked. The mayor of Indianapolis went to prison, as did the sheriff and a representative. Jackson, too, would have been prosecuted for bribery had he not been saved by the statute of limitations.

The Stephenson murder trial destroyed the Klan in Indiana and damaged it everywhere else. The backbone of the Indiana Klan were orderly, sober, lower-middle-class men who shunned violence. With Stephenson's fall, the Klan's moral pretensions crashed to the ground. By the summer of 1925, it was through.

Attempting to prove that it was not, some 50,000 Klansmen paraded down Pennsylvania Avenue that August, sixteen to twenty abreast. The parade took nearly four hours. Yet even this intended show of strength fell flat, for after the parade came the usual Klan rally. Hardly had the

---

* In the Evans-Simmons showdown Stephenson had supported Evans. The advantage of supporting the winning side was the marketing rights in twenty-three states. Stephenson became a millionaire within a year. Riches went to his head and he began to nurture ambitions that did not include Evans. The Imperial Wizard, in turn, ridiculed Stephenson as a man who picked his nose and ate his peas with a knife. His sensibilities affronted, Stephenson organized his own Klan.

rally begun when a violent thunderstorm burst directly overhead. Bedraggled Klansmen trailing sodden robes scurried away, seeking shelter.[43]

VI

Coolidge's inauguration was the first to be carried on radio and the most lackluster. It faithfully reflected his feeling that all ceremonial was a waste of time and money. Despite—perhaps at times because of—such puritanical idiosyncrasy Coolidge was the most widely admired political figure since Teddy Roosevelt at his peak twenty years earlier. People of every age, class, and region considered him a splendid President.[44]

Maintaining an appearance of flinty stoicism, he was overly sensitive to criticism. He labored assiduously to tame the press at his twice-a-week press conferences. These gatherings were held only under certain conditions; for example, if he refused to answer a question, that refusal was not to be reported. The correspondents could not even say that a press conference had been held, nor could they quote Coolidge directly. Yet he did win them over. A press conference in the Twenties was a small, fairly intimate gathering of the President and about a dozen reporters. Coolidge, like Harding, would think out loud on anything that took his fancy, something impossible to imagine now. He could not win over every Washington correspondent, but he enjoyed as favorable a press as almost any President in American history.[45]

Coolidge also took pains to court the public directly. At 12:30 each day anyone who wanted to shake the President's hand could do so. The doors to the Oval Office were opened and more than 1,000 people would pass through in half an hour. Coolidge's hand-shaking record was 1,900 in thirty-four minutes. It was a pleasure to do it, he maintained, and not a chore. Anyone who wanted his autograph had only to write and request it. He happily provided dozens each day.[46]

His amazing popularity stands in graphic contrast to the impression that clings to his memory of a dour, sour little man who never had much to say. Much of the time he *did* look sour.* The expression not of a bitter disposition, however, but a reflection of his chronic indigestion. Behind that impassive exterior he burned up vast amounts of nervous energy. And the iron self-control that he imposed upon a deeply sentimental nature frequently left him exhausted. He slept for up to twelve hours a day.[47]

This might seem to support the idea that Coolidge was a do-nothing President. The truth is, he worked diligently. On the farm crisis, to take

---

* Alice Roosevelt Longworth might have said that Coolidge "looked as if he was weaned on a pickle," but she didn't originate the expression. She picked it up at secondhand, from her doctor, who in turn had heard it from a patient.

only one example, he wrote personal letters to the editor of every farm journal in the country, seeking advice. He invited Hugh Johnson to come to the White House to explain "Equality for Agriculture" to him. He also "spent a good deal of time helping people who had complaints regarding claims, pensions, and government jobs. He did that whether or not they had political influence and often to the point where the work of his staff resembled that of a social service office."[48] A visitor who spent a week with Coolidge in the White House in 1925 left with the impression of a man who enjoyed being President and worked hard at it.[49]

He maintained an appearance of utter calm and stability. Yet he was fiercely jealous of his wife, the charming and gracious Grace Coolidge, and his treatment of her was tyrannical.* He had a blazing temper that he unleashed on subordinates and servants. He was suspicious and infuriatingly small-minded on occasion. Yet, although he could be a martinet toward those who worked for him, his friends found him devoted and thoughtful. There were no ex-friends of Calvin Coolidge.

For someone who had to work with Congress his attitude regarding politicians may have been a handicap; he despised them, in the main. They were both timid and vain, "twice spoiled . . . spoiled with praise and spoiled with abuse. With them nothing is natural, everything is artificial."[50] It was in his nature to expect little from Congress. It was also realistic. Congress was going to go its own way, regardless of what he said or did. The three Congresses he had to deal with would have resisted any attempt to lead them, by Coolidge or anyone else. He was content to maintain close personal relations with leading senators from both parties, which probably served him as well as any alternative strategy. The one major initiative he proposed was a tax cut, and in 1926 he got it.

In both Senate and House for most of Coolidge's presidency there was a roughly equal division between regular Democrats and regular Republicans. The balance of power was held by Progressives, most of them nominally Republican, but with little in common with Coolidge. These Progressives, most of them western senators, enjoyed remarkable independence. There were more voters in the Bronx than in Idaho, Montana, or South Dakota. A small but dedicated following could keep a man in Washington for a long time, and seniority would make him powerful. La Follette, going his own way, wielded as much power as anyone in the Senate in the early Twenties. These men came out of the frontier—plain-spoken, direct, contemptuous of formality, rank, bureaucracy, and bankers, believers in the common man and common sense. They caused the White

---

* She was irrepressible, however. She found her husband's nasal twang hilarious. On at least one occasion when he was delivering a speech Grace Coolidge had to hide behind a pillar while she broke up with laughter.

House endless trouble, whoever its occupant happened to be. Following La Follette's death in 1925, the most important of these Progressives was William Borah of Idaho.

An authority on the Constitution and a formidable debater, Borah's speeches on the Senate floor would fill the chamber, where most other senators' would empty it. His honesty and earnestness ill-equipped him for leadership because he could, and would, change his position overnight as the result of fresh thought on a subject. Politicians are expected to lead their followers around in circles, provided they do not do it too quickly. Borah, ostensibly a Republican, was more of a hindrance to Coolidge than any dozen Democratic senators combined. The senator from Idaho was against nearly everything that Coolidge was for, and the people Coolidge liked, Borah detested.[51] Coolidge had tried to put him on ice by offering him the vice-presidential nomination.[52]

Only a year later, Borah inflicted on Coolidge his worst defeat in Congress. In 1925 the President nominated Charles Beecher Warren as attorney general. Back in 1921, Borah had swallowed his doubts over Daugherty's fitness for office and regretted it at leisure thereafter. Warren as president and chief counsel of the Michigan Sugar Company had been criticized in the past for flouting the antitrust laws. Borah began to organize Senate opposition to Warren.* Coolidge refused to withdraw the nomination. Borah, beginning with virtually no support, managed to muster enough votes to tie those in Warren's favor, and Vice-President Dawes, still unfamiliar with voting procedures in the Senate, had by chance gone to his hotel to take a nap when the votes were cast.[53] Warren's nomination was rejected. When Coolidge resubmitted it, the Senate took umbrage at his persistence and overwhelmingly turned down Warren's appointment. Not for fifty years had the Senate refused to ratify a Cabinet nominee. His attempt to reward Wallace McCamant with a federal judgeship for his invaluable help in 1920 was similarly turned down.

For his part, Coolidge had no qualms about rejecting congressional handiwork. This reputedly do-nothing President vetoed fifty bills, compared with six vetoes by Harding and forty-four by Woodrow Wilson.[54]

Coolidge's election victory had been made inevitable by the recovery of farm prices when there were poor harvests all over the world and a good harvest in the United States. What was disastrous for La Follette was good for the President. But in 1925 wheat prices fell and there was a bumper

---

* It does not seem likely that the country lost a potentially great attorney general. Edmund Starling, Coolidge's Secret Service bodyguard, had a poignant recollection of Warren during this crisis: "He had been brought to Washington and hidden away at the Willard without being registered as a guest. He seemed a little apprehensive, for when I carried messages to him I always found him in bed with the covers pulled over his head." *Starling of the White House*, p. 228.

crop of corn. Then in 1926 cotton prices collapsed. McNary-Haugenism spread like an uncontrolled fire from the wheat and corn regions into the South. In February 1927, over the opposition of the leadership of both major parties, the McNary-Haugen bill was passed by both House and Senate. Coolidge promptly vetoed it, although he frankly admitted that he found the bill baffling, despite Hugh Johnson's help.[55] He simply feared that it would prove a money sink and leave the country with an enormous bureaucratic edifice it could do without.

Coolidge was more inclined to take the initiative in foreign than domestic affairs. But here he had to deal directly with Borah, who in 1924 succeeded Lodge as chairman of the Senate Foreign Relations Committee. Characteristically, Borah disliked diplomats. He preached the virtues of "open diplomacy." He was the ideal man to make foreign nations apprehensive. At least with Lodge they had known where they stood, even if they did not like it.

At the same time, Coolidge was no longer under the tutelage of the urbane and imposing Hughes, who filled out the four years he had intended to serve and then resigned. In his place Coolidge appointed ex-Senator Frank Kellogg of Michigan, a tiny, anxiety-ridden figure known to his colleagues in the Senate as "Nervous Nellie."[56] With his white hair, sightless eye, trembling hands, and obvious inferiority complex it was hard to believe that he had been president of the American Bar Association (even though his formal education stopped at the eighth grade), was a self-made millionaire, and a senator. He conscientiously read all of the reports that arrived from American ambassadors and ministers around the world, and then quivered with indecision each time something had to be done. He looked almost pathetically to Coolidge for leadership. When that failed, he was reduced to conducting foreign policy "by ringing Borah's doorbell."[57]

Kellogg succeeded in making bad relations with Mexico still worse by describing the Mexican leaders as Bolshevik dupes. It was the kind of utterance that went down wonderfully in Grand Rapids, but brought mobs into the streets in Mexico City. In this crisis Coolidge sent one of his friends from the Amherst class of '95, Dwight W. Morrow, another gnome-like figure, to Mexico. Morrow had become rich as a Morgan partner, and bored as million piled on million. Speaking his own quixotic version of Spanish, he hastened South. The Mexicans expected him to be merely a scouting party for the Marines.[58] In the end, however, Morrow's mission to Mexico provided Coolidge with his greatest foreign policy success.

II. That Old-Time Religion

I

By the early Twenties, American churchmen were embarrassed when they recalled their blessing on the declaration of war in 1917 and their promise of the wonders that victory would bring. The crisis of belief that created a million agnostics and 10 million doubting fellow travelers washed over all denominations, trickling down into the cracks appearing in a society under strain. In the cloistered calm of rich seminaries and the dusty streets of poor mill villages alike, religion was a burning issue. And in periods of religious upheaval a Newtonian principle seems to apply: to each religious action there is an equal and opposite reaction. The counterattack on doubt was led by the Fundamentalists. The term was coined by the Reverend Curtis Lee Laws in 1921.[1] Fundamentalism was as important to the Twenties as Prohibition.

At the simplest level it was a back-to-basics movement. The five fundamentals of belief were the infallibility of the Bible; the virgin birth of Christ; the Resurrection; that Christ died to atone for the sins of the world; and the Second Coming. By the mid-Twenties it was claimed that roughly one-fourth the population accepted the Fundamentalist creed.[2] Fundamentalist publications and organizations appeared with remarkable frequency. Fundamentalist Bible colleges flourished. The library, the town council, the schoolboard, and the newspaper were likely to hear from local Fundamentalists—often.

Although the Fundamentalist revival was strongest in the South, it

197

was also effective in the North. The most influential Fundamentalist pastor was William Bell Riley of the First Baptist Church of Minneapolis, acclaimed by William Jennings Bryan as "the greatest statesman in the American pulpit."[3] Some nights Carnegie Hall was filled with New York Fundamentalists, arguing over evolution.

Fundamentalism found most of its recruits among the Baptists, with a sprinkling of Methodists and Presbyterians. Its social roots were most apparent in the South where, in many a community, the only regular public gathering was the religious meeting. In such places, religion provided the only channel for unbridled emotional expression and the only stimulus to the imagination. Orgiastic religion swept the South, at times carrying ostensible Christians into rites not far removed from voodoo, such as belief in the magic handkerchief which had been blessed by some powerful preacher.[4] This hysterical religiosity came hard on the heels of industrialization, which was pushing hundreds of thousands of simple, impoverished country people into noisome factories and towns. Damned on Saturday night, they were desperate for salvation on Sunday.

II

An account of Tennessee published in 1922 described a state that had been stagnant since the Civil War. Its schools were backward, its agriculture impoverished, its industries few and inefficient, and its legislature the most benighted anywhere in North America. Intellectual and artistic life was virtually nonexistent. The state was by nature rich and beautiful. The people of Tennessee had done their best to change all that.[5] It seems natural, then, that it was in Tennessee where the historic clash took place between Fundamentalism and the modern world, for here, as everywhere else, the theory of what Tennesseans called *ee*volution was creeping into local schools in textbooks coming from the city. Local pastors never wearied of denouncing it.* But that seemed to do no good. What was needed was a law, or so it seemed to John Washington Butler, a Primitive Baptist from Round Lick, Tennessee. A kindly, agreeable man, he farmed 120 acres and spent his free hours as a part-time preacher. He was no puritanical fanatic, loving sports, music, and his fellowmen. He believed, however, that the Constitution was based on the Bible (which would have

---

* E.g., Rev. Z. Colin O'Farrell announced his sermon one week with a parody: "Backward, turn backward, O Time, in your flight; Make me a monkey again just for tonight." He proceeded to deliver a fervent denunciation of evolution, to the excited screeching of a chimpanzee he had brought into church tethered to a piece of broomstick. *Time*, September 1, 1924.

surprised half the men who signed it) and that Christianity was based on the literal truth of the Bible. Anything that weakened faith in the Bible as the word of God was therefore a threat to American society. In 1922 he ran for election to the state legislature on a single issue—*ee*volution. He won the election.

As a first-time legislator he had to spend two years learning how to translate desire into law. Reelected in 1924, he set about writing a bill. The Butler Act made it "unlawful for any teacher in any of the Universities, Normals and all other public schools of the state which are supported in whole or in part by the public funds of the state, to teach any theory that denies the story of the Divine Creation of man as taught in the Bible, and to teach instead that man has descended from a lower order of animals."[6]

Butler's bill attracted little overt opposition. When it came to a vote, it passed with ease. The governor, Austin Peay, was expected to veto it. At the critical moment, however, Peay's fellow Baptists put pressure on him to sign it, and he did so, trying to excuse himself by remarking, "Nobody believes that it is going to be an active statute."[7] It was certainly a curiosity, and like most freaks might well soon have expired. But its very oddity excited attention. A three-inch item about it appeared in the *New York Times*, and that in turn was brought to the notice of the ACLU.

A fund was raised to bring a test case, but no plaintiff could be found at long distance, a fact that the ACLU brought to the attention of the Tennessee newspapers. George W. Rappelyea, a young mining engineer with bushy hair and horn-rimmed glasses, saw the story in a Chattanooga paper. Originally from New York, he now worked in Dayton, Tennessee. He arranged a meeting at Robinson's drugstore with two local lawyers and John Scopes, recently graduated from the University of Kentucky, presently teaching science and football at Dayton High School. Scopes was a very reluctant defendant. After all, he explained, evolution was an essential part of modern biology. "But you have been violating the law," said Rappelyea. "So has every other teacher," the thin, bespectacled Scopes replied.

Robinson's drugstore was also Dayton's bookstore. Scopes fetched a copy of George Hunter's *Civic Biology* from the shelves. It was a book that the state textbook commission had approved. It included a thorough account of evolution. Rappelyea refused to be dissuaded. Wasn't the law a bad law? Scopes agreed that it was. Didn't responsible people have a duty to challenge bad laws? It took all of Rappelyea's persuasive powers, but Scopes eventually allowed Rappelyea to arrest him for violating the Butler Act.[8] Under indictment, Scopes went to New York to meet his lawyers from the ACLU, and was "dined and feted within an inch of his life."[9]

Scope's defense counsel included Dudley Field Malone of the ACLU, Bainbridge Colby, Arthur Garfield Hays (also of the ACLU) and Clarence Darrow. The ACLU had not chosen Darrow to lead the defense team. He had—for the only time in his long career—offered his services,[10] and Scopes had accepted them. Darrow was not at all what the ACLU had in mind. They wanted a nice establishment lawyer, a gentleman, say John W. Davies or Charles Evans Hughes. But the damage was done before they could stop it. To Darrow, the Scopes case was irresistible. His ideal recreation was a debate on religion. He enjoyed arguing religious questions so much that his friends were not entirely convinced of his agnosticism.[11] For several weeks in 1923 he had conducted an acrimonious debate on evolution in the pages of the *Chicago Tribune*. His opponent was William Jennings Bryan. And the Great Commoner had been appointed to the prosecution team that was to present the case against John Scopes.

With a major legal battle in the offing, Dayton, true to the booster ethic, turned itself upside down to capitalize on its sudden celebrity and warned nearby Chattanooga to keep its covetous hands off Dayton's trial. "On all roads into Dayton posters appealed to the skeptical: 'Where Will You Spend Eternity?' . . . others invited 'Sweetheart, Come to Jesus.' Hot dog, lemonade, and sandwich stands sprang up along the sidewalks. Little cotton apes appeared in windows, and stores offered pins reading, 'Your Old Man's a Monkey.' "[12] Meanwhile, Bryan strode around the town in a white pith helmet, fluttering a palm leaf fan and munching radishes.[13]

When the trial opened it became the first ever carried on the radio. Loudspeakers relayed the proceedings to the thousands of people who occupied the courthouse lawn, cooling themselves with fans reading "Do Your Gums Bleed?" distributed by a toothpaste company.[14] Inside, Arthur Garfield Hays discovered, "We of the defense had somehow acquired titles of 'Colonel.' Those on the other side were known as 'General.' "[15] The Judge, John T. Raulston, sat beneath a banner that enjoined, "Read Your Bible Daily."

Darrow saw the case for what it was: an important constitutional issue. He tried five times to get the case moved to a federal court, without success. What mattered was not whether Scopes had taught evolution, but whether the state had the right to forbid him to teach it. But he would never convince a Dayton jury of that. The defense was forced to depend on arguments that evolution was true. But the judge refused to allow the scientists the defense had imported as expert witnesses to take the stand. Their testimony, he ruled, could only be hearsay: they were not present when lower life forms evolved into human beings. At that point, Scopes's defense appeared to have collapsed. The trial seemed over. Many who had come to Dayton expecting a spectacle, such as H. L. Mencken, left.

In an inspired and desperate moment, Darrow decided to call to the stand the prosecution's chief helpmeet, Bryan, as an expert witness on the Bible. It was a brilliant stroke.

Bryan had spent the trial until now sitting at the counsel table without saying a word, sweating heavily, shredding the edges of his palm-leaf fan between false teeth. He had been interested in religious questions since childhood.* Bryan's theology was based less on study than on honing a debating point: "You believe in the age of rocks; I believe in the Rock of Ages." And, "I have as much right as an atheist to begin with an assumption, and I would rather begin with God and reason down than begin with dirt and reason up." His interest in religion became obsessive as he grew older, and by 1925 he had become a wholehearted Fundamentalist.[16] But he had not become conservative. He believed still in women's suffrage, government ownership of the railroads, the abolition of child labor, the regulation of business, and the abolition of the saloon—the entire Populist canon of the 1890s. The tragedy of Bryan's life (a tragedy in which he had the company of millions) was that the times had changed while he had not, could not. So when he took the stand Darrow had no trouble holding him up to ridicule and scorn.[17] Darrow repeatedly pressed him to defend the literal truth of the Bible. Each time he did so, Bryan tried to hedge. Having antagonized everyone who did not take the Bible literally, Bryan then managed to antagonize those who did. To Darrow's question, "Do you think the Earth was made in six days?" Bryan answered, "Not in six days of 24 hours."

The Dayton jury took all of eight minutes to find Scopes guilty. He was fined $100. The Tennessee Supreme Court upheld the Butler Act, but set aside Scope's conviction because the fine ought to have been set by the jury, not the judge. Scopes accepted a scholarship offered by a Tennessee businessman to send him to the University of Chicago for graduate study. In time he became an eminent geologist. He never went back to Tennessee.

A week after the trial ended Bryan died. He was buried at Arlington, mourned by millions of Fundamentalists as a martyr. The inscription on his tombstone reads, "He kept the Faith."

The struggle over, the teaching of evolution went on. Five states,

---

* A Baptist by temperament, he was frightened of water, so at the age of fourteen he became a Presbyterian.

including Tennessee, had passed laws against it. Not one was repealed. But nor were there any more prosecutions.

Fundamentalism pitted itself against fifty years of biblical scholarship. What it really amounted to, however, was a sad, distorted protest against the modern world, with its industrial disciplines, its lonely cities, and its economy of hard cash.

III

On Armistice Day a "Gospel car" had rolled into Tulsa, Oklahoma, with "Jesus Is Coming—Get Ready" painted down one side and "Where Will You Spend Eternity?" painted down the other. It was driven by a striking redheaded widow named Aimee Semple McPherson. The influenza epidemic had nearly killed her daughter, Roberta, in Philadelphia. Aimee headed west, seeking a more salubrious climate for the child.

The Gospel car (an open Oldsmobile) had to push its way along flooded river bottoms, its occupants had to make camp in the pouring rain, and snow closed the passes into northern California. A few days before Christmas, Aimee (everyone called her Aimee) arrived in Los Angeles "with ten dollars and a tambourine."[18]

The city did not fall to her at once. After a series of defeats she left the state and when she returned in 1921 she went farther south to San Diego. She could not have made a better choice. San Diego had the highest rates of sickness and suicide in any city in California, possibly in the United States. Her first meeting drew 30,000 people and produced her first "miracle." "When a middle-aged paralytic rose from her wheel chair and took a few stumbling steps, San Diego's legion of incurables, its sick and ailing, started for the platform."[19] The news spread quickly. Her healing revivals drew the crippled and afflicted from far and wide, clamoring for admission, creating pandemonium at the entrance to her tent. These riots of the sick filled the front page. Wherever she went, the lame, the blind, and the leprous struggled to seize her hand. Los Angeles now fell to her without a struggle. It was there that she would build her monument. No more tents for the leading revivalist of the era.

For most of 1921–22 she barnstormed the country, adding to her fame, raising money for the construction of Angelus Temple. To build a 3,000-seat arena with a stage that would do credit to a great opera house was an achievement. To keep those seats filled was another. But she possessed extraordinary vitality. She was attractive, if far from beautiful. Her body was broad and angular; her thick ankles were hidden behind very long skirts. She possessed a well-shaped head, clear skin, dazzling eyes, and a mass of shining hair. Her voice, trained at a thousand revivals, could play any tune she desired. Most of all, she exuded boundless energy. With her voice, her physical zest, and the boldness of her manner, she created an atmosphere of sexual excitement that many a conventionally beautiful woman could never hope to achieve.[20]

Women preachers were not unknown before the Twenties, but they were very rare. It was a prejudice she challenged head on. She had been called by God as she lay dying, and she told the story with enthusiasm and in detail. Men might be prejudiced against women preachers, she acknowledged, but God was not. "The religion she preached she called the Foursquare Gospel,* and it was a nonstop outburst of joy, joy, joy."[21] If anyone could fill 3,000 seats night after night with paying customers, Aimee could.

She trained a 100-voice choir and hired a 36-piece band. There were sewing circles for women and nurseries for children. The temple found jobs for men just out of prison and organized welfare services for the poor. It kept a sizable printing plant in full-time operation and ran its own radio station, KFSG (Kall Four Square Gospel). The station spread her influence from San Francisco to San Diego and as far east as Colorado and New Mexico. This powerful station swamped the airwaves, forcing Hoover to intervene. He shut down KFSG until she hired a qualified radio engineer named Kenneth Ormiston to monitor her signals.[22]

Meanwhile, on the vast stage she was mounting some of the most dramatic theatrical productions on the West Coast. Aimee wrote the scripts, choreographed the movements of her enormous cast, designed all the sets and costumes, and was the star of the show. She took the music from popular light operas, such as *The Merry Widow*. She dramatized Bible stories or moral themes, such as staging a battle between evil and good, complete with holy artillery, a blimp bearing the devil to the battlefield, and a scoreboard to keep track of the casualties.[23]

Not long after Ormiston had been hired, Sister Aimee could be seen, and heard, during services giggling into the telephone that connected her with the radio station above. Suddenly he left his wife and child. Mrs. Ormiston descended on the temple and made ugly scenes. Aimee decided to make a pilgrimage to the Holy Land. Her friendship with Ormiston appeared to be over.

When she returned from her travels she showed an unusual interest in putting money away. She began taking thousands of dollars each week

---

* It was a theological curiosity. It came to her in a vision. The Foursquare Gospel was belief in Regeneration, Divine Healing, the Second Coming, and the Baptism of the Holy Ghost.

from the collection for her own use. She also developed an unusual interest in swimming. On Tuesday, May 18, 1926, Aimee disported herself 100 yards offshore from the beach at Ocean Park, watched by her secretary, Emma Schaffer. With a cheerful wave to the nonswimming Miss Schaffer she plunged under the waves and disappeared. An intensive search was made for Aimee's body—and for Ormiston. But after a week he showed up, affable, relaxed, and sorry he could not be of more help.

Interest in Ormiston faded. Then a letter arrived, filled with gangland phrases, demanding $500,000 or else. The "or else" was that Sister Aimee would be sold into white slavery. Hardly had the contents of the letter been digested than the missing Aimee appeared in Douglas, Arizona, with a tale to tell, of kidnaping, brave resistance, and heroic escape. She came back to Los Angeles and a triumphant welcome. Thousands besieged the station to greet the train bringing her from Arizona. She was carried through the station in a flower-bedecked chair to shouts of joy and exultation.

A grand jury investigation into her disappearance failed to bring an indictment. The evidence, however, was very strong that her disappearance was a hoax. She had spent her nights, not in a desert shack, but in a Carmel bedroom with Ormiston. Both of them had been positively identified by people in Carmel.

In early 1927, with the threat of criminal prosecution behind her, she went east, to revive her spirits. In New York she made a foray into the Club El Fey. "She was tastefully gowned, demure and self-contained as she entered the club, which was crowded with revelers. At Tex Guinan's invitation she made a short speech. . . . Texas called on the crowd to 'give this courageous woman a big hand,' and was cheered for five minutes. She extended an invitation to all, chorus girls included, to come hear her at the Glad Tidings Tabernacle, and left amid more cheers."[24]

By this time Aimee was embroiled in a variety of law suits. She was to find that for her the road to heaven was paved with writs. Much of her huge income went in lawyers' fees. As her need for money grew, she involved the temple in real estate schemes, all of which reeked of snake oil, none of which succeeded. The temple congregation, however, provided a permanent flock, ready for fleecing.

Who were these faithful whose belief never faltered or failed? who never tired of filling those thousands of seats and the buckets in which the collection was taken? They were the uprooted. Each week some two to three thousand people arrived in Los Angeles to start a new life, as she had done. The annual Iowa Day picnic drew more than 40,000 celebrants.[25] Once, appearing on stage at the temple in a milkmaid's outfit and carrying a silver pail of foaming milk, she asked how many people there had ever lived on a farm. "The entire audience stood up."[26]

IV

The Protestant faith had been *the* American faith since Colonial times. Never was this identification more forcefully asserted than in the early years of the twentieth century, as Catholics and Jews poured into the cities and demanded a place in American life. The Protestant churches did not know how to respond to this crisis, a challenge that was more social than religious in nature. At the same time, there was the challenge to belief itself posed by modern science. And again the Protestant churches floundered against the incoming tide.

They had mounted spectacular fund-raising drives in the first two postwar years, copying the techniques of the war bond sellers. One Presbyterian campaign raised $35 million in a few weeks. A Methodist fund for missionaries raised $140 million in less than six months. Militant Protestantism, aroused with evangelical fervor and flush with cash, for an instant seemed poised to rout modernism and competing creeds alike.[27] After all, had they not just banished the saloon? It was a cruelly self-deceptive moment.

Throughout the Twenties there was a steady decline in the vitality of religious belief. Per capita gifts to religious charities dropped by 40 percent. The number of people coming forward to offer themselves for foreign missionary work fell from 2,700 in 1920 to barely 300 in 1927. Churches in both city and country reported declining attendance, forcing many of them to abandon Sunday evening services.[28] And there seemed nothing that could be done to reverse it. Religious faith appeared less and less relevant when set alongside the claims made by science, behaviorism, and psychoanalysis.

Among some young, liberally minded ministers the highest expression of faith remained direct action on social problems. The idea of a "Social Gospel" had been mooted among Protestant churchmen since the Civil War. In 1919 the United Textile Workers leadership abandoned a strike they had begun in Lawrence, Massachusetts, and decades of speculation turned into reality. Three young ministers—A. J. Muste, Harold Rotzel, and Cedric Long—assumed leadership of a strike the UTW considered lost.

The three clergymen adopted a policy of strict pacifism. When the police struck—and they did, hard—there was no muddying of the waters. The unprovoked, indefensible violence of the police was seen for what it was. Muste and Long were beaten up and jailed. But the strike was won. Wages were raised and the work week reduced by six hours; an astonishing result considering that the strike had begun as a protest against wage cuts.

Muste, Long, and Rotzel gave up their ministries. That was always the danger of the Social Gospel—the social was likely to overshadow the gospel. Muste continued his involvement in labor struggles, running Brookwood, the labor college at Katonah, New York. Brookwood was founded and financed by another former minister, William Fincke. But there were Social Gospel ministers who remained active in the church while being active elsewhere, such as Harry F. Ward. An eminent divine on the staff at Union Theological Seminary, he was also for much of the Twenties the head of the ACLU.

Within the church, liberal theologians such as Harry Emerson Fosdick were attempting to embrace modernism without discarding their faith to do it.[29] They accepted modern Bible scholarship. They stretched an ecumenical hand toward Catholics and Jews. But admirable and sincere though they might be, the fact remained that the Twenties saw the break-up of the self-confidence of Protestantism; the self-confidence, that is, of the traditional American faith.

12. The Golden Age of Bat, Club, Glove, and Ball

I

When the 1919 White Sox took the field for the World Series against the Cincinnati Reds, they were the strongest team that baseball had ever seen. Yet two days before the Series opened something strange had occurred: the odds had shifted in favor of the clearly underdog Reds. For no reason that anyone could see, someone was betting a fortune on Cincinnati. When the Reds took the nine-game Series by 5–3 the reason became apparent: the Series was fixed. Or so millions believed. Charles A. Comiskey, the owner of the White Sox, angrily denied it. He offered $10,000 for "a single clue."[1]

The rumors were a nine-day wonder. Americans believed that if there was one sport that was clean, that sport was baseball. Horse races were fixed, fights were fixed, but not baseball, never baseball. They were wrong, in fact, but the owners had always been able to cover up crooked games and the players who sold out to gamblers. When the 1920 season opened, all but one of the 1919 White Sox team were still playing for Comiskey. Toward the end of the season there was a rumor that a game between the Cubs and the Phillies had been fixed. A grand jury convened, and widened its investigation to include the White Sox. At which point Eddie Cicotte, who had won twenty-nine games for the White Sox in 1919, tearfully confessed that he had been bought off for $10,000. He did it, he explained, for the wife and kids. "Shoeless" Joe Jackson, a legendary hitter of the ball, admitted to being bought for $20,000, of which he was able to collect only $5,000. Cicotte and Jackson named six other players who had taken bribes to throw the Series.

The trial of the players and various gamblers took place eighteen months after the alleged crime. Much of the damning evidence had some-how been lost or stolen. The jury did not take long to acquit all the defendants. The owners had meanwhile hired a "Czar," federal Judge Kenesaw Mountain Landis, to clean up the game and keep it clean.[2] His decisions on the bench were based largely on impulse and vanity, but he passed for a folk hero. As one reporter described him, "The face of Kene-saw Mountain Landis is almost as familiar to the public as that of Charlie Chaplin."[3] His conduct in the courtroom was that of a ham actor, as he groaned aloud, "What shall I do?" seizing his white mane in his hands as he pondered what justice demanded. He managed the lighting in the courtroom to emphasize the cragginess of his features and the pure white-ness of his hair. When it came to image-building, the baseball owners had found just the man.

Landis made sure the seven White Sox players who were tried (the eighth indictment was dropped for lack of evidence) never played baseball again. He also added to his blacklist two players who had not even been indicted. The owners nervously worried that the fans would stay away in droves. Millions of dollars were poured into regilding the game's once untarnished reputation. What rescued the national game from the slough of despond, however, was not Landis or publicity gimmicks. It was a young Boston Red Sox player who, during spring training in Tampa in 1919, hit a baseball farther than one had ever been hit before, nearly 600 feet.[4]

He was one of the ugliest men ever to play the game, and one of the most lovable. He had a barrel torso, spindly legs, a strangely mincing pit-a-pat gait, an enormous head with tiny eyes, a squashed nose, and thick lips. Abandoned by his parents, he had grown up in a tough, shadowy world, without education, without love, and without illusions. He had known hunger. When he began to make a lot of money he became, and remained, a glutton. His pregame diet consisted of several hot dogs and a glass of water fizzing with bicarbonate of soda to help them on their way. Like many young ballplayers he had been nicknamed "Babe" when he joined the majors. But in his case, when the nickname spread from the dugout to the sports pages and then to the fans, it stuck. He was to be Babe Ruth for the rest of his life.

To the Red Sox, Ruth in 1919 was a star pitcher. To himself, he was a star hitter. Still pitching regularly, he began to fill Fenway Park by going after the all-time home run record of 27, set in 1884 by Edward Williamson of the Chicago Colts.* In his seven years to date in the majors Ruth had hit a total of 20 homers. This was still the era of "inside" baseball: "It meant playing for a run, a single run. You bunted safely, stole second, went to third on a sacrifice and scored on a fly ball to win 1–0."[5] Hitting was a lesser art than pitching; low scores were more admired than high ones. Ruth was about to change all that. By the end of the season he had hit 29 home runs, and brought out the crowds.

He demanded $20,000 for the 1920 season. The Red Sox were outraged. They sold him to the Yankees for $100,000 plus a loan of $300,000.† In cash and credit the Yankees were willing to part with ten times what any ballplayer had ever before been considered worth.

In 1920 Ruth hit 54 home runs. The runner-up in the American League boasted 19. The National League champion hit 15. His slugging average of .847 that year has never been surpassed. And the desire to see him hit a home run had become an obsession. When he was walked—as he often was—a thunder of angry boos rolled across the field.

The next year he took the Yankees to the first pennant they had ever won, in one of the most exciting American League races ever. He lifted his home run record to 59 and batted .378. Ruth epitomized a transformed game. The average for all major-league batters in the decade before 1919 was .250. By 1921 it had risen to nearly .290, where it remained for the next decade. As batting averages rose, so did scores. To the purists, this marked the cheapening of hallowed skills. But most fans are not purists. Then, as now, they wanted to see the ball belted out of the park, runners sliding into home, the bases loaded. Baseball in the Twenties gave them what they wanted. The ball became livelier.[6] Pitchers were deprived of the spitball. Baseball attendance doubled over prewar levels. At some grounds it rose threefold. Ruth made the Yankees the champions of the ticket booth before they became champions of the world. They became, in 1920, the first club to attract a million fans; 1,289,443 to be exact, twice their 1919 attendance. The Giants, who owned the Polo Grounds and allowed the Yankees to play there, were nettled by such lèse majesté. They suggested that the Yankees seek other accommodation. So in 1923 the Yan-

---

* The Colts that year played on a ground where right field was only 215 feet from home plate, and that was where 25 of Williamson's homers went. The next year, on a more conventional ground, he reverted to his usual home run tally, 3.

† This trade ruined the Red Sox. With Ruth they had won the World Series. In the eleven seasons following his departure they finished dead last nine times.

kees moved into their own ball park, Yankee Stadium, known to two generations of fans as "the house that Ruth built."

Ruth had become an object of national pride, like the Liberty Bell or the Grand Canyon, a hero far beyond the purlieu of New York. Which is not to suggest that he was slighted at home. The *New York Daily News* assigned a reporter, Marshall Hunt, to devote himself exclusively to writing about Babe, in season and out.[7] Yet the idol of millions was also the Bad Boy of Baseball. He drank, smoked, swore, chased anything in skirts, and had no manners. His blazing temper got him into trouble on and off the field. He was warned, fined, suspended. It made no difference. The strongest memory one sportswriter retained of Babe Ruth was of "a large man in a camel's hair coat and a camel's hair cap, standing in front of a hotel, his broad nostrils sniffing at the promise of the night."[8]

With a bat in his hand he remained lord of the diamond. Two Columbia University researchers tested his hand-and-eye coordination. It was almost uncanny. "If you needed someone to thread a needle by dim light in a moving automobile, Babe Ruth would be your man."[9] When he came to the plate he defied convention. Most pitchers try to keep the ball low. Ruth loved to see the ball coming in knee-high. To a pull hitter like Ruth, pitchers try to pitch outside. Ruth loved to make contact in front of the outside corner.* What then was a pitcher to do? "Pitch and duck," said one. "Pray for a single," said another.[10] There was another possibility, of course. In 1923 Ruth was walked more than half his times at bat. That year he batted .393 and led the Yankees to their first-ever World Series championship.

Fame and riches did not change him one bit. In some respects he would never grow up. Yet the youthful characteristics he carried into adult life—the earnestness, the sense of fun, the importance he attached to friendship, the complete lack of pretension—these made him a man whom other men found it easy to love. Alive with animal vitality, he raced around New York in a monogrammed roadster, bundled up in a raccoon coat, a huge cigar clamped between his teeth, as if determined to collect a speeding ticket a day. He radiated goodwill and sincerity. His delight in being "the Babe" was almost childlike. Wherever he was, he remained completely himself. On a scorching day when Harding came to see the Senators play the Yankees he was greeted in the Ruthian manner: "Hot as hell, ain't it, Prez?"[11]

Ruth symbolized a transformed game, and that transformed game

---

* The hitter on whom he modeled himself was "Shoeless" Joe Jackson, whose lifetime .356 average is the third-highest of all time.

itself symbolized a changed society. "The rage for Ruth was part of the shift from Puritan values," wrote Marshall Smelser. "Americans had become a consuming people who hungered for instant pleasures."[12]

II

Before the war, college football had been a minor sport, of interest to a small band of players, their friends, and their families. In 1900 Walter Camp could pick his All-American team simply by selecting the best players at Harvard, Yale, and Princeton. In the entire country there were perhaps a thousand people all told who played football.[13] So innocent was the game still that Harvard could go to the Rose Bowl on New Year's Day, 1920, and win.

In the Twenties, however, college enrollments more than doubled in a decade. As the number of students and alumni rose dramatically, so did attendance at football games. Thus began the golden age of stadium construction. Ohio State opened a 64,000-seater. Yale built a bowl that held 75,000. On the West Coast, Berkeley, Stanford, and Washington built 60,000-seat stadia. Universities discovered that although it was hard to raise faculty salaries, it was easy to raise a couple of million dollars for a football arena.

To serious people, college football was little more than a way of providing cheap thrills for a profit, like running a brothel or a speakeasy. Possibly worse, because it made a travesty of education.[15] To foster the belief that their *real* commitment was to learning and not to athletics, colleges refused to allow students to play on varsity teams during their first year.

The fact was, college football had become a big business. Many colleges and universities felt they could no longer do without it. By the end of the Twenties, college football games exceeded attendance at major league baseball games and took in more money.[16] The money that football brought in supported up to a score of minor sports, such as lacrosse and gymnastics, which would never pay their way. Football provided hundreds of students with occasional employment as ushers, ticket takers, and traffic guides. It paid off the bondholders who had financed the stadium.[17] And then there were the coaches. On average, they earned more than college professors.[18] They had to be paid, and so did some of the players. The goose got part of the egg.

It was not only in the colleges that football was flourishing. It was spreading rapidly into the high schools. By 1926 there were some 10,000 coaches and trainers in the schools and colleges supervising 200,000 players of the game.[19] It was from Wheaton High School in Illinois (from which the writer graduated) that there came the supreme football player of the 1920s, the man who did more than any other to turn it into a big-time, big-money sport, Harold "Red" Grange.

At the University of Illinois he played in 20 games and averaged 182 yards a game, at more than 10 yards each time he carried the ball. His masterpiece came in 1924 against one of the strongest teams in the country, Michigan. In the first 12 minutes of the game he carried the ball 4 times and scored 4 touchdowns, running 263 yards. To many football fans, this was for decades considered the greatest gridiron feat of all time. At the end of the first quarter the stadium crowd at Urbana gave him an ovation that held up the game for five minutes. The Illinois coach wanted to keep him on the bench for the rest of the game and leave his record of a touchdown a carry as a monument for posterity to marvel at.[20] Grange begged not to be rested. Records meant nothing to him; playing did. So the perfect record did not stand. He carried the ball half a dozen times more, and scored a fifth touchdown.

The next year, in 1925, Red Grange became the first athlete to grace the cover of *Time*.[21] For his final game for Illinois, played at Columbus, Ohio, against Ohio State, nearly 100,000 people traveled from all over the country to be there. "They had not come to see a football game," ran one account. "They had come to see Grange."[22]

Several weeks later he played his first professional football game. Before now, most big-name players were from the Ivy League. The logical step for an All-American was not pro football but becoming a bond sales-man. That changed with Red Grange. He showed that a top college player could draw big crowds and demand big money. His paycheck for his first pro game was $12,000. As the crowds kept coming, the price went up, to $35,000 a game. In three years he earned $1 million (about $1,000 for every minute he was on the field). Before he was thirty he had retired, heavy with honors and riches.

While Grange was making himself the supreme individual player of the Twenties, Knute Rockne of Notre Dame was being celebrated as the greatest coach the game would ever see. Rockne not only turned out some of the best teams in football history, but he was an innovator who helped to make the game explosive and exciting. Before 1920 there was resistance to the forward pass. It was legal, but so was picking one's nose. Not until Rockne's teams began to show how it could be used in a controlled, logical way to slice through a solid defense did the forward pass come into its own, pulling spectators to their feet as the ball rose high in the air.

III

All through May and June 1919 a crew of 500 men hammered and sawed from dawn until after dusk in Toledo, Ohio, to construct a 90,000-seat stadium that would be used only once and then dismantled. On July 4 the world heavyweight champion, Jess Willard, was to defend his title against a little-known fighter from the West, William Harrison Dempsey, whom everyone called "Jack."* When the day of the fight arrived the temperature soared to 106 degrees, and sap in the new lumber oozed all over the seats. At the gate, Bat Masterson collected spectators' knives and guns, assisted by Wyatt Earp.[23]

Four years earlier Willard had taken the championship from Jack Johnson in Havana. Standing six feet, five inches tall and weighing nearly 300 pounds, he was in the habit of beating smaller men senseless. He had killed one fighter. There were fears that he would kill Dempsey.

When the bell sounded to start the fight, Dempsey sprang from his corner, met Willard as he lumbered toward the center of the ring, and landed half a dozen punches that sent Willard to his knees. Nobody had ever hit harder than Dempsey. He knocked Willard down seven times before the first round ended. Willard returned to his corner with a broken jaw, spitting out six broken teeth. He was cut above and below both eyes. He was bleeding from the mouth. The right side of his face had been pounded into a crimson pulp.[24]

Dempsey, who was brown and hard, as if carved from mahogany, sat slumped in his corner between rounds, scowling at the canvas between his feet, his face unshaven, his forehead furrowed. He was all muscle and darkness. In each of the next two rounds he did more damage to Willard's body and face. When the bell sounded for the fourth round, a blood-smeared towel flew from Willard's corner, while Willard collapsed over his stool. Dempsey, like Byron, woke the next morning to find himself famous.

He had learned his craft in a thousand bars, hobo jungles, and mining camps, without gloves, referees, and rest intervals. As a skinny teenager with a girlish voice he would walk into the toughest saloon he could find and in piping tones announce: "I can't sing and I can't dance, but I'll lick anyone in the house!"[25] Within minutes he would be fighting for his life against the local arm-breaker. If he won, he passed the hat. If he lost, he

* There had been a great nineteenth-century middleweight by the name of Jack Dempsey. When another Dempsey haled into view he was, inevitably, called Jack.

crawled away to a flophouse to nurse his wounds and heal up for another town, another fight.

He grew stronger and fiercer every year, beating a succession of noted heavyweights without ever attracting much attention. Then, in 1917, his manager introduced him to a boxing promoter named Tex Rickard, who saw a million dollars in Dempsey's brine-soaked fists. These two men came out of the same background. Dempsey had been born in Manassas, Colorado, to pioneer parents who had gone west in a covered wagon. Rickard had grown up on the Texas frontier to become a cowpuncher, sheriff, lumberjack, gambler, and saloonkeeper. He promoted Dempsey heavily and got him what he longed for—the chance to fight Willard.

Dempsey was not a popular champion. Rumor had it that he had evaded the wartime draft. Rumor had it that a man could hit so hard only if his hands were enclosed in plaster of paris. In both cases the rumors were false, but they dogged him throughout his career. To Grantland Rice, as to many other people, Dempsey was "the oddest mixture of humanity I've ever known."[26] In the ring Dempsey bared his teeth like an animal as he hurled himself at his opponent. Outside the ring, he was gentle, quiet, and shy. He was almost desperate to be liked.

As the toast of Broadway, Dempsey did a lot of his training in nightclubs and bedrooms following the Willard fight. When he came to defend his title at Madison Square Garden in December 1920 against Bill Brennan he was long on confidence, short on preparation. Brennan beat him to the punch time and again, winning nearly every round. He split open Dempsey's left ear, which poured blood freely over the champion's back and chest. By the twelfth and final round only a knockout could save Dempsey's title. He knocked Brennan down with a right hook that first lifted the contender off his feet. Brennan got up from the canvas a second too late.[27]

Rickard was now able to transform boxing by creating the boxing millionaire, a far different creature from the pug who frequented low saloons and dined in greasy-spoon restaurants. His boxing millionaire was the aristocrat of the sporting world—the man who drove the most expensive cars, ate at the most expensive restaurants, lived in a movie-star mansion, and mixed with other aristocrats.* He would turn Dempsey into the first million-dollar champion. To see this demigod in action, Rickard calculated, people would pay almost any price.

Before this time boxing was presented in stuffy halls, the air blue with

---

* Among the rich and powerful men who would hang around the Dempsey training camp was J. Paul Getty, who was not much older than the champion and a keen amateur boxer. He begged to be allowed to spar for a round. He put up a creditable showing until, responding to the Getty command "Hit me a little harder, Jack," Dempsey knocked him out.

cigar smoke, the patrons rowdy and half-drunk, the fights spaced with tedious, unexplained delays. Brawls broke out over seats and tickets. Ushers were really bouncers eager to beat the recalcitrant into submission. Rickard put on fight programs that moved like clockwork, trained his ushers and private policemen as if they were an army, sold no more tickets than there were seats, and promoted his fights in large, well-ventilated halls. He brought the upper and middle classes out to the fights, and they brought their wives and sweethearts. The hall was clean, the staff courteous, the entertainment virtually nonstop. It was like going to the theater, only more exciting.

He built a 60,000-seat stadium near Jersey City to hold Dempsey's second title defense, on July 2, 1921. The gate was more than twice the size of that at any previous match, some $1.8 million. The contender was the light-heavyweight champion of Europe, Georges Carpentier. At 170 pounds he was really a beefed-up middleweight. Alongside Dempsey he looked undernourished. But he had the clear, ethereal face of a Greek statue. He was a war hero. He was adored. And he was certain to be beaten. This fact seems to have not escaped his notice. The only time that sportswriters ever saw him he was either on a rubbing table or eating at a restaurant. None ever saw him training.[28] As the fight drew near, Rickard grew terrified that Dempsey would ruin everything by killing Carpentier.[29]

This fight was the first important sports event ever broadcast.[30] It was listened to eagerly in thousands of speakeasies, poolrooms, lodge halls, barns, and living rooms up and down the East Coast. For the first and probably last time Americans wanted a foreign contender to beat an American champion. Dempsey won the fight with a fourth-round knockout. Carpentier won the adulation. "Over the result some men cried," said the *New Republic*, a journal not renowned for taking an interest in sport.[31]

Dempsey's fourth title defense, at the Polo Grounds in September 1923, was equally memorable for very different reasons. Dempsey's opponent was the Argentinian Luis Firpo, a fighter who disdained training as a waste of any grown man's time. Firpo carried all his possessions in a cardboard suitcase and had one suit of clothes. He was the most dedicated miser ever to take up boxing, pursuing his beliefs so devotedly that he refused to employ a manager.[32] He became a top contender solely on courage and strength.

When the opening bell sounded, Dempsey charged across the ring and threw a right hook at Firpo's jaw. For perhaps the only time in his life Firpo did it by the book. He sidestepped the right and threw a perfectly timed left uppercut that snapped Dempsey's head back. The champion's eyes glazed over, his knees shook, and he fell to the canvas. The Polo

Grounds turned into an indescribable bedlam. One man died of heart failure.[33]

What none of the screaming fans realized was that Firpo was fighting with a dislocated left arm.[34] Every blow he took on it, every blow he gave with it, was agonizing. His courage was almost inhuman. But this might be his only chance to fight for the championship. He held nothing back. Dempsey knocked him down three times in that first round, each time that Firpo bore in, fists flying. The fourth time he attacked, he hit Dempsey again with a left uppercut and knocked him clean out of the ring. In the confusion that followed, Dempsey was pushed back onto the canvas by the sportswriters among whose clacking typewriters he had crashed. Dempsey knocked Firpo down once again before the round ended. In the second round he knocked him out. This "thrilling, atavistic brawl"[35] was celebrated in one of the most famous of modern American paintings by George Bellows. It shows Dempsey being knocked out of the ring.

For the next three years Dempsey kept his title on ice. He could earn $500,000 a year without fighting. He was a vaudeville and movie star. Without even throwing a punch he could make more money than any other athlete in the world. But sooner or later he would have to defend his title, and the top contender now was a black fighter named Harry Wills. In vain did Wills plead, "If I were champion tomorrow, I'd be just as unassuming and peaceful as I am now. I wouldn't turn out to be another Jack Johnson."[36] There was pressure on Rickard not to promote a Wills-Dempsey fight. In 1910 Jack Johnson had taken the heavyweight crown from Jim Jeffries in Reno, Nevada. As news of Johnson's victory spread, there were race riots in every part of the United States. A dozen people were killed, scores badly injured. The promoter and referee of that Nevada fight was none other than George L. "Tex" Rickard himself. But the New York State Boxing Commission ordered Dempsey to fight Wills. Rickard convinced Dempsey that there was a way out—to fight another leading contender, a white one, someone who would also be easier to beat than Wills. The name Rickard came up with was that of Gene Tunney.

Before the war James Joseph Tunney had been a clerk in a Greenwich Village office. Tall, slender, good-looking in a boyish, Irish way, he seemed destined for a life of lower-middle-class obscurity. On his tenth birthday, however, he had been given a pair of boxing gloves. Growing up with a passion for physical fitness, he became an enthusiastic amateur boxer.[37] As a Marine at the Western Front during the war he fought his way to the AEF light-heavyweight championship. This made him the admired acquaintance of various upper-class veterans, and through them he met heiresses, charming debutantes who were as beautiful as he was handsome. A new world opened for him. But as Jay Gatsby discovered, rich girls do not marry poor boys. He would have to make himself rich first. He loved boxing, while loathing almost everything connected with it outside the ring. Like Gatsby, he would have to mix with people he disliked, make deals with gangsters, pursue a career that at bottom he despised, but he would do it, and come out clean as well as rich. In 1919 he began his quest to take the title from Dempsey.

He fought on the Dempsey-Carpentier card, winning a dull t.k.o., and everything he saw of Dempsey confirmed what he had suspected from descriptions he had heard: Dempsey had no answer to defensive boxing and speed. More important, he had no answer to a perfectly thrown straight right.

Tunney brought to his entire life a hunger for education that lesser men mocked and chose to dismiss as pretension. In the ring and out he was the exemplar of the self-educated man. He taught himself to box as earnestly as he pursued his love of literature. He learned to do what the book said, and what few fighters ever had the patience to master, the perfect straight left-hand leads that set up perfect straight right-hand crosses. He pickled his hands in brine to make them harder and chopped down trees to make them harder still. He was the first fighter to recognize that a boxer spends nearly half his time moving backward. So he prepared for that by running hundreds of miles backward each year. Technically, he was the best boxer the world had ever seen up to that time. And he was so in control of himself that he fought with a supernatural calm that began to unsettle his opponents. It was like fighting a machine.

By 1926 he had more than sixty fights behind him, and had lost only one of them (the man who beat him, Harry Greb, fought Tunney twice more; Tunney won each time). For seven years he was in training every single day. He never drank, never smoked, exercised constantly, ate all the things he was supposed to eat and none of those he was not. No one had ever seen a more dedicated athlete—dedicated, that is, to one fight. Even when playing golf he did not relax. "Gene would hit his drive, toss aside his club, and run down the fairway throwing phantom punches— left and right hooks—and muttering 'Dempsey . . . Dempsey . . . Dempsey. . . .' "[38]

When the two finally met at Sesquicentennial Stadium in Philadelphia on September 3, 1926, the champion had been out of the ring for three years. The chance to see Dempsey fight again brought a $2 million gate. At ringside sat serried ranks of millionaires: Andrew Mellon, a Rockefeller, a Biddle, two Roosevelts, a Whitney, Babe Ruth, Charlie Chaplin, William Randolph Hearst, Joseph Pulitzer, and scores more. The rain came down. The fight went on.

Tunney, the 4–1 underdog, feigned apprehension from the opening bell.[39] It worked. An overconfident Dempsey stepped straight into a perfectly timed right that nearly knocked him out. From that moment on, Tunney dominated the fight. It was not very exciting. Dempsey did not shatter but crumbled away. Tunney stripped him of his title bit by bit, round by round. At the end of the fight Dempsey staggered to his corner covered with welts and bruises. Behind him was Tunney, unruffled, unmarked, breathing easily. For the first time in history the heavyweight title changed hands on a decision.

As for Tunney, he was now rich. He could marry an heiress. It was a story too improbable for fiction. Gatsby had to fail. Not Tunney. And what price success? Well, Tunney said, "After the excitement in the dressing room had subsided, I went to a small hotel and had several pots of tea."[40]

IV

To those Americans who were even aware of its existence, tennis had always been the sport of the foppish and phony, the ideal diversion for people with money who gave themselves airs. On college campuses, where the game might have been respected, lawn tennis was mockingly known as "long penis." Those who took the game seriously were few, those who played the game well rarer still. The English, French, and Australians dominated tennis. It seemed likely they would do so forever. Each year half a dozen American players traveled with little hope to Wimbledon, mainly for the experience. Among the Americans who made the trip in 1920 was a twenty-seven-year-old from Philadelphia named William Tilden. He was tall, thin, aloof, and had a reputation for choking in big matches. He had never won a major championship. Nevertheless he spent his spare time in London writing a small book called *The Art of Tennis,** with all the confidence of a man who was, in his own mind, if nowhere else, the best player in the world.

Not from the moment he first took hold of a racket had Tilden shown any promise. At his prep school, Germantown Academy, he was a mediocre addition to an undistinguished team. At the University of Pennsylvania he failed to make the varsity. Supported by his rich parents, Tilden doggedly continued spending forty to fifty hours a week with a racket in his hand. In order to master the game, he had to change it. He created that tennis-as-art that is the epitome of the modern game, something fluid

---

* Dozens of tennis champions, including Bjorn Borg, have over the years cited this as the work that taught them most about the game.

and creative, in which intelligence and imagination win the kind of admiration that mere cunning and strength can never excite. Tilden went to Wimbledon having mastered every stroke, not only by learning the physical technique, but by thinking it out over and over again. "He could hold forth for an hour," says his biographer, "on nothing but how a ball spun."[41]

Tilden advanced flawlessly into the Wimbledon singles final. There, he beat the reigning Wimbledon champion, an Australian named Gerald Patterson, by three sets to one. He was the first American to win the men's singles title, and for the next six years, until he tore a cartilage in his left knee, he was invincible. No one before or since so dominated the game. He bestrode the tennis world, full of athleticism and daring. As an opponent, he was unfailingly generous and fair. A king at the court. Away from it, he was a desperately lonely man, shy, difficult, moving joylessly through the shadow world of homosexuality, seeking younger and younger boys as he grew older.

Tilden returned to Wimbledon in 1921 to defend his title, and the result was one of the most exciting five-set finals ever played. He won the match, having spent the preceding three weeks in a hospital bed and he was still not completely well. When the game ended, Tilden passed out. In following years he did not bother to travel to England each summer. He was the champion of the world. Everyone knew that. So why spend all that time going back and forth on ocean liners to prove it? Tilden preferred to wait until the Wimbledon champion appeared in the same American tournament with him, and then he beat the champion hollow.

As the man who had more or less invented the modern game and filled the courts with hundreds of thousands of paying customers, Tilden felt a duty to provide value for money. So he would allow his opponent in many a match to take a substantial lead. When all seemed lost beyond recall, he would signal that his comeback was about to begin by emptying a pitcher of water over his head. He would then play superbly, winning by the narrowest of margins. Tilden loved a cliff-hanger as much as the crowd.[42]

Tennis was still ostensibly an amateur sport. Yet he stayed at the best hotels, dined at the best restaurants, and was transported by limousine. The bills were sent to the tournament organizers who paid them gladly.[43] Tilden was doing for tennis what Dempsey was doing for boxing and Grange for football—turning it into a big-money sport.[44]

He also destroyed forever the image of tennis as a pastime for sissies. In 1922 he cut the middle finger of his right hand on a wire fence. The wound turned gangrenous and the fingernail fell out. He risked the loss of his entire arm by choosing to have only the first joint of the finger re-moved. But had the entire finger been removed, he would no longer have been able to play tennis. A second operation was necessary, but enough of the finger was saved for him to continue playing. For the rest of his life that stump of a finger pained him. At times it bled. But he could still play and still win.

In 1926, playing a Davis Cup match, he tore a cartilage in his left knee. Cartilage surgery was in its infancy. An operation would have left him with a permanently stiff knee. Tilden played in pain for the remainder of his life, with an unstable knee joint that vibrated so violently, said an osteopath who often watched him play, "it sounded just like a purring cat."[45]

In 1927 he returned to Wimbledon after a six-year absence. In the singles final he won the first two sets, but lost the next three by ever-wider margins. He was thirty-five years old. His stamina had gone. Having slid from the peak, he seemed certain never to scale it again.

V

American golfers could look back on a long record of disasters on British courses. To rub salt into the wound, British golfers would come to the United States each year and carry off some of the most glittering prizes. When Walter Hagen, the best American golfer by far, set off in 1920 to make an assault on the most prestigious tournament in the world, the British Open, he finished fifty-fifth.

Meanwhile, the child prodigy of American golf, a chubby adolescent from Atlanta by the name of Robert Tyre Jones, Jr., was destroying him-self and his game by throwing temper tantrums. When he played a bad shot, he hurled the offending club at a tree, kicked huge divots out of the ground, walked around in circles screaming curses, and lost his concen-tration. He would start off magnificently in one major championship after another and blow up before the last round. In the 1921 British Open (in which Hagen finished sixth) he did the last thing that any golfer ought to do. He picked up. Playing well for two rounds, he shot a forty-six for the first nine holes of the third. He played the tenth hole in silent fury, and shot a six. On the eleventh, an easy par three, he shot a five. Cursing and sulking, he picked up his ball and walked off the course. He quit in the middle of a match. And the course he had quit on was the most sacred in golf—St. Andrews. This was the bottom. He had never won an important championship, and if he could not control his temper, he never would.

In 1922 a chastened, reformed Jones entered the U.S. Open. As he forced impeccable manners on himself, his game improved dramatically.

He finished second. But why not first? he asked a friend. Because you stuff yourself with fried chicken, ice cream, candy, and pies, came the reply. Thereafter, Jones played on tea and toast. And that year Hagen won the British Open. He returned home to national jubilation. American golf had left the dark ages.

When the 1923 season began, Bobby Jones had nothing to show for seven years of highly competitive golf. He had not won a major prize. At twenty-one he was ready to give up the chase. But first he would make one more attempt on the U.S. Open. He went into the final round with a three-stroke lead over Bobby Cruikshank, an Englishman, and blew it. It was the kind of thing he had been doing for years. In the playoff the next day, Jones won the match on the eighteenth hole by a single stroke. It had taken seven years of struggle, but Bobby Jones was an overnight success.[46]

Having conquered himself, he had conquered his sport. Success made a superb player into a great one. In the next seven years he was to set a record that has never been surpassed. He did it, moreover, not by playing in dozens of tournaments each year as contemporary players do. He spent most of his time studying law at Harvard, then practicing it in Atlanta. He played in only half a dozen tournaments a year, sometimes fewer. In the seven years following his first U.S. Open victory, he won or made a playoff in nearly every tournament he entered. And he never took a dollar for it.

Bobby Jones was not dramatic or extroverted. He was not particularly noticeable; in fact, except for one thing: what he did looked as close to perfection as any human being could come in a sport. His playing was described as technically flawless. But it created the satisfaction that comes from great art when seen. He raised no objection when the press called him "Robot, the Mechanical Man of Golf."[47] He seemed to play the same impeccable game no matter what the course or the competition.

The moment he appeared on a golf course, some five to ten thousand admirers would swarm around him bent on adoring the Emperor Jones. Hagen's galleries had been good, but Jones's were phenomenal. His opponents played against him in comparative calm, whereas Jones had thousands trotting at his heels, patting him on the back, shrieking "Bobby! Bobby!" Yet his temper never cracked. He was unfailingly patient and courteous. He so liked to please that any duffer who could wangle the acquaintance of one of his many friends could easily get to play a round with Bobby Jones. He was no prig, no stuffed shirt. He smoked, swore, enjoyed ribald jokes, and drank corn whiskey. If it seemed that there was something unnatural about the calmness with which he played in even the hardest tournaments, there was.[48]

He was not the golfing machine the press witlessly conjured up. Between rounds he might have a cup of soup and not be able to keep it down. If he appeared to play with a grim expression, it was because he was trying to fight off nausea while playing the stroke. The cost of so much self-discipline was high. When a major championship began, he would become so nervous that he could not undo his tie. At the end of each round he would be emotionally exhausted. When it was finally over and the trophy presented, Jones would go back to his hotel room and collapse on his bed, crying as though his heart were breaking.[49]

To the sportswriters and untold millions of fans, Robert Tyre Jones, Jr., was "the champion of champions"—the man who was closer to perfection at his game than the other great athletes were at theirs. But the admiration in which he was held went beyond the flawless swing, the brilliant putt, and the shot from the fairway. At a time when people were losing faith in themselves, when money seemed the god to which all bowed down, he represented the triumph of character. Any thirteen-year-old boy could adore a Ruth, a Red Grange, or a Dempsey. Only a grown man could appreciate a Bobby Jones.

IV

It was in the Twenties that sport became the all-consuming interest that we know so well. Sporting heroes were no longer considered newsworthy only when they were competing for something. They were newsworthy all the time—at home, away from home, when they married, when they were divorced, when they behaved themselves, and when they were in trouble, when they changed managers, when they took a vacation, and when they did nothing much at all. People knew so much about their sporting heroes they might as well have been part of the family.

Freed from the exhausting work disciplines of the nineteenth century, Americans were, in fact, discovering sports directly. They had the time, the energy, and the money to play games. Their doctors encouraged them as well. Victorian-Puritan prejudices against grown men and women disporting themselves were suddenly banished. "For the first time in our history," wrote one scholar in some astonishment, "the crowds watching professional games are matched by the large numbers of people thronging the golf courses, tennis courts and playfields."[50] There was hardly any form of physical recreation that did not attract a million or more participants.

Before the Twenties there were only 300 private tennis clubs and a scattering of municipal courts. By the late 1920s there were nearly a thousand private clubs and enough municipal courts to accommodate 1.2 million players. "Tennis, anyone?" was a rhetorical question when Americans were wearing out 300,000 tennis balls each month.

More phenomenal still was the growth of golf. Before the war half a dozen states could not even boast a golf course, and nearly a score could boast only a few. "The popular conviction was that golf was a game for elderly professors and presidents of banks."[51] By 1927 there were 5,000 courses and 2 million players; the numbers of each rose rapidly every year. No sport in American history has ever caught on as golf did in the Twenties.[52] Most courses were still private, but the entrance requirements were not very daunting as a rule, and greens fees were reasonable. More remarkable, however, were the hundreds of municipal courses. So popular were many of these that an unbroken stream of players passed through them from dawn to dusk for half the year. "From sea-coast to sea-coast kidney-shaped traps were scooped out. . . . No land within thirty-five miles of a large city was safe, and if it had a winding stream and a hill suitable for a spreading clubhouse it was as good as under construction."[53]

This was the real glitter in the Golden Age of Sport. People were discovering sport for themselves. If there were more spectators to fill the huge new stadium and cheer some great athlete until they were dizzy and hoarse, it was because so many had, like him, taken up the bat, the club, the glove, or the ball. His agonies were their own, as were his victories.

13. We Are Amused

I

The Twenties in retrospect seem like one long party. That may be because in only a decade, at a time when most prices were stable, spending on amusement and recreation rose by 300 percent.[1] Each week about 100 million Americans went to the movies, a number equal to nearly the entire population. Mass entertainment had burst upon the world.

The upper class and the highly educated tended to despise the movies. But immigrants who knew little English could understand the silent films—they were the only harmless entertainment the poor could afford; and the lower-middle classes, trapped in dull jobs, were avid for escape. The movies rapidly killed off "the road"—the circuit of traveling theater companies—their only possible competitor. These companies had brought not so much culture as contempt, despising the provincial audience while trying to empty its pockets. Inferior productions at high prices, uncomfortable and shabby theaters, advertising that raised impossible expectations, were the earmarks of the road.

The movie palaces, with liveried attendants and overstuffed seats, although mocked by the sophisticated, catered to their audiences, something the traveling companies and provincial theater managers rarely attempted. And the movie theater offered all this comfort and glamor for a mere 50 cents. By 1926 there were more than 20,000 dream palaces offering celluloid refuge.[2] Those in the big cities strove to rival the fantasy world that flashed across the screen: lobbies that reflected, in gilt and

224

plaster, the rococo splendors of Versailles; enormous crystal chandeliers that sprayed ornate shafts of light; the thick and costly carpets favored by the most expensive hotels; fountains, lounging rooms, cathedral organs, thirty-piece orchestras, and seats covered in velvet. These metropolitan wonders set the standard that, on a smaller scale, spread to countless Main Streets.

The movie theater became the most recognizable building in town, dwarfing its neighbors, busy every night. A splendid new movie theater marked a town on the way up. George Babbitt felt it almost a duty to visit Zenith's premier picture palace, the Chateau. "With exclamations of 'Well, by golly!' and 'You got to go some to beat this dump!' " Babbitt admired it unreservedly.

A place like the Chateau was the epitome of modernity. Yet nineteenth-century ideas of comedy, morality, love, and adventure dominated the screen well into the Twenties. Film's greatest pioneer and innovator, D. W. Griffith, the man who had invented much of the modern film from close-up to fade-out, remained firmly under the spell of late Victorian dramatic conventions. Movie heroines were demure creatures with large luminous eyes and ringlets. Heroes were broad-chested stalwarts in white shirts and riding boots. Comedy films relied on nineteenth-century vaudeville traditions of knockabout. Not until about the mid-Twenties did the screen catch up with the world outside the movie theaters' doors. "Suddenly, the dimpled darling was partly replaced by the eager flapper. The stalwart hero was replaced by the smooth lounge lizard and attitudes to sex became somewhat more sophisticated."[3]

American film remained democratic, however, instead of selling out to art. All those movie theaters were going to remain filled. The distributors kept strong pressure on the studios to turn out films that told a good yarn. The artistic spirits among the moviemakers were thereby cast in the role of rebels. So when artistry did manage somehow to appear on the screen it always came as a surprise.

In Hollywood, life off-screen was also censored. In 1921 a bit player and *demimondaine* named Virginia Rappe fell violently ill at a party in San Francisco that was held in the hotel suite of the highest-paid star in movies, Roscoe "Fatty" Arbuckle. Miss Rappe died several days later, in great agony, from a peritonitis infection that had set in when her bladder ruptured. A folk legend instantly arose, persisting to this day, that Fatty Arbuckle had pushed a Coke bottle into Virginia Rappe's body during a sadistic sexual assault.

Far from being a libertine, the 300-pound Arbuckle was shy and gentle toward women; first, because he was self-conscious at being so fat;

second, because he was by temperament a sensitive, good-natured man. Wealth and fame had not turned him into a sadistic brute. He had not even attempted to have sex with Virginia Rappe. She had gone to him to beg for money. Arbuckle was a notoriously soft touch. She was pregnant, unmarried, and frightened. Her pregnancy was going badly and she needed to see a doctor. While pleading with Arbuckle, she began shrieking, fell on a bed, and in torment began to tear at her clothes. When a doctor arrived he had her taken not to a general hospital, but to a maternity hospital.

An attempt was made to blackmail Arbuckle. He resisted it. Local newspapers and prosecutors attempted to exploit the issue for their own aggrandizement. Arbuckle resisted them as well. This star of comedy found himself the center of a real-life tragedy. He braved prosecution for a monstrous crime rather than pay up. He was victimized by a district attorney's office that was desperate to please local voters. And he was tried by the gutter press in banner headlines that whipped up hysteria on palpably false evidence.

He faced three juries. The first stood 10–2 for acquittal. The second stood 10–2 for conviction. The third, which was the only one to hear his principal accuser directly, acquitted him in less than ten minutes and issued a statement that Arbuckle had been the victim of almost unbelievable injustice. They applauded his conduct in the face of a prosecution that was based almost entirely on perjury.[4]

By this time, the studio heads, like the baseball owners, had hired a "czar," in the slender, unprepossessing form of Will Hays, the chairman of the Republican National Committee. For $100,000 a year the nonsmoking, teetotaling, church-going Hays agreed to oversee the morals of Hollywood.

They seemed to be going from bad to worse. During Arbuckle's third trial a prominent movie director, William Desmond Taylor, was found murdered. A young actress with whom he had once been involved committed suicide a few days later. The Taylor scandal involved drugs and a collection of hundreds of pairs of panties, each tagged with the name of the original owner and the date the garment had been removed.

Moving quickly, the Hays Office drew up a list of nearly 200 people who were to be banned from films because they drank too much, took drugs, or were sexually promiscuous.[5] For a decade or so Los Angeles's growing army of prostitutes had been registering as studio extras to escape California's vagrancy statute which might otherwise have made life difficult for them. They were quietly prized off the register. And on the screen, a seven-foot rule was laid down for movie lovers: no kiss could run for more than seven feet of film. Actors and actresses found a "morals" clause in their contracts. If they did not behave, the studios could fine them. If they still did not behave, they could be fired and their contracts torn up.

In 1923 the Hays Office got around to Arbuckle. He was clean, they announced. Innocent of any wrongdoing. The studios were free to hire him at any time. Before that ghastly day in San Francisco he was Hollywood's biggest box-office draw. His salary was $1 million a year. So, with the blessing of Will Hays, Fatty Arbuckle waited for the offers to be made. They never came. He went around to the studios. He was politely and quickly shown the door.

Nervous studio heads had, in reality, little to fear. Scandal never seems to have discouraged ticket sales. If anything, it helped satisfy the voracious appetite for news about movie stars. Hollywood had created a new elite, a democratic aristocracy. It displaced the older elite that had dominated the popular imagination through its wealth and arrogance— Rockefeller, Vanderbilt, Gould, Morgan, and the like. The mansions on Fifth Avenue and the palaces at Newport, for decades the center of American social life, seemed dull and faded now. For everyone who took his or her social instruction from Emily Post's *Etiquette*, published in 1922, there were perhaps a dozen who took theirs from Cecil B. De Mille.

Between 1920 and 1926 there was no more influential film director. He set the style on screen and behind the camera. De Mille strode the set in open-neck shirts, puttees, a Louis XV hat, and knee-length pants. He puffed on an enormous drooping pipe and blew a silver bugle to send his extras into action.[6] His films were superficial, spectacular, and created long lines at the box office. They were pitilessly dissected on every lot in Hollywood, and they were carefully copied. The most important ingredient in them, the Hays Office notwithstanding, was sex.

"Cecil B. De Mille converted the bedroom into a boudoir, divorcing it from its familiar and literal associations with sleep. Largely because of him, the verb itself, as used by Americans, shed all suggestions of dormancy."[7] His films were given suggestive titles, such as *Male and Female*, *Forbidden Fruit*, *The Golden Bed*, and *Why Change Your Wife?* When women's clubs began to clamor against the prurience he was smuggling onto the screen, he outmaneuvered them. He ran a contest in the *Los Angeles Times* for movie ideas. The most common theme among more than 10,000 entries was religion.[8] And lo! he made *The Ten Commandments* and placed his sex orgies in a biblical setting.

De Mille's nonreligious films both reflected and shaped the life of the Twenties. He sought out leading dress designers, hair stylists, boot makers, and experts on makeup. He brought them to Hollywood and paid them well to keep them there. He intended to turn Hollywood into the place that dictated fashion to the lower 90 percent with as much authority as Paris dictated it to the upper 10 percent. To a remarkable extent, he succeeded. His films instructed millions in manners, dress, and hair styles. They portrayed a world of luxury and leisure, of moral freedom and hard-won success. "De Mille's films were, indeed, all the wish-dreams of the Twenties."[9]

The greatest film star of the age was, beyond any doubt, Charlie Chaplin. He was not an innovator in film as a craft, as Griffith was. Nor did he dazzle the public with spectacle, as De Mille did. It was as an artist that Chaplin reigned supreme. His tramp-clown was the universal symbol of American cinema. There was not a country in the world where Chaplin's creation was not revered. His disdain for the rich and love for the poor, his susceptibility to a pretty face, his stoical indifference to hardship made the tramp in baggy pants and derby hat the embodiment of ordinary people everywhere. He saw more spirituality in a prostitute than a society woman; more compassion in a convict than in his jailer.

Chaplin was the best-known man in the world in the mid-Twenties, and probably the best loved. When he went abroad "he traveled without a passport, for his face was known everywhere."[10] He was the only film-maker of the period, moreover, who consistently made films that were critical of the established, middle-class order.* His A Woman of Paris, released in 1923, was the most realistic, naturalistic film made up to that time. It told the story of a Parisian demimondaine and was based upon various recollections told to him by Peggy Hopkins Joyce.[11] There were no smitten breasts, no rolling eyes, no outthrown hands (without which, although tedious and ridiculous, until now no dramatic film was considered complete). In both the story and the treatment of it, A Woman of Paris, in which Chaplin did not appear,† was a landmark film. It abolished Victorian dramatic conventions.

Two years later came The Gold Rush, which did the same for comedy. This snowbound odyssey of Chaplin's little tramp made a mockery of Coolidge prosperity. The lust for riches was portrayed as the natural pur-

---

*A British writer, Beverley Nichols, stayed at Chaplin's home one week in 1926. One evening by chance he came upon his millionaire host standing on a stool in the kitchen delivering the most eloquent and dangerously convincing denunciation of capitalist economics and bourgeois morality he had ever heard. It put to shame every political professional that Nichols, in a wide acquaintanceship, had met. Chaplin's speech was loudly cheered by a dozen entranced servants and dinner guests. His kinship with the poor was no pose, but blood of his blood, bone of his bone.

† Except, unrecognized, for three seconds as a railroad porter.

suit of the stupid, the brutal, and the unprincipled. The little tramp searches instead for love. When he alters his aim and turns to prospecting he strikes gold. But by then he is friendless. The gold he finds signals defeat as surely as a white flag. The prospector's cabin, meanwhile, teeters on the brink of a precipice.

II

In 1919, broadcasting did not appear to have much of a future. The airwaves, under wartime powers, were still monopolized by the military. But before the war, radio had tried to carve out a place for itself. There had been news reports, weather forecasts, broadcasts of live music, poetry, drama, speeches, recorded music. Few people took any interest in it. Most looked on radio as a harmless eccentricity or as something practical only in the most narrow sense, such as communicating with ships at sea. Broadcasting was said to have been tried and to have failed.

The British, however, had a greater commitment to it. They had welcomed Marconi, and reaped benefits thereafter in a dozen ways. At the armistice they controlled most of the world's radio and cable communications. Both the American government and American business found this irksome. In 1919, with Washington's help, the Radio Corporation of America was formed.[12] Only American citizens could be directors or officers of RCA. Foreigners could not hold more than 80 percent of RCA's stock. And pressure was applied to force the British to sell all the equipment of the Marconi Company's American subsidiary to RCA. With the British grip broken, the military felt it safe at last to allow civilian broadcasting to resume in 1920. But would anyone be listening?

Experimental stations opened in New York, Cliffwood, New Jersey, and Long Beach, California, to find out. The Bureau of Standards in Washington began broadcasting music concerts once a week, as did an experimental station created by the *Detroit News*. Another station was opened by Westinghouse in Pittsburgh. No one seemed to have any but the vaguest ideas about what they were doing. They were all optimistic and enthusiastic, however, and it soon became evident that there were thousands, then tens of thousands, of equally zealous amateurs building crystal sets to listen in. At which point it occurred to Westinghouse that broadcasting did have a future after all. Its Pittsburgh station, KDKA, in October 1920, became the first to receive a government license, meaning that its amateur days were over. The parent corporation had, meanwhile, turned its attention to producing simple radio equipment, capable of picking up a broadcast clearly, with controls a child could operate.

The year 1922 brought the deluge. At the beginning of the year there were 4 licensed stations; at the end, 576. Tube sets were rapidly displacing crystal sets. Every week more and more stations went on the air, and transmitters grew more powerful.

The rush for broadcasting licenses included scores of colleges and universities, hundreds of churches, department stores, and newspapers. Some began as the hobbies of rich men. One was started by a stockyard (WAAF, Chicago), another by a laundry (KUS, Los Angeles). All were broadcasting on the same wavelength (833.3 kilocycles), which the government had set aside for "news, lectures, entertainment, etc." The confusion was indescribable. Patents were freely infringed. As radio grew, so did lawyers' business.

It was in 1922 that AT&T opened WBAY, New York. The station would provide its services to anyone who would pay for them. So began commercial radio. Hardly had WBAY gone on the air than it was followed by WEAF, which was owned by the Bell Corporation and boasted the most powerful transmitter in the western hemisphere. WEAF also had the most enthusiastic commitment yet to radio as entertainment. By 1923 it was the most popular station in America.

While the professionals were busy tending the equipment, the people on the air were still amateurs; if not exactly dragged in off the street, they were not far from it. Winifred T. Baur described how she broke into radio: "I was a regular WEAF listener, and having a holiday from my bank job on Washington's Birthday, 1923, I visited the studio out of curiosity where a hostess received me most cordially, and an engineer explained the equipment. While I was being conducted through the premises a singer arrived to begin a scheduled broadcast. The studio was in consternation because he had failed to bring an accompanist and there was no one in the studio who could play. So I volunteered to play the accompaniments."[13] And from that impromptu performance she went on to become the first female radio star. Many of the announcers in these early days were women. When not on the air, they were expected to act as hostesses for visitors to the station.

At about the time that Miss Baur stopped by at WEAF, so did Graham McNamee, during a break in jury duty. He introduced himself to the station's program director as the friend of a friend. The program director was taken with McNamee's mellifluous voice and on the spot offered him a broadcasting job. McNamee was both a trained singer and a semipro baseball player. By 1925 he was billed as "the world's most popular announcer." His was the best-known voice of the Twenties. He was equally at home introducing and discussing a concert of classical music or a fight between Dempsey and Tunney.

In 1926 the National Broadcasting Company was created by RCA in partnership with AT&T. This opened up the age of network broadcasting. The next year the Federal Radio Commission was created and a new radio law passed. Measures such as these were imperative for sorting out the chaos that nightly filled the ether as millions of people huddled in their living rooms, radio headsets covering their ears, deaf to anyone coming to the door,[14] trying to penetrate the cats' chorus of broadcasting.

Nothing had ever succeeded on so vast a scale in so short a time. The sale of radios had grown from $1 million in 1920 to $400 million in 1925. And it was not only the affluent middle class who enjoyed radio. By the late 1920s, reported a presidential commission, "On the roof of practically every tenement house on the lower East Side numerous radio antennae are in evidence."[15]

A challenge to radio was already on the horizon, however, in the shape of a screen no bigger than a man's hand. In April 1927 the image of Herbert Hoover's square, solemn face was transmitted from Washington to New York.[16] Television had made its American debut.

III

When the Civil War began, there was one southern state where much of the black population was free. Louisiana had nearly half a million "Freedmen of color," concentrated mainly in and around New Orleans. They owned property, including slaves. They were to be found in every trade and profession. They educated their children as well as they could afford, which for many involved studies in France. In virtually every material respect the freedmen of color lived in equality with whites.

The Civil War and Reconstruction ruined them. Jim Crow laws, designed to thwart the freedoms promised under the Fourteenth Amendment, were enforced against them just as if they were ex-slaves. For them, there was less freedom after Emancipation than before it. Nearly every avenue of self-expression was suddenly closed to them—except one.

The bands of the Confederate Army had broken up. All over New Orleans were stores whose windows displayed drums and gleaming trumpets. Long accustomed to providing music lessons for their children, the Creole freedmen bought up the Confederate Army's instruments. The music they made contained many strands: French, Italian, ballads from England and Scotland, work songs from the riverfront, but above all, African. It was the music of protest against injustice, the music of a spirit that flaunts its joy in the face of scorn and oppression. And that is how jazz was born.

It was music that was both black and American. Jazz could not have originated with whites. Nor could it have arisen in Africa. A decade after the Civil War ended, there were jazz bands parading the streets of New Orleans blaring out sounds that had never been heard before. Not a single note was written down, yet every musician seemed to know what to play.

At the same time that jazz was being born, the blues were coming into existence. They seem to have grown out of the work songs and field hollers from slavery days. As jazz became mainly the creation of black men, the blues became preeminently the music of black women.

Where the term "jazz" came from, no one knows. Perhaps it was a black slang expression for sexual intercourse. Or perhaps it stems from an early jazz pianist named Jasbo Brown, who would take a well-loved blues and, "hilarious with gin,"[17] would sing it at a wildly accelerated tempo and make sex jokes with the words to shouts of "More, Jas, more!"

Toward the end of the nineteenth century New Orleans decided, in the French manner, that although vice could not be stopped it could be regulated. A thirty-eight-block area was set aside for untrammeled fornication, drinking, and dope. The city councillor who proposed this reform was named Story. He was immortalized when his creation became known to the entire world as Storyville. It flourished, but what Storyville's brothels offered was what had been offered for time out of mind, sex. They needed a gimmick to turn every night into a free-spending party. They began to offer jazz music—hot, exciting, alive. The party lasted until 1917, when the navy closed Storyville down; or, more accurately, forced the hookers to scatter into other parts of the city.

The musicians scattered, too, but over a greater distance. For a decade and more they had been traveling up the Mississippi as far as Iowa, making music on the huge white riverboats carrying gamblers and cotton. Chicago nightclubs had even imported jazz bands from New Orleans before Storyville was closed down.[18] But now came the deluge. The time was right. The North was ready for jazz.

When Lt. James Reese Europe and the 369th Infantry Hell Fighters Band, fifty-strong and the first truly big band, arrived back in the United States in 1919 they created a sensation. This black musician was the toast of New York. At about the same time the Original Dixieland Jazz Band was making the first jazz recordings. The ODJB was a sextette; they were all white, and what they played was a tepid imitation of the real thing. But once white musicians started trying to play jazz, it ceased to be a quasi-folk music.

Ironically, when the golden age arrived for black musicians, the most creative figure in jazz was in the wrong place. Ferdinand "Jelly Roll" Morton was on the West Coast, leading his usual chaotic existence. All his life he claimed to have invented jazz. He was, in fact, the next best thing—the first jazz composer and one of the most innovative jazz pianists of all time. As early as 1902 Morton was using the term "jazz" to point out that what he was playing was not ragtime, which was a particular type of music. Jazz, he would explain, was not what you played, but how you played it. Anything could be turned into jazz. But ragtime was a particular kind of syncopation; it was a blind alley. Morton engineered an escape from it by his complete mastery of jazz form.[19]

He was born in New Orleans, a Creole, descended from freedmen of color. He never accepted his own blackness, which made him in turn a figure of contempt among most black musicians. They acknowledged his music while rejecting the man, with his olive skin, narrow, intelligent face, glistening black hair in tight, natural waves, gold rings on his fingers, and a large diamond set in gold in one of his front teeth. At fifteen he was a pianist in a Storyville brothel. He would play only in white bordellos where he did not have to mix with blacks. His nickname was a tribute to his sexual prowess.[20]

In 1904 he left New Orleans, aged nineteen, to travel through the South, living however he could. At various times he was a tailor, a cardsharp, a poolshark, a patent medicine faker, and a pimp. That is, he was mainly a hustler. Yet never far away was the piano. He had so mastered it that he could make it sound like an entire band, and he was composing some of the most famous jazz tunes, such as "Alabama Bound" and "King Porter Stomp." In time he began writing jazz arrangements, introducing European ideas of harmony. Morton was unusual among the early jazz musicians in his ability to read music easily and to write it down. Improvisation was the very soul of New Orleans jazz. Morton compromised by allowing each musician to make his own break (solo passage) in his own way. His ideas were copied countless times, but he made little from them. He spent much of the Twenties suing record companies, refusing to believe that no one can patent musical styles. When the golden rain began to fall, hardly any of it fell on him.

The turning point was the arrival in Chicago in 1920 of Joseph "King" Oliver's Creole Jazz Band. There was an audience waiting for them, the tens of thousands of southern blacks who longed to hear their own music again and were able to pay for it. When jazz moved to Chicago it "was no longer a New Orleans specialty; it became the music of the whole Negro people."[21] Gangsters also liked jazz. It was the music of outcasts, after all. But it also filled their speakeasies and nightclubs with a strident, brassy sound, creating an atmosphere of excitement that kept the customers coming. The jazzmen were expected to stay cool even when shooting broke out. Muggsy Spanier, a legendary New Orleans cornet player, saw two men shot at his feet one night at a speakeasy outside Chicago. He kept on playing, in a cold sweat, as though nothing had happened.[22]

The Creole Jazz Band numbered only six players, but every one of them was a superb instrumentalist. They proved for the first time that great jazz could be created by planning, organization, and discipline; they played with the freedom of one man, yet with the powerful sound of an ensemble.[23] After two years King Oliver decided to make the sound even more powerful by adding a second cornet. He sent for a young player he had taught for four years back in New Orleans by the name of Louis Armstrong.

Born in the poorest, blackest neighborhood in the city in 1900, Armstrong had been a connoisseur of trumpet styles by the age of ten. At twelve he fired a pistol in the street simply for the hell of it. He was placed in the Waifs' Home. It was there that he began to play the bugle.* Unlike most black musicians at that time, he was taught the proper physical techniques from the start. When he left the Waifs' Home two years later he sold coal by day (singing "My mule is white, my face is black / I sell my coal two bits a sack") and played cornet in honky-tonks at night.[24] In between times, he studied with Joe Oliver, who struck him on the knuckles with a stick each time he played a wrong note.

By 1922 no one had a better technique than Louis Armstrong, not even his mentor. Physically, he was almost born to play a brass instrument. He possessed, moreover, an ability to improvise that has never been surpassed by any musician on any instrument. His influence on other trumpet players can hardly be overstated.[25] Even his "jive" vocals were copied by scores of singers, most of them better able to sing than he.

While he played with the Creole Jazz Band, he played Joe Oliver's way, and the pupil was not allowed to outshine the master. Not a note was written down. When Lil Hardin (later Mrs. Armstrong) was hired by the band as its pianist, she asked for the music. "They politely told me they didn't have any. I then asked what key would the first number be in. I must have been speaking another language because [Joe Oliver] said, 'When you hear two knocks, just start playing.' "[26] That was how it was done: Oliver would make up a tune for a few bars, stamp his foot twice, and the band joined in. To the classical-trained Lil Hardin from Memphis it was an amazing way to do things.

In 1924 the Creole Jazz Band broke up, its missionary work done. All

---

* Captain Joseph Jones who ran the Waif's Home did not want it to seem like a prison, run to the sound of police whistles. He preferred bugle calls, reminiscent of a military school. Thus did Louis Armstrong have greatness thrust upon him.

across the country were scores of bands trying to follow where it had blazed the trail. The reasons for its breakup were as various as the players in the band. Louis Armstrong left, at the urging of his wife, to become the first of the great jazz soloists.[27] But for Joe Oliver, the Chicago years were the pinnacle. From here he slid down into penurious obscurity, smiling and friendly all the while, selling vegetables from a pushcart.

Jazz was going in directions which left the old New Orleans players far behind. Increasingly, jazz was nothing more than jazzed-up popular songs, and not genuine black music. That could still be found in some spirituals, in the blues sung in rural areas, and when some of the older players got together for their own enjoyment. It had gone back, in effect, to where it had come from.

Black jazz musicians began adopting European musical idioms, dropping the African elements—the complex polyrhythms, the playing very slightly off the beat, the improvisation—along the way. Jazz became swing. This was music that was smooth, rehearsed, increasingly melodic, and often sentimental. The blues were similarly transformed. As they moved into expensive nightclubs, they degenerated into a vehicle for dirty jokes. Sex had always been important in the blues, but now the sorrow was gone, the pathos slighted, the heartbreak reduced to a gesture. Very few urban blues singers sang of pain and failure out of pain and failure.

White musicians were taking over the name, the repertoire, and the instrumentation of jazz music. What came out, said the first serious jazz critic, was "a ridiculously jumpy conglomeration."[28] Their love of the music, however, was sincere. The new white style of jazz emerged inevitably in Chicago. Its first legendary player was Leon "Bix" Beiderbecke.

Growing up in Davenport, Iowa, he had heard the New Orleans jazzmen who came through the Tri-Cities on the Mississippi riverboats. In high school he was enraptured by the records of the Original Dixieland Jazz Band. By 1923, barely out of high school, he had his own band, the Wolverines. He played the cornet in a style that was all brilliance—perfectly shaped notes, one after another, that seemed to glitter as they fell. He could not swing the music as black musicians could, nor could he play in a soulful blues style. Yet what he had was undeniably effective and original.

Beiderbecke was interested only in music. Money, women, conventional success meant nothing to him. It was a lonely life. Absorbed in it, he propped himself up with bottles. Among his drinking pals was that other famous German-American of the era, Babe Ruth.

The sound that he was trying to create was somewhere between Chicago and Debussy. He would sit entranced at concerts of modern classical composers.[29] The struggle to reconcile what were fundamentally opposed ambitions reverberated throughout his life in his constant struggle to satisfy his parents, who wanted him to go to college (which he did, for eighteen days), and his own desire to be a jazzman. The booze helped to fill in the cracks.

As Beiderbecke's style became ever more plaintive and pretty he moved, almost inevitably, into the most successful of the white bands, the Paul Whiteman orchestra. This enormous bandleader, weighing 250 pounds and standing five feet, seven inches tall, was known throughout the Twenties as the "King of Jazz," although he knew almost nothing about it. Whiteman labored to create "symphonic jazz." The music was neither symphonic nor jazz, but what Whiteman played was what millions of people imagined jazz to be. It was, instead, transitional, and managed to crash between two very different traditions. Its one lasting masterpiece is George Gershwin's "Rhapsody in Blue," written especially for Whiteman's ensemble.

Whiteman himself had only the haziest idea of what he was after. At a Carnegie Hall concert in 1924 he played one number twice. First in his own symphonic jazz style and then in a vibrant, up-tempo parody of what he imagined black music would sound like. He was offering jazz his way and jazz the other way, or so he thought. The audience, however, failed the test. They politely applauded the first time and ecstatically cheered the second.[30]

White jazz bands provided a single, clear melodic line instead of the bewildering polyrhythms of the real jazz. That single line of melody made white jazz perfect for dancing, and the Twenties might with greater accuracy have been called "the Dance Age." Everybody with two good legs danced, whether the demanding tango or the enervated shuffle, in a narrow space known as "dancing on a dime." Modern dancing styles brought the dancers into close contact. People over forty were inclined to be disgusted, forgetting that nearly every objection—bodies too close, faces too close, music too fast and intoxicating—had been made in their childhood against the waltz.

Parties for young people abandoned nearly all the usual diversions, such as charades, card tricks, and recitations, to make dancing the entire evening program. Few hostesses dared give a party that did not include dancing. Churches used dances to attract the young. Schools taught social dancing to small children. The finer art of the dance, as exemplified on the stage by Russian artistes, flourished. There was a widespread interest in concert dances, à la Isodora Duncan. And square dancing, which had almost died out, suddenly enjoyed a remarkable rebirth.[31]

Flappers, drowning themselves in perfume, stuffing themselves with cakes and candy, almost lived for dancing. They knew every variation on the fox-trot, had mastered the ungainly camel-walk, threw themselves with abandon into the tango, relaxed with the infantile toddle,[32] and were always ready for something new. It came in 1924. It was called the Charleston.

Appearing first in a black revue called *Runnin' Wild*, this dance became for all time the step of the Twenties. It was an exhibition dance at first, considered too difficult for any but professionals to master, with its suddenly shifting rhythms and breathtaking pace.[33] Yet, within a year it had swept the country; in time it would conquer half the world. The Charleston remains frozen in the folk memory more than half a century later, like a pathologist's slide of an old cross section of tissue. When we think of the Twenties we pull out this slide and there is the age—flying beads, knock knees, and crossing hands.

14. Black Rose

I

On the streets of a dozen American cities a nation in exile was being formed, flaunting its existence in a tangible, visible reality. It sported titles and decorations, and strutting at its head, beneath a hat with white plumes, wearing a uniform in the purple, black, and green colors of the new nation, was its provisional president, Marcus Garvey.

West Indian blacks, such as Garvey, were as a rule more self-reliant and better businessmen than American-born blacks, who scorned them as people lacking in soul. Garvey was typical: assertive, articulate, and ambitious. The West Indians had grown up oppressed by poverty and racism. Yet, discrimination in the West Indies was subtler than in Alabama or even in New York and opportunities correspondingly greater. Harlemites grudgingly accepted them as the "shock troops" in the struggle to open the job market wider for urban blacks.[1]

They entered the United States through a side door: the unused quota places assigned to the colonial powers, to which they retained a remarkable loyalty. British West Indians flew the Union Jack in their windows, to the disgust of the entire tenement. French West Indians held Bastille Day dances. West Indians had the lowest naturalization rate of any immigrant group. Coming as they did from black societies that were rigorously patriarchal, they felt infinitely superior to the black matriarchy of Harlem.

The cause that Garvey preached, however, was blackness itself. He "set in motion what was to become the most compelling force in Negro life—race and color consciousness . . . the banner to which Negroes rally; the chain that binds them together."[2] He was not without competitors. On the one side were integrationists, such as the NAACP; on the other, revolutionaries such as the "Abyssinians," led by Grover Cleveland Redding. For a time Redding seemed likely to outshine Garvey.

Redding's Ethiopian Mission to Abyssinia began to attract large numbers of blacks whom Garvey was trying to recruit. Then, in the summer of 1920, Redding rode a white stallion through the South Side of Chicago. He was dressed in a toga of brilliant colors so that the horse did not capture all the attention. He ended his ride by setting fire to an American flag, and before it vanished completely in smoke, he emptied a pistol into it. Redding prepared to do the same with another flag, but this time a white sailor and a black policeman attempted to stop him. Redding instantly shot them down.

The Abyssinians raced down the streets to attack policemen, killing two of them, wounding half a dozen more, while terrified, law-abiding blacks hurried into their houses. Redding was seized, tried for murder, convicted, and hanged, his great dream of leading an "armed train" into the South unrealized.[3]

Garvey's Universal Negro Improvement Association grew apace. In each city where there were more than 10,000 members (New York, Chicago, Detroit, Philadelphia, Pittsburgh, Cleveland, and Cincinnati) the UNIA opened a Liberty Hall. There, weddings, funerals, cultural events and social gatherings were held almost every day. A Garveyite civil service handled such matters as UNIA passports. There were UNIA courts, dealing chiefly with domestic disputes. The Garveyites were trying to create a black nation by acting as though one already existed. The provisional president's fame was international, as the poet Langston Hughes discovered when he went to sea in 1923. "The name of Marcus Garvey," he found, "was known the length and breadth of the West coast of Africa."[4]

Like most West Indians, Garvey was proud of his blackness. There was not a single white ancestor in his family, he claimed. He gloried in being entirely black, a descendant of the Maroons, those escaped slaves who had fled into the mountains of Jamaica and there fought three generations of British soldiers to a standstill. According to Garvey, it had been a black nation, the Cushites, who introduced civilization into Egypt, Phoenicia, and ancient Greece. If God was made in man's image, then God had to be black for any black man to worship him, Garvey decided. Christ was similarly black. The emphasis on blackness was unrelenting. Any Garveyite who married someone white was immediately expelled. He ridiculed anyone who believed that blacks and whites could live peacefully within the same society. Whites were too thoroughly racist ever to be amenable to reasoned pleas for justice.

Garvey's ardent separatism won the praise of some white racists and led him into an amazing blunder. In 1922 he traveled to Atlanta to meet in secret with Edward Young Clarke. UNIA organizers were being harassed in the South. By making clear that the movement wanted separation, not mixing, perhaps the Klan would leave his organizers alone? Or so he seems to have reasoned. He could not have been more mistaken. Klan floggers were not interested in the finer points of black liberation.[5]

When the news leaked out that Garvey had supped with the devil, there was anguish among his million followers and supporters, joy among his many enemies. Garveyites and anti-Garveyites brawled on Harlem street corners. Several of Garvey's closest aides left him flat. Others remained within the UNIA to intrigue against him. Long-suppressed hostility between American blacks and West Indians broke into the open and nearly tore the UNIA apart.

Meanwhile, the UNIA's business ventures were about to collapse. In 1919 Garvey had launched a Negro Factories Corporation. It ran a chain of grocery stores, a publishing house, a restaurant, and various other businesses. He had proposed at the same time to create a black shipping line. The war had left the United States with thousands of ships for which there was no demand, and some were being sold for next to nothing. Garvey's proposed Black Star Line fired the imaginations of his followers as nothing else ever did. Before any attempt had been made to buy a ship, ticket requests, accompanied by money, poured into UNIA offices. Garvey had envisaged a line that would devote most of its efforts to carrying cargo between the United States and the West Indies, with passage to Africa for those who wanted to return to the ancestral land. The Back-to-Africa passion that surged through the movement was spontaneous.

The Black Star Line raised $750,000 through stock offerings, and only blacks were allowed to buy. This would have been enough to launch most types of business, but it was far from enough to create a shipping line. A succession of incompetent or crooked BSL officers succeeded in wasting most of the money anyway, or simply stole it. The BSL tried to operate its three ships with all-black crews. This proved impossible, so three white captains were hired. One of the ships sank, one was seized to satisfy a creditor, and the third was abandoned in Cuba after a fortune in repairs failed to make it seaworthy.

In 1923 Garvey and three other BSL officers were tried for using the mails to defraud in their sale of BSL stock. The government produced only one witness, who claimed to have been sold a $5.00 share by mail. The evidence consisted of an empty envelope. There was no letter on BSL or UNIA stationery, no stock certificate, no proof of payment. Garvey was convicted, his three codefendants acquitted, on the same evidence, the same testimony.[6]

The usual sentence for mail fraud was one year. Judge Julian Mack, a member of the NAACP, gave Garvey the maximum, five. His appeal was denied. In 1925 he entered Atlanta penitentiary to serve his sentence, utterly penniless. Although some of his aides in the UNIA had kept their fingers wedged firmly in the till, Garvey was an honest man.

II

Long after the war ended, the black migration northward continued at full spate. It involved more women than men.[7] For their entire history, blacks had been an agricultural people: the land was what they had known in slavery, the land was what they had known before slavery. In one generation they were becoming urbanized. Something new came into existence—the black ghetto in the heart of the city. "Church, lodge, respect of friends, established customs, social and racial, exercise controls in the small Southern community," observed Charles S. Johnson.[8] In the ghetto, these controls collapsed. The new freedom was both exciting and traumatic.

Supreme among all the new black communities stood Harlem. Until 1900 almost entirely white, it was by 1925 almost entirely black. A turn-of-the-century building boom had left the area with streets of empty apartments. Landlords began to take black tenants. After the war, as thousands of people migrated into New York from the South each week, there was a severe housing shortage. Real estate values rose sharply. Most of the buildings dated from a time when Harlem had been an upper-middle-class area, when large families lived in large rooms and were waited on by live-in servants. Few black families could live like that. Instead, they took in lodgers, partitioned the handsome, high-ceilinged rooms, and sang the words of a popular song, "What you gonna do when the rent comes 'round?" The lodgers were often the rootless and ruthless. In exchange for a little help with the rent, many a family got a lot of trouble.

Rapacious landlords, black and white, were making a killing out of what was turning into a slum boom. Working-class blacks earned less than working-class whites, yet were paying 50 percent more for housing.[9] Street after street in Harlem was filling up with ignorant, poor farm families, accustomed to living amid clutter and filth, innocent of urban ways, their desire for self-improvement completely satisfied by their translation to the city.

Wartime emergency housing laws, designed to control rents, provided

little relief. Landlords could always find ways to outflank them. Harlem's
permanent rent crisis gave birth to the rent party. Throughout the Twenties there were notices like this in Harlem store windows or tacked to
telephone poles:[10]

> If you're looking for a good time,
> Don't look no more.
> Just ring my bell
> And I'll answer the door.
>
>> Given by Charley Johnson and
>> Joe Hotboy, and How Hot!

Tickets cost anything from a nickel to a quarter. The admission fee produced less money, however, than the sale, once the party got going, of
illicit liquor and homemade soul food. Some parties were as exuberant
and picaresque as whites fondly imagined. Others ended in stabbings and
shootings.

Before the Twenties were out, New York had a black population of
300,000 or more. In the 1920 census there were not even 50,000.[11] Roughly
two-thirds of the city's black population was concentrated in Harlem. And
as Harlem was transformed into a slum, it became at the same time the
center of black cultural and intellectual life. It was the most diverse black
community in the world, and in history; peopled with Africans, West
Indians, blacks from the North, blacks from the South. It was probably
the most race-conscious place on the planet.[12]

White people also discovered Harlem, the new Harlem. They fled to
it as a refuge from the dullness, the orderliness, the narrowness of middle-
class life. And it was so convenient—only a taxi ride away for most New
Yorkers. There, whatever was forbidden elsewhere was easy to find—
marijuana, cocaine, sex. When the sun went down, Harlem was inte-
grated.[13]

By attracting nearly every black writer and intellectual, Harlem was
graced with what was known as the "Black Renaissance." It was characteristic of the place, the time, and the magnetic attraction that one of the
major works of this cultural outpouring was called *Home to Harlem*, yet
was written by a Jamaican, Claude McKay. His fellow Jamaican's newspaper, Marcus Garvey's the *Negro World*, was important to the Harlem
Renaissance. Garvey's paper circulated widely throughout the United
States and the West Indies. It was mainly a propaganda organ for black
nationalism. In the pages of the *Negro World* blacks for the first time were
able to see Africa portrayed in a flattering light. The *Negro World* spurned
the financial mainstay of the rest of the black press—advertisements for

hair straighteners and skin lighteners. And it opened its pages to budding black writers, such as Claude McKay.

With the awakening of black pride went a new interest in black history and art. There were even black dolls for black children to play with.[14] Ironically, however, there was only one important figure in the Harlem Renaissance who took an interest in jazz and that was Langston Hughes, Columbia dropout and onetime able-bodied seaman. For him this Renaissance had begun with the first all-black revue on Broadway, a show called *Shuffle Along*, which opened in 1921. "To see *Shuffle Along* was the main reason I wanted to go to Columbia," he confessed.[15]

A far different figure was Alain Locke, Rhodes scholar, professor of philosophy at Howard, something of a dandy, but with a gentle, reflective manner. His editing of *The New Negro*, which made much of the nation's intelligentsia aware of the profound changes taking place among blacks, and his energetic cheerleading for black intellectuals and artists made him the pope of the Harlem Renaissance. To people such as Locke, high culture was the perfect bridge between the races, not a barricade behind which a few gifted blacks might carve out a comfortable niche for themselves.

The trouble was that like every renaissance it depended on patronage. In this case, white patronage. When the novelty wore off, the Harlem Renaissance was suddenly over. It had never been an easy way to make a living. The best novel to come out of it, Jean Toomer's *Cane*, now widely conceded to be one of the best books of the Twenties, sold fewer than 500 copies in its first year of publication.[16] Toomer gave up writing.

Ray, the educated black man in *Home to Harlem*, typified the dilemmas faced by people such as McKay. Ray was crippled by education instead of being freed by it. High culture provided him with all the anxieties and doubts of the sensitive man, while denying him the emotional release of the ordinary black worker—cheap music, casual sex, rot-gut liquor, gambling, dope. Educated to middle-class ideas of what he should do with his life, he was nevertheless forced to work as a waiter, a mess boy, a railroad cook. The more he learned, the less he loved life.

III

The northward migration spread near-panic in the South. During the war most states passed "work or fight" laws. Men of draft age who were not in uniform had to take jobs. Southern towns and counties passed similar laws affecting everyone, regardless of sex, regardless of age. This legislation was never enforced against whites, only against blacks. It assured a large work force of domestic servants and field hands. What it amounted to was peonage in the guise of patriotism.[17]

To check the continuing outflow, labor agents were fined and imprisoned. Migrants who made their way to railroad stations were met by gangs of local thugs and terrified into turning back. "Many a colored farm tenant (had) to flee by night in order to come North."[18] Yet flee they did, despite intimidation. Black tenant farmers were systematically bilked by the white landowners who lauded the moral superiority of white culture and deplored the moral degeneracy of blacks. Cotton and tobacco continued to be grown under virtually the same conditions as under slavery.[19] These crops could be grown by the least skilled field hands; were cash crops; could not be eaten by man or beast; were easily stored and shipped; could be held against a poor market; were hand-cultivated and hand-harvested. They had wedded the South to slavery for more than 200 years; they kept it in a similar liaison into the Twenties.

But now southern blacks were beginning to inch their way up the economic ladder as education and ambition trickled down. Industry was beginning to appear in the South. And there were the alluring cities of the North which beckoned. As blacks began to move out and up, they became a challenge to the poor whites clinging to the rung just above that bottom rung that had been the black's appointed station in southern life for the past 300 years. Violent hatred of blacks was at its most intense and murderous as one descended the southern social scale.[20]

Hatred, however, threats, intimidation, even murder, failed to check the stirrings of hope that moved through black communities. There were jobs in the North; not enough jobs, true; not well-paid jobs; but better than being a domestic servant or half-starved handyman. The immigration laws created silent rejoicing in black communities.[21] American industry had for decades relied on cheap imported white labor. Almost overnight blacks became the reserve army of American industry, from which they had long been shut out, except during strikes. Blacks were also moving in large numbers into government jobs. Hoover, at a stroke, abolished segregation in the Commerce Department, putting pressure on other departments to do the same.

It was easier for black women to get jobs in the North than for men. Sixty percent of the women in Harlem went to work.[22] Even children seemed to stand a better chance of getting work than grown black men. Child labor was far more common among black children than among white.[23] But there can be no doubt that large numbers of blacks were entering industry at last. There was no mystery as to why the black population of Detroit doubled between 1920 and 1925 (from 41,000 to 82,000).[24]

The unions, licking their wounds from 1919 and losing their self-confidence, snubbed this new source of members. Only the UMW and the immigrant-dominated garment workers' unions welcomed black workers. By the late 1920s total black membership in AFL-affiliated unions came to little more than 40,000. Independent black unions boasted only 12,000 more.[25]

The most notable among these black unions was A. Philip Randolph's Brotherhood of Railroad Car Porters. As an elevator operator in his teens, the young Philip Randolph had tried to organize black elevator operators. He was discovered and fired. Then as a hotel waiter he had organized the Headwaiters and Sidewaiters Society of Greater New York. But again he was fired. With the help of a $10,000 gift from the Socialist party in 1925, he was able to launch the BRCP after dozens of porters asked him to create a union.

Pullman porters worked a 400-hour month. They asked for a reduction to 250 hours. The Pullman Company created a company union to fight the Brotherhood and claimed that the average porter earned $200 a month. Which was strange, seeing that the other demand of the porters was an end to tipping and a flat wage of $150 a month. Despite a combination of pressure and inducements, more than 7,000 of the Pullman Company's 11,000 porters voted to join the BRCP.[26] By the late Twenties, however, the company had virtually broken the union and rejected its demands.[27] The BRCP's experience was not one to encourage separate, black unions.

The world for black workers was a little wider than before. But work was still divided into black men's jobs and white men's jobs. On the railroads, for example, being a porter or a waiter was a job for a black man; being an engineer or conductor was for whites only. The time was still a long way off when blacks would be allowed to compete with whites for the same occupations.

IV

James Weldon Johnson, the secretary of the NAACP, in 1921 persuaded L. C. Dyer, a Republican from Missouri, to introduce a piece of legislation in the House that both of them knew stood no chance of becoming law. The Dyer bill would make lynching a federal crime. Dyer, though white, represented a St. Louis district that was largely black. The House passed the antilynching bill by a 2–1 margin. It was filibustered to death in the Senate.

Yet it was no vain gesture. The threat, however remote, that federal investigators would beat the backwoods and that federal prosecutors would bring local vigilantes into federal courts and charge them with murder pushed southern states into curbing mob violence. From 1922 the number of lynchings that were thwarted steadily outnumbered those that were successful.[28] The decline in lynchings was nothing short of spectacular. There had been 83 in 1919. There were 16 in 1924 and 18 in 1925.[29]

It was not only the threat of federal action that brought this steep fall. The NAACP's publicity campaigns brought to light actions that no one could justify. There was also the growing readiness of blacks to defend themselves. There was the northward migration, which resisted intimidation. Threats, in fact, could only hurry blacks out of the South. Finally, there was the rapid disintegration of the Klan. Natural disaster these days posed a greater threat to blacks than the manufactured violence of white mobs, as they discovered in the spring of 1927.

For nearly half a century levees had been built up and down the Mississippi, destroying the natural reservoirs carved out beyond the banks in the course of eons whenever the river was in flood. The levee builders argued, as they built the levees ever higher, that the river would bore a deep enough channel to contain itself. It failed to do as instructed.

When the spring floods came, after an unusually cold and wet winter, people in Memphis stared in awe as the Mississippi rushed by carrying a volume of water ten times as great as that going over Niagara Falls at its fullest.[30] This was the power that was unleashed on the lower delta. Rising higher and higher, the water broke over the levees and washed them away.

The river flooded its banks from Cairo, Illinois, to the Gulf. As the flood waters roared south, threatening to smash New Orleans to pieces, the levees north of the city were bombed. The water roared away from the city, and flooded St. Bernard and Plaquemine parishes. These two counties turned into a vast muddy lake in which hundreds of Cajuns and black sharecroppers drowned.

The Mississippi flood was the greatest natural disaster the country had suffered since the San Francisco earthquake. The dead numbered more than 500, the homeless more than half a million. There were 20,000 square miles of land under water, and property damage ran to more than $1 billion. Coolidge refused to call Congress back into session to vote an emergency appropriation. He relied instead on the Red Cross and Hoover. The Great Engineer knew about levees and rivers and emergency feeding. For three months he crisscrossed the area, organizing and exhorting, wading knee-deep in mud, living on his nerves.

By chance, Langston Hughes was traveling through Louisiana when the flood struck. Most of the victims were, like himself, black. And he remembered long after the face of Jim Crow humanitarianism: "The white refugees were brought down to the city (Baton Rouge) in steamers with cabins and covered decks to protect them from the elements, while the Negroes were transported in open flatboats. . . . The Red Cross housed the whites in a group of tree-shaded buildings. . . . The Negroes were housed in an open field in small tents, where the mud was ankle deep when it rained. The whites were given three hot meals a day, the Negroes two."[31]

About 80 percent of the flood refugees were black. Poor sharecroppers and tenants, reluctant to leave their shacks and tired land, they often had to be removed bodily by white National Guardsmen. Taken to camps for their safety, they had to endure being ordered about by white Red Cross women in faded wartime knickers. But when the flood water receded and they were free to leave at last, tens of thousands chose not to go back to their shacks to start anew. Instead, they went North to start anew.[32]

15. Help!

I

Most of the United States was not yet industrialized at the time of the armistice. Industry was heavily concentrated in half a dozen northern states. The South had virtually no heavy industry, nor had the West, and in the Midwest there were still large stretches where you could travel more than a hundred miles and never see a factory.[1] Throughout the Twenties the country's values remained largely those of a preindustrial people. This was true even in Greenwich Village, the epitome of urban sophistication.[2] Yet the social order in which those values made sense had almost vanished.

"The central theme of Progressivism was this revolt against industrial discipline," wrote Richard Hofstadter. "The Progressive movement was the complaint of the unorganized against the consequences of organization."[3] White-collar workers were the fastest growing part of the population, for as the factories reared blackly on the skyline and the cities spread out to pave over the farms, the world was swamped with paperwork. But this new middle class, raised with puritanical values of self-dependence, was swallowed up within huge organizations. The man who rose to the top in business was still admired. But the business he rose to the top of was viewed with suspicion.

The factories themselves were distasteful. They created noise, dirt, and population congestion. There was hardly a factory that was not an eyesore. And nearly every factory turned the streets around it into a slum. Factories fouled the air and poisoned the rivers. They displaced fields and turned men into cogs. More ominous still, the factory system—anonymous, ruthless, competitive—was becoming the model for modern society itself.

The most articulate protest came not from factory workers (it would be surprising if it did), but from writers. Max Eastman on his way to Russia in 1922 lamented, in a letter to Claude McKay, "I feel sometimes as though the whole modern world, capitalism and communism and all, were rushing toward some enormous nervous efficient machine-made doom of the true values of life."[4] The French writer Georges Duhamel, during his visit to the United States, awoke one night sweating heavily, terrified by a nightmare in which American gardeners reduced all the flowers in the world to a single, standardized bloom "that was specially profitable, and that lasted well."[5] Sophie Treadwell's play *Machinal* opened on Broadway in 1928. It combined elements of a famous love-and-murder case with criticism of the machine age. The play moved toward its murderous finale to incessant background sounds of machinery at work.

Middle-aged factory workers knew only too well how things were changing. In the late nineteenth-century factory it was easy for the boss and the workers to establish a personal relationship with one another. When visitors came to the plant they met the men. But as one worker bitterly complained in 1928, these days the men were ignored. Visitors were taken to admire the new machinery.[6] The new work disciplines imposed by the machines could strip men of their humanity. There were presses that punched sheet steel. All that the worker had to do was to insert the steel before the press descended and withdraw his hands quickly. But some men became fatigued, or surrendered to the numbness or monotony, or were simply careless. The machines cut off their hands. The solution that managers hit on was to handcuff the worker's hands to a lever, which pulled them away as the press came down. "Go to the press rooms today and you will see lines of workers standing before their presses," wrote one visitor, "their hands jerking away each time the presses move. . . . The individual workers do not control the movement of the presses, which are started and stopped by the foreman. . . . Even though they may be out of material, they have to stand before the press, their hands jerking back and forth. There they work, chained to their machines, as galley slaves were chained to their oars."[7]

Wherever the factories went up, there were workers who hated them. There was a Scottish steelworker named Frazear whom Mary Heaton Vorse met in Pittsburgh. Whenever he had enough money he would get drunk instead of going to work. Then he would go down to the mill gates and curse the mill, the mill boss, the mill slag, and the mill workers. He would rant against the molten steel, the white-hot fires, and the black smoke pouring into the sky. "His friends would follow him and watch him fearfully as he stood, huge, before the mill gates, cursing. . . . When he was drunk he thought the machines were alive; he thought they owned him and that he was their slave."[8]

Louis Adamic, a Yugoslavian immigrant, roamed the country from 1923 to 1927, taking jobs wherever he could find them. He worked in furniture, shoe, and textile factories, in steel mills, on farms and ranches, in a print shop, in a stone quarry, in a Detroit automobile plant, on construction sites, on the docks, in a grocery store, and virtually everywhere that he worked there was some form of sabotage. It had nothing to do with the IWW tactic of "striking on the job." It was, instead, an expression of defiance, of refusing to knuckle under to the machines. "In a shoe factory in Milwaukee a man was pointed out to me who was known to his fellow workers to be a *saboteur* . . . he hated the machines and had all sorts of devices to damage them. . . . I have seen men who—sometimes drunk, sometimes sober—cursed the machines and, passing by, shook their fists. . . ."[9]

To get the most out of the machinery that they were so eagerly arranging along the factory floor, managers had to turn the wheel full circle. They had to rediscover the humanity of workers. In 1927 Elton Mayo and his colleagues at the Harvard Business School were hired to study working conditions at the Western Electric Company in Hawthorne, Illinois, where telephones were made. Mayo's team introduced rest breaks, provided free refreshments, and shortened the work day. Productivity rose almost at once.

The rest breaks, the free refreshments, and the shorter day were all abruptly withdrawn. Productivity continued to rise. What Mayo had hit on was what might be called the experimentation effect: by taking a personal interest in these workers, Mayo's team had formed them into a cohesive unit in which self-respect and job satisfaction were high. That cohesion continued even after the old work routines were reestablished, because the experiment was still going on; the workers still felt that management was interested in them.[10] Happy workers turned out more than unhappy workers. An obvious lesson, perhaps, but now it had been proved by the latest scientific methods.

What made Western Electric ideal for this experiment was that the company seemed almost faultless by the standards of the time. It offered good wages, a company hospital, paid vacations, a subsidized cafeteria, and a pension plan. The Hawthorne findings would have been banal to the point of uselessness in the case of a bad employer. What Mayo had done was to show how far even the best employer needed to go to create a genuinely happy, highly productive work force.

Mayo's research remains a landmark in American industrial psychology, the starting point of a thousand personnel programs. Yet, he unearthed something that went far beyond the factory walls. Rapid industrialization was disrupting social organization, and one of the manifestations of that disorganization was acquisitiveness. It was not so much greed that was making society sick as a sick society making people greedy. After all, what else was there to justify their work, once they were stripped of their pride in their strength or skill, except money?[11]

II

In 1895 there were four automobiles produced in the United States and total automobile registration stood at four. In 1920 total automobile registration stood at 8.25 million, and by 1927 that figure had more than doubled.[12] The automobile was the supreme machine of the Twenties. The industry used so much of the country's steel, glass, wood, rubber, and gasoline that in one way and another it provided jobs for 5 million people. Its growth alone was enough to account for most of the annual growth of the labor force and to provide most of the Coolidge prosperity.

Bad roads and reckless driving, however, took a heavy toll. More than 25,000 people were killed each year and up to 600,000 were injured. Some 2,000 fatalities occurred at railroad crossings each year because many drivers, entering into the spirit of competition, delighted in trying to race the train to the crossing—and lost.[13] The states began to impose driving tests.

New York City, which endured more than 1,000 traffic deaths a year, tried another expedient, one that astonished an English visitor in 1920. All along Broadway, he reported, "at regular intervals there are high stands with posts like railway signals. At the top of these posts are lights. A red light is a warning, a white light stops the traffic, and a green light allows it to go forward." He was impressed, but he did not expect it to catch on: "I doubt whether it would be of any use in London."[14]

After several years, however, the idea spread to Boston. A tower nearly fifteen feet high was erected at the junction of Tremont and Boylston streets. From the top winked a dozen colored lights, ranging from purple, blue, and green to red, amber, and white. The resulting chaos at this junction was regarded with awe, it was so monumental. The display of lights flashed a bewildering range of instructions in four directions at once. One utterly mystified driver admitted, "I think they are over-estimating the intelligence of the Boston people."[15] He, too, did not expect traffic lights to have much of a future.

The world had not yet been completely remade for the car. In many a village and small town there was friction between car drivers and farmers when the old hitching posts and watering troughs were removed from the streets to help the flow of motor traffic.[16] Many farmers still relied on horses and mules, whose numbers had actually increased by 10 percent between 1910 and 1920.[17]

In 1919, Oregon, New Mexico, and Colorado hit on a new idea for building roads: they put a tax on gasoline. Within a decade every other state had done the same. The money raised was used to match federal road construction grants. There was no opposition to this policy anywhere. The gasoline tax was probably the most popular tax of all time. Under the 1921 Federal Highways Act each state built its own roads, and federal supervisors made sure that each system became part of a regional network. Thus, all-weather, hard-surface highways advanced across the landscape throughout the Twenties at remarkable speed. Those going east-west were given even numbers; those going north-south, odd numbers. There were 7,000 miles of concrete road in the United States at the end of the war. There were 50,000 miles by 1927, and the program was advancing at the rate of 10,000 miles a year.[18]

Before the Twenties the car was either a luxury (for the rich) or a necessity (for farmers and country doctors). But now it was part of everyday life, taking ordinary Americans to and from work, to and from leisure. They began to demand style, comfort, and reliability. In 1919 only 10 percent of cars were closed. By 1927 that figure had risen to 83 percent.[19] The closed car was an all-weather, all-purpose vehicle.

Along the spreading highway network thousands of auto camps opened for business. These forerunners of the motel provided crude toilet facilities and a cluster of tents. The tourist was expected to endure the rigors of camp life. And millions gladly did so. Early tourists formed their own organizations for mutual help and advice. One was the Tin Can Tourists' Association. Each member tied a tin can to the radiator cap of his car. Meeting one another along the highway, members of the TCTA would stop and exchange information about road conditions, detours, camp sites, and the best garage in the nearest town.[20] Automobile travel was to prove a powerful leveler, breaking down provincialism and advancing standardization in speech, manners and interests.

III

Back in 1908 a short, wiry, ebullient man named William Crapo Durant formed a company called General Motors in the course of one of the most bizarre careers in American business. It was in 1908 that Ford brought out the Model T. These two new ventures, launched by very different men at the same historic moment, were to prove to be the foundation of mass automobile production. Each man had seen the same opportunity. Each went about seizing it in his own way. That year only 65,000 cars would be produced. Most of them were no more than expensive toys. Durant and Ford saw a day, not far off, when cars would be sold in the millions.

Durant was a man of boundless optimism and irresistible impulses. While Ford created a centralized company, Durant's GM consisted of a dozen principalities. Where Ford aimed to sell the same car to all kinds of people, Durant aimed to sell all kinds of cars.

Durant could not even concentrate on the company he had created. He bought other companies with a profligate's abandon. Some of his purchases were farsighted. Yet he could also be so carried away by the enthusiasm of the moment that he paid $7 million (more than he had paid for Olds Motors and Buick Motors combined) to snap up a company whose principal asset was a patent application for a new type of tungsten lamp. When the Patent Office rejected the application Durant lost $7 million.[21]

Two years after he founded GM, Durant's masterpiece was virtually bankrupt. The price the banks demanded for rescuing GM was Durant's resignation from managing the company. He was allowed to remain on the GM board as a figurehead, nothing more. Durant turned his surplus energies to promoting Louis Chevrolet's new lightweight automobile. Durant bought up Chevrolet. By 1915 he had turned it into a very successful car. The next year, by swapping Chevrolet stock for GM stock, he regained control of General Motors. But by 1920 GM and Durant were once more so overextended that they faced a second collapse.

The recession of 1920 was forcing the price of GM shares down, along with every other blue-chip stock. Durant felt a personal commitment to the many people whom he had persuaded to buy GM stock. He bought heroically in a vain attempt to stop the slide in GM's share price, and lost his entire $20 million fortune in less than a week. As car sales slumped, every major automobile manufacturer but one slashed prices. Durant refused to lower the price of GM cars. Hundreds of GM dealers went bankrupt. Durant's impulsive ways had also lost the company the services of its greatest production engineer, Walter Chrysler. A strong-willed and temperamental figure, Chrysler had been driven to fury by Durant's haphazard ways. He eventually walked out, literally slamming the door behind him.

The House of Morgan rescued GM one midnight in the fall of 1920 as Durant's creditors prepared to move in for the kill. Pierre S. du Pont was installed as president of the company. Durant was forced out for the second time.[22]

No one had ever tried to run a company the size of General Motors. It resembled a beached whale—huge but helpless. In little more than a decade it had become the biggest private organization in the world. Its amazing growth threatened to prove its undoing. Du Pont and Alfred P. Sloan, Jr., set about reorganizing the company to take advantage of the flexibility that was the best part of the Durant heritage.

Billy Durant had meanwhile parlayed his reputation as the wizard of Detroit into a $7 million loan from a group of friends to create Durant Motors. The mismanagement techniques perfected at GM were transferred unsullied and intact to the new corporation—too many models, too many impulsive changes in direction, too little control over costs, too few able assistants willing to work in the midst of chaos. Nor had his ventures on Wall Street discouraged him. Durant headed a consortium of midwestern millionaires, and with their millions spent most of the Twenties diverting himself as the biggest bull on Wall Street. At times the group's holdings were reputed to have a paper value of $1 billion or more.

It was Sloan who remade GM so that each division was virtually self-contained. A separate unit handled nonproduction matters such as industrial relations, building construction, warehousing, and so on, freeing the divisions to concentrate on making cars. A variety of coordinating committees handled sales, research, and purchasing. An executive committee was created to reach up to the board of directors and down to all the production divisions and the other units and committees. Sloan liked to boast, "Policy may originate anywhere."[23] The structure was certainly remarkable in the room it made for objectivity and self-criticism. Large organizations all over the world, public and private alike, studied the GM formula and freely borrowed from it.[24]

By 1923 the reorganized GM was ready to take on Ford where he was strongest. The Model T accounted for nearly 60 percent of all car sales. GM's low-priced car was the Chevrolet, with 4 percent of the market. It looked like a hopeless chase, because to the first automobile generation automobiles were a four-letter word and that word was spelled FORD.

IV

At the age of sixteen Henry Ford walked away from the family farm in Dearborn, Michigan, to avoid a life of monotony and drudgery. He would be a mechanic and taste adventure. A mechanic of the 1880s was not like his counterpart a century later. In those days, he was a wanderer. A new world was springing up, full of new challenges, calling for new skills. A mechanic would skim the cream of experience from a job, then move on to another town. In his spare time, he would tinker in a barn, inventing something. For this was the great age of the individual inventor, and nearly all of them were farmers' boys.

Ford thought he could get rich by making cheap watches. But in 1892 Charles and Frank Duryea of Springfield, Massachusetts, made the first American automobile that actually worked. The next year Henry Ford built his first car, and knew that this was the adventure he sought, if only he could build enough of them.

Mass production already existed. Typewriters and sewing machines were produced by the thousands every week. But they involved only a few hundred simple parts. The automobile at the turn of the century needed 5,000 or more, many of them highly complicated, some of them machines in their own right. Ford's solution was part of his vision: he would devote all his efforts to a single car. Over the years he experimented and tinkered, and by 1908 he was ready to launch *the* car, the Model T. There was only one problem—it was too successful. Almost from the day it appeared, Ford could not keep up with demand for it. He called in one of Frederick Taylor's chief disciples,* Walter E. Flanders, and gave him a completely free hand. He could even set his own salary. He could have anything, if only he could raise production to more than 10,000 cars a year in a single plant. Flanders introduced line production. In his first year he exceeded Ford's goal.

At about the same time, Durant was trying to buy the Ford company and make it a GM subsidiary. Ford agreed to sell for $3 million cash. Durant could only offer stock. In 1909 he raised the offer to $8 million, part cash, part stock, Ford agreed to sell, but only for cash. The General Motors board decided that Ford Motors was "not worth that much." The deal fell through.[25]

Ford's obsession with mass production made his salesmen nervous, caused anxiety among his partners, and was laughed off by the 200 other automobile manufacturers in the United States with whom he had to compete. The machinery that he needed to fulfill his vision simply did not exist. Nor did the roads, the mechanics, the oil industry, the drivers, or the labor force.

Ford would listen to anybody who had an idea for increasing the production of the Model T. He was completely approachable and flexible. In 1913 two of his engineers turned their minds to the packinghouses of Chicago. There, beef carcasses were carried on moving chains past a line of meat dressers. Each man removed just one cut from each beef as it

---

* Taylor was the father of "scientific management," the virtual creator of management as a profession.

moved past him. Why not, they suggested, do the same thing, but in reverse? Ford built a moving belt assembly line.

The entire line moved, usually at six feet a minute. All raw materials, finished components, and cars under construction moved along at waist height to eliminate stooping or walking. Workers were forbidden to sit, whistle, sing, lean against the machinery, smoke, or talk while working. "Workers learned to communicate clandestinely without moving their lips in the 'Ford whisper' and wore frozen expressions known as 'Fordization of the Face.' "[26]

In less than two years the time taken to produce a Model T dropped from twelve and a half hours to ninety minutes. Ford had mastered mass production. But labor turnover reached 380 percent a year and created a crisis he had never foreseen—the perfect plant, and not enough workers to make it productive. His answer, which came from his partner, James Couzens, was to offer a wage of $5 a day. This one action made Ford the most famous manufacturer in the world. Men literally fought for the chance to work for him. Labor turnover dropped to less than 40 percent a year. Ford recouped his $5 by speeding up the line. Any man who complained would be shown the door—where there were half a dozen other men begging to be let in.

Production rose to 10,000 cars a week. Rackety Model Ts, all of them painted black, chugged through every city, town, and hamlet, creating a deep emotional attachment with the people who drove them. The Model T was balky, which created one problem after another. But it was also simple, which meant that with a little ingenuity the problems could be solved. Ford jokes became a staple of American humor. Ford had not included a speedometer, ran one joke, because you always knew what your speed was: at 15 mph the windshield rattled; at 20 the fenders rattled; at 25 your teeth rattled; and at 30 your fillings dropped out. Henry Ford rode into legend as the Model Ts rolled by.

He relished his role as folk hero. Even when Ford was the richest man in the world (and in constant money terms, he was probably the richest man ever, worth roughly $10 billion in current values) the common man identified with him, and Ford identified with the common man. He was proud to be a self-trained mechanic, trusting to instinct, trial and error, and hard work, in contrast to Alfred Sloan, who was of the modern breed, a college-trained engineer with a degree from MIT. Ford's disdain for book-learning kept him from sending his only son, Edsel, to college.[27]

When the war began, Ford declared himself a pacifist and internationalist. In 1916 he tried to sail a "Peace Ship" to Europe to persuade the belligerents to stop and was scoffed at for his pains. When the United States entered the war he announced that no "blood money" would stick to his hands; he would give back his share of the company's war profits. When the story got around that he had sent the Treasury a check running into millions of dollars to make good his pledge, he was happy to encourage it. The truth was, Ford welched on his pledge and took the "blood money" after all.[28] Both Ford and Edsel also insisted that if ever Edsel's services were considered more important in uniform, then Edsel would leap at the chance to serve his country. Meanwhile, Edsel claimed exemption from the draft. When his exemption was turned down in October 1917, he appealed. When the appeal was denied, Ford went to Wilson to keep his son at home. For years Ford had maintained that no man was indispensable to a large organization. During the war, it seems that Edsel was. Nothing, however, that Ford said or did shook the faith of ordinary people. They adored him. To a questioner who in 1919 asked him what he thought about history, Ford replied, "History is more or less the bunk."[29] The college-educated might scoff all they pleased. But the people who shared his distrust of intellectual pursuits were only bound more tightly to him. For here was the richest man in the world, yet he, like themselves, scorned bankers, parties, expensive clothes, rich men's hobbies, and snobs. At the age of sixty he would challenge ten-year-olds to a foot race; delighted in his ability to jump onto a waist-high table with two swift steps; and entered his office by the window.

His extreme individuality prompted the *Chicago Tribune* to call him an anarchist, and Ford sued for libel. When the trial opened at Mount Clemens, Michigan, in May 1919, correspondents from all over the world crowded into this small town, hitherto distinguished only by its medicinal springs. Ford spent eight days on the stand, jumping up from time to time to look out of the window as an airplane flew overhead or a bird sat on the windowsill. But they were really eight unhappy days during which he made his "History is the bunk . . ." remark, confused Benedict Arnold with Arnold Bennett, mixed up the Revolutionary War with the War of 1812, and proved what ought to have been obvious—that he was an imaginative mechanic with an eighth-grade education. He won the suit and was humiliated: the *Tribune* was fined exactly six cents.

That same year he bought out his remaining minority shareholders. General Motors was held by bankers. But Ford would be held entirely by Ford. Convinced that bankers owned and controlled the press (much of which seemed to be devoted to making him look foolish, or so he believed), he bought the struggling *Dearborn Independent*. Through Ford dealers, who diplomatically bought subscriptions for themselves, their friends, and their customers, the paper by 1921 enjoyed a "lead-pipe" circulation of 700,000 copies each week. The *Independent* railed at Wall Street, jazz, sexual freedom, rum, films, Turkish rugs, cities, and Jews.

When the 1920 recession struck, Ford was heavily in debt from buying out his partners, and repayment loomed in 1921 when he would have to find $75 million in cash. He refused to turn to the banks for help. Instead, he made his dealers become his bankers by forcing thousands of vehicles on them—vehicles they had not ordered, and for which they had to pay cash, immediately. It was they who went cap in hand to the bankers. Fortunately, the recession was soon over. Sales picked up and Ford emerged with his dealership network intact and Ford Motors entirely his own possession.

He emerged from these crises and adventures a changed man, however. The once open-minded, innovative visionary had become rigid and touchy. He began to discard the men who had helped make him great. Many of them went to GM, where they labored for revenge. Norval Hawkins, who had built up the dealer network from 15,000 car sales a year to more than 1 million, was too proud to grovel when Ford hoisted himself onto his pedestal, and Hawkins was forced out. GM hired him at $150,000 a year. William Knudsen, Ford's chief production engineer, had been invaluable in the struggle for mass production. But he could be dispensed with on a whim and was, in 1921. A year later he was hired by GM to take charge of Chevrolet.

Ford, throughout the Twenties, became increasingly tyrannical, suspicious, and isolated. He had always been a complex man.[30] While he was struggling to realize his dreams, the best elements in his nature seemed to thrive. Success, however, brought riches, adulation, power, and the pitiless exposure of his faults. It was a combination that brought out the worst side of Ford's nature. When he became dissatisfied with one of his departments, the eighty people employed there came to work one morning only to find their offices stripped to the walls and bare floor. It was his way of telling them they were fired. One executive who incurred Ford's wrath made the same discovery when workmen appeared, removed the roof of his office, and flung a tarpaulin over his desk. Another discovered that his desk had been chopped up with a fire ax.[31] Ford was both a Victorian eccentric and the head of a modern business corporation. He stood on the line where eccentricity and modernity met, and such bizarre events were the result. They would be unthinkable in the age of impersonal personnel departments and standardized firing procedures.

The Dearborn Independent was meanwhile carving out an unpleasant distinction for itself as the leading anti-Semitic publication in the world. When in December 1922 a New York Times correspondent visited the Munich headquarters of a rising young German politician, he found a strange shrine. "The wall beside his desk in Hitler's office is decorated with a large picture of Henry Ford. In the antechamber there is a large table covered with books, nearly all of them are a translation of *The Inter-national Jew . . .* published by Henry Ford."[32] Harding privately begged Ford to stop attacking Jews, and persuaded Ford's best friend, Edison, to make the same plea. For a time, it worked. There were no more long editorials blaming communism, labor unrest, and banking interests on the Jews. But in 1924 Ford took a deep dislike to Aaron Sapiro (he of the Sapiro plan) and the attacks started again. Sapiro sued for slander. And when Ford found that he could not evade another appearance in court unless the action was stopped, he chose to settle the case for an apology, a large sum in damages, and a promise never to slander Jews again.

The *Independent* was only a hobby, anyway. Ford's real interests were elsewhere, in building the Rouge plant. Before it caught his eye, the Rouge was simply a dull little tributary trickling into the Detroit river on the southeastern rim of the city. But in 1915 Ford decided to build a plant there that would startle the industrialized world. Not until he bought out the minority stockholders was he free to do it.

He placed the plant three miles upstream, dredged and widened the Rouge,and carved out a huge turning basin for ore carriers. A railroad (the Detroit, Toledo and Ironton) was bought and its lines fed into the site. The plant he built could be seen for miles, easily identified by the eight stacks rising 325 feet above the powerhouse. The Rouge plant occupied 2,000 acres. Its centerpiece was the foundry, where nearly 15,000 men worked by day and night. By 1924, when it was only two-thirds completed, it was being praised as a work of industrial art. Its arrangements were being copied from Tashkent to Tokyo. But Ford remained unsatisfied. Why bring steel to the Rouge? he asked. By 1926 a huge steel mill began to operate alongside the river, and by 1927 the entire plant was virtually complete.

Ford had bought forests for his wood, entire coal fields for his powerhouse, and he made his own steel. The Rouge plant was the highest expression of industrial organization in the world because it gave the fullest expression to the central idea of industrial production: uninterrupted flow. Ford had so completely mastered the challenge that from ore mines to car showrooms, he did not own or use a single warehouse.[33] His own fleet of ore carriers steamed down the Great Lakes to unload beside the huge foundry stacks, while other ships in Ford's fleet sailed out filled with Ford trucks, tractors, and Model Ts. Railroad cars clanked into the sidings with lumber and coal, as other railroad cars passed them bearing away yet more trucks, tractors, and Model Ts. Ford had brought everything together at a single site and on a scale no one else had ever attempted. The Rouge plant became to a generation of engineers far more than a factory. It was a monument.

It employed 75,000 men—some 5,000 of whom were hired simply to keep it clean. It was the brightest, safest, most rationally organized, highly mechanized plant anywhere. Yet, for the people who worked there, it was not a happy place. Ford's authoritarianism and crankiness kept his managers and executives in constant anxiety. His demands for more and still more production kept his workmen tense. The sheer size of the plant tended to make people feel overwhelmed. And the distance between managers and workers grew, both literally and figuratively.

The executives likely to find favor with Henry Ford these days were those whose approach to the workers was described by the former head of Ford's "Sociological Department" as "Treat 'em rough."[34] The popular idea on the shop floor, that if only the great man knew about the injustice and arbitrariness he would put a stop to it, was dead wrong. He knew. He ran the entire company from the top down with an iron hand.

At the same time, he remained color blind. He had lived and worked with black people most of his life. Among his friends were a number of blacks. By 1926 he employed more than 10,000 blacks, and many had been promoted into positions of responsibility where they hired and fired whites. Ford was also one of the very few industrialists who would hire thousands of people who were physically disabled. He took on men who were blind, limbless, deaf, dumb, or epileptic. His methods had removed the skill from the work that had to be done. A worker had to make the same one or two simple motions for hours on end. So a diligent person who was disabled could do the job. It was something that Ford was proud of. But he was not indifferent to the criticisms of repetitive work. He admitted, "Some of the operations are . . . so monotonous that it scarcely seems possible that any man would care to continue long at the same job."[35] He even condoned strikes.

Ford was almost unique among industrialists in preaching the virtues of high wages, claiming, "A low wage business is always insecure."[36] The work discipline in his factories was exacting, but as productivity rose, Ford raised wages without being pressed hard by labor to do so. In 1926 on his own initiative he revolutionized the work week. It had remained virtually unchanged at forty-eight hours for a generation. Ford announced the forty-hour, five-day week. The AFL fell on its knees and praised him, for where Ford went the rest of industry followed.

He could not always get his own way, however, In 1924 he bid for Muscle Shoals, on the Tennessee river, where the Wilson Administration had spent more than $100 million on a hydroelectric scheme. Originally intended to produce nitrates for explosives, the complex might be changed to produce nitrate fertilizer and enormous amounts of cheap electric power. Although his bid was far from being the lowest, he stood to get the contract simply because of his prestige. "Trust Ford" was the most effective argument his friends could make, because most people already did. The House passed a bill accepting Ford's offer.

He had not, in fact, offered very much. The improvements he asked for roughly equaled the price he was willing to pay. In effect, he would have been provided with virtually free electric power for his plants. The Senate bill to accept the Ford bid went to the Senate agriculture committee, chaired by George Norris of Nebraska. The senator was personally convinced that a great national asset such as Muscle Shoals ought to be turned to the benefit of the people who lived in that poverty-stricken region, and not given to the richest man in the world. The bill never emerged from committee.[37]

It was a loss that Ford easily shrugged off. He had realized his first dream, to flood the United States with cars, and his second, to build an empire. He had left the farm for adventure, and found it. Yet, "Henry Ford's interest in farming runs like a thread throughout his life."[38] Despite the huge plants he had built at Highland Park and beside the River Rouge, he tried to establish small factories in the fields. He dreamed of factories manned by men who were still farmers, and of farms worked by men who were factory hands. He dreamed, that is, of reconciling the two worlds. The six factories he set up in the countryside in the Twenties failed him. Every one ran at a loss.[39]

At Dearborn, which had now been conquered by concrete and roads, he built Greenfield Village, a memory of the world of his boyhood. He turned Sudbury, Massachusetts, into a showpiece of Colonial life. The millions he spent and the publicity he generated set off a nostalgic interest in Americana that persists to this day. The Terry clocks, the bean pots, the china hens for storing eggs, the settles, the spinning wheels that people had been throwing away since the 1890s were suddenly being zealously sought out in attics and barns and bid for handsomely in auction rooms. It is an ironic heritage from the man who considered history "the bunk."

Ford, with his passionate love of nature, plain food, hard work, folk songs, square dancing, family farms, and moral uplift remained a nineteenth-century man all his life. Yet he was also the greatest industrialist of the twentieth century. There were other production geniuses, such as Chrysler and Knudsen, and they followed virtually the same methods. Yet it was Ford who was reviled in print, in bars, on streetcorners, as the man who had turned his fellowmen into machines. It was Ford who was also hailed in his own country and abroad as a great social revolutionary. Either way, he had come to symbolize the triumph of the new industrial order as completely as Lenin symbolized the victory of communism.

16. Cross Words

I

After DeWitt Wallace had recovered from his war wounds he put aside his self-created hobby of condensing for his own amusement the newspaper and magazine stories that interested him. He went to work for Westinghouse's publicity department. When the 1920–21 recession struck, he was laid off. He borrowed $5,000 from friends and relatives and went into business for himself, hoping that what interested and amused him would interest and amuse others.

With his fiancée, Lila Acheson, to help him, Wallace set up his business in the basement of a Greenwich Village speakeasy. He managed to round up 1,500 subscribers, and in February 1921 the first issue of *Reader's Digest* went into the mail. Neither he nor Lila had ever worked on a magazine before they created their own. It was unique, too, in that it carried no advertising and it was not sold on newsstands. Yet, within a decade, its circulation would rise to half a million copies.

Like the Wallaces, neither Briton Hadden nor Henry Luce had any experience of magazine publishing. Yet they also managed to borrow enough money and find enough charter subscribers to create *Time*. The first issue went out (chaotically) in March 1923.

What Hadden and Luce possessed were youth, intelligence, and missionary fervor, and other, more experienced people, were ready to help them. *Time* took its news mainly from the *New York Times*, and the zealous, amateur heads of the magazine's departments rewrote it. Hadden and Luce were constantly skating up to the brink of financial disaster. The printing was poor. The photographs appeared, in Robert Benchley's phrase, to have been "engraved on pieces of bread."[1] The mailing lists were in the hands of debutantes, who treated the work as a lark and kept getting the lists mixed up. But by 1926 *Time* had reached solid ground. It began to make money.

It stumbled in the course of these early years into its true role—the substitute for a national newspaper. And "What was brilliant about it was less the idea than the execution."[2] *Time* was a reflection of Hadden's idiosyncrasies and passions. He affected to know nothing.* He expected his writers to inform him, not elevate him. Hadden had no interest in ideas, but he was always interested in people. *Time*'s inverted sentences (later parodied by Wolcott Gibbs: "Backward ran sentences till reeled the mind") reflected Hadden's boyhood enthusiasm for Greek. Wayward subscribers were sternly put in their place. One of Hadden's scrawled replies to a critical letter was eventually framed and hung for the admiration of a less forthright posterity: "Let Subscriber Goodkind mend his ways!"[3]

Hadden loved words such as "pig-faced" and "snaggletoothed," chortling over them in obvious delight. He loved to coin words, such as "cinemaddict" and "radiorator." *Time* revived recondite words and gave them new meanings, such as "tycoon" and "pundit." Not all the creations stuck. SCOTUS, for example, never replaced Supreme Court of the United States, whatever the charms of brevity. And *Time* alone referred to Houdini as "an ectoclast." But there were lasting additions to the language, such as "socialite."

Hadden, child of the times that he was, aimed to be a millionaire by the age of thirty and succeeded. But his second ambition, to be a great baseball player, had to fall by the wayside. He compensated by walking and talking like a ballplayer and setting his sights on owning the Yankees. He scoffed at what he considered effete amusements, such as golf and poker. He preferred to set up a shooting gallery in his living room. It amused him as well to startle his friends by wearing an asbestos fiber suit and putting out his cigarettes by grinding them against his knees and elbows.

---

* On a wide variety of subjects, this was no affectation. Hadden once sent his foreign editor a short newspaper clipping that announced the death of the last surviving British general to have served in the Crimean War, with a notation: "Great story. BH." The editor was puzzled. He came to Hadden's office, clipping in hand. "I don't understand this, Brit. Why's the death of this general such a great story?" Hadden, who wanted to be a pro baseball player, spoke with a Brooklyn accent, Yale or no Yale. "It ain't duh general," he said. "It's duh war." The editor confessed, "I still don't get it." "Tell 'em all about it," said Hadden, becoming impatient. "Tell 'em what de Crime was!"

Time was still fighting for its life when *American Mercury* made its debut in January 1924, edited by George Jean Nathan and Henry Louis Mencken. Their aim, they declared in No. 1, Vol. 1, was "to ascertain and tell the truth." They modestly admitted, "The Editors have heard no Voice from the burning bush."

The *American Mercury*, like *Time*, enjoyed testing its readers with obscure words such as "glabella" and "usufruct." Certain topics appeared frequently in its pages—Prohibition, censorship, Fundamentalists, boosters, the Klan. At 50 cents a copy ($2.00 in current prices) it was expensive. Yet it flourished from the start because of the reputation of its authors and because it had a winning feature, the section headed "Americana." Mencken each month diligently combed small-town newspapers for the bizarre, the grotesque, the plainly idiotic. "Americana" was "the 'enlightened man's' jokebook; he turned to it first, as the tired working man turned to the sports section of his daily newspaper."[4]

> Rise of civilized feeling in the Gulf littoral, as revealed by a placard in a Galveston museum:
>> DO NOT SPIT ON
>> THE BIRDS, MONKEYS
>> OR SNAKES!

> Disagreement over breakfast etiquette in Spokane:
>> Because at breakfast her husband milked milk from the goat's udder directly into his coffee, the wife is suing for divorce. She insists that neither she nor any person of refinement can stand such table manners.

> From an address before the Advertising Club of Portland by the Hon. George S. Fowler, advertising director of Colgate and Company:
>> 'I challenge you to find a boy with a clean mouth and a dirty heart. The boy who brushes his teeth twice a day doesn't go wrong. He can't.'

When the April 1926 edition of the magazine was banned in Boston for an article called "Hatrack,"* Mencken hastened north from his Baltimore home, to stand on Boston Common and there offer the offending bottle-green April issue to the Reverend Jason Franklin Chase, secretary of the New England Watch and Ward Society, who had been led there for that purpose by Arthur Garfield Hays. Mencken accepted a half-dollar from Chase, bit it hard, and grinned happily the while. Policemen, alerted that this transaction was going to take place, moved in and to Mencken's delight arrested him. Local magistrates spoiled everything by dismissing the case.

Other journalists regarded him with awe. He was loyal to fellow writ-

* See page 155.

ers at the risk of his own comfort and convenience, something rare among literary men. As an editor, he replied promptly to manuscript submissions, and a notice of acceptance came with a check pinned to it, something rare among editors. In the freemasonry of writers, no one stood higher than the short, moonfaced Mencken.[5]

In the wartime hostility to all things German he was at times insulted and shunned. But he restored himself at a single bound with the 1919 publication of *The American Language*. His wit, the ferocity of his judgments, and his honesty made him one of the most feared and one of the most admired men of the Twenties. His pronouncements were quoted, chuckled over, and passed into the mainstream of educated opinion. He was, as Walter Lippmann said, "the most powerful personal influence on this whole generation of educated people."[6]

He was not a powerful thinker. His gift was for exciting the emotions of people who thought as he did, and holding up to mockery the provincial, the bogus, and the banal. He specialized in the direct hit on the barn door. Every target he ever attacked was an easy target. Even then, he sometimes got it wrong. He dismissed the entire South as "the Sahara of the Bozart,"[7] unaware that a literary revival was about to flower that for thirty years would enrich American literature, and unaware that one of the leading artists of the Twenties, Georgia O'Keeffe, was living and working in Texas. He preferred to hail Chicago as "the literary capital of the world,"[8] just as the party was ending.

Mencken judged popular culture by the standards of high culture. He felt superior to nearly everything and to nearly everyone. So did his admirers. When at the end of the decade the preening had to stop, Mencken became passé almost overnight.

If the beer-loving, Baltimore-living Mencken appeared at times to be an unlikely candidate to bring sophistication into American life, he was easily surpassed by Harold Ross, who was the least likely candidate ever. Ross had been born in Aspen, Colorado, when it was a frontier town, full of silver miners. His father worked in the mines. Ross became a part-time sports reporter for the *Salt Lake City Telegram*. The turn of the century was the heyday of the tramp newspaperman. And that was what the rawboned, bucktoothed, shortsighted but muscular Ross became at the age of eighteen. They were a proud breed, who treasured freedom above security. Theirs was a life of talk, travel, printer's ink, poker, and hard drinking. His nickname for years afterward was Hobo Ross.[9] In those days he wore bright yellow high-button shoes and peg trousers. He was loud, profane, and ungrammatical. Rather than miss out on the war, he enlisted almost as soon as the United States entered it. In early 1918 he managed to talk his way onto *Stars and Stripes*. Private Ross suddenly discovered at the age of thirty that he was not a reporter after all. He was an editor.

In 1919, out of the army, he edited *Home Sector*—a *Stars and Stripes* for veterans. It failed to attract enough of them. After eight issues it folded. He then edited the *American Legion Weekly*, all the while yearning for a publication of his own, one which would cover life in the city as *Stars and Stripes* had covered life in the AEF. And then he met Raoul Fleischmann, heir to a fortune made out of yeast.

Ross and his wife would risk all their life savings, $20,000. Fleischmann would put up $30,000 for the new magazine. Ross wrote a brochure to attract potential advance subscribers, "The *New Yorker*," he promised, "will be the magazine which is not edited for the old lady in Dubuque." The magazine would be published for a metropolitan audience, and no other. He was not exactly offering sophistication, but "a jotting down in the small-town newspaper style of the comings, goings and doings in the village of New York."10

The first issue appeared February 21, 1925, and Ross was as good as his word: it was about as sophisticated as a small-town newspaper. So the *New Yorker* remained for some time to come. It was "the outstanding flop of 1925," said James Thurber," . . . and the only flop that kept on going."11 It was amateurish and brash. It lost money every week. After ten issues Fleischmann wanted to shut it down. The *New Yorker* came as close to folding as it is possible to come and still stay in business. Ross pleaded so persuasively that Fleischmann changed his mind and put up more money. This cycle—of virtual bankruptcy, Ross pleading, Fleischmann yielding—became a regular routine. By the time the magazine finally showed a profit Fleischmann had put up more than $500,000. But it then became, for its circulation, the most profitable magazine in the world.12

In these early years Ross hired almost anyone who asked for a job. The moment they did not produce what he wanted, he fired them. He could not himself produce what he wanted. But he knew it when he saw it. As the *New Yorker* found its feet it began to perform a great service. Ross was a compulsive perfectionist.* The magazine raised accuracy and clarity to a pinnacle never before seen in the American press. Yet the *New Yorker* style was casual rather than formal. Ross improved the country's prose, and by perfecting the one-line cartoon caption, sharpened its jokes.

---

* Ross disliked Alexander Woollcott (on whom *The Man Who Came to Dinner* is based) so intensely that even his perfectionism cracked. Woollcott was a self-important, self-celebrating figure. An illness in childhood had left him impotent. To compensate, he tyrannized and wounded anyone who crossed his path. His baroque literary style was the kind of thing that used to pass for fine writing. Ross loathed him. He deliberately misspelled Woollcott's name, which while Ross was alive always appeared in the *New Yorker* as Woolcott.

By the late Twenties what Ross was selling *was* sophistication. Yet he himself had changed very little. He remained contemptuous of college graduates and Eastern dudes. Cold drinks hurt his huge front teeth, so he drank them through a napkin. He was probably the worst-dressed editor in the history of American journalism (admittedly, he was pressed very hard by Briton Hadden). He dressed so badly, in fact, that when Walter Winchell wrote in his column that Ross never wore underwear, hardly anyone questioned it. Ross, stung by this slur, stormed into the *New Yorker* toilet, removed his underpants, and mailed them to Winchell.

Eventually it became a cliché to call the *New Yorker* "sophisticated." It was that, of course, and as its fame spread it was subscribed to in Dubuque and other points beyond the Hudson. But what it had chiefly brought to American journalism was not its air of wordly wisdom. The *New Yorker* stood for excellence. It was the best-written American publication of the twentieth century.

II

The new generation of writers broke with the past simply by getting out from under the English yoke. A third-rate English novel could easily displace a better American one before the Twenties. The judgment of English critics on American writers was considered vital. The judgment of American critics on English writers was considered impertinence. When young American writers had become expatriates (and many had, such as Pound, Frost, Eliot, Conrad Aiken, John Gould Fletcher, Hilda Doolittle, and Henry James) they went to London. In rejecting the past, the new generation had to break the continuity of Anglo-American literature.

They deplored the "puritanism" that colored it, knowing, as a rule, little about seventeenth- and eighteenth-century religious beliefs. What they were really protesting against was the bigotry and hypocrisy of the late nineteenth century, less Cotton Mather than Anthony Comstock. They derided the American village and small town. As a literary genre, this was not entirely new. But it felt new to a new generation of practitioners. And human beings are always rediscovering the wheel in some way. Growing up mainly involves finding out the already known.

Raking over the American past, American writers did make two important discoveries, however: Emily Dickinson and Herman Melville. Emerson, Thoreau, and Hawthorne were dusted off and their reputations regilded. But since that "Golden Day" (as Lewis Mumford termed it) on the eve of the Civil War they saw only fifty barren years.[13]

By rejecting the yoke of English literary authority, by shrugging off the fetters of provincial life, and by finding a few hard places on which to stand amid the slush of American literature, American writers were freeing themselves to write about the modern world in a modern way.

Even before the war ended an exodus to France—rather, to Paris— was expected.[14] And with the rising value of the dollar (worth eight francs in 1919; sixteen in 1923; twenty-five in 1926) living in France became dramatically cheaper each year. French literary models proved an inspiration in poetry, in fiction, in history, and in biography. The stream of consciousness novel, with its characteristic interior monologue, was contemporaneous with Freud. Its first full expression was Eduard Dujardin's *Les Lauriers sont Coupés* (1887), which greatly influenced James Joyce, living and writing in Paris. To young American writers, the gaunt, half-blind Joyce was a demigod.[15]

The battle line along which the break with the past raged was sex. The Twenties were punctuated with censorship fights. The first epic clash came with the publication in 1919 of James Branch Cabell's *Jurgen*, compared with whom Don Juan appeared to be a shy beginner. Almost forgotten now, Cabell was considered the best writer in America. "It was universally conceded that if the works of any writer of the time lived, they would be his."[16] *Jurgen* was banned from open sale for two years, until the courts ruled in Cabell's favor. Bootleg copies meanwhile brought fabulous prices.

Of greater importance was Sherwood Anderson's *Winesburg, Ohio* (1919), whose style made a lasting impression on American prose. It was laconic, yet sharp. The book had no plot, consisting of short stories set in a single town. Place and mood provided what unity the stories possessed. Winesburg was a thousand small towns. Anderson saw its limitations, and what it did to people. Yet he neither mocked nor scorned. It was enough to describe.

Although Anderson's writing was often crude or banal, he was able here and there to achieve effects which were so vivid that nothing like them had been seen before. It was this ability to put into one sentence or one briefly glimpsed scene an entire lifetime of feeling that made other writers sit at his feet. The spirit he brought to his characters—frustrated spinsters, repressed businessmen, pimply adolescents—was one of compassionate pessimism. And the chief thing on the minds of the inhabitants of *Winesburg, Ohio* was sex.

Anderson knew most of the better, younger writers of the Twenties, and left a deep mark on Hemingway, Faulkner, Wolfe, Saroyan, and Steinbeck, to name but five. He encouraged them, helped them to find publishers, and was surpassed by them.[17]

Only months after the appearance of *Winesburg, Ohio* came another account of the ghastliness of small-town life in the Midwest, Sinclair Lewis's *Main Street* (1920). "It was the most sensational event in twentieth-century American publishing history."[18] At a time when even the most popular novelist, Harold Bell Wright, sold about 1.5 million copies of his stories of high adventure and sexless romance, *Main Street*, with its account of misery in Gopher Prairie, sold 3 million. "No reader was indifferent to it: if *Main Street* was not the most important revelation of American life ever made, it was the most infamous libel upon it."[19]

Gopher Prairie was shown as it appeared to Carol Kennicott, who was transported there by the doctor she married. To him, it was the most wonderful place in the world. To her, it was just an ugly little prairie town, hardly better than the frontier camp made by its first settlers a century before. The people she met were decent, outgoing, and kind. They could make the flesh creep without even trying. The millions who read *Main Street* recognized themselves and the towns they lived in or had fled from. They were both shocked and enthralled. Gopher Prairie was the pyre on which dreams and hopes were burned. There was no beauty, no idealism, no room for the imagination, no intellectual life, anywhere; nothing on which dreams and hopes could live. In its own relentless way, it reduced them to ashes. And that is the flavor of the book—ashes.

Lewis's next novel, *Babbitt* (1922), was an even greater success. Novels with business settings had nearly always revolved around a tycoon, ruthless, heroic in his way, fabulously rich, whose smallest deeds were dramatic. Lewis created a new figure in fiction, the small businessman, or middleman, and far from being heroic this protaganist was almost certain to be faintly absurd. George Follansbee Babbitt, realtor of Zenith, was the first of the breed.

Lewis's affectionate satire fired a craze for Babbitt-spotting in public places. Babbitt became part of the language. Yet far from being insulted by Lewis's mockery, cities all over the Midwest competed for recognition as the original Zenith. Minneapolis tried to outpace its rivals by declaring a "Babbitt Week."

As for the original Babbitt, that was Lewis himself. Babbitt's creator had no alternative set of values, no deeper insights into human existence, no more elevated interests than dear old Georgie himself. Lewis's mockery was self-mockery. There is hardly a hint in the entire novel that the author might feel superior to his characters. In his own life, Lewis, like Babbitt, was embarrassingly hungry for success, love, and admiration, and just as crass in the pursuit of his desires. Lewis abroad was as gauche, as tiresomely patriotic, as sensitive to foreign sneers, and as provincially self-conscious as his Tired Business Man.

But Lewis was also the first American novelist to approach his craft almost as a social scientist. Moving easily through these midwestern towns, duck-hunting with the local Babbittry, he took voluminous notes, remarking in copious, accurate detail on every facet of small-town life. No one had ever portrayed everyday life in America with such veracity. As a result, he outsold all the other serious writers of the Twenties combined. It was Lewis, not Fitzgerald, who was considered the greatest novelist of his time. It was inevitable that he would be awarded the Pulitzer Prize. When it came, in 1926, for *Arrowsmith*, he astounded the country by turning it down, claiming that prizes were bad for serious writers. All his life, Lewis, his face pitted and empurpled by acne scars, fought a losing battle with an inferiority complex. But at this moment he was so celebrated he could spurn official recognition.

His fellow Minnesotan novelist, F. Scott Fitzgerald, was to tread an oddly similar path, yet Fitzgerald seemed to have little to feel inferior about. Five feet seven inches in height, slender, fair, he was androgynously pretty at Princeton. Fitzgerald would dress up as a girl at the drop of a purse. He could pass it off as an undergraduate jape. Yet his friendship with some of his male friends, especially those who played football or were in charge of something or other, who were leaders, dominant, powerful, was suffused with a romantic attachment that was both intense and obvious.

In 1917 Fitzgerald joined the army ("purely for *social reasons*," he informed his mother, lest she mistakenly think him motivated by heroism). He never went overseas and was defensive about it years afterward. He was discharged in early 1919 and went to work writing light verse for streetcar advertising (for the Muscatine, Iowa, steam laundry: "We keep you clean in Muscatine"). His evenings were spent writing and mailing out manuscripts, nearly every one of which was rejected. Fitzgerald decorated his room with 122 rejection slips.[20]

In the fall of 1919 he went home to St. Paul to live with his family while he tried to write a novel. If it succeeded, he might become rich enough at a stroke to win the girl he left behind from his days in a southern army camp, Zelda Sayre of Montgomery, Alabama. The novel was *This Side of Paradise*. When it appeared in the summer of 1920 it did not sell one-tenth as many copies as *Main Street*. It was, nevertheless, a sensation. *Jurgen* had celebrated sex; Lewis had squelched the small town; and Fitzgerald pitted youth against age. Three of the four corners of modern fiction were now in place.

This Side of Paradise was not a particularly good novel. Its best parts were clumsily lifted from Compton Mackenzie's *Sinister Street*; its worst parts were undiluted Fitzgerald. But it seemed very up-to-date. Freud appeared on page six. There was too much drinking and a fair sprinkling of recreational sex. It inspired a score of undergraduate novels, only one of which, *The Plastic Age* (1922) by Percy Marks, was any good. *The Plastic Age*, in fact, was better in every respect than *This Side of Paradise* without being in danger of being considered a great novel. The ground Fitzgerald had opened up was not in the end particularly fertile. But it did mark a new beginning. No one had taken college students seriously before. In the Twenties they were the object of avid curiosity.

In their private lives the Fitzgeralds seemed to feel a mission to personify life-glorifying youth. There was a deliberate element that made their supposedly irrepressible gaiety strangely joyless. The rides down Fifth Avenue on the roof of a taxi, the dancing on kitchen tables, the half hour spent in a revolving door, required an audience. The Fitzgeralds had to be seen to be the Fitzgeralds. Those who were not there were told about what they had missed in merciless detail.[21] The Fitzgeralds on their first trip to Paris bathed the baby in the bidet, unable to imagine what else it might be for.[22]

They partied as zealously as Twenties youth were supposed to do. In between parties they were kept busy writing notes to their friends to apologize, promising it wouldn't happen again. It was not that Fitzgerald drank a lot. The trouble was that he could get drunk on so little.[23] And when he was drunk he was obnoxious to perfection.

It was his 1922 collection of stories, *Tales of the Jazz Age*, that gave the Twenties their most famous tag. It was stories such as these, published mainly in the *Saturday Evening Post*, that made his name a household word, and made him one of the most highly paid writers in the world. In 1923 he earned $36,000, and managed to be broke at the end of the year. He could not even account for where nearly half of it had gone.[24]

Increasingly, it was the stories that became the source of his living. After *This Side of Paradise* each subsequent novel sank faster than its predecessor. When *The Great Gatsby* appeared in 1925 it was a critical success and a commercial failure. It would be nine years before Fitzgerald had the courage and self-confidence to write another novel.

Both Lewis and Fitzgerald drank in a reckless, self-destructive way; both lapsed easily into boorishness; both proved incapable of sustaining love or friendship; both were almost desperate for success. When it came, neither derived much satisfaction from it. Neither ever defeated the sense of inferiority that had driven each one so hard.

That may be why the writer Fitzgerald most admired was utterly different from himself, and that was Ernest Hemingway. No sooner had they met than Fitzgerald, one of the most famous writers in the world, appointed himself Hemingway's unpaid agent. At the time, Hemingway's first book, *Three Stories and Ten Poems* (1924), had just been published— all 300 copies of it.

Hemingway's first mentor had been Anderson, whom he had met in 1920. When Hemingway left for Paris in 1921 he carried with him an introduction to Gertrude Stein from Anderson. From afar, Anderson helped Hemingway to get *In Our Time* (1925) accepted by his own publisher, Horace Liveright.

It was a debt that Hemingway repaid by writing *The Torrents of Spring*, the sole purpose of which was to ridicule Anderson. When he finished it, he called one of Anderson's friends to come to the Closerie de Lilas. When she arrived, Hemingway, in a state of malicious excitement, insisted on reading the entire manuscript to her, gloating as he turned each page.[25] Hemingway's hardness was no pose. Fitzgerald adored him.

Hemingway was big and strong and brave. He boxed for recreation, skied, went hunting, wrestled bulls in the streets of Pamplona. During the war he had it both ways—drove an ambulance and came home a hero. He was wounded by an exploding shell while taking cover in a trench on a mission to take candy, cigarettes, and postcards to Italian soldiers. But then he tried to carry one of the badly wounded soldiers to safety and was hit in the right knee by a machine gun bullet.[26] No wonder Fitzgerald, sensitive about not serving overseas, stood in awe of him. Fitzgerald even confided to Hemingway his fears that his penis was too small. Hemingway took him into a cafe toilet to reassure him by letting him compare his organ with the hero's.[27]

For his part, Hemingway both liked and pitied Fitzgerald. He blamed his unpaid agent's troubles on Zelda, with her "hawk's eyes and thin mouth."[28] But he, too, eventually tired of Fitzgerald's drunken attempts at being amusing—such as urinating on the Hemingways' apartment door —and told his publisher never to let Fitzgerald have his address.[29]

Hemingway's prose style was spare, precise, without wasted words or gestures. Combined with an attitude of stoicism in the face of life's cruelty and stupidity, it captured perfectly the disillusioned spirit of the times, even if, reading it now, it seems almost as stylized as the prose of the Genteel Tradition it helped to make passé.

It was Hemingway, and to a lesser extent Fitzgerald, who provided the fourth corner of modern fiction, and that was resolution by violent death. With his war experiences and his delight in blood sports as the perfect recreation, Hemingway was as much an authority on this subject as Lewis was on Babbitt. And it is on these foundations—overt concern with sex, preferring the young to their elders, deriding small-town ways, and the murderous denouement—that modern American fiction has stood for half a century.

III

James O'Neill knew what a trap the American theater was. He longed to be a great actor and master the heroic/tragic roles of Shakespearean drama. He was conscientious in his craft, possessed presence and talent. Yet he chanced upon the title role in *The Count of Monte Cristo* and found that he could not get out of it. In this costume melodrama, fame and riches were his. The instant he sought another part no one was interested in him. *The Count* was what the theatergoing public wanted—predictable, noisy, full of good sword fights, all of it signifying absolutely nothing. And that was what James O'Neill was doomed to give them, in tour after tour, through hundreds of provincial towns. He had to live his tragic role offstage, made hollow by success. His wife took refuge from the endless touring in drug addiction. His eldest son took refuge from his parents' quarrels in the bottle and by eighteen was an alcoholic. His youngest son, Eugene, fled his family at seventeen. For the rest of his life he kept on running.

Dropping out of Princeton after his freshman year, the young O'Neill found a creed to match his pain—Nietzsche's *Thus Spake Zarathustra*. Its rejection of hope replaced the Catholic faith he had lost. He went prospecting for gold in Honduras; worked as an ordinary seaman on tramp steamers; was a down-and-out on the Buenos Aires waterfront; sold sewing machines; worked as a newspaper reporter; contracted TB; was married and divorced—all by the age of twenty-three.

He went to Harvard for a year to study playwriting and dropped out again. This time he became a Greenwich Village fixture, except that he was never in the same spot for long. He spent his time with bums, prostitutes, addicts, alcoholics, Wobblies, anarchists, pimps, gangsters, and bartenders rather than the intellectual and cultural figures in the neighborhood. The two were not always separate, of course. But O'Neill, who informed his family and friends that he was working as a dramatic critic, was drunk most of the time; too drunk to write, too drunk on occasion to drink, unless there was someone there to help get the bottle or glass to his mouth.[30] He lived on a dollar-a-day handout from his father.

The theater in which James O'Neill was held fast was meanwhile being challenged by German expressionism. Even serious theater—the theater of Ibsen and Shaw—depended on the old outward forms: proscenium arch, three acts (state problem, complicate problem, resolve problem), an array of costumes, recognizable settings, realistic props. Expressionists abandoned all of that. "For painted perspectives and glaring footlights they substituted simplified settings and spotlights. They made use of symbolic, suggestive and often distorted scenery. They introduced brilliant colors. And they rediscovered the mask."[31] The central aim of the old theater—whether in melodrama or serious plays—was to portray an objective reality. In the expressionist theater it was to express subjective states—the irrational, the violent, the absurd. Instead of the three-act, "well-made" play there were episodic, brief scenes. America's solitary expressionist theater in 1915 was not far from several of Eugene O'Neill's favorite bars. It was run by the Washington Square Players.

Dedicated though they were to avant-garde plays, the Players refused to stage a sex drama by George Cram Cook and his wife, Susan Glaspell, entitled *Suppressed Desires*. Cook and Glaspell broke away. With several friends they formed the Provincetown Players in Provincetown, Massachusetts. Their theater was a fishhouse at the end of a wharf owned by Mary Heaton Vorse. Their aim was to encourage avant-garde American playwrights. But after producing *Suppressed Desires* they were woefully short of promising scripts.

At that point fate sent Eugene O'Neill along the Provincetown beach, where he was staying in a shack with an alcoholic anarchist friend from Greenwich Village, to a meeting with his destiny.[32] The play he offered was *Bound East for Cardiff*. The Wharf Theater was 25 feet square. "Through the planks of its floor at high tide the bay could be seen and heard and smelled."[33] It was the ideal setting for a tale of tragedy aboard a tramp steamer.

Back in New York each winter, the Provincetown Players called themselves the Playwrights' Theater. O'Neill continued to write for them, winter and summer. For the first time in his life he could make a bare living by writing. But most of the time he was oppressed by money worries. And at the armistice O'Neill, aged thirty, was still only a "promising" playwright.

Unlike most of the people in the experimental theater, he did not despise Broadway as such (known in Greenwich Village as "The Great Trite Way"), only its methods, its values, and its pretenses. He wanted a Broadway success, but on his own terms.

In February 1920 he had his chance. The play was *Beyond the Horizon*. It had little plot, no melodrama, no surprises. It was naturalistic, and starkly tragic. O'Neill hid nervously behind a pillar to avoid recognition. The audience was unsure what to make of the play. Yet the theater critics had a feeling that something important was happening. To the surprise of everyone associated with it, *Beyond the Horizon* ran for 111 performances. It won the Pulitzer Prize, which O'Neill had never heard of until the telegram announcing the award reached him.

Six months later the Provincetown Players mounted *The Emperor Jones*, O'Neill's tale in eight brief scenes of a Pullman porter who became an African chief while on the run from a murder charge, only to be overthrown by his own fear and madness. Cook spent almost the entire treasury for the season ($502 out of a budget of $530) on this production, convinced that here was a masterpiece. The subject of the play was the state of mind of its protagonist. A black actor, Charles S. Gilpin, was for the first time given a starring role. The morning after the play opened, "the box office treasurer was greeted with the unprecedented sight of people lined up on MacDougal Street waiting to buy tickets."[34] It was the end of the Provincetown/Playwrights' days as an amateurish, experimental theater. It had so won the American theater over to innovation that it had lost its reason for existing. In a few years, it would go out of business.

For O'Neill, there were to be many years yet of success—and tragedy. At the request of George Jean Nathan he wrote a play for the *American Mercury*, but missed the first issue deadline. The play was *All God's Chillun Got Wings*. Its protagonists were a married couple—he black, she white. When the play prepared to open, O'Neill and the play's stars, Paul Robeson and Mary Blair, were bombarded with obscene and threatening letters.* O'Neill's script called for Miss Blair to kiss Robeson's hand. "Many white people do not like the idea," said *Time*, normally proud of its liberal views on race. "Neither do many black."[35] Riots were expected to greet the first public performance. Nothing much happened. O'Neill was disappointed.

All God's Chillun Got Wings remained true to the expressionist faith. The flat in which black Jim and white Ella tore one another to pieces became smaller and more claustrophobic with each scene. At the end, the ceiling was barely above their heads. They could hardly move without brushing against a wall. Two years later, in 1926, O'Neill demonstrated his complete mastery of the genre with *The Great God Brown*, in which all the characters wore masks. Thereafter, O'Neill moved back toward naturalism.

There were other serious playwrights and other serious plays on the American stage in the Twenties. But O'Neill towers above them all. Al-

---

* To one letter of protest from the Ku Klux Klan he replied by writing "GO FUCK YOURSELF" three inches high across it and mailed it back to Klan headquarters.

most singlehandedly, in just one decade, he brought American theater from melodramatic piffle to world prominence. He was no intellectual. What he was offering was not the theater of ideas. He had lived life intensely, so intensely that disaster was his lifelong companion. That was what his plays recreated—O'Neill's passions, disappointments, torments. His life was filled with Gothic horrors. Besides carrying the burdens of his father's failure-in-success, his mother's drug addiction, and the early death from alcoholism of his brother, there were his own children: Eugene, Jr., who cut his throat; Shane, who became a gutter crawler and heroin addict; and Oona, who was permanently estranged from him because at eighteen she married the fifty-year-old Charlie Chaplin. The fires that burned inside him were what O'Neill put on the stage. It was, in the most complete sense, living theater.

IV

The Twenties reaped the first fruits of free, universal secondary education. For the first time nearly the entire adult population could read, and did. Only a handful of magazines before the war reached a circulation of 1 million; in the Twenties there were a score or more. The tabloid, invented by Lord Northcliffe, had failed to catch on in the United States before the First World War. But when the New York Daily News began publishing in 1919, it succeeded beyond all its hopes. It became a very rich newspaper. The tabloid, with its small pages and large type, was ideal for reading in a crowded, rocking subway car. All it needed was enough people who had caught the reading habit.

By the mid-Twenties, New York was supporting three tabloids, with a combined circulation of 1.6 million. Other newspapers, losing circulation, began to ape the sensationalism of the tabloids.[36] The scandals and trivia that feature in nearly all accounts of the Twenties—from six-day bicycle races and dance marathons to the Hall-Mills murder trial, the death of Starr Faithfull, the execution of Ruth Snyder, the Peaches Browning case, and the trapped miner Floyd Collins—were the battles in these circulation wars. The present day did not invent media-hype: it is an inheritance.[37]

The Twenties was a time of fads: Mah-Jongg, seances, flagpole sitting, Babbitt-spotting, and the like. Like most fads, they seemed absorbing at the time but once the novelty wore off seemed tedious. Only one had any endurance, and that was the crossword puzzle. Two young men, Richard Simon and Lincoln Schuster, were trying to get into publishing, like quite a few young men of the time. They had little experience and little money.

So they began in a small way, publishing crossword puzzle books. They hired halls and organized crossword competitions, making up the rules as they went along. They cajoled newspaper editors into putting crosswords in their papers. They promoted crosswords so diligently that they sold 2 million copies of the *Cross-Word Puzzle Book*. Thus did millions of Americans come to know that there was an Egyptian sun god named Ra; that an eel was "a snakelike fish"; that one printer's measure was an "em," another an "en." It was confidently predicted that the fad would pass.

At all events, Simon and Schuster moved on to other things. It was a propitious time to go into publishing. The Twenties saw the creation of half a dozen major houses, including Morrow, Viking, Coward-McCann, and Harcourt, Brace. The number of new titles doubled in a decade, from 5,700 in 1919 to 11,000 ten years later.[38] It was also the age that saw both the Book-of-the-Month Club and the Literary Guild established within months of one another in 1926. The sale and distribution of books had long been little better than in Colonial times. The book clubs pioneered the mass distribution of books. Their success was instantaneous, the most convincing possible evidence that they were satisfying a deeply felt need —one that booksellers and publishers had not even realized existed.

And what were people reading? For two-and-a-half years the best-selling book was a volume called *Diet and Health*. Bruce Barton's *The Man Nobody Knows* sold almost as many copies as *Main Street*. It portrayed Christ as a businessman who gathered half a dozen top-flight salesmen together and created God's version of General Motors. Another best-seller was Chic Sale's *The Specialist*, which purported to be the reminiscences of a builder of outhouses. Although Americans were reading in unprecedented numbers, they seemed to be moving their lips as they did so.

In fact, the Twenties marked a revolutionary advance in literary taste. In the ten years from 1910 to 1920 the fiction best-seller lists were dominated by Zane Grey, Harold Bell Wright, Frances Hodgson Burnett, Ethel M. Dell, and Booth Tarkington. There was not one first-rate writer, not a single great novel, among the best-sellers. The next decade brought Lewis and O'Neill (with the text of *Strange Interlude*) into the top ten sellers, with Fitzgerald and Hemingway not far behind. The nonfiction best-seller lists were still more remarkable, because "there were no non-fiction 'best-sellers' at the turn of the century."[39] And it was the soundest works that tended to be the most successful. Not at all what one would expect from the frivolous jazz generation, giddy with bathtub gin.

17. The High Tide
of the Twenties—1927

I

Since the day of his return from the war, Billy Mitchell had thumped
three tubs: there would be another war in Europe, there would be war
with Japan, and both would be decided by air power. Mitchell was brash,
rich, and ambitious. He made enemies as easily as he made friends. He
fought his battles in the newspapers and in Congress and in 1921 he won
the public relations war. Mitchell pressured the navy into allowing him to
bomb a captured German battleship. He had to build a bomber force from
scratch while suppressing the miners' march in West Virginia. Specially
made bombs, bigger by far than anything used in the war, had to be
hurriedly built. But when films appeared in American movie theaters
showing the sinking of the "unsinkable" *Ostfriesland*, they created a sensation. Mitchell became a national hero.

His exuberant personality and unorthodox methods, however, made
the War and Navy departments more reluctant than ever to accept that
the bombing tests showed what Mitchell claimed—that airplanes made
battleships obsolete. This, in turn, made Mitchell more outspoken than
ever. In 1925 his unpopularity with his superiors cost him his post as
assistant chief of the air service. He was banished to a small airfield in
Texas, where he had almost nothing to do. The navy was meanwhile

about to show that it was as "air-minded" as the next service by sending three flying boats on a flight from California to Hawaii. Mitchell openly ridiculed it as a publicity gimmick. The PN flying boats were unwieldy, slow, and, flown by inexperienced crews, dangerous. One failed to take off. The second crashed shortly after takeoff. The third came down in the sea 400 miles from Hawaii.

Two weeks later came the loss of the country's aerial pride, the airship *Shenandoah*. It was touring midwestern state fairs: another publicity stunt. And dangerous, too, because September was the Great Lakes thunderstorm season. The navy brushed this objection aside, ignoring the reservations of the *Shenandoah*'s commander, Captain Zachary Lansdowne. The craft broke up in midair, hurling to their deaths the entire thirty-one-man crew. Souvenir hunters finished the damage the storm had wrought to the *Shenandoah*, and one among them tore from Lansdowne's lifeless hand his Annapolis class ring.

Mitchell was a deeply emotional man. He felt the deaths of young fliers very keenly. He lashed out at the War and Navy departments, accusing them of criminal negligence and a shortsighted view of national defense that he claimed was only marginally short of treason. In a 6,000-word indictment he touched on nearly every aspect of aviation, from meteorology to air-racing trophies. He was trying very hard to get himself court-martialed. He continued to speak out until he got what he wanted.

Coolidge drafted Morrow to head an air inquiry board to look into every aspect of American air policy. The War Department charged Mitchell with insubordination and "conduct prejudicial to good order and military discipline." When he arrived in Washington for his court-martial, Mitchell was met at Union Station by a cheering crowd 10,000 strong and a blaring drum and bugle corps.

A legend grew up afterward that Mitchell deliberately sacrificed his career for the sake of alerting his country to the need for modern air power. Instead, he went to his court-martial confident of vindication. Vindication not after fifteen or twenty years, but immediately, in full, leaving his critics confounded and discredited while he, Billy Mitchell, could then get down to the serious business of preparing the nation for the wars that he knew were coming.[1]

To a large extent, his court-martial pitted youth against age. In the modern world, nearly everyone was on the side of youth. After seven weeks of testimony, eight of the nine generals on the court found him guilty of insulting the army and navy. The ninth, who held out for acquittal, was his boyhood friend from Milwaukee, Major General Douglas

MacArthur. Mitchell was suspended from active duty for five years, lost his rank for five years, and forfeited all pay and allowances for five years. There was no official reprimand. It was a light sentence. But it was so far from vindication that it contained no crumb of comfort for Billy Mitchell. When Coolidge upheld the sentence, Mitchell resigned his commission. He began to tour the country, as a civilian, pleading for a third military service, an air force—crying, as he saw it, in the wilderness. Because the Morrow board, although it did much to support the development of civil aviation, flatly opposed a separate service devoted to air power.

The federal government was already supporting commercial aviation by providing a testing service for aviation equipment, by providing weather forecasts and navigational aids, and by letting mail contracts that amounted to heavy subsidies for the carriers. There was one young pilot on the airmail service who reflected ironically on some flights that the airline he worked for was making more money from the mail sacks and their big brass padlocks than from the letters inside, because the government paid by the pound. It was on one of these long, slow, solitary mail flights one night in the fall of 1926 from St. Louis to Chicago that it occurred to him he could fly from New York to Paris, if he had the right plane. He had plenty of time to think about what such a flight would involve. He was confident that he could do it. After all, "The flying couldn't be more dangerous or the weather worse than the night mail in winter."[2]

There was certainly no more dedicated pilot. Charles Augustus Lindbergh was only twenty-four years old, but he disdained alcohol, tobacco, and the girls who hung around airfields—anything, in fact, that might compromise the high standards he had explicitly set for himself, solemnly listing them (sixty-five items in all), including Alertness, Altruism, Balance, Brevity, Concentration, Diligence, Enterprise, Foresight, Honesty, Manliness, Orderliness, Reserve, Tact, Unselfishness, and Zeal.[3]

Alas, these qualities had not kept him from flunking out of the University of Wisconsin in his sophomore year. For a while he lived the precarious life of a barnstormer, but it was hard to make a living in the winter. His greatest ambition was to become a commercial pilot—but there was no commercial aviation to speak of. So he became an air cadet, learning to fly under expert instructors and being paid for it. In his class of 104 student pilots, only 18 graduated, with Lindbergh at the head of the class. With the government beginning to grant airmail contracts, there were jobs to be had at last. Lindbergh hardly received his commission before he resigned from active service. And now, as he flew back and forth between St. Louis and Chicago, a French ace, René Fonck, with 126 wartime victories in the air, was preparing to fly from New York to Paris, which made Lindbergh think of doing it himself.

Fonck was going to fly a trimotor craft with an American-French crew in pursuit of the prize put up by a French hotelier, Raymond Orteig. It was worth $25,000 for the first nonstop journey between New York and Paris. In the fall of 1926 Fonck's Sikorsky crashed on takeoff, killing two of the crew, leaving Fonck unscathed. The prize was still there for 1927, when the weather improved.

The conventional wisdom said that to fly the Atlantic required a plane with at least two engines, and at least two men to fly it. That was how the Englishmen, Alcock and Brown, had flown from Newfoundland to Ireland in 1919, a distance of 2,000 miles. From New York to Paris was almost twice as far, 3,600 miles. Lindbergh alone thought out the problem afresh. The solution he came up with was one man, one engine. Anything above the bare minimum—engines, crew, safety devices—exacted a penalty heavier than any advantage it conferred. All that was necessary was a plane filled with gasoline and a pilot who could stay awake for two days and two nights without losing his concentration.

Flying out of St. Louis, he had taken some of the city's leading businessmen—which meant some of its leading boosters—on sightseeing flights. Once the idea of trying to win the Orteig prize stirred in Lindbergh's mind, he knew where to try to raise the money. This lonely, shy young man spent the winter of 1926–27 in the most least likely guise he could ever assume: he became a hustler. He put up his savings, $2,000. A group of bankers and businessmen put up what amounted to a blank check, although he insisted he would need no more than $15,000.

Four other flights to Paris were planned for 1927, all of them more lavishly backed than Lindbergh's. At the Ryan Aircraft Company in San Diego, where a plane was being built to Lindbergh's specifications and on what amounted to a shoestring budget, almost all other work stopped to speed construction of the *Spirit of St. Louis*. Ordinary workmen, entering into the competitive spirit that seemed to rise all across the country as spring drew near, worked around the clock. As they drove themselves to exhaustion, Lindbergh silently turned pessimistic. He had started too late. Bigger planes and better-known pilots were about to take off before he was ready. For him to succeed, all of them would have to fail. And there was now proof that the thing could be done: two Frenchmen in March 1927 flew 3,200 miles nonstop from Paris to Tehran.

In mid-April, Commander Richard Byrd's trimotor, the *America*, took off from Roosevelt Field on Long Island. Destination—Paris. The *America* crashed, leaving Byrd with a broken wrist. Two weeks later an enormous yellow trimotor, the *American Legion*, flown by two of the Navy's top pilots, took off from Langley Field, Virginia, for Paris. The craft carried four tons of fuel. It rose seventy feet in the air, and crashed into a pond at the end of the runway, killing both pilots.

On May 9, the day before the *Spirit of St. Louis* was ready to be flown for the first time, Lindbergh read in the newspapers that two of France's best fliers, Charles Nungesser and François Coli, had taken off from Paris. Destination—New York. The details of their preparation convinced him they would succeed. All day long the news continued to come in—Nungesser and Coli had been sighted in mid-Atlantic, on course and on time. The next day, they were reported over the New England coast. In Paris, the celebrations had already begun. Lindbergh, sick at heart, began to think of making a flight in the opposite direction, from California to Hawaii.[4]

But fate was preparing his way. Nungesser and Coli perished somewhere at sea. When Lindbergh took off to fly the *Spirit of St. Louis* to New York, six men had died and three had been badly injured in pursuit of the Orteig prize. When he arrived in New York there were huge crowds to greet him, and two of his competitors, anxiously scanning the wet, gray skies. The tousled, six foot two inch Lindbergh, with his shy smile, became instantly the object of adoration. Around every other attempt to win the Orteig prize had been a dreary atmosphere of commercialism, petty bickering, stodgy bureaucracy, or rampant egotism. One of the best-prepared planes in the competition was still on the ground, held back by lawsuits. Lindbergh seemed almost a being from another world, another age.[5] Crowds followed him wherever he went. Reporters and photographers dogged his steps, bursting into his hotel room while he tried to catch some sleep before his flight, hoping to catch him in his pajamas.

Byrd, who had spent a lot of money preparing Roosevelt Field's long runway for his own flight, gallantly offered the use of it to Lindbergh for nothing. While his rivals waited for better weather, Lindbergh, asking himself if he would take off to fly the mail in these conditions, answered yes, and trundled down the runway, slowly, slowly, gathering speed. The ton of fuel around him weighed nearly as much as the aircraft itself. With very little to spare, he cleared the telegraph wires just beyond the runway's end and banked gingerly away to the northeast in a heavy rainstorm.

For most of the next thirty-six hours he needed all his skill and courage to keep his plane in the air, as he fought a struggle with tiredness that amounted to hand-to-hand combat with death. He had enjoyed no sleep the night before takeoff. It was an already tired man who took to the air. Fortunately, the *Spirit of St. Louis* was not a stable aircraft. The moment

Lindbergh's attention wandered, so did his plane, shaking him awake. Eventually he fell asleep with his eyes open, waking up again and again, and hallucinating.[6]

Thousands had seen Lindbergh take off. Newspapers and radio covered the flight more energetically than any event before. Every radio bulletin sent people scurrying to buy newspapers, which carried the details. And every flash extra sent them back to their radios for more up-to-date news.[7] The entire Western world seemed suspended—and unified— by a tiny airplane somewhere over the Atlantic. For an entire generation the most memorable day in their lives was the day they heard that Lindbergh had crossed the coast of France.*

By now he was alert; his tiredness suddenly vanished. He had so much fuel remaining he was tempted to pass over Paris, waggle his wings, and fly on to Rome. He circled the Eiffel Tower instead, took his bearings, and landed at Le Bourget. As he taxied to a halt, more than 100,000 people poured across the field, screaming deliriously, "Leen-bearg! Leen-bearg!" And all he had hoped for was an airport manager who might speak a few words of English, a quiet night, and a place to park his airplane.

There had never been a triumph like it. There has not been one since. The idea got around that he did not cash in on his fame. The unglamorous truth is that he did, at about $6,000 a testimonial, such as "I was able to carry very few things in my *Spirit of St. Louis* but I took special care not to forget my Waterman pen. . . ." He cashed in, without being obvious or tasteless about it, choosing carefully and demanding a high price.[8] No matter. He became for one dazzling historic instant the screen on which an entire nation projected its deepest wishes—for youth, for daring, for vision, for purity, for a spirit that could contain in harmony the simpler, old world and the complex, mechanical new one. He seemed to stand for all that was best in both what had been and in what the future held.

A cruiser brought Lindbergh and his aircraft home. As the *Memphis* steamed up the Potomac to band music, Lindbergh received the honor that had until now been reserved exclusively for heads of state—a twenty-one-gun salute. Coolidge received him in a ceremony of great national rejoicing. In New York, he received a welcome that outdid the armistice celebrations. As he rode in triumph through the packed canyons of New York, the ticker tape that swirled around him recorded stock prices at record levels.

---

* Robert Benchley sent a telegram to a friend in Paris: HAS LINDBERGH ARRIVED YET? HE LEFT HERE A WEEK AGO. The friend replied: DO YOU MEAN GEORGE LINDBERGH?

II

The summer of 1927 brought the nadir of Harding's reputation. The previous year Samuel Hopkins Adams's novel, *Revelry*, a thinly disguised account of a weak and womanizing president, had created a tremendous fuss. Adams's President Markham filled his Administration with crooked friends, got drunk regularly, and rather than face the unearthing of scandal, committed suicide. It was little more than pulp fiction, but it was eagerly read and probably believed. More devastating still, however, was a volume published almost in secret in June 1927 under the innocuous title *The President's Daughter*. Its author, Nan Britton, claimed to have been Harding's mistress; the proceeds of the book were to go to the Elizabeth Ann Guild—that is, to a little blonde girl named Elizabeth Ann, Miss Britton's child by Harding. No one reviewed the book. No reputable bookstore would carry it. At least, they would not carry it openly. "They kept it under the counter as if it were a collection of French postcards."[9] It never appeared on a list of best-sellers, yet probably sold close to 100,000 copies.

Miss Britton could produce little evidence to support her claims. She had none of the many letters she maintained that Harding had written. There was no provision for her or her child in Harding's will. The trouble with her book was Harding. Had she claimed that she had been Coolidge's mistress, no one would have believed her. But Harding's reputation was such that she was believed even without evidence. By her own account, however, it was she who had pursued Harding, rather than Harding who had taken advantage of an overawed innocent. The world was treated to any number of revelations: the President would not pay more than $5 for a pair of shoes; would not eat eggs for breakfast; had not slept with Florence for years; always gave money to blind beggars. The book carried photographs of such gripping memorabilia as a drawing by Elizabeth Ann, one of Elizabeth Ann's second-grade spelling tests, and Warren G. Harding's wallet. It read remarkably like *Gentlemen Prefer Blondes*.*

Some of her claims, such as making love to Harding in a closet off the Oval Office, were almost certainly false.[10] And the course of true love was not always smooth. On one occasion the senator had to pay off the house dicks; on another he had to hide in a wardrobe. When Nan became

---

* She never referred to Harding as "Warren." Lorelei Lee dealt with this delicate point in regard to Gus Eisman, the Button King: "Dorothy and I had quite a little quarrel because . . . she does not seem to realize that when a gentleman who is as important as Mr. Eisman spends quite a lot of money educating a girl, it really does not show revarance to call a gentleman by his first name. I mean, I never think of calling Mr. Eisman by his first name."

pregnant he brought her some of "Dr. Humphrey's No. 11 Tablets."[11] She took them. She stayed pregnant. In October 1919 she gave birth to Elizabeth Ann in Asbury Park, New Jersey.

The President's Daughter appeared just after Charlie Forbes left Leavenworth after serving twenty-one months of a two-year sentence; and just after Thomas W. Miller, Harding's Alien Property Custodian, went off to prison for corruption. The Senate investigation of Daugherty back in 1924 had more or less by accident unearthed the late Jess Smith's greatest coup: inducing Colonel Miller, war hero and seeming incorruptible, to sell a German-owned metal company worth $7 million at an 80 percent discount to a group of American businessmen. Jess's fee for services rendered came to $224,000. The disposition of this money strongly suggested that some of it had passed through Daugherty's hands by being paid into a bank owned by his brother Mal. But there was something singular about all this—the bank had no record of who paid the money in or to whom it was later paid out. All the records concerning this transaction had been burned, Mal Daugherty testified. By whom? he was asked. By my brother, he replied. Harry Daugherty flatly refused to testify.

Miller was convicted. The jury was deadlocked over Harry Daugherty's guilt. The indictment was dropped. Miller went to prison. Daugherty went home to Ohio.

The Teapot Dome trials were still winding their casual way through the federal judiciary. In February 1927 the government had won its civil suit against Doheny. The courts decided that the Elk Hills lease had been obtained by fraud. The government did not, therefore, have to reimburse him for the $12 million naval oil depot he had built at Pearl Harbor.

None of the Harding scandals had the least effect on the Coolidge Administration after Coolidge won election in his own right. He hardly deigned to notice any of them. He continued to play a more active role abroad than at home. Harding had brought the Marines out of Nicaragua. Coolidge sent them back in.

The elected president of that country had resigned in 1926. His liberal vice-president, Juan Sacasa, freely elected with him, had assumed his office. But in 1927 the Nicaraguan Congress, under the control of businessmen and large landowners, elected a conservative, Adolfo Diaz, to be president, plunging the country into civil war. The United States backed Diaz, claiming it was preventing communism in Central America. Sacasa had the support of a liberal-minded general named Sandino, and the 5,000 Marines Coolidge dispatched to Nicaragua were resisted by the Sandinistas. Borah for once was thwarted by Coolidge. The senator raged, but he could not order the Marines to come home.

Coolidge was meanwhile beginning to nurse doubts about "Coolidge prosperity." Strange things were happening. The economy was faltering in 1927. In some areas and industries, it was turning down sharply. Yet, on Wall Street, stock prices were rising dramatically. The year before, stock prices had gone up by about 10 percent, more or less in line with the economy. But in 1927 that rate had doubled, and the economy was running out of steam. The big bull market had begun. And Coolidge did not like it.

Every utterance Coolidge made in praise of business has been quoted against him for fifty years. The vast majority of his speeches, however, were concerned with other matters—peace, internationalism, morality, individualism, public service. These are almost universally ignored. Coolidge, the supposed champion of business, never showed any inclination to go in for it, never showed any interest in making money, and invariably found discussions of business boring.[12] His attitude was that it was for business to make the country prosperous, and he would no more instruct businessmen how to do that than he would tell a surgeon how to operate. Excessive speculation, nevertheless, went against his Puritan grain. Excess in anything seemed both immoral and dangerous.

In the spring of 1927 Coolidge sent for Professor William Z. Ripley of Harvard. The professor had recently published a book, *Main Street and Wall Street*, that was creating a stir. Coolidge and Ripley spent almost an entire day in earnest discussion, with Ripley describing the "prestidigitation, double-shuffling, honey-fugling, hornswoggling and skulduggery" behind the big bull market. Coolidge, deeply troubled, finally asked: "Well, Mr. Ripley, is there anything that we can do down here?"

"No," said Ripley, "it's a state matter."[13] And that, to Coolidge, was that. It was for New York State to regulate the stock exchange. Yet in his heart he knew that every stock boom ended in a crash. So he nursed his doubts and kept his silence, knowing that one wrong step by the President could bring the rickety structure down.

By his own lights, however, he was a conscientious executive, and not a do-nothing President. He did not simply veto the McNary-Haugen Act but sent it back to Congress with a long, closely reasoned, and somewhat angry message. He took sufficient interest in Garvey's case to order his release after two years' imprisonment. He gave seventy to eighty major addresses every year, and poured about 9,000 words a month into radio microphones.[14] In terms of public utterances, he was twice as forthcoming as Wilson, who was known worldwide as a mighty man of words. Three days out of four Coolidge was addressing a group on some matter or another. And in his press conferences he spoke with reporters three times a week.

His manner was formal and somewhat reserved. For visitors whom he did not know and who had more or less invited themselves to his office— presumably to ask for something or put him under the microscope—he kept a chair that squeaked each time they shifted their weight. "It was a chair which was calculated to induce an inferiority complex in even the most brazen one hundred per cent American," reported one victim.[15] He was extraordinarily hospitable, having twice as many people stay at the White House as his three predecessors combined.[16] Grace Coolidge strolled the South Lawn with her pet raccoon, Rebecca, and exchanged greetings with the people passing by. In the winter, the Coolidges introduced carol singing on the north portico of the White House. The Coolidge White House was not a cold and lifeless place.

Coolidge spent his elected term in office, however, in silent grief. In 1924 his eldest son, Calvin, Jr., while playing tennis on the South Lawn, developed a blister on one of his toes. The blister turned septic; blood poisoning set in. The boy died, aged sixteen. "When he went the power and the glory of the Presidency went with him," said Coolidge.[17] He had never ceased to grieve for his mother, who had died when he was twelve. For the rest of his life, Coolidge grieved for his dead son. He would stand at the White House window that looked onto the tennis court and see the boy playing there still.[18]

In July 1927 Coolidge went west on vacation with a secret in his heart. He stopped off at Hammond, Indiana, to dedicate a war memorial. But his mind was still on the economy. He delivered a speech calling attention to the unskilled workers who were not enjoying the benefits of "Coolidge prosperity," while paper fortunes were being run up on Wall Street.

On vacation in the Black Hills of South Dakota he fished in white gloves. He did nothing but hold the rod. "Bait was put on for him and any fish he caught were likewise taken off the hook for him."[19] To avoid hurting people's feelings he made himself look even more foolish by donning Indian war bonnets and cowboy's chaps with CAL emblazoned on them in huge, glittering letters.

On August 2, the fourth anniversary of Coolidge's accession to the presidency, the thirty reporters assigned to cover the presidential vacation made their way through unseasonable cold and drizzle to the Rapid City High School for a press conference. Coolidge would meet them in the mathematics classroom. As they filed in, he told them, "The line forms on the right." As each man passed by him, Coolidge handed him a slip of paper, two inches wide. On it was typed: "I do not choose to run for

President in nineteen twenty-eight." There was no explanation; not a word. The reporters stared at their slips of paper, dumbfounded, then they rushed as one man for the doorway, jamming it, in a fierce struggle to reach a telephone.[20]

III

Following the conviction of Sacco and Vanzetti, the defense committee moved from Beacon Hill to 256 Hanover Street: "a third-floor garret anteroom leading into a small inner office,"[21] at the top of a narrow, buckled staircase. Fred Moore dedicated himself to raising money, persuading prosecution witnesses to recant their testimony, and to keeping the cause alive. But his freebooting, free-spending ways angered Felicani, Sacco, and Vanzetti. Moore broke away in 1924, setting up a Sacco and Vanzetti New Trial Committee, which the two convicted men would have nothing to do with. It was as though Sacco and Vanzetti were the dispensable element in Moore's campaign. But so long as it kept going, it kept Moore solvent. Sacco's last letter to Moore concluded, "Your implacable enemy, now and forever, Nick Sacco."[22]

William G. Thompson took over the defense, and the McAnarney brothers were at last able to withdraw. Thompson was one of the most imposing members of the Boston bar, Harvard-educated, welcome in all the best houses, conservative, old money, upper class. Vanzetti instinctively disliked him. Sacco would accept almost anyone after Moore. At first, Thompson was cool and formal in his relations with his new clients. But within a year he had become so convinced of their innocence that his entire practice was taken up with the challenge of saving these two anarchists' lives. He won their trust completely. "Ha! To have known you 6 years ago!" wrote Vanzetti. "I would never have been a convict."[23]

Sacco and Vanzetti refused to seek a pardon or mercy. They wanted a new trial. While Thompson tried to secure one, they stayed in jail: Vanzetti in Charleston, serving his first sentence; Sacco in Dedham, on the murder conviction. With a wife and two children to brood on, Sacco's nerves frayed, then broke. When he was finally given work in the prison shoeshop the once-skilled shoe trimmer proved so accident-prone he had to be restored to forced idleness. He beat his head against the furniture in his cell, crying out, "I am innocent! There is no justice!" Four men were needed to hold him back from crushing his skull. He longed to die. He was removed to the Bridgewater Hospital for the Criminally Insane for six months, until he regained his self-control.

Vanzetti occupied his time by engaging in a vast correspondence (largely with women), learning English, reading voraciously, talking to other prisoners, and making license plates. In some ways, Vanzetti seemed to thrive in prison; it was both school and pulpit. At the end of 1924, however, Thompson's motion for a new trial was denied. Vanzetti had always been prey to bouts of depression. He now plunged into paranoid fantasies, barricading his cell door against imaginary assassins, smashing his cell furniture, raving that the air in his cell was filled with electricity that was burning him up. In January 1925 he was taken to Bridgewater asylum, where he remained for four months.

While he was there, the Dedham jail received an epileptic, half-blind prisoner named Celestino Madeiros, twenty-two, convicted of killing a cashier during a bank robbery. For several months Madeiros was held in a cell next to Sacco's. Suspicious of all the prisoners in adjoining cells being police spies, Sacco paid no attention to Madeiros. In time, Madeiros was moved to another cell. One afternoon in mid-November Madeiros handed a note to one of the jail trusties, asking him to give it to Sacco. The trusty took the note to the floor above, where Sacco was held, and passed a convict who had a magazine he wanted Sacco to have. The note was slipped into the magazine, and the magazine handed to Sacco. A short while later the trusty passed the cell. Sacco was leaning against the wall, crying. In one hand was the note. "What is this?" he asked the trusty, shaking the note in his trembling hand. "Can't you read English?" the trusty replied. But Sacco understood what the note said. It was a confession by Madeiros, saying that he had been part of the gang at the South Braintree robbery, and Sacco and Vanzetti were innocent.[24]

Madeiros's confession was less than the whole truth. His account of how he was recruited for the robbery by several men he met in a bar only the night before the crime, his claim that he could not remember any of their names, his inability to describe what they looked like, and his statement that he never saw any of them again after the payroll money was divided prompted disbelief. Yet the rest of the confession, concerning the robbery and the getaway, is coherent and credible. Madeiros was trying to get Sacco and Vanzetti off the hook without impaling the real gang on it.

He told just enough, however, for one of Thompson's staff to track them down. The gang worked out of Providence, Rhode Island, and was headed by Frank Morelli. Madeiros had said, for instance, that the gang had been looting freight cars of shoes and textiles before the payroll robbery. When the Morelli gang was investigated, it turned out that in 1920 they were facing nine federal indictments for stealing from railroad cars. Five of the thefts occurred at South Braintree station, consisting of shoes made at the two factories in front of which the payroll guards were shot.

One of the gang members in 1920 was seen driving a Buick that matched exactly the description of the getaway car. It also turned out that this lead had been dropped in Moore's lap in 1923. A Dane named Emil Moller was then sharing an Atlanta penitentiary cell with Frank Morelli. After lights out, Morelli would brag about his crimes, and one of his proudest achievements was the South Braintree robbery, for which two innocent men were taking the rap. Wasn't *that* a clean getaway![25] Moller wrote a letter and addressed it to "The Sacco-Vanzetti Case, Boston, Massachusetts." It was delivered to Moore. But nothing came of it. Moore dismissed Moller's story as hearsay. There was one other remarkable element in the Madeiros confession and the trail it led to Frank Morelli: Sacco and Morelli could have passed for twins. Prosecution and defense witnesses shown photographs of Morelli at once identified them as being photographs of Sacco.[26]

As Felix Frankfurter summarized these developments in an exhaustive review of the evidence, "The Morelli theory accounts for all members of the Braintree murder gang; the Sacco and Vanzetti theory for only two. . . . The Morelli theory accounts for all the bullets found in the dead men; the Sacco and Vanzetti theory for only one. The Morelli explanation settles the motive . . . whereas the Sacco and Vanzetti theory is unsupported by any motive."[27] A motion for a new trial was once again presented, based on the Madeiros confession, new evidence developed by investigation of the confession, and on a claim that the trial judge had been prejudiced. And who was the judge assigned to rule on this motion? None other than Thayer himself. He examined the record and boldly exonerated the trial judge of prejudice. Motion denied. An execution date was finally set, for July 10, 1927.

Vanzetti was brought to Dedham jail, under the same roof at last with Sacco, for whom imprisonment was death without dying. He would go gladly to the electric chair, for only then would his wife's suffering cease. Sacco took no more interest in his defense. Vanzetti remained full of fight. What had begun as an obscure criminal case in a small American town had become by the spring of 1927 an international cause célèbre. Nothing had so divided American opinion since slavery.

The pressure on Alvan T. Fuller, the governor of Massachusetts, to do something was irresistible. Fuller, a Packard dealer, was the richest man in the state, worth an estimated $40 million. A caricature parvenu, he wore a gold signet ring with a Fuller crest unearthed by mail order. During his four years in Congress, he had not shown himself a man able to keep his head when other men were losing theirs. When the Red Scare was at its height in November 1919, Congressman Fuller's solution, he informed the House of Representatives, was "the execution of the whole red scum brood of anarchists, Bolsheviks, IWWs and revolutionaries."[28] As the crisis rolled down upon him in 1927, he wanted to do the right thing—and be seen to do it. The Republican nominating convention was only a year away. A governor of Massachusetts might set his sights realistically on the vice-presidential nomination.

Fuller interviewed Sacco and Vanzetti, talked to the witnesses, the jurors, and the lawyers on both sides. The more he considered it, the more complicated it was. He decided to do as many have done when similarly perplexed: he would create a committee. He chose the president of Harvard, A. Lawrence Lowell; the president of MIT, Samuel W. Stratton; and a former probate judge, Robert A. Grant. The Sacco and Vanzetti Defense Committee was overjoyed. Yet Lowell was one of the luminaries on the Immigration Restriction League; Stratton had no training in the law and, appointed on Lowell's recommendation, was expected to follow Lowell's lead; and Grant, with no experience in criminal law, had given it as his considered opinion that the Italians were a nation of thieves.[29] The execution date was changed to August 10 to allow the Governor's Advisory Committee time to hold its hearings and report back to Fuller.

Dedham jail was small and relaxed, bright with fresh paint and polished brass. It reflected the penological ideas of Sanford Bates. The warden knew his sixty to seventy prisoners by name and treated each as an individual. With its tidy lawn and curving driveway, Dedham jail resembled a slightly careworn private school. In a reception room with oak benches and shelves filled with books, Sacco and Vanzetti received a steady stream of visitors without bars or screens to intervene and no guards to eavesdrop on their conversation. They sat there on hard plain chairs, Vanzetti expansive and fluent, Sacco quiet and pessimistic. Vanzetti was proud to show off the results of his daily exercises, a symbolic rebuke to the waiting electric chair. Like a growing adolescent, he would flex his biceps, as if through his strength he could cling to life.[30]

On June 30, with the Governor's Advisory Committee about to open its hearings, they were moved to Charleston prison, where Massachusetts maintained its death row. Almost from the first day of the hearings it was obvious that the committee saw its role as defending the prosecution's case. Thompson wanted to withdraw from what was a sham. Frankfurter convinced him that it was too late—withdrawal now would be interpreted as lack of confidence in the innocence of Sacco and Vanzetti. But they were free to show what they thought of the committee's fairness: they went on a hunger strike.

The Governor's Advisory Committee held secret hearings from which the defense lawyers were excluded; insinuated that three of Sacco's alibi witnesses had perjured themselves (only to have this attempt blow up in their faces); and accepted as reliable "in this case" the identification testimony of a woman the prosecution had not dared to put on the stand because of her evident mental instability. The committee charitably called her "eccentric." It completed its work by publishing a censored, truncated transcript, clumsily edited to cover up its mistakes.[31] Fuller was given carte blanche to let the execution go ahead.

As August 10 neared, protestors began arriving in Boston from other cities. They could find no one who would rent them a hall to hold their meetings. On August 10 Sacco and Vanzetti prepared to die at midnight. At 11:23 P.M. Fuller stayed execution for another twelve days so that the blizzard of writs and motions before various state and federal courts could be settled. Coolidge in the Black Hills was bombarded with telegrams. There came no reply.

Back in 1920 the Communist party had refused to have any part in the Sacco and Vanzetti defense. As they moved toward the electric chair, proclaiming that they were about to die as martyrs of the proletariat,[32] the Communists began to take an interest. In 1926 the party's legal branch, the International Labor Defense, offered its full support for the Sacco and Vanzetti Defense Committee. In 1927 it organized protest demonstrations around the world against the pending execution. The ILD sent Fred Beal to Boston to supervise its campaign there—the same Fred Beal mentioned earlier (see chapter 1).

American intellectuals, galvanized largely by the *New Republic* and *Nation*, were for the first time ever drawn in large numbers into organized protestations. Boston's police stations steadily filled up with singing, chanting protestors, most of them neatly dressed and well-spoken.

When Monday, August 22, dawned, Boston was like a city under siege. Every public building was under armed guard. Police and militiamen appeared in force on nearly every street. The tension in the city rose with every hour. Thousands of people gathered on the Common, arguing heatedly. Busloads of workers rolled into the city from New York, bearing huge signs that read SACCO AND VANZETTI MUST NOT DIE! and festooned with red streamers.[33]

As evening fell, Fred Beal tried to lead a march on Charleston prison, unaware that all the streets within half a mile of the prison were cordoned off. A charge of mounted police broke up the march. At midnight Beal was in a police station cell, bleeding from a lip split open by a truncheon blow. In Charleston prison, Madeiros was on his way to the electric chair. His execution had been postponed in case Sacco and Vanzetti were retried and his testimony about the robbery was needed. But he need tarry no longer. When they were set down to die, so was he.

Madeiros went to the chair calmly, saying nothing. In death as in life, Sacco went before Vanzetti. He was weak as the result of his long fast, but walked unaided. In the chair, he cried out "Long live anarchy!" He bade farewell to his wife and children and died with "Farewell *mia madre*" on his lips. Vanzetti died last, calmly stating again that he was innocent. His last words were of forgiveness.[34] At 256 Hanover Street the telephone rang twice—the prearranged signal that the executions had been carried out. "There was a terrible scene then," said an eyewitness, "as these comrades and friends of Sacco and Vanzetti shouted and cried and threw themselves on the floor."[35]

The funeral march five days later covered eight miles, from Scollay Square to Forest Hills; a blaze of crimson wreaths and open cars banked with scarlet flowers on a cold, wet day in August when dead leaves fell from still green trees. Along the route of march drummed the hoofs of police horses, as lines of mounted policemen in black raincoats and shiny hats rode by. The marchers, some 50,000 strong, wearing red armbands, followed the cortège in step. It might have been the burial procession of a king.

When the police saw this spectacle unfold before them, they became enraged. They rode in fury down upon the marchers, scattering them. Roadblocks were thrown up along the route of march. Traffic was diverted into it. Very few mourners reached the cemetery gates. And there, they were turned aside.[36]

IV

Dempsey defeated was more popular than Dempsey victorious. The more sportswriters and boxing fans saw of Tunney, who treated them with disdain, the more they liked the plain, unvarnished Dempsey, who would not be seen dead with a book of poetry in his fist. "I goaded and gloated," Tunney admitted. "I richly deserved what I got."[37]

Dempsey set out to regain his title. He never trained harder. He, who had chosen his opponents with care, earned the rematch he could have had by right and fought the number one contender, Jack Sharkey, first. Sharkey looked like the Dempsey of 1919. He had never lost a fight. He hit with devastating power. He was utterly fearless. And he was five years younger than Dempsey. He entered the ring a 2–1 favorite.

By the end of the first round he had stunned Dempsey with a left hook that split the former champion's lower lip and sent blood flowing down his chest. In the third he cut Dempsey over the left eye. Sharkey took the first four rounds. The next two rounds were even. In the seventh, Sharkey made a mistake.

Dempsey liked to test an opponent with a punch to the testicles, to see what kind of man he was up against. According to the boxing editor of the New York Times, James P. Dawson, who was in a perfect position to look up and see what was happening, Dempsey tested Sharkey four times.[38] Sharkey turned to protest to the referee. That was his only mistake in the fight. He did not get to make another. The moment he took his eyes off Dempsey he was knocked out by a left hook that might have stunned an ox. Sharkey fell to the canvas clutching his shorts.

Interest in the rematch with Tunney now rose to such a fever pitch that the fight set for Soldier Field in Chicago on September 22, 1927, became an event of national importance. Rickard managed to wedge 150,000 people into a stadium built for 100,000. More than half the people at the second Dempsey-Tunney fight would see hardly anything of it. No matter. Being there was all that counted. The gate receipts came to $2,658,000 (more than $8,000,000 in 1982 prices). A decade earlier, the record gate had stood at $200,000. There had been only five million-dollar fights. Dempsey fought in all of them, Rickard promoted all of them:* Carpentier, Firpo, Sharkey, and Tunney twice.

And the Firpo fight was to haunt Dempsey still. In that fight, he refused to go to a neutral corner each time he knocked Firpo down. In the school where Dempsey learned to box, you hovered over a fallen man, staying slightly behind him, where he could not see you clearly. Then, as he rose, you could smash him half a dozen times before he was ready to defend himself. Tunney's handlers laid down strict conditions on this point. The referee could not begin the count until the fighter who had knocked his opponent down retired to a neutral corner. It seemed pretty academic. Tunney had never been knocked down.

From the opening bell on the night of September 22, Dempsey fought a better fight than he had at Philadelphia. Tunney fought as coolly as ever. Dempsey hit him in the testicles, as he had done at Philadelphia. As before, Tunney kept his temper, and kept his eye on Dempsey. By the seventh round, Tunney had only a slight lead. Then Dempsey knocked him down. He stood over Tunney, panting. "I couldn't move," he later told a friend. "I just couldn't. I wanted him to get up. I wanted to kill the son of a bitch."[39] The referee pushed Dempsey toward a neutral corner.

---

* Between 1927 and 1961 there were to be only four million-dollar fights. Not until the advent of Muhammed Ali would there be a fighter as colorful as Dempsey.

It was five or six seconds before he began to count. When he called, "eight," Tunney stood up.[40]

Dempsey charged in. Tunney parried a looping left, circled Dempsey, and staggered him with a blow to the temple. To Dempsey's fury, Tunney spent the next two minutes backpedaling, instead of slugging it out. Dempsey at thirty-one could not move forward as fast as Tunney moved backward. At the end of the round, however, Tunney stood his ground. As Dempsey bore in, Tunney hit him with a straight right to the heart. It was the hardest blow Dempsey had ever taken in a fight. He said later, "I thought I was going to die."[41] Tunney took the next eight rounds and kept his title.

Tunney's share of the gate worked out at $990,445. He made up the difference so that Rickard could give him a paycheck for $1,000,000. As for Dempsey, he never complained about the long count. Where he came from, you did not crow when you won, you did not whine when you lost. He retired from the ring to save his eyes from further damage. He left it adored, the last of the old frontier brawlers, the first of the fighting millionaires.

V

The best thing about American movies was their beauty. With very rare exceptions, they kept one eye on the Hays Office and another on the dime novels which had flourished since the turn of the century. Good always triumphed over evil. Seducers of young girls always paid heavily for their pleasure. Crooked businessmen were invariably ruined in the last reel. A happy marriage could be secured only by the wedding of two virgins. Sex outside marriage had to lead to disaster. Adultery ditto, in spades. Money was not important. Character was.

This romantic nonsense was beginning to wear thin by the late 1920s.[42] Audiences were ready for something new. There was a feeling among a few moviemakers that what they were ready for was sound.

Edison had synchronized sound and film back in 1894. Lee De Forest had put sound waves directly onto the margin of film strip in 1921, and in 1924 made several electioneering talkies for Coolidge's campaign. Griffith, too, had experimented with a sound version of *Dream Street*. But no one seemed to like it, so the film was released as a silent. To rush into sound might drive people out of the movie theaters, reasoned the always nervous moguls of Hollywood. The Big Five (MGM, Universal, Paramount, First National, and Producers' Distributing Corporation) made a pact: no one would make a sound movie unless they all made sound movies. Which seemed to stop the idea dead.

William Fox, however, had fallen in love with sound. Fox was one of the biggest movie theater operators in the world. Two young engineers named Theodore Case and Earl Sponable put on a demonstration for him of a sound system they had developed. On the screen, a canary trilled its heart out. The theater filled with clear, high notes. Fox could hardly believe his ears. He searched the projection booth for a hidden canary or skulking bird whistler. Fox gave Case and Sponable his backing for their system and named it Movietone.

The Warner Brothers studio, meanwhile, was working on another system, called Vitaphone. In 1926 they released a sound film called *Don Juan*. It sank like a stone. A few musical shorts were released, but they seemed more an extension of the record business than a new departure for the movies.

The enthusiastic Fox was nevertheless converting all his theaters to sound. He was a born gambler, determined to win big or lose spectacularly. All he could use his sound system for was his Movietone newsreels, which were little more than fillers between the feature films. And then, at the end of May 1927, he sprang a sensation: a film of Lindbergh taking off for Paris, and the *Spirit of St. Louis*'s engine roared into life, filling the darkened theaters with its powerful drumming as the tiny aircraft thundered down Roosevelt Field and into the air. Audiences gasped and cheered. In a hundred feet of film Fox had put drama and reality into sound movies.[43]

Warner Brothers already had in production a full-length sound movie based on a Broadway play, *The Jazz Singer*. The star of the play was George Jessel, who held out for more money than Warners considered him worth.* The part went instead to Al Jolson, who was not exactly cheap but was so famous that he could make the movie a success all by himself. Which to Jolson was the way it ought to be.

His ego was in a class of its own in a profession where egotism flourished. He would stop the orchestra in the middle of a show, advance to the footlights, and ask the audience whom they had really bought tickets to see. When they cried out, "Al! Al! Al!" he would order the rest of the cast to get off the stage. He would continue to perform, alone, until well past the show's advertised running time.[44] His way of following a big-name act was to come on stage and announce, "You ain't heard nothin' yet." He even dared to introduce himself this way the night he had to follow Caruso (who thought this was hilarious and could be heard laughing in

---

* The oft-told, widely believed story that Warner Brothers were on the brink of bankruptcy and risked their all on *The Jazz Singer* is just that, a story. So long as they were backed by Goldman, Sachs they were never in danger of folding.

the wings).[45] Jolson modestly billed himself "The World's Greatest Entertainer."

The plot of *The Jazz Singer* was so treacly that audiences risked death by gagging. The son of a cantor joins a theatrical troupe as a black-faced singer-comedian, to the dismay of his father, who considers this the waste of a great gift from God, his son's marvelous voice. The parents grieve for their errant son. The son becomes rich and famous. The father dies. The son sees his tinsel existence for what it is. In the last reel he is seen singing Israel's woes before the Sopher Torah in his father's synagogue. On October 6, 1927, *The Jazz Singer* had its New York premiere. It attracted more interest than any other film since Griffith's *Birth of a Nation* more than a decade before.

Although it was billed as the first all-singing, all-talking, full-length feature film, *The Jazz Singer* contained titles linking the episodes.* In production, Jolson was expected only to sing. But in the true Jolson style, he did what he wanted, which was to steal the film. Audiences expected him to say at some point, "You ain't heard nothin' yet," which he did just as if it were a live show. What the script did not call for and Jolson added was an outburst of ad-libbing with Eugenie Bessemer, who played the mother. For the first time the screen offered dialogue that built up to an emotional crescendo. As a work of art, it was rubbish. As a movie, it was a triumph.

And so throughout the fall of 1927 long lines formed wherever it was shown; lines of witnesses to a revolution. There was no doubt about it. The movies had been born again.

VI

On the roads of 1927 there were more Model Ts than all the other cars combined. And the buyer got more than transportation. "Its motor power, transmitted by simple attachments while the rear wheels were propped on jacks, filled silos, operated portable sawmills, and ran feed-cutters, grinders, churns, and small power tools."[46] Yet the Chevrolet would soon overtake the Model T.

General Motors was not trying to undersell Ford. That would have been the perfect formula for going broke. The Model T of 1908 had sold for $845; the Model T of 1927 was $290 f.o.b. Detroit. No one else could even make a car for less than $300. What GM offered was a lot more car for only an extra $80 to $90. The Chevrolet included, for example, a self-

---

* Ironically, there was, in *The Jazz Singer*, no jazz: not a bar.

starter—no more standing in the cold and the rain cranking and cursing. And Ford played into Chevrolet's hands. GM's policy of an annual model change was a promise of yearly improvements. Ford's policy was to promise more of what already existed. He was also in competition from an unexpected source—the used car dealer. For virtually a generation the first car was a Model T, bought from Ford. Now it was a used Model T, bought from someone else. A decent used car, without excessive mileage, could be found for $100 or so. Even Ford could not undersell that.

Increasingly, the country grew disenchanted with the car that had done more than any other machine to shape its manners, its morals, its cities, its farms, its work habits, its buying habits, and its prosperity. It suddenly seemed hopelessly out-of-date. What modern driver, curious to know how much fuel remained in his gas tank, wanted to be obliged to bend under the front seat, where the tank was located, and poke about with a stick or a screwdriver? The lights worked off a magneto, which made them glow or fade depending on the engine speed. "On stormy nights in strange places, Ford drivers were fed up with the maneuver of coming to a dead stop and racing their engines in order to see what lay ahead."[47]

By the time the Model T's race was run, so was that of Ford the innovator. He was surrounded these days with courtiers, private detectives, and public relations men. The man on the shop floor now who thought he had a better idea on how to make cars was advised to keep it to himself and just do as he was told.

To the despair of his dealers, Ford resisted installment sales. As early as 1919 Durant had seen that the automobile industry could not grow very large on a cash-on-delivery policy. He created the General Motors Acceptance Corporation to provide billions of dollars in credit.[48] One reason Ford was so passionate about reducing the price of the Model T was his puritan's dread of anything involving debt.

In 1926 Ford's total sales dropped from the 2 million a year level, where they had remained for three years, to 1.6 million units. Tractor and truck sales remained high. But the Model T was falling spectacularly. Scores of Ford dealers facing collapse went over to GM and began selling Chevrolets. Two or three more years like this and Ford would be ruined.

In May 1927 he simply shut down the Model T line. He and Edsel climbed into the last one, numbered 15,007,003, as it came off the assembly line and drove home to Dearborn in the cold and rain.

His plants laid off 40,000 workers while a new car was designed and the lines changed over to produce it. Unemployment in Detroit rose by more than 60,000. A lot of people not employed directly by Ford depended on the wages paid to Ford workers. It was a changeover without advance planning. Yet public confidence in Ford stood so high that half a million models of the new car were ordered sight unseen, price unknown.

In August the prototype of the Model A was ready. At GM, Sloan had built up a research department and a test track. Ford had no research department and the nearest road was his test track. He stepped up to the prototype, declared, "Somebody must represent the public,"[49] climbed in, and drove off at high speed, heading for a field littered with rocks and fallen timber to see how the new car held up.

During the evening of November 30, 1927, crowds began to assemble outside the New York Ford showroom on Broadway. They waited patiently throughout the night to see the Model A at its debut on the morning of December 1. When the throngs proved too great to handle at the showroom, the car was put on display at Madison Square Garden. In Kansas City, the crowds were so vast that the car could not be seen until platforms were built for it in Convention Hall. The masses gazed up from below in awe, as if it were a deity. In Cleveland, the crowds spilling into the streets around the showrooms were so great that mounted police had to be sent to control them. And so it went, in city after city, at the end of that feverish year.

PART III

BELSHAZZAR'S FEAST

18. Hail to the Chief

I

Orphaned at an early age, shuttled back and forth among a variety of relatives, Herbert Hoover had grown up with a determination to be independent that matched in fervor the faith of the Christian martyrs and the single-mindedness of the Conquistadors. He possessed no great natural gifts. When he applied to Stanford at the age of seventeen, he failed the English part of the entrance examination and was admitted mainly because he did well on the mathematics paper. Throughout his life he remained more at ease with figures than with words. He enjoyed no academic distinction. Stanford at the turn of the century was not as demanding as it is now. Yet Hoover, one of its most diligent students, never received an A in his four years there. He had to distinguish himself in other ways. He became a student leader by bringing order to the normal chaos of student finances and by improving the administration of student affairs.

During vacations, he went to work for the Geological Survey with a mule, a knife, and a blanket in which he slept in the wilds through all weathers. When he graduated, the only job he could find, despite his engineering degree, was pushing ore cars in a Nevada silver mine. There may have been nights when, aching in every part of his body, listening to the drunken brawls and shooting sprees in the streets of a frontier town, Hoover wondered about his chosen career as a mining engineer. Yet he had joined the right profession at the right time. The demand for cheap metals and fossil fuels became voracious as the machine age reached maturity. Engineering was the fastest growing profession in the United States. There were only 10,000 professional engineers when Hoover entered Stanford in 1891; there were nearly 250,000 by the late 1920s. They were drawn mainly from the skilled working class and from family farms. Hoover was typical of the breed—democratic and humane in his sympathies, repelled by political radicalism, skeptical of social panaceas.

Hoover rose rapidly in his chosen profession. He showed a gift for reorganizing production methods so that a losing mine could on occasion be made profitable. And if he could not make it profitable, he wasted no time closing it down. He avoided get-rich-quick ventures in gold and diamonds, preferring the more useful business of extracting low-grade ores such as zinc and coal.[1] It was an adventurous life, nevertheless, taking him to wild, remote parts of the world—to China, to Australia, to Malaya. Mining engineers were then the glamorous figures in an otherwise unglamorous profession.* And by 1914, when Hoover reached his fortieth birthday, he had become a multimillionaire. He became famous as the man who repatriated stranded Americans from Europe when the war broke out, and he cemented his fame as the man who staunched famine in Belgium.

His greatest success, however, was in his role as food administrator after the United States entered the war. "Managing the army or navy or the shipyards gives you excellent chances for trouble with soldiers or sailors or labor unions," wrote Vernon Kellogg in 1918. "But managing food gives you the supreme opportunity for trouble with everybody."[2] Hoover could not have made a greater success. The entire country by the time of the armistice knew that " 'to Hooverize' meant to economize, to save and share."[3] He had also come to typify something new in American life: the businessman who rises to the top of his profession, then devotes the rest of his life to public service. It was something neither the Founding Fathers nor the Robber Barons would ever have understood. In effect, Hoover entered government service not to become richer, nor to protect the possessions of his rich friends, but to start a new career.

The greatest prize of all might possibly have come his way very quickly had he not ruined his political chances by announcing in March 1920, "I am an independent progressive. . . . I still object as much to the reactionary group in the Republican Party as I do to the radical group in the Democratic Party."[4] Having managed to alienate the guiding lights of

---

* The brave, resourceful hero of John Buchan's most famous thriller, *The 39 Steps*, was Richard Hannay, a mining engineer. Around 1920 this amounted to typecasting.

both major parties with a single utterance, he had taken himself out of the 1920 nomination stakes, possibly without realizing that he had done so.

But he was well content to be made secretary of commerce, and in his new career he retained an emotive link with his dazzling past. The man in charge of any major mining operation was invariably known to everyone on the site as "the Chief." When Hoover left the mines for public service he brought with him a score of former associates. To them, he was now, as he had always been, the Chief. The appellation stayed with him through all his years in Washington. So journalists were surprised when they went to meet this wonder at his painful, almost unbelievable shyness. His handshake was limp. Asked a question, he would deliver a terse, matter-of-fact reply, without any display of emotion in what he said or the way he said it. Most of the time he was speaking, he stared hard at his shoes. "The casual guest obtains only a hazy impression of his appearance," reported one bemused visitor.[5]

This shyness led Hoover to hire press aides, out of his own pocket, who were themselves well-respected journalists. They came to admire him, and long after they left his service to return to journalism they remained devoted to the Chief. It was only by so indirect a public relations strategy that Hoover could ever become the towering public figure that he was by 1928. To the Washington press corps, Hoover's shyness soon lost its importance. For in comparison with most of the politicians they had to deal with, Hoover shone like a good deed in a naughty world.[6] Yet Hoover disliked seeing his name in print. Odd as it may seem, it upset him to read paragraphs of praise. It was the work that mattered; never the man. Publicity was necessary for Belgian relief to succeed. Publicity was essential to the success of the Food Administration. He evidently believed that the Commerce Department would also need a fair wind of public support to reach its destination. So Hoover cultivated the press, while trying to keep his name out of it.

He built up a large press bureau, held frequent press conferences in his office, and generally made himself the best news source in Washington. He was informal, forthright, accessible. In pursuit of policy ends, he organized 250 national conferences on major social and economic issues. Every one of these meetings was conducted in a blaze of publicity. They were not held to generate new ideas. They were held to generate support for reform. It was here, in these conferences, that Hoover fondly believed the world could find an example of voluntary collective action to solve social problems. Government experts would provide encouragement and advice. But they exercised no control over these meetings; there would be no new tier of federal bureaucracy.

Hoover brought with him to the Commerce Department the internationalism nurtured by long residence abroad. He believed in the League, with its evident imperfections. Isolationism struck him as a brand of self-delusion. He was committed to disarmament and played an important behind-the-scenes role as unofficial adviser to Charles Evans Hughes at the Washington Naval Conference. Although the United States remained nominally isolationist, Hoover worked diligently at the Commerce Department to promote the exporting of American goods, money, and know-how.

His engineer's concern with waste and inefficiency found new scope. His first months as secretary of commerce brought a typical Hoover triumph. An investigation of housing revealed that there were sixty-six sizes of bricks. He was overjoyed when he talked the brick manufacturers into reducing this to forty-four.[7] His obsession with waste led to the creation of the Division of Simplified Practices within the Bureau of Standards. Between 1921 and 1928 the division held more than 1,200 conferences on the elimination of inefficiency in industrial production at every stage from design to distribution. "Unnecessary varieties of everything from the sizes of cans and bottles . . . to toilet paper, blackboards and all kinds of bolts, pipes and nuts were reduced in number."[8] To Hoover, the elimination of waste, the rejection of unnecessary duplication, meant lower production costs. This, in turn, meant a fairer, more just distribution of consumer goods—that is, a fairer, more just society. And through the Commerce Department's Division of Building and Housing he promoted the adoption of uniform building and zoning laws in nearly forty states. This meant better, safer family homes and, to Hoover's way of thinking, happier families.[9]

He turned his department into one of the most active agencies in the federal government. He gave the Bureau of the Census a lot more to do than count heads every ten years. He waged a stubborn, increasingly successful fight against foreign cartels in raw materials such as rubber, silk, and nitrates. He played a central role in the creation of the National Academy of Sciences. He took over much of the conservation work that would have been done by the Interior Department had it not been run by the profoundly anticonservationist Albert B. Fall. He devoted much of his energies to the promotion of two infant industries, aviation and radio.

His Quaker and Progressive background made this shy, seemingly aloof man remarkably sensitive to the plight of Indians, blacks, women, and children—all of them, for various reasons, vulnerable. Nor did he forget the jobless during the heady years of Coolidge prosperity. He consistently, and persistently, argued that the right way to fight an economic downturn was to maintain wage rates and to expand public works programs. He asked Congress to create a public works reserve fund of $3 billion. But not even congressional Progressives seemed able to grasp what Hoover was driving at. George Norris, who would have been canonized long since if democracies had saints, sneered, "We had better let God run (the economy) as in the past, and not take the power away from him and give it to Hoover."[10]

Hoover's role as the Great Humanitarian continued to flourish even in his Commerce Department years. When the Mississippi flood struck in the spring of 1927, more than a million people were made homeless. There was only one man whom the country could imagine taking charge of relief operations on this scale. It took two months for the crest of the flood to travel the thousand miles from Cairo to the Gulf. Once Hoover had set relief operations in motion, an army of relief workers toiled abreast of, sometimes ahead of, the crest.* Tent cities rose on hundreds of hilltops. Sawmills worked around the clock to make 1,000 crude wooden boats. An impromptu fleet was formed to rescue the stranded and evacuate the endangered. Admiral Hoover's pride was his collection of forty aging paddle steamers. He seemed to be everywhere at once, the various parts of his nature fulfilled. The shy and earnest Hoover was swept aside in the haste to get things done. It was a rejoicing Hoover who was caught by cameramen in Opelousas, Louisiana, "beaming over newborn triplets named Highwater, Flood and Inundation."[11]

II

Alfred Emanuel Smith stood only five feet, seven inches, but he was a sturdy figure, with a glowing pink face beneath his brown derby, expressive blue eyes, a self-assertive, voluble manner, expensive suits, and a habit of spitting on the carpet in between deep puffs on his corona.[12] Born into poverty, he had made his way up from the slums through a dozen menial jobs. He spent several years as a process server, hardly a promising occupation. But he stayed in favor as a young Tammany Hall activist and by the time he was thirty was rewarded with a seat in the New York legislature. He stayed honest. In 1916, however, Tammany gave him his reward by making him sheriff of New York, a sinecure worth $50,000 a year.[13] There was no law that said an honest politician had to stay poor.

---

* It was noted in chapter 14 that there were complaints of white relief workers discriminating against the hundreds of thousands of black victims of the flood. When these were brought to Hoover's attention, he responded promptly and largely succeeded in halting such practices.

In 1918 he was elected governor of New York. At Albany, he made a reputation as a bold innovator, not least for his novel approach to patronage. Low-ranking appointments were filled in the time-honored fashion —they went to deserving Democrats. But the top jobs were actually dispensed on merit. This could not save him from the Republican landslide of 1920. But two years later, in November 1922, he was reelected governor, unseating the man who had unseated him.

He was moved by the right impulses, but was hardly a brilliant or resourceful politician. The routine work of administration bored him. Unlike other men similarly placed in state government, he made no complaints and diligently got on with it. He did not fritter away his time on poker, girls, moneymaking, or heroic drinking. Set against the standards of state government circa 1920, this was enough to make him a statesman. His achievements later seemed modest. At the time, they seemed magnificent. The true nature of his success, however, was obvious to at least two of his admirers: "In Albany, as in New York, he was building up a following that rested on his personality."[14] Al Smith was congenial, straightforward, unassuming, a wonderful teller of jokes, a man you would enjoy having a drink with.

He had returned to Albany with the largest plurality any governor had ever won in the history of New York. He was beyond any doubt the people's choice, and no longer a machinemade man. He secured repeal of the Lusk Laws. He encouraged the legislature to repeal New York's Baby Volstead Act, and after a brief crisis of nerves over signing the repeal legislation, put his name to it. He attempted to introduce legislation that would set minimum wages and maximum hours for the employment of women and children; to control rents and promote low-cost housing; and to ban injunctions in labor disputes. Such legislation was already in force in Wisconsin, where La Follette held sway. But an outcry went up in New York that this kind of thing was socialism and might even be communism. It was actually overdue. And it was far more important for New York, fast becoming an urban and industrial state, to adopt such legislation than for an agricultural state such as Wisconsin to do so. He got very little of the legislation he asked for. By taking this stand he nevertheless spoke for urban America against the rural and agricultural interests which had dominated state government since the founding of the Republic.

His most important achievement was his reorganization of New York's state government. Back in 1919 he had appointed a Reconstruction Committee to oversee demobilization. It busied itself with the problems posed by converting men and institutions, businesses and veterans to peacetime pursuits, but it was also wise enough to take up the long-stand-

ing matters aggravated by the war, such as the shortage of housing, chaotic public transportation, rudimentary public health programs, and bad
industrial relations. The Reconstruction Committee proved so useful that
it was kept in business long after the armistice, and in 1923 Al Smith
invited it to reorganize New York's state government. In 1925 its recom-
mendations were accepted by constitutional amendment. Politicians in
other industrial states were impressed.

Al Smith's reputation for decisive action was one of his greatest assets
when, in 1924, he began to campaign for the Democratic nomination.
That same year, New York made the governorship a four-year post, and
Smith took solace in reelection. Yet the decisive governor of New York
depended heavily on a circle of advisers, of whom the closest, in every
respect, was Belle Moscowitz. The short, plump, motherly Mrs. Moscowitz could be found most days sitting in the governor's office, placidly
knitting, and from time to time, when a decision had to be made, Al Smith
would swivel around to ask, "What do you think, Mrs. M.?"[15] After swear-
ing that he would do this and do that to secure a child labor amendment
to the Constitution, he did nothing. He spoke out against the use of
injunctions in labor disputes, but never used his powers as governor to
discourage it. The commissioners he appointed to oversee public utilities
and public services might have been appointed by Mellon or Coolidge.
For these and other lapses, he was increasingly viewed with suspicion by
liberal Democrats as the 1928 election approached.[16]

He was regarded with suspicion elsewhere because of his lifelong
connection with Tammany Hall. Outside New York City, Tammany was
hated and feared. Nast's cartoons of half a century earlier, showing the
Tammany tiger mauling a young woman in a flimsy white chiton under
the approving beady eyes of a bloated Boss Tweed, had lost none of their
force. Few seemed aware that Tammany was a fraternal order, not limited
to Democrats. While it supported the Democratic party, it was not necessary to belong to Tammany to rise high in the party. Tammany's 50,000
members were simply foot soldiers who got out the vote on election day,
mainly in Manhattan. Tammany supported immigrants in a city of immigrants. It had opposed imprisonment for debt in a city filled with the poor.
It worked for the regulation of business. During Reconstruction it had
stood for reconciliation with the South. It opposed the grants of public
lands to the railroads. Tammany had played a vital role in the direct
election of senators and the establishment of the progressive income tax.
Tammany men had created Central Park, Riverside Drive, and the Brooklyn Bridge. It supported the City College of New York, the Metropolitan
Museum, and the five-cent subway fare.[17] It had made Al Smith great.

But for every vote it assured him in New York, it would almost certainly cost him two outside.

Someone who had risen high without joining Tammany Hall was Michael Hylan, since 1918 the mayor of New York. He was not noticeably bright or competent. That was tolerable, as far as Al Smith was concerned. But Hylan danced to the tune of William Randolph Hearst, and that was not. "Red" Mike was so much Hearst's puppet that to beat him was the next best thing to beating W.R. himself.*

Hylan, a onetime motorman on the elevated railroad, made his sole claim to the loyalty of city voters the proud boast that he had kept the subway fare at a nickel. This was a dangerous ploy, because the mayor had no more power over subway fares than the ducks in Central Park. If the voters ever discovered they had been tricked—and Al Smith intended to make sure they did so—Hylan could count on taking a knockout at the polls. Al Smith's chosen replacement for Hylan was a dapper little state legislator named James J. Walker, known to everyone as Jimmy. Walker's natural milieu was less city hall than a Broadway dressing room. As the lyricist of a hundred mediocre songs (a Cole Porter he was not) he was show biz dabbling in politics rather than politics out on the town. If he ever had a serious political thought in his life, there is no record extant. But in 1926 he easily defeated Hylan in the race for mayor.

The governor now reigned supreme throughout New York; city and state were his. He had no illusions about Walker's wayward lifestyle. His only illusion was that having put Walker's spat-clad feet on the straight and narrow path he could keep them there.

It was obvious by this time that Al Smith was so far ahead of every other potential Democratic nominee for 1928 that the question of his religion, long kept in the background, broke into open, public debate. Methodist Bishop Adna W. Leonard of Buffalo, president of the New York Anti-Saloon League, issued a sinister warning in August 1926: "No Governor can kiss the papal ring and get within gunshot of the White House."[18] From this moment on, Al Smith's Catholicism became an issue of the most intense public interest, long before he declared his candidacy for the nomination.

He kept his peace until the spring of 1927 when the *Atlantic* ran "An

---

* In 1919, dairy farmers and New York City milk retailers were in dispute. The result was a serious milk shortage in the city for more than two weeks. The worst of it was inevitably felt by the poor. The Hearst newspapers ran atrocity photographs of dying, skeletal infants purportedly on the Lower East Side, but almost certainly Armenian victims of Turkish genocide. The starvation that the photographs so vividly portrayed was blamed on Al Smith. It was an episode that made Smith, not by temperament a man given to hating, a lifelong enemy of Hearst.

Open Letter to the Honorable Alfred E. Smith." It was written by a corporation lawyer named Charles C. Marshall, and suggested politely that even a Catholic president would be burdened with "a dual allegiance." The governor was indeed as devout as Marshall assumed. He kept a picture of the pope on his office wall. When a group of cardinals visited New York he gladly knelt and kissed the papal legate's ring. But there had never been the least action in his political career that could be interpreted as showing favor to his church. Religion was one thing; politics another. And when it was pointed out to him that public demonstrations of his faith could hurt him politically, he was both puzzled and enraged.[19]

His advisers drafted a reply to Marshall, which appeared in the May issue of the *Atlantic* as "Catholic and Patriot: Governor Smith Replies." It argued that in faith and morals, every Catholic had a duty to obey the pope. But this was a personal matter. The pope had no more authority to advise him on politics than anyone else. He believed, the article concluded, in freedom of conscience, separation of church and state, and support for the public schools. Far from ending the dispute over Al Smith's religion, however, the exchange in the *Atlantic* brought the issue to the attention of the entire country. In effect, the 1928 election campaign had already begun.

III

In February 1928 the Senate by a vote of 56–26 approved an anti-third-term resolution, just in case Coolidge changed his mind. It was unnecessary. When the Republican convention met at Kansas City at the beginning of July, Coolidge sent his secretary, Everett Sanders, to make sure that no attempt was made to force the nomination on him.[20] It was doubly unnecessary, in fact, because Hoover was so plainly the convention's choice.

There was strong opposition within the Republican party hierarchy to Hoover's nomination. The rich, inflexible old guard suspected him of being a Democrat at heart. Had he not served under that man Wilson? Had he not favored membership in the League? He was pro-British, they grumbled, and called him "Sir Herbert." Hoover, meanwhile, did nothing to win the nomination beyond allowing his name to be entered in the primaries. His nomination really did come from the grass roots. He was especially popular with women voters on his reputation as a great humanitarian. When the first ballot was cast, Hoover collected 80 percent of the votes.

In his acceptance speech, at Stanford stadium on August 11, he reviewed the country's achievements since 1920: a 45 percent increase in national income, while population rose by 8 percent; 2.3 million new families, and 3.5 million new houses; a 66 percent rise in high school enrollment, a 75 percent rise in college enrollment. After spraying his audience with more figures than they could expect to comprehend as they sat sweating under a broiling sun, he summarized what the figures meant: "We in America today are nearer to the final triumph over poverty than ever before in the history of any land. The poorhouse is vanishing from among us. We have not yet reached the goal, but, given a chance to go forward with the policies of the last eight years, we shall soon with the help of God be in sight of the day when poverty will be banished from this nation."[21]

Hoover's entire campaign was to consist of seven such speeches. He delivered them head bent, as if in rapt contemplation of his navel, left hand in left trouser pocket, nervously jiggling his keys, right shoulder working up and down. His eyes never left the page as he read in his midwestern monotone a thousand words sweated out over many hours by Hoover alone. They invariably sounded more like official reports than emotional perorations.[22]

Al Smith enjoyed a similarly easy passage to the nomination. In September 1927 McAdoo announced that he would not be a candidate, which virtually assured the governor the nomination nine months in advance. To prepare the Democratic party for the impending struggle, he brought in one of his rich friends as party chairman, John J. Raskob, a vice-president of General Motors. In 1924 Raskob had voted for Coolidge, and admired him still.[23] But he was a Catholic, and that led him into the services of Al Smith. His origins were as humble as the governor's, his rise as dramatic. Raskob had begun in business as a stenographer and became Pierre S. du Pont's typist. He rapidly became Du Pont's closest adviser. When Du Pont became a major shareholder in General Motors in 1918, Raskob was installed as chairman of the all-powerful Finance Committee and with Durant created GMAC.

Since the disastrous 1920 election the Democratic party had virtually fallen apart, leaving only a pile of unpaid bills to mark its existence. It no longer had a national headquarters or a publication of its own. The Women's National Democratic Club had to save the party's archives from becoming a banquet for mice and stored them away in the club's attic.[24] One of Raskob's first actions on becoming party chairman in 1928 was to open a Democratic National Committee headquarters in the General Motors Building on Broadway.

Ironically, the enfeebled state of the party made it easier for Al Smith to win the nomination. There was no alternative candidate of proven ability. The convention was opened in Houston, and Franklin D. Roosevelt for the second time delivered his Happy Warrior nominating speech. Smith won the nomination on the first ballot. He was the choice of bosses and rank-and-file Democrats alike. Yet there was no attempt to make the nomination unanimous. Several southern states were sure to refuse. For his running mate, Smith was given Senator Joseph T. Robinson of Arkansas, probably the most obscure figure in the Senate, but from Arkansas and a bone-dry Methodist.

Having won the nomination, Al Smith sent the convention a telegram that ignored its carefully drawn plank on Prohibition. He pledged to enforce the law (under the presidential oath he would have had no choice about it). At the same time, he ardently preached the virtues of temperance over Prohibition. He attacked the Volstead Act, arousing the ire of prohibitionists all over the United States, and there were many prohibitionists within his own party. It was not an auspicious beginning, even though everyone already knew that Al Smith was wet. His career in politics had begun in a saloon.* Nowadays he merely favored an occasional drink, and was firmly against the revival of the saloon.[25] But he had inadvertently encouraged a powerful whispering campaign. According to this, the governor rarely passed a sober day. He was not simply wet, but a hopeless alcoholic.[26]

More damaging, however, was his Catholicism. It far outweighed every other issue in the campaign.[27] There was a long history of anti-Catholicism in American politics. It was always a powerful force at the polls.[28] Even an impeccable old Progressive like William Allen White was upset by Smith's nomination: "The whole Puritan civilization which has built a sturdy, orderly nation is threatened by Smith."[29]

The Protestant churches led the attack on the governor. It was not unusual for a church to try to influence American politics. The Baptists in the South and the Methodists in the North had been major political instruments for more than a century. And six months before the Houston convention, a Methodist Bishop, James Cannon, was touring the South trying to organize an anti-Smith bloc to deny him the nomination. On the eve of the election the *Memphis Commercial Appeal* carried an advertisement urging, "Vote as You Pray."[30] At the request of the Republican National Committee, Mabel Walker Willebrandt, assistant attorney general, went to Cincinnati to address a gathering of Methodist ministers.†

---

* Although in his memoirs, *Up to Now* (New York, 1928), it became a "café."
† She was known as "the inevitable Mrs. Willebrandt," she spoke at so many gatherings.

Hoover had studiously avoided any mention of religion. Mrs. Willebrandt, however, was carried away by the sight of 2,000 divines at her feet. "There are 2,000 pastors here," she exulted. "You have in your charge more than 600,000 members of the Methodist Church in Ohio alone. That is enough to swing the election."[31]

Besides the burdens of his wetness and his religion, Al Smith suffered from what has been aptly termed "his urban provinciality."[32] The United States was not yet a predominantly urban nation. It was, rather, on the cusp. What made an impression in the city was likely to horrify the country. And the governor was noticeably ill at ease outside his own domain. His accent was against him. Thanks to radio (raddio), listeners far beyond New York were able to hear him for the first (foist) time, as the governor spoke to them personally (poisonally) on such matters as work (woik) and research (reesoich). And there was snobbishly cruel prejudice in those upper-class drawing rooms where all it took to provoke laughter was for someone to say, "Can you imagine Mrs. Smith in the White House?"[33]

The final blow to his hopes was Al Smith's own failure to give his campaign a coherent strategy. He could have stressed the economic issue —pointed to the yawning gaps in prosperity, the high levels of unemployment, the disparity of gains between stockholders and workers. Instead, he genuflected before the graven image of business success. He might have attacked American intervention in Latin American countries. He maintained an impenetrable silence instead. His campaign was lackluster and issueless. And when he tried to make something out of the agricultural crisis, he soon got lost. He feared alienating the conservative Democrats by accepting McNary-Haugenism. And he feared alienating the farmers by rejecting it. Here was the most divisive issue in the Republican party, but he made nothing of it. When it became obvious that he really did not understand either the nature of the problem or its proposed remedy, he beat a rapid, ignominious retreat.[34]

With Smith running for the White House, the New York Democratic leadership had to find a new candidate for the governor's mansion. The choice narrowed down to four men: Robert F. Wagner, Herbert H. Lehman, Owen D. Young, and Franklin D. Roosevelt. Both Wagner and Lehman were more interested in running for the Senate. Young preferred to continue as he was, running both RCA and General Electric. And Roosevelt was afraid, he said, of jeopardizing his recovery from the polio attack that had left him with paralyzed legs.

Roosevelt did, however, intend to run for governor in 1932. From there, he would make his own bid for the White House in 1936, at the end of Hoover's second term. That was the strategy that he and Louis Howe had agreed on. But if Roosevelt had one weakness it was his inability to say no and make it stick. The state Democratic leadership wore down his resistance. He was persuaded to run, however reluctantly.* Lehman was similarly pressured into running for lieutenant governor.[35]

In the closing weeks of the election campaign, the press and the country seemed more interested in Gene Tunney's wedding, the deaths of thirty New Yorkers in a single weekend from drinking bad liquor, the arrival of the dirigible *Graf Zeppelin*, and the World Series between the Yankees and the Cardinals, than in Hoover or Smith. The man of the hour was neither of these, but Babe Ruth, who hit three home runs in a single World Series game.

On election day, however, nearly 70 percent of eligible voters went to the polls, a vast improvement on 1924's 51 percent. Al Smith gained almost twice as many votes as Davis had won. For the first time the Democrats had spent almost as much as the Republicans, and had courted big business with as much zeal.[36] Yet the Democrats paid heavily for being divided over Prohibition, the Klan, Smith's religion, and rural poverty versus urban prosperity. These four issues—drink, nativism, Fundamentalism, and money—had become a seamless web of discontent.

Hoover sat tight and reaped the benefits. The sole issue in the Republican campaign was the economy. Republican campaign workers stood on street corners handing out copper coins that bore the legend: "The Hoover Lucky Pocket Piece—Good for four years of prosperity." The utterance that Hoover is often claimed to have made, of promising "two chickens in every pot and a car in every garage," was never made by Hoover. It was written by a copywriter for a Republican party advertisement.

On election night he set up a blackboard in the living room of his Palo Alto home and methodically chalked up the results as they came in throughout the evening. To Al Smith's 15 million votes, he had won 22 million; to Smith's 87 electoral votes, a record 444. Al Smith did not even carry his own state. And Hoover had broken the Solid South, winning Kentucky, Tennessee, North Carolina, Virginia, Texas, South Carolina, and Florida.

Around Smith a legend grew up that he had been beaten by his religion. There is no doubt that it cost him millions of votes. Yet a greater handicap was the fact that he was a Democrat. There was not a Democrat alive in 1928 who could have beaten Hoover. Smith had done as well as anyone was likely to have done on the Democratic ticket that November. Even a dry Protestant would have taken a drubbing.[37]

Another, much subtler, myth grew up, and over the years encrusted

---

* His closest political adviser, Louis Howe, promptly sent a telegram to Warm Springs: MESS IS NO NAME FOR IT.

the 1928 election, that Al Smith in defeat had laid the foundations of the modern Democratic party. For the first time, the legend runs, the big cities became a force in national politics. This story is even more remarkable in a way. Because there is nothing at all to support it except imagination.[38] The cities had been overwhelmingly Democratic for a decade. The moment the Democratic party pulled itself together, the mass of urban voters would achieve the power their numbers implied. Al Smith did not pull his party together. He went a long way toward tearing it apart. He lost half a dozen states in the South that no Democrat since the Civil War had come close to losing. He managed to make the farm vote safe for the Republican party despite the agricultural depression. And he failed to win the votes of ordinary blacks. A few black leaders went with Al Smith. The rank and file cast their ballots for Hoover. Although Al Smith won millions more votes than Davis or Cox, Hoover won far more than Coolidge or Harding. For one thing, the electorate was growing; for another, 1928 was a controversial election, generating far more interest than most. A blazing building attracts more interest than a fire in a wastebasket.

The myth of 1928 as a turning point was, in the end, a myth of consolation, whose force would only grow as the facts grew hazier in the memory, and Al Smith seemed more and more the good guy who lost.

IV

Coolidge prepared to leave Washington secure in the knowledge that whatever posterity had to say about his presidency he had left a lasting mark on the capital, thanks to the Plan of 1926. Coolidge had discovered that it would be cheaper for overcrowded government bureaus to build new offices than to rent them. He and Mellon, in the name of economy, determined with the aid of various architects and planners to save the nation's capital from the grip of the tawdry and banal. Most of Pennsylvania Avenue was as dreary as any small town's Main Street. Congress was coaxed into voting $275 million and granting sweeping powers to implement the plan. The Mall was to be made over and cleared of minor structures. Along the south side of Pennsylvania Avenue seven vast new government buildings were to rise, in chaste white marble and to a simple design, to house the Departments of Commerce, Labor, and Justice, the Internal Revenue, and a score of important agencies. The temporary buildings of World War I, standing for more than a decade, were to be torn down. Entire blocks filled with ramshackle hotels, shops, gas stations, and diners were to be razed. A new Supreme Court building was to rise across from the Capitol. The Court had been sitting since Reconstruction in a cramped room between the House and the Senate. Within a decade, under the Plan of 1926, Washington would look like one of the great capital cities of the world. At present, it was about as grand as Youngstown, Ohio.

Coolidge left Washington without regrets. He had done his duty, so far as he could see it. And his entire adult life had been filled with nostalgic longing for New England. Even in the White House his thoughts turned constantly to Vermont. He was content to leave the great world to its business and sit in a rocking chair on the Plymouth porch, wearing a battered old hat and shapeless old clothes, and live on small-town gossip. Or, when moved to more demanding pastimes, he would go into Northampton, Massachusetts, and occupy himself with the Northampton Literary Society.

His successor occupied himself between election and inaugural in an unprecedented way. Instead of hanging around for four and a half months with little to do, Hoover went off to South America on a goodwill tour. On his return he stopped in Miami for a few days to visit with old friends. He was the man of the hour, returning triumphant, to a nation ready for strong leadership after five years of nondirective therapy. One evening, standing in front of the huge open fire in J. C. Penney's mansion, Hoover turned to his friends and in an unguarded moment gave voice to his anxieties. "I have no dread of the ordinary work of the Presidency," he said. "What I do fear is the result of the exaggerated idea the people have conceived of me. They have a conviction that I am a sort of superman, that no problem is beyond my capacity. If some unprecedented calamity should come upon this nation I would be sacrificed to the unreasoning disappointment of a people who had expected too much."[39]

By Inauguration Day, a cold, wet day in March, he seemed to have put such thoughts behind him. He took the oath with a firm "I do!" instead of the "I affirm" that was expected of a devout Quaker.* He gave an address calling for a "New Day," a tacit acceptance of the need for strong leadership. Then he rode to the White House in an open car despite the rain that pelted down.

Hoover placed a telephone on the President's desk for the first time; employed five secretaries rather than one; put the presidential yacht in mothballs; closed the presidential stables; and gave his salary away. Mrs. Hoover, meanwhile, was redecorating nearly every room in the White House and filling them with antiques.

---

* A devout Quaker, but not a strict Quaker: he smoked, took a drink on occasion, swore like an ore car pusher, and disbelieved in pacifism.

During his first six months in office Hoover took decisive action in almost every conceivable direction. He ordered publication of all large tax refunds; authorized direct quotation of his press conferences; put an end to sales and leases of government oil lands; changed Mellon's tax policies by proposing large cuts at the lower end, small reductions at the top; asked for the names of all political prisoners and, on learning there were none, began issuing pardons to all former political prisoners who requested one; sought to help get Tom Mooney out of San Quentin but was hampered by his own attorney general, William D. Mitchell; secured the resignation of Mrs. Willebrandt;* secured a large increase in appropriations for Howard University, so that Howard could operate an accredited law school; entertained blacks at the White House for the first time over howls of outrage from half the Republican party; and refused to allow the police to interfere with Communist demonstrators outside the White House. He secured a 20 percent increase in funds for the Indian Bureau. He launched the first White House Conference on Children. He asked Congress to create a cabinet-level Department of Health, Education, and Welfare. He chose a dedicated conservationist, Ray Lyman Wilbur, to run the Interior Department. He asked Congress for a St. Lawrence Seaway bill, in vain. He set in motion the building of Boulder Dam, and 75 percent of the power it generated was to be sold cheaply to publicly owned power companies, to the fury of privately owned power companies. He also busied himself with reforming the apparatus of federal justice, from the courts to the prisons. He acted like a man with not a moment to lose. Yet in the end much of what he sought would have to be approved and financed by Congress. The two administrations in which he had served had been constantly embroiled in fights with Capitol Hill. And "by the time Hoover reached the White House he and many prominent Congressmen were old antagonists."[40]

Like Harding, Hoover took office with the farmlands in turmoil. Like Harding, he called Congress into special session to deal with the crisis. McNary-Haugen had been amended in 1928 to include all farm products, all surpluses, whether seasonal or not. In this form, it was passed by both houses, vetoed by Coolidge, and passed again over his veto. But before it could be implemented, the Administration went out of office.

There was no chance that Hoover would accept McNary-Haugen. He had called Henry C. Wallace a "fascist" for proposing it.[41] By which he

---

* She stayed on in Washington in a very well-paid job as counsel to Fruit Industries, a California grape growers' cooperative that made grape concentrates used for making—guess what? The federal government was persuaded to make a $20 million loan to Fruit Industries, so the taxpayer subsidized home winemaking during Prohibition on an impressive scale.

meant that that was the logic of using the powers of government to fix wages, prices, production targets, and distribution methods. Its model was Mussolini's Italy. Even Peek had lost much of his belief in the plan. He had been lobbying for the past year or so for marketing cooperatives, aided with government credits and exemptions from taxation.

Farmers regarded Hoover with the deepest misgivings. During his service as food administrator, he had kept wheat at less than $2.50 a bushel when it could have sold for as much as $4. They were convinced that he wanted them to stay poor so the cities could thrive on cheap food. And when he preached to them that they could solve their postwar problems themselves by cutting production, well, that only showed what a son of a bitch he really was. It was like telling them to cut their throats.[42] So it was ironic that while Harding and Coolidge absolutely refused to accept permanent federal responsibility for the welfare of farmers, it was Hoover who capitulated.

He proposed to the emergency session of Congress a Federal Farm Board, which would advance money for purchasing, storing, and marketing farm products; it would provide farmers' cooperatives with both money and advice; it would curb waste by taking marginal land out of production; and it would develop agricultural by-products for industry. The FFB was meant to stand as a monument to the voluntary approach. On July 15, 1929, it opened for business. There was an advisory committee for every crop, to take responsibility for production control. "The theory was that the producers, once told what they should do for their own good, would act individually and without coercion."[43] Under the FFB were various "stabilization corporations" that would buy up whatever "exportable surpluses" still existed after exhortation and common sense had been applied. These surpluses were not expected to be so large that they would seriously affect the world price for them, and so would be fairly easy to dispose of.

The emergency session took up the related matter of the tariff, as its predecessor had done eight years before. Both parties in the election had promised tariff revision, by which they meant revision upward. The flexible provision in the Fordney-McCumber Tariff had proved to be flexible the way a knee is—it flexed one way. Thirty-two of the thirty-seven tariff changes since 1921 had been upward. Not even this was enough to satisfy farmers or manufacturers.

The proposed Hawley-Smoot Tariff was so high it amounted to a declaration of trade war. One thousand American economists collectively petitioned Hoover not to sign it into law. Hoover, however, knew that with his signature or without it, Congress would enact this tariff. He tried to portray it as an aid to agriculture, fought to retain the principle of flexibility, and finally endorsed this smash-and-grab approach to international trade.[44]

Hoover made good on another campaign pledge, to launch a thorough, dispassionate inquiry into Prohibition. He established a committee under George W. Wickersham, Taft's attorney general, and widened the scope of its investigation to include crime of all kinds. As far as Hoover's own views went, "Prohibition had to be defended not because it was Prohibition but because it was the law."[45] He never called it "a noble experiment."

The drys remained a force to be reckoned with in Congress. If anything, they became more implacable as popular resistance rose. In 1929 they succeeded in passing the "Jones Five and Dime Law" (after Senator Wesley L. Jones of Washington, a longtime friend of Hoover). This raised maximum penalties for first offenders under the Volstead Act to five years in prison and a $10,000 fine. First offenses also became felonies. The Jones Act succeeded in further discrediting Prohibition by making it ludicrously draconian.

The new President meanwhile delighted in his role. Around him swirled a bustle of activity not seen in Washington since wartime. Energy seemed to radiate from the White House. Every day began on a vigorous note. The President had invented Hooverball. This involved throwing an eight-pound medicine ball over a net ten feet high, on a court set out as if for tennis. The scoring was much the same as in tennis.[46] At seven each morning the game began promptly, regardless of the weather. For half an hour as many as eighteen middle-aged Cabinet members, generals, congressmen and White House aides scampered back and forth like boys, laughing and sweating, while the Chief kept score as he ran.

19. Worked Up

I

Mass production meant hard times for millions of workers. Once its techniques had been mastered, up to 200,000 workers a year were replaced by automatic and semiautomatic machinery.[1] A new phrase entered the language—"technological unemployment."[2] For the first time in a hundred years employment in manufacturing struck a plateau, then turned down. Yet the labor force as a whole was rising in the Twenties much faster than the rate of population growth, from 41.5 million to 48 million.[3] When Harding's Conference on Unemployment met in 1921, it assumed that it was dealing with a temporary crisis. It was, in fact, convening at the dawn of an era of permanently high unemployment.

A later presidential conference agreed that at no time in the 1920s did the rate drop below 5 percent, and admitted that this was erring on the side of caution.[4] Estimates varied wildly. In entire industries—construction, mining, agriculture, the retail trades—there were no reliable figures on income and employment. Those that were reliable came from factories and the railroads and were collected by the government. If these figures rose or fell, the percentage involved was applied to the entire work force. This ignored the shift toward services; population growth, which was adding more than half a million job-seekers a year; and the hundreds of thousands who left the farms to look for work in the cities. The result was that government figures on unemployment were not even half right.

To find its true rate of unemployment, Baltimore, in 1928, sent its policemen out to visit every family in the city. The rate was 42.5 percent. Across the country, the AFL said that nearly 18 percent of union members were out of work; and union members were usually better at finding and keeping jobs than non-union members.[5] Robert S. Lynd and his wife, Helen, were surveying Muncie, Indiana, in 1923–24 for their famous study, *Middletown*. Ostensibly a thriving industrial town, Muncie surprised them: "It was a time of considerable local unemployment."[6]

There were entire industries that were in a depression for the whole of the Twenties, such as coal mining, where unemployment for the decade was 30 percent, after peaking in 1922 at 50 percent.[7] There were entire regions that remained permanently depressed, such as the textile and shoe towns of New England. Before 1920 they provided a living. Wages were low, but there were always jobs to be had for the asking. By 1929 nearly all these towns had lost mills and factories and much of their population. Massachusetts saw little of the fabled Coolidge prosperity. And so the very state where Coolidge had made his political career, solidly Republican for nearly a century, became increasingly Democratic. The road that the Commonwealth was following was being traveled, at a slower pace, throughout the urbanized, industrialized Northeast.

There were other indicators. Welfare agencies in every part of the country reported "acute local unemployment" in 1928. Tens of thousands of workers took wage cuts. In the Bowery, breadlines formed, two blocks long.[8] The Department of Labor insisted that there were only 1,874,000 out of work; Senator Hendrick Shipstead of North Dakota, who counted more than factories and railroads, said there were more like 8 million.[9]

With the Model A in full production, Henry Ford announced at Christmas that in the new year he would be hiring an extra 30,000 men.[10] On the first hiring day, January 2, 1929, more than 25,000 men surrounded the Rouge plant in bitter cold, clamoring for work. The temperature was −14 degrees. Many of these thousands had waited all night. Those felled by exposure were hurried to a hospital. As panic set in, the crowd pressed hard against the employment office. Fire hoses were brought to bear, the water turning quickly to ice on drenched men. This shivering, jobless army was drawn from a dozen states. Only 600 found work that day.

II

Those who had jobs could count themselves lucky, even though the average worker did not enjoy paid vacations, paid public holidays, or sick pay. What mass production had done was to take skilled jobs and break them down into the simplest operations. A worker then learned one of those operations, not the whole skill. The job he did could be mastered in less than a day, sometimes in less than five minutes—tighten a nut, slip in a bolt, strike a nail. Modern production was based on a paradox: high technology depending on an army of unskilled labor. Yet this unskilled work paid far more than a broom-pusher's wage. So workers counted themselves lucky to get it.

Wages, however, were not all that high in the land of high wages. Most workers had to struggle to earn a decent living. An Australian labor leader, who came to marvel at the land of prosperous workers, went home feeling they would be better off moving to Australia, where wages were higher and working conditions easier.[11] There was no minimum wage in the United States by the late Twenties. Before 1919 some seventeen states had enacted minimum wage laws. But in 1923 the Supreme Court struck down a Washington, D.C., statute that fixed a minimum wage for women, finding that it hindered the bargaining freedom between employers and workers. It was therefore unconstitutional.[12] The decision, in effect, redefined labor as a commodity. The Court did not see, or chose to ignore, the fact that bargaining power is not invariably equal between employers and workers (and in the Twenties, with unemployment above 10 percent even at the best times, it was unlikely ever to be equal). This decision, *Adkins v. Children's Hospital*, was the most important labor decision of the decade. State after state repealed its minimum wage law.

The average industrial wage rose from 1919's $1,158 to $1,304 in 1927, a solid if unspectacular gain, during a period of mainly stable prices.[13] Most "minimum health and decency" budgets worked out in the Twenties, however, were around $2,000 a year for a family of four. How then did they make up the difference? Usually by sending the wife to work. The average family had 1.6 income earners, which brought it up to the $2,000 mark.[14] So most of them got by, just.

Women now made up a quarter of the work force. But the world of work was divided into women's jobs and men's jobs, and women's jobs paid a lot less. Even where men and women did the same work, whether in the professions or unskilled toil, women received only two-thirds to half of men's earnings.[15] The usual justification was that women worked for "pin money" and married women were doing it for luxuries. The truth is they were more likely to be doing it for groceries. Among women looking for work the competition was therefore ferocious, especially where the women (often girls in their teens) were unskilled. Two hundred would apply for three or four vacancies. They begged desperately for jobs that paid $13–$14 a week, for six days of nine and a half hours a day.[16] Where wives and daughters could not secure even badly paid jobs like these, their families did not get by. In the mid-1920s there were some 26 million American families. Roughly 6 million were "chronically destitute."[17]

Yet, for others, there was a sense of unheralded prosperity. Real incomes in 1920 were less than 5 percent above the incomes of 1899. The Twenties brought an average increase in income of about 35 percent. But the biggest gains went to the people earning more than $3,000 a year.[18]* The number of people with six-figure incomes doubled between 1920 and 1928. The number of millionaires had risen from 7,000 in 1914 to about 35,000 in 1928. While there was so much wealth at the top of the social tree, however, the average saver of 1927 increased his savings that year by all of $11.[19]

III

The AFL had gained handsomely from its wartime pact with the government; its membership doubled. By 1920 there were 4 million AFL members, twice as many in 1916. Industrialists, however, resented strong unions, and the strikes of 1919 convinced many of them that the unions would have to be broken. Manufacturers' groups, meeting in Chicago in 1921, launched what they termed "the American Plan." Its stated purpose was opposition to the closed shop. Its real purpose was union busting. Tactics varied from industry to industry, but its success rate was very high. Some of the American Plan's overwhelming victories were over the building trades in major cities, such as Chicago and San Francisco. Contractors who refused to operate an open shop found it impossible to obtain bank credit and building supplies.[20] In retrospect, the steel industry's total victory in the steel strike of 1919 had given the postwar anti-union drive a running start.[21] The momentum was maintained by a 1922 Supreme Court decision, *United Mine Workers v. Coronado Coal Company*, which ruled that a union was legally responsible for the actions of its members. The union could be sued and damages collected from it.[22] This was a potential threat to the very existence of unions—a stick held over their heads.

There was a carrot—the company union. By the late 1920s, company unions had enrolled a million members. Workers joined in such numbers because the company union offered a measure of health and safety insurance they would otherwise lack; probably contained grievance machinery that would otherwise not be provided; and for many workers traditionally

---

* In the mid-Twenties only about 6 percent of the gainfully employed earned more than $3,000 a year.

ignored by the established unions (blacks, women, clerical workers, recent immigrants) more representation than they had ever enjoyed before. So workers joined company unions of their own free will, even though they did not see them for a moment as being *real* unions. They were known throught American industry as "Kiss Me Clubs."[23]

The fate of the real unions was typified by the United Mine Workers, which in 1920 was one of the biggest, best-run, most powerful unions in the AFL. Danger alone was enough to justify the miners' claim for high wages. Each year some 2,000–2,500 miners were crushed to death by falling rock or slate; were run over by machinery on rails or wheels; were fatally mangled by still other machinery; were burned to death; or died in underground explosions. And yet they resigned themselves to wage cuts. What they sought chiefly was the assurance of steady work and the protection of a strong union. Steady work meant a six-hour day at the coalface, week in, week out. A strong union meant national wage bargaining, not local and district bargaining, which permitted low-cost mines to undercut the rest.

The UMW made yet another attempt to organize the hundreds of non-union West Virginia mines, where miners worked for as little as $2.00 a day. The strike was beaten into the ground the day a federal court granted the coal companies an injunction. It was an injunction to the striking miners and their families to starve, restraining the UMW from "furnishing the inhabitants of said tent colonies or to those who may hereafter inhabit the same, any sum or sums of money, orders for money, merchandise, or orders for merchandise, or any other thing of value. . . ."[24]

With coal-cutting costs falling steadily as the mines became mechanized; with most of the available work going increasingly to non-union miners; with legal disasters draining the treasury and lowering morale; racked with internal dissension; the UMW saw its membership fall from half a million in 1920 to barely 75,000 only eight years later. Yet, the union continued paying dues to the AFL on the basis of a membership topping 400,000 rather than swallow its pride and admit that it had been routed.[25]

As the unions reeled from one defeat after another, they were reduced to holding only their traditional territory of a generation earlier—building, printing, railroads—that is, where crafts were entrenched and mass production almost unknown. But the machinery was becoming more sophisticated every year. Even Gompers' own trade, cigarmaking, was being mechanized at the time of his death in 1924. (He was succeeded as president of the AFL by William Green, secretary-treasurer of the UMW).

American unions were remarkable for the lack of opposition they posed to the introduction of machinery. They "accept the position that the worker must be efficient," noted one foreign visitor, surprised.[26] There was a much-heralded experiment in union-management cooperation on the Baltimore and Ohio Railroad that was held out as a model for the rest of American industry. The essence of the experiment, noted an approving presidential committee, "is the assumption *by the union* of responsibility for efficiency and output"[27] (italics added).

Labor's response to the rapid proliferation of machinery was to demand a shorter work week. In the decade up to 1919 it had shrunk steadily, despite the war. In the 1920s, however, the work week stayed virtually the same, around fifty-one hours, no matter how much machinery was brought into the plant.[28]

The unions also took what amounted to a Victorian approach to unemployment insurance—they were against it. Gompers, like Coolidge, thought it would rot the moral fiber. In 1928 only 37,000 wage earners out of more than 30 million enjoyed any form of unemployment insurance. They were more exposed to job insecurity than any other industrialized work force. That might have made them eager to obtain unemployment insurance. But it did not. They believed, with Coolidge and Gompers and the Chamber of Commerce, that if they encountered hardship they had only themselves to blame. Economists and social workers who saw the need for unemployment insurance were baffled by the resistance put up to it by the very people who stood to gain most.[29]

The hostility of unions to the welfare state played into the hands of employers, who could present themselves unchallenged as the sole source of security for the working class. And some employers began to establish what were the rudiments of a private welfare state. What, then, did any union have to offer when the employer provided not only a job, but health care, a pension fund, and group insurance? All the union did was take your dues.[30]

"The AF of L machinery has practically collapsed," wrote a despondent official. "AF of L organizers have forgotten how to organize. They may be effective as lobbyists, negotiators or public speakers, but their usefulness in organizing the disorganized has almost ceased."[31]

IV

Unions were weak for many reasons: the rising number of women in the labor force; the growth of the service sector; the reluctance of migrant workers to join unions; the unions' hostility to blacks. By 1929 only one wage earner in eight belonged to a union, the lowest percentage by a large margin of any industrialized country. And there was nothing American unions could do to change that so long as business remained prosperous enough to fight strikes, and unemployment was too high for workers to make their strikes effective.

The injunction, devised centuries before to protect a man's fields, was stretched so widely now that it could outlaw pickets, boycotts, and most of the armory of striking workers. Faced with a strike, said Felix Frankfurter and Nathan Greene, "the extraordinary remedy of the injunction has become the ordinary legal remedy, almost the sole remedy."[32] As a rule, they were granted without notice to the defendants and without offering them any opportunity to be heard. Having chanced upon this quick, cheap strike-buster, business resorted to it on an amazing scale: nearly 1,000 injunctions were granted in labor disputes in the 1920s, as many as in the preceding forty years.

Mass arrests were another anti-union tactic. During a garment strike in New York in 1926 nearly 8,000 people were arrested. In the 1928 New Bedford textile strike there were 2,000 arrests. Prolonged legal battles were also useful for depleting union treasuries. In 1929, after a decade of costly litigation, the AFL's strike fund amounted to $55,000.

Finally, there were the workers. The militant spirit of 1919 had quickly passed into history, an extension of the fevers of the war. The rapidity of industrialization, its energy, its swift creation of great wealth, its giddying swings between boom and recession, its layoffs one year and high wages the next, its exhausting work disciplines and permanent job insecurity, had overwhelmed a formerly agrarian people. "The working class is mystified by the whole fateful business," the Lynds reported from Middletown.[33]

And so 1928 brought the smallest number of strikes on record, 629. The next year, 1929, brought the smallest number of strikers, 230,463. In effect, the strike had become little more than a museum piece,[34] except to the Communist party, which more or less rediscovered it.

V

Passaic, New Jersey, was a textile town. The millworkers were mainly Hungarians and Poles. Most spoke little English. Their homes were dark, cramped, airless, and damp. At thirteen, children went to work, because the wages paid by the mills ranged from $9.00 to $15.00 a week. It was only with three or four wage earners that these families managed to exist.[35] "These textile slaves all work," wrote one shocked visitor, "all, all, father, mother and children, half the family by day, the other half by night."[36]

There was no other industry nearby that would take these unskilled workers, and they were too poor as a rule to move in search of work. When in October 1925 Botany Mills imposed a 10 percent wage cut, it was a calamity for these hard-pressed people. In vain did they look to the AFL's United Textile Workers for protection. The UTW had organized only 30,000 of the 1 million American textile workers: the most skilled, best paid 3 percent.

In November the Communist party's National Textile Workers Union moved into Passaic in the person of young, bespectacled Alvin Weisbord, recently graduated from Harvard law school. He began to sign up members for the NTW. In December the new NTW members were fired. The textile workers responded by walking out en masse at the beginning of the new year. The Passaic strike was a landmark in American labor history—the first major strike openly under Communist party direction.[37]

Weisbord was energetic, idealistic, and completely committed to the welfare of the strikers. He also knew next to nothing about the textile industry, trade unions, and strikes. Starting at Botany Mills, the shutdown spread rapidly throughout Passaic. Some 16,000 workers struck. But not the AFL's elite. The strike consisted largely of pitched battles, because the police from the outset considered it their role to break up the strikers' meetings with clubs and tear gas, fire hoses and fists.[38] Nearly a thousand people were arrested. Picket lines were broken up by force. Union property was destroyed. By September 1926 the strike was faltering. Public support had never been very strong, because of the Communist direction of the walkout.

The governor of New Jersey, Harry Moore, offered to mediate the dispute if Weisbord withdrew. Rather than prevent a settlement, Weisbord agreed. But Moore found the textile companies immovable. Weisbord resumed direction of the strike. But then the UTW offered to take control, and Weisbord once again withdrew.[39] On March 1, 1927, the Passaic strike finally ended, without wage cuts. There was little rejoicing among the millworkers, however. They had lost a year's wages. Many, in fact, would never get back their jobs.

The Communists, however, were greatly encouraged by Passaic. They had put together and run a strike for the best part of a year. There were nearly a million millworkers ripe for organization. In 1928 the Communist party adopted a policy of dual unionism—where the AFL was vulnerable (in mining, textiles, and the garment industry) the CP, by dividing the American working class, might conqueror it still. As the new policy went into effect it was turned, inevitably, toward the least organized, most badly exploited of all industrial workers, the millhands of the

South. On January 1, 1929, Fred Beal arrived in Charlotte, North Carolina, on a mission that would nearly cost him his life.

VI

While the Communist party's National Textile Workers Union was moving into the South, twelve southern intellectuals and writers were at work on a volume to be published as *I'll Take My Stand*. This "agrarian manifesto" maintained that industrialism was inimical to the arts, education, religion, social life, and the natural environment. In the end, it was antihuman. The South had held out against the industrial tide longer than any other region. The Agrarians called on it to do its duty and remain true to its agrarian past. In doing so, it could lead a national return to the old virtues of plain living, right thinking, and social harmony.*

The truth was, industrialism was not being forced on innocent southerners. They clutched at electrification as drowning men are presumed to clutch at straws. A twelve-day Southern Exposition held in New York in 1925 offered every inducement short of free beer to attract new industry southward. "For most Southerners the overriding theme of the 1920s was, very simply, expansion."[40] The industry that was wooed most vigorously was textiles. The advantages that were usually touted were abundant cheap labor and water power. The rapid growth of textile mills by the late Twenties left the South with overproduction. To keep costs down, labor was sweated. Few mills earned large profits.[41]

The early mills, those founded before the World War I, had been run on much the same lines as the old cotton plantations. In theory, the mill was a business owned by shareholders. "In practice, the difference came to little, for the active head of the mill usually had practical control of the corporation itself."[42] But after the war the mills were much bigger. The old paternalistic, personal style of mill ownership was supplanted by absentee owners, and day-to-day operation was in the hands of managers trained at business schools—the kind of men millworkers, used to the old system, disliked on sight.

The millworkers were themselves the most despised of southern whites. Whole families drifted from tenantry into mill villages, where they would live in a mill-owned house for a few dollars a week, buy at the mill-owned store, and provided the entire family worked, there was security,

---

* None of the twelve Agrarians is known to have been able to milk a cow, plough a field, or look after pigs. Had they actually been forced to take a stand it would have been in Washington Square or Montparnasse.

after a fashion. Soon the family could not afford to move. They had become, in effect, serfs. Other poor southerners showed their contempt of the millworkers by calling them "lint-heads." "One gets the feeling when he sees these long, emaciated figures, wan and sleepy-looking and without any vividness or interest, that it were far better that they had remained on the farm and scratched the soil with their nails," wrote Frank Tannenbaum, shaken by the weeks he had spent among them. "It were far better that they had starved on bitter roots or killed one another in long family feuds. . . ."[43] The mill village offered no real escape from the exhausting work in the mill; only drugs, incest, venereal disease, promiscuity, and corn likker. It was a world apart, isolated from other towns and villages. Its people intermarried and sent their children into the mill.

There, parents and children alike worked ten to twelve hours a day. The temperature was usually around 90 degrees. They moved listlessly amid the deafening roar of the looms. To wring the last measure of production out of workers and equipment alike, the mills worked around the clock, and in the late Twenties the mill managers began to impose the "stretch-out" on more and more mills. The stretch-out was the textile version of the assembly-line speedup. It made each millhand operate a larger number of machines without any increase, or a trifling increase, in pay. The stretch-out created bitterness and anger among a traditionally docile work force. It was "an agricultural psychology grappling with a manufacturing problem; a planting culture conflicting with an industrial economy."[44]

When the textile workers looked to the AFL for support in their protests, the AFL leadership, chary of defeat, held back, impotently pleading with millowners to relent in their demands. Nowhere was the resulting crisis more desperate than in Gastonia County, North Carolina, by 1929 "the leading textile county in the South."[45] And Fred Beal, organizing millworkers around Charlotte, was repeatedly told that if he could only organize the Loray mill in Gastonia, "you'll organize the South."[46] In mid-March he moved to Gastonia.

Despite the cynicism of the Communist party's involvement in the Sacco and Vanzetti case, Beal had come to feel that it was the sole organization completely committed to the working class. He had few illusions about its competence or its independence. As a result, his party membership was from the first skeptical and turbulent. The party tried to tell him how to run the strike he was organizing. He was told to make "the Negro Question" the principal issue, rather than wages and conditions. He pointed out that there were no blacks in the mill. The party leadership informed him that he had to obey orders. Beal simply ignored them.

The United Textile Workers had organized a strike in Gastonia in

1919. It was trounced. Since then the UTW had been careful to leave Gastonia alone. "The textile workers therefore joined the only union that offered them an application blank,"[47] which was the NTW, in the person of Fred Beal, aided by Alvin Weisbord. On March 5, a week after Beal began organizing, the Loray mill fired five workers whom he had recruited in secret. On April 1 a majority on both the day and the night shifts refused to work. The strike was on.

Strikes were breaking out elsewhere in the Piedmont. More than 5,000 workers had struck the rayon mills of Elizabethton, Tennessee. Textile workers at Greenville, South Carolina, had come out, and there were other clashes. In nearly every conflict the immediate cause of grievance was the stretch-out. In reality, there was an accumulation of ills long borne in silence.

Organizing in Gastonia meant teaching workers how to picket by marching them around the union hall and teaching them to sing union songs. When the strike began, local sentiment was strongly behind it. But as more and more organizers arrived from the North, that support began to weaken.

The strikers demanded a minimum weekly wage of $20.00, an end to the stretch-out, screen doors and bathtubs for the company-owned houses, equal pay for women and children (who did the same work as the men, but for as little as $7.00 a week), and union recognition. The Communist party approach to strikes, however, went beyond demands of this kind—demands that any union might make. To the Communists, strikes were an important part of the education of the working class. Communist party organizations descended on the Gastonia strike as if it were a carcass to be devoured by carrion. The Young Communist League, the Young Pioneers, the International Labor Defense, the Workers' International Relief, and other CP fronts sent their recruiters south. A "women's organizer" arrived to take up the challenge of what was considered the uniquely taxing work of raising the consciousness of working-class women.[48]

Beal had seen many strikes, but never one like this. At the outset, nearly 2,500 millhands came out. Then, as food ran out, hundreds went back to work, only to come out again a few weeks later. Most workers were also related to one another, thanks to inbreeding. The scabs and strikebreakers were not hated or vilified, because they were not a breed apart. The strikebreaker who entered the mill in the morning was likely to show up at the strike meeting that night. Beal developed a new tactic: organizing the scabs to stage sudden walkouts as an expression of solidarity with the strike.

In the evenings, the strikers talked far into the night. Beal would tell them of life in the Soviet Union, where everything a worker might want had already been won. Not that he had ever seen life in Russia. But most of all there was singing to keep up spirits. Ella May Wiggins, the mother of five children, thin and exhausted although not yet thirty, who had worked in the mills since the age of fifteen, became the strikers' balladeer. "She would stand somewhere in a corner, chewing tobacco or snuff and fumbling over notes of a new poem scribbled on the back of a union leaflet. Suddenly some one would call for her to sing."[49] Her ballads were set to old tunes, with new words, simple and direct:

> How it grieves the heart of a mother,
> You every one must know.
> For we can't buy for our children,
> Our wages are too low.

Local deputy sheriffs wrecked the union hall one night and then ransacked the relief store next door where flour, sugar, potatoes, and other foodstuffs had been stocked for the strikers' families. The food was thrown into the street and under the eyes of cowed millhands was sprayed with kerosene. Another day, more than 100 families were evicted from their run-down company shacks, their pitiful possessions dragged out into the muddy, unpaved street and trampled on. The evicted strikers looked on helplessly, surrounded by weeping women and children, offering no resistance.

Fred Beal organized a mass walkout of scabs for the night shift on June 7. The plan was betrayed by a company spy. On the evening of the seventh a dozen policemen shot up the union hall. Some of the strikers were armed and returned the fire. In the gunfight one of the strikers was wounded, and the Gastonia chief of police, D. A. Aderholt, was killed. Beal, several of his assistants, and a dozen strikers were indicted for conspiracy to murder.[50] *

The trial was held in Charlotte. The prosecution adopted a tactic from a movie called *The Trial of Mary Dugan*, where a murder conviction was won by putting a life-size dummy of the deceased before the jury at a crucial moment in the trial. A shrouded model of Chief Aderholt, constructed in secret at a cost of $1,000 and dressed in his blood-stained uniform, was wheeled into the courtroom. The shroud was dramatically pulled away.

---

* One of the defense lawyers at the subsequent trial, Arthur Garfield Hayes, knew where Beal and the other CP organizers were when Aderholt was shot: lying flat on their stomachs. But "they resented admission of the fact, since it was supposed to be an undignified position for a revolutionist while a shooting was going on." Arthur Garfield Hayes, *Trial by Prejudice* (New York, 1933), p. 285.

Reporters howled with laughter. The dead man's widow and daughter shrieked hysterically. The judge shouted, "Take it out!" The prosecutor, John G. Carpenter, fussed with the chief's collar and lifted Aderholt's hat until the painted eyes stared at the jury. "I just wanted to . . . ," he started to explain. The judge shouted again, *"Take that out!"* At last, it went, wobbling on its wheels.[51]

The trial of the Gastonia strikers did something their strike had never achieved. It turned events in Gastonia into a historic labor struggle. It put heart into the entire labor left-wing, drew liberals from far and near, and filled the news columns of important papers. Following the dummy episode, the judge declared a mistrial.

A mob singing "Praise God from Whom All Blessings Flow" and led by the Loray mill's lawyer, Major Bulwinkle, rushed the boardinghouse where some of the union organizers lived. Several men were seized, ordered to kiss the flag, beaten, whipped, then taken into the country to be hanged. The lynching party was interrupted at the last moment by a group of possum hunters.[52] A protest rally was called to publicize this attempt at mass murder. A truckload of millworkers driving to the rally was stopped on the outskirts of Gastonia by a group of armed men, who raked it with a rifle and pistol shots. Ella May Wiggins remained on the truck, while the others ran for cover. She slumped forward, shot in the breast, and fell on the truck floor, dead.[53]

The ACLU had managed the defense in the first trial, despite the unwanted "help" forced on it by the International Labor Defense. But it refused to shoulder this double burden twice and pulled out of the case, leaving the second trial to the ILD. The Communists proceeded to destroy the defense. Their star witness was put on the stand to make a plea on behalf of revolutionary violence. The jury showed what it thought of revolutionary violence by returning a verdict of guilty of murder in the first degree. The judge had to remind them that the defendants were charged with second-degree murder. The jury had to think again. All the defendants were convicted, and all drew long prison terms. Fred Beal was sentenced to twenty years at hard labor.

During this second trial, the United Textile Workers called a strike in Marion, North Carolina. The entire Piedmont was by this time swept with labor strife. With strikes falling almost into disuse, this impoverished, virtually union-free region saw fifteen major strikes in 1929. At Marion, the state militia was sent in to crush the strike. Pickets were dispersed at bayonet point. When workers again tried to picket the mill, the Marion police fired tear gas into the line of pickets and opened fire. Six strikers fell dead with bullet wounds in their backs.[54] The strike was crushed.

On the same day that Beal and his codefendants (who by the second trial had been reduced to six) were found guilty, another jury sitting in Gastonia heard six witnesses identify one Horace Wheeler as the man who had shot Ella May Wiggins. The Gastonia jury swiftly acquitted him of murder.

Beal was ordered by the Communist party to flee to the Soviet Union. He did as he was told, not because he feared prison, but because he was intensely curious to see the "workers' paradise" whose praises he had sung unseen. Behind him was a mixed legacy of the purest idealism and Communist chicanery, of heroism and defeat. Possessing almost nothing but his own courage and intelligence, he had journeyed into the poorest, most recently industrialized part of the country, bearing hope. Southern mill-hands were the newest, most wretched part of the modern proletariat. Their only hope of a better life was through organization. Yet not even the AFL would dare to try to bring it to them in Gastonia. Fred Beal had dared, and for four months had held the strike together. Like the Charge of the Light Brigade, it seemed a glorious act of folly that far outshone many a soberly won success. When Fred Beal fled to the Soviet Union in October 1929, the very name Gastonia stood for the most famous strike of the Twenties. Like Passaic, it was to become a landmark in the struggle to create industrial unions.

20. The Business of America

During the Great War, businessmen, seconded by their companies, went to Washington to help the war effort at a dollar a year and said feelingly that *this* was the life. Simply making more and more money was boring; public service, that was where satisfaction was to be found.[1] But when the war ended, they went back to the company and boring riches. Service, however, was not completely forgotten, for a somewhat skeptical world was now given to understand that business was itself a form of public service, possibly the best form of all. "The word *service* began to appear in innumerable mottoes—it was on the lips of every Rotarian, advertising man, and every supposedly progressive business leader. . . ."[2]

Only a generation earlier big business had loomed as the chief threat to democracy. The business of American politics (and the muckraking press) in the days of Roosevelt and Wilson was the curbing of the corporation. The last great legislative landmark of this era was the Federal Trade Commission, established in 1914. It aimed to curtail unfair competition. The practices it attempted to outlaw ranged from sabotage to outright fraud. Fair competition was supposed to make it possible for small business to flourish and the evil of bigness to lose its power. The FTC was not founded to regulate monopolies. "Its concern was the prevention of monopolies."[3] By the mid-Twenties the business lobby in Congress had gutted the never-very-robust FTC. First, by keeping it on a starvation diet; second, by blocking the appointment to it of anyone not acceptable to business. Most Progressive appointees had by 1925 resigned in frustration.

Hoover as Secretary of Commerce preferred the voluntary approach anyway. His favored panacea was the trade association. It sprang from the most respectable Progressive premises: make business aware of its wastefulness, its inefficiency, and its irrationality, and businessmen would, in a spirit of self-interest, set matters right. In his first four years at the Commerce Department Hoover had the satisfaction of seeing 400 trade associations come into existence. As a good Progressive, he believed in the assiduous collection and publication of facts. So too, it turned out, did the trade associations. "What was ultimately accomplished was the exchange among competitors of information relative to prices, sales, stocks and shipments sufficient to achieve open, intelligent, uniform price-fixing."[4]

There had been a steady and marked decline in competition since the Civil War. Up to 1914 it was characterized by the growth of monopolies and trusts. Now it was based on oligopoly, nonprice competition, the setting of prices for an entire industry by a single price leader (for example, US Steel), and by informal market sharing under the supervision of trade associations. The result was a concentration of economic power that must have had a million dead Progressives spinning in their graves. Hardly a month went by without half a dozen mergers between major corporations. Thus did the big grow rapidly bigger.[5] And during the Twenties nearly 20 percent of the entire national wealth of the United States was shifted away from private ownership to corporate ownership. In time, all that individuals would own would be their houses, their cars, some furniture, and a little cash. Legal title to nearly all the wealth-producing property would before long be held by corporations.[6] At the same time, stock ownership was becoming so widely dispersed that no individual stockholder was likely to own even 1 percent of the outstanding stock. The twenty biggest owners of the Pennsylvania Railroad in 1929 held all of 2.7 percent of the stock between them; at US Steel the twenty biggest held a more impressive 5.1 percent.[7]

What made it possible for these huge corporations to be run effectively at all was "scientific management," which had "so routinized business procedures that a number of commonplace men together could handle situations that had grown too complex" even for a Carnegie or a Rockefeller to handle alone.[8] Nervous energy, quick thinking, an indomitable will, had been the answer to every difficulty in the old corporation. In the new one, management was the answer—in selling, in budgeting, in research, in financing new ventures, in abolishing old ones, in hiring and in firing. Schools of management were being founded. Management practices were becoming standardized. Yet it was still a comparatively new growth; something transitional. Many of the new methods were experimental; many of its assumptions untested.[9] It was only after 1922 that large numbers of businesses introduced budgets, for example, even though it is hard to imagine a large business now without one.[10]

Managers and corporate executives discovered in the Twenties that business was that coveted thing, a "profession." And to prove it, there was the lavishly endowed, newly founded Harvard Graduate School of Business Administration. Opened in 1924 with a gift from George Fisher Baker,* it boasted twenty-three handsome buildings occupying a lovely site on the Charles River across from the university. Harvard reciprocated by giving Baker an honorary Ph.D.

Business was proud and self-confident.[11] It hardly seemed remarkable that Thomas N. Carver, Harvard's professor of political economy, could contemplate the gleaming new buildings on the other side of the Charles and preach that the young man who wanted to serve society best would go straight into investment banking.[12]

II

All over the country the old prime movers from the early industrial age were being scrapped. The steam engines, the water wheels, the stationary internal combustion engines of the type that had dazzled Henry Adams back in 1893 were being ripped out. They gave way to steam turbines run by electrical generators. The sale of electricity doubled in less than ten years, while consumption of fuel oil more than doubled, and of gas quadrupled. America in the Twenties developed a voracious appetite for energy.[13] As energy poured into industry, goods poured out. There was a productivity revolution.†

Horsepower per wage earner increased by 50 percent in 1920–29;[14] manufacturing output rose by 64 percent.[15] Most of this increased output came after the 1921–22 recession. For the six years 1922–27 the economy as a whole grew by 7 percent a year—the best peacetime growth rate the United States has ever achieved.[16]

Employers credited the upsurge in productivity to Prohibition, which

---

* President of First National Bank of New York, and the largest shareholder in both AT&T and US Steel.
† There were five major productivity surveys in the 1920s. No two came to the same conclusion. What they did agree on was the magnitude of the increase. They were based on the Census of Manufactures, issued after 1919 in alternate years. A wide variety of enterprises was not included in the Census of Manufactures. Nor did the figures allow for new products, changes in working hours, or improvements in quality.

had cut down sharply on absenteeism, especially on Monday mornings.[17] Much was also due to the better organization of factory work, with continuous line production, moving assembly lines, and a coherent flow of raw materials for processing.[18] Scientific management extended not only to the factory floor but changed packaging and distribution, and so moderated the swings from good years to bad ones. Personnel departments began to hire men and train them in a systematic fashion. In a decade, labor turnover dropped from 100 percent a year to less than 50 percent.[19] Finally, the transformation of the high school at the turn of the century, when a majority of American teenagers were for the first time sent to school instead of to work, provided modern industry with an educated work force. It was not highly educated, yet it was more flexible, more educable and more literate than any other in history. And this alone accounted for much of the productivity revolution of the Twenties.[20]

Where business remained competitive and productivity increased sharply, prices tumbled. A tire and inner tube, for example, cost more than $30.00 in 1914. In the late 1920s a better tire and inner tube cost only $15.70.[21] But workers' earnings lagged far behind the productivity increases that made such price cuts possible. The extreme example was auto workers, whose productivity rose by 1,300 percent between 1900 and 1926. Their real earnings in the same period rose by 44 percent.[22] Across industry as a whole, wage increases lagged far behind productivity increases, which inspired one of the most important myths of the Twenties—that business hogged nearly all the gains and left the workers the crumbs. What happened was much subtler. The real earnings of all workers rose by only about 25 percent between the armistice and 1928. But the earnings of unskilled workers did not rise at all in real terms. The skilled workers on the other hand saw their real earnings rise by about 50 percent—not that far out of line with the overall increase in productivity.[23]

The market for unskilled labor was depressed and remained that way throughout the Twenties. Although European immigration had been curbed, millions of agricultural laborers moved into the cities; large numbers of Mexicans crossed the border freely in search of work; and hundreds of unskilled married women sought part-time jobs each year. The productivity of such workers was low at best.

It was true, however, that business profits rose by an average of 7.3 percent a year from 1922 to 1929, considerably faster than the increased earnings of skilled workers in the same period.[24] Profits, that is, went up even faster than productivity, and earnings from common stock went up at an average of 16.5 percent a year. And business as a whole appeared to be thriving.

Reports of record profits filled the business pages of the daily press and cast around business the aura that always accompanies success. Yet important sectors of the economy were obviously depressed—agriculture, shipping, the railroads, coal mining, textiles. In the way that prosperity was divided up, business was not so very different from the population at large. Some 100 corporations accounted for 50 percent of total industrial net income. The rest was divided among more than 90,000 corporations.[25] In January 1929 the president of the National Manufacturers Association, John E. Edgerton, expressed his anxiety. Nearly half of the country's factories were running at a loss, he announced. The productivity revolution was leading them to the abyss by producing far more than the country could consume.[26]* It was not only industrial corporations that were in trouble. During the boom year of 1928 nearly 700,000 businesses of all types filed income tax returns. One in four showed that it was operating at a loss.[27]†

Hoover's Conference on Recent Economic Changes, however, saw no reason to fear overproduction, referring enthusiastically to "the expansibility of human wants and desires . . . [and] one want satisfied nearly always makes way for another."[28] They pointed to huge markets waiting to be satisfied: nearly all farms lacked electricity; two-thirds of homes lacked vacuum cleaners or washing machines; 95 percent were without refrigerators; and despite the amazing growth of radio, 70 percent of American homes in 1927 had no radio. "We seem only to have touched the fringe of our potentialities," they declared.[29] A statement that was both true and false at the same time.

Throughout the nineteenth century five generations of Americans, moved by the Puritan ethic of work and thrift, had saved assiduously. Those savings provided long-term investment capital for the basic industrial and transportation networks that came to maturity around 1915. The infrastructure was complete. Yet large numbers of people went on saving as diligently as ever their parents and grandparents had done. The need now was for new long-term investment opportunities. This soft spot in the economy turned into a sore. Its obvious effects were the ever greater riches at the top of the social scale and the widespread unemployment and underemployment at the bottom. Despite whatever protestations a Mellon or a Coolidge might make, government—federal, state, and local

* Lindbergh's flight had made the United States "air-minded" in various ways, including a sudden increase in aircraft manufacturing companies. In 1927, aircraft production was 1,650, more or less in line with demand. In 1929 it jumped to 6,000—far more than could be sold.
† Some of this was doubtless tax evasion. But the general picture is supported by other figures.

combined—was drawn irresistibly into the marketplace. By 1929 government used more capital and employed more people than any of the basic industries.* It was not a conscious policy decision. It seems rather to have been an unconscious form of self-defense by a society under strain, in the same way that male birthrates are likely to go up in times of war.[30]

The savings ethic did, in time, begin to lose its traditional hold. As the Twenties wore on, speculation became rife. The old structure of income distribution and old ideas on what to do with surplus income first became irrelevant and then became dangerous. Under the economic and social order that was coming into being, there had to be either new long-term investment opportunities or a redistribution of income. There was neither.

III

The Puritan ethic ran to homilies rather than proverbs or epigrams. Its best-known example was "business is business," and everyone knew what it meant: in business, whatever succeeded was right. But the homily had by the Twenties become double-edged. It was a shorthand expression for the stronger taking advantage of the weaker. One of the first things any new trade association did to refurbish the image of its membership was to adopt a code of ethics, "and in 1926 there was almost an epidemic of books on business ethics."[31]

Besides glorying in the role of business as a profession and its activities as service, businessmen increasingly gave public blessings on the doctrine of high wages. As a rule, however, "they believed in other employers paying high wages."[32]

There was, nevertheless, a growing sense of responsibility for the welfare of employees. The identification between the best interests of a large corporation and its work force was demonstrated in the most convincing possible way when Chevrolet changed models in 1928. From the last production model of its old four-cylinder car to production of the new six-cylinder Chevrolet, only six weeks elasped. There were no massive layoffs, and in those six weeks Chevrolet dealers cleared their showrooms of old stock. In contrast to Ford's changeover from the Model T, it was virtually flawless. After four months Chevrolet was once again working at full capacity, something that had taken Ford eighteen months. In the meantime, Chevrolet had overtaken Ford and won the race it embarked upon back in 1922.

---

* For all the talk of economy, total government spending increased every year, from $8.4 billion in 1921 to $11 billion in 1929.

Although manufacturing output rose dramatically in the Twenties, manufacturing employment fell by only a few percent.[33] Most manufacturers preferred to retain their existing work force as output increased and, with the same number of workers as before, reap the benefits of greater total sales. Demands for a shorter work week instead were nearly always rejected.

Scientific management stressed the need for good relations between managers and workers, combined with hostility toward labor unions. When the American Plan was launched, business sang the praises of the "open shop." To the public at large and to most politicians that was a good thing, because they assumed it meant freedom of choice in union membership. What it meant to most businessmen, however, was something else again. It meant the right to stop unions from organizing. To stop them, that is, from offering workers the choice of membership. Nor did the new codes of ethics put an end to strikebreaking by hiring armies of thugs. Many "private detectives" were men with criminal records. Often they were being sought by the police in some other city.[34]

What emerged in the Twenties in labor relations was really a new form of paternalism. The welfare capitalism of the modern corporation was presented as the last word in enlightened personnel policy, but it was intended mainly to counteract the impact of unions. The management of the leading exponents of welfare capitalism (such as General Electric and Bethlehem Steel) congratulated themselves on their intelligence and humanity. And in comparison with labor relations a decade earlier, there were some startling improvements. But the number of workers involved remained comparatively small, perhaps embracing 5 percent of the whole.

One of the most admired, most publicized ventures was the attempt to stabilize production. The model was Procter and Gamble's guarantee of forty-eight weeks of employment each year. It was highly praised. Personnel experts flocked to see this marvel in action. The program, however, applied only to the soap factories. The demand for soap is unseasonal; people are always in need of a wash. Procter and Gamble also enjoyed the dominant position in the market. The guarantee of forty-eight weeks' work was not extended to the P&G workers in the South and Southwest who were processing vegetable oils—a highly competitive product susceptible to severe fluctuations in sales. Security was extended only to those who already had it.

A more popular scheme was the stock-purchase plan. Several hundred companies encouraged their employees to buy the company's stock. These plans were zealously promoted. They made good advertising, for one thing. For another, they helped to ensure employee loyalty. And for a third, "The use of employees' savings furnished a new source of capital on easy terms and from a group of investors not critical of financial statements."[35] There were perhaps a million employees who joined these stock-purchase plans. This was hailed as proof that "the people" were grasping the reins of capitalism.

There were also many employers torn between the old cavalier ethic of "business is business" and the new ethic of welfare capitalism, typified by William M. Wood, president of the American Woolen Company, one of the largest textile corporations in the world. Back in 1912 it was Wood and his mills who provided the focal point of the famous Lawrence textile strike. In 1922 he confided to Clarence Barron (publisher of the *Wall Street Journal* and founder of *Barron's Weekly*): "American Woolen Company showed $9 million net last year, but we really made $14 million. Our policy this year will be to show as little profit as possible. If you show big earnings you will never get them; your employees will insist upon an advance in wages."[35] Yet only three years later he put 25 percent of his company's cash surplus into building a model village for his workers, at a cost of $6 million.*

IV

Two young men who did well during the war were Oris and Mantis Van Sweringen of Cleveland. These two inseparables (lifelong bachelors, they slept side by side on narrow beds in a mansion they shared with their two unmarried sisters) had built Shaker Heights. The armistice saw them with $500,000 in cash and nothing much left to do. They decided to build a high-speed electric railway to join Shaker Heights more closely to Cleveland. The site they picked out for their terminal proved to be promised to the New York, Chicago and St. Louis Railroad—known as the Nickel Plate. They could see only one solution: buy the railroad.

They borrowed an extra $500,000 from friends, but this was far from enough. At that point they went to see their bankers again, who suggested that the Van Sweringens set up a holding company—to be called Nickel Plate Securities Company—and sell shares in it to the public, while retaining enough shares in their own hands to keep control. Within weeks they raised more than $7.5 million. At a single bound they were in the railroad business through discovering the holding company. Virtually overnight the Van Sweringens lost interest in real estate, which, compared with what a holding company could do, was merely dirt.

---

* This project was managed largely by his son, whom Wood adored. In 1926 Wood's son died. A few months later the still grief-stricken Wood shot himself to death in Florida.

A holding company could, they discovered, be organized so that control could be retained with as little as 1 percent of the stock.[36] And that was how they spent the Twenties, piling holding company on holding company. Starting with a mere $500,000, they built up a railroad empire covering eight Class I lines with 30,000 miles of track and a value of $1 billion, all without ever having to put up another dollar of their own money. The structure was so complicated, however, that it took batteries of lawyers and accountants to try to explain to the Senate Banking Committee how it worked.[37]

What the Van Sweringen brothers had stumbled upon was the major invention by which modern corporations had slipped the net fashioned for the control of business by the turn-of-the-century Progressives.[38] The holding company was particularly popular with railroads and utilities before 1920 as a way of eluding the ICC and state public utilities commissions. Its very complexity could be a form of defense against regulation. In the Twenties, it grew prodigiously. By 1929 virtually every one of the leading American corporations was a holding company. Standard Oil of New Jersey (reputed to be the best-run company in the United States) owned seventy subsidiaries. The New York Central Railroad owned the stock of nearly 100 lesser corporations.[39] But in 1929 *the* holding company was spelled I-N-S-U-L-L.

Only Ford was more famous than Samuel Insull in the ranks of the self-made businessmen. Insull, born in England, was the epitome of a thousand Victorian novels, starting as an office boy, rising to the top of the business world by working twenty hours a day. Self-taught, self-willed, and a teetotaler, he had learned to master any subject that interested or affected him. He read as he ran, held down three jobs rather than one, and when opportunity came his way, Insull grabbed it with both hands. At nineteen he had, as Victorian youth was expected to have, a hero. Insull's hero was Thomas Edison. As chance would have it, Insull went to work for a man he believed was a banker, but who turned out to be Edison's man in Europe.

Insull promptly taught himself more about Edison's European affairs than Edison's representative had ever known. His devotion to Edison's interests was absolute. There was no task too trivial or too demanding. Before long, Insull was on his way to New York to become Edison's secretary.

The title hardly described the job. He woke Edison up every day, made sure he ate his meals, made sure he was properly dressed, wrote his letters, signed his checks, did everything short of wiping his nose.[40] Edison's inventions were pouring forth—the stock ticker, the phonograph, the mimeograph machine, electric lighting, motion pictures, electric power stations, and scores more. All had to be financed and, when perfected, marketed. Insull at the age of twenty-one was managing all of Edison's businesses and created new ones, the greatest of which was Edison General Electric. As Insull's biographer would later remark, "Insull had been in the electric business as long as there had been an electric business."[41] In time, the name Edison was dropped and Insull's creation became simply General Electric.

The tireless Insull characteristically expanded the new company too quickly. As its debts mounted, it became ripe for a takeover, and to Edison's dismay it fell into the hands of the embodiment of the plutocracy he despised, J. P. Morgan. Insull made the blow bearable, however, by ensuring that Edison came out of this deal with $5 million in cash. The Morgan board was sufficiently impressed to offer Insull effective control of GE under a Morgan-appointed company president. He turned it down for a job that paid only one-third as much, but where he would be the top man in every respect, as president of the Chicago Edison Company. He left New York with a bitter boast that he would build a small generating station in Chicago into a company that would dwarf General Electric.[42]

When he arrived in Chicago in 1892 there were more than thirty electric light and power companies. By 1895 he had wiped out this opposition. He intended from the first to create a monopoly, not because he wanted to force people into paying high prices, but because he had a mission. Edison had once prophesied, "We will make electric light so cheap that only the rich will burn candles." Insull's mission was to make the prophecy come true. By 1900 he was running the largest power station in the world, on Harrison Street. It was still the largest in the world forty years later.

Insull more or less created the modern system of gas and electric utilities based on local monopoly; revolutionized the marketing of securities; invented cost accounting; played a major role in the development of mass production; and created modern systems of nationwide product distribution. He was a master of public relations, and to an entire generation he was the greatest living example of the tycoon as patron of the arts. He was also the benign employer. Insull's workers enjoyed a shorter work week and higher pay than almost any other work force in the country. They received free medical care, company-financed night schools, cheap loans, regular bonuses, plus unemployment insurance and a genuine profit-sharing plan. He was a model employer in another respect—blacks were hired in numbers and treated exactly the same as whites.[43]

General Electric, meanwhile, had got out of the business of providing electricity. Instead, it built generators to Insull's ever-greater specifications for his ever-expanding domain. Chicago was flooded with huge quantities of cheap electricity, to the envy of nearly all other cities. Insull had shown the way to create millions of happy customers, eager to electrify almost everything. By World War I the entire electric industry was following dutifully in Insull's footsteps. There was not a single part of it where he had not left his mark. Even the countries that set up government monopolies in electricity, such as Canada and England, asked Insull to show them how to do it. And he did all this at a time when there was an acceptable alternative to electric lighting. Before 1914 electricity had an established rival in gas, which had been in general use for more than a century.

Insull in 1920 looked the part of the Victorian business giant: white walrus mustache, spats, silver-topped cane, pince-nez, ruddy complexion, and a pair of enormous brown eyes that sparkled or dominated, as the need might be. Having made his fortune, he proved a famously soft touch, favoring Englishmen down on their luck in America, out-of-work actors, journalists, and drunks willing to take the pledge. Better still, however, was assuming the Dickensian role of Unknown Benefactor, like Magwitch in *Great Expectations*: the Englishman who has made a fortune in the colonies and in old age delights in doing good, anonymously, for the deserving poor.

Living mainly at his 4,000-acre estate at Libertyville, Illinois, he indulged himself in the gentlemanly and expensive pursuit of horse-breeding. And out of the pleasant hours spent in the countryside came another mission—rural electrification. Until this passion seized Insull, electric light and power had been, like paved streets, something only for cities and large towns. With his devotion to cheap power and mass markets already crowned with success, Insull dedicated himself to driving transmission lines across the gently rolling farmlands of the Midwest.*

Old age, however, also had its torments. In 1912, Insull's beautiful, petite wife had closed her bedroom door on him forever. She had always considered sex revolting, as a respectable woman of her generation was expected to do, and this was her counterrevolution. Insull, bewildered and rejected, became in the years that followed a different man. No longer the ambitious graduate of the Samuel Smiles–Horatio Alger school of honest success, but a lonely man lusting for power. Money he already had in abundance. As more money piled up, he gave it away. It was power

---

* It is worth noting that nearly every electric power company in the United States shied away from rural electrification between the wars; that not until the 1960s was rural electrification completed, and then only after twenty-five years of government intervention.

alone that interested the transformed Insull. He got what he sought. By 1929 he was by any measure the most powerful businessman in America. He dominated Chicago in a way that Ford had never dominated Detroit. He was, in fact, a power in thirteen states, not one.[44]

But he was not invulnerable. During the 1921 recession some of the provinces of the Insull realm were in danger of crashing. Money was hard to come by, and since his defeat by the House of Morgan he maintained a burning hatred for the bankers of New York. Insull hit on a new way of selling securities: to the masses, rather than the few. His cash crisis was quickly solved, such was Insull's fame. In weathering this crisis he managed to save a company that seemed absolutely certain to go bust, People's Gas, Light and Coke Company. It was not an Insull creation. He was actually drafted onto the company's board of directors under false pretenses by people who were in need of a miracle. Insull delivered it. With the crisis past, he had a nervous breakdown.[45]

By 1928 he presided over a utilities empire worth $3 billion, serving 4 million customers. In his hands were 221 active companies, and 27 that existed mainly on paper. His various enterprises had 600,000 stockholders and almost as many bondholders. Insull's companies turned out as much electricity and gas as was consumed by a major industrial country such as Great Britain or Germany. And he had built all of it himself, starting with nothing but his own intelligence and zeal. Along the way he had become a folk hero to millions of ordinary people. These days even the bankers wooed him, for fear of missing out. "They would call us up the way the grocer used to call my mamma," said Insull's bookkeeper, Phil McEnroe, "and try to push their money at us. 'We have some nice lettuce today, Mr. McEnroe; we have some nice fresh green money today, Mr. Insull. Isn't there something you could use maybe $10,000,000 for?' "[46] *

In December 1928 Insull was suddenly gripped with anxiety that Cyrus Eaton, a Cleveland banker and industrialist, was about to make a raid on his empire and wrench away some of his most flourishing provinces. Insull formed a gigantic holding company to protect it. When stock in Insull Utility Investments went on sale in January 1929, there was something approaching panic in the scramble to buy it. Before long the value of all Insull securities, spread among five large holding companies, was rising by $10 million a day, every day. The structure of all these

---

* Traditionally, bankers had lorded it over businessmen and had to be courted into granting loans. There was a joke passed down through three generations about the would-be borrower who discovered that his town's biggest banker had a glass eye. A friend to whom he disclosed his discovery asked him how he detected it. He replied, "That eye looked sympathetic."

holding companies and their subsidiaries was so complicated, however, that not even Insull could explain how each part related to all the rest.[47] It was enough to him that all the strings led back to his own hands. The centerpiece of the structure was the biggest holding company in the world, Middle West Utilities, with its 111 subsidiaries and assets worth $1.25 billion.

Insull by this time was providing electricity and gas to nineteen states. He owned the streetcars of Milwaukee. He also, it was often claimed, owned senators and city halls. No businessman in 1929 had more reason to be pleased at what he had created, or to be more confident in the future, than Samuel Insull. There was no more modern industry than electric power, and if one man had built it, that man was he.

21. Wait Not, Want Not

I

There was a formula for business success believed in for a hundred years despite all the evidence against it. It was known as "oil for the lamps of China," or "a shirt on the back of every Chinaman." From New England to Lancashire, merchants loaded ships with oil and shirts and sent them off to win the fabled riches of the East by peaceful trade. Typhoons often sank more than a few of the ships. Intrepid traders died of strange ailments. Vast fortunes disappeared without trace. Hardly anyone got rich by selling oil or shirts to the Chinese. By a cruelly ironic twist of history, however, the Chinese were looked on as the first consumer society simply because there were so many of them. Too few merchant-adventurers paused to wonder how the Chinese would be able to buy their shirts and oil.

While this folly lasted, mass markets were coming into existence in the West. Around the time of World War I, businessmen woke up. Long used to looking along the street and seeing their fellow citizens mainly as potential workers, it suddenly dawned on them that what they were looking at was an army of potential customers. The argument made by Ford and others was unassailable: high wages would raise mass purchasing power, increase demand, and lift the volume of production enough to bring unit costs down. Paradoxically, high wages did not necessarily mean higher prices. Workers were still workers, of course. But they now had to be courted as consumers. And under the modern factory system, within a generation wives ceased to be homemakers and became mere purchasers of manufactured goods and processed foods.

By tradition, "business looked upon the 'market' as something beyond its control."[1] Since the Middle Ages selling had been the part of business where personal experience, quick wits, and individual charm were expected to prevail. If business had an artistic side to it, selling was it. It was all-important, and presumed to be unteachable beyond an elementary level. The moment business looked out and saw a world of consumers walking the streets with money in their pockets, that changed. The Twenties saw "costly investigations of 'consumer appeal,' of advertising 'pull,' of 'sales resistance,'" reported Hoover's Conference on Recent Economic Changes in 1929. "The very terms would have been unintelligible to our fathers."[2] Once people were regarded chiefly as consumers, nothing was exempt. Even when they were not doing anything very much, they qualified. Leisure itself became something "consumable." And although the work week remained more or less unchanged throughout the Twenties, thanks to the automobile, people insisted on having more leisure time than their parents had dreamed of. Around 1900 hardly anyone took regular vacations. In 1929 the two-week (unpaid) summer vacation was part of American life.[3]

Americans were like Molière's M. Jordan, who was surpised to learn that he spoke prose, after he had spoken it for years. It was only in the late Twenties that the world's first consumer society discovered that was what it was and had been for some time. It came about through the publication in 1927 of a book called *Your Money's Worth*, written by an accountant named Stuart Chase and an economist named Frederick J. Schlink. *Your Money's Worth* sold 100,000 copies. It was the first articulate expression of the interests of a consumer society. It protested at length against wastefulness, fancy packaging, outright fraud, profiteering, and quackery. *Your Money's Worth* made a complete identification between political liberalism and everyday consumerism. In 1928 Schlink founded Consumers Research (later to become Consumers Union) in White Plains, New York, to provide consumers with objective information on all manner of products.* He was convinced that no government bureau would or could provide such a service—it would always be susceptible to outside pressure, unlike a laboratory financed solely by consumers themselves.[4]

Chase became one of the leading writers on social problems caused by economic disorder. He came to believe that production had ceased to

---

* The National Consumers League founded in 1891 was a feminist organization. When feminism faded into insignificance in the Twenties, so did the NCL. By 1923 it existed almost entirely as a letterhead.

matter. If anything, the United States produced too much. It needed only 50,000 gas stations, but had 160,000. Its factories could turn out 900 million pairs of shoes each year, but its people bought only 300 million pairs. What a waste of capital, he cried, what a waste of plant![5] And businessmen agreed. "Since 1920 it is pre-eminently the problem of marketing, and especially the creation of demand, which has held the attention of business executives," said the Conference on Recent Economic Changes.[6] It was a problem to which two solutions were offered: advertising and credit. Together, these formed the chrysalis out of which sprang the Mark I Consumer Society.

II

Around 1900 Albert Lasker was the boy wonder of advertising; at twenty-three he was a partner in Chicago's Lord and Thomas, earning $1,000 a week. By 1912 Lasker, aged thirty-two, owned Lord and Thomas. By the late 1920s modern advertising was his creation more than that of anyone else.

Lasker had thought out the basis of advertising as no one else had ever done. He was the leading exemplar of the hard sell—copy that was forthright and positive. He invented "reason why" advertising, which gave the reader an explicit reason for trying the product. To make his methods more effective, he created the first training program for advertising copywriters. And under Lasker, Lord and Thomas became the training ground for an entire generation of advertising men, most of whom were hired away from the firm for small fortunes or set up agencies of their own; encouraged, perhaps, by Lasker's example—in 1920 he was paying himself $1 million a year.

Before 1917 nearly all the top advertising men had come up by way of patent medicine copy.* Advertising was "a marginal, grubby business."[7] It was transformed by Lasker, by the rise of radio, and by the growth of genuinely mass magazines.† Harvard Business School acknowledged the new importance, and respectability, of advertising by creating its annual Advertising Awards in 1923. It had also become a big business in a very short time, moving from total expenditures of around $400 million a year before the war to $2.6 billion in 1929.[8]

It had become one of the most important tools of mass persuasion, not a mere seller of goods. It was effective because it had quickly found its

---

* Strictly speaking, a patent medicine was one whose formula was on file at the Patent Office. Most, however, were concoctions peddled as if they contained a magic ingredient by men who kept a healthy distance between themselves and government officials.

† Before World War I, only the *Saturday Evening Post* had a circulation above 1 million.

best method—to aim at the emotions instead of the mind; to regard the average consumer as one would a fourteen-year-old. The old style of advertising ran to bald, factual statements (even fraudulent patent medicine copy made the wildest claims in a sober manner). Modern advertising made an effort at creating "human interest," or tried to stir the emotions with a striking layout. And the hard-sell approach became a way of life. The real world vanished under a hail of superlatives.

There was probably less advertising that was blatantly dishonest. As if by way of compensation, there was a lot that was blantantly cynical. One of Lasker's biggest accounts was Lucky Strike cigarettes, and the copy for Luckies suggested that smoking made people slimmer; when the S.S. *America* saved thirty-two Italian seamen in 1929 the heroism of the *America's* crew was attributed to their smoking Luckies. The Twenties saw the rapid rise of the paid testimonial, in which famous people happily lied for money to mislead the credulous. It was the Twenties, too, that saw the phony white-coated doctors and dentists offering "medical" advice to millions. People were encouraged to brush their teeth with toothpastes heavily laced with potassium chlorate, eight grams of which would kill a human being. (There was at least one case of suicide by eating toothpaste for the poison it contained.)[9] To guard their health, they were advised to eat All-Bran, which inflamed their bowels; and to give cod-liver oil to their children, although there was no vitamin D in most cod-liver oil preparations. "Nerve tonics" were heavily promoted, and were useless. Sanatogen, the most popular of these, consisted mainly of liquefied, flavored, and colored cottage cheese. Virtually all the better-known antiseptics were useless; some were even dangerous. The advertising of such products was designed to get around the unpleasant truth and still make it seem good for you, even though it might really be poison.

Spurred on by advertising, the Twenties saw some remarkable discoveries. Fleischmann in 1919 discovered that yeast was a "health food"—a remedy for constipation, bad skin, indigestion, and other minor but unpleasant ailments. An entire generation of magazine readers was introduced to society matrons looking cheerful and active, and reporting: "Last fall I felt tired and worn out with a lack of energy caused by constipation. I was also troubled with pimples and blackheads."* Two yeast cakes a day saved their lives.

Advertising prospered by exploiting the deepest anxieties, especially

---

* Judging by the advertising of the time, the entire country lived in terror of constipation. *Time* in January 1925 carried a full-page ad for a course in "Spinal Motion." The copy contained this edifying paragraph: "I asked about constipation. He gave me another motion —a peculiar, writhing and twisting movement—and fifteen minutes later came a complete evacuation!"

among women. "Halitosis" was dug out of medical dictionaries to excite fears of bad breath and sell Listerine. B.O. (for "body odor") was the staple of Lifebuoy's copy. The favorite affliction was probably pyorrhea. Nearly every toothpaste and toothbrush manufacturer invoked this menace. The prize went to a toothpaste called Forhan, whose advertising read: "Pyorrhea steals upon you like a thief in the night. . . . Pyorrhea seizes four out of five!"[10]

All of which reinforced the twentieth-century obsession that people have with their bodies, part of which is a terror of germs. Yet when Ernest Mahler invented Kotex in the early Twenties, it sold very poorly, even though it was far more comfortable and disposable than other sanitary napkins. It posed an advertising dilemma even in the age of post-Victorian frankness about the body, because absolutely no one would carry an advertisement that used the terms "menstruation" and "sanitary napkin." And even if women knew what Kotex was for, they were shy about going into a drugstore and asking for it. Lasker rose to the challenge. He wrote ads which made the purpose of Kotex clear without ever using the banned words. Then he put what looked like poor boxes in thousands of drugstores, next to huge stacks of Kotex, which came in a plain wrapping. All a woman had to do was drop fifty cents in the box and pick up a package. The rest is history. In a world frightened of germs, Mahler's invention of 1924, Kleenex, was an even greater success, without any of the problems.

Lasker made another lasting impression on American life. People had for years been eating oranges. But they did not eat enough to keep up with the supply pouring forth from the new orange groves of California. So he launched a campaign to get people to drink orange juice, daily if possible. That, too, is history.

There was absolutely no escape from advertising by the late Twenties short of taking up residence in a cave. Radio "took advertising where advertising had always striven to get it, directly into the home. Radio infiltrated defenses once virtually impregnable."[11] A generation earlier, newspapers had consisted almost entirely of news. Now they became mainly vehicles for advertising. This was even more the case with mass magazines. Billboards sprouted on every street, a form of advertising we now take for granted but which then excited vehement hostility, "because of its blatant conspicuousness in an urban society whose memories and esthetic values were rooted largely in a rural environment."[12] The response was advertising on behalf of advertising; attempts to portray it as a public service, a folk art, a source of information and ideas, a spur to consumer demand and thereby a vital cog in the great prosperity machine.

This kind of general advertising spread rapidly. Expensive campaigns were launched, not to sell this or that product, but to generate goodwill toward a business, such as banking, or to promote a city or state. Whole industries set out to "educate" consumers to buy their fruit or soap or cotton goods rather than this brand or that.[13]

What advertising as a whole was selling was a way of life, one that centered on the home (preferably owned) and the family (invariably healthy and limited to no more than three children)—a way of life that was made worthwhile by romantic love. And love required staying young, or at least looking young, regardless of age. It was a lifestyle that was overwhelmingly middle class and urban. It depended on abundant leisure, and on a willingness to spend without counting the cost.

III

Between 1890 and 1930 the population had virtually doubled (from 63 million to 123 million). But the rate of increase had dropped sharply since the war, and by 1930 the United States had what amounted to zero population growth.[14] This, combined with the shortage of new long-term investment opportunities, spread an urgency akin to terror into the nooks and crannies of American life. The boosterism, which to us seems so strident and naïve; the domination of the hard sell in all forms of advertising; the religious fervor of businessmen's conclaves; the feverish worship of business success; we may smile at it now, or turn away in disgust. But somewhere in those murky recesses in the human mind where no sensible historian would dream of going, I think that millions of people heard the ice cracking. They responded in different ways, as people always will. Some took to the hills to become self-sufficient.[15] Others did nothing. For the rest, it was spend, spend, spend. Around 1900, Americans had discovered mass production. Around 1910 they discovered mass distribution. Around 1920 they discovered mass finance.

Until the war, houses were about the only items that respectable people bought on credit. Book agents, sellers of kitchen utensils, and proprietors of dry-goods stores allowed deferred payments. Sewing machines and pianos were often sold on installment plans. But all of these plans combined amounted to only a few hundred million dollars a year.[16] What transformed installment buying was the automobile.

Up to 1919 the typical buyer showed up at the dealer's showroom with cash in hand or a check and drove off happily in his new car, with an unfettered sense of ownership adding to his pleasure. Durant and Raskob, however, could see that this proudly Puritan approach to car ownership would never cover the country with mass-produced cars. To create millions of new customers, they formed the General Motors Acceptance Corporation. Before this, "facilities for consumer credit on a national basis did not exist," Alfred Sloan, Jr., noted with pride.[17] By 1927 two-thirds of all automobile sales were on time payments.[18] In Middletown, reported the Lynds, it was as high as 90 percent.[19] Even Ford had to capitulate (his dealers had been creating sub rosa installment plans for years in conjunction with the local banks). In 1928 he launched the Universal Credit Corporation, modeled after GMAC, to finance Ford dealers and customers. But he was careful to keep his own name out of it, now that Henry Ford the Common Man had become Henry Ford the Banker.

A mortgage had not been considered *real* indebtedness, because it involved an asset whose value was almost certain to rise. But a car began losing its value from the moment it took to the road. It was the automobile which thus smashed the traditional dam, the time-honored inhibitions about going into debt. And once the habit caught on, it spread in a dozen directions at once.

The growth of finance companies in the Twenties astonished financial journalists.[20] Companies such as Beneficial Finance and Household Finance had quietly conducted a small-scale business in half a dozen northeastern cities before the war. In the Twenties they grew by 30 percent a year.[21] That Puritan homily "waste not, want not" had been remade in a decade into "wait not, want not." By 1928, 85 percent of furniture, 80 percent of phonographs, 75 percent of washing machines, 70 percent of refrigerators, and more than half of all sewing machines, pianos, and vacuum cleaners were bought on credit.[22] Personal debts were rising two and a half times faster than incomes.[23]

By 1929 providing consumer credit had become the tenth biggest business in the United States. The amount involved had risen to $7 billion a year. Roughly one-fifth of all retail sales now depended on credit. And yet, as one authority on the subject anxiously remarked, "In spite of its enormous size and the social consequences bound up in it, mass credit is still a dark continent. Economists have left it almost entirely unexplored. Government statistics have almost completely ignored it."[24]

Hoover's Conference on Recent Economic Changes, reporting in 1929, emphasized instead the growth in savings accounts. It was not all spend, spend, spend, they reported. The amounts saved had doubled in a decade, and a larger proportion of Americans than ever before had savings accounts.[25] All of which was true as far as it went. Savings deposits in banks rose by 7 percent a year in 1922–29.[26] But for one thing, most people did not have savings accounts. And for another, there were millions of families who prudently saved a couple of hundred dollars while running up a thousand dollars in debts. Savings alone do not a cautious citizen make. The Lynds, researching in Middletown, found it virtually impossible to meet a family that was not in debt; something that Middletowners ruefully admitted would have been inconceivable a generation earlier, when people borrowed only in an emergency.[27] "It is the undeniable fact," wrote Joseph Schumpeter, one of the leading economists of this century, "that during the twenties households habitually overspent their current receipts . . . or that the algebraic sum of household savings throughout was negative, the deficit being covered by borrowing and drawing on speculative gains."[28]

Hard-sell advertising and the democratization of credit were the Twenties' answer to overproduction, low population growth, a shortage of new industries, and a static structure of income distribution. But all they could do was keep the party going a little longer. It was Belshazzar's feast all over again. The writing was as plainly on the wall as the message *Mene Mene Tekel Upharsin* written, according to the Book of Daniel, by a disembodied hand. In both cases, the message was the same: "You have been weighed in the balance and found wanting." Yet like Belshazzar and his feasting courtiers, none of the partygoers of 1929 was able to figure out what the message said.

22. Rose like a Rocket...

I

Back in 1919 Charles Ponzi was forty-two years old, an ex-forger, ex-vegetable dealer, employed for the present as a clerk at J. P. Poole, a foreign trade house in Boston. The five foot, two inch Ponzi was dreaming, however, of greater things than peaceful obscurity at $20 a week. He had decided to become a financier, nothing daunted by the fact that he had little more than $100 in cash. The Great Ponzi, as he styled himself, had other assets—a complete lack of scruples, and a keen awareness of human greed.

He opened the Old Colony Foreign Exchange Company. By exploiting the postwar upheavals in foreign exchange markets, he claimed, he was able to buy international money orders in one country at a low price and sell them within weeks or days in some other country at a much higher price. Ponzi promised to pay $15 for every $10 left in his care for ninety days.

Money trickled in for a couple of months, then virtually stopped. Ninety days after opening for business, Ponzi began paying out as promised, without hesitation. Reporters hastened to the Old Colony Foreign Exchange Company, and Ponzi became famous in days. Within six months he was taking in $1 million a week. Ponzi lived out the fantasies of sudden riches: he bought a big house, hired servants, rode around Boston in a chauffeured limousine, took over J. P. Poole, and fired his former boss. Crowds followed him in the streets. One admirer shouted out,

"You're the greatest Italian of them all!" Ponzi modestly disagreed. "No, no. Columbus and Marconi. Columbus discovered America. Marconi discovered the wireless." "So what?" said the admirer. "You discovered money!"[1]

The newspapers had made Ponzi. Only one journalist, Edward Dunn, city editor of the *Boston Post*, troubled to find out how many foreign money orders were sold. In 1919 those sold in the United States had a total value of $58,560. That would absorb only the smallest fraction of the money Ponzi had taken in. As doubts began to grow about Ponzi's scheme, the unsavory facts about his past emerged, such as his prison terms in Atlanta and Montreal.

Despite these revelations, despite the proof that he was operating a swindle, the lure of easy riches was irresistible. The money kept coming in. But to keep his bizarre con game going Ponzi had to keep paying out on his ninety-day notes. The end came on August 16, 1920, when the Old Colony Exchange Company went out of business with assets listed at $0 and liabilities totalling $2,122,000. Ponzi had taken in $15 million, and actually paid most of it out to his "investors." Ponzi went to jail once more for using the mails to defraud.

Before the Twenties were over, other men would operate more successful swindles and never see the inside of a prison cell. Ponzi however deserves pride of place. Because he was the first in the new era to exploit boldly, publicly, and on a vast scale the get-rich-quick fever that swept through the Twenties as Saint Vitus's dance had swept through Germany in the fourteenth century.

II

The fastest-growing city in the United States in the 1920s was Miami by a wide margin. A hamlet boasting only sixty inhabitants in 1896, it was a city of 60,000 in 1924. Telephones were being installed at such a rate that the phone company was making its plans on the assumption of a permanent population of 300,000 by 1940. Yet up to World War I, Miami consisted mainly of mangrove jungle and malarial swamp. But then came Carl G. Fisher, who marveled at the climate and was undaunted by obstacles. He and his partners cleared the jungle, drained the swamp, built a seawall, built up the beach, erected a three-and-a-half-mile causeway linking beach and mainland, and saw their dreams of riches realized. In 1924 lots in the former swamp sold for $20,000 and more. Artificial islands were now being built in the shallow waters of Biscayne Bay on which millionaires' mansions would rise one day.

Fischer had not simply made himself and his friends rich. By developing Miami, he had made it possible for others to get rich too. At first, they were merely lucky, like William Jennings Bryan, who in 1912 had bought a modest house in Miami where he could keep his aging bones warm each winter. Eight years later Bryan sold his house and to his amazement realized a profit of $250,000. It came as a revelation. For the rest of his life Bryan devoted much of his energies to orating on the miracles of Florida real estate. When he died in 1925 the Great Commoner went to his rest a millionaire.[2] It was not only in Miami that riches were to be had. One C. W. Bingham arrived in Palm Beach in 1896 and bought a piece of ocean-front property half a mile wide for $4.65 a front foot. By the time of the armistice it was selling for $160 a front foot as rich families from the cold cities of the North started to discover the joys of Christmas at 80 degrees. By 1925 its value had risen to $3,300 a front foot.[3] The Florida land boom was on in full cry.

It matched the fervor of the Yukon gold rush. Every other business in the state appeared to be selling land or options to buy. "Whoever remains longer than a week and does not buy a lot must be an incorrigible iconoclast, or blind, deaf and paralyzed," Bruce Bliven reported from the front lines. "There is no other subject of conversation but buying and its potentialities."[4] The boom rolled up to ever-dizzier heights on the free bus trip. Simply by expressing an interest in real estate anyone could travel from one end of Florida to the other and back, absolutely free, with free lunches every afternoon. Busloads of potential buyers lurched out from the coastal cities each morning into the arid, dreary hinterland, to look over "the property." This usually consisted of several hundred acres of burned-over land, some of it still smoking. Under a circus tent the company's best spellbinders would deliver passionate speeches about how easy it was to get rich in real estate, so foolproof that even babes in arms could do it were it not for the law. Then came the free (bad) lunch, and after that the afternoon was entrusted to the salesmen. With a 10 percent down payment you reserved your Florida lot. You could then sell this option—known as a "binder"—and make a profit without ever putting up more than the original 10 percent. The market in selling binders was in some places more active than in selling the actual lots.

The climate brought the first generation of Florida boomers; the chance to get rich brought the next. But there were other charms as well. Miami was not far, after all, from wet Havana, wet Bimini, wet Nassau. Bootlegging was disguised as fishing. "Any visitor may see the cheering spectacle of twenty huge limousines waiting in line at the entrance to a 'fish wharf,' their owners supposedly so overcome by the craving for piscatorial delicacies that they insist on driving home with the fish, wrapped in square packages."[5]

So for their various reasons, thousands each week poured into the state. "Lots were bought from blue prints. They look better that way," reported the vice-president of an Atlanta finance company. "Then the buyer gets the promoter's vision, can see the splendid curving boulevards, the yacht basin, the parks lined with leaning coconut trees, and the flaming hibiscus."[6] The lots, meanwhile, were likely to be under water or to consist of foul-smelling swamp. Such lots were sold "pre-development." And they were given exotic names, usually Spanish, like Boca Raton (which means Rat's Jaw) and Los Gatos (a more prosaic choice, meaning The Cats).

The architecture was also vaguely Spanish. The architects who designed it came from all over the United States. They knew next to nothing about Florida, yet right away they had to create buildings with a "Floridian" character. Much of what resulted was on a par with that other bastard architecture of the age, the big-city picture palace, running as it did to the grotesque and melodramatic. The doyen of this crew was Addison Mizner, the creator of Boca Raton. An upper-class con man, he went to Florida to get rich in real estate and decided to get rich in architecture instead. He taught himself the subject in a week or two, in between charming rich people into offering him commissions. In return, he gave them million-dollar mansions in a style later known as "Bastard-Spanish-Moorish-Romanesque-Gothic-Renaissance-Big Bull Market-and Damn the Expense."[7]

The Florida land boom was not unique. Cities all over the country were trying to grow as fast as they could. Huge tracts were being divided into lots for subdivisions. High-pressure selling was the usual technique for disposing of the thousands of lots the average subdivision produced. In Florida and elsewhere, the development of these subdivisions was often premature and chaotic. Most of the lots would remain undeveloped and in time would revert to the city or county in lieu of unpaid taxes.

But while the game lasted, it was the hottest game in town. It was a natural for a Ponzi. And after he got out of prison, he went straight to Florida to recoup his fortunes. He set up the Charpon Land Syndicate, which offered land "near Jacksonville." Near in this case meant sixty-five miles. Ponzi tried to raise the money to finance his land syndicate by selling "unit certificates of indebtedness" for $310 each. He guaranteed a 200 percent return within three months. This venture collapsed in April 1926 when Ponzi was convicted of violating Florida's trust laws. A more imaginative scheme was set in motion by Ben Hecht, who coauthored that minor classic of the Twenties stage, *The Front Page.* He found someone who had already made a million dollars out of the Florida boom and was greedy for more. With this millionaire's backing, Hecht set up a swindle to sell the malarial jungle swamp that made up most of Key Largo by faking the discovery of a hidden pirate treasure. In his youth, he had faked dozens of sensational newspaper stories. With this background, he played the buried-treasure story into the headlines. The suckers came in droves.[8] His millionaire backer, however, had made such a shambles of his other ventures that all the gains from this swindle were lost in another.

By 1925, people were pouring into Florida faster than food could be shipped in, and that summer, famine threatened. A ban was placed on incoming shipments of building materials, household goods, bottled drinks, even chewing gum, so that trucks, trains, and steamships could bring in more food. The ice plants broke down under the strain of trying to keep up with demand; the ice that remained could only be bought with a doctor's prescription.

But nothing seemed able to abate the land fever. A journalist who arrived in Florida that summer to write about the foolishness of it all, Gertrude Mathews Shelby, was swept away instead. With a $2,500 down payment she bought a binder on thirty-four and a half acres. She then sold the binder before the first installment was due, and cleared $13,000 in one month.[9] Everyone who entered Florida, for whatever reason, was "a prospect." The center of the real estate boom was the seventy-two-mile strip between Miami and Palm Beach. But the creed ran, "Buy anywhere. You can't lose." Yet everyone Mrs. Shelby talked to was convinced that one day the boom would go bust. They all expected to get out before then. This was the same mentality that kept the money coming in after Ponzi was revealed as a con man—get in, get rich, get out.

So the boom rolled on. Miami continued to grow so fast its inhabitants called it "the Magic City." The *Miami Herald*, serving a city smaller than Toledo, carried more advertising than any other paper in the world.[10] There was little to fear from nature because the Magic City was north of the "hurricane belt," said the real estate men. And the people kept coming, rolling down the Dixie Highway, so the boom would run for a few years yet.

Then, one night in mid-September, 1926, the barometer reading in Miami fell to 27.75—the lowest ever recorded in the United States. A gale that raced along at 130 miles an hour tore through the city. More than 100 people drowned. Some 40,000 were made homeless. Hundreds of boats were sunk or smashed to bits. The streets were clogged with uprooted palm trees and littered with glass. There was virtually no food that was still edible. Thousand-ton ships were stranded in the streets. There was no electric power. Miami was as shattered as a city attacked and looted by an army.[11]

Throughout southern Florida, the death toll ran to 400; property damage came to $300 million. State government had so lost its sense of proportion, however, that the governor, John Wellborn Martin, and other officials did virtually nothing to help the relief operations. They minimized the extent of the damage because the truth would hurt the price of real estate. While the Red Cross tried to aid the injured and homeless, the state government sent its men and supplies to help repair property damage instead.[12] Yet the hurricane had blown away the miles of ropes and flags that marked out in swamps the promised thoroughfares of promised cities. Ocean-front properties that had sold for $2,000 a foot dropped to $1,000, and then to $700. With the collapse of the boom came hundreds of bankruptcies, thousands of foreclosures. For tens of thousands who had come to get rich, unemployment and hardship were what they got. Miami became by 1928 one of the cheapest cities in which to live. It had been hard to find a studio apartment for less than $50 a week in 1925. A year after the hurricane it was possible to rent an entire furnished house on Biscayne Bay for $50 a month.[13]

The city, however, lived on to survive other hurricanes and grow as Fischer had imagined it growing. No gale can blow away a city. What the hurricane of 1926 had blown away was the illusion that there would always be another sucker who would come along, buy you out, make you rich, and be left holding the bag.

III

The Liberty Loan campaigns of the war did more than raise money for the government. They introduced the entire country to the securities market. By the armistice some 65 million people had become the owners of government bonds. In the meantime they had become familiar with the machinery of stock markets, something with which few people had any contact before. The war had made the world safe for securities salesmen.

As the price of everything shot upward in 1919 and early 1920, there was a rush to cash in on the stock market. Call money went up to 25 percent, which helped to complete the revolution Liberty Loans had begun.[14] Until now, most of the money borrowed for stock purchases had been arranged through time loans, where the borrower had to put up collateral of 20 percent or more and the loan had to be renewed every thirty, sixty, or ninety days, depending on the agreement reached. A call loan (or demand loan) was good for just one day, but renewable at the option of both parties from day to day. Speculators liked call loans, despite the daily fluctuations in the call-money interest rate, because that was how the speculators played the market—day by day. They did not want the cash they had invested to be tied up. The banks also woke up about the same time to the charms of the call-loan market. A 25 percent rate of return brought them running. On a call loan, there was no minimum amount of collateral. That did not worry the banks, because payment on a call loan could be demanded virtually within hours after the market turned down. In the meantime, they would be employing their resources to the full, at a high rate of return.

Not even the market slump in the 1921 recession frightened them away, when the call-loan rate dropped to a humble 5–6 percent, for Wall Street was still a lively place. "Even the reputed 'wickedness' of the Street gave it a certain glamor in the twenties,"[15] one of its least likely recruits, Matthew Josephson, discovered.

Stocks were of two kinds: common and preferred. The differences were that preferred carried no voting rights but promised a fixed dividend, while common carried voting rights and made no promises about dividends. Investors had traditionally preferred preferred, with their guarantee of 6, or 7, or possibly 8 percent. Each year, after a corporation had paid off its bondholders and the owners of preferred stock and settled its tax bill with the government, if there was a surplus left over, it was divided among the holders of common stock. As a result, business had to depend on the capital markets if it wanted to raise money for new investment. But during the war the utilities companies began holding back part of their surplus so they could finance expansion from within. The Liberty Loans were simply mopping up most of the money in the capital market.

By the early 1920s most large corporations were copying the utilities' precedent. They financed their new investment out of earnings. They kept the holders of the common stock happy by paying a small but regular dividend. The dividend was increasingly paid, not in cash, but in a new stock issue, after a 1920 Supreme Court ruling that this kind of dividend was free from income tax.

While these changes in relations between corporation and shareholder were unfolding, the embrace was made tighter still. The shareholder of 1925 was so eager to increase his holdings, the corporation found, that it could issue still more stock and he would buy it, in vast amounts, if it was offered to him first at slightly below the market price. And this produced even more money for new investment. The upshot of all these changes was that in less than ten years common stock became the truly preferred stock, and preferred was seen as being fit only for widows, orphans, the managers of pension funds, and other people afraid to get their feet wet. By 1925 common stock was more than preferred: it was irresistible.

With new stock issues being ground out in a hopeless attempt to appease the growing public demand, the brokerage houses hired thousands of eager young customers' men to sell the new issues. They were quickly trained, then thrown into the fray. They hastened forward, without caution or doubt, never having known a major panic or even a bad bear market. "In effect, uninitiated brokers were selling stocks to an uninformed public."[16]

New possibilities in finding both investors and investments were discovered in the creation of the investment trust. They were imported from Britain, where they had been in existence for a generation. The first modern American investment trust was the International Securities Trust of America, formed in 1921. Through such a trust, an investor with only a few hundred dollars to risk could participate in a portfolio of investments covering dozens of the most glamorous and successful names in American business. The big bull market of the Twenties was the ideal environment. From 1923 to 1929 investment trusts sprang up like mushrooms after rain. By 1929 a new one was opening every day.[17] It was a common practice for an investment trust to own shares in other investment trusts. They were piled on top of one another, like holding companies. They were also ripe for picking. In Britain, a more sedate country, management costs were about 0.5 percent of total assets in the average investment trust. In the United States management absorbed 10–20 percent, sometimes more.[18] They were likely to know what they were doing, however, because many an investment trust was set up by people who had securities to sell. Once the trust was formed and the investors lined up, the trust took their money and used it to buy those securities. It was a thriving field. By 1929 the various investment trusts held portfolios with a combined estimated value of $4.5 billion.

Matthew Josephson had meanwhile gravitated from life among the French Surrealists and the editorship of an avant-garde magazine (which folded) to becoming a financial analyst for a major Wall Street firm of stockbrokers. "My office adjoined the board room," he later wrote, "a spacious clublike room, furnished with upholstered chairs, and having on one wall a large stock board where a clerk rapidly chalked up stock quotations as they came in on the ticker tape, and at the other end a glass-enclosed booth where an order clerk received orders to buy or sell and telegraphed them to our floor broker on the Exchange. A crowd of day-to-day speculators sat here always watching the panorama of the stock board, making a buzz of talk or sometimes expressing themselves in laughter, jeers, or oaths, depending on how the wheel of fortune turned for them. The tickers' metallic voices sputtered steadily, telephones rang repeatedly, customers' men shouted prices into telephones for clients and rushed to the window of the order clerk with their orders on little slips of paper. The board room was the heart of the firm's business."[19] And this scene was repeated every business day in a thousand brokerage houses. The atmosphere was like that at a racecourse, and the firms were no more likely to lose than bookies are. In this atmosphere of excitement and male competition, customers were traded in and out of securities without much trouble. And whether their stocks went up or down, the house gathered in its broker's fee of $15 on every hundred shares.

The liveliness of Wall Street in the Twenties was often credited to a new breed of big-time plungers, the westerners (only we would nowadays call them midwesterners). For the first time, "outsiders were able to capture the public imagination, exert leadership, and change the Wall Street Point of View while assuming direction of the great bull market."[20] The names of these men were almost legendary in the boardrooms—Billy Durant, the Van Sweringen brothers, the seven Fisher brothers from Detroit, Jesse Livermore, Arthur W. Cutten. They dealt in millions and went with their instincts, ignoring the caution of easterners, raised on limited horizons.

Livermore was "a speculator pure and simple."[21] He maintained a string of mansions and mistresses to inhabit them. He drove around New York in a huge yellow Rolls-Royce. Operating on a vast scale, pretending to sources that did not exist and information that he could not possibly possess, he was an impressive phony.[22] Men who really were very rich, such as Doheny, laughed at him; and so did men like Clarence Barron, who had forgotten more about the stock market than Livermore would ever know. But in those boardrooms, Livermore's was a name to conjure with. He was the Street's most famous bear.* He made his first million in the crash of 1907. He made another million in the 1921 recession. Since then, he had played both sides of the market, sometimes a bull, sometimes a bear.

If Livermore was the most flamboyant of the new breed, Arthur Cutten was decidedly the least so. A middle-aged Chicago bookkeeper, with high stiff collars and a pince-nez, he came to New York in 1925 with $10 million—his gains in only two years at the Chicago corn pit. He arrived without fanfare. By 1928, however, he too was famous in the brokerage house boardrooms, the envy of a hundred thousand speculators. Cutten

---

* All stock sales are a form of betting. A bull is betting that the shares will go up in value; a bear that they will come down. A bear agrees to sell a certain amount of stock, borrows it (usually from a broker), and delivers it at once to the buyer. He has an agreement to replace the stock he has borrowed after a specified time, say thirty days. If the stock drops in value, he can then replace it for less than he received at the time of the sale. The difference in the two prices is his profit. If the price of the stock goes up, however, he has to suffer the resulting loss.

was an incurable optimist, buying on a heroic scale all across the board. Almost everything he bought went up sharply in the big bull market. The fact that Cutten was buying a stock helped push the price up still further.[23]

The most famous of the bulls was, of course, Billy Durant, running his syndicate of midwestern millionaires in pursuit of ever-greater riches. Ironically, had Durant stayed out of the stock market and simply held on to his GM stock, instead of frittering it away in 1920, he would by 1927 have been worth $500 million.[24] In the same camp with Durant was the country's leading columnist, the Hearst press's Arthur Brisbane, whose "Today" column was carried by more than 1,000 newspapers. Brisbane was one of the biggest boosters of Florida real estate and common stocks. He wrote, he liked to say, "for the tired brain or the lack of brain."[25]

IV

In the Twenties the Federal Reserve System was still a fairly new and untried creature, put together by Wilsonian Progressives to break the "Wall Street money trust." It was a reform like woman suffrage and Prohibition, to bring sweet reason into the hurly-burly life of a frontier people. Its dominant figure in the 1920s was the governor of the crown jewel of the system, the Federal Reserve Bank of New York, the aptly named Benjamin Strong.

He came of a solidly middle-class family based on Puritan stock which ran heavily to theologians and politicians. Yet when he reached eighteen the family was momentarily hard-pressed. He alone of four brothers was unable to go to college. He went to work instead as a clerk on Wall Street. He rose rapidly in the world of investment banking. His private life, however, was dogged by tragedy. The wife to whom he was devoted for ten years took her own life in a fit of postnatal depression.[26] He remarried two years later. In 1916 his second wife left him. By 1920 his chief, virtually sole interest in life was the Federal Reserve. His loneliness was relieved only by his close friendship with the head of the Bank of England, Montagu Norman, with whom he spent his vacations (and frequent convalescences) in the south of France.

Harding's appointments to the Federal Reserve Board ranged from the barely adequate to the obviously appalling. In Strong, however, the system possessed at least one figure of world stature. He, more than anyone else, took the amorphous creature brought to life by the Federal Reserve Act and turned it into the Federal Reserve System. Its chief role was to ensure that industry, agriculture, and commerce secured the credit they needed on terms that were reasonable. Only when inflation or stock market speculation or exchange rate instability began to interfere with the smooth operation of the money supply was the Fed expected to respond to them. That is, it was not set up to deal with inflation, speculation, or exchange rates, but it had to watch them closely.

The Federal Reserve had two ways of influencing the money supply. It could buy or sell government securities on the open market, which increased or decreased the reserves of all the member banks in the system; it was their reserves which formed the base of the money supply. The other way was for the Fed to raise or lower the rediscount rate *—the rate, that is, it charged member banks when they borrowed from it. At the time, this was a novel and imaginative system, untried but full of promise. In essence, it is how the Federal Reserve works to this day, except that it no longer accepts commercial paper as collateral. The fact is, however, that despite every assumption that such measures allow the Federal Reserve to control the money supply, they do nothing of the kind. All they can do is work indirectly upon it. If banks and individuals are willing to borrow at high rates and spend freely, the Federal Reserve's policy is not going to stop them, or the resulting inflation.

Limitations such as this become apparent only with experience, alas (and not always even then). Benjamin Strong, however, was under few illusions about the Fed's powers. He disliked what was happening on the stock market, yet, he pointed out, there was almost nothing the system could do to curb speculation except to deflate the entire economy.[27] Too much like hunting flies with a fire ax. Abroad, Strong believed deeply in promoting international economic stability, a generation ahead of his time. To him, international reconstruction was both a humanitarian duty and in the best interests of the United States. A poor and hungry world was a dangerous place in which to live.

He and Norman together engineered Britain's return to the gold standard, in a strong mutual conviction that gold would restore stability to exchange rates and exert a restraining influence on governments. So far as it went, the idea was sound. But the pound was pegged, for reasons of pride, at its prewar value of $5.00, even though the British economy had been badly weakened by the war. The British propped it up with high interest rates, while Strong labored to keep American interest rates low, both to help the British and to help other devastated countries—France, Belgium, Poland, Italy, and Germany—revive their economies with

---

* This was the term used in the Twenties, when the member banks used commercial paper as collateral for their loans from the Fed. Thus a bank could make a loan to a business one day, and the next day take this promissory note to the Federal Reserve Bank in its region and raise new cash on it. The note was "rediscounted." But this meant the money supply expanded *automatically* in good times, and contracted just as automatically in bad. In 1935 the system changed its rules and stopped rediscounting commercial paper.

American loans. Easy-credit policies in the American money markets, however, were inevitably vulnerable to speculative forces. In 1924 Strong warned Norman that if speculation became unacceptedly rampant the easy-credit policies would have to come to an end. For the present, at least, the Federal Reserve was happy to follow Strong's lead, because European recovery might revive demand for American agricultural exports and relieve the crisis in the farmlands.[28] It was largely foreign demand that set the price of American farm products.

Low American interest rates might also help to stem the flow of gold into the United States. The net outflow of gold was weakening foreign currencies and steadily making the dollar stronger; good for expatriate writers living in Paris but not so good for American exporters. It was also producing inflation at home. Between 1922 and 1927 the United States gold stock increased by $900 million, mainly because of gold imports. Nearly two-thirds of this ended up in the reserves of American banks. The banks could lend up to $13 for every $1 they held in gold. These imports, therefore, represented a powerful inflationary force, expanding the money supply by $6 billion.[29] And there was little the Fed could do about it so long as economic uncertainty created a nervous hankering for gold.

The state of American banking alone was enough to make people nervous. Hardly a day passed in the 1920s without one to three banks going bust. In 1926 nearly 1,000 banks failed; even in supposedly prosperous 1928 nearly 500 failed. Of the 25,000 banks in operation thousands were hair-raisingly mismanaged.[30] Most of the failures were in rural areas. When the farms went bust, so did the banks. The banks that were members of the Federal Reserve System made up the top half of American banking; they were bigger, better-run, and had the support of the system behind them. The lower half was, literally, something else again.

But the behavior of even the upper half was enough to give a sober individual pause. Because the banks, too, were caught up in the whirling ticker-tape parade to endless riches. The pace was set by the richest bank in the United States, National City Bank of New York, gray, conservative, boring—all that the most apprehensive depositor could ask for. In 1921, however, Charles E. Mitchell was installed as President. Mitchell was not a gray, conservative, boring banker. He was a securities salesman who had made his way up, as Strong had done, from a humble clerkship. At thirty, Mitchell was the head of his own firm, at forty, head of the National City Company, the National City Bank's security selling subsidiary. Mitchell's rapid promotion to the presidency of the bank itself marked a break with the past in both spirit and method. Under his leadership, "the National City Bank grew to be not merely a bank in the old-fashioned sense, but essentially a factory for the manufacture of stocks and bonds, a wholesaler and retailer for their sale, and a stock speculator and gambler."[31] It was work that paid well. In 1928 Mitchell as president of the bank received a comparatively modest $25,000 salary. But his bonuses from the National City Company came to $1,316,634.14.[32]

Many of National City Company's most profitable ventures were overseas. For them, and for countless other sellers of securities, foreign loan markets were the nearest thing known to Christmas every day. The world was literally crying out for dollars. They were happy to find people willing to lend, at a (high) price. National City Bank's own agents reported that Peru had a record of bad debts, for example; it had no prospects of economic growth, and government in Peru was a sometime thing. National City nevertheless floated loans for Peru totaling $90 million, and collected extra millions as its own commission. There was never a hint to investors that they were taking a chance.[33] On the contrary, Mitchell's salesmen praised Peru as a wonderful investment.* It was a story that was repeated with minor variations ad infinitum. American holdings of foreign securities and promissory notes more than doubled between 1919 and 1929, from $6.9 billion to $17 billion, on loans ranging from the unwise to the suicidal.

The banks like everyone else did not want to miss out on the action. And like the brokerage houses, they were being stirred by new men, such as Mitchell, with new ideas. Even the citadel of conservative banking—investment banking—succumbed. For a century, any major company looking for a really big loan had turned to the oligopoly of the half dozen famous banking houses that clustered around Wall Street. Their very existence, their role in the country's history, their conservatism, all created a comforting illusion of stability. Their day, however, had passed. No oligopoly of famous firms could hope to raise money on the scale that modern corporations demanded, nor could expect to handle the tidal wave of securities that poured onto the market after 1921.[34] New, more aggressive firms, such as Dillon, Reed and Company, came into existence and wrested a large piece of the action away.†

Any lingering doubts that a new day had dawned came in early 1929

---

* Would anyone be surprised to learn that these loans went into default in fairly short order?

† In the late Twenties, Clarence Dillon was the Boy Wonder of Wall Street. In his early forties, he was friendly and expansive in a manner true to his Texas origins, yet impeccably Harvard in his education. He had created Youngstown Steel and Tube. He had created a major banking house (specializing in foreign loans). He had beaten the House of Morgan in the bidding for the Dodge Corporation and thus helped create Chrysler. He took over National Cash Register when it became too big for the founders' family to manage. He was hailed as a genius.

when the House of Morgan finally capitulated. There was no more conservative banking house in the world. Morgan scrutinized its depositors as
carefully as it scrutinized its borrowers. To leave money at the House of
Morgan was a privilege and an honor. It required an introduction, preferably from the chairman of the board of one of the top 100 corporations.
To Morgan, riches spelled rectitude. But in 1929 the fever somehow blew
in through an open window. Morgan began to launch holding companies,
so it, too, could cash in on the stock market boom.

V

The matters covered since the beginning of this chapter were the kind
of thing Professor Ripley had in mind when he described Wall Street to
Coolidge in 1927 as a scene of "prestidigitation, double-shuffling, honey-
fugling, hornswoggling and skulduggery." And that was before the big bull
market really got rolling. Ripley, raised in more conventional times, was
shocked by the insider dealing, the corporate secretiveness, the speculative fever, the growth of holding companies and investment trusts, the rise
of management control, and stockholder indifference. Despite blue-sky
laws, ICC regulations, stock exchange disclosure rules, and the like, sharp
practice permeated the securities market. To him, it could have only one
result—a monumental, God-awful crash, for one very simple reason: "In
the end, the truth is bound to prevail."[35] What is remarkable, however, is
not the prognostication or its eventual fulfillment, but that his book, *Main
Street and Wall Street,* was widely reviewed, sold 50,000 copies, was
quoted from by countless financial journalists, brought an invitation to
the White House, spelled out clearly what was going on—and nothing
happened. It was as though the stock market led a life all its own. And in
a way, it did.

There seemed to be endless ways to get rich. New securities gushed
forth, more and more each year. New issues amounted to $30 million a
month in 1926; up to $800 million a month in early 1929.[36] Many of the
choicest offerings barely trickled down to the ordinary shareholder, because the banks which handled them built up "preferred lists" of people
they would like to please—such as Coolidge, Raskob, Bernard Baruch,
McAdoo, Lindbergh. Not only were the chosen few given first choice of
each plum offering, they could buy their shares at a lower price than the
ordinary players of the game who were hanging around the boardrooms
sweating with excitement. A Johns-Manville offering of 1927, for example,
went to preferred list customers for as little as $47.50 a share, while what
was left over went to the general public for $79 a share.[37]

Another way to get rich was by belonging to a speculators' pool. The pool would concentrate on a particular share or cluster of shares and then drive up their value by bribing financial journalists on all the best newspapers, such as the *Wall Street Journal*, the *New York Times*, and the *New York Herald Tribune*.[38] The press, too, did not want to miss out on the action. It fawned on and flattered the big men on Wall Street. A Billy Durant or a Jesse Livermore was covered as if he were a baseball star.

The most glamorous stock of the Twenties was RCA, known as Radio. In 1921 it had traded at $2.50 a share. By 1927 it had reached $85.00, even though it had never paid a dividend. In early 1928 a small group was formed to make a killing in Radio. They agreed to buy 1 million shares, which represented a large part of what was potentially available, because GE and Westinghouse held large blocks of RCA stock that would never come onto the market. The group brought in one New York Stock Exchange member, Michael J. Meehan, to run the operation day by day. Employing a variety of legal but deceptive maneuvers, Meehan managed to generate enough interest to push Radio from 90 to 109—at which point the group sold out. They divided nearly $5 million, of which 10 percent went to Meehan as his fee. It was little more than a confidence game.[39] The players included Raskob, Wilson's secretary, Joseph Tumulty, a Rockefeller, the wife of David Sarnoff, and Walter P. Chrysler. When they pulled out of Radio, the stock dropped to 87. It was a fleecing that took all of one week. It was a classic example of a "stock pool" at work.* The big bull market saw dozens of them.

There were also hundreds of outright stock swindles. They were a very big business, running to an estimated $600 million a year or more.[40] There were fashions in stock swindles. Oil was a big favorite in the early Twenties; phony mine stocks were all the rage in 1927.[41] Fraudulent bankruptcies were also thriving, to the tune of half a billion dollars a year or thereabouts.[42] Any impression that what was wrong with Wall Street in the Twenties was simply that speculation got out of hand is plain wrong. It was a place where crookedness of all kinds flourished.

Although Wall Street had prospered steadily as the economy recovered from the 1921 recession, it was not until late 1927 that the big bull market really hit its stride. In 1926 stock prices and stock sales had gone up by 11 percent, faster than productivity but nothing to be alarmed about. In 1927 stock prices rose by 20 percent and stock sales by 24 percent. Yet the economy went into a slight recession that year. After five

* "The point of a stock pool manipulation was simplicity itself: it was a way of inducing the Stock Exchange ticker tape to tell a story that was essentially false, and thus to deceive the public." John Brooks, *Once in Golconda* (New York, 1969), p. 69.

years of sustained high growth, industrial production flattened out. Prices fell. Unemployment rose. With Europe facing a similar recession, the Federal Reserve responded to pleas from home and abroad to stimulate the American economy. It bought large amounts of government securities, and it cut the rediscount rate from 4 percent to 3.5 percent. It was bad luck rather than bad management that this otherwise sensible and modest spur was applied just when the stock market was parting with reality. The result was the biggest boom in history.

Almost every passing month now brought a record day for share sales, leaving brokers exhausted by the three o'clock gong that ended trading. In the early Twenties a 2-million-share day was a good day; in the mid-Twenties 3 million shares could create excitement. By 1928 the 4-million-share day passed almost without comment, and the 5 million barrier was quickly broken. And the scene at the New York Stock Exchange was being played out at all the other stock exchanges—in Chicago, Los Angeles, St. Louis, and San Francisco. Fueling most of this buying and selling was the astonishing growth in the call-money market.[43]

At the start of 1928 a terse announcement from the New York Stock Exchange that brokers' loans had reached $4.4 billion set off a wave of nervous selling. Coolidge was asked if he thought the level of these loans was too high. He confessed, as he often did on complicated economic questions, that it was all very difficult, he was unfamiliar with the details, etcetera, etcetera.[44] In the end, he simply tried to sound reassuring, without saying anything specific. The market steadied, and rose again.

Where were the brokers getting so much money to keep the game going? About a third was coming from the banks. A large slice came from investment trusts, as attractive securities rose into the stratosphere and then out of sight. "This money was loaned to speculators, who often used it to purchase shares in the same investment trust that had loaned the money initially!"[45] Large corporations, too, began to steer some of their huge cash reserves into call loans. Standard Oil of New Jersey, for instance, provided $110 million. By the end of 1928 the amount of money brokers had out in loans to their customers was approaching the total for all the currency in circulation in the United States—$6.4 billion.[46]

Strong had meanwhile become deeply apprehensive. In the spring of 1928 he began putting up the rediscount rate in New York, raising it to 4 percent. The rest of the system followed suit. By October 1928 he had raised it to 5 percent. This in turn pushed the call-money rate to 10 percent, and still the boom continued unabated. It was a bitter disappointment. For the last two years Strong's labors had been wrung by an iron will from a body wracked with pain. He was dying from tuberculosis, suffering from shingles, and lived in constant agony from diverticulitis of the colon. An operation to ease this last condition led to a severe hemorrhage. In October 1928 Strong died, at the age of fifty-five. With his death, the Federal Reserve lost the one man who might have found a way out of the box it was now in. At present, it could do nothing right. If it pursued low interest rates, it added fuel to the fires of speculation. And if it pursued high interest rates it did exactly the same thing, because each time the rediscount rate went up, so did the call-money rate, and each time that went up, the banks, the investment trusts, and the large corporations hurried forward to press money on anyone who wanted to play the Wall Street endless riches game.

Who, then, were the players? There was a belief at the time, later set in the concrete of popular myth, that, in the words of a Twenties song, "Everybody's doin' it." As a typical account puts it, there "were chauffeurs, taxi drivers, speakeasy bartenders, elevator operators, waiters and barbers, who got into the market on tips from the people they served."[47] Some accounts put the number of shareholders as high as 15 million. The Treasury's chief actuary, Joseph McCoy, in 1928 found only 3 million shareholders, however. Some were involved in hundreds of stock transactions each year, and were counted over and over again. Most shareholders were urban and upper middle class. They paid cash for their purchases, and put them away in safe deposit boxes. Fewer than half of all shareholders held "active" accounts. Here there was more duplication, because a speculator might easily hold half a dozen separate accounts, and a Livermore might have as many as fifty. It was the speculators moreover who bought their shares on margin (putting up, on average, 30 percent of the price and borrowing the rest from their broker). There were only 500,000 margin accounts, held by somewhat fewer people.[48] It was that 0.4 percent of the entire population that was creating the ferment on Wall Street.

Common stocks were now selling at prices where they would return dividends of only 2–3 percent for years to come. Selling such stocks had become a form of pyramid selling. As Ponzi and others had already discovered, the game would go on only as long as the supply of suckers lasted. There was simply no other way to justify borrowing money at 10 percent to buy something that would yield only 2 percent, except perhaps for the excitement of the moment, the delicious sensation of flirting with danger for very high stakes.

23. ...Fell like a Stick

I

Since 1921 there had been one of the biggest construction booms in history. The United States was making up the wartime housing backlog. As automobiles covered the landscape, so did hard-surfaced roads. As business boomed, so did the construction of factories and office buildings. As school and college enrollments shot up, so did new classrooms. For seven years the volume of construction rose by more than 6 percent a year.[1] Once the backlog had been caught up, however, the building boom was bound to slow down, quickly. Construction has always been volatile. Hoover, as Secretary of Commerce, tried to make it more stable by cutting back on government building programs when the industry was growing, and expanding them at the first sign of a downturn. But during the 1922–28 construction boom it had seemed a fairly academic proposition.*

Residential construction led the way into this boom, and out of it. There was a slackening of residential construction all through 1928. In the first quarter of 1929 the entire construction industry suffered a slump, and then went over the edge. From March 1929 to the end of the year there was an unprecedented drop in building permits—65 percent in only ten months.[2] Construction fell back to the levels of 1921, when the country had been in a deep recession.[3] The sudden downturn in construction worked a depressive effect all across the economy.

---

* This was another boom the banks did not want to miss out on. Although not allowed to speculate directly in real estate, they dealt themselves in by lending munificently to construction companies.

The other side of the building coin was mortgage indebtedness. Between 1922 and 1929 it more than doubled, from $13 billion to $27.1 billion.[4] In the same period, family incomes had risen modestly. It was a heavy burden of debt to have taken on so quickly. It represented a massive bet on sustained prosperity.

That prosperity was, in turn, dependent to a large degree on automobile sales. One of the nightmares of the Twenties was that cars would reach "saturation point." Even Alfred P. Sloan, Jr., was known to be worried.[5] But year after year sales held up, and in April 1929 they rose to their highest point ever—650,000 passenger cars sold. Monthly sales had never before topped 500,000. It was a delirious experience. It did not last long. Car sales plummeted for the next six months.[6] It was a sickening descent after so heady a rise.

Ever since 1922 the production of consumer durables such as housing and automobiles had been rising by 5.6 percent a year, while the production of nondurables rose at half that rate. This was a remarkable disparity, completely without precedent.[7] Durable goods possess a fairly long life. They can be accumulated in one period, and maintained for years thereafter. In other words, the overall demand for them is bound to be unstable, unlike the demand for nondurables, such as food and fuel. And "the larger they bulk in consumers' purchases, the larger is the element of instability. This effect is reinforced by the fact that purchase of durable goods is more extensively financed on credit than are those of perishable ones."[8] A simultaneous downturn in construction and cars was therefore very bad news. It was the kind of thing we would notice nowadays almost the moment it happened. In 1929, however, only a handful of people paid any attention to it at all.

Except, that is, among the working class. In August the automobile factories began laying off thousands of men each week. Everyone knew it was going to be a hard winter. Even the wives of men who still had jobs spent that summer looking for work, just in case.[9] Sure enough, factory employment fell steadily for the last five months of 1929; as much in those five months as in "the two years from the end of 1925, when employment was at a temporary peak, to the end of 1927, when the recession was at its lowest point."[10] There were 3 million or more out of work that fall, with more certain to be laid off by Christmas.[11] Whatever was happening on Wall Street, that was what was happening in the real economy.

II

"Wall Street's bull market collapsed [yesterday] with a detonation heard round the world," ran the report in the *New York Times.* "Losses ranged from 23½ points in active Stock Exchange issues to as much as 150 in stocks dealt over the counter. . . . Individual losses were staggering. Hundreds of small traders were wiped out." Selling orders poured in from all over the United States. The floor of the Exchange saw scenes of near-panic as stock prices crashed all across the board. And all of this happened on June 12, 1928.[12] Two weeks later the market stabilized, and by August the losses had been recovered. The big bull market rolled on. What violent gyrations like this demonstrated was how volatile the boom was. It lived entirely on the nerves of the speculators. Every other week someone or some event sent a tremor through the market simply by suggesting that the end was nigh.

Following the 1928 election came the "Hoover Market." In a single week—five days of trading—more than 30 million shares changed hands. In a month average share prices rose 50 percent. Each day, the ticker was running two hours behind the market at the close of trading.[13] And lo! having shot up, the Hoover market just as suddenly fell like a stick. In a single week in mid-December paper losses amounted to $6 billion. Thousands of traders went under.

The financial editor of the *New York Times*, Alexander Dana Noyes, greeted the New Year with a categorical prediction that 1929 would bring a stupendous crash that would end the bull market once and for all.[14] The *New Republic's* financial expert, George Soule, similarly warned Hoover on the eve of his inauguration that one of the first tasks the new Administration would have to face would be a massive stock market collapse.[15]

Hoover was only too well aware of the danger that loomed. Shortly after entering the White House he spoke individually with dozens of influential editors and publishers, urging them to editorialize against stock market speculation. He prevailed on Mellon to advise people to convert their holdings from stocks into bonds. An emissary was sent to New York to ask the major banks to concentrate more on banking and less on selling securities. Hoover sent for the vice-president of the New York Stock Exchange, Richard Whitney, owner of his own brokerage and brother to a Morgan partner, to plead for restraint. All in vain.[16]

Academic economists remained bullish almost to a man.[17] So too did virtually all the principal investment advisory services. And the *Wall Street Journal* never flagged in its self-appointed role as principal cheerleader.

What stirred Wall Street in the spring of 1929 was something very much like panic—a panic buying of stocks, for fear of missing out. Once the stocks were bought, there was a panicky fear of selling out. It was the kind of emotional vice that keeps people glued to roulette tables or welded to a slot machine.

Many of the stocks they hungered for—blue chips such as Coca-Cola

—almost never appeared on the big board. Other speculative favorites, such as Insull Utilities, were traded out of town or on the curb. There was far less sound stock around than all the activity would suggest. The entire boom was based on a fairly narrow range of stocks, perhaps 200 at the most, widely quoted, with well-known names. There were hundreds of humble, respectable stocks that hardly moved from one year to the next. But so much feverish speculation began to make Congress nervous. In February 1929 the Senate passed a resolution asking the Federal Reserve for guidance if it became necessary for legislation to be written to curb speculation. And in the House the Banking and Currency Committee was preparing to investigate the big bull market during the next session of Congress.

There were even important figures in Wall Street who were urging the Federal Reserve to raise the rediscount rate. The Fed was reluctant to act. For one thing, there was nothing in its charter that authorized it to dampen the stock market. Nor did it possess any method of selective credit control or credit rationing. The Fed embodied the best thinking of a generation back, as nearly all institutions do. And finally, the more it tried to curb speculation by raising interest rates, the more money it created for brokers' loans. It was a dilemma to which the Federal Reserve had no answer.[18]

In March it issued a public warning that stock prices were highly inflated and called for a voluntary reduction in the call-money market. Stock prices dropped sharply. Then Charles E. Mitchell revived them by announcing that the National City Bank would make an extra $100 million available for brokers' loans. "The stock market was clearly victorious in its combat with the Reserve Banks."[19]

It was with evident reluctance, and no conviction that much good would come of it, that the Fed in August 1929 finally raised the rediscount rate to 6 percent on a Thursday afternoon. When the Stock Exchange opened on Friday the floor was crowded with sellers even before the opening gong sounded. The scene was chaotic from start to finish. Average share prices closed nearly $10.00 down, a new record for a one-day decline.[20] But by Monday nerves had recovered. Stock prices turned upward once more.

These summer months were hectic, to say the least. In London, the collapse of a cardboard financial empire pasted together by a swindler named Clarence Hatry triggered the crash of the overextended London Stock Exchange. There was turmoil in foreign markets generally. The Germans in 1928 had run out of American loans with which to finance reparations, which dampened the market for more foreign loans. Foreign trade had been propped up largely by American money and goods all through the Twenties. That trade was now grinding slowly to a walking pace, and British banks, to cover themselves in the wake of the London crash, were selling off large holdings of American stock.[21]

On September 1 the American Bankers' Association, at its annual convention, passed a resolution for an investigation into brokers' loans, which, the bankers declared, had put the stock market on the brink of catastrophe.[22] Issues of new securities had reached $1 billion a month. The call-money rate touched 16 percent. Week by week, the market began to slide from one sharp break to another. Between the breaks came half-hearted recoveries.

There was a general decline in prices all through the week starting October 14, but no panic. When the New York Stock Exchange opened on Monday October 21, however, even the glamour stocks slumped badly. Tuesday and Wednesday were equally bad. Fear began to grip the entire Street. On Thursday morning, "A crowd rushed to the visitors' gallery overlooking the Exchange floor,"[23] in anticipation that something momentous was going to happen. They were not disappointed. After nearly an hour's trading there were millions of stocks offered for sale—and no buyers. It was the nightmare come true—one that will wake a stockbroker in the middle of the night in a cold sweat. Bedlam broke out on the Exchange floor as brokers shouted themselves hoarse. Some broke into tears, knowing they were ruined. In the gallery, there was hysteria. The visitors were hurriedly cleared out by the police to prevent a riot.

The answer to a crisis like this, all wise men knew, along with the rest of the population, was for the banks to stand together. If they kept their nerve, they could break a panic. The last time anything like this had occurred was in 1907, when J. Pierpont Morgan the elder had made them see their duty, instead of scurrying away, every man for himself (and his depositors). "He made the New York bank heads sign on the dotted line. They gave him control of all of their assets. They protested all night. . . . They said they were too proud, and J. Pierpont Morgan said that he would ruin the man who would not sign. They said it was against the law, and he damned the law. They said it would not work, and he said that he would make it work. They said the people would not believe, and he said that he would fill the banking windows of New York with milled gold and make the people believe. He saved the situation."[24]

But that was in an earlier day, a different world. The banks of October 1929 had $8.5 billion out in loans to stockbrokers.[25] More than $6.5 billion came from member banks of the Federal Reserve in New York City. When buyers could no longer be found at any price for millions of stocks that

Thursday morning, virtually every bank in the city was at that moment technically insolvent. For the collateral for those loans was stock, and all of it had a formally fixed "lending value"—an assigned value, that is, below which it could not fall. Stocks were referred to as having "an intrinsic value." It was a myth. The true bottom line for stocks was nothing. And that was where many of them were at 11:00 A.M. on Thursday, October 24. Others were well below their assigned values, with little chance of recovery.

Shortly before noon, the bankers acted. Charles E. Mitchell and George F. Baker slipped into the offices of J. P. Morgan and Co. They were soon followed by Albert Wiggin, the president of Chase National, and Seward Prosser, the head of Bankers Trust. They had all been summoned by Thomas W. Lamont, a senior Morgan partner. Out of this meeting came a pledge that six investment trusts owned by the various banks represented at the meeting would each put up $40 million, "to fill the air pockets," as Lamont termed it.[26]

At 1:30 P.M. Richard F. Whitney, who was known to be the Morgan broker, strode in his usual imperious manner through the horde of traders milling about the floor in controlled desperation. Whitney made for Post 2, where US Steel was traded. It was a stock which before the September slide had reached 261. It had opened on October 24 at 205½, since when it had dropped to 193½. In a clear ringing voice Whitney offered 205 for 25,000 shares of Steel. Those who heard the bid broke into cheers. The price was flashed on the big board. Other blue-chip stocks rallied. The good news spread down the telephone wires to boardrooms all around the country (the ticker was hours behind, swamped with orders to sell). That afternoon the bankers' consortium used up $100 million or so of its resources—not that more than a dozen people were even aware of its existence. In a way, it was really a general stockpool, rather than a single stockpool, shoring up the market until its aims were achieved.

Its aims in this case meant getting rid of huge amounts of stock held by their affiliates and writing down the assigned lending value on tens of millions of shares. On a rational basis, Whitney's bid for Steel was a blunder the veriest tyro would not make: he had offered $300,000 more than he needed to if all he wanted was 25,000 shares. It was a ploy, nothing more, nothing less. On Friday the market was steady. The banks busily adjusted assigned lending values,[27] and quietly pulled out of the market.

When Monday morning arrived for the start of another week's trading, thousands of brokers learned that the collateral that secured their clients' loans had lost half or more than half of its assigned value. The banks leaned on the brokers, the brokers leaned on their customers, and the customers rounded up what cash they could. If they did not do it fast enough, or did not come up with enough, the brokers sold them out. The stock market collapsed again, and this time there was no bankers' consortium, no artificial recovery. The game was finally over.

III

The Crash gave rise to an outpouring of puritanical glee. Hoover, Coolidge, John Maynard Keynes, Henry Ford, and scores of other public figures welcomed it as a necessary chastisement of recklessness and speculation. It was the first stock market crash in memory that saw no failure of a big bank or a major corporation. "It was considered purely financial. Plungers, gamblers and other disreputable people had lost their money; others were still in good shape."[28] Sanity would return to Wall Street. Those who had lost deserved to lose. Business itself was sound, Hoover and Mellon insisted. This was not complacency. It was what almost everyone with any knowledge of the subject believed.

On past form a major market crash might cut production and employment by about 6 percent, however, as business held back on investment and waited for the shock wave to pass.[29] Hoover refused to allow this "natural" sequence of events to take its course. On November 21 he launched his counterattack by convening a meeting of leading industrialists at the White House. He urged them to maintain their payrolls. They agreed to a man, and Ford returned to Detroit to announce the introduction of the $7.00 day. From labor leaders, Hoover won a pledge to discourage strikes and demands for wage increases. He wrung a promise from the heads of public utilities to invest $1.8 billion in new construction and repairs in 1930. A committee was set up to educate the American public on the heretical doctrine that the time to increase government spending was during a slump, not during a boom as they supposed.

Hoover wrote personally to every state governor, pleading with them not to cut back on state spending. Instead, he urged, they ought to speed up their public works to help absorb the unemployed. And he set up a committee under Julius H. Barnes, the chairman of the U.S. Chamber of Commerce, to make sure that business kept its promises.[30]

The Federal Reserve System was also acting to ward off the impending slump. The New York Federal Reserve Bank had been headed since Strong's death by George L. Harrison, by training a lawyer, who had joined the Federal Reserve in 1914 as its legal counsel. He served as Strong's deputy after 1920 and labored after Strong's death to act as he believed the great man would have done. In the last week of October,

Harrison cut the rediscount rate in New York to 5 percent and bought $160 million worth of government securities, even though he had authority to buy only $25 million worth a week. The Federal Reserve Board chided him for his independence but followed where he led. When Harrison asked for authority to spend up to $200 million a week to buy government securities, the Washington board rapidly agreed to his request.

On December 5 Hoover held a highly publicized conference with 400 of the country's leading business executives. He pleaded with them not to cut back on their investment plans. A seventy-two-man body, the National Business Advisory Council, was created to keep a check on them. He had already ordered the pace of federal public works to be speeded up, and raised federal public-works spending plans for 1930 by $420 million. He ordered the Shipping Board to increase ship construction. He got Congress to cut taxes by $140 million. In these various ways, he hoped to counter the expected postcrash recession, and keep it short. His decisiveness, his ready acceptance of governmental responsibility, won him the praise of liberals and Progressives who until now had been inclined to portray him as a tool of business interests.[31]

The crash had come at the worst possible time. Unemployment always rose sharply in November. Relief agencies had their largest caseload from November through March. But there was hope that once the winter was past, Hoover's measures would bring the country through to full recovery in the fall of 1930. For the present, the conferences, the pledges, the committees, were designed to do one thing above all: to maintain confidence. As Barnes said in January 1930 of Hoover's efforts all during November and December, "It was obvious that the thing to be feared most was fear."[32]

IV

The path of the storm was littered with spectacular wrecks. The seven Fisher brothers had descended on Wall Street in 1923, after selling Fisher Body to GM, with $300 million to play the market. The crash was said to have left them $200 million poorer.[33] Jack Dempsey, the first millionaire athlete, was a millionaire no longer. He was broke. The crash had cost him $3 million.[34] Among those utterly wiped out was Greenwich Village's famous millionaire bohemian, Robert Clairmont. He was probably the only person who meant it when he said he did not care if he was poor. When he was rich he was besieged by his neighbors, as they clamored for handouts. Some crawled up the ice chute to make their pitch. Simply living in the Village the past few years had cost him $800,000 in hand-outs.[35] He looked forward to a life of peaceful poverty.

All through the winter the standard response to the cocktail party greeting "How's things?" was "Caught short." The lucky ones had been caught short only to be bailed out. At National City Bank nearly $2.5 million of the shareholders' money was put by Mitchell and his board into a "Morale Loan Fund" to help the 100 or so bank executives who had been caught short. The money was loaned without collateral. It was never repaid.[36] Insull, the model employer, bailed out his employees who were caught short by dipping into his own huge stock portfolio, so that they could put up more collateral and avoid being sold out.[37]

For the bears, the crash was no disaster but a chance to get rich. There was a Wall Street legend that George F. Baker at the age of eighty-nine had roused himself from his sickbed, pushed hovering doctors and nurses aside, exulting "This is my ninth panic. I have made money in every one of them!"[38] Baker with his huge muttonchop whiskers was a figure out of the past; a Victorian in the Forsyte mold. He had outlived his great contemporaries in finance—Morgan the elder, James J. Hill, Andrew Carnegie—and turned First National City Bank from a neighborhood business into the third largest bank in the world. It was true, nevertheless, that Baker knew how to do well in a panic.

By the end of December average stock prices stood where they had been in early 1927, before the big bull market took off. All the gains of two and a half years had been wiped out. And all the stocks that were overvalued back in the summer were by the same criteria undervalued now. Men who had pulled out then, such as Joseph P. Kennedy, came back for a little bargain hunting. So did Jesse Livermore, betting that the market would fall still farther. He was bitterly hated. Many a ruined speculator blamed his misfortunes on Livermore's selling the market short. Even Livermore was surpassed however by Bernard "Sell 'Em Ben" Smith, an ex-sailor, ex-used-car salesman. On Black Thursday he reportedly ran into his broker's office screaming, "Sell 'em all. They're not worth anything!" After the crash he organized a bear pool. He and his backers got rich betting the market would continue to fall.[39] And Albert Wiggin, the head of Chase National Bank (now Chase Manhattan) managed to make $4 million between September 11 and December 11, 1929 by selling short the stock of his own bank.[40]

There was no general mood of anxiety, however. When at the end of 1929 the *New York Times* looked back on the year, it chose as the most newsworthy event of the past twelve months the expedition of Commander Richard E. Byrd to the South Pole.[41] Looking ahead, there was at

least one source of cautious and objective advice on the economy—the
bond rating services (Moody's, Poor's, Fitch, and others). Their 1930 rat-
ings were cautious, pointing to a modest recession lasting nine months or
so, followed by a strong recovery.[42]

Business was a major source of news in the Twenties—far more than
the business department at Time could ever use. This led Henry Luce to
toy with the idea of a business magazine. A dummy issue of Luce's brainchild, to be called Fortune, was produced in September 1929. Then came
the crash. Luce and his executives had to decide whether the project
ought to be pursued. They agreed to go ahead. "But we will not be over-
optimistic," they said. "We will recognize that this business slump may
last as long as an entire year."[43] In February 1930 the first issue, totaling
30,000 copies, went out to subscribers. It carried features such as a history
of RCA and "A Budget for a $25,000 Income in Chicago."

That same month the New York Times carried an editorial which
noted with satisfaction that "the patient" was on the road to full recovery.[44]
The crash had been a sobering event, it conceded; but business looked on
it as being long overdue and salutary. Some parts of industry were at the
moment sluggish, but others were doing very nicely. And they were right.
Iron prices and output, for instance, had long been considered a good
"barometer of trade," because they responded quickly to changes in the
economy. In the first half of 1929, production of pig-iron and steel ingots
had risen sharply, and plummeted from September onward as the bull
market went bust. In the first quarter of 1930 prices and output revived
vigorously.[45] The number of building permits issued was also rising every
month.[46] From January to May automobile sales recovered and matched
the sales for the same period in 1925–28.[47] Blue chip corporations in February and March were reporting their 1929 profits. Most of them had
achieved record highs, and the US Steel report was examined with awe:
$21.18 a share, which was nearly $10 above the previous record set in
1928. Reports such as these led to predictions of a new bull market in the
fall of 1930, once the recession was past.

Businessmen by and large were sticking to the pledges they had made.
Wages were being maintained. Insull led the utilities' heads and raised
$200 million for new investment in his own companies in 1930.[48] Overall,
business in the first six months of 1930 was as good as its word: investment
was $500 million up on the first half of 1929. Government spending was
also slightly higher. The Federal Reserve was playing its part by reducing
the rediscount rate to 3½ percent, then 2½ percent, and keeping its member banks solvent by buying large amounts of government securities. Over
much of the country, in the cities that were not financial centers, the

crash seemed remote.[49] And in the cities that were financial centers, no important bank had closed its doors, no large corporation had gone under. By every reasonable standard, the economy seemed certain to revive.

Yet social workers in the Bowery that winter of 1929–30 noticed that the breadlines seemed longer than usual. And there was another difference: ". . . there are many young men, still clean, still not too pasty of face, among the old timers."[50] These new unemployed were also a more militant breed. There were demonstrations of the unemployed in New York, Los Angeles, and Chicago, broken up by the police with tear gas and night sticks, supposedly justified by Communist involvement in organizing the unemployed. But that was hardly illegal.[51]

In April 1930 Hoover ordered a house-to-house census of unemployment. This found 3.2 million out of work. But Hoover decided that at least half a million were not *seriously* interested in finding a job and another million were seasonal workers in between jobs. One way and another, he could find only one million "families without breadwinners."[52] The Progressive who believed in collecting the facts had started massaging them to make them look better.

The Census Bureau's definition of unemployment was narrowly drawn to begin with. People who had worked at a plant that closed down were not counted as unemployed if they said they expected the plant to reopen. Nor were elderly out-of-work miners who expressed (vain) hopes that they might one day be taken on by a mine. The bureau excluded anyone who did not put down "a gainful occupation," which drew a veil over hundreds of thousands of unskilled workers who drifted from job to job, and were drifting the day the Census Bureau enumerator showed up. So in Philadelphia, for example, the bureau could find only 73,275 jobless. A combined city/University of Pennsylvania study done at the same time unearthed 105,000.[53] In April 1930 the true figure of unemployment was probably close to 5 million.

Hoover's insistence, that bad as unemployment was, it was about to get better, convinced no one. Because by the end of April it was becoming evident that the recession was going to be deeper and longer than almost anyone had thought possible.[54] At the end of April 1930 the stock market fell sharply. A pall of gloom began spreading over the entire economy. By June, when employment ought to have been rising, it was the number of families seeking relief that was rising instead.[55]

Attendance during the 1930 baseball season was 6 percent up on the figure for 1929. But attendance at college football games fell for the first time ever, by 6 percent.[56] Baseball was played in the spring and summer, when confidence was still largely intact, and the future seemed reasonably bright. By the fall of 1930, however, when the football season began, that confidence was falling apart, leaving empty seats in the stands as wage levels finally began tumbling down and a wave of bank failures shook dozens of American cities.

Something had gone badly wrong. But what?

V

The usual, popular view is that because the Depression came after the crash it was somehow caused by the crash. But as the past few pages have shown, that was not what happened, nor is there any economist who sees the crash as anything more than one factor among many in the Depression. The popular interpretation is a perfect example of one of the most enduring of all fallacies—after this, therefore because of this.*

Virtually all serious theories on what caused the Depression blame either business or government. They may find blame on both sides,[57] but one is usually allotted the lion's share. The dominant view is largely Keynesian: by 1929 there was overcapacity in a wide range of crucial industries, notably automobiles, textiles, and construction, while money was being poured into the coffers of American business for new investment. The opportunities for large-scale investment, however, were drying up. Of the $8 billion raised in 1929 through the sales of stocks, bonds, and notes, only $2 billion went into real investment, such as plant and equipment. Most of the rest went into the call-money market or cash reserves or somewhere else.[58] The downturn in key industries in the spring and summer of 1929 was proof that a recession had already begun. An even sharper business contraction was inevitable. It makes more sense, according to this approach, to say that the economic downturn caused the crash than that the crash caused the downturn. The crash was only the extension to the stock market of a faltering economy, in which agriculture, construction, and automobiles were already in deep trouble. In other words, the recession caused the Depression.[59]

The alternative view is that there was no depression in the offing in the winter of 1929–30, only a recession, much like the recession of 1921, perhaps not even as bad as that one had been. The Administration and the Federal Reserve had done all the right things to counter the effects of

---

* A favorite item in courses on logic, where it is known by its Latin name *post hoc, ergo propter hoc*. The usual illustration is the shaman who, around the end of February each year, dons a costume of green and does a ritual dance. Sure enough, a few weeks later the trees turn green. After this, therefore . . .

a recession, and thereafter sat quietly by while the economy proceeded to fall apart. Having assumed there would be no Great Depression, they produced one.[60] Six valuable months were simply wasted, while necessary reforms on the stock market and in the banking structure were blindly neglected. Came the fall of 1930 and banks began to fail. And there is nothing to spread panic among ordinary people faster than a wave of bank failures.

The Federal Reserve is a prime target for criticism. After doing the right things in the immediate aftermath of the crash, it was doing nothing right thereafter. It cut the rediscount rate, but not quickly enough. It bought government securities, but not enough of them. This is the interpretation advanced most forcefully by monetarists.[61] The Fed's actions reduced the supply of money at critical moments, making recovery impossible and bank failures certain. Every bank panic both reflected loss of public confidence and encouraged it, in the monetarist view.

Hoover is often saddled with responsibility for steering the country straight from the crash into the Depression. This theory at its most charitable runs that he had done everything any president could do to ward off a depression, except for one thing—he did not commit all the federal government's resources to maintaining demand. With a chorus of praise ringing in his ears, Hoover did not, perhaps could not, recognize in time that he had made a monumental blunder. It was the mistake Napoleon had made with the Imperial Guard at Waterloo—when they were finally thrown into the battle, it was already lost.[62]

Hoover was to live to a very old age, and spent much of it propagating his own theory, which was that the Depression was imported from abroad. European economies reeled from disaster to disaster for ten years after the armistice; were propped up again and again by the United States; wasted the time thus secured for them; wasted the money they borrowed; and finally went under as all profligates must. The trouble was they were clutching at Uncle Sam's pockets at the time and he fell over when they did.

European economists replied by maintaining that the Depression was like the phyloxera plant louse that ravaged the vineyards of France—imported from the USA. For fifty years they have argued that the first fatal step was the reduction in American foreign lending in 1928, which pushed a dozen hard-pressed countries into bankruptcy. World trade promptly went into a slump. Then came the crash, which completed the collapse of international trading and lending. As the United States went under, it dragged the rest of the world with it.[63]

There is something to all these theories. But even if all these interpretations were rolled into one overarching explanation, there would still be something vitally important missing from them. Neither individually nor together do they provide the central mechanism by which the economic events of 1929 turned into the Great Depression of late 1930 and after. But of that, more anon.

The stock market structure of 1929 was certainly dangerous. Stock prices were not as a whole wildly inflated—some were, others led a very quiet existence. There was no Securities and Exchange Commission, however, to probe, to caution, to regulate. With results that have already been described. The massive crookedness along Wall Street in the Twenties made sure that when a collapse did come its effects would be magnified and recovery made more difficult. Margins were too low by present standards; on average, margin traders put up only 30–50 percent of the value of the stock they bought, instead of the present 75–90 percent. The Federal Reserve did not possess the wide range of powers it needed to control speculation. Big institutional investors were not as powerful as they are in our day, when they can do more to shore up the stock market than any old-time bankers' consortium ever achieved. There is no arguing with the Keynesian emphasis on the weakness of the market structure, the problem of finding new investment opportunities, and the impending recession signaled by the fall in car sales and construction. But a recession is all that these factors pointed to then, or would point to now.

Monetary theory assumes that the money supply determined the amount of money in use, without reference to the demand for money. The Federal Reserve is criticized for cutting the rediscount rate to 2½ percent in May 1930. Too high, says Milton Friedman. But even if the rate had been 1½ percent it might still have been too high. Money cannot be forced on people who are afraid to borrow, no matter what the rate. Borrowing does not take place in offices and banks. It takes place in a society. The Friedman theory also assumes that the stock of money available determined incomes in 1930. It is just as plausible, however, to turn the argument around and say that the money stock fell because of a fall in demand—a fall occasioned by a fall in incomes and consumer spending. Besides, the actual money stock declined by only 2.6 percent between October 1929 and October 1930.[64]

The bank failure theory has its merits, if only because it fills an important place in the social psychology of the early Depression. But there was no run of bank failures in Britain or Canada, and both of them had a depression on the American scale.

During the Twenties the United States had become the world's biggest exporter, by a large margin. This hardly squared with the argument made to justify the Hawley-Smoot tariff, that American manufacturers needed protection against unfair foreign competition. Nor was there the least chance that it would help American farmers. American exports had, in fact, been rising, while imports remained stable. A new high tariff was almost certain to provoke retaliation. That was the argument made by the 1,000 economists who petitioned Hoover in April 1930 to veto the bill. They might have raised another point: to hamper world trade in the middle of a worldwide recession was crazy. Yet Hoover was right to point out that other countries had made a shambles of their own affairs. The British, for example, by pegging the pound at $5 purely for reasons of self-esteem; the French for their ludicrous and dangerous policy of bleeding Germany white, and keeping it that way.

International trade, however, was only a small part of American business. The total volume of exports and imports amounted to less than 5 percent of the Gross National Product. And while the effects of the fall-off in foreign lending were being felt abroad in early 1930, those effects had not yet been reexported to the United States. When they arrived, in the winter of 1930, the Depression had already taken hold.

It is my contention that what turned an unavoidable recession into the Great Depression was the spectacular fall in consumer spending in the first half of 1930; that this was the essential mechanism that turned a mere downturn into a collapse. Banks, business, government, all may have been less than perfect. We live with that kind of unwisdom every day. But even had they all played their allotted roles—allotted by hindsight, that is—to perfection, the drop in consumer spending would have still produced a depression. What is extraordinary is that no one—no economist, no historian—has until now given this element its rightful due.

Generally speaking, all spending comes under one of three headings: Investment-Consumption-Government. The balance between these three shifts from time to time, but the structure remains. In the first six months of 1930, investment was higher than in the first six months of 1929. Ditto government spending.[65] Consumer spending fell by $2.7 billion. (In 1982 terms, allowing for both inflation and the vastly larger economy of the present day, the comparable figure would be around $54 billion.) If the crash could not have come at a worse time from the point of view of employment, the recession could not have arrived at a worse time from the point of view of consumer spending: it is nearly always weaker in the first two quarters of the year than the last two quarters. This is how consumer spending broke down in Quarters I and II of:

	1929	1930 (in billions)
Perishables	$13.720	$12.992
Durables/Semi-durables	$10.967	$ 9.441
Services	$13.510	$13.161

Spending on perishable commodities, such as cigarettes, food, gasoline, paper products, and so on had fallen by $730 million. Spending on services was down by $350 million. But spending on durables and semi-durables was down by more than these combined, by $1.5 billion in all.[66]

A period of heavy buying of durable goods leads inevitably to a period when such buying tapers off sharply. Propelled along by the rapid proliferation of installment plans in the Twenties, sales of durables were almost certain to come to a sudden slowdown, as people gave their incomes a chance to catch up with their commitments. To double one's debts from $500 to $1,000 was the work of a few minutes. But to double one's income might well take a decade. And as we have seen, the Twenties had seen an extraordinary increase in personal indebtedness. That mountain of debt is also part of the missing link. Failure to recognize its importance has been one reason why the fall in consumption has generally been overlooked.

The most recent full-length inquiry into the causes of the Depression demonstrates what I mean. It points to the incontrovertible fact that those who had lost heavily on the stock market had lost fortunes that existed only on paper, plus the cash they had actually put up in the first place. This made them poorer than they would otherwise have been, and therefore forced them to cut back on their spending.* "But something else happened to depress consumption in 1930. At the current state of our knowledge, the unexplained fall in consumption is larger than the part we can explain, but the magnitude of the total fall is incontrovertible. It is worth emphasizing that the fall in consumption was unusually large in 1930, because the conventional literature assumes that it was investment that experienced the unusual fall. . . . The Depression was not caused by a dramatic collapse of investment."[67] The puzzlement of this economist is plain: he has seen what happened, but cannot explain it.

Nearly all accounts of the crash and the Depression have been written either by economists, who stick to the same set of figures and turn it this way and that, as if it were a kaleidoscope (and indeed, depending on how you turn it around, it does make different patterns), or by historians, who tend to leave the hard economic questions alone. What is lacking is the

---

* I suspect that most of this money would have gone straight back into the stock market had there been no crash.

necessary social dimension. To put it crudely, Americans were in hock up to their ears. They were already beginning to catch their breath from their prolonged spending spree when the recession arrived, and it scared the daylights out of them.

Consumer flight accounted in large part for the 1921 downturn, when inflation combined with recession to terrify consumers. When prices tumbled, the consumers came back in droves. The recession was soon over, and a boom underway.[68] Prices fell in 1930, but not by much until the end of the year. It would be wrong to suggest that Americans simply stopped buying durable goods. The real decline came in areas where demand was momentarily close to being satisfied, and borrowing had created a huge amount of debt—namely, cars and houses. Refrigerators, still a novelty in the late 1920s, were in strong demand throughout the entire Depression; their sales grew every year, no matter what.[69]

But many millions of families were carrying a burden of debt that was unprecedented; this was the first generation that was heavily dependent on credit, and thus the first of its kind that ever had to face a recession. This, I believe, made people feel unusually vulnerable, and easily frightened them into tightening the purse strings. They carried far less personal debt than we do. But they were far more conscious of the debt they carried.* So when the boom ended they tried to be careful, and created a disaster.

They were really in the best position to create one. Although nearly every theory on the cause of the Depression blames business or government, the plain fact is that consumers accounted for 92–94 percent of the nation's spending. Much of the controversy over the Depression, however, has been a political argument, conducted in terms of economic theory, but ideological for all that—perhaps because of it. In 1929 total consumer spending was $78 billion. In 1930 it fell to $70.5 billion.[70] Had both federal spending and business net investment risen 50 percent that year, they would still have failed to make good that $7.5 billion shortfall. What is more, they would probably have simply created a high rate of inflation on top of high unemployment.

The flight of ordinary Americans away from the marketplace began in the first nine months of 1930, when wage rates held up comparatively well. There was a decline in overall earnings, most of it suffered by farm-

---

* Between 1922 and 1929 the debts of farmers, railroads, and public agencies remained more or less stable. But business borrowed heavily, and so did the last important category of borrowers, individuals. Personal debts increased by 50 percent in seven years. Debt servicing alone in 1930 accounted for nearly 10 percent of Gross National Product. Throughout the Depression Congress was awash with proposals to bail out people who could not pay their debts. Charles Merz, "Debts—Public and Private," *New York Times*, January 29, 1933.

ers and factory workers. But in some areas (public utilities, distribution) earnings increased.[71] The general drop in earnings did not come until the last quarter, and it was spectacular.* In earlier recessions, wages had dropped almost from the start. Hoover had gained a year. And, it now seemed, utterly in vain. The last months of 1930 brought a wave of mortgage failures and broken banks. Output fell, unemployment rose, investment was heavily slashed.

This book might be expected in the normal course of such accounts to end at this point. But bear with me a while yet, reader. The story that I set out to tell is far from finished. No one at the time believed for a moment that the crash marked the beginning of a depression, let along *the* Depression. No one knew it. No one acted as if it was true. For the vast majority of Americans, life in 1930 was much like life in 1929. Or as one of the notable survivors from the period later remarked, "The 1920s didn't end with the Wall Street crash . . . or the last day of December 1929. The moral atmosphere of the boom continued after the boom had ended. . . ."[72] So let us see this age through to its natural conclusion.

---

* Lionel Robbins's by now classic account, *The Great Depression* (London, 1931), has for fifty years helped to throw economists off the right track. Robbins criticizes Hoover's strenuous attempts to maintain wages because it encouraged consumption. He asserts that consumption actually rose in 1930–31 and thereby deprived business of vital capital. His evidence for this claimed increase is limited to less than a dozen items, most of them verging on the whimsical, such as "silks and velvets," "infants' wear," and "cheese."

PART IV

PURPLE TWILIGHT

24. Crime and Punishment

I

One morning in the spring of 1929, Mellon sent for Elmer Irey, who ran the Treasury Department's Special Intelligence unit. Mellon asked Irey if he had heard about the Medicine Ball Cabinet that met on the South Lawn at seven each morning. Irey said that he had read about it. "Well, when the exercising starts, Mr. Hoover says to me, 'Have you got that fellow Capone yet?' " said Mellon. "And when exercise is done and everybody is leaving, the last thing Mr. Hoover always says is 'Remember, now; I want that man Capone in jail.' "[1] With that, Mellon dropped the ball squarely into Irey's lap.

Capone stood at the summit of organized crime in the Twenties; he remains the most famous big-time mobster in history. But summits are not scaled in a day, and Capone's hold on Chicago had its origins before World War I, when Capone was still a juvenile delinquent. Modern organized crime really began in 1909, with Big Jim Colosimo, a saloonkeeper and whoremonger. As his business prospered, Colosimo felt the need for reliable help. He sent for his nephew, Johnny Torrio, to come to Chicago. Torrio had served his apprenticeship in crime with the Five Points gang, a murderous bunch of young thugs who spread terror throughout the Lower East Side of New York for several years. Yet Torrio was short and highly nervous, disliking violence, claiming never to have fired a gun. He preferred to organize the violence, and to be somewhere else when it was being dealt out. Within a few years, with Torrio's organizing gifts to rely

393

on, Colosimo was a brothel-and-saloon millionaire, presiding over his empire from Colosimo's Restaurant. In his white linen suits, huge black
mustache, diamond stickpin, and vast bulk, he seemed cheerful and vulgar; hardly a man to spread fear. He relied instead on buying up policemen
and politicians. And then one afternoon in 1920 he was gunned down in
his own restaurant. There were no witnesses, no clues. At his funeral the
honorary pallbearers included three judges, two congressmen, a state senator and nine Chicago aldermen.[2] Torrio, the odds-on bet in Chicago as
the organizer of Uncle Jim's sudden demise, took over the empire.

Only a year earlier Torrio himself had been in search of reliable help
as he built up his own organization inside his uncle's. That was when he
had sent to New York for an amiable, ambitious young cutthroat who
went by the Anglo-Saxon moniker Al Brown, but was otherwise known as
Alphonse Capone. The most serious threat to Torrio's inheritance came
from the Dion O'Bannion gang, which controlled much of the North
Side. O'Bannion was the most improbable gangster ever: short, moon-
faced, and limping, he was a florist most of the time. He handled the floral
arrangements of some of the biggest gangster funerals, such as that of
Frank Capone, gunned down in 1922.

O'Bannion had an understanding with Torrio that amounted to a
spheres-of-influence agreement between rival states. The trouble was that
O'Bannion loathed Italians. So while the agreement held for three years,
he could not resist making a fool of Torrio by selling him a 25 percent
share in a brewery that he, O'Bannion, knew was going to be shut down.
He stung Torrio for $500,000. What Torrio found intolerable was not the
loss of the money but O'Bannion's gloating. In 1924, shortly after this
transaction, O'Bannion was shot dead among his flower arrangements by
three professional gunmen. O'Bannion's funeral cost $100,000, and in-
cluded twenty-six truckloads of flowers. He was buried in a section of a
Catholic cemetery reserved for persons of mixed marriages or otherwise
in official disfavor. But his underlings were pleased. It was, said one of
them, "the funeral of funerals; just what Dion would have wanted—simple but lavish."[3]

With their chief buried, O'Bannion's gang could then get back to the
war. They ambushed Torrio and left him seriously wounded. He lived,
only to get out of town, handing over all his crime interests to Capone.
Between 1924 and 1928, Capone devoted his efforts to consolidating his
inheritance of whorehouses, distilleries, speakeasies, and gambling dens
by destroying the other major gangs in the city. The organization he
headed had been one of the biggest crime conglomerates in the United
States long before the Volstead Act. The belief that Prohibition created

organized crime is wrong. It is likely, in fact, that the speakeasies and brothels run by Capone did no more business than the saloons that Prohibition had closed down. Crime and corruption had flourished in Chicago when Capone was still wearing short pants.

But Capone's larger-than-life personality filled the newspapers day after day. And that was new for a crime boss. Capone cultivated the press as if he were running for office. A Capone mobster could be identified (when not working undercover, as it were) by his pearl gray felt hat, a narrow band of black silk circling the crown. The Twenties saw color return to men's clothing after a century of increasing drabness, and Capone in his lime-green suits and silk ties of dazzling hue was a peacock. General Motors, than which no business was more respectable, was perfectly happy to build a special Cadillac for the Big Fellow: seven tons in weight, with an armor-plated body, steel-encased gas tank, bullet-proof glass half an inch thick, and a special compartment behind the rear seat for carrying guns. The windows were designed so that those inside the car could shoot at pursuers without exposing themselves unduly. It was obviously a gangster's car, its design made sense only in one context for a private citizen—the commission of crime. GM did not even pause to consider the matter. They simply sent in their bill for $30,000.[4]

No one had any illusions about Capone. By 1929 the Capone gang was credited by police officials with at least 300 murders.[5] On February 14, 1929, the struggle for control of the North Side produced a killing that could shake a city grown accustomed to gang wars. George "Bugs" Moran had built up a gang based on what was left of the O'Bannion organization (not that there was much left). The Moran gang was lured to a garage and taken inside by men disguised as policemen. There, they were lined against a wall and shot down with tommy guns. By a fluke Moran escaped the St. Valentine's Day massacre, but seven other men died. Then and ever after, it was considered typically Capone.

The Chicago police seemed—perhaps were—completely helpless. A group of eminent Chicagoans, however, formed themselves into a body known only as the Secret Six to finance a counterattack on Capone. They had visited Hoover shortly after his inauguration. They helped pay the bills of Irey's investigators. And they supported another group, a ten-man squad formed in 1929 from within the Justice Department's Prohibition Bureau, under the leadership of Eliot Ness, who called themselves "The Untouchables." It was certainly true of Ness. He had worked as a Prohibition agent in Chicago for two years and never took a bribe. Unable to buy him off, Capone tried to have him killed. Ness survived three assassination attempts. His bodyguard was murdered.

His strategy was to smash the chief source of Capone's income, the network of secret breweries. The Untouchables located and shut down more than thirty and arrested more than one hundred people (all of whom needed lawyers and bail money), seized more than fifty trucks, nearly all brand-new; and smashed millions of dollars' worth of brewing equipment. Beer had been trucked openly through the streets of Chicago in the Twenties. In 1930 it was becoming hard to find and was delivered in passenger cars a couple of barrels at a time.[6]

Irey was also closing in. Back in 1926 an Internal Revenue agent in Chicago had talked Ralph "Bottles" Capone, Al Capone's brother, into filing income tax returns for 1922–25, by convincing him that it would save him a lot of trouble if he did so. "Bottles" obliged by filing returns that embroiled him in endless litigation and led to the discovery that he had thriftily salted away $1,751,840 in various accounts. All of which cast serious doubt on Bottles's sworn statement that he was broke. The net that caught Bottles was gradually cast wider, snagging Al Capone's cousin and "enforcer," Frank Nitti, and his "treasurer," Jake "Greasy Thumb" Guzik. The pressure on Capone was carefully being raised by Irey's T-men.

With the heat on from the St. Valentine's Day massacre, and Moran somewhere unscathed and plotting revenge, Capone saw fit to travel eastward. He was arrested in Philadelphia and charged with carrying concealed weapons. He was swiftly tried, convicted, and sent to Moyamensing prison to serve his one-year sentence. Capone seemed oddly unperturbed by these events, like a man looking for refuge.

Hardly had he returned to Chicago in 1930 before Bottles, Nitti, and Guzik went to prison with eighteen-month sentences for tax evasion. But Capone acted like a man without a care. When the Depression took hold in the fall of 1930, a huge South Side building was turned into a soup kitchen, under a banner reading FREE FOOD FOR THE WORKLESS. Capone financed it at a cost of $2,000 a week. That Christmas he bought and gave away 5,000 turkeys. To himself, and to millions of others, he was a modern Robin Hood. Was he involved in murder? Well, they said, the victims were themselves murderers. Was he a bootlegger? Well, it was a stupid law anyway. To much of the urban working class, Capone was an example of style, derring-do, and big-money success.*

The government astonished Capone by demanding millions in back taxes. "They can't collect legal taxes from illegal money," he protested.[7]

---

* The college-educated middle class took a different view. When in 1931 he went to see Northwestern play Nebraska at football, word of his presence spread quickly through the crowd. He was booed unrelentingly for three quarters, until he left the stadium.

But they could. He decided to square these complicated matters by making a statement. The government wanted to know the source of his income. It came, said the statement, from an organization which kept no books. "The taxpayer" (Capone) received one-sixth of the profits. Exhaustive, patient digging turned up a ledger from a gambling den in Cicero, a district of Chicago, which had been raided in 1924. The ledger listed large payments to someone named "Al." The cashier was traced and (surprise!) induced to talk. He identified Capone as the Al of the ledger. An indictment was brought swiftly and in secret, beating the statute of limitations by forty-eight hours. According to the ledger, this single gambling operation cleared nearly $300,000 a year—and one-sixth of that came to $1,000 a week, at a time when Capone's sworn statement claimed he was making less than $75.

When the indictment became public, Capone was calm. He expected to go away, as Bottles and the "Enforcer" had gone away, for eighteen months. The United States district attorney was asking for only two and a half years. The night before he went to court, Capone held a lavish going-away party. In the morning he went before the judge and entered a plea of "guilty." Federal Judge James Wilkerson (he of the notorious Wilkerson injunction of 1922, see pp. 133) refused to be bound by the district attorney's recommendation of a moderate sentence in exchange for a guilty plea. Capone was outraged, and chose to go to trial.

"In eleven days," Irey noted with evident satisfaction, "the government proved Al had it, he spent it, he admitted making it, and paid no taxes on any of it."[8] The defense case was that the evidence merely proved what everybody already knew—Al was a big spender. So why was the government wasting millions to persecute one man when it could spend its money a lot better on soup kitchens. Convicted on some counts, Capone was acquitted on others. He still expected a light sentence. He choked on his cough drop when Wilkerson gave him eleven years.[9]

Hoover was satisfied; Mellon was satisfied; Irey was satisfied. For Ness there was the pleasure of taking Capone to the train station and putting him aboard the Dixie Flyer for Atlanta Federal Penitentiary.

II

In April 1922 the creator of that greatest of all fictional detectives, Sherlock Holmes, arrived in the United States on a lecture tour. The first thing that Arthur Conan Doyle discovered was that "New York was in the throes of a crime wave. . . . This remarkable wave of crime was not confined to New York but was even greater in Chicago, and greater still, I was informed, in St. Louis."[10] It was a crime wave fanned, however, largely by the press and the police commissioner. Citizens were banding together for self-defense. The streets were unsafe, they cried, and they blamed it on the war.[11] By 1927 an element of defeatism had taken root and there were magazine articles such as "Our Permanent Crime Wave."[12] Americans in the Twenties believed that the war and Prohibition had saddled them with a massive increase in crime, and it was here to stay.

Yet many of the crime figures for Chicago were remarkably lower in the mid-Twenties than in 1919. Payroll robberies were down by 50 percent; so were other armed robberies; so were burglaries.[13] And in New York, the records at Sing Sing showed a heavy drop in crimes against property since 1890, offset to some extent by crimes against the person, such as assault and rape.[14] The homicide rate nationwide had doubled between 1900 and 1919. In the Twenties it rose hardly at all.[15] There was virtually nothing in the relevant data to show that crime in the 1920s was more prevalent than it had been a decade before, or a generation before. If anything, they showed a slight decrease overall.[16]

What had altered was awareness of crime as the old society gave way to the new. On the frontier, people had left their houses unlocked even when they went away for several weeks or months. "If a stranger came by, he might go in and feed himself or sleep in the house, clean up afterward, and go on his way."[17] Even crooks could be nostalgic about the safe old days. Ernest Booth, an armed robber who spent most of the Twenties in San Quentin, remembered working in a general store in Mendocino, California, around 1910. "Often when the owner was not in the store, customers would help themselves and leave behind a note or the cash-payment on the counter."[18]

It is unlikely that people and property had been much safer in the old days. But people felt safer, and it was the feeling that stayed on in the memory. The watershed was Colosimo's funeral on May 15, 1920; the first of the gaudy, flower-bedecked gangster's funerals that became part of the folk-imagery of the new age. The parade that saw Big Jim go to his rest advertised the Chicago alliance between crime and politics. There were 5,000 mourners, and at the front, judges, aldermen, and congressmen walked side by side with convicted white slavers, dope peddlers, stickup artists, murderers, and extortionists. The old illusion that authority stood as a shield between the citizen and the gangster took a beating that day.

It took another one night in April 1926 when William H. McSwiggin, an assistant state's attorney, was sitting in a car outside a Cicero saloon with two known gangsters, and two gunmen riddled the car with Thompson submachine guns.* A great many people were curious to know what a prosecutor was doing at nine in the evening in the company of gangsters.[19] They never found out. And two years later a United States senator, Charles Deneen, went home to Chicago to walk a mile and a half in the rain at a gangster's funeral. The deceased, one "Diamond Joe" Esposito, had been a power in Chicago's Little Italy up to the time of his swift and brutal death. Deneen's involvement with the likes of Diamond Joe was not without its drawbacks. Following the funeral, hand grenades exploded on the steps of the senator's Chicago home.[20]

For much of the Twenties the governor of Illinois was Lennington Small. He was a crook. So, it turned out, were many of his friends. In 1922 he was tried for corruption on what looked like very convincing evidence. He was acquitted, to some astonishment in other states, but none in Illinois. He staved off further prosecution by handing back two-thirds of the million dollars he had stolen.[21] Chicago's mayor for most of these heady years was William "Big Bill" Thompson, who boasted, "I'm wetter than the middle of the Atlantic Ocean,"[22] and promised to punch the king of England on the nose if that worthy ever dared to penetrate the Chicago city limits. This kind of electioneering made Thompson the most popular mayor the city ever elected. Thompson was already rich, thanks to his parents. But he had nothing against a dishonest dollar,[23] and had no objections to other peoples getting rich however they chose to go about it.

A lot of them went about it in a very public way. Chicago's beer wars raged from 1922 through 1927 and left at least 260 gangsters dead at the hands of other gangsters. It was not only the mobsters who killed prodigiously, however—so did the police, who killed a further 220 in 1922–27.[24] The record holder was Lieutenant Frank Reynolds, with a personal score of eleven.[25]

Illinois was far from being alone either in political corruption or in open gang warfare. Indiana and Pennsylvania were notoriously at the mercy of thieves and fixers. And although Chicago seemed to get most of the publicity, one New York editor observed that New York could hardly be a more violent or cold-blooded place. "New York has the type of gunman who would shoot his grandmother in the back and lay bets on which way she would fall."[26] The political ties were blatant even in the reign of Good Guy Al Smith. When Robert P. Brindell, the head of New York's construction unions, went to prison for a multimillion-dollar swindle, he went not to a humble cell, but to a house in the prison grounds. There he

---

* The second most famous weapon in history (after the atomic bomb); invented in 1919–20 by Brigadier General John T. Thompson to give foot soldiers an answer to the murderous defensive machine-gun fire of World War I.

entertained his friends, ate well, carried on his business affairs, and relaxed while time passed. The day he finished his (minimum) sentence the Honorable Al Smith gave him a pardon.[27]

The New York Police Department's Vice Squad was running one of the dirtiest rackets imaginable—shaking down hundreds of women and girls, some as young as fifteen, by framing them on prostitution charges.[28] The investigation of this scandal merged with another: at least half a dozen judges in the magistrates courts had either bought their appointments for hard cash or their appointments had been bought for them by big-time racketeers. Police, city officials, magistrates, more than twenty lawyers and dozens of bondsmen had conspired for years to shake down helpless women, who found themselves facing planted evidence and paid perjurers if they got into court. Terrified, they handed over their savings to stay out of prison.[29] But this was only one operation. The number and variety of corrupt enterprises involving police, prosecutors, and judges defies belief. They involved sham lawyers, known mobsters, stolen documents, perjured testimony, vanishing witnesses, tens of millions of dollars, and the complete disappearance in August 1930 of Justice Joseph F. Crater of the New York Supreme Court. The judge first virtually emptied his bank accounts of $5,100 before disappearing. Mrs. Crater said she knew nothing, while "showgirl June Manners, said to be his friend, also was reported missing."[30]

Despite these sensations elsewhere, Chicago remained firmly entrenched in the public imagination as the crime capital of the universe, where enormous black limousines cruised with intent down crowded streets, tommy guns blazing briefly into a storefront or another limousine, and roared away, tires squealing as they disappeared from sight around a corner. In Chicago it seemed that murder had become a public spectacle, a free (if dangerous) entertainment. The city had always been a frontier town, where North met South, East met West. Its history was one of unbroken violence. Its wealth made it a magnet for crooks all over the country. Its reputation as a crime capital, therefore, was not without basis. But it was wildly exaggerated. Better than 90 percent of its crime was not committed by the Capone gang, the O'Bannion gang, the Moran gang, the Terrible Gennas, or others whose names filled the newspapers. It was committed by adolescents and young men under twenty-five. If they belonged to a gang, and many did, it was probably a neighborhood gang that had begun as a playgroup some years before.[31]

As a murder capital, Chicago was again overrated. Murder did rise spectacularly in some areas in the Twenties: in places with rapid population growth—Florida, for instance, where the murder rate quadrupled during the 1919–26 land boom.[32] But in Chicago the population increase was gradual, and so was the increase in killing. Even the gang wars had only a marginal effect on the city's homicide rate. And Cicero, supposedly the most wide-open part of a wide-open town, where there were indeed some amazingly public shoot-outs and ambushes, had a murder rate in 1925 of 3.68 per 100,000 inhabitants. The beer wars were in full swing. Yet Cicero's murder rate was on a par with that of New Haven, Connecticut, and Waterville, Maine.[33] Alas for myth, Memphis and Miami were vastly more murderous than the streets of Chicago in the days of Al Capone.[34]

There is no denying, though, that some kinds of crime had gone public—mainly bank robberies. Between 1885 and 1914 there was not a single daylight bank robbery anywhere in the United States. Banks *were* robbed, but at night. Torch-proof safes, time locks and burglar alarms put most of the safecrackers out of business. To rob a bank it became necessary to hold it up in broad daylight. And there were 1,100 bank holdups in 1915–28.[35] In Texas, the banks fought back in frontier style. Every bank carried a sign on behalf of the Texas Bankers Association in a prominent place. It read:

$5000 REWARD
DEAD BANK ROBBERS WANTED
$5000 cash will be paid for
each bank robber killed while
robbing a Texas bank.[36]

It was an idea that spread to other states.[37]

Appalled by what they saw as a permanent crime wave, Americans were nevertheless fascinated by gangsters. In 1930 Warner Brothers released *Little Caesar*. Its central character, Ricco, played by Edward G. Robinson, was obviously based on Capone. The film was such a success that 1931 saw the release of fifty gangster films. The studios piously disclaimed any desire to glamorize crime. Intentional or not, that is what they did. The early Thirties also saw a cycle of films in which corruption was ritually condemned while it was made interesting. These "shyster" films dwelt on corrupt lawyers (*The Mouthpiece*), corrupt newspapermen (*The Front Page*), and corrupt politicians (*The Dark Horse*). It was far removed from the sentimental and melodramatic world of the movies only ten years before. The modern fascination with big-time crime is another part of the Twenties.

III

Organized crime did not begin with Prohibition; instead, it was given a powerful incentive to become much better organized. The fortunes of men like Big Jim Colosimo had been based on saloons, brothels, and gambling dens; on their political connections; on the murderous battles between employers and workers. There were mobsters long before Prohibition. What happened under a Torrio was that gangsters began to look on crime as a branch of business. Capone rose to the top of that business by being as ruthless as anyone else in it, while being far better organized. The attention to detail that characterized a Capone killing was what also kept the Big Fellow alive.[38]

Before the war, the Black Hand had flourished in Chicago's Italian neighborhoods. It was mainly an extortion racket. With the advent of Prohibition, hundreds of Blackhanders went straight into bootlegging. It was far more profitable than shaking down corner storekeepers or the local spaghetti factory.[39] Similarly with the Unione Siciliana. Before 1920 it was devoted to helping immigrants, which often meant fighting the Black Hand. By 1920 the gangsters had penetrated it. The Unione now had two sides. One continued the traditional good works; the other provided an organizational framework for extortion, white slavery, armed robbery, union racketeering, bootlegging, and murder. Either way, it was dominated by Capone.

On the South Side of Chicago the dominant gang was the Terrible Gennas. They built a model community to help their fellow Sicilians there. At the same time, they kept hundreds of families in Little Italy ministering in the family kitchen to the needs of a portable still, turning corn sugar into alcohol for a retainer of $15 a day. "The tenement flats, houses and back rooms of stores with the required apparatus ran into the thousands, and over the entire community hung the stench of fermenting mash."[40]

Prohibition worked similar organizational wonders in New York. "Dutch" Schultz (real name: Arthur Flegenheimer) was only a bartender as late as 1928 when he opened his first speakeasy. Schultz found that he had an unsuspected gift for organization. Within two years he had a speakeasy chain, running to eleven establishments. Dutch sought new worlds to conquer and took over dozens of numbers rackets in Harlem. As Bismarck had brought unity to a jigsaw puzzle of petty states, so did Dutch Schultz consolidate forty competing operations into a single mighty force.[41]

Public resistance was tempered by the fact that the modern crime gangs provided quality booze. If the customer complained, his money was refunded or he was allowed to exchange the unopened bottles for a different brand. The big bootlegging outfits operated much as any reputable business would act in a competitive field—they cultivated the customer.

Most of the bad booze came from the independents, and their stuff could be, literally, poison. The gangs ruled by force and murder, yet they rarely posed any threat to ordinary citizens. Despite the rattle of gunfire and the thunder of exploding bombs, ran one commentary, "it is a war in which the non-combatants are safer than they were in Belgium."[42]

The gangsters were themselves becoming tired of the constant warfare. It was obviously bad for business. In December 1928 Sicilian-born mobsters from a dozen cities met in Cleveland. What they discussed is open to conjecture. But the fact that such a meeting took place indicated movement toward the creation of some kind of confederation. Then, in May 1930, a bigger meeting was held in Atlantic City, involving Italians, Jews, Irish, and Slavs; thirty major gangsters were there, including Capone. Torrio, freshly returned from a prolonged sojourn in Italy, chaired the meeting. "The main subjects were disarmament, peace and amalgamation on a nationwide scale."[43]

Hoover, meanwhile, was making Prohibition enforcement more effective, by appointing aggressive federal prosecutors and upgrading the staff of the Prohibition Bureau. Coolidge had taken advantage of Wheeler's death to bring the bureau under Civil Service regulations. At a stroke, 1,500 employees were dismissed because they failed normal civil service standards of education, honesty, and competence. The resignation of Roy Haynes in 1926 had been another step toward greater effectiveness. "Spending more hours on the lecture platform than in Washington, Haynes seemed to prefer sanctification of the dry laws to their enforcement."[44] His successor, Brigadier General Lincoln C. Andrews, concentrated on the task at hand. The Jones Five and Dime Act of 1929 was also the first law with sufficiently stiff penalties to frighten people away from bootlegging. And then came Hoover.

There was little, however, that anyone could do about people making their own liquor. Production of corn sugar had risen from 150 million pounds in 1921 to nearly 1 billion pounds in 1929.[45] No one had any illusions about the reason for this astonishing increase. Almost all of the supply of corn sugar was being distilled into homemade booze. It was cheap—$5.00 for a 100-pound bag; made high quality alcohol; produced very little odor; and left only a small amount of mash behind. Yet there were still millions of people drinking the most bizarre and dangerous concoctions in their search for an alcoholic good time. A woman in Atlanta, Annie Marino, for instance, convicted in 1930 of public drunkenness readily named her poison—mothballs dissolved in gasoline.[46] Ginger extract, freely available at drugstores, was mixed with sweet syrup to cut the spicy taste and produced a cheap, legal intoxicant. But in 1930 a large batch of adulterated Jamaican ginger extract found its way into circulation. It left 20,000 people in varying states of what was known as "jake paralysis." Dozens died. Cincinnati alone had 300 cases of jake paralysis.[47] The victims were mainly poor. The adulterant (tri-ortho-cresyl phosphate) had been added to increase the potency of the ginger extract; it was normally added only to varnish or shellac. Among those who did not die were dozens who were blinded for life and hundreds who were permanently crippled. Yet even while this was happening, the gangsters were bringing in more and more decent liquor and the price was coming down.[48]

The Wickersham Committee was toiling diligently at its appointed task, and at the end of 1930, after nineteen months of conscientious effort, it produced a report that opposed repeal of the Eighteenth Amendment. But seven of the eleven members expressed individual opinions in favor of modification to allow the sale of beer and wine. Hoover's attempts to accept the report without accepting its conclusions created both bewilderment and disgust. The double-talk that surrounded this episode was a blow to the President and the drys. And Hoover, by making Prohibition enforcement more effective, was probably hastening the repeal of the Eighteenth Amendment. The number of liquor convictions annually in the federal courts had doubled. Jail sentences had quadrupled. And the demand for repeal became both clamorous and well-organized.

When Tex Guinan was tried in a New York federal court in 1929 for selling liquor, the courtroom had been packed with supporters. Huge crowds milled in the street outside. The jury voted for her acquittal, to an outburst of cheering. She returned to her club behind a brass band and threw a victory party that ran for days.[49]

Two nights after Christmas, 1929, a rumrunner, the *Black Duck*, had been caught in Narragansett Bay by a Coast Guard cutter as she tried to bring in 500 cases of whiskey for New Year's Eve. When the *Black Duck* made a run for the open sea, the cutter opened fire. Three of the four men aboard the *Black Duck* were killed, the 500 cases seized. An angry crowd formed outside Faneuil Hall to protest against the deaths, then went on a rampage on Boston Common and beat up a Coast Guard recruiter.[50]

With public opinion shifting so heavily against the drys, the Association Against the Prohibition Amendment had become a propaganda organ as strong as the Anti-Saloon League. In 1929 the AAPA gave birth to a women's auxiliary, the million-strong Women's Organization for National Prohibition Repeal. Rich society women threw themselves into the cause of repeal as they had done in other days for charity. Prohibition could no longer be defended as the sure protection of American women—not after repeal became fashionable with the Junior League.

Hardly a week went by without some important defector from the dry side, such as John D. Rockefeller, Jr. Dwight Morrow, running in the New Jersey senatorial primary in May 1930, roundly condemned the Eighteenth Amendment, called for repeal, and urged that Prohibition be given back to the states to decide, each for itself. City and state bar associations had come out by the dozen for an end to Prohibition. In November 1930 the American Bar Association came out against the Eighteenth Amendment by more than 2–1.

What was wrong with Prohibition was brilliantly summarized in a poem by Franklin P. Adams, widely reproduced, called "The Wickersham Report":

> Prohibition is an awful flop;
> We like it.
> It can't stop what it's meant to stop.
> We like it.
> It's left a trail of death and slime,
> It don't prohibit worth a dime,
> It's filled our land with graft and crime;
> Nevertheless, we're for it.

IV

Sanford Bates reformed the Deer Island prison. He set up a school and a debating society. A form of self-government was introduced. A moneymaking piggery was created. Deer Island prison became the best prison in Massachusetts, yet turned back a sizable part of its annual appropriation each year. Coolidge, before becoming Vice-President, appointed Bates Massachusetts' commissioner of corrections.

When Hoover took office in 1929, he found the federal prisons on the verge of collapsing back into the conditions of the eighteenth century. Thanks to the Harrison Act and Prohibition enforcement, the federal prison population had grown in ten years from 3,900 to more than 13,000.[51] In those ten years not a single new federal prison had been built, but there was constant agitation for reform. Espionage Act prisoners, released and pardoned, had been atypical convicts—educated, articulate, organized. They had endured/enjoyed a middle-class education on prison conditions. What they wanted was known as the New Penology. In 1929 they got it: Hoover appointed Bates to reform the federal prisons.

At present, each (overcrowded) prison had only one doctor. There was virtually no work to be done, little exercise and fresh air, an appalling diet, and ill-trained guards. Hoover and Bates drew up plans to reform these prisons and build new ones. Work was to be found, recreation provided, the diet improved, and prison staff properly trained. Prison employees came under the civil service at last. Public health service doctors were made responsible for the health of prisoners. A new parole system virtually doubled the number of men paroled, and many more were placed on probation.[52] Open prisons and work camps were created, and thousands of prisoners were transferred to them.

Bates's principal achievement was to set a standard of penology against which all other American prisons would have to be judged. The need for new federal penitentiaries provided him with the chance to show what he was driving at from scratch. When the new federal penitentiary at Lewisburg, Pennsylvania, opened in 1932, it was spacious, airy, secure, but dignified rather than forbidding. There was a large school, a well-stocked library, spacious grounds, a pleasant setting, and rooms instead of cells. Prisoners were actually encouraged to raise their grievances, either with the warden or by writing to Washington.

With Hoover's enthusiastic backing, Bates created the Federal Bureau of Prisons. The example it set of humane treatment became a model at home and abroad. And it was certainly needed at home, because the conditions that prevailed in most American prisons and jails in the Twenties were enough to make a reasonable person rage.

Attempting to stem the supposed crime wave, New York had in 1925 adopted a measure proposed by an upstate legislator, Caleb Baumes, to brand anyone with four felony convictions a "habitual criminal" and send him to prison for life. The Baumes law quickly filled New York's prisons with petty offenders, the kind of people who commit dozens of minor, nonviolent crimes, such as burglary or shoplifting. Its effect on criminals who went in for such offenses as murder, armed robbery, and rape was virtually nil. The petty criminals sent away for life carried with them a deep sense of injustice and hopelessness. They had nothing left to lose. They became a constant source of friction and unrest. The habitual-criminal law was, nevertheless, copied by other states.*

To the surprise of no one who was aware of conditions in American prisons, 1929 saw a wave of riots that left twenty guards and prisoners dead and more than 100 injured. Overcrowding and desperation led three prisoners at the Ohio state penitentiary at Columbus to start a fire in one of the workshops in April 1930. Huge crowds gathered to watch the blaze. Firemen refused to fight the flames without police protection, while prison officers refused to open the cells for fear of a mass escape. By the time the

---

* In Michigan they sent a thirty-year-old mother of three to prison for life, automatically, for her fourth prohibition conviction.

guards and the firemen had worked out a satisfactory arrangement, much of the prison had burned down. The death toll of prisoners was 322 burned to death, and one of the three who had started the fire hanged himself in remorse.[53]

Police brutality was enshrined in a phrase that is with us yet—"the third degree." The first degree of pressure was to be arrested. The second degree of pressure was to be taken in. The third degree came in the back of the station house when the police went to work on the suspect. "I have seen a man beaten on the Adam's apple so that blood spurted out of his mouth," said one crime reporter. "I have seen another put in a dentist's chair and held there while the dentist, who seemed to enjoy his job, ground down a sound molar under a rough burr."[54] In Seattle the third degree involved an electrically wired carpet, covering the floor of one cell. The chief of police described what happened when the current was turned on: "Sparks fly and the prisoner leaps, screaming in agony, into the air. It is not fatal, its effects are not lasting, and it leaves no marks."[55] Torture was an integral part of police investigation, applied mainly when a suspect was poor, uneducated, and friendless.

Nor was it limited to the back of police stations. Flogging was a commonplace in state prisons. Even at a "good" prison, such as Jackson in Michigan, a prisoner would receive thirty to forty lashes with a heavy, water-soaked leather strap for a trifling offense.[56] And Delaware had a whipping post at which offenders were publicly flogged. Crowds would gather to watch a flogging and were disappointed that the prison warden charged with applying the whip did not have much heart for his task.[57]

Nearly every prison had pitch-dark cells where recalcitrant prisoners were kept alive on two slices of bread and one cup of water every twenty-four hours. Prisoners in dark cells were handcuffed to the wall virtually the entire time. But in some prisons the handcuffs had been replaced with an iron cage which could be adjusted to fit almost anyone. Once inside this cage, the prisoner had to stand upright. He could not bend his knees or turn around. His hands were forced against his body. It was impossible for him to move his arms. And so he stood like a post, day and night, in utter darkness, except for the minute or two that it took to feed him bread and water through the bars of his cage.[58]

The "water-cure" was as popular in prisons as in mental asylums. A prisoner (or a patient) who became violent was stripped naked and placed in a narrow, tiled enclave. He was then pounded into submission by a thudding jet of water from a fire hose. Even very strong men would collapse, exhausted and struggling for breath, after two or three minutes.

Aimed from only ten feet away, the hose would cover a man with bruises and ruin his kidneys. Guards wielding clubs made sure he did not move out of the enclosure.[59]

Bad as conditions were in state prisons, they were even worse in city and county jails,[60] unless you happened to be rich. Then it was almost as good as a rest home, as Harry F. Sinclair was to discover.

Acquitted during his joint trial with Albert B. Fall, Sinclair had nevertheless been convicted for contempt of Congress when he refused to turn over all his records to the Walsh subcommittee. He received a sentence of ninety days. Subsequently, he received six months for trying to interfere with the jury during his trial with Fall. Sinclair disproved the folk wisdom that said it was impossible to put a million dollars behind bars. On the night of May 6, 1929, a three-limousine cavalcade pulled up at the District of Columbia jail. Sinclair started serving his time.

Major William L. Peak, the jail superintendent, let it be known that Sinclair would enjoy no special treatment. "The jail isn't like it used to be," announced Peak. "We'll put him to work and hope he likes it."[61] Sinclair, worth $50 million or more, was the richest person ever to be imprisoned in the United States, and he certainly was making no complaints. He turned two rooms of the jail hospital into the boardroom of the Sinclair Oil Corporation, slept in pink silk pajamas, dined on filet mignon and hothouse strawberries, sent his laundry to New York by courier, and enjoyed the devoted ministrations of a dozen prisoner-servants, including a bootblack by the name of Herbert Hoover.[62]

V

Remember Robert E. Burns? He was last seen in chapter 1, just discharged from the army, only to find that his sweetheart had married someone else and his job had been given to another accountant. These blows came after a year as a front-line medic and pushed him into a nervous collapse. He drifted aimlessly from job to job and place to place. He arrived in Atlanta in 1922, penniless and in rags. At a Salvation Army hostel he met two other down-and-outs. They involved him in a holdup of a store that netted $5.80. For this he received a six- to ten-year sentence on the chain gang.

He was given a suit of "stripes" and a pair of boots; no underwear, no socks. A large shackle was riveted around each ankle, and the shackles were joined with a chain of thirteen links. Another chain, three feet long, was attached to the middle of this chain, and in order to walk, the end of this three-foot chain had to be carried in the hand. The chain between his ankles, moreover, was comparatively short. A man could not take a normal stride. Chains and shackles together weighed twenty pounds. At night all the prisoners were attached to yet another chain which ran around the barnlike room in which they slept. Each time a man got up to urinate, the entire room reverberated to the sound of clanking metal, and every man was tugged awake.

The day on the chain gang began at 3:30 A.M. By five they were down at the quarry with sledgehammers, breaking stone. They worked thirteen hours a day. Their food consisted of corn pone, pork belly, and red beans, spiced with sand and worms. There were no washing facilities, except for a basin of cold water—no soap, no towels. Each evening, after dinner, the guards would pick out that prisoner on each twenty-man work gang who had done the least work that day; even if all had worked themselves to exhaustion, someone had to come last. In front of the other convicts these men were pinned to a bench, their trousers were pulled down, and they were flayed with leather straps until the blood ran down their legs. There was no treatment for their gaping wounds. The day ended with the convicts climbing wearily into their cots and being chained together once again. Throughout the night their sleep was troubled by the groans of the men who had been whipped.

The shackles that Burns wore were round. He became friendly with a black prisoner, who wielded a sledgehammer with such skill that he could hit a pin with his eyes closed. Burns asked him to knock his shackles into an elliptical shape, and braced them against a boulder. A single miscalculation and Burns's ankles would have been shattered. He would have been crippled for life. The black man hit both shackles perfectly. Burns stepped out of them. The black prisoner stood to gain nothing from this, and risked his life if the guards discovered what he had done. Burns's escape was his only reward.

Burns ran into the swamp, followed, as he knew he would be, by bloodhounds. When the dogs caught up with him he showed no fear, but treated the chase like a game. Instead of tearing him to pieces, the dogs responded to his gentle talk and did not give him away, as they had been trained to do, by howling at his heels. Burns got clean away, arriving in Chicago in 1923 with exactly 20 cents.

From 1924 to 1929 he was the publisher of a successful real estate weekly called *The Greater Chicago Magazine*. He led a blameless life. He got married. The marriage failed. He became interested in another woman. He asked his wife for a divorce. She gave him her answer by tipping off the Georgia authorities. Georgia asked for his extradition. Convinced that if he did not fight extradition the authorities would set aside the balance of his sentence, he returned to Georgia. He was immediately put in chains once more.

He was the most famous prisoner in the South. Crowds would come out to see his short, stocky figure laboring on the Campbell County chain gang. Then, as his money ran out and interest in him dwindled, he was transferred to the hardest chain gang in the states, building roads fifteen and a half hours each day, swinging a pickax for Georgia through an entire year. In September 1930 he escaped for a second time and wrote the most influential work in the history of American prisons, *I Am a Fugitive from a Georgia Chain Gang*. It aroused public opinion against the brutality of American prisons as nothing else had ever done.

Burns had to take what comfort he could from that. For he had escaped straight into the Depression, his savings and his business gone. "I am sitting in my plainly furnished room, alone, writing this record of events with hands horny from heavy toil," he wrote at the end of his book. "I am now John Pashley—an itinerant laborer, friendless, weary in body and mind. . . ."[63]

VI

Lindbergh remained the greatest hero of the age. In 1928 he was *Time*'s first ever "Man of the Year." His picture was hung up in a million homes. "It stares at you from over the reception desks of Midwestern hotels. It is hung at the entrance to railway stations, draped in flags. It smiles at you from the inside of taxi-cabs, it is stuck to the walls of elevators, it brightens the desks of countless stenographers. It is placed in schoolrooms, side by side with Lincoln and Washington."[64]

On a flying goodwill tour of Mexico he had met, and later married, one of Dwight Morrow's daughters. They had a son, and in 1932 Charles Augustus Lindbergh, Jr., was the most famous baby in the land. The Lindberghs were staying at their new home in New Jersey at the end of February that year. On the night of February 29, Anne Morrow Lindbergh and the child's nurse put the baby to bed, then closed and bolted all the shutters except one pair, which had become warped and would not close.[65] That night, someone entered the house (ironically named Hopewell) through that single unshielded window and kidnaped the child.

Kidnaping was hardly a novel crime, but the kidnaping of children was rare.* Until the Depression it was a crime limited almost entirely to

---

* "Charlie Ross, the original nonpareil, is a national hero eclipsed in popularity only by Jesse James, albeit their distinctions are divergent," wrote *Time* in 1927. "Every year someone claims to be Charlie. . . ." In 1874 the four-year-old Charlie Ross had become the first child ever kidnaped in the United States for money. He was never restored to his family. He vanished without trace, the most famous child of his time.

men who demanded comparatively small sums—say, a thousand dollars —for the return of a successful small businessman in a Sicilian neighborhood; who couched their ransom demands in a parody of the flowery language of Latin diplomacy; and who signed the ransom note "La Mano Nera" or stamped it with a crude black hand. After 1930 almost anyone seemed a potential victim. A Broadway playwright, Charles Rosenthal, was kidnaped in 1931 and released for a ransom of $50,000. In Oklahoma City an oil millionaire, Charles F. Urschel, was kidnaped. Another victim was William Hamm, the brewer. In St. Louis, Adolphus Busch Orthwein, the grandson of the famous brewer, was kidnaped. Altogether, 1931 saw at least 300 kidnapings, of both grown men and small children.[66]

For the generation of the Twenties the kidnaping of Charles Augustus Lindbergh, Jr., was "the crime of the century" (as the assassination of John F. Kennedy has been to our own time). On the morning of March 3, nearly every daily newspaper in the United States carried on its front page the baby's diet, for the benefit of his abductor. "The Lindbergh kidnaping is not only a harrowing private tragedy," wrote the New Republic, "it is also a public event."[67] For weeks it overshadowed the Depression.

The passionate involvement of the entire country in the case led to the swift passage of the "Lindbergh Act," which made kidnaping a federal crime. Even before the act was passed, Hoover offered the aid of virtually every agency in the federal government. Al Capone, in Cook County jail awaiting transfer to Atlanta penitentiary, made an offer: the child's safe return in exchange for freedom. Irey conveyed Capone's proposal to Lindbergh, who turned it down flat. "I wouldn't ask for Capone's release— even if it would save a life."[68]

For ten weeks there was hardly a meeting, from boards of directors down to PTAs, that did not begin with a prayer for the return of the Lindberghs' baby.[69] On May 12 a black truckdriver stopped to relieve himself in some woods only a mile from Hopewell. He found the decaying remains of an infant half-hidden in the underbrush. Charles Augustus Lindbergh, Jr., had died within minutes of being abducted. Not since the assassination of Abraham Lincoln had any crime so shaken the country, and after ten weeks the trail had gone cold.

25. Built Wright

His strong-willed, independent-minded mother had hung the room of the infant Frank Lloyd Wright with ten large engravings of famous English cathedrals to provide him with his first lessons in the human creation of beauty. She intended him to grow up to become a great architect. Not even the departure of her husband, never to be seen again by wife and son, deflected her. At the cost of great privation she put Frank through three and a half years at the University of Wisconsin. But the education the university offered seemed so shallow and pointless that without waiting to be graduated, Frank Lloyd Wright dropped out. With seven dollars to his name he left for Chicago.

He arrived in the office of the most exciting architect of the Gilded Age, Louis Sullivan, by a roundabout course, but almost as if fated to do so. Wright rapidly antagonized virtually the entire drafting room, with his long hair and modishly bohemian clothes. Two of his tormentors he beat into submission in a boxing match that degenerated into a brawl. A third was goaded by Wright into a murderous rage. By the time Wright had felled him with a hastily seized large T-square, there were eleven stab wounds in Wright's back and his shoes were squishy with blood running into them.[1] Yet he determined to stay with Sullivan, and rose high enough to fire all his antagonists.

Almost from the start, he was Sullivan's star pupil. In return, Wright for the rest of his life referred in his Victorian-romantic way to Sullivan as "the Master." Modern construction methods and new materials were making it possible to build structures far taller than anything that had ever existed this side of the pyramids. Buildings inevitably grew. But that was all that most of them were—tall. Almost every possible device was employed to make them appear less tall than they were. And they were as overdecorated and banal as the mass of late Victorian architecture. Sullivan was the first architect to *emphasize* the verticality of tall buildings, and he abolished much of the clutter. The result was the first collection of modern skyscrapers—tall, unified, daring. It was Sullivan, too, who coined the expression "Form follows function"—meaning that a building needed to be designed from the inside out; that it was more than the search for a pretty face. He laid the foundations for most of the good architecture of the twentieth century. Wright sat at his feet for six years, becoming while he did so one of the three best draftsmen in America.[2] He had his own office adjoining the Master's. They became inseparable friends. Yet he quarreled, inevitably, with the man he adored. "I threw down my pencil and walked out . . . ," he later wrote.[3]

His private life was another arena enlivened with conflict and drama. At a time when respectable people stayed out of debt, he was in debt up to his ears and beyond, familiar from the first years of marriage with bill collectors, bailiffs, and begging merchants. He shrugged such cares away. "So long as we had the luxuries, the necessities could pretty well take care of themselves."[4] The father of four children, he loathed no sound more than the piping tones of a child framing the word "papa." Domestic life alternately bored and infuriated Wright.

But in his work, he was a man with the mark of genius about him. Offered four years in Paris to study at the Beaux Arts, courtesy of rich admirers, he turned the offer down. The style was too impersonal, he said. He refused almost certain success to pursue his own vision. It was a vision of what domestic architecture ought to be, of homes built in a coherent, unified style, filled with space and light. He reduced interior walls, put in larger windows and fewer of them. He rapidly took up new materials. Concrete was just becoming easily available at the turn of the century. Wright's Unity Temple in Oak Park was the first large structure ever made from concrete and wooden forms. His evolving vision of "organic" architecture grew out of a continuous study of nature. The houses he was building on midwestern prairies were all horizontal lines, like the prairie itself. He stressed the importance of human proportions; in this case, his own proportions. Wright stood five feet eight and a half inches tall. A Wright house was built for a man of exactly that height. Had he been a six-footer who knows what they would have been like?

It was a struggle to get his houses built. Bankers did not like to lend money on them. Contractors did not know how to build them. He turned the construction of a house into an epic struggle, while telling his clients, "You'll live like a king and queen!"[5] By which he meant that they would live a more elevated life simply by living in a Wright-designed home. Like Ruskin, Frank Lloyd Wright considered architecture an exercise in morality.

So the houses got built somehow. But he was choking to death on domesticity. Two years earlier he had designed a house for Mamah Borthwick Cheyney and her husband. In 1909, at the age of forty, Wright eloped with Mrs. Cheyney. They fled to Italy.

When they returned two years later, Wright found that running away with a client's wife had cut the flow of new clients to a venturesome trickle. His mother gave him a hillside property in southern Wisconsin which she had inherited. It was there that Wright built his refuge from the world, Taliesin. He set up his studio, built a house alongside it, and settled there with his new family and assistants. Taliesin was one of his greatest triumphs: a complex of buildings that was not on the hill but *of* it. One night, when Wright was in Chicago, a servant went berserk. He murdered Mamah Cheyney and one of her children with an axe and locked six people in the dining room, which he set ablaze with gasoline. He then swallowed acid and took his own life. When Wright arrived home he found only smoking ruins and seven dead. To save himself from going mad with grief, Wright threw himself into designing and building Taliesin II, on the black hole in the hillside filled with the ashes of the first Taliesin.

His debts were staggering, his commissions few. With time on his hands, he returned, as he did again and again, to where all great art begins —in the study of nature. He devoted himself to it, and in it he included human beings. Just as he studied light, open spaces, rolling hills, so he studied the human spirit. It was this clear-eyed, steady observation of the natural world that enabled him to see everything around him as no one else saw it. To people who had forgotten how to see, his work seemed radical and at times bizarre. But they had less time to spend on looking than he had.

With his love of nature went complete acceptance of the machine. If the architecture of the Machine Age was rubbish, he said with passion, that was not the fault of the machine: ". . . the Machine is only the Creature, not the Creator of this iniquity! . . . the Machine is itself the victim of Artist-impotence."[6] Simplicity, clarity of surface, renewed ability to make the best of the inherent quality of materials, were machinery's gifts to architecture; gifts spurned by men without vision to see them. Instead, they were used to turn out imitations or debased variations on the safe, respected, and dead, such as fake Gothic cathedrals, hung on steel skeletons and air-conditioned.* Machine-made glass however had already destroyed classical architecture, with its recesses of stone and its gloomy interiors where daylight rarely penetrated. Cheap, clear glass, flooding any interior, no matter how large or deep, with bright sunlight had abolished the fake Greek temples, the copies of Roman basilicas. That reinforced Wright's faith. He saw architecture being reborn because of glass and steel.

In 1916 a Japanese commission was touring the United States in search of an architect who could introduce modern architecture to Japan by designing the Imperial Hotel. When the commission reached the Midwest it saw some of Wright's houses more or less by accident. The job was his, and he was glad to have it. He arrived in Japan shortly before the United States entered the war. Wrieto-san did not return until 1921.

He responded wholeheartedly to Japanese art and architecture, admiring its clarity, its organic unity, its directness. There was no clutter in a Japanese building, no straining for effect. He set out to create a building that would be thoroughly modern, yet harmonious with the Japanese architecture he admired so intensely. The story of the building of the Imperial Hotel was to be pure melodrama from beginning to end. Wright overcame one challenge after another, wearing out a dozen devoted assistants and interpreters. He floated the hotel on the sixty feet of mud beneath it, instead of trying to make it secure in the eight feet of earth that overlay the mud. He put the hotel on eight-foot pins, instead of pouring a concrete foundation. This was the technique used in Chicago's Loop, where the soil was sludgy. Wright used it in Tokyo, however, because of the risk of a major earthquake.

As often happened with a Wright design, the costs began to rise far beyond the original estimates. The consortium building the hotel insisted on at least one economy measure—to scratch the vast pool Wright had designed. He was adamant that it stay. When the earthquake struck, he argued, the pool's water would save the hotel from the fires raging all around it. No pool, he concluded, no Wright. The pool remained.

On September 1, 1923, virtually the entire city fell down.† Wright's hotel became a shelter for thousands of the homeless; hardly a corner of it was damaged. And what saved it from burning down was the water in

---

* When James Gamble Rogers finished building Yale's masterpiece of fake Gothic, the Harkness Tower, in 1918, he had the steps ground down with machinery to create the impression that they had been worn away by centuries of constant use.
† To this day the Emperor of Japan goes into mourning on September 1 each year.

the pool that Wright had built. The survival of the Imperial Hotel made Wright the most famous architect in the world.*

His private life was as chaotic as ever. After ten years of separation his wife agreed to divorce him. Wright married the woman with whom he had lived for four years. Shortly afterward, she walked out on him. A year later, when he was financially and emotionally recovered, a fire destroyed half of Taliesin II in the middle of a raging thunderstorm. Wright stood on the roof, a garden hose in his hands, feet scorched, his eyebrows burned off, fighting the flames in vain.[7] He had not paid off the cost of building Taliesin II before he immersed himself in building Taliesin III.

Although legally separated, his second wife chose to pursue him remorselessly when he began living with another woman (destined in time to become the third, and last, Mrs. Wright). Under a barrage of lawsuits and debt collectors, he and his new love fled, to give his lawyers time to save Taliesin III from the bank and to escape the gutter press, which howled at his beautifully designed door. By driving into Minnesota he unwittingly violated the Mann Act. (Sweet irony! Senator James R. Mann had been one of his neighbors in Oak Park.) Betrayed like Christ for cold cash, he was surprised in the middle of the night by a posse of photographers, lawyers, and sheriffs, forcibly seized, and thrown into jail.

In desperate financial and legal trouble, he incorporated himself, selling shares in his future earnings to friends and admirers. The going price for one genius in good working order in 1926 was $75,000. Most of this was swallowed up by his divorced second wife and her lawyers. She still pursued him with an insane fury, and was to spend her last months in a mental hospital.

Wright was the most famous underemployed architect of the Twenties, partly because of these domestic dramas, and partly because his ideas were radical and untried. He earned a living mainly by designing half a dozen houses in and around Los Angeles. The most interesting thing about them was the way he took the most humble building material since clay and wattle, the lowly concrete block, and used it to build houses of extraordinary charm, completely harmonious with their settings.

He spent 1928 and 1929 in the Arizona desert, designing a resort to be known as San-Marcos-in-the-Desert. It was another challenge. Not since the pharaohs had anyone tried to build great architecture on burning sands. The crash ruined any chance of financing the San Marcos project. For Wright, it seemed the very end of the road. He was sixty years old, flat broke,[8] and the only Wright buildings erected since 1926 were the

---

* The hotel survived until 1968, when it was demolished.

structures in which he and his assistants lived and worked in the desert, made from canvas and green wood. His failure was made complete by official *un*recognition: he was dropped from *Who's Who in America* in 1929.

II

The Twenties saw the American discovery of the fine arts.[9] Until 1900 Americans were too busy filling in a continent; art was something European, effete, pointless. Culture was left to the women, like jam-making. There was a National Academy, but it was a feeble, derivative place for feeble, derivative artists. At the turn of the century, however, Robert Henri led a revolt against the National Academy and brought forth the first school of American realist painters. No great artist himself, Henri was an inspired teacher and promoter. His most important artistic principle was that there was no right or wrong subject. It was for the artist to paint or draw anything he chose, because there was beauty in everything. "You can find it anywhere, everywhere," said Henri.[10] Among the pupils who imbibed this doctrine were George Bellows, Edward Hopper, and Rockwell Kent. The school itself became known (in the Twenties, after it had passed its peak) as the Ashcan school of painting.

Bellows was its first star pupil. Arriving in New York, he rapidly became "a true creature of the city . . . [prowling] every street from the Bowery north to Riverside Drive."[11] He shared a cheap apartment with Eugene O'Neill, and did drawings of the hordes of urban poor for *The Masses* during the heady Village days just before the First World War. As a painter, his grasp of technique was no more than workmanlike. It was the manner that was everything—frank, assertive, and completely in tune with its subject matter. The colors were lurid, the brushwork vigorous. Instead of trying to ignore the vulgar, strident life around him, he tried to capture it. If the streets were drab, the people tired, that was how he showed them. It came as a revelation, the kind of thing that people find both disturbing yet convincing. The crudeness of execution in a Bellows painting was one with the crudeness of the life he was trying to portray— each was a reflection of a country too energetic to worry about refinement, whether in its boulevards or its painters.

Bellows's popular reputation was based on his prize-fight canvases, of which there are five. (One, *Introducing John L. Sullivan*, has no fighting in it.) The *New York World* commissioned him to cover the Dempsey-Carpentier fight. The *New York Evening-Journal* commissioned him to cover the Dempsey-Firpo fight. His artistic reputation was equally high.

He won major prizes, was given large commissions, exhibited as often as he wished, and was a member of the National Academy. He was considered in his time the first great painter the country had produced. And he was all-American. Bellows had never gone abroad in his life. His death in 1925 at the age of forty-three from an infected appendix, which he had neglected in devotion to his art, was lamented as a national tragedy.

But the Ashcan school was by now as passé as the settlement house of the same era. Of its practitioners only one was to make the transition successfully to later forms of realistic art, and that was Edward Hopper. And he did it by going his own way, into bleakness and despair. The post-Ashcan school of realism was really to be found in the works of Charles Sheeler, who found it impossible to make a living as a painter for most of his life. Sheeler earned his living as a photographer, and not because he considered it a subsidiary of the fine arts. He took photographs of buildings for architects to use.

The idea of artistic photography was all soft-focus and spreading shadows. Sheeler's photographs went in the opposite direction, with sharp definition, hard colors, and a brilliant clarity that would seem completely up-to-date in 1982. Sheeler also did something that was reckless in its day —he absolutely refused to retouch his photographs. He helped to make photography honest.

In 1927 Sheeler spent six weeks at the Rouge plant, photographing the Machine Age equivalent of the Taj Mahal. The result was thirty-two photographs, which were reproduced all over the world. And out of them came Sheeler's famous "industrial" paintings, such as *Upper Deck* and *American Landscape*. It is pointless to try to describe paintings. All I can say is that they celebrate machinery in such a way that at one moment they appear realistic, at another abstract. However they are viewed, they convey Sheeler's complete mastery of color and form. In the end, Sheeler has to be counted as a representational painter, but one who is utterly unsentimental. There is a coolness to Sheeler's finest work that shades into Hopperian bleakness.

For warmth and excitement, you have to look to Joseph Stella's masterpiece of 1919, *Brooklyn Bridge*, another of the great paintings of the time. It is both abstract and representational. It borrowed from both cubism and futurism, and yet was undeniably a painting of the bridge at its most glamorous and obvious. In this single canvas, Stella made himself a major transitional figure, embracing European and American painting, the past and the future, the abstract and the realistic.

There was warmth, too, in the paintings of Georgia O'Keeffe, who was as thoroughly all-American as Bellows. Not until she was sixty-five did she visit Europe. Her paintings of 1919–32 were alive with a passionate intensity. Many were of flowers or of parts of flowers. The lines were sinuous, the colors bold, the shapes vaguely sexual. Instead of trying to flatten everything out in the modern manner, however, she tried to suggest three dimensions and emphasized space. Hers was an art that was highly personal, yet thoroughly modern in temper; deeply felt and uniquely American. And depending on how the viewer looked at it, an O'Keeffe painting was either abstract or representational.

While she and others were trying to come to grips with abstraction, expressionism, and new approaches to realism, there were artists who went to the opposite extreme, such as Thomas Hart Benton, John Steuart Curry, and Grant Wood. They adopted an artificial naïvety and celebrated the American past. Out of this movement came the most famous American painting of the twentieth century, Grant Wood's 1930 double portrait called *American Gothic*. In those two pinched, plain faces, so easily mocked, so hard for us to understand, there is an honest tribute to the humble and obscure farm people who had turned a wilderness into a country. It is an elegy in paint to a world we never knew.

III

In 1921 the *Chicago Tribune* invited 300 leading architects from around the world to enter designs for what was to be the most important architectural competition in a generation. One of the first to be invited was James Mead Howells, a successful New York architect with dozens of commissions. The problem for Howells was that he was too successful. He could hardly find time to work up a competition entry.

Passing through Grand Central Station one afternoon he encountered Raymond Hood. Howells and Hood had been fellow students at l'Ecole des Beaux Arts in Paris fifteen years earlier. But while Howells had gone on to fame and riches, Hood had gone on to poverty and semipermanent unemployment. At forty-one, Hood had failed as thoroughly as Howells had succeeded. Howells mentioned the competition to his old friend, saying that he could not see where he would find the time for it. A thought suddenly struck him. How would Hood, who had time to spare in plenty, like to work up an entry in Howells's office? The organizers were paying all expenses.

In 1922, when the results of the competition were announced, the Howells-Hood design won first prize. The Tribune Tower they designed was a backward-looking piece of pseudo-Gothic flummery, based largely on the Tour de Buerre at Rouen. There were massive doors that would not have looked out of place at Chartres. At the top was a crown of huge, useless flying buttresses. That such a building was considered appropriate for Chicago, the home of the skyscraper, was astonishing.* For Hood, however, it was salvation. Broke and already in debt, he borrowed enough money to buy an overcoat and a train ticket to go to Chicago and collect his prize.[12]

The *Tribune* competition created a fad for building towers of all kinds —as the central feature of a department store, as a monument to the war dead, as a carillon. The most admired of these towers was Bertram Goodhue's Nebraska state capitol, built 1924–26. Goodhue rejected the tradition which for more than a century had decreed domes for capitols. He put up a dramatic, phallic shaft. From the top the bronze figure of a sower perpetually scatters seed on the fruitful plains below.

The Twenties also saw the continuation of the neoclassical revival which began around 1900, only to be slowed down by the war. It was given fresh impetus as Washington began to take on the appearance of an imperial capital. It is possible that between 1900 and 1933 more marble went into American public buildings than was ever used in the Roman Empire. The style was really Classic Eclectic—that is, Greek with other things stuck on. The Lincoln Memorial, completed in 1922 after fifteen years of labor, and designed by Henry Bacon, illustrates the point. Its principle exterior features are thirty-six Doric columns; one for each state of the Union during Lincoln's presidency. But instead of having the flat Greek temple roof that belongs with these columns, there is a recessed attic story, for no particular reason whatever. The building is as dead as Lincoln. The statue inside however *lives*. The work of Daniel Chester French, a prolific hack, it is beyond doubt the most successful sitting statue in the history of sculpture. Hard by is the Arlington Memorial Bridge, built in 1929–30, harmonizing perfectly with the monument, yet in its own right a beautiful and functional structure based on graceful, low arches.

The styling struggles that raged all through the Twenties were at bottom an attempt to break forever the tenacious hold of High Victorian picturesque eclecticism, which happily mixed fake Gothic with fake Moorish with fake classical and almost anything else it could lay its hands on. The result was almost invariably an overelaborate, heavy, enervating pile. The modern architects pinned their faith on materials developed by the late Victorians, and neglected by them: ironwork, concrete, and plate

---

* Hood believed the prize ought to have gone to the highly modernistic design by the Finnish architect Eliel Saarinen, which received second prize.

glass. To the people who had developed them, such materials offered only economy and safety, not artistic possibilities. Iron facades, for example, were developed around 1800. And they were diligently painted to look like wood. Modern architects saw themselves fighting for truth against lies; and for light against darkness.

In the midst of these struggles came the equivalent of throwing in the towel. When the American Institute of Architects was invited to participate in the 1925 Exposition Internationale des Arts Decoratifs et Industriels Modernes at Paris, the AIA declined to accept. The United States had nothing to show, it said.

The movement that the Paris show both enshrined and promoted was the most important movement in design of modern times. Yet the United States had nothing to show. What an admission! But no art style "so rigorously formulated ever imposed itself so universally. . . . With justice, so far, we can describe it as the last of the total styles."[13] And not even the United States could escape it. It appeared in the design of beauty parlors, ocean liners, handbags, shoes, lampposts, book covers, cigarette lighters, ashtrays, dresses, ties, hats, hotels, furniture, hip flasks and factories. Art Deco borrowed from a dozen sources, from Art Nouveau and cubism to the Russian ballet, African masks, and Aztec temples. It was a strange combination of disparate elements improbably roped together by complete acceptance of the Machine Age. It featured new materials, such as Bakelite and stainless steel. Its aim was to break down the traditional divisions between art and industry, craft production and mass production. Art Deco colors were brilliant. Fashionable people who had lived their entire lives with subdued walls suddenly decided to paint them scarlet, or yellow, or jade green, or, best of all, orange. The power of man was represented by machinery, usually shown in relief—airplanes, ships, cranes, oil rigs. The power of nature was shown with zigzag lightning bolts.

Although officially unrepresented, the 1925 Paris Exposition had a greater impact on American architects than upon any others. No city in the world during the next ten years surrendered to Art Deco more completely than New York. There was a building boom already under way. More office buildings were constructed in New York in 1926 (thirty) than in any year before or since.[14] And in the years that followed, Art Deco literally rose to great heights.

Color had gone out of architecture.[15] Art Deco brought it back, with shaded brick, terra cotta, polished aluminum, and black marble. Raymond Hood's American Radiator Building, finished in 1924, anticipated the trend. This black-and-gold building was the first of the colored skyscrapers. The masterpiece of the genre, however, was Walter Van Alen's

Chrysler Building, the tallest building in the world (at 1,048 feet) when it
was finished in 1930. The 150-foot spire that crowned the building was a
cascade of polished aluminum that shone gold and silver in the sun. At
the base of the tower ran a frieze of stylized hubcaps and mudguards.

Even before the Chrysler building opened it was about to be overtaken by the Empire State Building, rising on the Fifth Avenue site where
the old Waldorf-Astoria Hotel had been torn down in 1929.* From an
architectural point of view, the Empire State Building was completely
banal; so standardized that at one time it was rising by more than a story
a day. When it was finished in 1931, however, it was a great success with
visitors for the thrilling views it provided. Its 1,250 feet were topped with
an 80-foot steel lance for mooring dirigibles. But the city would not allow
a dirigible to come near it.

The Empire State Building was not simply the tallest building in the
world for more than thirty years; it was also the biggest ziggurat ever
constructed. A 1916 New York zoning law forced skyscrapers to be built
in tiers, each set back from the one below it. On the four tiers that the
setback law required, a tower of any height might be constructed. The
intention was to keep skyscrapers from blocking out all the sunlight and to
allow air to circulate freely at street level. The setback law gave a unique
character to American skyscrapers for half a century, and it imposed a
formal discipline that kept big buildings from being only that—big. New
York in the Twenties looked like Babylon revisited as ziggurats rose from
Harlem to the Battery, not only in skyscrapers, but in warehouses, apartment buildings, and hotels.

Architecture was, as Hoover's Committee on Recent Social Trends
acknowledged, "America's most distinctive contribution to the arts,"[16]
mainly because of the skyscraper, partly because of Frank Lloyd Wright.
American architectural ideas had been exported to the rest of the world,
and in the late Twenties were being reimported from Europe with the
arrival of architects such as Richard Neutra and the publication in English
of Le Corbusier's influential *Vers une Architecture*. The hard-edged,
clean-line style that was coming into existence eschewed ornamentation;
it accepted the machine-made look, the lavish use of glass, and imperson-
ality. Its earliest completed works on American soil were houses rather
than large buildings. Its leading text provided it with a name, *The International Style*, by Henry-Russell Hitchcock and Philip Johnson.

Hood had meanwhile become the most successful architect of the
Twenties. Small and shy, he was ambitious and bold. When Joseph Medill

* Al Smith's rich friends installed the former governor as president of the Empire State
Building Corporation. The structure was unkindly referred to for years as "Al Smith's last
erection."

Patterson, publisher of the *New York Daily News*, came to him in 1928 with a moderate request for a six-story printing plant, Hood talked him into a better idea. Profoundly impressed by Le Corbusier, Hood persuaded Patterson to build a monument to modern architecture. The publisher may have been influenced by a defensive moral certainty that the *Daily News* was trash. The more dismal the product, the more imposing the package. Patterson was completely won over to Hood's proposal.[17]

From a technical viewpoint, the challenge of the new building was that it stood on a very narrow site. Hood's solution was a design of unbroken verticality and unprecedented simplicity. In a moment of weakness, however, he tried to play safe. He put a soaring Gothic fantasy at the top, as he had done with the Tribune Tower and the American Radiator Building. Wright dropped by and found Hood brooding over a plasticine model of the Daily News Building, not completely happy with it. Wright steeled Hood's nerve. "Ray, cut the top off," said Wright. "Just cut it off."[18] Which is what Hood did.

The result was a bold and handsome design. There were windows on every side of the tower, even though that meant sacrificing valuable (that is, rentable) ground space. He intended his skyscraper to be surrounded by space, not hemmed in by other buildings. The verticality of the Daily News Building, when it was finished in 1930, was emphasized by bands of brown, black, and white brick. A warm effect was achieved by putting orange-brown shades in the windows. The only ornamentation was the huge granite plaque over the entrance, incised with a crowd scene that seemed to mirror the bustle in the street it fronted. Here was the least ostentatious big building in New York, and the most admired.

Hardly had the Daily News Building been completed before ground was broken for Hood's next major work, the McGraw-Hill Building on West 42nd Street. The company had decided to press ahead with construction in the confident belief that the economy was about to right itself. In October 1931 the building was finished, and an astonishing structure it was. Hood had combined Art Deco with the international style; it was a skyscraper—all thirty-four stories of it—yet it emphasized horizontal rather than vertical lines; and it was the most zigguratic shape this side of a genuine Babylonian temple. The entire building was colored blue—dark blue at the bottom, shading off into azure blue where it met the sky. The windows, in strong horizontal bands, were sea green.

And ground was now being broken for Rockefeller Center, a $250 million gamble that the Depression would pass. Most of the design was entrusted to Raymond Hood—not bad for a man who only ten years before had been too poor to own an overcoat.

26. Aspiring

I

People who had been abroad for twenty years or so were astonished at the sight that greeted them when they steamed into New York harbor in the mid-Twenties. What they remembered was the way the Statue of Liberty towered above the harbor. But now the eye was drawn farther along the calm, green, sheltered waters, and the heart was this time moved by the skyline of lower Manhattan, where tall office buildings clustered around still taller skyscrapers. What they remembered was "a low-browed place, with its various churches as quite conspicuous landmarks."[1] Here was an enormous city, crammed with vast buildings, criss-crossed with huge avenues, its rivers spanned by enormous bridges. New York represented a revolution in scale among the world's great cities.

Ford Madox Ford remembered how as late as 1906 "New York had a quality of littleness and a quality of age. Then there were boardinghouses where men in shirtsleeves and lady guests in white shirtwaists sat on the steps of houses on Madison Avenue right down to 24th Street. . . . In those days the air was more clear than it was possible for air to be."[2] These days, smoke dirtied the air; buildings crowded in upon people; there was no "quality of littleness" left. There were New Yorkers, such as Edmund Wilson, who were horrified by what was happening to their city. "I could remember when New York was as bracing, as electrical and full of light as San Francisco had been," he lamented.[3] In 1930 the last farm on Manhattan (located at Broadway and 213th Street) was turned into a miniature golf course.[4]

424

The Commonweal in 1925 looked ahead to 1950, when New York and its environs were expected to have 20 million inhabitants, and shuddered. It was all very well for businessmen to see the "Supercity" in terms of huge new markets hungering for democratized luxuries. "But they never really think of the misery and essential loneliness of the wretched millions who will, or may, endure these fearful luxuries. . . . They will be scientifically fed. . . . They will all think the same things. . . . They will be taught to walk at the same uniform pace. . . ."[5]

There was hardly a city in the Twenties without a downtown where, against a backdrop of rubble, freshly painted signs proclaimed: "On this site will be erected . . ." No city that was a city was without a skyscraper. But Frank Lloyd Wright, who had been in almost at the birth, was among those who were crying "Enough!" Advertising men and landlords had battened upon a wonderful creation and ruined it. The skyscrapers rising in American cities were not the tall, clean buildings Sullivan had envisaged. These were elephantine money-machines, crushing the natural life out of those who worked in them, had to live among them, and had to move around them. The skyscrapers were never meant to be crowded together in one part of the city. Nor were their straight lines meant to be compromised by setbacks or decoration. "Today all skyscrapers have been whittled to a point, and a smoking chimney is usually the point. They whistle, they steam, they moor dirigibles, they wave flags, or they merely aspire. . . ."[6] As the buildings rose toward the sky, so did a chorus of protest. Edison and Ford, the *New York World*, the editor of the *Journal of the American Institute of Architects*, and countless local officials agitated for a ban on skyscraper construction.[7] There was a pointed protest in poetic/graphic form:[8]

<pre>
                THE
        S   K   Y   -
        SCRAPER
        T   A   L   L
        I   S   A
        WONDER
        TO   ALL
        A   THING
        TOADMIRE
        BEYOND
        QUESTION
</pre>
Butoh!downbelowwherepedestriansgo
itcertainlyaddstocongestion

And this chorus of protest arose before the crash. It was in the three years following the crash that the skyscraper boom actually came to its peak, as the projects planned in the last exhilarating years of prosperity moved from drawing boards to construction. These buildings, wrote Elmer Davis in 1932, "changed the skyline more in the last three years than anything that was done in the two decades before."[9] Yet above the twelfth floor of these great buildings, the offices were empty. In the streets down below passed tens of thousands of homeless, jobless men. The faith which had built the skyscrapers was dying, overtaken by events.

II

If a population of 10,000+ is taken as the measure of a genuinely urban community, then the United States in 1930 was still less than half urbanized (47.6 percent).[10] And a community had to contain at least 10,000 people before most specialized stores could be found there; a store, for example, that sold nothing but men's and women's shoes.[11] Even if one takes the cutoff mark for urbanization at the former standard of 8,000 inhabitants, it was not until 1933 that half the population of the United States was truly urbanized.[12]

But there is no denying that cities grew prodigiously during the Twenties, and the pacesetters were generally those that had become cities only in the last generation. The two fastest-growing big cities were Detroit and Los Angeles. Both became for the next half century notable sites of bizarre social change.

As cities grew, community declined. Among the Italian-American population of Chicago, for example, there was rapid growth despite the new immigration laws. But young Italian-Americans were abandoning their parents' ways, marrying non-Italians and moving into non-Italian neighborhoods.[13] There was the same pattern in other ethnic neighborhoods in cities all across the United States. When the break came with the old neighborhood, the old friends, even with parents, it was not complete, however. Millions became what might be termed residual ethnics, knowing only a few Italian phrases, observing only a few of the Jewish rites, clinging to only a handful of the old Scandinavian or German customs, but considering themselves in some way still Italian or Jewish, Norwegian or German.

The decline in community was marked, ironically, by the growth at the heart of nearly every city of a noncommunity—the "rooming house" area. These districts teemed with people who were simply passing through. Isolation and despair took a heavy toll. In these areas the suicide rate tended to be higher than anywhere else in the city.[14]

Cities took shape around a variety of communities based mainly on ethnicity, income, or education. There were in New York easily identified neighborhoods dominated by the Irish, the Italians, the Jews, students, bohemians, upper-middle-class professionals, or down-and-outers. And when these various communities impinged on one another, as they did in Greenwich Village, there was virtually no contact between them.[15] It was a pattern of geographical proximity and social division that was becoming typical of all the big cities. There was nothing to show movement toward a new social order; there was only a drifting away from the past social orders of the different populations that had in the years since the Civil War poured into the major American cities.

As social cohesion declined, social dislocation grew. Around 1900 juvenile crime had been almost unknown. "The juvenile criminal was regarded as a prodigy with a capacity for crimes," said Clarence Darrow. "Something of the attitude obtained in regard to him which attaches to the child chess player or the child mathematician."[16] It was the city, he decided, which created juvenile delinquency.

In large part, it was surely due to the growth of urban slums. And the slums were created because the cities grew so fast, destroying buildings as well as communities faster than they could be replaced. "In Chicago this transition (from village to city) took place in a single generation."[17] What made life endurable to many who had to live in these urban slums was alcohol, even when it involved the risk of blindness, death, or paralysis. And, said one authority, "Dope is liberally peddled in the slums."[18]

The cities also exacted a heavy price from the middle-class urbanites. The popular view of divorce was that it was due to the growing economic independence of women; or to the decline in religious belief; or to easier divorce legislation; or to the drop in age at marriage. When all these factors were held constant, however, the major cause for the dramatic increase in divorce rates was urbanization. City life both pushed down the birthrate and increased the breakup of marriages.[19]

The country's housing problem was mainly a city problem.[20] Before the war the solid middle class had generally shunned apartments—too much like tenements, they said. An apartment *might* be all right for a bachelor, but it was no place to raise a family. It lacked privacy, it was too noisy, there was nowhere safe for the children to play, and so on. In little more than ten years hostility to apartment life collapsed. In the cities it was the family house that now faced an uncertain future. An apartment was likely to be both cheaper and more convenient when servants became hard to find, as during World War I. So huge apartment blocks sprang up all over the major cities in the Twenties, and the apartments in them were smaller than those of a decade before: the average size of the New York and Chicago apartments built in 1915 was four-and-a-half rooms, the 1925 average had fallen to three-and-a-half—because urban families were small families, and urban rents were high.[21]

About 75 percent of the urban population was working class, and in Middletown at least half the working class in the Twenties came straight off the farm.[22] In one generation these farm-bred families had to make the transition to an entirely new way of life. And the life into which they were moving excited criticism from, among others, Lewis Mumford. "We have had the alternative of humanizing the industrial city or dehumanizing the population," he wrote in 1922. "So far we have dehumanized the population."[23] The sheer size of a modern city seemed not only to create problems of the kind just described, but to make solutions to them almost impossible, leading to predictions that cities would inevitably fall apart from their own weight.[24]

To millions of people, this destruction was a prospect to be welcomed. The people of rural America in the Twenties regarded the cities with a loathing so fierce, so all-encompassing, so bitter, that it virtually defies belief. It was not simply that city people were different and modern (that is, disgusting and corrupt) but they threatened everything that rural people considered worthwhile.[25] Traditional farm values were nonmaterialistic going on antimaterialistic. The chief sin that the farmer laid at the city's door was its money-grubbing. And yet . . . and yet . . . The farmer wanted—*needed*—a Model T, a tractor, electricity, a steady cash income, a radio, a refrigerator, and a lot of other things. Here was a conflict of values not so much between city and country as a conflict *inside* half the population, yearning to cling to its simpler ways and values, yearning to enjoy the comforts of modern life. In the Twenties this conflict, which had been building up for a generation, became unbearable. As it exploded, it spread poison and bitterness. Something like hysteria gripped rural America and created recruits for the Klan, the Anti-Saloon League, and Fundamentalism. This was the resistance before the surrender; the last ditch that proves to be the great divide. They wanted the old values and the new machinery. It was the kind of thing we have since come to recognize in the hysterical contortions of other modernizing nations. It was in the Twenties that rural America went through the fire and in the end came to accept that it could not pick and choose.

III

The population of the cities with more than 30,000 people rose by 1 million a year throughout the Twenties.[26] As they grew, so did city government, in both expenditures and responsibilities. It was the rapid rise in spending at the local level—the "social wage"—that helped raise living standards even among the poor and unskilled in this period, an era of transition between the end of laissez-faire capitalism and the beginning of the welfare state.[27] The fast-growing cities set higher and higher standards of public service. "If a large city, for example, had no better sanitation than the average rural district," said one authority in 1926, "it would soon be overwhelmed by epidemics. If it had no better protection against fire it would soon be in ashes. If it had no better facilities for transporting goods its people would starve. . . . It must make more and better provision for all these things as the price of its existence and progress."[28]

While the federal government in the Twenties accounted for 10 percent of public-works spending, the cities accounted for 65 percent.[29] Some of the projects undertaken in the Twenties are crucial to the cities that we know today. Before 1927 people crossed the Hudson more or less as the Dutch had crossed it 300 years before—by ferry. But that year saw the opening of the Holland Tunnel * and the beginning of the construction of the George Washington Bridge. On the other side of the continent, a commission set up by Hoover announced in 1930 the construction of two further monuments of heroic engineering—the Golden Gate Bridge and the San Francisco-Oakland Bay Bridge.

Projects on this scale, however, required federal help. For as the cities took up their mounting burden of responsibilities, many of their most prosperous citizens were moving out to the suburbs, "removing themselves from the political city while remaining within the sphere of influence of the economic and cultural city."[30] The cities of the 1920s contained in microcosm the urban crisis that we know so well. But the suburbs were different from those of today. They were mainly for the upper middle class; almost unbelievably spacious by our standards. In the suburbs adjoining the sixty-eight largest cities, population density in 1925 was one person to every two and a half acres of land.[31]

In the cities, meanwhile, overcrowding was becoming steadily worse as the slums were torn down. Using their powers under eminent domain, city departments razed entire blocks of rotting buildings. These then became parks or were simply left as open space. Armed with the power to tear down for "public use," no city government possessed a legal right to build housing for public use. Many people resisted the whole idea of public housing. Yet housing remained the most pressing problem the

---

* Unusual among heroic public works for being named, not after a war hero or a politician, but for an engineer, Clifford M. Holland. He solved the principal problem that the tunnel posed, which was ventilation.

growing cities faced. Milwaukee under its Socialist mayor tried in 1919 to create municipal housing, but dared not to do it directly. A housing corporation was set up, and the city bought stock in the corporation. It was a small-scale venture that produced 100 houses. Massachusetts tried a different scheme, financed out of unclaimed bank deposits. In all, twelve houses were built.[32] In 1926, New York passed a state housing law which aimed at providing low-cost housing in New York City by offering private builders such inducements as tax exemptions and the use of eminent domain. After five years, however, the legislation remained virtually unused.

It was a problem that seemed to defy solution. Before the war a third of the population had enjoyed good housing, a third had fair housing, and the remaining third were in obviously bad housing—the kind of "housing" that consisted of a room without windows off a hallway where rats stirred, or several rooms without running water, bath, or toilet. The slump in domestic construction from 1917 to 1922 increased the stock of bad housing. The subsequent building boom had restored the former state of affairs. By 1930 the United States was one-third badly housed.[33] And with the rise of the cities there had actually been a decline in home ownership since 1900.[34]

All classes short of millionaires were affected by these changes. The business executive on $10,000 a year could eat well, travel, play golf, drive an expensive new car, but if he lived in the big city he would almost certainly live in an apartment that was too noisy, too expensive, and too small. A new family house in New York in 1930 would cost around $35,000 —roughly twenty times the average income, and too much even for the $10,000-a-year executive. In the suburbs, a family house with four bedrooms and half an acre of land could be bought for $20,000 or so, and that was where he was going.[35]

"*Babbitt*, as a saga of the age, was not realism," said *Fortune* in 1932, "but rich, luxurious romance. . . . For the one thing certain about the great majority of Americans . . . is that its members do not inhabit Mr. Babbitt's world. They don't wash in Mr. Babbitt's bathroom. An incredible percentage of them don't wash in any bathroom at all."[36] Many millions had to share a toilet in the hall, use a privy, or resort to "the north exposure of a tree." Their kitchens were not decked out with electrical appliances. They did not have—and had never seen—a gleaming tiled bathroom. And these were not simply the poor. They included ordinary people with full-time jobs. "For the truth is," concluded *Fortune*, "that *less than half the homes in America measure up to minimum standards of health and decency.*" The minimum they had in mind was electricity, a bathtub, inside running water, dry walls, regular garbage removal, and an inside toilet.

It was not only the big-city slums that were filled with malodorous housing. Des Moines, for instance, had nearly 19,000 dwellings. Of these, 5,000 lacked running water and sewerage. In Zanesville, Ohio, 40 percent of the homes lacked baths. And so it went in nearly every small city, small town, and village in the United States. Up to half the population was badly housed *before* the Depression took its toll.

Unable to do much about housing, cities had more success providing relief from the rigors of overcrowding. Recreation became as essential to a well-run city as sewers and streetlights. Before World War I municipal parks and public playgrounds were concentrated in a handful of northeastern cities. By 1930 virtually every city with 25,000 people or more had parks and playgrounds. In a decade public playgrounds increased by more than 60 percent and the acreage of municipal parks doubled.[37] There was a dramatic increase in municipal beaches and a doubling of municipal swimming pools.[38]

Nor was this boom in recreation held within the city limits. The urban population was a mobile, car-owning population. The Twenties saw the fastest growth in history of state parks and forests, and of national parks and forests. The earliest had been set aside in response to pressure from conservationists. But the Twenties saw a philosophy of use arise and fill the parks and forests with camp sites, hunting areas, hiking trails, boats, siwmmers, and fishermen. Visitors to national parts and forests in 1915 numbered 5 million; in 1931 they numbered 40 million.[39] There was a passion for camping that was a form of nostalgia for the pioneer life so recently vanished. What had begun in the late nineteenth century as a way of getting city children out into the country air became in the Twenties a stampede of several million adults bearing guy ropes and canvas. Such was the result of city life providing the motive and the Model T providing the means.

The chief symbolic monument to this city-bred hunger for escape stirred first in the mind of Robert Moses, in a vision of half a dozen splendid parks across Long Island, linked by fast, wide roads leading to Jones Beach.[40] Moses' ambition meant protracted warfare with the Long Island rich, who considered all choice sections of real estate in their own demesne, even if they did not own them. In the legislature and the courts, Moses, with the enthusiastic backing of Al Smith, drove his dream toward realization. By 1929 he had won. The masses of New York had, within a forty-five-minute drive, a glittering expanse of white sand and booming surf entirely at their pleasure.

IV

In St. Louis, Cleveland, Pittsburgh, and dozens of other American cities soft coal filled the air with smoke. Up to four tons of solid matter—soot—rained down each day in neighborhoods close to industrial centers.[41] In New York, the smoke robbed the city of 20 percent of its sunlight; in Cleveland the loss was 50 percent. This loss of sunlight produced rickets in thousands of children.[42] Nearly every city had laws regulating the burning of soft coal. But the laws were hardly ever enforced. "Oh, the two daily baths are not an affectation in a land where the sky sheds more soot than light!" said a visiting Frenchman.[43]

Yet, paradoxically, life expectancy was rising dramatically as a result of city living. It was far safer to be born in Chicago than in some spruce little hamlet back of beyond. One grew older in Detroit than in Appalachia. Life expectancy was decidedly longer this side of the frontier. In the 1920s it rose by five years, from fifty-five to sixty, the largest gain ever made in a single decade,[44] and doctors could have added a further five years and raised the average to sixty-five had they been given the resources.[45]

These dramatic gains were due mainly to public-health programs, which were almost entirely run by city government.[46] At the turn of the century (when life expectancy was forty-eight years) city water supplies were a leading cause of death, spreading typhoid to millions. Diphtheria was a major cause of infant deaths. But by the late Twenties typhoid fever was a problem only in rural communities, and diphtheria had almost vanished in heavily industrialized states.

As late as 1910 tuberculosis was the leading cause of death, referred to as the Great White Plague. By 1930 it was not even in the top ten. TB had become an illness of the very poor, still rampant among Indians and blacks, and among immigrants from cold, damp, northern European countries. There had never been so dramatic an advance in public health, yet no one could say just how it came about. A higher standard of living, safer factories, a better diet, better medical care—all may have played a part.[47] What was undeniable was that the swift fall of TB as the chief cause of death marked a rapid upsurge in the health of Americans, indicating a more vigorous, more disease-resistant, more health-conscious people.

The most popular of all public-health programs was the struggle against VD. In the early Twenties syphilis affected 10 percent of the population, and gonorrhea was the second most common of serious infectious diseases (second only to measles).[48] Syphilis caused mental illness in thousands each year. Gonorrhea was among the leading causes of blindness. Syphilis with its degenerative effects was held largely to blame for the shorter life expectancy of blacks, which was twelve years lower than that of whites.[49]

As infectious diseases lost their place as the leading causes of death they were supplanted by heart disease and cancer.[50] Before 1920 neither had caused much concern; cancer's meteoric rise to second place among the causes of death spread that modern terror that we know so well. To the first cancer-conscious generation there seemed something insidious, almost evil, about it.*

Public-health programs could not take all the credit for longer life spans and better health. Diet doubtless played an important part. As Hoover's brother Theodore once remarked about growing up in Iowa in the 1870s, there was plenty to eat, yet there was also plenty of malnutrition, because the diet was bad. As a result, so were teeth, bowels, and kidneys.[51] The War Food Administration had made it patriotic to eat less and to eat sensibly. The habits the WFA promoted had a lasting effect among millions. Consumption of starch fell; consumption of fresh fruits and green vegetables rose sharply. Americans in 1925 ate seventy-five pounds of food less a year than they had eaten only ten years earlier. The acreage of fruit and vegetable crops virtually doubled in the Twenties.[52]

The shift from farm to city life, however, had brought a spectacular increase in sugar consumption. The craving for sweet, sugar-laden things had turned diabetes mellitus from a minor cause of death in the nineteenth century into a major killer in the twentieth. Between 1900 and the 1920s the incidence of diabetes deaths in New York City more than doubled.[53] Sugar had traditionally been a luxury. Now everyone ate it; on average, 115 pounds a year—three times what their grandparents had consumed.[54] Diabetes was a luxury disease; it flourished in American cities. The same nervous needs that created a craving for sweet things similarly raised cigarette consumption from 15 billion in 1915 to 100 billion in 1928,[55] destroying the health of countless thousands.

The cities also spawned drug addiction. There were fantastic rumors about the extent of the addiction, and part of the folklore of the Twenties was that the AEF had refused to fight without being doped up.[56] The draft uncovered comparatively few addicts. But addiction was probably more common among working-class white women than among men in 1918.[57] Throughout the Twenties large amounts of narcotics were smuggled into

* The *New York Times* was under instructions from Adolph S. Ochs to devote its first six pages to news of a cancer cure when it was found, no matter what other news had been made that day, whether of war or peace.

the United States, usually through East Coast ports. Opium was heavily in demand, and more than a ton a year was seized by U.S. Customs. The seizures represented a small fraction of the total drug traffic.[58] Most of the opium that came in was turned into heroin and injected. Morphine, also injected, was even more popular than heroin.

Drugs were not hard to obtain, despite the Harrison Act. There were an estimated 1 million drug addicts.[59] Doctors were allowed to prescribe for addicts provided they gradually reduced the dosage. But most addicts were supplied by doctors and pharmacists who were either venal or unable to resist the pleadings of an articulate addict. Few in the large army of junkies had to resort to street-corner dope dealers. As a result, the quality of their drugs was high, dosage controlled, and drug deaths rare. Nor was there a large involvement of organized crime. Instead, there were figures like the elderly doctor in Scranton, Pennsylvania, dispensing eighteen pounds of morphine a year—enough for 830,000 average doses.[60]

The American Medical Association, however, was absolutely opposed to the ambulatory treatment of addicts. As part of its on-going campaign against quackery it managed to get heroin banned from patent medicines, and it pressed energetically for federal control of narcotics.[61] Internal Revenue agents began arresting doctors and druggists for supplying drugs freely, instead of as part of a cure. The only effective treatment, however, was detoxification in confinement. These arrests gradually frightened doctors away from addiction treatment and led to the criminalization of what was really a public-health problem.

The shift to city living had other lasting effects on American medicine. The cities were rich, and they were filled with people concerned with their bodies to the point of obsession, as we have seen. Inevitably, the doctors got rich. As late as 1916 the average physician's income in New York was a modest $1,200 a year. Medicine at the turn of the century had been, as one doctor remembered, "a free-and-easy, altruistic, anything but businesslike profession."[62] No longer. It had become openly materialistic and commercialized. It was also becoming specialized, with thousands of surgeons who devoted their careers to one organ—the gall bladder, perhaps, or the vermiform appendix—and its removal. And many of these operations, it was claimed, were unnecessary, undertaken to provide the surgeon with the standard of living which he felt was due him.[63]

Health insurance was still a new field, covering less than one percent of the population. As the cost of doctors and hospitals rose out of sight, people of average means joked bitterly that only the rich and the poor could afford medical care.[64] When Doctors Hospital in Manhattan opened in January 1930 it was both the most expensive hospital in the country and the shape of things to come. There were no wards, only private rooms, and each of these had its own bathroom, carpet, refrigerator, and individual decor. The entire establishment felt more like a hotel than a hospital, a sensation reinforced by the presence of barbers, stenographers, tailors, florists, and a French chef supervising the kitchen.

The other direction in which hospital care was moving was to be found in the Columbia-Presbyterian Medical Center, which took most of the Twenties to build. It was not one hospital but thirteen hospitals, placed one above the other and sharing certain common services, such as heating and maintenance. Yet each hospital had its own laboratory and its own kitchens. The services that might be termed "personal" to each patient were literally close at hand. The services that might be termed "general" to all patients were centralized. In this approach to organization, it was a radical departure. But it was radical, too, in its assumption that the center's main purpose was not caring for the sick, but keeping people out of the hospital. To do that, it maintained a score of out-patient departments and clinics.

Despite the gains in recent years, there was still much that could be done. There were only two prenatal clinics in operation in the United States in 1928, in New York and Detroit. In both cities they brought about a spectacular decline in infant mortality rates.[65]

The gains in longevity remain, however, the most impressive feature of the shift to city life, because they represent the virtual salvation of the American working class. Given that the *average* life expectancy in 1900 was forty-eight years, that of the upper class was almost certainly above this figure, and that of the lower classes well below it. That was why public-health programs, by democratizing health care, were able to score such astonishing gains so quickly. Longevity among the rich did not rise by very much. Among the working class the results were startling, raising life expectancy this side of the frontier by fifteen years or so in a single generation.

V

"In the 36 years from 1890 to 1926 the population of the continental United States increased 86%; the college and university enrollment increased about 550%; and the secondary school enrollment increased almost 1100%."[66] This was the transformation of American education— when education became genuinely democratic; the fulfilment of a movement that went back a century to the creation of the first public high schools in Massachusetts.

At the end of the war only one-fourth of the population of high school age was receiving secondary education. By 1930 that figure had risen to more than half. It seemed incredible that only a generation earlier there had been heated opposition to compulsory education from families and from employers. As the Lynds discovered in Middletown in 1924, secondary education had become an article of faith among all classes.[67] A changing age structure, the rapid increase in machinery, the productivity revolution, and the decline of agriculture, all helped to reduce the demand for child labor, and the attitudes of parents changed as families grew smaller and the struggle for existence eased. "Withdrawal of children from school is now thought of as an offense against nature," wrote one surprised observer, "whereas formerly child labor was regarded as a legitimate means of compensating parents for the care which they had bestowed on their families."[68] Every state in the Union by 1930 had compulsory attendance laws. They expressed one of the profound social changes that marks off the modern world from that of the nineteenth century—the belief that education is a right, something that no parent can withhold from a child.

It was a change that outran the pace of school construction. In 1923 there was a shortage of 2 million seats in American schools. Classes were set up in basements, held on the stairs, in corridors, under trees.[69] The education explosion was at its most obvious in the cities. By 1930 there were twenty-nine high schools with enrollments above the 5,000 mark and one, New York's DeWitt Clinton, that exceeded 10,000.[70] At the end of the war there were nearly 200,000 one-room schools. As the Twenties wore on, thousands of these closed every year, replaced by consolidated schools. Consolidation raised educational standards and to some extent equalized opportunity by bringing poor districts into union with prosperous ones. Between 1918 and 1930 the number of consolidated schools more than tripled, from 5,300 to 16,200.[71]

The Twenties backed up its new faith with money. Educational expenditures more than doubled in the decade; between 1910 and 1920 they had barely kept pace with inflation.[72] And teachers, by tradition badly underpaid, made such gains after the armistice that they outpaced the rest of the working population in increased earnings.[73]

As the schools grew and money was poured into them, they were transformed in other ways. The National Education Association, between 1915 and 1920, issued four bulky reports on how to make education more efficient—its contribution to the national obsession with waste. These reports were full of concrete advice, right down to the positioning of elbows on desks during handwriting lessons. Throughout the 1920s there were zealous attempts to make pedagogy a science. The result was a riot of well-meant scientism. Meanwhile, the Progressive Education Association had come into existence, founded in Washington, D.C., in 1919. Its roots were in the Progressivism of the Goo-Goo era. But that era had passed. The Progressive education of the Twenties had little connection with political radicalism.[74] There was, in fact, no unifying thread beyond a vague commitment to experimentation. Different teachers, different school boards, meant different things when they spoke of "progressive education."

This was the period that saw the first widespread development of "the child-centered school" and the "project method." John Dewey was held responsible for both, when he was directly responsible for neither.* Dewey was highly critical of the attempts being made to put the entire responsibility for a child's intellectual development on the child. It was in the Twenties when schools became miniature communities, in which there was far more on offer than lessons: there were clubs, dances, elections, and "home rooms" where the social graces were to be practiced. The school was no longer where children spent a few hours a day for half the year until they were thirteen or fourteen. It had become the focal point of their life from the ages of six to sixteen. Home and church had for centuries borne the responsibility of turning children into members of society. The school was now expected to relieve them of most of that burden.

The two most influential developments of the Twenties were the Gary Plan and the Dalton Plan, which were copied around the world. Under the Gary (Indiana) Plan the schools were open for nearly the entire year, the curriculum was widely extended, and most courses became elective. Under the Dalton (Massachusetts) Plan, lessons were downgraded. Instead, each student was given assignments which might last from a week to a semester, involving a wide range of reading, leading to a written report which was made the basis of group discussion. The Dalton Plan spread to a wide variety of countries, including the Soviet Union.†

Rapid growth and widespread experimentation created a nearly universal conviction among teachers, school administrators, and parents that more meant worse; that the general level of intellectual ability in the democratic, nonselective high school of 1925 was markedly lower than in the much smaller, quasi-selective high school of 1900.[75] The emphasis that was placed on physical education and instruction in health seemed to

---

* Dewey was like the ancient sage *quem discipuli trucidaverunt stylis suis*—that is, whom his disciples murdered with their pens.

† In Russia it provided the plot of a well-known comic novel, *The Diary of a Communist Schoolboy*, by N. Ognyov. The students in the novel soon hate the new method because it seems to transfer all the work from teachers to students. They revolt and burn the assumed inventor of the plan, a reactionary aristocrat called Lord Dalton, in effigy.

bear out their doubts. The United States was the only country in the world to consider physical education a specialty like art or music instruction.[76] There had been a steady shrinkage in the amount of time spent each week on literacy and numeracy, and an equally steady rise in the time spent on domestic science, typing, and shop. Yet this did not necessarily mean there was any less teaching of the three Rs, because the school year had grown by eight weeks or more since 1900. There was no solid evidence at all to show that intellectual standards had fallen.[77] There was instead a lot of evidence to show that the intellectual aspirations that parents held for their children, and that children held for themselves, were at last being served. That evidence was the brand-new high school that stood at the end of the Twenties in thousands of cities and towns all across the United States.

All the more tragic, then, that many were graduating their first class straight into the Depression.

27. Plumbing the Depths

In August 1930 every bank in Toledo but one failed. The next month thirty-nine Philadelphia banks went bust. In October the biggest investment house in Tennessee collapsed, dragging down scores of banks across the upper South.[1] All that fall, banks in the South and West toppled over as cotton prices plummeted. The northeastern banks that failed were usually the victims of mismanagement or looting, such as the Ohio State Bank run by Mal Daugherty. He robbed his 4,000 depositors on a vast scale and his bank was among those that folded in September 1930 when the Depression took hold. The former attorney general's brother went to prison in 1931. Another notable victim was the portentously named Bank of the United States.

This bank was based on the Lower East Side, from whose poverty and hardship Bernard K. Marcus, president of the bank, had long since escaped. When banker Marcus traveled to Europe each summer it required a specially built van to carry his thirty trunks and suitcases down to the pier. He sailed aboard the most expensive ships, ensconced in the most expensive cabin. He could afford to indulge himself. Simply by stock transfers between his bank and two of its security-selling, real estate-dealing subsidiaries he had once made a million dollars overnight. The bank's depositors, the bedrock of the Marcus millions, were by contrast the kind of people who acquired money at a snail's pace, a dollar this week, two dollars next week, and sometimes only a few cents. But they saved seriously, year in, year out. And they trusted the Bank of the United States, not only for its imposing name but because it was *their* bank, run by Bernie Marcus, who came from these very streets.

Marcus and two of his partners, however, were using the bank's deposits for speculation, and the profits derived therefrom went not to the depositors, but to the bank president and his pals—which was actually legal. The New York State Banking Department knew, however, as early as July 1929 that the bank was being mismanaged and was in danger of collapse.[2] Nothing was done about it. The state's superintendent of banks, Frank H. Warder, gave the bank a clean bill of health. The stock market collapse came soon after, wiping out all the paper gains of Marcus and his partners. They felt deeply aggrieved. Someone ought to make good their loss, and the someone they chose was the depositors. They took $8 million from their own bank and replaced it with stock in the subsidiary corporations—stock arbitrarily assigned a value of $8 million. It was the same old shell game, after time had been called.

On the night of December 11, 1930, the bank folded. Huge crowds formed in the street outside; thousands of men, women, and children, milling about in the pouring rain, crying, beating their fists in frustration at the cold wet walls for the dollars, and the hopes, that were gone. It was a piteous scene, repeated at many another bank failure in the years to come. For some, like George Gelies, it was the end. Gelies, a janitor, had saved $1,000. It had taken him forty years to save that much. With it, he intended to become his own boss and open a chicken farm. After two days and two nights of waiting outside the Bank of the United States, he was hungry, soaking wet, and delirious. He stumbled home and hanged himself from a steam pipe in the basement where he lived and worked.[3]

Marcus and three of his partners went to prison for seven years. Warder was later sentenced to five to ten years for corruption. With its 59 branches and 400,000 depositors the Bank of the United States was the biggest bank that had ever gone bust in America. Its failure sent a tremor through millions of depositors. People began holding on to their money. Bank deposits began to fall drastically.

A fall in deposits always occurs in a depression. The banks began selling off bonds to improve their liquidity. That was what the conventional wisdom said they had to do to revive public confidence. This, however, was a different world from that of the earlier depressions. These days 90 percent of the country's currency was in bank checks. Businesses and individuals alike held comparatively little cash. Nine transactions out of ten were, in effect, on credit. That meant 90 percent of the country's currency was only as good as the banks on which it was drawn. The banks, in turn, were only as good as the collateral on the loans they had made, because that was where most of the banks' assets had been placed. On the face of it, there was nothing much wrong with most loans. The trouble was, the country as a whole was overextended, as we have seen. Once the economy began faltering badly, the rot quickly set in. The last six months of 1930 saw a spectacular increase in mortgage foreclosures. In Philadelphia, there had been 737 sheriff's writs issued for foreclosure in 1929; the figure for 1930 was 11,918.[4] Income was falling, but the debts of yesteryear had to be paid at yesteryear's interest rates. By 1932, interest payments alone would comsume 20 percent of national income.[5] This was hardly a setting in which the public would bravely forget about bank failures and go on a borrowing spree.

As banks built up their cash reserves to two and three times their usual levels, the less profitable the banks became. A totally liquid bank would, in fact, soon go broke. Its fixed expenses would be much greater than earnings from the cash, call loans, and bundle of government securities it held. Nevertheless, the banks dug in. In doing so, they chopped away at the underpinnings of a strong economy: confidence and credit. And the more they dug in, the more nervous the depositors became.

Events only seemed to justify their apprehension, for during the years 1929–32 nearly 6,000 banks closed; one in five was a member of the Federal Reserve. Nearly $3 billion of depositors' money was lost. "Contemplating an average of more than 120 bank closures every month for 48 months in succession, the depositor still uncaught might well prefer socks, mattresses and buried pots to banks."[6]

It was less a matter of rational economics than of irrational social psychology. Up to $10 billion had been invested during the boom in real estate bonds. There was wholesale defaulting in 1931 on these investments. Up to $6 billion had been lost, and there was no remedy open to the bondholders. The losses far exceeded the losses of failed banks, yet they passed almost unnoticed.[7] People who played the stock market or the real estate boom knew they stood a risk of losing their money. No one ever puts money into a bank on that basis. It is the one place where people expect absolute safety, even if no such thing has ever existed.

There was in the spring of 1931 a moment when recovery seemed possible. The Depression had bottomed out, said the optimists. Then Austria's largest bank, the Credit Anstalt, went under, sending a shock wave through international financial markets. And in September the British admitted defeat in their effort to prop up the pound at a rate of $5.00. Their gold reserves were being sacrificed to this folly. Britain went off the gold standard. It was a step long overdue. It could also hardly have come at a worse time, creating turmoil in American banks as the pound tumbled down. Americans, discovering at last that in modern finance there is no "abroad," rushed out once more to withdraw their money from the banks and tried to convert it into gold, or simply stuffed it into an old boot.[8]

II

It was not until the spring of 1931 that Wall Street, where legend has it that the Depression began, saw its first serious collapse. For a year and a half brokerages weeded out the players who had lost (known in the parlance of customers' men as "pushing the dead ones overboard"). The market was not as exciting a place as it had been, but the commission on selling was the same as the commission on buying. Contrary to cherished folk wisdom, it was as safe as it had ever been to walk down Wall Street; there was little danger of being struck on the head by a falling stock broker. But in April 1931 Pynchon and Company, one of the biggest, most respected firms, went bust. To many on Wall Street this was almost as stunning as the crash itself.[9]

There were still fortunes being made in the stock market. Astute bears were searching out companies that were likely to go lower in trading, sold them short, and in the Depression that alone was enough to make any but the very soundest stocks take a nose dive. It also made recovery of the market virtually impossible. In October 1931 the New York Stock Exchange banned short sales of stocks that were already falling (a rule that is still in force). This did not end bear raids, but it made them more difficult. The Exchange however continued to ignore other forms of market manipulation and insider dealings. Hoover pressed the Senate Banking and Currency Committee to hold public hearings, to expose the chicanery which had helped produce the crash and was now impeding recovery from the Depression. Under the law, it was for the governor of New York to act, as Ripley had reminded Coolidge. But Roosevelt studiously left the Stock Exchange alone. Hoover hoped that exposure would force Roosevelt's hand, or lay the basis for federal regulation should that fail.[10]

While Hoover was trying to clean up Wall Street, Insull was trying to save the country's largest financial empire from collapse. In 1930 he had sought to perfect its defenses by buying out Cyrus Eaton's holdings of Insull securities. To buy them, he had to borrow $48 million, half of it from New York banks. He consoled himself with the knowledge that he was buying out Eaton at postcrash stock prices, but he still detested having to do business with New York. He came out of this deal with five huge holding companies whose assets totaled more than $2.5 billion. And all that Insull had put up of his own money to create this structure was $1 million.[11]

A grim struggle now ensued to break the market in Insull securities, force him to default on his loans and then pick up the pieces of his empire, a money-spinner if ever there was one. For at the base of this gigantic pyramid were the 255 operating companies, all of them soundly managed, possessing modern plants. Insull had spent the past forty years scorning Wall Street and Morgan banks, ridiculing them in private and in public. And now, the instant he was vulnerable to attack, the bears moved in to drive the price of Insull securities down, to zero if need be.

Insull's instinct was to save the value of his securities. He began buying to keep the price up. It was a game he could only lose—the bears had more cash than he. The day he could not go on buying the price would fall and the bears would clean him out. One of his assistants came up with a brilliant counterploy: the preemptive short sale. That is, if People's Gas was at $300 he would sell short; say 50,000 shares at $290. He would stop buying, let the stock drop to $270, buy the promised 50,000 at that price, and make the delivery at the promised price of $290. He would clear $1 million on the transaction. Had this operation continued Insull would have cleared about $1 billion in cash and broken several New York banks—assuming, that is, they really were determined to drive the value of Insull's securities down to zero.

This brilliant strategy was in operation and working splendidly before Insull heard of it. No man ever had salvation so sweetly spiced with revenge handed to him on a platter as was offered to Insull. Yet he spurned it, would not even consider it. He detested his enemies too much to become like them. Insull loathed bears and short selling. He ordered the operation to be stopped. "We can't do that," he said. "That would be immoral."[12] With those words he delivered himself over to his enemies, hands bound, and with an apple in his mouth. A few months later, when the British went off the gold standard, the stock market panicked and Insull's securities went down with everything else.

The Chicago banks, seeing the way things were going, allied themselves with the New York banks after decades of standing by Insull. But most of the Chicago bankers who had helped him in the past were dead; he had outlived too many of his friends. There was a new, younger breed in their place with whom he had little in common. So when the spring of 1932 came around and he needed $10 million in cash to pay various bills, they turned him down cold.

The holding companies which were to have saved what he had built up were about to destroy him. A holding company's value was based on the value of the securities it held; a different thing from the property values of the operating companies under its aegis. "A good (utilities) company, protected by regulatory laws which pretty nearly guarantee profits, doesn't have to worry about the market value of its plant, its property. But a holding company . . . has no asset value save the market value of the stock it owns. It is possible for it to collapse even though the companies controlled are sound."[13] Which is exactly what happened to Insull.

All the cash he could get his hands on was going to pay off earlier loans and to support the price of holdings. There was not even enough left over to pay the printing bills. On April 14 the Lincoln Printing Company of Chicago filed a petition of receivership. For want of a mere $10 million, Insull's billion-dollar empire was lost. He was forced off the boards of more than sixty corporations in a single day, June 6, 1932.

It was the biggest business crash in American history. The loss to the millions who had bought Insull securities ran to $1 billion. "There was hardly a petit-bourgeois family in Chicago that did not possess at least one bond or stock certificate bearing the imprint of an Insull company."[14] And Insull himself went under—"too broke," said one of his friends, "to go bankrupt."[15] Indicted for mail fraud, he fled to Greece.

III

As farmers contemplated their ripening crops in the fall of 1930 they knew that what they were about to reap was disaster. Wheat, cotton, and corn prices had all collapsed. Throughout the Twenties farm acreage and the number of farms both fell steadily. Farm families fell from being a third of the population to being one-fourth. Yet productivity had risen so that farm output was as high overall in 1930 as in 1920.[16]

Few farm families could any longer make a living from farming. They had to develop a sideline—a roadside stand, a gasoline station, running a village store, putting the eldest daughter to work teaching school, sending one of the sons to work at a sawmill—or sell off part of their property, such as the timber or the breeding stock. The Depression only made it harder to make a living in agriculture. Yet it also stemmed the flight from the land. Hundreds of thousands of people even returned to it, for with land they could at least grow their own food. As a result, American farms in 1932 had more people on them (32.5 million) than they had ever had.[17]

It was not the collapse of the stock market in 1929 that brought the Depression to rural America, but the collapse of farm prices in the fall of 1930, busting banks as farmers defaulted on their loans.[18] To farmers the name of salvation was "dollar wheat," referred to reverentially as if it were the Holy Grail of agriculture. But with wheat selling for 60 cents a bushel it was a long way off.

Hoover's rejection of McNary-Haugenism was predictable. His alternative, the Federal Farm Board, was in retrospect equally predictable, because it embodied the Hooverian faith of cooperative action. The FFB set up scores, then hundreds, of farmer-owned, farmer-controlled marketing cooperatives, to which the various stabilization corporations—which were to buy up farm surpluses—were mere adjuncts. McNary-Haugenism aimed at raising farm prices; the Federal Farm Board aimed at stabilizing them. The Cotton Stabilization Corporation, the Grain Stabilization Corporation, and the Wheat Stabilization Corporation bought up the surpluses and happily held on to them, just waiting for that wonderful day when prices rose and all their surplus cotton, wheat, and corn could be unloaded without knocking the market dead.

Alexander Legge, the FFB chairman, spent the summer and fall of 1930 touring the wheat belt offering what he called "Legge Shows." No scantily clad girls to be seen, though. Only Legge, red in the face, sweating heavily, giving a profane speech on the need to cut wheat acreage by at least 20 percent. The Legge shows managed to achieve a reduction of about 3 percent.[19] Discouraged, Legge resigned.

With the Cotton Stabilization Corporation stuffed to bursting point with surplus cotton, his successor as FFB chairman, James C. Stone, watched the 1931 cotton crop ripening with deep anxiety. The price had dropped from 18 cents a pound in 1929 to 8.5 cents a pound at the end of 1930. Another large cotton crop would drive it to next to nothing. Stone wired a desperate plea to the governors of cotton-growing states "to immediately mobilize every interested and available agency . . . to induce plowing under every third row of cotton now growing."[20] To describe the recipients of this message as being incensed would be an understatement. The *New York Times* flatly called Stone's proposal crazy.[21] The price of cotton dropped to 3.5 cents a pound.

Far worse than falling prices, however, was the drought. Throughout the spring of 1930 farmers had waited for the spring rains to fall. Week after week passed, and from Virginia to the Gulf, from Ohio to the Rockies, hardly a shower was seen. "Streams dried up and rivers idled past cracked mudbanks. The long green leaves of corn shriveled, turned brown, curled up in despair, and rustled mournfully while burning winds swept the plains."[22] Millions of farm animals, driven mad by starvation and choking dust storms, were slaughtered. A million farm families faced a fate almost as grim. This was the worst drought in American history. It covered most of Kentucky, much of Illinois, Missouri, Virginia, Ohio,

Tennessee, Mississippi, Louisiana, and virtually the entire state of Arkansas. When a massive natural disaster struck, the Red Cross was sent in, much like the cavalry riding to the rescue of beleaguered homesteaders under Indian attack.

The Red Cross was a semiofficial body; its head was chosen by the President, it administered various forms of federal aid. It was a system of emergency relief which men such as Hoover believed in with all their hearts as being the fairest, most enlightened approach open to a free people, in which citizens helped each other and brotherhood, not bureaucracy, flourished. It was a nice, romantic idea of the best High Victorian kind. The drought of 1930–31 knocked it stone-dead.

The Red Cross launched its inevitable appeal to aid these drought-stricken tenant farmers and sharecroppers. It asked for $10 million. But the Depression had absorbed nearly all the charity available. It took months to reach the $10 million figure that it expected to reach in ten days. Its forte, moreover, was the disaster that struck tens of thousands, confined to a comparatively small area, who needed aid for two weeks to two months. The Mississippi flood of 1927 had stretched it to its limit. The drought was a disaster that lasted more than a year, covered an area the size of Europe, and involved six or seven million people.[23]

For many of the Red Cross workers the drought came as a revelation. It brought a large number of educated, upper-middle-class northerners into direct contact for the first time with millions of the poorest white people in the United States. It came as a shock which, once the surprise wore off, became a stimulus for reform.[24] In the Cumberland Mountains were a people, they found, who had rarely needed money except for clothes. The mountaineers lived on a few meager crops and spindly animals that they raised themselves; on "meat, milk, and molasses," as the local expression ran. But then came the drought—and the Red Cross, with its forms, its questions, and not enough money. It doled out $3.00 a week for a family of five, just enough to avoid starving to death, but not enough to keep hunger at bay. In England, Arkansas, 500 poor farmers descended on the town's grocery stores and demanded food at rifle point.[25] In Henryetta, Oklahoma, hundreds of starving people raided the sixteen grocery and provision stores in town.[26]

Attempts in Congress to fill the breach by direct federal aid were bitterly resisted by the Red Cross, jealous of its empire of the poor, and discouraged by the White House. The Senate found a way out of this impasse by making a $20 million appropriation to the Agriculture Department for "agricultural rehabilitation" in the drought area. Farmers could borrow from this fund for seed, fertilizer—or food. Even so, they had to put up their property as collateral. Those who lacked collateral were as dependent as ever on the Red Cross, itself virtually broke.

IV

Business more or less kept to the pledges made to Hoover in the wake of the crash to maintain wage rates, until the last quarter of 1930. Even then, if rates were maintained the number of hours worked were likely to fall. For the year as a whole, there was a drop in income of about 10 percent, its effects somewhat offset by a 5 percent drop in prices.

Not until the spring of 1931 did outright wage-cutting set in,[27] limited at first to a comparative handful of companies. Then, in the summer, US Steel cut dividends without cutting wages; the reverse of what it had done in the 1921 recession. There was general surprise, verging on astonishment. But on October 1 it ran up the white flag: salaries and wages alike were cut by 10 percent. The common-labor wage rate of US Steel was the most important single wage rate in American industry. It set the pattern for thousands of employers. Two million workers—three times the number in the steel industry—saw their wages drop as a result.[28]

These wage cuts came after a year of vague threats of labor turmoil if they were imposed, and after months of boardroom agonizing.[29] But when they came, they were grudgingly accepted. Even a badly paid job seemed better than a breadline. When the next year's output reached its Depression low it was actually higher, by a whisker, than it had been at the bottom of the 1921 recession,[30] yet now there was far more unemployment. Thanks to mass production, scientific management and a better educated work force, the same amount could be produced by several million fewer workers.

As the Depression bore down in 1931–32, some of the big corporations did try to help the people they laid off by giving them loans, regular deliveries of groceries, or generous payoffs. But companies such as these (Goodyear Rubber, International Harvester, Standard Oil of New Jersey, Westinghouse, US Steel) were in a decided minority. A few companies, such as Eastman Kodak and General Electric, had their own unemployment insurance plans in operation. But after a year or two they simply ran out of money. The Depression revealed the true nature of welfare capitalism: as business slackened, wages were eventually cut, men were fired, benefits were withdrawn, work-sharing was introduced ("the poor supporting the poor").

No one knew for certain how many people were without work. The government claimed "only" 2.5 million in the winter of 1931–32; but the figure most people raised in conversation was 10 million[31]—roughly 25 percent of the work force—a figure which that famous left-wing revolutionary publication *Fortune* considered the absolute minimum of the totally unemployed.[32]

Not even acceptance of wage cuts and work-sharing had staved off massive suffering. Few people any longer believed that business could, or ever would, pull the country out of the Depression.

V

The years of prosperity had done nothing to diminish Urbain Ledoux's passionate involvement with the dispossessed. Each winter he ran a canteen called "The Tub" near St. Mark's Place on the Bowery. A man could come in and eat as much as he wanted for a nickel, which removed the stigma of charity, even though the real cost of the meal might be as much as 50 cents. The sick paid nothing, and the utterly destitute were fed for nothing and given a nickel. In the winter of 1929–30 The Tub provided 250,000 meals, about what Ledoux had expected.

Ledoux would close down his canteen in the late spring of each year, once it grew warm enough for men to sleep in the parks and people walked sunny streets in a giving mood, ripe for the plea of panhandlers. Ledoux would return to the business world, running sales campaigns for manufacturers. What he earned in these months underwrote The Tub during the next winter.[33] It was the very model of enlightened individual charity. Came the winter of 1930, Ledoux's canteen had competition.

When a line formed on a New York street that winter it was probably for a bank or a breadline. There were more than eighty breadlines, some of them stretching for blocks. The meals they provided were Lucullan— cheese sandwiches and coffee; beans, bread, and coffee; stew and bread; or oatmeal and milk. In a few lines there was cash to be had; a nickel, perhaps as much as a dime. The breadline became, and remained, a crucial part of the folk imagery of the Depression. It was, in fact, limited largely to New York, patterned mainly on Ledoux's Tub. Cities such as Detroit, Los Angeles, Baltimore, Washington, Pittsburgh, and Milwaukee had no breadlines.[34] Most cities had no soup kitchens.

The vast majority of men in the breadlines and soup kitchens of New York, and to a lesser degree Chicago, were chronic deadbeats—the kind of people Ledoux had been seeing through the winter for years. But now, going from line to line, they could eat up to twelve times a day, and collect as much as 20 to 30 cents for their trouble.[35] Most of the people thrown out of work by the Depression avoided the breadlines and the humiliation they represented.

Women especially shrank back in horror, like Meridel Le Seuer. "I've lived in cities for many months, broke, without help, too timid to get in breadlines," she wrote in the winter of 1931. "I've known many women to live like this until they simply faint in the street from privations, without saying a word to anyone. A woman will shut herself up in a room until it is taken away from her, and eat a cracker a day and be as quiet as a mouse . . . [she] will go for weeks verging on starvation, crawling in some hole, going through the streets ashamed, sitting in libraries, parks, going for days without speaking to a living soul, shut up in the terror of her own misery. . . ."[36]

Public officials and Chambers of Commerce turned aside criticisms of existing relief programs with the phrase "No one has starved." New York, for example, admitted only two starvation deaths in 1930, and one was senile, the other evidently an eccentric. An independent investigator, however, checked with four major hospitals in the city and found twenty deaths that year attributed to starvation.[37] Besides, people weakened by starvation are prime candidates for a fatal bout of pneumonia. Even before the Depression, at the height of Coolidge prosperity, a lifelong hobo had offered an expert opinion: "Many people believe that a man can't starve in an American community. They are wrong. Men have died of hunger within sight, almost, of food. I have seen men so close to starvation that they no longer had the energy to look for food. But they were men who had missed their calling."[38]

To prefer starvation to humiliation is an individual choice. For people with children there is no choice. The writer Louis Adamic and his wife were sitting down to breakfast in Brooklyn one morning in January 1932 when the doorbell rang. Adamic went to answer it, expecting to find the postman. "Instead of the postman, however, I was confronted by two children: a girl, as we afterwards learned, of ten and a boy of eight. Not very adequate for the season and the weather, their clothing was patched but clean. They carried school books. 'Excuse me, Mister,' said the girl in a voice that sounded older than she looked, 'but we have no eats in our house and my mother said I should take my brother before we go to school and ring a doorbell in some house'—she swallowed heavily and took a deep breath—'and ask you to give us something to eat.' "[39] It was a practice he had heard of, but he had absolutely refused to believe it.

The extent to which people would go to cling to the last shreds of self-respect was epitomized by another part of the folk-imagery of the Depression, apple-selling on street corners. It amounted to a tragicomic hoax.

The International Apple Shippers Association, a growers' marketing co-operative of the type admired by the Federal Farm Board, hit on a way to dispose of the apple surpluses building up in the Pacific Northwest: it would allow an unemployed man to take a crate of apples on a credit of $1.75 to sell them at 5 cents each. The crate would hold 100–120 apples. There were soon thousands upon thousands of streetcorner apple vendors, and as demand rose the IASA put up the price of a crate to $2.25. This calculated exploitation of the poor reduced the amount of surplus that would otherwise have been left to rot, because there was no apple stabilization corporation to buy it up. For the streetcorner vendors who sold half a crate or less, there was nothing.

This was a depression that did not simply cast millions of working-class people onto the street as former depressions had done. By 1931 it was claiming hundreds of thousands of victims among white-collar workers. The women (secretaries, bookkeepers, teachers) would refuse to surrender by seeking relief until eviction was only two or three days away; single white-collar men held out until after eviction. "Time was when a white collar case was an event in a social worker's life," wrote a social worker. "Not so today. . . . The old pattern of the poor has completely changed."[40]

No other industrial country was half so unprepared for a tragedy on this scale because no other country clung so tenaciously to the wrong parts of the past. European visitors could hardly credit what they found: "Despite its abounding prosperity and amazing civilization," wrote one of them in 1925, "the social organization is right back in the Victorian Age. . . . She has no pensions for her old people; no medical benefits for her workers; no unemployment insurance for any trade."[41] The vast majority of Americans detested the idea of the dole—it made people dependents of the state: that seemed to a pioneer nation both unnatural and faintly sinister. The entire history of the country was flatly against it. And the dole smacked of helplessness: once dependent, always dependent.

It was a belief that had existed side by side with some of the worst slums, the harshest poverty, anywhere in the world. Jacob Riis's *How the Other Half Lives* was one of the great works of protest of the late nineteenth century, with its detailed descriptions of daily life in the New York slums. There were families like that of Michael Gold, who also wrote a famous book, *Jews Without Money*. He grew up on the Lower East Side in the years before World War I. His family lived for years without either an income or charity after Gold's father broke both his legs in an accident at work. That they could live without any money at all was possible only because, even in a desperately poor neighborhood, people shared what little they had, were close to the suffering of their neighbors, and gave most where it was most needed. It was not simply the scale of the Depression that made state intervention on a vast scale imperative; it was the decline of these urban neighborhoods, once as close-knit as a village.

For the moment, however, the urban middle class was pinning its hopes on "work relief." This went back to 1914 when William H. Matthews was working for the Association for Improving the Condition of the Poor. He put six men to work one day with rakes and shovels at the Bronx Botanical Gardens. In the years that followed he became the country's foremost practitioner of work relief. In 1930 he was running the Emergency Work Bureau of New York. He planned to hire several hundred people each day when winter arrived. As early as May, however, he had up to 700 people at work each day. When winter set in as many as 1,500 a day came looking for jobs. Wall Street businesses raised $8 million to help the EWB through the winter (jokingly calling it "Bolshevism insurance").[42] But even this sum, far more than Matthews expected to spend in an entire year, was still not enough.

Meanwhile, visitors to the parks were greeted with the sight of men in good overcoats and hats inexpertly wielding in their soft white hands a hoe, a rake, a shovel. And indoors, "All the charitable institutions, the churches and the museums of New York are having such a cleaning this winter as they never had before."[43] Work relief had been transformed from a minor form of help into the great white hope of relief. At its peak the EWB took on a maximum of 37,000 people a week. The city had at least 300,000 unemployed.

Relief was still considered largely the business of private agencies, financed by special appeals or the community chest. The first community chest was launched in Cleveland in 1913 and established that people gave more freely when organized to give. By 1930 there were 363 community chests.[44] The Depression raised the degree of organization another notch: virtually everyone in the phone book received several pleas in the mail each week to give for unemployment relief.

In most communities the fund-raising operations were run by local bankers and prominent businessmen, backed up by massive publicity campaigns. In 1930 they raised $80 million for community chests. Compared with the size of the problem, it was like using a peashooter to stop a rhinoceros. Workmen's compensation alone disbursed more than twice as much as the community chests. The voluntary—"American"—principle might possibly have worked, had Americans been half as generous as they believed they were. Most of the money raised by community chests was given by company employees, who handed over their dollar or two with resignation rather than enthusiasm. Only 3 percent of the population gave money to the Red Cross. Jews reputedly took good care of their own, yet in New York only one Jew in thirty ever gave money to a Jewish charity. Major corporations, whose executives extolled the virtues of giving, gave only derisory sums for relief, yet some held huge cash surpluses built up in the Twenties.[45]

As for the recipients of relief, they loathed it. "One's neighbors were kinder. Tammany Hall was kinder. Starvation was kinder," said one Michael Gold. The Emergency Relief Bureau of New York made a house-to-house survey in February 1932 of 6,300 families where the breadwinner was no longer a breadwinner. Not one of these 6,300 families was known to any welfare agency, yet in 81 percent there was a shortage of food, 88 percent were behind with the rent, nearly 40 percent were without winter clothing, and 25 percent could no longer heat their homes.[46]

Ironically, the American system of relief was far closer to the traditional dole, far more like charity, than the British and European systems of unemployment insurance, in which the beneficiaries had earned the right to assistance by their former contributions. "We are the only industrial nation really on the dole," Abraham Epstein discovered. "There are no breadlines in the whole of Europe, for all its relative poverty."[47]

What the voluntary principle amounted to was badly organized charity, detested by the very people it was supposed to help, and providing little more than a grudging handout. It is possible, in fact, that the most important form of private help never appeared in any of the figures on relief. Stereotypes of grasping landlords to the contrary, the Depression saw rent forgiveness on a monumental scale. Millions of unemployed simply stopped paying their rent. There was no widespread wave of evictions.[48]

The voluntary principle said that people ought to do all they could to help themselves before resorting to charity, and that is just what many did in various ways. "Garbage eating was reported at Cicero and 31st Street, at 35th and La Salle Streets, at the loading platform on South Water Street, at the I.C.C. Railroad at 25th Street, at Fulton and Randolph markets, at 40th and Ashland, and at the large dump at Summit. These nine places by no means exhaust the list," reported the University of Chicago's Special Committee on Garbage Dumps in 1932. "Around the truck which was unloading garbage and other refuse were about thirty-five men, women and children. As soon as the truck pulled away from the pile, all of them started digging with sticks, some with their hands, grabbing bits of food and vegetables. . . ."[49]

VI

Many a town or city responded to the crisis by issuing a "work or starve" proclamation, backed up with work relief. But when half a dozen applicants applied for every job the authorities provided, it hardly seemed reasonable to expect the five men who were turned away to starve. City officials were literally at their wits' end.

In Dallas, men put on work-relief projects were paid only in food. The city argued they would spend cash wages on liquor.[50] Oklahoma City's approach to the unemployed men was to arrest them, charge them with vagrancy, convict them, then order them to get out of town.[51] In Midland, Texas, the city council turned over public land to the unemployed, so they could grow their own food. The Red Cross provided seed. "The volunteer fire department offered to hold its weekly practices by those gardens that needed to be watered."[52] In Pittsburgh and Minneapolis, the Depression was fought by the outright rejection of machinery: tens of thousands of men were engaged in public works that were restricted to hand labor.[53]

The city which had for a generation been considered the most generous toward the unfortunate was Boston. Heavily Catholic, heavily Irish, it was spared the puritanical creed that saw moral worth in riches and moral disgrace in being poor. Its mayor for most of the interwar period, James Michael Curley, was another of the major transitional figures of this strange and tempestuous time. A romantic, intelligent crook, he saw clearly that the old-style welfare system based on the city-hall machine and the ward boss—the timely load of coal, the big basket of groceries—was no longer enough. He believed in deficit spending and increased public works. Yet he also revered business success and deplored government programs of direct relief, including unemployment insurance. It was the dole, he said with relish, that turned the English from empire-builders into "servile mendicants."[54] Even so, public relief in Boston was more generous than in almost any other city in the United States. By the end of 1931 Boston was virtually bankrupt.

The resourceful Curley set up an Emergency Unemployment Relief Committee. To get its fund drive underway, "The Mayor orchestrated a full-scale burial of General D. Pression. An effigy, enclosed in a black pine coffin, arrived at Battery Wharf atop a municipal garbage truck bedecked with bunches of carrots, beets and turnips. Workers lowered the General onto the ferryboat *Flaherty* and Curley pushed him off. . . . Two dozen chorus girls and a brass band led the multitude in a rendition of

'Happy Days Are Here Again,' the sirens of harbor craft sounded, and jets of water spouted skyward from city fireboats."[55] The fund drive reached its target of $3 million; enough for three months of relief. But it could not be repeated every three months. That it reached its goal at all was only possible by heavy exactions from city employees. And Boston, generous Boston, was helping one jobless person out of every four; the other three had to fend for themselves.

Its place as the most giving of cities had already gone to what was perhaps the worst-hit city of all, Detroit. Its relief rolls in 1929 carried 17,000. In February 1931 more than 210,000 people applied for relief. Ford's pledge to Hoover had completely broken down. He had cut his payroll by 70 percent, and he was by far the biggest employer in the area. (Not in the city—he put his plants a few feet on the other side of the city line to avoid paying city taxes.) Frank Murphy had run for mayor of Detroit in the fall of 1930 on a commitment to help the unemployed and won easily. Almost from the outset of the Depression the city accepted the welfare burden it created.

Detroit under Murphy provided jobs and direct relief on a scale not matched anywhere else. It fed and housed 12,000 jobless men each day; found employment for thousands more; provided welfare for 50,000 families; and paid for the free distribution of crackers and milk in the schools. Murphy maintained that measures such as these were not charity; they were as much a part of running a city as keeping the streets clean and lighted.[56] But by the end of 1931 Detroit, like Boston, was broke.

Chicago was bankrupt even before the crash. In 1929 the city simply ran out of money to pay its teachers, its firemen, its policemen, its nurses, its welfare workers, its street sweepers, or almost anyone else. Hardly surprising, then, that a visitor reported in 1932: "I found the suffering among the jobless in Chicago immeasurably worse than in any other section or city."[57] Conditions so desperate gave rise to farce mixed with tragedy: "In Chicago, James D. O'Reilly, a municipal employee, saw his home auctioned off because he had failed to pay city taxes of $34; the city owed him, in unpaid salary, $850."[58]

The nation's premier city counted itself a generous place. Yet the most that a family on relief in New York could expect to receive was $5.00 a week. With 30 percent of the working population unemployed, that was all if could afford. The entire system of public relief in New York was riddled with graft, anyway. Help went first to the members, former members, and friends of members of the local political club. The fabled generosity of the ward boss to the neighborhood poor was at bottom just one more political racket. And when New York ran out of money in 1931, as

Boston and Detroit had done, it clamored for help from the state capital. There was a more receptive ear in Albany, however, than in most state capitals.

Roosevelt was not a reforming governor in the Al Smith mold. Yet his approach to the Depression was direct, pragmatic, and free from ideological dross. As he told an audience of college students in the spring of 1932: "It is common sense to take a method and try it; if it fails, admit it frankly and try another. But above all try something."[59] When New York, Buffalo, and other cities ran out of money for relief in 1931, he persuaded the state legislature to vote an extra $20 million for them and won a further supplement in 1932.

The disbursement of this money was entrusted to the newly created New York State Temporary Relief Association, run by Harry L. Hopkins, social worker extraordinaire. In a generation a new profession had come into existence almost unnoticed—social work. Trained social workers rejected all the old notions of worthy and unworthy poor; rejected, too, the traditional charity organization view that relief had an inherent tendency to pauperize the recipient. Slowly but surely they took control away from well-meaning, upper-middle-class volunteers. By the late Twenties the United States had 25,000 trained, full-time social workers.[60] It was the Depression that saw them come into their own. They became "the voice of the unemployed. . . . Nothing was hidden from social workers. Their work was within, beyond the facades erected by pride. . . ."[61]

A polite but bitter guerrilla war was raging, however, in hundreds of New York towns between this modern form of organized morality and the traditional system—that is, between the town "poor officer" and the trained social worker. A town poor officer was, as he had been for 200 years, part of local government; local relief was, as it had been for 200 years, part of local politics. And now the poor officers and the ward bosses were being pushed aside by social workers, who were forever wanting to investigate things, who talked about "adequate budgets," and referred to something called a "social service index." The poor officer was used to doling out a bucket of coal here, a bag of groceries there, buying this person a pair of shoes, some old person a pair of glasses, and even on occasion handing over two or three dollars. He did not need to investigate: he *knew* who needed help and who was faking. With the state government putting tens of millions of dollars into relief, however, it forced social workers on these towns to administer it. If they wanted the one, they had to accept the other.[62]

By 1932 there was hardly a city or town that was not broke. Revenue from property taxes had fallen as people became delinquent or went bankrupt. Expenses had risen phenomenally, thanks to relief. Cities that tried to borrow their way out of the crisis found that the market for municipal bonds had collapsed. Local banks welcomed municipal paper about as much as they welcomed notes reading, "Hand over the money." American cities began to fire thousands of municipal employees each week in a hopeless attempt to live within their shrunken incomes.[63]

In June 1932 Frank Murphy called James Curley and other big city mayors to a conference. The whole point of the meeting was to petition the federal government to provide a grant of $500 million to the cities for relief programs that winter, plus a $5 billion public-works program in 1933. There was nowhere else left to turn. The cities, like the charities, had been swept away.

VII

There were strikes even at the bottom of the Depression. In the fall of 1931 the mill workers of Paterson, New Jersey, came out against wage cuts and for the eight-hour day. After two months they not only won the eight-hour day but wage *increases*.[64] For every success, however, there were a dozen, perhaps a score, of failures. In Lawrence, Massachusetts, that same fall 20,000 mill workers struck against a 10 percent wage cut. The strike was as solid as a strike could be. But the strikers had no savings. When the New England winter set in around the middle of November, they shivered and hungered and accepted defeat.[65]

The textile mills of the South were in turmoil, as they had been on the verge of the crash. The biggest and oldest major southern textile firm, the Riverside and Dan River Cotton Mills of Danville, Virginia, had escaped the earlier troubles. But in 1930 a 10 percent wage cut was imposed. Even the company unions resisted this. These mills were reputed to be the best-run, most enlightened, best-paying in the South. Yet when the wage cut was resisted, 2,500 union members in the Dan River work force were fired. In September 1930 the United Textile Workers called a strike.

The strike held for two months. The state militia was sent in to beat the strikers into submission. Still the strike held. But in January 1931, facing starvation, the strikers went back, with nothing to show for their four months away.[66] It was a defeat that discouraged textile strikes in the South for years to come.

In the next-door state of West Virginia, an armed truce had prevailed in the coal fields since the epic struggles of 1921. But with the Depression the truce began to break down, leaving dead men in its wake. Payrolls were being cut, families evicted once again. And the soft-coal miners of western Pennsylvania and eastern Ohio went on strike in desperation in the summer of 1931. Desperate because even the men who had work were hungry. Relief programs in the coalfields had become a bone fought over by Communists, Socialists and the UMW, each seeking to win the loyalty of hungry families. When the strike came, the Communists used soup, bread, and beans to bolster it. He who did not strike, neither did he eat.[67] It was a violent strike, with organizers being murdered in the night and pickets being clubbed to the ground. When the Communists' money ran out and there was no more free soup, the strike collapsed.

In "Egypt" conditions were equally desperate. An impoverished Chicago could buy less and less coal. The effect was devastating. In Franklin and Williamson counties dozens of banks closed. Hundreds of storekeepers went bankrupt. Entire towns were abandoned. In those which were not, the streets were filled with idle men. A visitor to Coello in 1932 could find only two men who still had jobs.[68] On April 1 that year the miners of southern Illinois went on strike. It seemed superfluous, so few of them were working. It was the expression of anguish of a community that was dying. Men murdered one another over straws.

Bloodier still was Harlan County, Kentucky. The Twenties had brought it a fleeting taste of prosperity as the coal operators expanded the nonunion soft-coal mines of the border states. Isolated, independent, poverty-stricken mountaineers abandoned their shacks up muddy trails for life in a coal camp, where there were streetlights and company movie theaters instead of darkness and boredom; where there were doctors instead of old women casting spells, They gave up a kind of freedom for membership in the industrial working class. Whatever the hardships of the miners' lives, they were fairly content. In 1929 the average Harlan County miner earned $1,200 a year—far more than many a mountaineer had ever expected to see.[69] The Depression broke the demand for coal that underlay such wages, and the drought destroyed the crops that made their wages go far enough to keep a family. By 1931 their earnings had dropped to $800. The number of children dying from malnutrition-induced illnesses had virtually doubled since 1929. Then, in February 1931, the coal operators cut wage rates by 10 percent. The miners chose to resist. They demanded a union.

The UMW had been driven out of Harlan County almost a decade earlier. When it returned in 1931 it returned in the night. Its meetings were held in secret, in abandoned mines and deep woods. The companies fired anyone suspected of joining the union and evicted them from their homes. Hundreds of miners were not even fired; they were locked out. The shutdown in Harlan County was more a spontaneous revolt than an organized strike. It could not have come at a worse time, because local relief supplies had just run out. The drought had blighted the crops. The UMW was virtually penniless. Gangs of armed miners began raiding company stores for food.

The miners had nothing left to lose. They turned to the Communist-run National Mineworkers' Union even though the NMU had just been trounced in the Pennsylvania coalfields. It was a case of the beaten leading the beaten. The NMU moved into Harlan County, launched a national publicity campaign, and opened seven soup kitchens.

The Red Cross refused to supply relief to miners' families, claiming that this would amount to interference in an industrial dispute. Local doctors refused to treat the miners and their families. Injunctions against the strike flowed from local courts. A soup kitchen feeding hungry women and children was blown up with dynamite.[70] Two journalists who came to report on the strike left with bullet wounds.[71]

The International Labor Defense persuaded Theodore Dreiser to organize a group of noted non-Communist radicals to go to Harlan County and see for themselves the bloodiest strike since the steel strike of 1919. And among the eleven-man delegation headed by Dreiser was Charles Rumford Walker, ex-United States Cavalry, ex-steelworker, currently associate editor of the radical journal *Independent*. Dreiser at sixty took two of his mistresses with him. When an attempt was made to convict him of "immoral behavior," Dreiser's defense was that he was "finally, totally and utterly impotent," which made his friends smile.[72]

The Dreiser committee could not save the hopeless strike of starving miners in a county where civil liberties had been virtually eradicated; where union organizers were murdered with impunity; where outsiders who came to investigate conditions could expect to be shot. But the publicity it generated renewed the relief effort and led the United States Senate to open hearings on conditions in Harlan County in May 1932. This one small, dreary spot in southeastern Kentucky became to an entire generation a byword for brutality.

And there seemed almost nothing that the unions could do about it, in Harlan County or anywhere else. Union membership in 1929 had stood at 3.4 million; by 1932 it had fallen below 3 million. Organizers were laid off, union officers' salaries were cut and cut again, strike funds dried up, conventions were postponed or cancelled, union newspapers shrank to a few pages or failed to appear. The few initiatives on labor-management cooperation that were launched in the days of prosperity withered. Some unions had been corrupt before 1930. But now the demoralized AFL was penetrated at a hundred points by racketeers.

For decades the social outlook of American unions had been much like that of orthodox capitalists—the state should keep out. Trade unions reflected the ideals of self-reliance and independence of a pioneer people. By late 1932, however, they had taken such a thrashing and were so completely dispirited that to many, perhaps most, union members there was only one way for unions ever to pick themselves up from the floor— with a hand from the government. The state had been historically portrayed as the natural, the inevitable, enemy of the working class. In 1932 the state was filled with working people figuratively on their knees begging it to save them. Union leaders had knees that bent less easily. They damned in hollow, ritual tones the introduction of unemployment insurance. With nearly one-third of the work force out of work this opposition seemed perverse. In November 1932 the rank and file of the AFL forced its leadership to abandon the sacred doctrine of voluntarism, received direct from Gompers's hands, and demanded unemployment insurance.[73]

VIII

Howard Scott went to work for a while at Muscle Shoals after his spell as intellectual guru to the Wobblies. But his true milieu was not the pinched, muddy towns along the Tennessee River, and he went back to Greenwich Village. There he fell in with Thorstein Veblen, the beau ideal of non-Communist radicals of the Twenties. Scott, however, was no mere disciple; he was a fertile source of ideas in his own right. He was also one of the best-known figures in the Village; a huge man (six feet five inches tall, weighing more than 200 pounds), he strode its streets in a broad-brimmed black hat and long leather coat, with a red kerchief around his neck. His nights were spent in Village cafes, extolling the role of the engineer.

He had virtually no standing among reputable engineers. But when the Depression took hold, with the entire country desperately searching for new ideas, Scott at last came into his own: he was taken up by Walter Rautenstrauch, chairman of the Industrial Engineering Department at Columbia. Rautenstrauch had been an early disciple of Frederick Taylor, the father of "scientific management." With financial help from the president of Columbia, Nicholas Murray Butler, Scott and Rautenstrauch launched the Committee on Technocracy in 1931. They had found the way to defeat the Depression, they said, nothing less.

Technocracy combined scientific management, a variety of ideas drawn from Veblen (who had died in 1929), a conception of energy as the true measure of all things, and acceptance of the engineer. The idea of energy as the proper yardstick of all economic activity was not exactly new. As early as 1921 Edison had been arguing for an "energy dollar"—a

currency based on the amount of energy the country produced and consumed each year.[74] The Depression, however, made serious people for the
first time take the idea seriously. The Committee on Technocracy began
an energy survey of North America.

Scott these days had cast away his former garb and walked around the
Village in expensive, well-cut suits. But this did not shake the faith of his
admirers. Technocrats who saw him coming would throw back their
shoulders and salute smartly as he passed.[75] For decades to come American parks featured graying men on soapboxes arguing the merits of
Technocracy.

Technocrats propounded both an energy theory of value and an energy theory of history. Because the amount of energy available per capita
had not increased much between 4000 B.C. and A.D. 1800 these were "six
thousand static years."[76] It was not politics or mere economic and social
developments that caused societies to change; it was technology. But
when technology fell into the wrong hands—bankers', politicians', soldiers'—it was wasted, used for inhuman ends, and led eventually to a
crash. The price system of modern economies was, moreover, a delusion,
created so that some people could have more than their share, at the
expense of the rest. When all prices were based on the amount of energy
that went into the production of goods or the provision of services, social
justice would prevail for the first time in history.

The world the Technocrats described included a $20,000 a year aver-
age income, and an average work week of sixteen to twenty hours. Technocracy committees sprang up in every city in the United States. But the
energy survey proved impossible to carry out; it was far too ambitious.
Without it there could be no practical plan.[77] As realization of this sank
in, Scott and Rautenstrauch fell to quarreling and the movement rapidly
disintegrated; another blighted promise of an age littered with promises.

For many American intellectuals and writers, the solution already
existed. It was to be found in following the Soviet Union. The execution
of Sacco and Vanzetti had proved a turning point in that it more or less
created a community of American intellectuals for the first time. Until
then, they were isolated figures, such as Veblen, or existed within small
coteries clustered around radical journals. The Sacco-Vanzetti protest
brought them together for the first time, made them aware of their numbers, and made the country aware of them. It was they who did most of
the organizing and found they had a gift for it. The Depression revived
them and sent them into action once more. They did not necessarily
embrace communism when they lauded the Soviet Union, but rather
state planning of all production.

There was a deeply utopian streak to many of these radicals. They argued keenly among themselves and adopted a variety of stances. Yet in nearly all the most prominent figures—Max Eastman, Floyd Dell, Mike Gold, Upton Sinclair, Robert Minor, and Waldo Frank—there was a utopian innocence that is touching, until one reflects that they were grown men, in middle age. No one agitated more zealously for the Communist cause without being a Communist than the aging Lincoln Steffens. He admired the Soviet rulers for their toughness, and scorned the squeamishness of liberals. Bloodshed and torture had to be accepted in creating the new order. There was a lot of that kind of reasoning in the Depression. Of course, it was not Steffens's blood that was being spilled, or his wife's, or his child's; not his genitals that were being crushed or his fingernails that were being torn out in the name of a higher stage of human development.

To Edmund Wilson, the old order, based on nationalism and capitalism, had completely collapsed. People who were hardly ever troubled by ideas were these days talking about the prospects of revolution. The only way out was for the liberals to take over the aims of the Communists, without embracing communism. He wanted American democracy plus state ownership of all means of production, industrial representation in government instead of regional representation.[78] At the very moment when several million Kulaks were being murdered, he described the Soviet Union as being "fairly and sensibly run."[79]

The American working class was less impressed. Even Fred Beal, whose radical texts were Edward Bellamy and Jack London, found the party line hardly to his taste, and in his reading preferences he was probably typical of many working-class radicals of his generation. He said of the Communist leadership in the late Twenties and early Thirties: "Their method of education consisted of distributing Marxist literature. When we got their pamphlets and papers, full of such words as proletariat, ideological, aggrandizement, manifestations, capitulate and orientate, we pretended to understand what it all meant, and let it go at that."[80]

The vast majority of American workers were simply stunned by what was happening to them. Their passivity was the most striking thing about them. Sherwood Anderson drove around the country to talk to people at the bottom of the Depression. Again and again he heard the same apology from the unemployed. " 'I've failed in this American scheme. It's my own fault.' That's the tone. 'I failed. I failed. It's my own fault.' You get it on all sides. There may be stupidity in it, but there is also humility."[81]

The Communists however were convinced that their time had come. "If ever there was a situation that conformed to the classical Marxist vision of an exploited and suffering proletariat in opposition to heartless capitalists, this was it."[82] The Communist party of the United States saw membership rise from 6,500 in 1929 to nearly 20,000 in 1932. William Z. Foster, by assiduously licking Stalin's boots, had secured his "election" as head of the party in 1929. Foster had actually won only 10 percent of the vote, but that result was set aside on Stalin's orders.

The CP created unemployed councils in various cities in 1930–32 and enrolled 20,000 adherents. They might have enrolled many more had they not adopted slogans such as "Defend the Soviet Union!" and "Down with Yankee Imperialism!" which did not seem particularly relevant to people who were simply looking for work.[83] The Communists also surrendered to a cult of proletarian toughness. Communist union organizers were able to call on several hundred "sluggers," eager to use knives and clubs. When demonstrations of the unemployed were organized, there was instruction in street fighting.[84] Far from fearing police brutality, it was welcomed and, on occasion, deliberately provoked.[85] The slogan of these demonstrations was "Starve or Fight!" Highly emotive, it was coined by someone unlikely to do either—a millionaire's widow.

The years 1931–32 saw dozens of food riots, unemployment riots, eviction riots, and other violent acts of protest organized by Communists or Communist sympathizers. Most were crushed by the police or militia.[86] The most famous and bloodiest clash occurred on March 7, 1932, when Communist sympathizers organized a hunger march on the supreme temple of the Machine Age, the Rouge plant.

Three thousand marchers assembled in downtown Detroit with police permission and marched to Dearborn, on the other side of the city line. Trouble flared the instant the marchers crossed into Dearborn. The Dearborn police tried to break the line of marchers coming on four abreast by firing tear gas. Gasping and choking, the line held, and the police ran out of gas canisters. Some marchers began throwing stones at the police, who responded by drawing their guns and opening fire. The marchers surged up to the gates of the Rouge plant, in a swirl of tear-gas clouds, brickbats, and pistol fire. The Ford police drenched the marchers with fire hoses, while Ford's security chief, Harry Bennett, drove his car at speed through the gates and into the marchers. Bennett stepped from his car and was felled by a brick.

As Bennett's inert form was being carried off to the Ford hospital, the Ford police opened fire on the marchers at point-blank range. Four marchers lay dead, twenty more lay wounded in the street, in spreading pools of blood. Not a single policeman was injured.

Proletarian toughness was one more nonanswer to the Depression.

28. The Wound-Dresser

I

The death of the nineteenth century in the First World War, and the failure at Versailles to bury the corpse, pushed every Western nation into the kind of ventures undertaken only *in extremis*. Different countries responded in various ways, according to their history and character. In Italy, Fascism arose; in Germany, National Socialism; in France, the Popular Front; in Britain, the National Government; and in the United States . . . well, we shall see.

A tangled skein of problems was simplified by the Depression into one overriding issue: what was the proper role of the federal government in a modern society? All discussion of the causes of the Depression and the way to defeat it centered on the relationship between rulers and ruled.

The years since the war were shrugged off as wasted years, a static time, and something of that circa 1931 mentality still prevails. But normalcy, Coolidge, and Mellon to the contrary, the federal government had grown inexorably. By 1925 the postwar retrenchment was finished, yet taking federal, state, and local government together, the business of government employed twice as many people as before the war.[1] Federal spending was five times the level of 1916; the national debt was twenty times as high.[2] In real terms, federal spending virtually doubled between 1915 and 1930, and the pattern was much the same in the states and cities.[3]

Washington had begun to take up the burden of direct responsibility for assuring the people's welfare, but it could do so only piecemeal while the country remained in the (fading) grip of its pioneer past. In 1921 Congress passed the Sheppard-Towner Act, the first-ever federal social-security measure, providing money to the states for maternity and infancy programs. Coolidge, before going out of office, declined to ask for the program to be continued. It lapsed in June 1929. The dam however had been breached.

The Supreme Court was another formidable obstacle, bound, as courts must be, by what had been, until events clearly showed that what had been had lost its moral force. The first child-labor law had invoked the power of Congress to regulate interstate commerce,* a power that had been used to curb white slavery, adulterated food, and lotteries. In 1918 the Court ruled that using this power to curb child labor was unconstitutional.[4] Congress passed a second child-labor law, putting a 10 percent tax on goods made by child labor. The Court had sanctioned prohibitory taxes on narcotics, phosphorous matches, and yellow margarine, but the line evidently had to be drawn somewhere because the Court in 1922 drew it at child labor.[5] The only course open now was a child-labor amendment.

The proposed amendment would grant Congress the power "to limit, regulate and prohibit the labor of persons under 18 years of age." Business interests lobbied against it. Rumor had it that the parent who ordered his seventeen-year-old son to mow the lawn could end up in court, as could the mother who ordered her fifteen-year-old daughter to do the dishes. Newspaper routes—that traditional educational service—would be banned. And so on.[6] It was an issue that generated much passion for most of the Twenties, yet by 1932 only six states had ratified the Child Labor Amendment. The states however had enacted a wide variety of statutes to discourage or ban the employment of children and there was a considerable decline in child labor after 1920. As for Hoover, there was no issue that moved him more deeply than the rights of children. In the Cabinet and in the White House, he pressed for adoption of the Child Labor Amendment. But by setting the upper limit at eighteen instead of sixteen, the amendment's congressional sponsors had made defeat almost certain.[7]

Throughout the Twenties issues such as this were kept alive, despite indifference and hostility, by social workers, aging Progressives, modern

---

* One of the great legislative triumphs of the Progressives, it was passed at a time when nearly 10 percent of the work force was made up of children under sixteen and Progressive journals carried this quatrain:

The golf links lie so near the mill
That almost every day
The little children may look out
And see the men at play.

liberals, and others. They never ceased to press for a wide range of reforms: housing projects, old-age pensions, minimum wage laws and maximum hours, unemployment insurance, and a ban on child labor. And in
1926 Robert F. Wagner was elected to the Senate from New York, dedicated to the idea of making government the employer of last resort. The
German-born Wagner inherited a Bismarckian view of social welfare: to
help a hungry man was both a moral act and discouraged him from throwing bricks at policemen. Wagner arrived at the Senate determined to help
the masses of urban poor. The best single thing that could be done for
them was to provide them with full employment. Wagner was, as one
reporter discovered, "the only real product of the American city in that
rural and suburban body, the United States Senate."[8]

With the Depression throwing millions out of work, Wagner in 1931
introduced a bill that would have created a system of federally supported,
state-run employment agencies. The United States Employment Service
was still in business, but limited mainly to placing 500,000 migratory farm-
workers each year. This was an area where the problem was not finding
jobs, but finding workers willing to do them. The Wagner system of employment offices, on the other hand, "would correct the practice of telling
a hundred men in Chicago that there is a job in Milwaukee and collecting
$5 from each—with either a single position or a purely fictitious one
available when the whole hundred spend their last nickel in reaching
Milwaukee."[9] Congress passed Wagner's bill. Hoover vetoed it, with a
stinging rebuke that made no sense at all. He referred to USES as an
adequate alternative, placing up to 1.3 million workers each year. His own
Unemployment Commission urged him to sign the bill. It is possible that
he vetoed the measure rather than see the Democrats in Congress make
the running on the struggle to stem the Depression.[10]

As the Depression threw into stark relief the plight of the unemployed, so it cast a brilliant light over the aged, revealing to much of the
nation the graying of America. The United States, with its high living
costs, probably needed to do more for its old people than almost any
country in the world, yet did the least. Pioneers were expected to drop in
their tracks.

The first symbolic breakthrough had been forcing the 5 million men
and women who served in the war to take out government insurance. But
they were given no incentive to keep their policies in force when the war
ended, and more than 99 percent allowed their policies to lapse. At the
state level, only judges had a decent pension plan. Rare was the city that
provided adequately for its retired clerks, policemen, and firefighters. Half
of all teachers in the public schools had no pension plan, and the other

half were covered by plans of doubtful worth. Among workers, a tiny elite of the most skilled men alone could contemplate retirement with equanimity.[11] Company pension plans usually required at least twenty-five years of continuous service. The business cycle made it unlikely that any more than a small fraction of the work force would stay with one employer that long. Every downturn, such as in 1921 and 1930–32 led to massive layoffs, and the end of pension rights. Of the 7 million people over sixty-five in the United States in 1931, some 180,000 enjoyed state old-age pensions; a further 140,000 received company pensions. Most of the rest were destitute.[12]

The federal government had in 1920 tried to set a positive example by inaugurating a compulsory old-age and sickness insurance program for civil servants, financed by a 2½ percent payroll deduction. Reformers cherished hopes that the sight of 500,000 civil servants enjoying old age and sickness coverage would spur cities, states, and business to follow suit, and that workers would demand it. It never happened.

Nor did the fact that 40 million European industrial workers in 1929 were covered by unemployment insurance impress Americans. Even those in favor of such schemes could see only the unions or employers running them. The idea that government might do it was unthinkable.[13] Without unemployment insurance every sizable rise in unemployment brought a sharp drop in demand, depressing the economy still further and threatening to produce yet more unemployment. Hoover, however, clung like a limpet to a romantic view of private insurance, in which insurance companies bravely took on everyone, including the sick and the aging and the likely-to-be-fired and insured them for moderate sums. Anything the government provided to those who fell outside the private insurance net should be no more than "a bare subsistence."[14]

There was the same tunnel vision when it came to relief. Despite his own experiences in Belgium and Russia, Hoover insisted on relief that was locally administered, to cope with local distress; intoned that responsibility lay with the individual, the family, the employer, the landlord, and—perhaps—the local community. Any attempt to move responsibility from the local level to the federal was a body blow to self-esteem and democratic institutions alike.

Yet his belief in individualism was not of the dog-eat-dog variety. Caught off-balance by the unexpected turn of events in 1930, he assumed complete responsibility for rolling back the Depression from the late fall of 1930 onward. With winter approaching, he set up the President's Committee on Unemployment Relief, with Colonel Arthur Woods, former police commissioner of New York, as its chairman. Its aim was to promote and coordinate local relief efforts. Under the committee's guidance, 3,000 local relief offices were opened, which "were given the responsibility to see that no one went hungry or cold."[15] These local offices reported to Wood, and through him to Hoover, that they were doing a wonderful job —naturally. Yet that winter shantytowns sprang up on open ground in the major cities where the cold and the hungry huddled in misery and squalor; obvious eyesores known as Hoovervilles.

Some of Hoover's close advisers in 1931 urged the President to create a corporate state, in which businesses would have to participate or be heavily fined; workers would be guaranteed job security for life and old-age and sickness insurance; business would set the nation's production targets and fix prices.[16] The U.S. Chamber of Commerce countered with a proposal to lift virtually all government restraints on business, including antitrust legislation. In return, business would be required to pull the country out of the Depression.[17]

Hoover rejected both kinds of advice. He detested the welfare state. But he also detested the price-fixing cartel and unregulated business. The fatal flaw of nearly all the recovery measures that were proposed to Hoover was that they would inevitably have increased the role of government and added to governmental bureaucracy. Hoover was deeply convinced that bureaucracy was living death to a democratic society. And while the scope of government activities did, in the end, grow much wider and more profound under Hoover, the number of federal employees actually *dropped* (from 573,000 to 565,000). He created forty commissions and committees, but only four were permanent.

Meanwhile, as we have seen, local and state relief funds were rapidly drying up. With half the country turning to Washington, Congress responded. In the winter of 1931 Senators Robert La Follette, Jr., and Edward P. Costigan opened hearings on relief in the cities. Day in and day out, the testimony that was heard established beyond any lingering doubt that there was massive, unprecedented suffering; and that the relief agencies—public and private alike—were at the end of their resources. The executive director of the community chest optimistically expected to raise $100 million in 1932, yet said he really needed $400 million. The only remaining remedy, he argued, was direct federal assistance. The U.S. Catholic bishops endorsed federal relief. The Jewish charities did the same. So did the AFL. From city after city, state after state, came officials and relief authorities to testify that there was no money left, and the need desperate. Only Wood's successor, Walter S. Gifford of AT&T, argued that there was no one hungry or cold.[18]

In February 1932 La Follette and Costigan introduced a bill that would provide $375 million to subsidize local relief. Congress seemed ready to pass a major relief bill. There were other congressmen with relief measures of their own to be submitted. Their various authors refused to stand aside while La Follette and Costigan reaped all the glory. Unable to agree on a relief bill, these Democrats and Republicans did their opponents' work for them.

But this did not spare Hoover from a nation's scorn. His prolonged resistance to federal involvement in relief damned him then and ever after. It made him appear—wrongly—a man indifferent to suffering; the ultimate and unanswerable rebuke to his reputation as the great humanitarian. This emotive issue has led two generations of otherwise reasonable and fair-minded scholars to regard Hoover with loathing. When the dullards and the charlatans who have occupied the White House from time to time have all been forgotten or forgiven, Hoover will still be held fast in the stocks of American history, his square, serious face plastered with egg.

II

The President took what might be termed the patriotic view of the crisis—he blamed it on foreigners. The crash was long overdue, and not necessarily a bad thing, ran the Hooverian theory. But all the crash caused was a recession. The Depression on the other hand was a worldwide phenomenon, afflicting a dozen important countries, and their economies had broken down *before* the crash. By the winter of 1930–31 the American recession had run its course and the country was on the verge of recovery when the European economies fell over like pins in a ten-strike, and *that* was what dragged the United States into the Depression.[19] Only when sanity returned to the world economic order would the American economy be able to recover. Hoover became obsessed with restoring the international gold standard as the ladder up which everyone, Americans and foreigners alike, would be able at last to climb out of this pit.

It was certainly true that ever since Versailles the economies of the world's five or six largest economies were so interrelated that not one of them could sneeze without some other catching a cold. Yet, if Hoover had noticed that a dozen countries were depressed before the crash, why had he signed the Hawley-Smoot Tariff in 1930? The United States hardly needed protection from the exports of countries going on the rocks. Within a year of the Hawley-Smoot Tariff becoming law, twenty-five countries retaliated by raising their tariffs on American goods. They all denied that this was what they were doing. Even if this were true in some cases, the general effect on international trade was devastating. By 1932

American exports had fallen to the level of the 1890s, before the United States had become a major trading nation.[20]

Nor had the strange, triangular loans-reparations-debt repayment structure survived recent vicissitudes. From the 1924 Dawes plan to 1929 there was remarkable enthusiasm to lend money to Germany. Loans floated in the United States were oversubscribed by up to 1000 percent. Private American investors in the Twenties loaned the Germans $1.5 billion, and American banks loaned about $3 billion more.[21] But in 1929 Germany defaulted again on her reparations. Owen D. Young was despatched to write a new plan. Like Dawes before him, he scaled down the sum owing, and annual payments were sharply reduced.

The Young plan came into effect in the spring of 1930, over German protests that it was still too much. In May 1931 the United States ambassador to Germany, Frederic M. Sackett, returned to Washington and warned the President that Germany was on the brink of revolution. If Germany fell into chaos, the shock would be felt throughout Europe. For the next six weeks Hoover worked tirelessly to keep Germany from the bankruptcy which threatened to destroy its government. Not being a party to the reparations agreement, the United States could not lift the reparations burden directly. Hoover decided to declare a one-year moratorium on the American collection of war debts, provided the Allies would make a similar suspension on reparations. He won the agreement of the British and Italians easily, but not of the French. They would not say yes, and they would not say no. The French felt no obligation to rescue the Germans from disaster. Only after seventeen days of talks and Hoover's eventual decision to act without their agreement if necessary were the French forced to agree.[22]

The debt moratorium was one of Hoover's greatest public successes. Hoover publicly admitted what no responsible American official had before acknowledged: the direct connection between debt repayments by the Allies and reparations payments by the Germans. He presented the moratorium as a measure to beat the Depression by reviving world trade. And while admitting the connection, he would not admit making the admission. "Reparations," he blandly maintained, "is necessarily a wholly European problem with which we have no relation."[23] Yet Hoover hoped that the moratorium would continue indefinitely, ending this snarled and poisonous business once and for all.

III

Unable to promote recovery by restoring the international gold standard, Hoover sought desperately to save the American structure of credit from collapsing completely. When the British dashed his hopes by going off the gold standard, American bankers were in terror that the billions of dollars they had out in foreign loans were about to be lost. Terrified bankers are not much use in a crisis. On Sunday, October 4, as dusk settled on Washington, the President slipped out of the White House and went to Mellon's home on Massachusetts Avenue for a secret meeting with forty of the country's most important bankers and insurance company executives.

Hoover, in effect, told them to pull themselves together. He browbeat them into creating the National Credit Corporation, which would make loans on paper the Federal Reserve was not allowed to accept, to a total of $500 million. Bankers, however, do not make loans to create confidence; they make them because they are confident. The same rule applies to borrowers, in spades. Launched to editorial praise in October, by December the NCC had loaned $150 million and was as good as finished. But by this time Hoover had something else up his sleeve.

Throughout 1931, analogies had been made between the Great War and the deepening Depression. Hoover himself began to employ the same kind of language, and on December 8 he sent a message to Congress asking for the creation of a body plainly modeled on the War Finance Corporation, to be known as the Reconstruction Finance Corporation.

The President, meanwhile, had begun to take a profound dislike to his secretary of the treasury. As the Depression ruined Hoover's reputation, so it blighted Mellon's. He was mocked on the Senate floor as "The greatest Secretary of the Treasury since the last one. . . ."[24] Any idea that he was a financial genius had vanished without trace. Mellon was absolutely and completely baffled by the Depression. When Hoover looked to him for ideas, he got platitudes in reply. The banalities that had passed for wisdom during prosperity were infuriating once that prosperity had gone. Despite Hoover's evident desire to see him leave, Mellon remained where he was, smoking his cheroots and looking frailer, more spiritual, every day. But in January 1932 Dawes, whom Hoover had made ambassador to Great Britain (over Dawes's vigorous protests; he hated fancy dinners and formal receptions), resigned his post. Hoover promptly shoved Mellon into it and appointed the very rich Ogden Mills, the undersecretary of the treasury, to succeed him.

Once the Reconstruction Finance Act had been passed and the RFC stood ready to begin operations, Hoover once more dragged Dawes from Chicago and made him head of the RFC. On the very first day of its existence, Dawes put through a $15 million loan in a matter of minutes to save the Bank of America.[25] Which was exactly the kind of thing it was supposed to do. The RFC perfectly embodied what Hoover was trying to do, and made certain that he would be maligned for it. He was convinced that indirect relief could save the country, and that direct relief would impoverish it permanently. He chose to inflate the economy through the banks, the insurance companies, the railroads, and the trust companies instead of printing more money and giving it away; that is, by direct inflation.

Inevitably, this was described as helping the rich and ignoring the poor. Yet, if recovery were to be achieved, indirect inflation stood a better chance than the direct variety, because the machinery for doing it could be quickly created, the methods involved were well established and, what is more, widely accepted. In the short term, moreover, they prevented the breakdown of credit. The RFC saved the railroads, and probably saved the banking system. Before it began operations, bank failures were running at seventy a week. Within three months the failure rate was down to one a fortnight.

As Hoover drafted the RFC Act it could have done much to revive cities, farms, and industry, by authorizing loans for slum clearance, farm improvements, and the modernization of plants. The Democratic leadership in the House, however, struck these provisions from the bill.[26] Hoover had also proposed to set up Federal Home Loan Banks. These would have been financed by the RFC but operated by the savings and loan associations and banks that normally offered mortgages. The Home Loan Banks were intended to save the homes of the hundreds of thousands, possibly millions, who had bought homes in good times and risked losing them now. These banks would have refinanced virtually every mortgage at risk of default. It was a popular measure, but Congress took nine months to bring this law into effect, by which time many homes were lost.

Occupied as he was with these initiatives, Hoover had not forgotten Wall Street. For more than a hundred years Wall Street and Washington had enjoyed a comparatively amicable relationship, with only the occasional brief clash to keep it interesting. That tradition ended abruptly in January 1932 when Hoover summoned Whitney, recently elevated to the presidency of the New York Stock Exchange, for a meeting. It turned into a stiff lecture from a very angry man. If the Stock Exchange did not promptly and thoroughly reform itself, Hoover threatened, then he would take control of the Exchange by federal law and do the job himself. From this moment on there was bitter hostility between Wall Street and Washington, and it lasted for many years thereafter.[27]

The White House, while urging bankers to lend money, was at the same time running an antihoarding campaign. A frightened people were hoarding large bills and gold to an estimated value of $1.3 billion. Hoover pleaded with them to take their money and gold to the banks and thereby make credit easier, recovery more likely.[28] His main concern, however, was the Federal Reserve. The mechanism which had proved its ability to stimulate business in good times was proving unable to do the same in bad. A legend was already taking hold, in fact, that the Federal Reserve in its profound unwisdom was strangling the money supply and, with it, the system of credit.

There is no doubt that the money supply was falling sharply. But in May 1931 the Federal Reserve Bank of New York cut the rediscount rate to 1½ percent, the lowest rate ever offered by a central bank anywhere. It had all the impact of a ripe banana hitting a tank. The Fed could only lower interest rates. Its charter did not authorize the governors of the Federal Reserve to descend on local bankers, seize them by the scruff of the neck, and drag them off to the nearest Federal Reserve Bank, their pockets stuffed with high-grade commercial paper, ripe for rediscounting. Instead, the governors had to sit tight, in attitudes of exasperation, while the local bankers beavered away at *reducing* their borrowings from the Federal Reserve. Terrified of bank runs, they improved their liquidity, just in case a crowd began forming outside their doors. The Federal Reserve could take no credit for Coolidge prosperity or blame for the Depression, and for the same reason—it had not the ability to do much about either.

The Reconstruction Finance Corporation was one way to get around this dilemma. The Glass-Steagall Act was another. Drafted in the Treasury Department and the White House, this bill allowed the Federal Reserve to use government bonds as security for new issues of currency. At a stroke it would free $750 million from the gold reserves and expand the money supply by $2 billion. Credit was to be increased still further by authorizing the Federal Reserve to accept as collateral low-grade commercial paper that would not usually be considered eligible for loans at a central bank.

Hoover had to talk long and hard to persuade the octogenarian Senator Carter Glass of Virginia, "father of the Federal Reserve," to sponsor this measure, which seemed to bring the system down to one notch above pawnbroking. But in the end Glass relented, and Henry Steagall of Alabama, chairman of the House Banking and Currency Committee, introduced it in the House in February 1932. "In an urgent mood comparable to wartime, Congress put everything aside for the Glass-Steagall bill."[29] It became law in just two weeks.

IV

The 1930 election was a Republican disaster. More than fifty House and eleven Senate seats were captured by Democrats. When the Seventy-second Congress convened it was almost evenly divided between the two parties, with a nominal Republican majority of one in the Senate and two in the House. Up to ten Republican senators however voted as a rule with the Democrats. Hoover suggested to the Republican leadership in the Senate that it allow the Democrats to organize it, "and thereby convert their sabotage into responsibility."[30] It must have seemed a bizarre idea.

In the event, the Seventy-second Congress tried to kill him with kindness. Both parties gave Hoover nearly everything he asked for. Only a few presidents have ever had so compliant a Congress. If recovery failed to come, they were making sure that Hoover got the blame.

Ogden Mills, freshly installed as Mellon's successor, was both diligently drinking himself to death (he got there in 1937 with the aid of a bottle of gin gulped down in less than an hour) and trying to persuade Hoover that taxes had to be raised. To the modern mind raising taxes in the middle of a massive depression—and in an election year, to boot—is something that nobody would think of while sober. But now is now, and then was on the borderline.

There had been a moderate budget deficit in 1930, followed by a billion-dollar deficit in 1931, and worse was projected for 1932. The Treasury, in 1931, had floated an $800 million bond issue to cover the shortfall in government revenues caused by the Depression; the biggest bond issue since the war. Hoover, however, did not believe in the sanctity of balanced budgets. The Depression was like a war, he reasoned, and the normal rules did not apply. Mills nevertheless was able in the end to persuade him to ask Congress to enact a federal sales tax.

This was an age when Americans almost to a man (and woman) deplored deficit spending, and this was as true of liberals as of the Chamber of Commerce. Walter Lippmann, for example, strenuously attacked high government spending in 1932, calling it a hangover from the boom years, excusable in prosperity, madness in a depression. Total government spending had risen eightfold in the past twenty-five years. "They have to deflate. . . . The American nation is not eight times as rich. The reform of government finance is one of the urgent inescapable tasks in the program of recovery."[31] Journals such as the *New Republic* and the *Nation* were running editorials with titles such as "Taxes Should Be Raised."[32] When Ogden Mills went to tell the House Ways and Means Committee that the government had to raise at least $1.25 billion in new taxes, almost no one in Congress disagreed with him. The danger that faced government at every level was that, if it went to the bond markets too often with government securities to cover its deficits, the day might come when there were no takers. Taxes had to be raised to save the government's credit, ran this line of argument. For if the government's credit were to collapse, no one could answer for what might follow.

The Democratic leadership in the house therefore supported the Administration's tax bill. But it severely miscalculated the mood in the House. Willing to support Hoover's recovery measures, it was not in favor of fresh exactions from the mass of the people. La Guardia organized a revolt on the floor of the House. In a scene of utter pandemonium the sales tax proposal was rejected by 253–153.[33] It was a triumph La Guardia was to follow up a few months later when, in partnership with Norris in the Senate, he won passage of an act that virtually abolished the use of injunctions to crush strikes. Hoover, with evident reluctance, signed the Norris-La Guardia Act into law.

Hoover had meanwhile presented another tax measure, this time putting surtax on very large incomes, raising corporate income taxes by 1¾ percent, raising estate taxes, and introducing a wide range of excise taxes. The Revenue Act of 1932 was to become one of the most important of Hoover's legislative achievements; it "essentially set the tax structure for the entire period up to the Second World War."[34]

It was one of the Depression's ironies that almost from the outset there was what amounted to a Keynesian consensus: wages had to be maintained; the railroads and utilities had to continue their investment programs; commodity prices had to be shored up; business had to buy new plant and equipment; public works had to be expanded. Aggregate demand had to be maintained. What was missing at first was any comprehension of the scale of what was required. And once it became clear that the scale involved was five, ten, twenty times what anyone would have imagined in the winter of 1929–30 there was hardly anyone, in Washington or elsewhere, who really had the reckless courage that was called for, *if* the Keynesian theory was right. Because only government could now provide the stimulus that was needed. Savings had more or less vanished. This traditional source of money for new investment was but a shadow of what it had been. Incomes had fallen by more than 30 percent since 1929. One worker in four was without a job. Consumer spending was flat. Only government could create new demand, new investment. As things stood in 1932, however, it would have required spending at least eight times its present income to make good the shortfall in demand.

Where was the money to come from? Any government that announced that it was going to increase its spending by 800 percent would be signing its death warrant. Everything except gold, guns, and food would immediately lose its value. Even doubling its spending would increase deficits so much that business would be terrified into spending less (possibly nothing); farsighted workers would buy wheelbarrows in which to collect their wages; and cemeteries would be raided for the teeth of the dead.

The comparatively modest efforts to sustain demand by increasing federal spending in 1930–32 were offset by cuts in state and local government spending as revenues fell. Even the Democratic leadership in Congress wanted to fight the Depression by cutting all federal salaries by 10 percent and by firing 10 percent of all federal employees. Hoover called sixteen leading Democrats into the Oval Office, one at a time, to inform them that this idea was "heartless and medieval."[35]

Hoover came to office committed to increasing public works long before the Depression began. He distinguished, however, between what he termed "nonproductive" public works and "reproductive" public works. The nonproductive kind were paid for by the Treasury, out of the taxpayers' money. They involved such projects as building post offices and widening rivers. Once finished, they generated little or no income. Reproductive works, on the other hand, generated revenue or created new jobs after completion, as the San Francisco-Oakland Bay Bridge would do. For projects such as this the federal government provided financing while private business managed the construction. There are no prizes for guessing which type of public works project Hoover preferred.

Nevertheless, spending on nonproductive public works rose to nearly $1 billion a year under Hoover. He ran a public building program that was three times greater than those of the seven previous Presidents combined.[36] But Hoover had no illusions about how much was being achieved. To give half the estimated unemployed jobs on public works would have cost $10 billion a year, when the entire federal budget amounted to $3.2 billion. Where would the money come from? And what would happen to the other half? All that he could do for the unemployed was provide bandages, like those tenderhearted men during the Civil War who, acknowledging their helplessness to stop the killing, became wound-dressers at army hospitals.

Congress, however, was snowed under with proposals to expand public works. In May 1932 the House passed a bill offered by the Democratic minority leader, John Nance Garner. The Garner bill would have built more than 1,000 brand-new post offices. In June the Senate voted for a bill offered by Wagner to provide the RFC with $3 billion to be spent on public works. A House-Senate conference stitched the two bills together in July. Hoover vetoed the result. La Guardia in the House and Costigan in the Senate introduced a bill to create a United States Exchange Corporation, with a capital of $500 million to make loans of up to $500 to anyone who needed money. It was a poor man's RFC. It died in committee.[37] Another bill was passed, however, that directed the RFC to make loans "for any conceivable purpose on any conceivable security to anybody who wants money."[38] Hoover vetoed it.

He disliked relief as much as he had ever done. "Direct relief to individuals from the Federal government," Hoover intoned, "would bring an inevitable train of corruption and waste. . . ."[39] (Who would now deny it?) Yet while he was vetoing the Garner-Wagner public-works bill, the Administration was pressing Congress to pass the Emergency Relief and Construction bill as an amendment to the RFC Act. It amounted to a $2.1 billion package. The RFC was authorized to lend up to $1.5 billion to the states and cities for "reproductive" public works, including slum clearance. A further $320 million was to be loaned by the Treasury for public works, such as building post offices. And there was $300 million to be loaned to the states for direct relief among the unemployed. No one in Congress or outside it had any illusions about this provision. This $300 million "loan" would never be repaid, was not expected to be repaid. Congress passed the bill quickly. When it arrived at the White House, Hoover, having dictated the terms of his own surrender, signed it into law.

V

Walter W. Waters, a slender man with wavy blond hair and piercing blue eyes, went overseas with the 146th Field Artillery, served as a medic, rose to the rank of sergeant, and was discharged from the army in June 1919. He spent the next six years drifting from town to town and job to job in the Pacific Northwest. Then he married and settled down to a regular job in a cannery outside Portland. By 1930 Waters was assistant superintendent at the cannery, had $1,000 in the bank, and was content with life. That December the cannery laid off half its employees, including Waters. By December 1931 he was destitute—savings gone, possessions pawned, hunger a fact of life, and work impossible to find.[40] The one thing he possessed that still had cash value was his Adjusted Compensation Certificate, better known as "the bonus."

Enacted over Coolidge's veto in 1924, the bonus bill had created a twenty-year endowment policy, which matured at death or in 1945. The bonus provided each veteran with $1.25 for every day served overseas, $1.00 for every day of service in the United States, plus 4 percent compound interest up to the date of encashment. Some 3.5 million veterans received adjusted compensation certificates. The average value was $1,000. There was a part payment provision, but any veteran who applied for it (to a maximum of 50 percent) had to wait up to two years for it to come through. Waters, and many another veteran down on his luck, felt he could not wait that long. Congressman Wright Patman of Texas agreed.

In December 1931 Patman introduced legislation that would authorize full payment before 1945. News of the Patman bill stirred Waters and other veterans into life, but not until May 1932, when the Ways and Means Committee shelved the bill, did it occur to the veterans of Portland to march on Washington. In the middle of May they set out, three hundred strong, with less than $30.00 between them. They shuffled along to the sound of a borrowed drum, older and grayer than the last time they had marched. When dissension broke out several days later, Waters, who discovered an unsuspected gift for oratory, took control of the group with the aid of a bugler. He offered the discipline they had once been accustomed to obeying.

What most of the bonus army really wanted was a job. To some extent their cross-country journey was a hunger march, of which the capital had by this time seen quite a few. In December 1931 the Communist party had led 1,600 hunger marchers to Washington. Hoover's attitude toward Communists was detached and disdainful. He was determined, moreover, that their right to protest and organize should be respected. He ordered that tents, blankets, a field kitchen, and medical facilities be provided for the hunger marchers. The Washington chief of police, Brigadier General Pelham D. Glassford, on his big blue motorcycle, personally led the marchers down Pennsylvania Avenue, as they sang the *Internationale* and carried scarlet banners. Hoover accepted a petition that set out their demands.[41]

In January 1932 a Roman Catholic priest from Pittsburgh, James R. Cox, led 10,000 unemployed men to the capital in a motorcade eight miles long. Hoover ordered the army to feed them, while they petitioned Congress for jobs. Cox was invited to meet Hoover, who listened sympathetically to the priest's pleas for expanded public works and higher taxes on the rich.[42]

But Hoover was hostile to the bonus army riding the rails toward Washington as spring shaded into summer. To him, the veterans were a special-interest lobby, who were in truth privileged, not deprived. And he had done well by them. In 1930 he had reorganized veterans' services and created the Veterans Administration. In 1932 veterans' benefits would account for 25 percent of the federal budget, the largest item in it. Hoover invariably vetoed bonus bills, but he did for veterans what no other president had ever attempted: all needy and sick veterans were made eligible for disability allowances. This more than doubled the number of veterans receiving VA pensions (from 370,000 to 850,000). He also made sure that a 100 percent service-connected disability pension was higher than the average wage. Far from slighting veterans, he took the initiative on their behalf. To pay the bonus, however, would have cost $2.3 billion, and he was not going to inflate the economy on that scale for a group he regarded as privileged. Most people appear to have agreed with him.

Still the Bonus Expeditionary Force came on, riding the rails as far as St. Louis. There, the Baltimore and Ohio Railroad simply stopped running east-bound trains until the BEF left the railroad yard. Local veterans organizations drove them to Indiana. For most of the way after that they were ferried across each state by the National Guard. The manner in which state and local authorities helped the bonus army on its way symbolized the change the Depression had wrought: "It was much simpler to pass the problem on to Washington than to deal with it locally."[43] And at every stop the marchers' ranks were swelled. When it arrived in Washington, Waters led an army 15,000 strong, with more men arriving every day. The BEF eventually numbered 60,000 men.[44] And it found a champion it could never have expected—the chief of police.

Glassford stood six feet three inches tall, a distinguished-looking man with an adventurous nature. He had spent his army leaves unconventionally; his idea of rest and recreation was to get a job as a circus roustabout. Retired from the army, he spent his evenings with beautiful women and his days roaring about the District on his enormous motorcycle. To Glassford, the men who marched so sadly into Washington that June were poignant figures, shadows of the men he had led on the Western Front. Special-interest nothing; they were hunger-marchers as far as he was concerned. He went to Capitol Hill to testify for them. He became the secretary-treasurer of the BEF. With his help, the BEF set up twenty-seven encampments, mainly in the northeastern section of the District. The largest was strung along the mudflats of the Anacostia River, where 15,000 made homes from packing cases and canvas sacks. Men began bringing their families with them, and the BEF had a contingent of women and children numbering more than 2,000. Anacostia may not have been much, but it provided friendship and, ironically, security—no bill collectors came to call, no landlord was demanding rent.

Hoover's original hostility had meanwhile melted. But the march was by now unpopular in both Congress and the press. Patman would have nothing to do with the bonus army; nor would the leadership of the American Legion, although some local posts supported it. Hoover reversed his earlier position in private. He authorized the provision of tents, cots, field kitchens, and the sale at giveaway prices of army rations. Federal property was made available to squatters. When it became evident that the BEF camps were rife with illness, he secretly ordered the army reserve to set up a field hospital. All these things were done over vehement opposition from Patrick J. Hurley, the secretary of war. Publicly, however, the President maintained an aloof attitude, not wanting to encourage more arrivals or to make himself a target for criticism, of which he already had a historically large share.[45]

With the overt help of Glassford and the covert help of Hoover the BEF turned into the largest protest demonstration the capitol had ever seen. It lasted two months. Glassford staged fund-raising events. Evalyn Walsh McLean arrived one day with 1,000 sandwiches. American Legionnaires raised $5,000 for the BEF. Well-wishers sent in nickels and dimes from all over the country. Each day there were rallies of some kind. "But they do not sing," reported Gardner Jackson, "not even on their formal demonstration marches up Pennsylvania Avenue. Short rations discourage singing."[46]

The Patman bill was brought out of committee. It was passed by the House. It was overwhelmingly rejected by the Senate, by 62–18. The BEF had failed, as most of the men in it had known it would. And with Congress about to adjourn, their protest seemed increasingly pointless.[47] Hoover persuaded Congress to offer loans to BEF members so they could ride the cushions home. The bonus army began to break up. Some 10,000 or so stayed on, however, for one reason or another. They were being egged on to militant action both by the comparatively small number of Communists among them and by Waters, who did not intend to let the Communists steal this protest from under his nose.

A dozen of the buildings being used by the BEF were scheduled for demolition under the Coolidge-Mellon Plan of 1925 (see page 316). The demolition contractors were becoming impatient, losing money as the good weather of summer passed and the buildings stayed up. They began to press their friends in government, now that the Patman bill was dead, to get the squatters out. Glassford, however, resisted every attempt to make his police force carry out evictions. He negotiated an agreement with Waters to have the squatters leave peacefully and move to other sites.

On the morning of July 28, a group of forty men, led by several

Communist organizers and following an American flag, tried to reclaim one of the evacuated buildings. The police at the site were outnumbered and surprised. They were forced to retreat under a hail of bricks and stones. Glassford hurried to the scene and fell stunned to the ground. One of his aides, Edward G. Scott, who had won the Medal of Honor in 1918, attempted to shield the prostrate Glassford until he, too, was struck on the head by a barrage of bricks and collapsed with a fractured skull.[48] Waters appears to have gone into hiding once violence broke out. Police reinforcements rescued Glassford and Scott and cleared the site with minimal force. Six policemen were removed to hospital.

Later that same day, as bonus marchers continued trying to reclaim the government buildings, two policemen, George Shinault and Miles Zamanezck, were cornered on a half-demolished second floor. To a shout of "Let's get 'em!" the policemen were rushed,[49] and Shinault was seized. While being punched and choked he drew his revolver and fired six shots. Three men fell wounded, two of them fatally. And three more policemen were hospitalized for their injuries at the hands of the BEF. The District of Columbia commissioners now decided that the situation was no longer under police control. They asked for federal troops.

Hoover refused to consider their request until it was put in writing and endorsed by Glassford. Hours later a written request was delivered to the White House, with a report from five senior police officials that they could not contain the riots that were breaking out "except by the free use of firearms."[50]

Hoover had to act, as any president would act, to save life. He gave very precise orders to Hurley, however, and through him to the army chief of staff, Major General Douglas MacArthur. The troops employed were not to be armed.[51] The bonus marchers were to be cleared from the downtown area and escorted to their various camps. Any who resisted were to be arrested and turned over to the police. The operation the President authorized was no more than military support of the police power.[52]

MacArthur ignored Hoover's orders. Resplendent in jodhpurs and all his medals, the general could hardly be troubled with clearing a couple of blocks of a handful of malcontents. He chose to clear the entire District of the BEF, taking no prisoners, and driving the marchers out of their camps. To the surprise of his aide, Major Dwight D. Eisenhower, MacArthur assumed personal command of an operation that, had Hoover's orders been followed, an infantry battalion under a lieutenant colonel could have handled in two or three hours. To Eisenhower, the appearance of the chief of staff on the streets was both unseemly and provocative.

To widen their freedom of action, Hurley and MacArthur asked Hoover for a proclamation of a state of insurrection. He politely told them not to be absurd. As afternoon gave way to dusk on July 28, MacArthur's forces moved into Pennsylvania Avenue, bayonets glittering in the sunshine, the treads of five tanks squeaking and clanking. The bonus army jeered and began throwing rocks. The soldiers fired tear gas in reply, and a small force of horsemen, led by Major George Patton, charged down Pennsylvania Avenue in the last mounted engagement of the United States Cavalry.[53]

The bonus army shattered under the onslaught of tear gas and sabers. Weeping and choking, the veterans fled to their camps. As night fell, MacArthur's force reassembled at Anacostia Bridge. He gave his men an hour to rest and eat dinner before attacking the camp on the other side of the river. Hoover, learning of this, ordered Hurley to stop MacArthur from crossing the bridge. Major General Van Horn Mosley, the deputy chief of staff, personally took the order to MacArthur not to cross Anacostia Bridge. MacArthur finished his dinner and ordered his men to attack.[54]

As the army moved into the Anacostia camp, tearing down some shacks, setting fire to others, and firing tear gas in every direction, the bonus marchers acknowledged their defeat by finishing what the soldiers had begun: in a final gesture of defiance, they razed their own camp. By dawn, the bonus army had vanished. For MacArthur, the Battle of Anacostia Flats ended in total victory. For Hoover, the routing of the bonus army was a catastrophe. Unwilling to make a public issue of MacArthur's insubordination, he took responsibility for everything that had happened, while lamely asserting the BEF "was largely organized and managed by Communists."[55] The flames that lit up the Washington sky that summer's night, the pall of smoke drifting over the District next morning, marked the funeral pyre of Hoover's reputation.

It was a fall from grace as complete as any in classical tragedy.

VI

Between the 1928 election and the 1932 convention at Chicago the Democratic party, deeply in doubt about itself and badly split among its various elements, was kept going as an organization with money and direction from the very rich, very conservative Raskob. He put the party into the hands of professional managers for the first time, perhaps hoping that Al Smith might eventually change his mind. But in 1929, in 1930, and in 1931 the former governor of New York maintained that he had no interest in running for the White House again. He was heavily in debt, he said, and besides, no Catholic could win that election for at least another generation. Yet, when the Democratic convention drew near, he began to flirt with fantasy and grew bitter. He had never thought much of Roosevelt, and this upper-class lightweight was being cried up by half the party as the man who would win both the nomination and the election, while a man of real ability, a Smith, was denied the White House by bigots and fanatics. It was too unjust for a proud man to bear. Two weeks after Roosevelt announced his candidacy in January 1932, Smith declared that he too was running.

Relations between them had never been easy or close. The social gulf had always made itself felt, in small ways rather than important ones, but a reminder, nonetheless, that they came from very different worlds.[56] It was Roosevelt's good luck, however, that the friendlier Al Smith became with Raskob and other multimillionaires, the cooler the relations between the former governor and Tammany Hall had become. On the other hand, he had to do something about that other son of Tammany, Mayor Jimmy Walker. Roosevelt had never been a Tammany man. To carry his state at the convention he wanted Tammany's support.

Walker was by now known to New York as the "Late Mayor." He never rose before noon, and was never on time for appointments. The scandals surrounding the magistrates' courts had led to other inquiries which revealed extensive corruption in city government and a knack the mayor had for getting people to give him large sums of money in exchange, he insisted, for doing nothing at all. Roosevelt, under persistent prodding from good government types, reluctantly set out to remove the mayor from office. When the issue of whether the governor had this power came to court, judgment was given for the governor. Rather than face more questions from Roosevelt, Walker resigned and sailed away.

Walker's resignation cost Roosevelt Tammany's support, while stilling few of the doubts about Roosevelt's ability. The governor was blessed with typical American gifts: optimism, energy, compassion, and physical courage. But he lacked others of these gifts: openness, idealism, conviction. He trusted no one; perhaps because no one could trust him. Roosevelt was as much an actor as John Barrymore, and was never offstage. His mind was not deep, but his intelligence was quick, his interests broad. He was both affable and aristocratic. He was a big man physically, with a dominating personality. Even though crippled he had presence.

There can be no doubt about his determination to help the victims of the Depression. He was the first governor to press for direct relief by the states and one of the first to support unemployment insurance. Economists who suggested that the Depression be allowed to run its "natural" course were dismissed with contempt for their callousness.[57] When the state legislature resisted his anti-Depression measures, Roosevelt used radio to appeal directly to the voters for their help. He reformed New York's state penitentiaries, built new prisons to ease the overcrowding which had triggered the riots of 1929–30, and made the Baumes law less draconian.

The Walker affair, however, left him with a reputation for evasiveness and vacillation. When he declared his candidacy for president, Walter Lippmann wrote an appraisal of Roosevelt that was widely circulated at the time and for many years thereafter. Lippmann could find nothing in Roosevelt's three years as governor to suggest that he held firm convictions about anything. He concluded, "Franklin D. Roosevelt is no crusader. He is no tribune of the people. He is no enemy of entrenched privilege. He is a pleasant man who, without any important qualifications for the office, would very much like to be President."[58]

When the convention opened in July in Chicago, Roosevelt proved to be far ahead of Al Smith. On the first ballot he won 666 votes to Smith's 201. A large majority, but not two-thirds. Roosevelt was 100 votes short, and he stayed that way on the next two ballots. The key to victory was held by Garner, who, supported ardently by William Randolph Hearst, had won the Texas and California primaries. Garner held more than 90 votes. Hearst disliked Roosevelt less than he disliked Smith, and Garner had no intention of deadlocking the convention. They agreed to release Garner's votes to Roosevelt. But to make the Texas delegation vote for Roosevelt, Garner had to accept the vice-presidential nomination. He would have preferred to be Speaker of the House, but he did his duty.[59]

As word spread through the hall that Texas and California were going to switch to Roosevelt, there was a fourth-ballot stampede that carried Roosevelt to victory. The governor made history by introducing aviation to politics and by delivering his acceptance speech to the body that had given him the nomination. "Roosevelt did not relish flying, but there was no time for him to get there by train."[60]

Roosevelt's campaign began with his acceptance speech. He declared in ringing tones, "I say to you that from this date on the Eighteenth Amendment is doomed!" As for the Depression, he vowed to put 1 million unemployed men to work as soon as he took office. What would they do? They would plant trees. It did not make a lot of sense,* but it *was* a promise of jobs.

The man Roosevelt was challenging for the White House held more

---

* One man can plant up to 1,000 trees a day. With 1 million men doing it, it would be possible in theory to plant a billion trees in twenty-four hours. As there were only several hundred million seedling trees available in 1932, Roosevelt's vast army of tree-planters would have enjoyed about a morning's employment.

power over the United States in peacetime than Wilson had possessed during the war. Hoover had also concentrated the power of the federal government so that almost everything seemed to lead into or out of his office. Despite his unprecedented role, defeat was certain. The animus that Hoover's name excited cannot be exaggerated. So much more had been expected of him than of almost anyone ever elected to the presidency, and the country had never fallen so low. He was derided with a hatred that went beyond hate. The Republicans, moreover, had taken all the credit for the prosperity of the Twenties. They had thereby saddled themselves with all the blame for the Depression when it came.

Various Republican senators and representatives nursed vain hopes that Coolidge might be talked into campaigning for the White House again, knowing that if they had to run on the same ticket with Hoover, it meant leaving the government payroll and joining the unemployed.[61] Hoover knew what to expect: "I had little hope of re-election but it was incumbent on me to fight it out to the end."[62] So his name went forward inexorably to the nominating convention.

The love affair with the press with which he had come to office had long since ended. The two press conferences a week at the start fell off to a press conference a month. "Two years in the White House has greyed his hair, accentuated the pastiness of his complexion, deepened the lines in his round, boyish face," reported *Time* in 1931. "Losing faith in the Press, he has come to think of himself as a martyr in a hair shirt, misunderstood and misinterpreted by the People."[63] A campaign was launched by his advisers and friends to "humanize" Hoover, on radio and in the newspapers. It was a doomed venture, with a nauseating stress on Hoover's love for dogs and small children.

He was nominated in the same hall in Chicago that saw Roosevelt's triumph. But Hoover's nomination was acclaimed by a hall that was one-third empty and by a band that tactlessly played "California, here I come / Right back where I started from."

VII

Roosevelt's campaign consisted mainly of blaming Hoover for the Depression. He committed himself to balancing the budget and reducing "the cost of Federal government operations by 25 per cent."[64] In rural areas he introduced himself as a "farmer."[65] In short, Roosevelt presented himself as the safe, solid, middle-of-the-road amateur in politics who would take good care of the taxpayers' money and make sure that bureaucracy was kept in check.

Yet it was Roosevelt who made the most impressive appraisal in the 1932 campaign of where the country stood, addressing the San Francisco Commonwealth Club in September. An era had ended, he said. "Equality of opportunity as we have known it no longer exists. Our industrial plant is built; the problem just now is whether under existing conditions it has not been overbuilt. Our last frontier has long since been reached; and there is practically no more free land. More than half of our people do not live on the farms or on lands and cannot live by cultivating their own property. There is no safety valve in the form of a Western prairie to which those thrown out of work by the Eastern economic machine can go for a new start. We are not able to invite the immigrant from Europe to share our endless plenty." While opportunity was ending for the worker, so were horizons shrinking for the independent businessman. The economic life of the country was increasingly under the control of huge corporations. The age of expansion was over, never to return. The challenge now was to create a new order, one that was both efficient and just. It could only arise, however, if the role of government was radically changed.

What Roosevelt was moving toward was outlined in one of the best-selling books of 1932, Stuart Chase's A New Deal.* A modern government, said Chase, could manage the economy simply by inflating or deflating the money supply. "If the government borrowed or inflated for a bold program of public works which absorbed two or three million of the unemployed directly—thus feeding huge new streams into the river bed of purchasing power—thus stimulating industry—thus causing more of the unemployed to be absorbed as food and clothing workers—thus adding to purchasing power again—thus checking the domestic price fall— thus strengthening the banks . . ." the result would be a new deal all around.[66] There were other things as well—lower tariffs, higher taxes on the rich, unemployment insurance for workers—but the first thing had to be economic revival.

Radicals and liberals however did not flock to Roosevelt's side. To the New Republic he was "an untried jockey on a very lame horse."[67] The Depression had revived the Socialist party, and that was where the New Republic placed its bet.

From 1924 to 1928 the Socialist party was "all but dead."[68] But in 1928 the party had nominated for president an obscure forty-four-year-old Social Gospel minister, Norman Thomas. Even within the Socialist party he was virtually unknown outside New York. He drew 275,000 votes that

---

* The expression "a new deal" derived from frontier poker games.

year. With the Depression, disaffected liberals who had no faith in either Communism or the Democratic party were won over by Thomas, who was a superb public speaker. This onetime newsboy for Harding and the *Marion Star* attracted an entire generation of college students into radical, non-Communist politics. But the Socialist party he led was a very different creature from that led by Debs, with few farmers, few industrial workers. It was like Thomas himself, educated and middle class.

Yet it failed to attract the educated, middle-class radicals who had become hooked on the somewhat diluted, Americanized brand of Joe Stalin virility drops. More than fifty writers and intellectuals (including Edmund Wilson, Sherwood Anderson, Sidney Hook, Matthew Josephson, John Dos Passos, Langston Hughes, and Lincoln Steffens) published a pamphlet called "Culture and Crisis," subtitled "An Open Letter to the Writers, Artists, Teachers, Physicians, Engineers, Scientists and Other Professional Workers of America." It called on them to vote Communist in the November election.

Hoover, meanwhile, was running for reelection on the basis of speeches that sounded like detailed reports from the chief accountant. How anyone stayed awake through them is hard to imagine.[69] Hoover could not win the ongoing argument no matter what he said. He was damned for running a deficit budget every year. Yet he was also damned for not spending more on public works—and it was his public works that were running up the deficits.

In the last week of the campaign, he traveled from Washington to Palo Alto on a speaking tour, most of it through the farmlands. And there the harvest was in, prices crashing. Wheat had been selling for most of the year at 50 cents a bushel. In Nebraska it now sold for 18 cents, in Montana for 12 cents.[70] Corn prices had also collapsed. Cotton was selling for 3 cents a pound. By this time the Cotton Stabilization Corporation had spent nearly $130 million on cotton that was worth about $40 million—provided it stayed off the market. Most of the cotton, like most of the wheat being held by the Federal Farm Board, was simply given quietly to the Red Cross for relief. Hoover's belief that farmers would cooperate to stabilize production had never stood the least chance of success. What he had done by creating the FFB was to make certain they would raise output, because he had provided them with an ultimate buyer—the taxpayer. When this unpleasant truth was finally admitted, the FFB was wound up, a $370 million failure. McNary-Haugenism, against which Hoover had fought hard and long, might have been cheaper. And the farmers were going to vote for Roosevelt, anyway.

To William Allen White, traveling west with Hoover, the memory of the 1929 inaugural address came flooding back—the vision that had seemed so bright, of a government that was competent and compassionate; of a country growing richer and happier than almost anyone had the right to imagine. He recalled excitement and joy so strong that not even the cold and rain of that March day could affect them. Then, less than four years later, Hoover was once more speaking into a microphone, once more was addressing his countrymen, this time from a railroad train halted in the Nevada desert, a mere speck in a vast white landscape ringed with black mountains. "His weariness shows in his slumping torso. His eyes lack luster and are red-rimmed with care. And over the radio, to his friends and supporters, his voice comes tired—how infinitely tired!—and his words how hollow and how sad in disillusionment. He has fought the good fight—and lost."[71]

On election night he went to bed early, knowing he had been defeated, and for the first time since entering government service Hoover slept for eleven hours.[72]

29. Loose Ends

I

The election of 1932 saw the victory of what soon became known as the New Deal coalition—western and southern, urban and rural, blacks, Catholics, and Jews. It set the shape of American political life for the next forty years, in which the Democratic party was, in effect, the "natural" party of government. It was the most epochal victory since the election of 1860, which brought Lincoln to power on a pledge to save the Union.

Roosevelt's campaign had, by way of contrast, made no monumental promises; merely the repeal of Prohibition and a 25 percent cut in federal spending. Nor did he win by holding a mirror up to nature in which the American people could see themselves as they were—harried, depressed, impoverished. What Roosevelt held up was a piece of blank canvas on which they could outline for themselves their desire for a different world.

Whatever the future really held was as much a mystery to Roosevelt as it was to everyone else. Yet no coup d'etat, no revolution, no civil war, could have marked a break with the past more clearly than this election. The voting booth is a blunt instrument. It offers crude choices, it gives crude replies. Political commentators and political scientists pore over most election results, looking for the meaning, like Roman haruspices sorting through the entrails of slaughtered sheep.

The meaning of the 1932 election, however, is plain: it marked the overt acceptance of the modern world, no matter what that involved. The Twenties was a no-man's land, torn between the nineteenth century and the twentieth. As this book has amply shown, this split ran clear through American life. The frontier was cheek by jowl with the Machine Age. In

1926 a band of Apache Indians crossed the border into Arizona and attacked the ranch of Francisco Fimores, killing his wife and kidnaping his son. With an armed band of a dozen friends and neighbors, Fimores chased the Apaches deep into Mexico. Just as in the movies, the rescue party was ambushed and only one survived to tell the tale.[1] In November 1929 a Union Pacific train was derailed in the middle of Wyoming. Out from the bushes came a nervous man with fair hair and a .38 revolver. He proceeded to hold up the passengers, took $800 from them, and galloped away. He lacked the style of Jesse James but the general approach was the same.[2]

In a state such as South Dakota, many of the original white settlers were still alive in the Twenties. In Oklahoma, a state only since 1907, governors were regularly impeached, and frontier "justice" flourished. Orderly government involved habits not learned overnight.

The same split between two worlds, two centuries, prevailed in the realm of ideas. If there was one point on which all economists agreed, it was that economies had built-in elements that made them bob up like corks, no matter how far down they were dragged. This was certainly true of nineteenth-century economic orders. They did right themselves after a while with virtually no help from government. But a modern economy, with its complicated debt structure and its constant need for new long-term investment, is a different matter. Savings virtually disappeared in 1931, as people began struggling to pay off their debts. Result—investment virtually disappeared in 1932. And without new investment there could be no recovery. The modern economic order had come into existence almost unnoticed. But it was there, ticking away alongside outworn economic ideas.

The same was true of social values. Americans believed in self-help and the caring, close-knit community. Yet most people now depended on wages, and communities had come unraveled. Besides, pioneer America was both a young country and a country of the young. The Twenties saw the graying of America. The over-sixty-fives were the fastest-growing part of the population. In a wage-based economy provision had to be made for them. Recognition of that fact, however, was a long time in coming.

The Depression made it impossible to continue the tug-of-war between two worlds that had given tension and form to the Twenties. Much of what we think of as the New Deal had been created by Hoover or anticipated by him before Roosevelt's election. In the Reconstruction Finance Corporation the government intervened directly in the peacetime economy for the first time; its creation marked the beginning of the mixed economy. In the Emergency Relief and Construction Act the federal government for the first time assumed responsibility for relief. By 1933 it was funding 80 percent of state and local relief spending. With the creation of the Federal Farm Board the federal government assumed responsibility for making up the incomes of farmers with taxpayers' money. The Federal Home Loan Banks made the federal government an active partner in promoting home ownership. The most important change, however, the one from which the others flowed, was the changed role of the presidency.

Hoover presided over a country that expected him to beat the Depression. No president had ever assumed responsibility for managing the American economy. The business of government since 1776 had been limited to war, diplomacy, and foreign trade. It was not expected to create prosperity. Even a president as committed to reform as Wilson was able, up to 1917, to do all his work in four or five hours a day.

Hoover assumed complete responsibility for overcoming the Depression. Alas, there was no solution to it. The banks were shaky, business paralyzed, farmers impoverished, charities inadequate, unions demoralized, cities and states broke, intellectuals misled, and all were looking to the federal government to play the role of the knight in shining armor. There was no escape, not even in escapism. In the movies made during the Depression local government is invariably shown as ineffective and corrupt, whereas the federal government is a benign, incorruptible deity. But there was no knight in shining armor. Had there been a way to beat the Depression, Hoover or Roosevelt would have found it.

Hoover was described by Henry Stimson as being "capable of more prolonged and intense intellectual effort" than any president he knew,[4] and Stimson served under every president from Teddy Roosevelt to Harry Truman. Roosevelt was pragmatic and flexible. In the Brain Trust he enjoyed the dedicated service of some of the most capable men ever brought into American government. But no twitching of the reins of power would ever conquer the Depression, and for one overriding reason: to restore demand on the scale required by government action would have first destroyed money and then would have destroyed the government. It would have had to borrow at least $20 billion a year for several years, at a time when the entire nation's income had fallen to $39 billion a year. Unable to borrow so much from so little, it would have had to run the printing presses until the money turned out was worth less than the paper used. Roosevelt, like Hoover, became a wound-dresser; he did, however, apply the bandages with greater flair.

Small doses of inflation could help to ease the agony and, here and there, put people back to work. In 1936 the bonus was paid, a $2.3 billion boost that fueled the mild upturn of 1937, followed by the downturn of 1938. What made the Depression so appalling a human tragedy was that it could be overcome only by an event as awesome, as terrifying, and as irresistible as the Depression itself. And that was the Second World War, a conflict that was not contrived, but part of the bedrock of the twentieth century. Only with the onset of the war was borrowing and spending on the scale required finally possible. A government can create money; it cannot create belief in it. Hoover could not overcome the Depression, nor could Roosevelt, nor could any man.

The important things that Hoover did were done because they had to be done, but Hoover, with one foot in the nineteenth century, hated having to do them. In trying to defeat the Depression he had created the modern presidency—the presidency of wildly inflated expectations: the "manager of the economy" presidency; the "toughest-job-in-the-world" presidency; the crisis-management presidency. When Hoover left office, William Allen White wrote a dispassionate farewell under the title, "Herbert Hoover—The Last of the Old Presidents or the First of the New?" The short answer is, "Both."

II

For four years Harding's drumlike memorial stood undedicated in isolated splendor outside Marion, Ohio. Coolidge would not go near it. It fell to Hoover to do the decent thing, and on a warm June day in 1931 he made a hurried visit, dedicated the memorial, and spoke of how Harding's tragedy had been giving his trust to false friends. Harry M. Daugherty, sitting in the first row of seats, seemed to flush angrily during Hoover's brief peroration.

As for Fall, the wheels of justice ground so slowly that he did not go on trial until the week of the crash. Found guilty of corruption, he was sentenced to a year in prison and a fine of $100,000. He appealed, and lost. He entered the state prison at Santa Fe, New Mexico, in July 1931. Doheny had meanwhile been tried for giving the bribe Fall had been convicted of taking. But Doheny was acquitted. Intent is a crucial element in any bribery conviction. Doheny was always an excellent witness for himself. There was nothing in the evidence to disprove his contention that he had never intended to bribe Fall; simply to help an old friend in a pinch. In the course of his long life, no one ever pinned a lie on Doheny.

There were many people, moreover, who believed that Fall had been too harshly treated. He refused to take the stand in his own defense. He had admitted to a lie, when he named Ned McLean as the source of the $100,000 loan. He had shown appalling judgment in awarding the Elk Hills lease without competitive bidding. He had associated with Sinclair, who was involved in various operations that smacked of fraud. Fall, such people believed, was the victim of bad luck and bad judgment, not an out-

and-out crook. What he had done in granting the leases was to live up to his anticonservationist views. He was going to lease the oil lands. That had been obvious well in advance.

Fall went to prison penniless. The government never collected the $100,000 fine. Doheny's oil company foreclosed on the Three Rivers Ranch and evicted Fall from his home. The company was no longer run by Doheny, who had vowed that Fall would never want for anything. Doheny's son, the bearer of the little black bag containing the money for Albert Fall, had died in a bizarre shooting in a Washington office. Doheny grieved for his dead son until he went insane.

The Great Ponzi went to prison in 1926 for larceny and mail fraud connected with his Florida real estate swindle. Released in 1934 he went to Italy, became active in the Fascist party, and was in time appointed manager of LATI, the Italian state airline.

From Greece, Insull resisted efforts to extradite him, to no avail. In 1934 he was returned to the United States and tried for mail fraud. It took the jury five minutes to decide that he was innocent. The indictment arose mainly from a Depression-born hunger for business villains on whom the country's misery could be blamed. Attempting to revile him for his wealth, the prosecution produced his income tax returns, showing that he had earned $500,000 a year from his directorships. It backfired when the defense produced receipts to show that he gave more than $500,000 to charity each year.

The prosecutions continued, however. In 1935 the state of Illinois prosecuted him on a charge of embezzlement. He was once again acquitted. Three months later he was back in federal court, charged with violating the Bankruptcy Act. And again he was acquitted. The fact was, Insull had never been a crook. The methods by which he did business were legal and, to his mind, ethical. These acquittals notwithstanding, Insull became the scapegoat for an entire generation of financiers who straddled the old order and the new.

Although the Insull crash was the biggest business failure in American history, the operating companies went on selling electricity and gas at a profit. Eighty percent of the various Insull securities were in time redeemed. Even his personal creditors lost only a modest fraction of the $16 million he owed at the time he went bankrupt. The utilities empire he had created was still producing nearly 15 percent of the country's light and power at the time of his death, in poverty, in a Paris Metro station in 1938.

William Durant's last automobile venture, Durant Motors Incorporated, went into liquidation in 1933. The man who founded General Motors was at last out of the automobile business. He was broke and became the proprietor, with the help of friends, of a lunch counter.

In 1936 Richard Whitney, president of the New York Stock Exchange and longtime treasurer of the New York Yacht Club, took $150,200 of the club's bonds and used them as collateral for a loan he desperately needed. That is, he stole $150,200. He was meanwhile looting the NYSE's Gratuity Fund, which was supposed to look after the families of deceased Exchange employees. In 1938 his malefactions caught up with him and Whitney was convicted of embezzlement. He was for several years one of Sing Sing's "model" prisoners.

Larry Fay was also a model of sorts. It was he who had created the fashion among Twenties gangsters for wearing solid-color shirts with loud neckties and very expensive suits. Fay spent a fortune every year on clothes. As the years went by, he survived numerous brushes with both the law and mobsters, only to fall victim to the share-the-work movement of late 1932.

On December 30 he posted a notice in the Club Casa Blanca, successor to the padlocked Club El Fey, which informed all employees that their pay was going to be cut and their hours shortened to create jobs for other people. Two nights later Fay's doorman, Edward Maloney, arrived at the club evidently drunk and brooding on the impending cut in his $100-a-week pay. He began arguing with Fay, pulled out a gun, and shot him dead.

As for Tex Guinan, she barely survived the repeal of Prohibition. She died in November 1933.

In July that same year the *New York Times* had begun to offer something different in news services. It ran a front page box under the heading *The Kidnaping Situation*. A regular feature for some time thereafter, it carried an up-to-date summary of recent abductions—the names of those kidnaped, ransoms paid, victims released or found dead, kidnapers caught.

The Lindbergh kidnaping remained unsolved, although one of Irey's agents, Arthur Madden, three times told the investigators of the crime how to find the man they were looking for. Money from the ransom had been found circulating in the Bronx. The New York Traffic License Bureau kept its Bronx registrations at the Bronx County Courthouse, separate from all the other boroughs. The ransom notes were in so strange a hand that it would have been comparatively easy to discover if the person who had written the notes had ever registered a car in the Bronx. Nothing was done to follow up this suggestion.

In 1935 Bruno Richard Hauptmann was tracked to his Bronx home after passing more of the ransom money. Portions of the ladder left at Hopewell had been cut from wood in Hauptmann's attic. The bulk of the ransom money was found in his garage. His handwriting matched that on the ransom notes, and was on file at the Bronx County Courthouse. Hauptmann was convicted of kidnaping and murder and was executed for his crime.

In May 1928 an attempt was made to blow up the Queens home of Robert G. Elliott, official executioner of New York, New Jersey, Pennsylvania, and Massachusetts. It was Elliott who had executed Sacco and Vanzetti. The explosion wrecked the front of his house, but Elliott and his family were unscathed. Four years later, in 1932, a bomb shattered Judge Thayer's home, inflicting terrible injuries on his wife.

The court interpreter, Joseph Ross, whom Vanzetti had accused of being favorable to the prosecution (Ross even named his son Webster Thayer Ross) had gone to jail for trying to bribe a judge. Fuller's chief legal adviser, Attorney General Arthur K. Reading, had been removed from office for corruption. Reading had taken a $25,000 bribe. The presence in a capital case of proven crooks did not inspire confidence in the result. Even the very conservative president of the Massachusetts bar, George R. Nutter, in December 1928 protested at the low standards of justice in the Commonwealth, where judges and public alike "accept defects in judicial procedure as an imposition of Providence. . . . The Sacco-Vanzetti case showed serious imperfections in our method of administering justice." Ten years later Massachusetts responded to such criticisms by revising its appellate procedures so that had another case like that of Sacco and Vanzetti come up before its courts they would have received a new trial. This was at least a partial admission that they had not received full justice. In 1977 the Massachusetts legislature, by resolution, acknowledged that an injustice had been done.

Released from Atlanta penitentiary, Marcus Garvey returned to Jamaica. His burning ambition to lead a return to Africa which would both free Africans and realize the destiny of all black peoples remained unrealized. When he died in London in 1940 he was destitute and virtually forgotten. But twenty-five years later, following Jamaican independence, his remains were taken back to his native soil for a state funeral. The Jamaican government created the Marcus Garvey Prize for Human Rights. Its first recipient was Martin Luther King, Jr.

Aimee Semple McPherson died in 1944, of a drug overdose. Frank Lloyd Wright spent the early 1930s giving speeches and lecturing from time to time at the New School for Social Research. At sixty-five Wright was widely scorned, and his career seemed at an end. Yet the audiences he drew—and whom he addressed for thirty-five or forty dollars—sustained his faith. Wherever he went the hall was sure to be packed with young men and women; intelligent, enthusiastic, critical, yet eager to learn about "Organic Architecture" or "The Natural House."

The city of Chicago was planning a Century of Progress Exhibition for 1933, Depression or no Depression. The architects chosen to design it did not include Wright, to the fury of Wright's growing body of admirers. Protest meetings were held at the University Club and the New School for Social Research. At a stormy meeting at Town Hall in New York, Raymond Hood, one of the members of the commission to select architects for the project, explained why Wright had been excluded. He was, said Hood, "too much of an individualist."

In the summer of 1932 Wright created the Taliesin Fellowship, which would bring more than twenty apprentices to work at Taliesin III, each of them paying a fee of $650. The first class assembled on October 1, 1932. If Wright could not make the future one way, he would do it another.

Briton Hadden might have become rich enough to own the Yankees had he not died in February 1929 at the age of thirty-one. He died in effect as the result of a bad cold. His resistance was lowered, he picked up a streptococcal infection, and succumbed to pneumonia. A decade later one shot of penicillin would have saved him.

In the world of belles lettres, Sinclair Lewis in 1930 became the first American to win the Nobel Prize for Literature. There was surprise even among his admirers. Few of his fellow writers felt that American letters had been honored by Lewis's award. By 1933 he was back where he was before he wrote *Main Street*, hacking away, but the sums these days were much larger.

Fitzgerald also earned more money when the Depression was at its worst than at any other time of his life; all of it earned from short stories. In the spring of 1932 he moved into a rambling, ramshackle mansion set in twenty-eight semirural acres outside Baltimore. The huge, ugly old house was named La Paix, and with Zelda's madness peace was something Fitzgerald sorely needed. Yet, thought the adolescent son of the owner of Fitzgerald's new home, "To the once famous but temporarily eclipsed author La Paix must have seemed the end of the line." Zelda roamed the grounds in sleeveless summer dresses and ballet slippers, or sat beside a small, wind-up Victrola, playing over and over again one of the great song hits of the Twenties, "Valencia."

The fate that Fitzgerald dreaded most, with his intense nature a natural fear perhaps, was what he called "emotional bankruptcy." And in the way of the world as it is, that was of course to be his fate, a burnt-out case at the time of his death in 1940 at the age of forty-four. Hemingway had meanwhile written *For Whom the Bell Tolls*, arresting the decline of his reputation. He had become, in fact, a larger-than-life figure, the heavyweight champion of American literature.

After beating Dempsey for the second time, Tunney was still under contract to fight for Rickard at least once more. Dempsey, offered the fight, refused it. In August 1928 Tunney defended his title against a New Zealand blacksmith named Tom Heeney, known as "the Hard Rock from Down Under." Heeney was scientifically beaten to a pulp for eleven rounds before the referee stopped the fight. For this Tunney received $525,000. When it turned out that Rickard had lost $155,000 on the fight, which had failed to attract much interest, Tunney offered to make up half the loss! Rickard, sporting in his own way, declined to accept Tunney's money. Having earned $2 million for three championship fights, Tunney quit the ring forever. After announcing his retirement he broke into a jig and shouted exuberantly, "I am free, free, free!" A few months later he married Polly Lauder, twenty-one, a Greenwich, Connecticut, heiress to a steel fortune.

In January 1929 Rickard died at the age of 58. Dempsey was holding his hand. A dandy in life, sporting a wide-brimmed fedora, a gold-topped cane, and huge Havana cigars, Rickard in death lay in state at Madison Square Garden in a huge bronze "gangster's special" coffin, while thousands of fight fans reverently filed past. Dempsey, cleaned out by the crash, went into the restaurant business and became a New York landmark for nearly half a century.

For Bobby Jones, the bottom of his career had been the day he walked off the course at St. Andrews in 1921 and quit in the middle of a round. The top came appropriately at St. Andrews, nine years later, when he won the hardest tournament of all, the British Amateur, with its seven elimination rounds and the thirty-six hole showdown that determined the winner. That year, 1930, he was to win the grand slam, golf's "Impregnable Quadrilateral"—the U.S. Amateur, the U.S. Open, the British Amateur, and the British Open. With no kingdoms left to conquer, he retired from competition. Bobby Jones left golf as everyone wanted to see him go—as undisputed champion.

There was one last glorious chapter for Tilden as well before the book was closed. In 1930 he went to Wimbledon for what was certain to be the last time. He was thirty-seven years old and considered washed-up. Yet he went on to win every match he played, becoming the oldest Wimbledon singles champion ever. It was the perfect ending to his amateur career. After that he turned professional, playing hundreds of meaningless games against other aging players.

As Tilden grew older, he became less cautious. There were towns that he could not go back to, clubs from which he was tacitly barred. In 1946 the Los Angeles police arrested him in a car whose other occupant was a fourteen-year-old boy named Bobby with an unbuttoned fly. Over the despairing pleas of his lawyers to plead "not guilty," Tilden did the sporting thing and freely confessed. He was sentenced to a year in the county jail. In 1949 there was another arrest, another spell in jail. In his last years he literally stank. Once so fastidious, he ceased to take showers or bathe, even after a tennis match. He pawned his trophies to pay for food, slept on the couches of his few remaining friends, and died in 1953 at the age of sixty from a heart attack.

The sporting hero of the Twenties had seemed washed up all the way back in 1925. Ruth's overeating, heavy drinking, and late nights with a dizzying number of women brought on a physical collapse, the breakup of his marriage, a $5,000 fine from the Yankees' manager and the threat of indefinite suspension. Faced with losing forever the one thing that he really loved—the chance to play baseball—Ruth rose like a phoenix from the ashes of illness and disgrace. Ruth between the ages of thirty-two and thirty-seven put on a display of hitting that has never been surpassed. In those six years he averaged 50 home runs a year, a batting average of .354 and 155 runs batted in. In 1927 he hit 60 home runs in 154 games (a record which still stands), and the Yankees that year were probably the greatest baseball team ever.

By 1932, however, as with all athletes as they approach forty, the legs were beginning to go. More and more, Ruth had to leave a game in the seventh inning to let a younger player take over in center field. His last World Series came that fall, when the Yankees played the Cubs. The Yankees won the first two games at home before traveling to Chicago. When they arrived, Ruth and his second wife were spat on as they entered their hotel. In pregame practice at Wrigley Field, Ruth was pelted with lemons. The real struggle was not between the Yankees and the Cubs, but between Ruth and the Cub fans.

When he came up to bat third in the first inning the stands erupted with cries of "Potbelly!" "Fatso!" "Bastard!" Even "Nigger!" To the Cubs fans, Ruth alone stood between their team and victory. Ruth proceeded to hit a three-run homer. When he came up to bat in the fifth inning the score was tied 4–4. The Cubs crowded the dugout steps, screaming at Ruth. The 50,000 fans raised a terrific din when strike one was called, followed by two balls. The next delivery was a strike. Ruth, grinning, held up two fingers. The Cubs began spilling out of the dugout.

Ruth waved them back and called out to the pitcher, Charlie Root, "I'm gonna cut the next pitch right down your fuckin' throat!" The gesture he made to punctuate this statement, pointing at Root, has gone down in baseball legend as the time Babe Ruth called a home run. The pitch from Root was a change-up, curving low and away. Ruth reached for it and hit a line-drive homer deep into the center-field bleachers. An overjoyed Ruth trotted around the bases, hands clasped over his head, laughing and exulting, "You, lucky, lucky bum!" From a box near home plate, Franklin D. Roosevelt, Yankee fan and presidential candidate, looked on, laughing, applauding, following Ruth's progress with evident glee. The Yankees won the game and later the Series 4–0.

Ruth's drinking pal, Bix Beiderbecke, meanwhile had lost himself in countless bottles. In 1929 Whiteman had sent him home to Davenport to dry out. When the boy wonder of jazz tried to get back to work in 1930, however, he found he was just one more unemployed musician; one of thousands. In 1931 he died of pneumonia, aged twenty-eight. It was really the liquor that killed him.

Jelly Roll Morton finally had a chance to put his genius on record and the discs he made with his Red Hot Peppers in the late 1920s stand as proof of his incomparable talent. To many jazz enthusiasts, this was by far the best band of the era. But in 1930 it broke up. Jelly had never been an easy man to work with. By 1932 the diamonds he had sported (even on his underwear) had gone into pawn. He eked out a living substituting for pianists who drank too much to show up every night. He died in Los Angeles in 1941, poor, but with a growing reputation among serious jazz critics.

And Fred Beal, with whom this book began, was in Russia, deeply disenchanted with the workers' paradise. What he found was a reality he could never have imagined—hordes of orphaned children, mobs of beggars in rags, rapacious Communist officials, near-starvation among the working class; worst of all was the cruelty, cynicism, and savagery of Soviet power. He and the people who had fled with him from North Carolina sought to return to the United States, and prison, only to find themselves already prisoners in their supposed haven.

It took a press campaign mounted by the ACLU to force the Comintern to let them go. Back in the United States, Beal was so horrified by what he saw of the Depression that he allowed himself to be talked into going back to Russia. Nothing he had seen weakened his devotion to the cause in which he believed. So he returned, this time to work in a tractor plant in the Ukraine. There he saw the true nature of collectivization— the murder of 4 million kulaks ("rich" peasants who owned perhaps two cows and a plot of land the size of a tennis court). Murder was the basis of Stalinist rule, the logical and inevitable development of all Communist government. By a ruse, Fred Beal slipped out of the Soviet Union in 1933. After five years in hiding, in which he wrote his autobiography, denouncing communism, he was betrayed to the police. In 1938 he entered the North Carolina penitentiary. He was pardoned and set free in 1942, soon slipping back into the obscurity in which he had spent that other war, which now seemed so far, far away, part of another age, a different world.

Notes

CHAPTER 1

1. The epidemic's course at Camp Devens is followed in Alfred W. Crosby, Jr., *Epidemic and Peace, 1918* (Westport, Conn., 1976), pp. 4–11.
2. Louis Weinstein, "Influenza—1918, A Revisit," *New England Journal of Medicine*, May 6, 1976. The virtually simultaneous appearance on opposite sides of the world of this deadly and still unidentified virus has led the British astrologer Sir Fred Hoyle to suggest in recent years that life may have been brought to Earth from outer space, and that life forms still reach this planet from other parts of the universe.
3. Crosby, op. cit., pp. 205–206.
4. One noted demographer maintains that at least 20 million died in India alone: Kingsley Davis, *The Population of India and Pakistan* (Princeton, N.J., 1951), p. 41.
5. Francis Russell, *The Great Interlude* (New York, 1964), pp. 25–26.
6. Ruth Rosen and Sue Davidson, eds., *The Maimie Papers* (Old Westbury, New York, 1977), pp. 412–13.
7. Fred E. Beal, *Proletarian Journey* (New York, 1937), pp. 66–67.
8. Ibid.
9. Sanford Bates, *Prisons and Beyond* (New York, 1937), p. 3.
10. Burl Noggle, *Into the Twenties* (Urbana, Ill., 1974), p. 14.
11. Quoted in Frederic L. Paxson, *Postwar Years, Normalcy 1918–1923* (Berkeley & Los Angeles, 1948), p. 7.
12. Niven Bush, *Briton Hadden* (New York, 1949), pp. 40–43.
13. Burke Davis, *The Billy Mitchell Affair* (New York, 1967), p. 3.
14. Beal, p. 69.
15. Charles Rumford Walker, *Steel: The Diary of a Furnace Worker* (Boston, 1922), p. 2.
16. Arthur Walworth, *Woodrow Wilson*, vol. 2 (New York, 1965), pp. 268–69.
17. Francis Russell, *Tragedy at Dedham* (New York, 1962), p. 83.
18. Arthur M. Schlesinger, Jr., *The Crisis of the Old Order* (Boston, 1957), p. 30.
19. Quoted in Arthur Link, *Wilson: The New Freedom* (Princeton, N.J., 1956), p. 69.
20. J. M. Keynes, "When the Big Four Met," *New Republic*, December 24, 1919.
21. The mild stroke theory is advanced in Edwin A. Weinstein, "Woodrow Wilson's Neuro-

logic Illness," *Journal of American History*, September, 1970. A brain thrombosis—not quite the same thing as a stroke—is posited by Gene Smith, *When the Cheering Stopped* (New York, 1964), pp. 100–101.

22. According to Wilson's valet, Irwin Hood Hoover, *Forty-Two Years at the White House* (Boston, 1934), pp. 98–99: "He went to bed ostensibly with a cold. When he got on his feet again he was a different man . . . he was never the same after this little spell of sickness."
23. Herbert Hoover, *Memoirs*, vol. 1, *Years of Adventure* (New York, 1951), p. 461.
24. David M. Burner, *Herbert Hoover: A Public Life* (New York, 1979), pp. 116–18.
25. J. M. Keynes, *The Economic Consequences of the Peace* (London, 1919), p. 257 f.
26. Herbert Hoover, op. cit.
27. Eugene Lyons, *Herbert Hoover* (New York, 1940), p. 133.
28. Louis Adamic, "The Assassin of Wilson," *American Mercury*, October 1930.
29. Edmund W. Starling, *Starling of the White House* (New York, 1946), p. 152.
30. Smith, op. cit., pp. 77–79; Mrs. Wilson admitted that she was in tears—but only because her husband's lofty speech had moved her deeply. Edith Bolling Wilson, *My Memoir* (Indianapolis, 1939), p. 338.
31. Ibid., pp. 343–44; Irwin Hood Hoover, op. cit., pp. 100–103.
32. Josephus Daniels, *The Wilson Era: Years of War and After 1917–1923* (Chapel Hill, N.C., 1946), p. 513.
33. Wilson, op. cit., p. 357; Smith, op. cit., pp. 126–28; Hoover, op. cit., p. 105.
34. Dixon Wecter, *When Johnny Comes Marching Home* (Boston, 1944), pp. 284–86.
35. Kenneth S. Davis, *The Hero* (Garden City, N.Y., 1959), p. 89.
36. *New Republic*, July 27, 1921.

CHAPTER 2

1. Harold A. Littledale, "Our Debt of Honor," *Nation*, November 17, 1920.
2. On the principal limitations of the Vocational Rehabilitation Act and the Federal Board for Vocational Education, see James R. Mock and Evangeline Thurber, *Report on Demobilization* (Norman, Okla., 1944), pp. 213–15.
3. On the ceremonies welcoming returning veterans, see Dixon Wecter, *When Johnny Comes Marching Home* (Boston, 1944), pp. 300–304.
4. *Survey*, April 5, 1919.
5. Maurice R. Davie, *Problems of City Life* (New York, 1932), p. 203.
6. On the wartime inflation, see U.S. President's Conference, *Recent Economic Changes* (Washington, D.C., 1929), vol. 1; Elmus R. Wicker, *Federal Reserve Monetary Policy 1917–1933* (New York, 1966), pp. 21–23.
7. *Recent Economic Changes*, p. 849.
8. Len De Caux, *Labor Radical* (Boston, 1970), p. 38.
9. Paul F. Brissenden, *The Earnings of Factory Workers 1899–1927* (New York, 1929), p. 46.
10. Gerald Rosenblum, *Immigrant Workers* (New York, 1973), pp. 67–68.
11. *Time*, March 17, 1923; *Nation*, April 9, 1924. More than a dozen states had child-labor laws which kept the under-14s out of the factories, but not out of the fields. Farmers relied heavily on cheap child labor, and most state legislatures were highly responsive to farmers' interests.
12. *Nation*, January 3, 1920.
13. Charles C. Chapman, *The Development of American Business and Banking Thought 1913–1936* (New York, 1936).
14. Louis Witte, *The Government in Labor Disputes* (New York, 1932), p. 183
15. Sidney Howard and Robert Dunn, *The Labor Spy* (New York, 1924), p. 18.
16. Robert L. Friedheim, *The Seattle General Strike* (Seattle, Wash., 1964), p. 11.
17. Anna Louise Strong, *I Change Worlds* (New York, 1935), pp. 74–75.

18. His own account of the strike modestly understates his role in it: Harvey O'Connor, *Revolution in Seattle* (New York, 1964).
19. William McDonald, "The Seattle Strike and After" *Nation*, March 29, 1919; Friedheim, op. cit., p. 113.
20. Robert Morss Lovett, "The Trial of the Communists," *Nation*, August 14, 1920; Friedheim, op. cit., p. 118.
21. A fact that Darrow used to show up Hansen as a charlatan: "Arguments of Clarence Darrow in the Case of the Communist Labor Party in the Criminal Court, Chicago." (Chicago, 1920).
22. *Survey*, Jan. 15, 1924.
23. Communists did try, however, to involve themselves in the strike: Benjamin Gitlow, *The Whole of Their Lives* (New York, 1948), pp. 55–56.
24. Morris Markey, "The Strange Death of Starr Faithfull," in Ishbell Leighton, ed., *The Aspirin Age* (Garden City, N.Y., 1949).
25. Francis Russell, *The Great Interlude* (New York, 1962), pp. 45–46.
26. Donald R. McCoy, *Calvin Coolidge* (New York, 1967), p. 92.
27. Claude M. Fuess, *Calvin Coolidge* (Boston, 1940), p. 227.
28. "Boston union labor refused to make new uniforms for them": Wecter, op. cit., p. 375; cf. Robert K. Murray, *Red Scare* (New York, 1965), p. 133.
29. Mary Heaton Vorse, *Men and Steel* (New York, 1920), p. 21.
30. According to the Interchurch World Movement: "In some plants even the 36-hour turn is not unknown." *Report on the Steel Strike* (New York, 1920), p. 47; the average week in steel in 1919 was 69 hours; for men working at blast furnaces it was 82 hours. Ibid., p. 54.
31. Kirby Page, "The US Steel Corporation," *Atlantic*, May 1922.
32. Charles Rumford Walker, *Steel: The Diary of a Furnace Worker* (Boston, 1922), p. 51.
33. U.S. Senate, Committee on Labor and Education, *Investigation of the Strike in the Steel Industry*, Sixty-sixth Congress, 1st session (Washington, D.C., 1919), p. 163.
34. Living conditions in steel towns were so bad that deaths from pneumonia were as common as deaths from accidents in the mills. Horace B. Davis, *Labor and Steel* (London, 1933), p. 55.
35. Theodore Draper, *The Roots of American Communism* (New York, 1957), p. 311.
36. On the origins of the National Commmmittee for Organizing Iron and Steel Workers, see William Z. Foster, *Pages from a Worker's Life* (New York, 1939); and David Brody, *Labor in Crisis: The Steel Strike of 1919* (Philadelphia, 1965), pp. 61–63, 96–97.
37. Selig Perlman and Philip Taft, *Labor Movements*, vol. 4, *History of Labor in the United States 1896–1932* (New York, 1935), remark that Fanny Sellins "was killed under especially revolting circumstances." p. 464. For a detailed account, which throws light on the tactics of company thugs in this period, see Elizabeth Gurley Flynn, *The Rebel Girl* (New York, 1973), pp. 291–92.
38. Foster's organizing tactics are described in the Interchurch World Movement, *Report*, pp. 156–59.
39. Brody, op. cit., casts doubt on this figure, p. 113. It came from the National Committee and may well have been inflated. To have brought out the number Brody favors— 250,000—would nevertheless have been an unprecedented achievement.
40. Yet men would walk miles through snow and in freezing temperatures to reach the nonsteel towns where union meetings were being held. Interchurch World Movement, *Public Opinion and the Steel Strike* (New York, 1921), p. 35.
41. Survey, November 8, 1919.
42. Vorse, op. cit., p. 160; on the reign of terror, see chap. 3, "Civil Rights in Western Pennsylvania," in *Public Opinion and the Steel Strike*.
43. Irving Berstein, *The Lean Years* (Boston, 1959), p. 51.
44. On the silence of the newspapers, see *Public Opinion and the Steel Strike*, pp. 85–98.

45. An estimated 30,000 black strikebreakers were brought into the mills: Brody, op. cit., p. 162.
46. S. Adele Shaw, "Closed Towns," *Survey*, November 8, 1919.
47. Vorse, op. cit., p. 82.
48. Arthur Gleason, "Company Owned Americans," *Nation*, June 12, 1920.
49. Arthur Gleason, "Private Ownership of Public Officials," *Nation*, May 29, 1920.
50. Ibid.
51. On the wave of forcible evictions in Mingo County after the UMW launched its 1920 organizing drive, see Winthrop D. Lane, *Civil War in West Virginia* (New York, 1921), pp. 47–48.
52. Ibid., p. 48.
53. Neil Birkenshaw, "Labor's Valley Forge," *Nation*, December 8, 1920.
54. Perlman and Taft, p. 481.
55. *New York Times*, August 29–September 4, 1921.
56. Winthrop Lane, "West Virginia—Civil War in the Coal Fields," *Survey*, November 5, 1921; James M. Cain, "The Battleground of Coal," *Atlantic*, October 1922.
57. Melvyn Dubovsky and Warren Van Tine, *John L. Lewis* (New York, 1973), pp. 76–78.
58. *International Organization etc.* v. *Red Jacket C.C.&C. Co.* 18 Fed. (2nd) 389 (C.C.A. 4th, 1927).
59. McAlister Coleman, "Herrin," *Survey*, October 1, 1924.
60. The most thorough, the most reliable account of the Herrin massacre is Paul M. Angle, *Bloody Williamson* (New York, 1951), pp. 3–11.
61. *Time*, March 10, 1923, reported 22 deaths, but Angle's figure of 23 includes one man who died a slow death from his wounds that day.
62. Herbert Feis, "Kansas Miners and the Kansas Court," *Survey*, February 25, 1922.
63. *New Republic*, December 1, 1920.
64. George Soule, *Prosperity Decade* (New York, 1940), p. 97.
65. Paul Douglas, *Real Wages in the United States 1890–1926* (Boston 1930), p. 563.
66. Veterans were believed to be especially hard hit during this labor shake-out because employers found them too independent-minded for comfort. *New Republic*, August 16, 1922.
67. William L. Chenery, "Mr. Zero," *Survey*, October 1, 1922.

CHAPTER 3

1. Wilson wanted to put the editor of the *Star* in jail for having printed her letter. David A. Shannon, *The Socialist Party of America* (New York, 1955), p. 113.
2. Zechariah Chafee, Jr., *Free Speech* (New York, 1920), pp. 302–10.
3. *New Republic*, August 18, 1920.
4. None of the 20 went to prison—two died, two fled, and the remaining 16 were pardoned by Governor Len Small. Arthur Weinberg, ed., *Attorney for the Damned* (New York, 1957), pp. 155–61.
5. *Nation*, April 17, 1920.
6. Mark Sullivan, *Our Times*, vol. 6, *The Twenties* (New York, 1935), p. 156.
7. Robert K. Murray, *Red Scare* (New York, 1964), pp. 74–76.
8. *Washington Post*, May 7, 1919.
9. *New York Times*, May 1, 1919.
10. Stanley Coben, *A. Mitchell Palmer* (New York, 1963), p. 202.
11. *New York Times*, June 4, 1919.
12. The Roosevelts had driven into R Street only moments after the explosion. Frank Freidel, *Franklin D. Roosevelt: The Ordeal* (Boston, 1954), p. 29.
13. Allen F. Davis, "Welfare, Reform and WWI," *American Quarterly*, fall 1967.
14. Charles Merz, "Progressivism, Old and New," *Atlantic*, July 1923.

15. Debs was remarkable among political figures in that almost without exception every friend he ever made, he kept, as his biography shows. Ray Ginger, *The Bending Cross* (New Brunswick, N.J., 1949).
16. On the fragmentation of the Socialist party in 1917, see Shannon, *op. cit.*, pp. 99–125.
17. *Writings and Speeches of Eugene V. Debs* (New York, 1948), p. 437.
18. Coben, op. cit., p. 203.
19. Shannon, op. cit., pp. 132–140.
20. Benjamin Gitlow, *The Whole of Their Lives* (New York, 1948), pp. 26–28.
21. There is a complete translation of this forgery in Oliver M. Sayler, "Bolshevik or Anarchist," *New Republic*, March 1, 1919.
22. Granville Hicks, *Where We Came Out* (New York, 1954), p. 25.
23. Bernard Baruch, *My Memoir* (New York, 1939).
24. William Preston, Jr., *Aliens and Dissenters* (Cambridge, Mass., 1963), pp. 11–13, 18.
25. Ibid., pp. 210–11.
26. Chafee, op. cit., p. 242.
27. *New York Times*, November 9, 1919.
28. Quoted in Murray, op. cit., p. 207.
29. Ella Reeve Bloor, *We Are Many* (London, 1941), pp. 162–63, provides an eyewitness account of the raid on the Finnish Hall in Worcester, Massachusetts.
30. Murray, op. cit., p. 214.
31. Frederick R. Barkley, "Jailing Radicals in Detroit," *Nation*, January 31, 1920.
32. *Nation*, May 15, 1920.
33. Louis F. Post, *The Deportations Delirium of 1920* (New York, 1921), p. 278.
34. Roberta Strauss Feurlicht, *Justice Crucified* (New York, 1977), p. 8.
35. For Vanzetti's account of his life in the United States before 1919, see Marion D. Frankfurter and Gardner Jackson, *The Letters of Sacco and Vanzetti* (New York, 1930); cf. John Dos Passos, *Facing the Chair* (Boston, 1927), pp. 60–62.
36. Post, op. cit., p. 95.
37. Herbert B. Ehrmann, *The Case That Will Not Die* (New York, 1969), p. 68.
38. Francis Russell, *Tragedy in Dedham* (New York, 1962), p. 97.
39. Ehrmann, op. cit., pp. 145–49.
40. Feurlicht, op. cit., p. 282.
41. The entire trial transcript, plus supplementary material, is available. Bernard Flexner and Charles C. Burlingham, eds., *The Sacco-Vanzetti Case*, 6 vols. (New York, 1929).
42. "In the case against Vanzetti there was nothing to show any connection with the actual shooting, nor even anything to show he had knowledge that shooting might take place. Vanzetti was found guilty of participating in a conspiracy to rob under circumstances which would be likely to result in murder." Osmond K. Fraenkel, *The Sacco-Vanzetti Case* (New York, 1931), pp. 530–31.
43. See the photographs in Ehrmann, op. cit., appendix.
44. The evidence that the Wall Street bomb was planted by anarchists is circumstantial but persuasive. There was a mailbox at the corner of Cedar and Wall, several blocks from Broad and Wall. The mailbox had been cleared at 11:30 A.M. The next collection was due at 11:58. Sometime between 11:30 and 11:58 someone dropped five sheets of loose, badly smudged paper into the box. Each sheet bore a message that had been crudely printed with rubber stamps:

> Remember
> We will not tolerate
> any longer
> Free the political
> prisoners or it will be
> sure death for all of you
> AMERICAN ANARCHIST FIGHTERS

The bomb exploded at 11:58. See Edmund Gilligan, "The Wall Street Explosion Mystery," *American Mercury*, September, 1938.
45. *New York Times*, September 21, 1920.

CHAPTER 4

1. Arnold S. Rice, *The Ku Klux Klan in American Politics* (Washington, D.C., 1962), pp. 11–12.
2. The Klan may have been revived because of Prohibition. Georgia had voted for local option, and then tried to wriggle out of actual dryness by means of the Locker Law. This said that a man who belonged to a club that owned lockers could keep as much liquor as he liked in the locker assigned to him. Following which nearly every fraternal organization in Georgia became a locker club, and others were created in a hurry. There was money to be made from promoting locker clubs. One day Simmons appeared at Atlanta City Hall to call on City Clerk Walter Taylor with the prospectus for a new locker club. Simmons had thought up what he considered a magnetic name for recruiting members: the Ku Klux Klan. Taylor said it would never work. And a few weeks later Georgia went bone dry, repealing the Locker Law. Simmons, however, still thought he could make something of his brainchild, without lockers or bourbon. Ward Greene, "Notes for a History of the Klan," *American Mercury*, June 1925.
3. Charles C. Alexander, *The KKK in the Southwest* (Paducah, Ky., 1965), p. 6.
4. Leroy Percy, "The Modern Ku Klux Klan," *Atlantic*, July 1922.
5. Kenneth T. Jackson, *The Ku Klux Klan in the City 1915–1930* (New York, 1967), p. 8.
6. Frederic Paxson, *Postwar Years: Normalcy 1918–1923* (Berkeley and Los Angeles, 1948), p. 72.
7. Alexander, op. cit., p. 7.
8. Jackson, op. cit., p. 82.
9. John Anthony, ed., "The Klan Holds a Klavern," *Best News Stories of 1923* (Boston, 1924).
10. Hiram Evans in *The Kourier Magazine*, February 1933.
11. Emerson Loucks, *The Ku Klux Klan in Pennsylvania* (Harrisburg, Pa., 1936), p. 87.
12. Rice, op. cit., p. 18.
13. John Mecklin, *The Ku Klux Klan* (New York, 1922), p. 107.
14. Alexander, op. cit., p. 21.
15. Loucks, op. cit., p. 36.
16. Chicago, for example, had an estimated 40–80,000 Klansmen. Jackson, op. cit., p. 125.
17. *Time*, October 1, 1923.
18. *Nation*, January 2, 1924.
19. John Anthony, ed., *Best News Stories of 1924* (Boston, 1925), pp. 233–43.
20. John Higham, *Strangers in the Land* (New Brunswick, N.J., 1955), p. 299.
21. David M. Chalmers, *Hooded Americanism* (New York, 1976), pp. 60–63.
22. "The Mer Rouge Case," in *Best News Stories of 1923*.
23. Ibid., p. 124.
24. Lowell Mellett, "Klan and Church," *Atlantic*, November 1923.
25. In Ishbel Leighton ed., *The Aspirin Age* (Garden City, N.Y., 1949) pp. 113–14.
26. Ibid.
27. Alexander, op. cit., p. 10.
28. Chalmers, op. cit., pp. 37–38.
29. Ibid., pp. 101–104.
30. Andre Siegfried, *America Comes of Age* (New York, 1927), p. 146.
31. Cf. Arthur Sweeney "Mental Tests for Immigrants," *North American Review*, May 1922; Celia James Cannon, "American Misgivings," *Atlantic*, February 1922.
32. Robert A. Divine, *American Immigration Policy 1924–1952* (New Haven, 1957), pp. 11–14.

33. *New York Times*, February 20, 1921.
34. Kate H. Claghorn, *The Immigrant's Day in Court* (New York, 1923), pp. 5–17.
35. Ibid., pp. 159–77.
36. *Survey*, January 29, 1921.
37. Louis Adamic, *My America* (New York, 1938), p. 239.
38. Higham, op. cit., p. 264.
39. *Nation*, December 8, 1920.
40. Howard Zinn, *La Guardia in Congress* (Ithaca, N.Y., 1959), p. 85.
41. Roy L. Garis, *Immigration Restriction* (New York, 1927), p. 150.
42. *Time*, September 17, 1923.
43. Ibid., October 8, 1923.
44. Harold Spender, *A Briton in America* (London, 1921), p. 31.
45. *New Republic*, March 1, 1919.
46. Quoted in Chicago Commission on Race Relations, *The Negro in Chicago* (Chicago, 1920), p. 89.
47. *New Republic*, May 3, 1919.
48. *Jackson Daily News*, June 26, 1919.
49. William M. Tuttle, Jr., *Race Riot* (New York, 1970), pp. 25–29.
50. Ibid., p. 153; Sterling D. Spero and Abram L. Harris, *The Black Worker* (New York, 1931), p. 112.
51. Carl Sandburg, *The Chicago Race Riot* (New York, 1919), p. 8.
52. Tuttle reports an interview with one James Harris who claims to have been aboard the raft, pp. 6–8. Harris, however, waited 50 years before telling this story to anyone and some of the details in it are simply wrong.
53. *New Republic*, September 10, 1919.
54. Seligmann, op. cit., p. 156; Tuttle, op. cit., pp. 169–70.
55. Walter F. White, "The Race Conflict in Arkansas," *Survey*, December 13, 1919 and "I Investigate Lynchings," *American Mercury*, January 1929; Walter Wilson, "The Cotton Kingdom," *New Republic*, December 16, 1931; Seligmann, p. 220, passim.
56. *Nation*, June 26, 1920.
57. *New Republic*, June 22, 1921.
58. *New York Times*, July 23, 1919.
59. *Time*, July 2, 1923.

CHAPTER 5

1. Andre Siegfried, *America Comes of Age* (New York, 1927), p. 43.
2. Nels Anderson, *The Hobo* (Chicago, 1923), p. 92.
3. Clifford Shaw, *The Jack-Roller* (Chicago, 1930), p. 137.
4. Anderson, op. cit., p. 40.
5. Panzram's autobiography, a minor classic of criminal psychopathy, is the basis of Thomas E. Gaddis and James O. Long's *Killer* (New York, 1970).
6. *Literary Digest*, April 21, 1923.
7. Robert L. Tyler, *Rebels of the Woods* (Eugene, Ore., 1967), pp. 89–90.
8. Rexford G. Tugwell, "The Casual of the Woods," *Survey*, July 3, 1920.
9. William D. Haywood, *Bill Haywood's Book* (New York, 1929), pp. 91–94.
10. Paul F. Brissenden, *The IWW* (New York, 1920), pp. 40–42.
11. Ibid., pp. 57–70.
12. Ralph Chaplin, *Wobbly* (Chicago, 1948), p. 147.
13. Theodore Draper, *The Roots of American Communism* (New York, 1957), p. 24.
14. Robert W. Bruère, "The Industrial Workers of the World," *Harper's*, July 1918; L. P. Edwards, "Manufacturing Reds," *Atlantic*, July 1920.
15. Chaplin, op. cit., p. 194.
16. *New Republic*, September 26, 1924.

17. The oath appears in full in Tyler, op. cit., p. 103; also, see *Survey*, May 1, 1920.
18. Tyler, op. cit., p. 156.
19. Haywood, op. cit., p. 355.
20. Robert K. Murray, *Red Scare* (New York, 1964), pp. 183–84; Thomas S. McMahon, "Centralia and the IWW," *Survey*, November 29, 1919.
21. Chaplin, op. cit., p. 294.
22. *Portland Oregonian*, November 23, 1919.
23. Robert Joyce Tasker, *Grimhaven* (New York, 1928), pp. 190–93.
24. Chaplin, p. 296.
25. On how and why the Communists organized Haywood's flight to the Soviet Union, see Benjamin Gitlow, *The Whole of Their Lives* (New York, 1948), pp. 46–47.
26. Leo Pasvolsky, "Civilization and Oil," *Atlantic*, February 1923.
27. Gerald Forbes, *Flush Production* (Norman, Okla., 1942), pp. 53–55.
28. Samuel W. Tait, *The Wildcatters* (Princeton, 1946), p. 137; *New Republic*, October 3, 1923.
29. Boyce House, *Oil Boom* (Caldwell, Idaho, 1938), pp. 153–54.
30. Ibid., p. 149.
31. Max Bentley, "Smackover and the Seekers of Oil," *Harper's*, December 1923.
32. House, op. cit., p. 120.
33. Ibid., p. 70.
34. Robert S. Lynd, "Done in Oil," *Survey*, November 1, 1922.
35. Calvin Coolidge, *Autobiography of Calvin Coolidge* (New York, 1929), p. 29.
36. Oswald Garrison Villard, "The New Fight for Old Liberties," *Harper's*, September 1925.
37. Veronica and Paul King, *The Raven on the Skyscraper* (London, 1925), p. 40.
38. Arthur Conan Doyle, *Our American Adventure* (London, 1923), p. 17.
39. Norman H. Clark, *Deliver Us from Evil* (New York, 1976), p. 66.
40. For an imaginative and scholarly appraisal of this trinity on the eve of the war, see Henry F. May, *The End of American Innocence* (New York, 1959).

CHAPTER 6

1. Mrs. Wilson states flatly that Lansing was dismissed for calling the Cabinet meetings, which she terms "agitation to put his Chief out of office." Edith Bolling Wilson, *Memoirs* (Indianapolis, 1939), p. 359.
2. Edmund W. Starling, *Starling of the White House* (New York, 1946), p. 157.
3. John A. Garraty, *Henry Cabot Lodge* (New York, 1953), pp. 348–49.
4. Even within Lodge's family there was complete disagreement on what the Senator really wanted. From what he said *en famille* he was plainly in some confusion himself. Denna F. Fleming, *The United States and the League of Nations* (New York, 1932), pp. 475–77.
5. William A. White, *The Autobiography of William Allen White* (New York, 1946), p. 550.
6. On Lodge's alliance with the Irreconcilables, see Ralph Stone, *The Irreconcilables* (Paducah, Ky., 1970), pp. 90–91, 94–95, 122–23, 157; and Garraty, op. cit., pp. 357–90.
7. William Hard, "The Irreconcilables," *New Republic*, March 31, 1920.
8. Lodge's discomfiture led him to write his last book, which is little more than a tortuous attempt to salvage his reputation as a man who served his country well: *The Senate and the League of Nations* (New York, 1925).
9. The standard, pro-Wilson account of this complex and unhappy episode is Thomas A. Bailey, *Woodrow Wilson and the Great Betrayal* (New York, 1945).
10. *Nation*, June 5, 1920.
11. Ibid., June 19, 1920.
12. Wesley Bagby, *The Road to Normalcy* (Baltimore, 1962), pp. 39–40.
13. Harry M. Daugherty, *The Inside Story of the Harding Tragedy* (New York, 1935), p. 25.

14. *New York Times*, June 21, 1920.
15. Adams, op. cit., p. 131.
16. Mark Sullivan, *Our Times*, vol. 6, *The Twenties* (New York, 1935), pp. 37–38 n.
17. *New York Times*, February 21, 1920.
18. Adams, op. cit., p. 140.
19. Daugherty, p. 39, rejects this story.
20. Robert K. Murray, *The Harding Era* (Minneapolis, 1969); Bagby, op. cit., pp. 97–101.
21. For the embittered view of one unreconciled Wood delegate, however, see White, op. cit., pp. 586–87. To delegates like himself, in their disappointment Harding's nomination inevitably appeared the result of a fix.
22. Donald R. McCoy, *Calvin Coolidge* (New York, 1967), p. 120.
23. See poll in *Literary Digest*, June 12, 1920.
24. Walter Lippmann, *Men of Destiny* (New York, 1927), p. 113.
25. *Nation*, July 17, 1920.
26. Andrew Sinclair, *The Available Man* (New York, 1965), p. 86.
27. Gene Smith, *When the Cheering Stopped* (New York, 1964), pp. 155–56.
28. George McAdam, "Harding," *World's Work*, October 1920.
29. Sullivan, op. cit., p. 30.
30. He could nevertheless make an impression. Harding chaired the Senate investigation into the bitter IWW-led Lawrence strike. The radicals who were called to appear before the committee expected a hostile reception. They were surprised. "I could see," recalled one of them, later to be famous, "that he was in sympathy with my vehement replies." Margaret Sanger, *An Autobiography* (New York, 1939), p. 82.
31. Adams, op. cit., pp. 93–94.
32. Murray, op. cit., pp. 23–24.
33. Sinclair, op. cit., pp. 109–11.
34. *Saturday Evening Post*, October 21, 1923.
35. Bagby, op. cit., p. 124.
36. Murray, op. cit., p. 52.
37. *New York Times*, July 21, 1920.
38. Adams, op. cit., p. 181; Mrs. Wilson on the other hand says that Tumulty was jubilant over the Chancellor genealogies and that the President refused to allow the Democratic party to use them in the election campaign, *Memoirs*, p. 365.
39. Adams, op. cit., p. 183. He was one of the reporters at the Chancellor press conference and admits to feeling embarrassed for the hapless professor.
40. Robert K. Murray, *The Politics of Normalcy* (New York, 1973), p. 9.
41. Robert K. Murray, *The Harding Era*, p. 25.
42. Adams, op. cit., pp. 194–95.

CHAPTER 7

1. Preston Slosson, *The Great Crusade and After* (New York, 1930), p. 196 n.
2. John D. Black, *Agricultural Reform in the United States* (New York, 1929), p. 440.
3. U.S. Bureau of the Census, *Fourteenth Census*, 1920, vol. 5, *Agriculture*, p. 512.
4. U.S. Federal Trade Commission, *National Wealth and Income* (Washington, D.C., 1926), table 49, p. 110.
5. James H. Shideler, *Farm Crisis 1919–1923* (Berkeley and Los Angeles, 1957), p. 38.
6. Gilbert C. Fite, *George N. Peek and the Fight for Farm Parity* (Norman, Okla., 1954), p. 9.
7. Elmus R. Wicker, *Federal Reserve Monetary Policy 1917–1933* (New York, 1966), pp. 21–23.
8. "The agricultural West and South were in fact bankrupt; the resources of their banks were tied up in non-collectible paper." Alfred Noyes, *The War Period of American Fi-

nance (New York, 1926), pp. 405–406. It was only the Fed's policy of lending freely to member banks, but at the then high rate of 7 percent, that contained the catastrophe.

9. Andrew A. Bruce, *Non-Partisan League* (New York, 1921), pp. 60–61.

10. Shideler, op. cit., p. 50; Fite, op. cit., pp. 19–20.

11. Robert K. Murray, *The Harding Era* (Minneapolis, 1969), p. 279.

12. Shideler, op. cit., p. 187. The *New York World*, April 9, 1922, was aghast: "This is not a partisan tariff but a lunatic tariff."

13. James Peter Warbasse, "Cooperation: The People's Business," *Nation*, November 17, 1920.

14. Arthur Capper, *The Agricultural Bloc* (New York, 1922), p. 9.

15. On farm income in the 1920s, see Black, op. cit., p. 8.

16. One farmer in 10 had been foreclosed or had simply left without waiting for the formalities. Albert B. Genung, *The Agricultural Depression Following World War I* (Ithaca, N.Y., 1954), pp. 14–15.

17. Murray, op. cit., p. 91.

18. *New Republic*, March 2, 1921.

19. Samuel Hopkins Adams, *Incredible Era* (Boston, 1939), p. 197.

20. Daugherty asked outright for the appointment, and Harding could see no way to refuse it. Bascom Timmons, *Portrait of an American* (Boston, 1953), p. 203.

21. Three-fourths of America's war dead—some 45,000 bodies—were eventually brought home at their relatives' request and reburied.

22. *Nation*, January 12, 1921; *New Republic*, January 19, 1921.

23. William A. White, *The Autobiography of William Allen White* (New York, 1945), p. 598.

24. Mark Sullivan, *The Great Adventure at Washington* (New York, 1922), pp. 18–34.

25. *New York Times*, June 22, 1923.

26. Murray, op. cit., pp. 353–54.

27. Paul A. Carter, *Another Part of the Twenties* (New York, 1977), p. 171.

28. *Nation*, October 26, 1920 and November 10, 1920.

29. James Weldon Johnson, "Self-Determining Haiti," *New Republic*, August 28, 1920.

30. Harding told Hoover how he overcame the objections of Penrose and Lodge: "He had told them, 'Mellon and Hoover or no Mellon.' " Yet Harding was supposedly a spineless creature, dominated by stronger men. Herbert Hoover, *Memoirs*, vol. 2, *The Cabinet and the Presidency* (New York, 1951), p. 36.

31. Quoted in Robert K. Murray, *The Politics of Normalcy* (New York, 1973), p. 33.

32. *New York Times*, July 23. 1921.

33. David Hinshaw, *Herbert Hoover* (New York, 1950), pp. 106–107, 113–14.

34. Joseph Brandes, *Herbert Hoover and Economic Diplomacy* (Pittsburgh, 1962), p. 16.

35. Kirby Page, "The U.S. Steel Corporation," *Atlantic*, May 1922; Philip Cabot, "Judge Gary," *Atlantic*, May 1921.

36. *Survey*, March 5, 1921.

37. Hoover, op. cit., pp. 103–104; David Burner, *Herbert Hoover: A Public Life* (New York, 1979), p. 174.

38. U.S. President's Conference, *Recent Economic Changes* (Washington, D.C., 1929), table 8, p. 879.

39. John S. Commons et al., *History of Labor in the U.S. 1896–1932*, vol. 3, *Working Conditions and Labor Legislation* by Don D. Lescohier and Elizabeth Brandeis (New York, 1935), pp. 134–36, 173–74.

40. Thomas W. Lamont, "Problems of the Incoming Administration," *Harper's*, March 1921.

41. Solomon Fabricant, *The Output of Manufacturing Industries 1899–1937* (New York, 1940), table 1, p. 44.

42. Charles Pierce Butler, "The Cost of Progress," *Harper's*, May 1923.

43. Stanley Coben, *A. Mitchell Palmer* (New York, 1963), pp. 186–88.

44. On the background to this strike, see Selig Perlman and Philip Taft, *Labor Movements* (New York, 1935), p. 517.

45. Harry M. Daugherty, *The Inside Story of the Harding Tragedy* (New York, 1932), pp. 304–309 reproduces the Wilkerson injunction in full.
46. Hoover, op. cit., pp. 47–48.
47. *Survey*, February 28, 1920.
48. Mark Sullivan, *Our Times*, vol. 6, *The Twenties* (New York, 1935), p. 143.
49. Bruce Bliven, "Charlie, Warren and Ned," *New Republic*, May 28, 1924.
50. Adams, op. cit., pp. 296–97.
51. Ibid., p. 236.
52. Murray, op cit., p. 104.
53. Sullivan, op cit., p. 232; Murray, *Harding Era*, pp. 435–36.
54. Even a crusty egocentric such as Lodge could not help admiring Fall. John A. Garraty, *Henry Cabot Lodge* (New York, 1953), p. 421 n.
55. Adams, op. cit., p. 341.
56. O. P. White, "Five El Paso Worthies," *American Mercury*, December 1929.
57. Daugherty, op. cit., pp. 76–77.
58. Burl Noggle, *Teapot Dome* (Baton Rouge, La., 1962), p. 93.
59. *New York Tribune*, August 3, 1923.
60. *New Republic*, October 20, 1920. His Secret Service bodyguard described him as "the kindest man I ever knew." Edmund Starling, *Starling of the White House* (New York, 1946), p. 171.
61. Cf. William A. Crawford, "A Week in the White House with Harding," *World's Work*, May 1921.
62. Starling was present at most of these poker sessions, and how decorous they were! Harding had a bad stomach and was restricted to one highball. Most of the players were rich, and played for penny ante stakes. At 11:45 the game promptly stopped. Starling, op. cit., p. 170.
63. Sullivan, op. cit., pp. 97–103.
64. David Burner, *The Politics of Provincialism* (New York, 1968), pp. 103–104.
65. *New Republic*, June 28, 1921.
66. Daugherty, op. cit., p. 113, claims that he recommended Debs's release. The Harding papers show that he did no such thing: Andrew Sinclair, *The Available Man* (New York, 1965), pp. 227–28.
67. Ralph Chaplin, *Wobbly* (Chicago, 1948), p. 322.
68. Sinclair, op. cit., p. 286.
69. Starling, op. cit., pp. 192–93, relates passing a letter from a friend concerning the oil leases to the President, and his anguish over its contents.
70. Calvin Coolidge, *The Autobiography of Calvin Coolidge* (New York, 1933), p. 173.
71. Ray Lyman Wilbur was one of the doctors who attended Harding at San Francisco. Wilbur had also been at the 1920 convention and received the news of Harding's nomination with disbelief because, to his physician's eye, Harding was so obviously suffering from heart disease he stood little chance of living another four years. He describes the course of Harding's collapse and death in *The Memoirs of Ray Lyman Wilbur* (Palo Alto, Calif., 1960), pp. 378–82.
72. Lorena A. Hickok, "The Funeral Train at Honey Creek," in Joseph Anthony, ed., *The Best News Stories of 1923* (Boston, 1924).
73. Sullivan, op cit., p. 253.

CHAPTER 8

1. The two minor classics produced by the moral crisis of the Twenties, and offering extended commentaries on it, were Joseph Wood Krutch, *The Modern Temper* (New York, 1929) and Walter Lippmann, *A Preface to Morals* (New York, 1929).
2. Harold F. Stearns, ed., *Civilization in the United States* (New York, 1922), p. vii.
3. James Truslow Adams, *Our Business Civilization* (New York, 1929), p. 190.

4. Cf. Louis Raymond Reid, "The Small Town"; Duncan Aikman, "The Home-town Mind," *Harper's*, November 1925.

5. Charles Merz, "Sweet Land of Secrecy," *Harper's*, February 1927.

6. Quoted in Hugh Grant Adam, *An Australian Looks at America* (London, 1928), p. 2.

7. Cf. Robert M. Crunden, *From Self to Society 1919–1941* (Englewood Cliffs, N.J., 1972), p. 28; Caroline F. Ware, *Greenwich Village 1920–1930* (Boston, 1935), p. 6.

8. Henry F. May, "Shifting Perspectives on the 1920s," *Mississippi Valley Historical Review*, December 1956.

9. Frederic Hoffman, *The Twenties* (New York, 1955), p. 316.

10. For Freud's impact on American thought between the wars, see Nathan Hale, Jr., *Freud and the Americans* (New York, 1971); Frederic J. Hoffman, *Freudianism and the Literary Mind* (Baton Rouge, La., 1957); David Shakow and David Rapoport, *The Influence of Freud on American Psychology* (Cleveland 1968).

11. John C. Burnham, "On the Origins of Behaviorism," *Journal of the History of the Behavioral Sciences* (April, 1968); Lucille Birnbaum, "Behavioralism in the 1920s," *American Quarterly*, spring 1955.

12. Robert H. Elias, *Entangling Alliances with None* (New York, 1973), pp. 6–7.

13. John B. Watson, *Behaviorism* (New York, 1925), p. 104.

14. Stuart Chase in the *New York Herald Tribune*, June 21, 1925.

15. Robert Littell, "Emile Coué," *New Republic*, January 24, 1923.

16. Emile Coué, *Self-Mastery Through Conscious Autosuggestion* (New York, 1922), p. 19.

17. Matthew Josephson, *Life Among the Surrealists* (New York, 1962), pp. 142–44.

18. Emily Hahn, *Romantic Rebels* (Boston, 1966), p. 254; cf. Thomas Parry, *Garrets and Pretenders* (New York, 1960), pp. 320–21.

19. Hahn, p. 236.

20. Joseph Freeman, *An American Testament* (New York, 1936), p. 244.

21. Josephson, op. cit., p. 315.

22. Winifred Kirkland, "The New Death," *Atlantic*, May 1918.

23. J. Spengler, "When Population Ceases to Grow," *Harper's*, September 3, 1930.

24. Cf. the symposium "The Case Against the Younger Generation," *Literary Digest*, June 17, 1922.

25. Dixon Wecter, *When Johnny Comes Marching Home* (Boston, 1944), p. 342; G. Stanley Hall, "Flapper American Novissima," *Atlantic*, June 1922.

26. Mark Sullivan, *Our Times*, vol. 6, *The Twenties* (New York, 1935), p. 396; A Professor, "The Young Person," *Atlantic*, February 1925; Adams, op. cit., p. 63; and all of Ben B. Lindsey and Wainwright Evans, *The Revolt of Modern Youth* (New York, 1928).

27. This is clear from the case studies contained in Robert L. Dickinson and Lura Beam, *A Thousand Marriages* (Baltimore, 1931).

28. Edmund Wilson, *The Twenties* (New York, 1975), p. 43.

29. F. Scott Fitzgerald, "Echoes of the Jazz Age," *Scribner's*, November 1931.

30. *New Republic*, November 28, 1928.

31. Robert L. Dickinson and Lura Beam, *The Single Woman* (Baltimore, 1934), p. 396.

32. Ibid., chapter 16.

33. Katherine Bement Davis, *Factors in the Sex Life of 2200 Women* (New York, 1929), table 1, p. 97; table 3, p. 249.

34. E.g., M. J. Exner, *The Sexual Side of Marriage* (New York, 1929), still in print after a dozen editions.

35. *Time*, January 30, 1928.

36. Howard B. Woolston, *Prostitution in the U.S.* (New York, 1921), p. 38.

37. Willoughby C. Waterman, *Prostitution and Its Repression in New York City 1900–1931* (New York, 1932), pp. 58–76.

38. George E. Worthington, "The Night Clubs of New York," *Survey*, January 1, 1929.

39. Walter C. Reckless, *Vice in Chicago* (Chicago, 1933), pp. 15–16, 25–26.

40. Waterman, op. cit., pp. 126–27.

41. *New Republic*, May 26, 1926.
42. Beverley Nichols, *The Star-Spangled Manner* (London, 1928), pp. 64–68.
43. *New Republic*, April 29, 1925.
44. *Time*, March 1, 1926.
45. Harvey Zorbaugh, *The Gold Coast and the Slum* (Chicago, 1929), p. 104.
46. Page Smith, *A Letter from My Father* (New York, 1975), is an edited version of the 10,000-page diary.
47. Lindsey and Evans, op. cit., pp. 66–70.
48. Krutch, p. 67.
49. Ben Hecht, *A Child of the Century* (New York, 1954), p. 47; he was a police reporter at the time.
50. *Survey*, December 1, 1924.
51. Francis Perkins, "Do Women in Industry Need Protection?" *Survey*, February 15, 1926.
52. The entire issue of the *Survey* for Dec. 1, 1926, is devoted to the condition of working women in the Twenties.
53. *Nation*, January 20, 1926.
54. Elizabeth Breuer, "Feminism's Awkward Age," *Harper's*, April 1925.
55. Dorothy Dunbar Bromley, "Feminist-New Style," *Harper's*, October 1927.
56. William Henry Chafe, *The American Woman* (New York, 1971), pp. 37–41.
57. Ware, pp. 258–60.
58. "The struggle for women's rights ended during the 1920s," says William L. O'Neill, *Everyone Was Brave* (Chicago, 1969), p. vii; a judgment echoed by Chafe, pp. 51–57; and Anne Frior Scott, "After Suffrage: Southern Women in the Twenties," *Journal of Southern History*, August 1964.
59. Dickinson and Beam, op. cit., p. 397.
60. Louis Dublin, *Health and Wealth* (New York, 1928), p. 180; Ira S. Wile, ed., *The Sex Life of the Unmarried Adult* (New York, 1934), p. 47.
61. Alfred Cahen, *A Statistical Analysis of American Divorce* (New York, 1932), p. 21.
62. Ibid., p. 111.
63. *Atlantic Monthly* in 1922–1923 ran five articles on this subject, e.g., Joseph Fort Newton's "What God Hath Not Joined" in the issue for June 1923, which lamented "the riot of divorce has become almost an orgy . . ." Similarly, *Harper's* frequently agonized over divorce, e.g., Beatrice Hinckle's "The Chaos of Modern Marriage," in the issue for December 1925.
64. *Time*, September 15, 1930, and March 16, 1931.
65. Leading all the rest on this theme was V. F. Calverton's *The Bankruptcy of Marriage* (New York, 1928). To read it is to master the entire intellectual-radical catechism against marriage popular in the Twenties. It has a very contemporary ring more than 50 years later.
66. Ben B. Lindsey, *Companionate Marriage* (New York, 1927).
67. Emanuel H. Lavine, *"Gimme": How Politicians Get Rich* (New York 1931), p. 13.
68. Calverton, op. cit., pp. 179–80.
69. Margaret Sanger, *My Fight for Birth Control* (New York, 1931), p. 4.
70. Ibid., pp. 55–56.
71. Ibid., p. 60.
72. Margaret Sanger, *An Autobiography* (New York, 1939), p. 128.
73. David M. Kennedy, *Birth Control in America* (New Haven, Conn., 1970), p. 31.
74. Ibid., pp. 78–80.
75. Ibid., p. 96.
76. Ibid., pp. 34–35.
77. Margaret Sanger, *Happiness in Marriage* (London, 1927), pp. 165–66.
78. Calverton, op. cit., pp. 130–31.
79. *Time*, March 22, 1926.
80. Hamilton, op. cit., table 51, p. 120.

81. Davis, op. cit., table 1, p. 14.
82. Lippmann, op. cit., p. 272.

CHAPTER 9

1. Andrew Sinclair, *Era of Excess* (Boston, 1962), p. 77.
2. James H. Timberlake, *Prohibition and the Progressive Movement* (Cambridge, Mass., 1963), p. 40.
3. Sinclair, op. cit., p. 71.
4. Norman H. Clark, *The Dry Years* (Seattle, 1965), p. 56.
5. The different social values of the various groups working for prohibition are examined at length by Joseph Gusfield, *Symbolic Crusade* (Urbana, Ill., 1963).
6. The dry Progressives of one region—the Southwest—are the subject of Lewis L. Gould, *Progressives and Prohibition* (Austin, Texas, 1973).
7. Jimmie Lewis Franklin, *Born Sober* (Norman, Okla., 1971), pp. 83–85, 89–90.
8. Burton J. Hendrick, "Frightfulness Against the Saloon," *Harper's*, September 1918.
9. Herbert Asbury, *The Great Illusion* (Garden City, N.Y., 1950), p. 136.
10. *The Outlook*, January 7, 1920.
11. Sinclair, op. cit., p. 91.
12. Asbury, op. cit., pp. 175–77.
13. Elmer Irey, *The Tax Dodgers* (Garden City, N.Y., 1949), pp. 22–23.
14. Ibid., p. 18.
15. Izzy Einstein, *Prohibition Agent No. 1* (New York, 1932), p. 2.
16. Asbury, op. cit., p. 211.
17. Sinclair, op. cit., p. 188.
18. Charles Merz, *The Dry Decade* (New York, 1931), p. 150.
19. Clark, op. cit., p. 153.
20. *New York Times*, March 2–4, 1924.
21. Norman H. Clark, *Deliver Us from Evil* (New York, 1976), p. 163.
22. Malcolm F. Willoughby, *Rum War at Sea* (Washington, D.C., 1964), pp. 151, 162.
23. Stanley Walker, *The Night Club Era* (New York, 1932), p. 159.
24. Oliver H. P. Garrett, "Why They Cleaned Up Philadelphia," *New Republic*, Feb. 27, 1924.
25. Arthur H. Lewis, *The Worlds of Chippy Patterson* (Philadelphia, 1960), p. 240.
26. *Time*, January 4, 1926.
27. Frederic F. Van de Water, *The Real McCoy* (New York, 1931), pp. 21–23.
28. Ibid., p. 37.
29. This was the Coast Guard's estimate. Willoughby, op. cit., p. 17.
30. Ibid., p. 31.
31. Clark, *Dry Years*, p. 173.
32. Clark, *Deliver Us from Evil*, p. 162.
33. Asbury, op. cit., pp. 172–73.
34. Ibid., pp. 221–23.
35. Caroline F. Ware, *Greenwich Village 1920–1930* (New York, 1935), p. 71.
36. Homer Turner, "Notes of a Prohibition Agent," *American Mercury*, April 1928.
37. U.S. Treasury Dept. *Statistics Concerning Intoxicating Liquor* (Washington, D.C., 1930), p. 52.
38. *Time*, March 12, 1928.
39. Carl Jones in Frank Brookhauser, ed., *These Were Our Years* (Garden City, N.Y., 1959), p. 120.
40. Alice Roosevelt Longworth, *Crowded Hours* (New York, 1935), p. 315.
41. Niven Busch, *Briton Hadden* (New York, 1949), p. 214.
42. *New Republic*, June 30, 1926.

43. Morrow Mayo, "Night Life in San Francisco," *New Republic*, Aug. 14, 1929.
44. Stephen Graham, "The Bowery Under Prohibition," *Harper's*, February 1927.
45. Asbury, op. cit., pp. 190–91.
46. John C. Burnham, "New Perspectives on the Prohibition 'Experiment,' " *Journal of Social History*, no. 2, 1968.
47. Clark, *Dry Years*, p. 136.
48. See the various estimates in U.S. Dept. of Health, Education and Welfare, *Alcohol and Health* (Washington, D.C., 1971); Vera Efron and Mark Keller, *Selected Statistics on the Consumption of Alcohol 1850–1968* (New Brunswick, N.J., 1970), table 2, p. 4; and Joseph R. Gusfield, "Prohibition," in John Braeman et al., *Change and Continuity in the 20th Century* (Columbus, Ohio, 1968).

CHAPTER 10

1. Donald McCoy, *Calvin Coolidge* (New York, 1967), p. 149.
2. William A. White, *A Puritan in Babylon* (New York, 1933), pp. 242–43.
3. Edwin G. Long, "Calvin the Silent," *New Republic*, September 28, 1921.
4. White, op. cit., p. 222.
5. His bodyguard found Coolidge garrulous: Edmund Starling, *Starling of the White House* (New York, 1946), p. 211; so did the founder of *Barron's Weekly*. Arthur Pound and Samuel T. Moore eds., *They Told Barron* (New York, 1930), p. 258.
6. The liberal, anti-Coolidge press was as eager as Mellon to see the national debt reduced, convinced that public borrowing would ruin the economy. Cf. *New Republic*, July 2, 1924.
7. Walter Lippmann, *Men of Destiny* (New York, 1927); and in the same vein, Beverley Nichols, *The Star Spangled Manner* (London, 1928), pp. 114–18.
8. Albert B. Genung, *The Agricultural Depression Following WWI* (Ithaca, N.Y., 1958), p. 16.
9. Gilbert C. Fite, *George N. Peek and the Fight for Farm Parity* (Norman, Okla., 1954), pp. 37–38.
10. Betty M. Glad, *Charles Evans Hughes and the Illusions of Innocence* (Urbana, Ill., 1966), pp. 312–27.
11. Herbert Hoover, *Memoirs*, vol. 2, *The Cabinet and the Presidency* (New York, 1952), pp. 177–78.
12. Arthur Brisbane's "Today" column was carried in more than 1,000 newspapers, and Brisbane often claimed that Japan would one day attempt to seize the Philippines and Guam. Hector C. Bywater's *The Great Pacific War* (Boston, 1925) foretold with remarkable accuracy the general course of the war with Japan when it came. Equally prophetic was Fredrick Palmer, "Where the Next European War Will Start," *Harper's*, November 1925. See also *New Republic*, July 13, 1921, and December 10, 1924.
13. Roy L. Garis, *Immigration Restriction* (New York, 1927), p. 197.
14. U.S. Bureau of the Census, *Statistical Abstract: 1950* (Washington, D.C., 1950), p. 97.
15. Burl Noggle, *Teapot Dome* (Baton Rouge, La., 1962), p. 51.
16. White, op. cit., pp. 274–75.
17. Mark Sullivan, *Our Times*, vol. 6, *The Twenties* (New York, 1935), pp. 319–21.
18. Barron knew Doheny well and trusted him. He gives Doheny's explanation of the oil leases in Pound and Moore, op. cit., pp. 164–65.
19. *Time*, July 7, 1924.
20. *New Republic*, June 11, 1924.
21. Arnold Rice, *The KKK in American Politics* (Washington, D.C., 1962), p. 13; but Kenneth T. Jackson, *The KKK in the City* (New York, 1966), puts Klan membership at little more than 2 million, p. 236.
22. Charles Alexander, *The KKK in the Southwest* (Paducah, Ky., 1965), p. 96.

23. Viz., "Roughly 10 percent of the public officials and policemen in every California city were identified as members of the Invisible Empire." Jackson, op. cit., p. 190.
24. *Time*, July 7, 1924; Robert K. Murray, *The 103rd Ballot* (New York, 1976), p. 123.
25. Lawrence A. Levine, *Defender of the Faith* (New York, 1965), pp. 311–13.
26. Murray, op. cit., pp. 126–27.
27. Quoting Wordsworth was a suggestion that Judge Joseph Proskauer, an ardent Smith supporter, pressed on a reluctant Roosevelt. Matthew Josephson, *Al Smith* (Boston, 1969).
28. Murray, op. cit., p. 131.
29. E.g., *Harper's*, June 1924; *Nation*, June 12, 1924.
30. Murray, op. cit., pp. 207.
31. Andre Siegfried, *America Comes of Age* (New York, 1927), p. 295.
32. Robert Littell, "La Follette for President," *New Republic*, July 16, 1924.
33. Kenneth McKay, *The Progressive Movement of 1924* (New York, 1947), p. 145.
34. Mellon's tax policies were largely inherited from his predecessor, David F. Houston, and he retained Houston, a Democrat, as assistant secretary to help him put them into effect: David E. Koskoff, *The Mellons* (Cleveland, 1979), pp. 171–72.
35. Noggle, op. cit., p. 174 n.
36. Karl Schriftgeisser, *This Was Normalcy* (Boston, 1948), p. 213.
37. *Time*, Nov. 17, 1924.
38. Lowell Mellett, "Klan and Church," *Atlantic*, November 1923.
39. Isabel Leighton, ed., *The Aspirin Age* (New York, 1949), p. 116.
40. David Chalmers, *Hooded Americanism* (New York, 1976), p. 163.
41. Rice, op. cit., p. 11.
42. Leighton, op. cit., pp. 125–26.
43. *New York Times* and *Washington Post*, August 9, 1925.
44. Bruce Bliven, "The Great Coolidge Mystery," *Harper's*, December 1925.
45. The hostile (minority) view was summed up and given forceful expression by Frank Kent of the *Baltimore Sun* in "Mr. Coolidge," *American Mercury*, August 1924.
46. Calvin Coolidge, *An Autobiography* (New York, 1933), p. 202.
47. Irwin H. Hoover, *Forty-Two Years at the White House* (Boston, 1934), p. 268.
48. McCoy, op. cit., p. 288.
49. Myron M. Stearns, "Gentlemen, the President!" in Paul A. Carter, ed., *The Uncertain World of Normalcy* (New York, 1971).
50. Coolidge, op. cit., p. 229.
51. Cf. *New Republic*, July 1, 1925; *Nation*, March 14, 1928.
52. Leroy Ashby, *The Spearless Leader* (Urbana, Ill., 1972), pp. 155–59.
53. His version of the tie-vote affair is in Charles G. Dawes, *Notes as Vice President* (Boston, 1935), pp. 183–84.
54. *Information Please Almanac*, 1977.
55. Howard H. Quint and Robert Ferrell, eds., *The Talkative President* (Boston, 1964), pp. 119–20.
56. *Time*, September 28, 1925.
57. L. Ethan Ellis, *Republican Foreign Policy 1921–1933* (New Brunswick, N.J., 1968), p. 46.
58. One Mexican newspaper even carried a banner headline that translated "After Morrow Come the Marines": Harold Nicholson, *Dwight Morrow* (London, 1932), p. 326.

CHAPTER 11

1. Maynard Shipley, *The War on Modern Science* (New York, 1927), p. 29.
2. Ibid., p. 3.
3. Quoted in Kenneth K. Bailey, *Southern White Protestantism in the 20th Century* (New York, 1964), p. 50.

4. W. J. Cash, *The Mind of the South* (New York, 1941), pp. 289–92.
5. Ernest Gruening, ed., *These United States* (New York, 1923), pp. 143–54.
6. Ray Ginger, *Six Days or Forever?* (Boston, 1958), p. 3.
7. Quoted in ibid., p. 7.
8. Arthur Garfield Hayes, *Let Freedom Ring* (New York, 1937), pp. 25–26; Ginger, op. cit., pp. 19–20.
9. *New Republic,* June 25, 1925.
10. Clarence Darrow, *The Story of My Life* (New York, 1932), p. 244.
11. Irving Stone, *Clarence Darrow for the Defense* (Garden City, N.Y., 1941), p. 423.
12. Norman F. Furniss, *The Fundamentalist Controversy 1918–1933* (New Haven, Conn., 1954), p. 7.
13. Ginger, op. cit., pp. 84–85.
14. On Dayton during the trial, see Frank R. Kent, "On the Dayton Firing Line," *New Republic,* July 29, 1925, and H. L. Mencken, "The Scopes Trial," *Baltimore Sun,* July 13, 1925.
15. Hayes, op. cit., p. 36.
16. Lawrence Levine, *Defender of the Faith* (New York, 1965), pp. 246–51, 258–59.
17. Arthur Weinberg, ed., *Attorney for the Damned* (New York, 1957), reprints Darrow's clash with Bryan in full, pp. 193–227.
18. Lately Thomas, *Storming Heaven* (New York, 1970), p. 20.
19. Isabel Leighton, ed., *The Aspirin Age* (New York, 1949), p. 57.
20. A German labor leader who visited the Angelus Temple was only one of countless men who were entranced. Ernest Toller, *Which World, Which Way?* (London, 1931), pp. 37–38. He forecast that her evident sexual vitality would prove her undoing.
21. Thomas, op. cit., p. 26.
22. Herbert Hoover, *Memoirs,* vol. 2, *The Cabinet and the Presidency* (New York, 1952), p. 142.
23. For eyewitness accounts of various productions, see Leighton, p. 60; Toller, p. 41; and Sarah Comstock, "Aimee Semple McPherson," *Harper's,* October 1927.
24. Thomas, op. cit., p. 67.
25. Gruening, op. cit., p. 223.
26. Leighton, op. cit., p. 78.
27. Donald B. Meyer, *The Protestant Search for Political Realism 1919–1941* (Berkeley and Los Angeles, 1960), pp. 7–12.
28. Robert T. Handy, "The American Religious Depression 1925–1935" *Church History,* vol. 29 (1960).
29. Robert Moats Miller, *American Protestantism and Social Issues 1919–1939* (Chapel Hill, N.C., 1958), pp. 34–40.

CHAPTER 12

1. Harold Seymour, *Baseball: The Golden Age* (New York, 1971), p. 295.
2. The idea originated with an advertising wizard, Albert Lasker. John D. Gunther, *Taken at the Flood* (New York, 1960), p. 122.
3. Henry F. Pringle, "Portrait of a Bench Warmer," *Harper's,* April 1927.
4. Robert Creamer, *Babe* (New York, 1974), p. 190.
5. Ibid., p. 217.
6. Seymour, op. cit., p. 423.
7. Karl Wagenheim, *Babe Ruth* (New York, 1974), p. 62.
8. Quoted in Creamer, op. cit., p. 221.
9. Marshall Smelser, *The Life That Ruth Built* (Chicago, 1975), p. 139.
10. Ibid., p. 181.
11. Creamer, op. cit., p. 181.

12. Smelser, op. cit., p. 170.
13. Grantland Rice, "The Real All-American," *Collier's*, Nov. 20, 1926.
14. *Survey*, December 1, 1922.
15. *Nation*, November 6, 1929.
16. Georges Duhamel, *America, the Menace* (London, 1931), pp. 153–54.
17. Douglas P. Haskell, "Football as Big Business," *New Republic*, January 19, 1927.
18. Abraham Flexner, *Universities: American, English, German* (New York, 1930), p. 206.
19. Rice, *op. cit.*
20. Alison Danzig and Peter Brandwein, *Sports' Golden Age* (New York, 1948), pp. 121–22.
21. *Time*, October 5, 1925.
22. Ibid., November 30, 1925.
23. Jack Dempsey and Barbara Piatelli Dempsey, *Dempsey* (New York, 1977), pp. 113–14.
24. Randy Roberts, *Jack Dempsey* (Baton Rouge, La., 1979), p. 62.
25. Dempsey and Dempsey, op. cit., p. 25.
26. Grantland Rice, *The Tumult and the Shouting* (New York, 1954), p. 89.
27. *New York Times*, December 21, 1920.
28. Rice, op. cit., p. 91.
29. Roberts, op. cit., p. 122.
30. Karl A. Bickel, *New Empires* (Philadelphia, 1930).
31. *New Republic*, July 20, 1921.
32. Roberts, op. cit., pp. 173–74.
33. Ibid., p. 185.
34. Nat Fleischer, *Fifty Years at Ringside* (New York, 1958), pp. 122–24.
35. Paul Gallico, *Farewell to Sport* (New York, 1935), p. 16.
36. *Time*, June 4, 1923.
37. Gene Tunney, *A Man Must Fight* (Boson, 1932), pp. 7–11.
38. Rice, op. cit., p. 110.
39. Tunney, op. cit., p. 233.
40. Ibid., p. 234.
41. Frank De Ford, *Big Bill Tilden* (New York, 1977), p. 30.
42. Ibid., pp. 16, 79.
43. John R. Tunis, "The Lawn Tennis Industry," *Harper's*, February 1928.
44. *Time*, February 18, 1929.
45. Quoted by De Ford, op. cit., p. 147.
46. Herbert Warren Wind, *The Story of American Golf* (New York, 1956).
47. *Time*, September 22, 1930.
48. Gallico, op. cit., p. 73.
49. Wind, op. cit., pp. 215, 292.
50. Steiner, op. cit., pp. 61–62.
51. Charles Merz, *The Great American Bandwagon* (New York, 1928), p. 91.
52. Steiner, op. cit., table 20, p. 71.
53. Wind, op. cit., p. 231.

CHAPTER 13

1. Jesse Steiner, *Americans at Play* (New York, 1933), p. 192.
2. Lewis Jacobs, *The Rise of the American Film* (New York, 1939), p. 414.
3. Charles Higham, *The Art of the American Film 1900–1971* (Garden City, N.Y., 1973), p. 4.
4. David A. Yallop, *The Day the Laughter Stopped* (London, 1976), p. 103.
5. Ibid., p. 261.
6. Jacobs, op. cit., p. 340.
7. Lloyd Morris, *Not So Long Ago* (New York, 1949), p. 174.
8. David Robinson, *Hollywood in the Twenties* (New York, 1968), p. 89.

9. Ibid., p. 88.
10. Jacobs, op. cit., p. 240.
11. Charles Chaplin, *My Autobiography* (London, 1964), p. 322.
12. Eric Barnouw, *A Tower in Babel* (New York, 1966), pp. 57–60.
13. William Peck Banning, *Commercial Broadcasting Pioneer* (Cambridge, Mass., 1948), p. 105.
14. Edmund Starling, *Starling of the White House* (New York, 1946), found it impossible to get his friends to answer the doorbell on Sunday evenings; cf. "The Ether Will Now Oblige," *New Republic*, February 15, 1922.
15. U.S. President's Conference, *Recent Economic Changes* (New York, 1929), p. 322.
16. Harris Gaylord Warren, *Herbert Hoover and the Great Depression* (New York, 1967), p. 4.
17. Alain Locke, ed., *The New Negro* (New York, 1925), p. 219.
18. Rudi Blesh, *Shining Trumpets* (London, 1958), pp. 217–19.
19. See Martin Williams, "Jelly Roll Morton," in Nat Hentoff and Albert McCarthy, eds., *Jazz* (New York, 1959).
20. Alan Lomax, *Mister Jelly Roll*, 2nd ed. (Berkeley & Los Angeles, 1973), pp. 144–145.
21. Ibid., p. 181.
22. Kenneth Allsop, *The Bootleggers and Their Era* (Garden City, N.Y., 1961), p. 177.
23. For an eyewitness account of the Creole Jazz Band in these years, and the effect it had on Chicago's aspiring jazz musicians, see Milton "Mezz" Mezzrow and Bernard Wolfe, *Really the Blues* (New York, 1946), pp. 25–26.
24. Martin Williams, *Jazz Masters of New Orleans* (New York, 1967), p. 167.
25. Richard Hadlock, *Jazz Masters of the Twenties* (New York, 1974), p. 46, lists more than a score of famous trumpeters who borrowed heavily from Armstrong.
26. Nat Shapiro and Nat Hentoff, eds., *Hear Me Talkin' to Ya* (New York, 1955), p. 90.
27. Frederic Ramsey, Jr., and Charles Edward Smith, *Jazzmen* (New York, 1939), pp. 74–75.
28. Hugues Panassié, *The Real Jazz*, rev. ed. (New York, 1960), p. 60.
29. Shapiro and Hentoff, op. cit., pp. 144–46.
30. For an eyewitness account, see Burton Rascoe, *A Bookman's Daybook* (New York, 1929), p. 236–37.
31. Preston Slosson, *The Great Crusade and After* (New York, 1930), p. 282.
32. G. Stanley Hall, "Flapper Americana Novissimus," *Atlantic*, June 1922.
33. Gilbert Seldes, "Shake Your Feet," *New Republic*, November 4, 1925.

CHAPTER 14

1. Alain Locke, ed., *The New Negro* (New York, 1925), p. 345.
2. Roi Ottley, *New World A-Coming* (New York, 1943), p. 81.
3. Theodore G. Vincent, *Black Power and the Garvey Movement* (Berkeley, 1972), pp. 85–87.
4. Langston Hughes, *The Big Sea* (New York, 1940), p. 102.
5. David Cronon, *Black Moses* (Madison, Wis., 1955), p. 189.
6. Robert Morss Lovett, "The Emperor Jones of Finance," *New Republic*, July 11, 1923.
7. Locke, op. cit., p. 290.
8. Ibid., p. 285.
9. Gilbert Osofsky, *Harlem: The Making of a Ghetto* (New York, 1966), p. 136.
10. Quoted in ibid., p. 139.
11. Konrad Bercovici, "The Black Blocks of Manhattan," *Harper's*, October 1924; *New York Times*, December 10, 1928.
12. *Survey*, March 1, 1925. The entire issue is devoted to "Harlem—Mecca of the New Negro."
13. For a vivid, firsthand account of Harlem night life as seen by a white visitor in 1927, see Beverley Nichols, *The Star-Spangled Manner* (London, 1928), chap. 9.
14. Preston Slosson, *the Great Crusade and After* (New York, 1930), p. 262.

15. Hughes, op. cit., p. 224.
16. Nathan I. Huggins, *Harlem Renaissance* (New York, 1971), p. 238.
17. " 'Work or Fight' in the South," *New Republic*, March 1, 1919.
18. Herbert Seligmann, *The Negro Faces America* (New York, 1922), pp. 149–50.
19. Frank Tannenbaum, *Darker Phases of the South* (New York, 1924), p. 127.
20. Cf. Andre Siegfried, *America Comes of Age* (New York, 1928), p. 97.
21. Locke, p. 412.
22. Ibid., p. 290.
23. John Commons et al, *A History of Labor in the U.S.* (New York, 1935), vol. 3, p. 41.
24. Sterling D. Spero and Abram L. Harris, *The Black Worker* (New York, 1931), p. 152.
25. Ibid., pp. 78–79.
26. *Time*, June 18, 1928.
27. See Spero and Harris, p. 457.
28. W. J. Cash, *The Mind of the South* (New York, 1945), p. 300.
29. Walter White, *Rope and Faggot* (New York, 1929), pp. 231–32.
30. *Nation*, May 11, 1927.
31. Hughes, op. cit., p. 288.
32. Adam Kellogg, "Behind the Levees," *Survey*, June 1, 1927.

CHAPTER 15

1. Cf. *Survey*, July 1, 1924.
2. Caroline Ware, *Greenwich Village 1920–1930* (Boston, 1935), p. 4.
3. Richard Hofstadter, *The Age of Reform* (New York, 1955), p. 214.
4. Max Eastman, *Love and Revolution* (New York, 1964), p. 285.
5. Georges Duhamel, *America, the Menace* (London, 1931), p. 187.
6. Quoted by Stuart Evans *Captains of Consciousness* (New York, 1976), p. 11.
7. Ralph Borsodi, *This Ugly Civilization* (New York, 1929), pp. 149–50.
8. Mary Heaton Vorse, *Men and Steel* (New York, 1920), p. 30.
9. Louis Adamic, *Class Violence in America* (New York, 1931), pp. 390–91.
10. Elton Mayo, *Human Problems of an Industrial Civilization* (New York, 1933), pp. 67–75.
11. Ibid., pp. 146–47.
12. National Automobile Chamber of Commerce, *Facts and Figures* (New York, 1931), pp. 15–16.
13. Herbert L. Towle, "The Motor Menace," *Atlantic*, July 1925.
14. Harold Spender, *A Briton in America* (London, 1921), p. 42.
15. *Survey*, January 15, 1925.
16. Edmund DeS. Brunner et al., *American Agricultural Villages* (New York, 1922), pp. 98–99.
17. There were 24 million horses and mules on farms in 1910; 26.5 million in 1919: U.S. President's Conference, *Recent Economic Changes* (New York, 1929), vol. 2, table 2, p. 558.
18. Harold U. Faulkner, *From Versailles to the New Deal* (New Haven, Conn., 1951), p. 109.
19. *Recent Economic Changes*, table 1, p. 323.
20. Lloyd Morris, *Not So Long Ago* (New York, 1949), p. 388.
21. Alfred P. Sloan, Jr., *My Years with General Motors* (Garden City, N.Y., 1963), p. 27.
22. For Durant's version of his downfall, see Arthur Pound and Samuel T. Moore, eds., *They Told Barron* (New York, 1930), pp. 102–105.
23. Sloan, op cit., p. xxiv.
24. R. L. Duffus, "The Rise of a Billion-Dollar Corporation," *New York Times*, November 18, 1928.
25. Keith Sward, *The Legend of Henry Ford* (New York, 1948), p. 29.

26. James J. Flink, *The Car Culture* (Cambridge, Mass., 1975), p. 87.
27. Samuel S. Marquis, *Henry Ford: An Interpretation* (Boston, 1923), p. 180.
28. Allan Nevins and Frank E. Hill, *Ford: Expansion and Challenge 1915–1938* (New York, 1957), pp. 71–73.
29. *New York Times*, May 20, 1919.
30. Cf. Marquis, op. cit., pp. 7, 49, 168. Marquis was both a personal friend and the head of Ford's Sociological (personnel, that is) Department.
31. Sward, op. cit., p. 183; Nevins and Hill, op. cit., p. 276.
32. *New York Times*, December 20, 1922.
33. Charles Merz, *And Then Came Ford* (New York, 1929), p. 267.
34. Marquis, op. cit., p. 177.
35. Ibid., pp. 259–60.
36. Ibid., p. 127.
37. Richard Lowitt, *George W. Norris* (Urbana, Ill., 1971), pp. 197–214; Donald McCoy, *Calvin Coolidge* (New York, 1967), pp. 227–28.
38. Raymond Wik, *Henry Ford and Grass Roots America* (Ann Arbor, Mich., 1972), p. 142.
39. Nevins and Hill, op. cit., pp. 227–30.

CHAPTER 16

1. Quoted by Theodore B. Peterson, *Magazines in the 20th Century* (Urbana, Ill., 1964), p. 236.
2. Niven Busch, *Briton Hadden* (New York, 1949), p. 64
3. Wolcott Gibbs, "Time . . . Fortune . . . Life . . . Luce," *New Yorker*, November 28, 1936.
4. Frederick Hoffman, *The Twenties* (New York, 1955), p. 311.
5. For an example of his courage and loyalty, see Ben Hecht, *A Child of the Century* (New York, 1954), p. 180.
6. Walter Lippmann, *Men of Destiny* (New York, 1927), p. 61.
7. H. L. Mencken, *Prejudices: Second Series* (New York, 1922).
8. Quoted by Dale Kramer, *Chicago Renaissance* (New York, 1966), p. 309.
9. Dale Kramer, *Ross and the New Yorker* (Garden City, N.Y., 1951), p. 11.
10. Quoted by James Thurber, *The Years with Ross* (Boston, 1959), p. 25.
11. Ibid., p. 20.
12. Kramer, op. cit., p. 100.
13. Van Wyck Brooks, "The Literary Life," in Harold Stearns ed., *Civilization in the United States* (New York, 1922); Lewis Mumford, *The Golden Day* (New York, 1926).
14. Ernest Dimnet, "The Real Paris," *Atlantic*, August 1918.
15. The literary editor of the *New York Times*, Burton Rascoe, kept meeting young writers in the early Twenties who had just read *Ulysses* and were in despair of ever writing again: Burton Rascoe, *A Bookman's Daybook* (New York, 1929), p. 27.
16. Irene and Allen Cleaton, *Books and Battles* (Boston, 1937), p. 20.
17. As Alfred Kazin judiciously put it, Anderson turned out to be both "a visionary" and "a minor figure": Alfred Kazin, *On Native Ground* (New York, 1943), p. 216.
18. Mark Schorer, *Sinclair Lewis* (New York, 1961), p. 268.
19. Ibid., p. 269.
20. Andrew Turnbull, *Scott Fitzgerald* (London, 1962), p. 93.
21. Nancy Milford, *Zelda* (New York, 1970), pp. 68, 121.
22. Ibid., p. 98.
23. Arthur Mizener, *This Side of Paradise* (Boston, 1959), p. 84; Turnbull, op. cit., pp. 64–65.
24. F. Scott Fitzgerald, "How to Live on $36,000 a Year," *Scribner's*, April 5, 1924.
25. Kramer, *Chicago Renaissance*, p. 378.

26. Carlos Baker, *Ernest Hemingway* (New York, 1969), p. 69.
27. Ernest Hemingway, *A Moveable Feast* (New York, 1964), p. 171.
28. Ibid., p. 162.
29. Matthew J. Bruccoli, *Scott and Ernest* (London, 1978), p. 73.
30. Arthur and Barbara Gelb, *O'Neill* (New York, 1962), p. 294.
31. Mardi Valgemae, *Accelerated Grimace: Expressionism in the American Drama of the 1920s* (Carbondale, Ill., 1972), pp. 7–8.
32. Hutchins Hapgood, *A Victorian in the Modern World* (New York, 1939), p. 396.
33. Gelb and Gelb, op. cit., p. 307.
34. Jack Poggi, *Theater in America* (Ithaca, N.Y., 1968), p. 113.
35. *Time*, March 17, 1924.
36. E.g., in February 1928 an "artistic dancer" by the name of Mademoiselle Roseray staged a fake suicide attempt in Central Park pond, as a publicity stunt. Both the *New York Times* and the *World* carried the "story" on their front pages.
37. Cf. the central portion of W. A. Swanberg's *Hearst* (New York, 1961) for lavish details on the gutter press at work in the Twenties.
38. Mark Sullivan, *Our Times*, vol. 6, *The Twenties* (New York, 1935), p. 352.
39. Oliver Sayler, *Revolt in the Arts* (New York, 1930), p. 113.

CHAPTER 17

1. Burke Davis, *The Billy Mitchell Affair* (New York, 1967), pp. 250–51.
2. Charles A. Lindbergh, *The Spirit of St. Louis* (New York, 1954), p. 15.
3. Leonard Mosley, *Lindbergh* (Garden City. N.Y., 1976), p. 51.
4. Lindbergh, op. cit., p. 72.
5. *Time*, May 23, 1927.
6. Lindbergh, op. cit., pp. 195–96.
7. Karl A. Bickel, *New Empires* (Philadelphia, 1930), pp. 44–45.
8. Kenneth Davis, *The Hero* (Garden City, N.Y., 1959), pp. 217–19, 269; Mosley, op. cit., p. 118.
9. Paul Sann, *The Lawless Decade* (Cleveland, 1960), p. 71.
10. "He may have made love to Nan Britton, but not while he was in the White House. That I know for certain": Edmund Starling, *Starling of the White House* (New York, 1946), p. 170.
11. Nan Britton, *The President's Daughter* (New York, 1927), p. 80.
12. Claude Fuess, *Calvin Coolidge* (Boston, 1940), p. 374.
13. William A. White, *A Puritan in Babylon* (New York, 1937), pp. 335–38; cf. Starling, p. 263.
14. Charles Merz, "The Silent Mr. Coolidge," *New Republic*, June 2, 1926.
15. Beverley Nichols, *The Star-Spangled Manner* (London, 1928), pp. 110–11.
16. Fuess, op. cit., p. 367.
17. Ibid., p. 351.
18. Irwin Hood Hoover, *Forty-Two Years at the White House* (Boston, 1934), p. 131.
19. White, op. cit., pp. 359–60; Fuess, op. cit., p. 395.
20. Francis Russell, *Tragedy in Dedham* (New York, 1962), p. 222.
21. Marion D. Frankfurter and Gardner Jackson, *The Letters of Sacco and Vanzetti* (New York, 1930), pp. 23–24.
22. Ibid., p. 187.
23. Roberta Feurlicht, *Justice Crucified* (New York, 1977), p. 311.
24. It is reprinted in full in John Dos Passos, *Facing the Chair* (Boston, 1927), pp. 25–27.
25. He made the same boast on his deathbed many years later to a Boston mobster named Vincent Teresa, Vincent Teresa, *My Life in the Mafia* (Chicago, 1972).
26. Feurlicht, op. cit., p. 320.

27. Felix Frankfurter, *The Case of Sacco and Vanzetti* (Boston, 1927), p. 100.
28. *New York World*, August 9, 1927.
29. Feurlicht, op. cit., p. 359.
30. Bruce Bliven, "In Dedham Jail," *New Republic*, June 22, 1927; Russell, op. cit., p. 117.
31. Herbert B. Ehrmann, *The Case That Will Not Die* (New York, 1969), pp. 379–92.
32. Elizabeth Glendower Evans, "Sacco and Vanzetti," *Survey*, June 15, 1926.
33. Ella Reeve Bloor, *We Are Many* (London, 1941), pp. 207–208; Russell, op. cit., pp. 1–2.
34. William G. Thompson, "Vanzetti's Last Statement," *New Republic*, February 1, 1928; Russell, op. cit., p. 450.
35. Bloor, op. cit., p. 211.
36. Jeanette Marks, *Thirteen Days* (New York, 1929).
37. Gene Tunney, *A Man Must Fight* (Boston, 1932), p. 239.
38. In Alison Danzig and Peter Brandwein, *Sports' Golden Age* (New York, 1948), p. 76.
39. Randy Roberts, *Dempsey* (Baton Rouge, La., 1979), p. 259.
40. For the views of the two principals regarding the "long count," see Tunney, op. cit., pp. 268–70; Jack Dempsey and Barbara Piatelli Dempsey, *Dempsey* (New York, 1977), p. 219.
41. Tunney, op. cit., p. 280.
42. Charles Higham, *The Art of the American Film* (Garden City, N.Y., 1973), p. 85.
43. Alexander Walker, *The Shattered Silents* (London, 1978).
44. Robert Benchley in *Life*, Jan. 13, 1925, describes Jolson's impact on his audience.
45. Walker, op. cit., p. 36.
46. Allen Nevins and Frank Hill, *Ford: Expansion and Challenge* (New York, 1957), p. 434.
47. Keith Sward, *The Legend of Henry Ford* (New York, 1948), p. 197.
48. James J. Flink, *The Car Culture* (Cambridge, Mass., 1973), p. 117.
49. Nevins and Hill, op. cit., p. 450.

CHAPTER 18

1. Hoover's engineering career was later inflated out of all reasonable proportion by his friends and ridiculed with vituperative zeal by his enemies. The most evenhanded appraisal is probably Geoffrey Blainey, "Herbert Hoover's Forgotten Years," in *Business Archives and History*, February 1963.
2. Vernon Kellogg, "Herbert Hoover as Individual and Type," *Atlantic*, August 1918.
3. Harris Gaylord Warren, *Herbert Hoover and the Great Depression* (New York, 1967), p. 23.
4. *New York Times*, March 11, 1920.
5. Henry F. Pringle, "Hoover: An Enigma Easily Misunderstood," *World's Work*, June 1928.
6. Craig M. Lloyd, *Aggressive Introvert* (Columbus, Ohio, 1973), pp. 60–66.
7. David Hinshaw, *Herbert Hoover: American Quaker* (New York, 1950), pp. 125–26.
8. Joan Hoff Wilson, *Herbert Hoover, Forgotten Progressive* (Boston, 1975), p. 180.
9. Herbert Hoover, *Memoirs*, vol. 2, *The Cabinet and the Presidency* (New York, 1952), p. 125.
10. Quoted in David Burner, *Herbert Hoover* (New York, 1979), p. 166.
11. Ibid., p. 193.
12. William A. White, *Masks in a Pageant* (New York, 1928), p. 464.
13. Richard O'Connor, *The Last Hurrah* (New York, 1970), p. 89.
14. Norman Hapgood and Henry Moscowitz, *Up from the City Streets* (New York, 1927), p. 73.
15. Robert A. Caro, *The Power Broker* (New York, 1974), p. 93.
16. E.g., *New Republic*, September 5, 1928.
17. William L. Chenery, "So This is Tammany Hall!" *Atlantic*, September 1924; Joseph McGoldrick, "The New Tammany," ibid., September, 1928.
18. *New York Times*, August 9, 1926.

19. Matthew and Hannah Josephson, *Al Smith* (Boston, 1969), pp. 361–62.
20. Calvin Coolidge, *The Autobiography of Calvin Coolidge* (Boston, 1929), p. 233; Donald R. McCoy, *Calvin Coolidge* (New York, 1967), pp. 388–89.
21. *New York Times*, August 12, 1928.
22. Hinshaw, op. cit., p. 144.
23. Roy V. Peel and Thomas C. Donnelly, *The 1928 Campaign* (New York, 1931), p. 39.
24. David Burner, *The Politics of Provincialism* (New York, 1968), p. 148.
25. For his views on booze, see Josephson, op. cit., p. 292.
26. Edward A. Moore, *A Catholic Runs for President* (New York, 1956), pp. 127–28.
27. The most recent in-depth study on this hotly argued point is Allen J. Lichtman, *Prejudice and the Old Politics* (Chapel Hill, N.C., 1979).
28. Moore, pp. 1–18, provides a useful summary.
29. *New York Herald Tribune*, July 15, 1928.
30. Quoted in Kenneth Bailey, *Southern White Protestantism in the 20th Century* (New York, 1964), p. 93.
31. *New York Times*, September 8, 1928.
32. Wilson, op. cit., p. 132.
33. Moore, op. cit., pp. 158–59.
34. Gilbert C. Fite, *George N. Peek and the Fight for Farm Parity* (Norman, Okla., 1954), p. 216; *New Republic*, August 1, 1928.
35. Bernard Bellush, *Franklin D. Roosevelt as Governor of New York* (New York, 1955), pp. 6–9; Oscar Handlin, *Al Smith and His America* (Boston, 1958), p. 142; Frank Freidel, *Franklin D. Roosevelt: The Ordeal* (Boston, 1954), pp. 253–55.
36. Peel and Donnelly, op. cit., pp. 48, 79–80.
37. Richard Hofstadter, "Could a Protestant Have Beaten Hoover in 1928?" *Reporter*, March 17, 1960; Ruth C. Silva, *Rum, Religion and Votes* (College Park, Pa., 1962), pp. 2–12.
38. Lichtman, op. cit., pp. 200–201.
39. Willis J. Abbott, *Watching the World Go By* (Boston, 1973), p. 345.
40. Jordan A. Schwartz, "Hoover and Congress," in Martin Fausold and George T. Mazuzan, eds., *The Hoover Presidency* (Albany, N.Y., 1974).
41. Hoover, op. cit., p. 174.
42. Fite, op. cit., p. 126.
43. Warren, op. cit., p. 172.
44. The details at every stage of the enactment of the Hawley-Smoot tariff are to be found in E. E. Schattschneider, *Politics, Pressures and the Tariff* (New York, 1935), the definitive account of this legislation.
45. Warren, op. cit., p. 212.
46. Hoover, op. cit., p. 327.

CHAPTER 19

1. John R. Commons et al., *History of Labor*, vol. 3 (New York, 1935), p. 111.
2. Henri Dubreuil, *Robots or Men?* (New York, 1930). Chapter 5 is titled "Technological Unemployment."
3. Commons, op. cit., table 1, p. 35.
4. U.S. President's Conference, *Recent Economic Changes* (New York, 1929), table 8, p. 879; cf. Stanley Lebergott "Annual Estimates of Unemployment in the U.S. 1900–1954," *The Measurement and Behavior of Unemployment* (Princeton, N.J., 1957), p. 215, putting it at 1.9 percent in 1926.
5. *Time*, March 12, 1928.
6. Robert Lynd and Helen Lynd, *Middletown* (New York, 1929), p. 66.
7. Paul Douglas, *Real Wages in the United States* (Boston, 1930), table 170, p. 437.
8. *Survey*, March 1, 1928.

9. *New York Times*, March 28, 1929.
10. William M. Leiserson, "Henry Ford's Want Ad," *New Republic*, March 6, 1929; *New York Times*, January 3, 1929.
11. Hugh Adam, *An Australian Looks at America* (London, 1928), pp. 45–47.
12. *Adkins v. Children's Hospital*, 261 US 525 (1923).
13. Paul F. Brissenden, *Earnings of Factory Workers* (New York, 1929), table 20, p. 53.
14. Louis I. Dublin, *Health and Wealth* (New York, 1928), p. 188.
15. William Henry Chafe, *The American Woman* (New York, 1972), p. 61; J. Stanley Lemons, *The Woman Citizen: Social Feminism in the 1920s* (Urbana, Ill., 1973), pp. 140–41.
16. Margaret Lindsay Sutherland, "A Student Factory Hand" *Nation*, February 3, 1926.
17. Rexford G. Tugwell et al., *American Economic Life*, 3d ed. (New York, 1930), pp. 120–21.
18. *Nation*, April 27, 1927; Douglas, table 24, p. 108.
19. Abraham Epstein, "Darker Phases of American Prosperity," *New Republic*, February 6, 1929; Daisy Lee Worthington Worcester, "This Amazing Prosperity," *Survey*, November 1, 1928; Lewis Corey, "Who Owns the Nation's Wealth?" *New Republic*, August 10, 1927.
20. Selig Perlman and Philip Taft, *Labor Movements* (New York, 1935), pp. 506–11.
21. Irving Bernstein, *The Lean Years* (Boston, 1959), p. 148.
22. *United Mine Workers v. Coronado Coal Company* 259 US 344 (1922).
23. Bernstein, p. 173.
24. *United Mine Workers v. Red Jacket Consolidated Coal and Coke Company*, 18 Fed. (2d) 839 (1927).
25. Melvyn Dubofsky and Warren Van Tine, *John L. Lewis* (New York, 1973), pp. 133–34.
26. Adam, op. cit., p. 73.
27. *Recent Economic Changes*, p. 482.
28. Douglas, op. cit., chart 16, p. 117.
29. See Israel Mufson, "As Labor Sees Unemployment Insurance," *Survey*, October 15, 1928; Theresa Wolfson, "Trade Union Insurance," ibid., April 1, 1929.
30. Abraham Epstein, "Outwitting American Unionism," *New Republic*, April 6, 1927.
31. Louis Stanley, "The Collapse of the AF of L," *Nation*, October 8, 1927.
32. Felix Frankfurter and Nathan Greene, *The Labor Injunction* (New York, 1930), p. 32.
33. Edwin E. Witte, *The Government in Labor Disputes* (New York, 1932); p. 84 provides a decade by decade breakdown.
34. Stanley, op. cit.
35. Bernstein, p. 90.
36. Beulah Amidon, "An Old-Fashioned Strike," *Survey*, April 1, 1926.
37. Joseph Freeman, *An American Testament* (New York, 1936), p. 399.
38. *Time*, March 15, 1926.
39. Most of the strike organization was under the direction, behind the scenes, of Benjamin Gitlow. He explains how it was done. Benjamin Gitlow, *The Whole of Their Lives* (New York, 1948), pp. 130–32.
40. George B. Tindall, *The Emergence of the New South 1913–1945* (Baton Rouge, La., 1967), p. 71.
41. Merryle Stanley Rukeyser, "The Challenge to Labor Standards," *Nation*, Aug. 14, 1929.
42. W. J. Cash, *The Mind of the South* (New York, 1941), p. 201.
43. Frank Tannenbaum, *Darker Phases of the South* (New York, 1924), p. 70.
44. Tom Tippett, *When Southern Labor Stirs* (New York, 1931), p. 5.
45. Tindall, p. 75.
46. Fred E. Beal, *Proletarian Journey* (New York, 1937), p. 120.
47. Tippett, p. 84.
48. Beal, p. 131.
49. Ibid., p. 159.
50. Ibid., pp. 187–188.

51. Ibid., p. 183.
52. Nell Battle Lewis, "Anarchy vs. Communism in Gastonia," *Nation*, vol. CXXIX (1929), pp. 321–322.
53. Beal, p. 193.
54. Tippett, p. 138.

CHAPTER 20

1. Robert W. Bruère, "The New Nationalism and Business," *Harper's*, March 1919.
2. Charles C. Chapman, *The Development of American Business and Banking Thought 1913–1936* (New York), 1936, p. 100.
3. Thomas C. Blaisdell, Jr., *The Federal Trade Commission* (New York, 1932), p. 179.
4. Dwight L. Dumond, *Roosevelt to Roosevelt* (New York, 1937), p. 334.
5. Adolphe A. Berle and Gardiner C. Means, *The Modern Corporation and Private Property* (New York, 1932), appendix D, pp. 320–21.
6. A. A. Berle and V. E. Pederson, *Liquid Claims and National Wealth* (New York, 1934).
7. Berle and Means, op. cit., p. 47.
8. Thomas C. Cochran and William Miller, *The Age of Enterprise* (Cambridge, Mass., 1942), p. 407.
9. U.S. President's Conference on Recent Economic Changes, *Recent Economic Changes* (New York, 1929), p. 344.
10. The work which persuaded them to take this step is a modern business classic, J. D. McKinsey's *Budgetary Control* (New York, 1922).
11. Louis Galambos, *The Public Image of Big Business in America 1880–1940* (Baltimore, 1975), pp. 195–216, 220; and Edna Lonigan, "Wanted: A New Criticism of Business," *New Republic*, June 26, 1929, voiced a general liberal lament when she wrote, "There is no longer any active criticism of business."
12. Thomas N. Carver, *The Present Economic Revolution in the United States* (Boston, 1926), pp. 192–94.
13. Walter N. Polakov, *The Power Age* (New York, 1933), pp. 73–77.
14. Harry Jerome, *Mechanization in Industry* (New York, 1934), table 25, p. 257.
15. Solomon Fabricant, *The Output of Manufacturing Industries 1899–1937* (New York, 1940), table 2, p. 48.
16. Edward F. Denison, *The Sources of Economic Growth in the U.S.* (New York, 1962), table 2, p. 17.
17. An argument accepted by Paul Douglas, *Real Wages in the U.S. 1890–1926* (Boston, 1930), p. 567.
18. See Jerome, op. cit., p. 37.
19. Sumner H. Slichter, "The Secret of High Wages," *New Republic*, March 28, 1928.
20. Denison, op. cit., pp. 70–76.
21. U.S. Department of Labor, *Monthly Labor Review*, December 1932.
22. Douglas, op. cit., table 185, p. 512.
23. *Recent Economic Changes*, pp. 104–105; Douglas, op. cit., chart 81, p. 511.
24. Frederick Mills, *Economic Tendencies in the United States* (New York, 1932), table 192, p. 482.
25. *Time*, March 12, 1928.
26. Abraham Epstein, "Darker Phases of American Prosperity," *New Republic*, February 6, 1929.
27. *Nation*, Jan. 7, 1931.
28. Recent Economic Changes, pp. xv, xviii.
29. Ibid., p. xix.
30. Cochran and Miller, pp. 298–300.
31. *Recent Economic Changes*, p. 496.

32. John Commons et al., *History of Labor*, vol. 3 (New York 1935), p. 91.
33. Jerome, op. cit., p. 382.
34. Clinch Calkins, *Spy Overhead* (New York, 1937), pp. 140–42.
35. Arthur Pound and Samuel T. Moore, eds., *They Told Barron* (New York, 1930), p. 133.
36. Robert Sobel, *The Great Bull Market* (New York, 1968), p. 83.
37. U.S. Senate Committee on Banking and Currency, *Stock Exchange Practices* (Washington, D.C., 1932–1934), pp. 715 et seq.
38. James C. Bonbright and Gardiner C. Means, *The Holding Company* (New York, 1932), p. 7.
39. John T. Flynn, *Investment Trusts Gone Wrong!* (New York, 1930), p. 20.
40. *Time*, November 29, 1926.
41. Forrest McDonald, *Insull* (Chicago, 1962), p. vii.
42. Ibid., p. 54.
43. Ibid., pp. 112, 192.
44. *New Republic*, March 16, 1927; *Time*, op. cit.
45. McDonald, pp. 205–13.
46. Ibid., p. 278.
47. "Following the tribes of begetters through Genesis is a simple matter when compared with the Insull maze": Herbert Gaylord Warren, *Herbert Hoover and the Great Depression* (New York, 1967), p. 81.

CHAPTER 21

1. Charles C. Chapman, *The Development of American Business and Banking Thought, 1913–1936* (New York, 1936), p. 129.
2. U.S. President's Conference, *Recent Economic Changes* (New York, 1929), pp. 864–65.
3. Robert S. and Helen M. Lynd, *Middletown* (New York, 1929), 261—62.
4. "If there had existed a militant organization of consumers with a staff of commodity experts, this book would not have been written": Stuart Chase and F. J. Schlink, *Your Money's Worth* (New York, 1927), p. 229.
5. Stuart Chase, *A New Deal* (New York, 1932), pp. 18, 77.
6. John Gunther, *Taken at the Flood* (New York, 1960), p. 96.
7. Eric Barnouw, *A Tower in Babel* (New York, 1966), p. 202.
8. Neil Borden, *The Economic Effects of Advertising* (Chicago, 1942), table 3, p. 57; Robert Sobel, *The Great Bull Market* (New York, 1968), p. 43.
9. Arthur Kallett and F. J. Schlink, *100,000,000 Guinea Pigs* (New York, 1933), p. 65.
10. Philip Wagner, "Mouth-Conscious America," *New Republic*, July 21, 1926.
11. James Playsted Wood, *The Story of Advertising* (New York, 1958), p. 413.
12. Otis Pease, *The Responsibilities of American Advertising: Private Control and Public Influence 1920–1940* (New Haven, 1958), p. 140.
13. Chase and Schlink, op. cit., p. 65.
14. Louis I. Dublin, "Statistical Bulletin," Metropolitan Life Insurance Co. (New York, 1932).
15. The leading exponent was Ralph Borsodi, whose text, *This Ugly Civilization* (New York, 1929), was a Twenties best-seller.
16. Evans Clark, *Financing the Consumer* (New York, 1930), pp. 12–13.
17. Alfred Sloan, Jr., *My Years with General Motors* (Garden City, N.Y., 1963), pp. 302–303.
18. "Facts and Figures on the Automobile Industry," U.S. Chamber of Commerce (Washington, D.C., 1929).
19. Lynd and Lynd, op. cit., p. 255.
20. Arthur Pound, "The Land of Dignified Credit," *Atlantic*, February 1926; see also Orrin C. Lester, "A Dollar Down and Ten to Go," *Survey*, November 1, 1928.
21. Clark, op. cit., pp. 49–55.

22. W. C. Plummer, "Social and Economic Consequences of Buying on the Installment Plan," *Annals*, vol. 129, supplement 3.
23. Temporary National Economic Committee, *Verbatim Record of Proceedings* (Washington, D.C., 1939), vol. 1, Reference Data Section III, p. 41; Evans Clark, *The Internal Debts of the United States* (New York, 1933), p. 16; Frederick Lewis Allen, *The Lords of Creation* (New York, 1936), p. 403.
24. Evans Clark, "Mass Credit," *Survey*, October 1, 1930.
25. *Recent Economic Changes*, op. cit.
26. Frederick Mills, *Economic Tendencies in the United States* (New York, 1932), table 172, p. 435.
27. Lynd and Lynd, op. cit., p. 46.
28. Joseph Schumpeter, "The American Economy in the Interwar Period: The Decade of the Twenties," *American Economic Review*, May 1946.

CHAPTER 22

1. Robert Sobel, *The Great Bull Market* (New York, 1968), p. 18.
2. Lawrence W. Levine, *Defender of the Faith* (New York, 1965), pp. 238–41.
3. Arthur T. Pound and Samuel Moore, eds., *They Told Barron* (New York, 1930), p. 270.
4. Bruce Bliven, "Where Ev'ry Prospect Pleases," *New Republic*, March 26, 1924.
5. Ibid.; cf. Lucy J. Chamberlain, "Behind the Boom in Florida," *Survey*, February 1, 1926.
6. Aaron M. Sakolski, *The Great American Land Bubble* (New York, 1932), pp. 338–39.
7. John Burke, *Rogue's Progress* (New York, 1975), pp. 205–29, describes Mizner's career as con man/architect.
8. Ben Hecht, *A Child of the Century* (New York, 1954), pp. 446–55.
9. Gertrude Mathews Shelby, "Florida Frenzy," *Harper's*, January 1926.
10. *Time*, August 3, 1925.
11. *New York Times*, Sepetember 19–23, 1926.
12. *New Republic*, October 27, 1926; *Time*, Oct. 11, 1926.
13. Henry S. Villar, "Florida Aftermath," *Nation*, June 6, 1928.
14. Alexander Dana Noyes, *The War Period of American Finance* (New York, 1926), p. 36.
15. Matthew Josephson, *Life Among the Surrealists* (New York, 1962), p. 278.
16. Sobel, op. cit., p. 65.
17. Ibid., p. 92.
18. John T. Flynn, *Investment Trusts Gone Wrong!* (New York, 1930), pp. 96–98.
19. Josephson, op. cit., p. 276.
20. Sobel, op. cit., p. 60.
21. Earl Sparling, *Mystery Men of Wall Street* (New York, 1930), p. 52.
22. Pound and Moore, op. cit., pp. 46–48.
23. Sparling, op. cit., pp. 84–85.
24. Pound and Moore, op. cit., p. 101.
25. *Time*, August 11, 1926.
26. Lester V. Chandler, *Benjamin Strong, Central Banker* (Washington, D.C., 1958), p. 30.
27. Ibid., pp. 427–35.
28. Elmus R. Wicker, *Federal Reserve Monetary Policy 1917–1933* (New York, 1966), pp. 112–13.
29. U.S. President's Conference, *Recent Economic Changes* (New York, 1929), pp. 668–69.
30. Herbert Hoover, *Memoirs*, vol. 3. See also *The Great Depression* (New York, 1952), p. 21; Virgil Willits, "The Banks Go Chainstore," *American Mercury*, May 1930; *Nation*, February 26, 1930.
31. Ferdinand Pecora, *Wall Street Under Oath* (New York, 1935), p. 77.
32. U.S. Senate Banking and Currency Committee, *Stock Exchange Practices* (Washington, D.C., 1932), p. 206.

33. Pecora, op. cit., pp. 100–102.
34. Giulio Pontecorvo, "Investment Banking and Security Speculation in the 1920s," *Business History Review*, summer 1958.
35. Walter Ripley, *Main Street and Wall Street* (New York, 1927), p. 352.
36. Federal Reserve Board, *Banking and Monetary Statistics* (Washington, D.C., 1943), pp. 488–89.
37. *Stock Exchange Practices*, pp. 173–74.
38. Sobel, op. cit., pp. 72–73.
39. Gordon Thomas and Max Morgan-Witts, *The Day the Bubble Burst* (New York, 1979), pp. 104–106, 114–24.
40. Stuart Chase, *The Tragedy of Waste* (New York, 1925), p. 78.
41. Keyes Winter, "Fools and Their Money," *Harper's*, August 1927.
42. E. H. Smith, "Our Biggest Tax—The Cost of Crime," *Literary Digest*, July 5, 1924.
43. Charles Merz, "Bull Market," *Harper's*, April 1929; *Time*, November 26, 1928.
44. Howard H. Quint and Robert H. Ferrell, *The Talkative President* (Boston, 1964), pp. 137–38.
45. Sobel, op. cit., p. 95.
46. *Time*, October 22, 1928.
47. Caroline Bird, *The Invisible Scar* (New York, 1966), p. 10.
48. Robert Sobel, *Panic on Wall Street* (New York, 1968), pp. 356–57; the Senate Banking and Currency Committee could find only 1,548,707 stockholders in the entire country in 1929, and only one in three held a margin account—*Stock Exchange Practices*, p. 13. In the mid-Twenties the Federal Trade Commission had surveyed 1 million stockholders. Their average holdings of common stock were worth $7,000; their preferred, $5,200. The market was hardly a place for "everybody." FTC, *National Wealth and Income* (Washington, D.C., 1926), p. 6; and for one example of rejection at the time of the idea that large numbers were involved in the stock market, see *New Republic*, June 26, 1929.

CHAPTER 23

1. Frederick C. Mills, *Economic Tendencies in the United States* (New York, 1932), table 106, p. 246.
2. W. Floyd Maxwell, "The Building Industry Since the War," *Review of Economic Statistics*, May 1931, chart 1.
3. Mills, op. cit., table 112, p. 267.
4. Ibid., table 179, p. 453.
5. *New Republic*, January 12, 1927.
6. Joseph L. Snider, *Business Statistics*, 2nd ed. (New York, 1932), charts 3 and 4, p. 125.
7. Mills, op. cit., table 114, p. 270.
8. George Soule, *Prosperity Decade* (London, 1947), p. 148.
9. Helen Hall, "When Detroit's Out of Gear," *Survey*, April 1, 1930.
10. Federal Reserve Board, *Bulletin*, February 1930.
11. John R. Commons et al., *History of Labor in the United States*, vol. 3 (New York, 1935), p. 142; there had been confident forecasts that unemployment would rise sharply even if prosperity continued, e.g., William Leiserson, "Unemployment, 1929," *Survey*, April 1, 1929.
12. *New York Times*, June 13, 1928.
13. *Time*, November 26, 1928.
14. *New York Times*, January 1, 1929.
15. *New Republic*, February 27, 1929.
16. Herbert Hoover, *Memoirs*, vol. 3, *The Depression* (New York, 1952), p. 17.
17. Robert Sobel, *The Great Bull Market* (New York, 1968), p. 127.

18. Elmus R. Wicker, *Federal Reserve Monetary Policy 1917–1933* (New York, 1966), pp. 129–30, 136–37.
19. Harold Reed, *Federal Reserve Policy 1921–1930* (New York, 1930), p. 152.
20. *New York Times*, August 9, 1929.
21. Irving Fisher, *The Stock Market Crash—And After* (New York, 1930), p. 20.
22. *New York Times*, September 2, 1929.
23. Sobel, op. cit., p. 135.
24. Herbert Corey, *The Truth About Hoover* (Boston, 1932), p. 43.
25. Federal Reserve Board, *Banking and Monetary Statistics* (Washington, D.C., 1943), p. 494.
26. *New York Times*, January 16, 1930.
27. Burton Rascoe, "The Grim Anniversary," *New Republic*, September 29, 1930.
28. Robert Sobel, *Panic on Wall Street* (New York, 1969), p. 384.
29. Otto T. Mallery, "How to Keep the Wheels Turning," *Survey*, December 15, 1929.
30. Hoover, op. cit., pp. 43–44.
31. E.g., *New Republic*, November 27, 1929.
32. Julius H. Barnes, "Business in the New Year," *Review of Reviews*, January 1930.
33. Earl Sparling, *Mystery Men of Wall Street* (New York, 1930), p. 178.
34. Jack Dempsey and Barbara Piatelli Dempsey, *Dempsey* (New York, 1977), p. 228.
35. Albert Parry, *Garrets and Pretenders* (New York, 1960), p. 319.
36. Ferdinand Pecora, *Wall Street Under Oath* (New York, 1935), p. 127.
37. Forrest McDonald, *Insull* (Chicago, 1962), p. 283.
38. *Time*, May 11, 1931; John Brooks, *Once in Golconda* (New York, 1969), p. 120.
39. Sobel, *Great Bull Market*, p. 157.
40. Pecora, op. cit., p. 153.
41. *New York Times*, December 31, 1929.
42. Peter Temin, *Did Monetary Forces Cause the Great Depression?* (New York, 1973), pp. 79–82.
43. Theodore B. Peterson, *Magazines in the 20th Century* (Urbana, Ill., 1964), p. 238.
44. *New York Times*, February 12, 1930.
45. Snider, op. cit., p. 80.
46. W. Floyd Maxwell, op. cit.
47. Snider, op. cit., charts 3 and 4, p. 125.
48. McDonald, op. cit., p. 285.
49. Robert C. Cottner et al., *Texas Cities and the Great Depression* (Austin, Texas, 1973), pp. 11–16.
50. *Survey*, April 1, 1930.
51. *New Republic*, March 12, 1930; *Nation*, April 9, 1930.
52. Hoover, op. cit., p. 49.
53. Charles E. Persons, "Census Reports on Unemployment in April 1930," *Annals*, March 1931.
54. *Time*, April 28, 1930.
55. *Survey*, Aug. 15, 1930.
56. Jesse F. Steiner, *Americans at Play* (New York, 1933), pp. 84, 88.
57. John Kenneth Galbraith, *The Great Crash, 1929* (New York, 1962), pp. 178–79; cf. the exchange between Schumpeter and Gardner C. Means in *American Economic Review*, May 1946.
58. Pontecorvo, op. cit.
59. Temin, op. cit., pp. 62, 185–91.
60. Sobel, *Great Bull Market*, pp. 151–52.
61. Milton Friedman and Anna Schwartz, *The Great Contraction 1929–1933* (Princeton, 1965), pp. 63–71; Wicker, op. cit., p. 196.
62. Albert U. Romasco, *The Poverty of Abundance* (New York, 1965), p. 44.

63. Lionel Robbins, *The Great Depression* (London, 1931), pp. 10, 44; Derek H. Aldcroft, *From Versailles to Wall Street 1919–1929* (London, 1977), pp. 281–82.
64. Friedman and Schwartz, op. cit., pp. 11, 55.
65. Harold Barger, *Outlay and Income in the United States 1921–1938* (New York, 1942), table 10, pp. 106–107.
66. Ibid., table 9, p. 94.
67. Temin, op. cit., p. 172; cf. Lewis Corey, "Wall Street and Hard Times," *New Republic*, March 26, 1930, on the real money losses from the crash.
68. Harry W. Payne, *Business Behavior 1919–1922* (Chicago, 1942), p. 213; Snider, op. cit., p. 251.
69. Neil Borden, *The Economic Effects of Advertising* (New York 1942), table 102, p. 418.
70. Barger, op. cit., table 3, pp. 50–51.
71. Ibid., table 13, p. 150.
72. Malcolm Cowley, *Exile's Return* (New York, 1956), p. 301.

CHAPTER 24

1. Elmer T. Irey, *The Tax Dodgers* (Garden City, N.Y., 1949), p. 43; Herbert Hoover in his *Memoirs*, vol. 2, *The Cabinet and the Presidency* (New York, 1952), says that he had hardly been sworn in before a delegation of prominent Chicagoans came to plead for his help in ridding their city of Capone, p. 277.
2. Herbert Asbury, *The Gem of the Prairie* (Garden City, N.Y., 1942), p. 315.
3. Joseph Anthony, ed., *Best News Stories of 1924* (Boston, 1925), p. 31.
4. John Kobler, *Capone* (New York, 1971), p. 135.
5. Eliot Ness, *The Untouchables* (New York, 1957), p. 39.
6. Ibid., p. 234.
7. Kobler, op. cit., p. 269.
8. Irey, op. cit., pp. 66–67.
9. *Time*, November 2, 1931.
10. Arthur Conan Doyle, *Our American Adventure* (London, 1923), p. 23.
11. *New Republic*, April 19, 1922.
12. Edward Hale Bierstadt, "Our Permanent Crime Wave," *Harper's*, December 1927.
13. *New Republic*, Oct. 17, 1923.
14. Lewis E. Lawes, *Life and Death in Sing Sing* (New York, 1929), p. 50.
15. Harry Elmer Barnes, *Battling the Crime Wave* (Boston, 1931), p. 209.
16. U.S. President's Committee on Recent Social Trends, *Recent Social Trends* (New York, 1933), p. 1165; Harry L. Best, *Crime and the Criminal Law in the United States* (New York, 1930), pp. 153–61.
17. William D. Haywood, *Bill Haywood's Book* (New York, 1929), p. 53.
18. Ernest Booth, *Stealing Through Life* (New York, 1929), p. 48.
19. John Landesco, *Organized Crime in Chicago* (Chicago, 1929), pp. 10–23.
20. *Time*, April 9, 1928; see also Oliver H. P. Garrett, "Politics and Crime in Chicago," *New Republic*, June 9, 1926.
21. Ibid., June 13, 1927.
22. Kenneth Allsop, *The Bootleggers* (Garden City, N.Y., 1961), p. 123.
23. *Time*, July 2, 1928.
24. Landesco, op. cit., pp. 97–98.
25. *Time*, July 2, 1930.
26. Stanley Walker, *The Night Club Era* (New York, 1933), p. 158.
27. Emanuel H. Lavine, *Gimme: or How Politicians Get Rich* (New York, 1931), pp. 19–21.
28. *New Republic*, June 25, 1930.
29. William B. Northrop and John A. Northrop, *The Insolence of Office* (New York, 1932), pp. 20–23, 41–53.

30. *Time*, September 22, 1930.
31. Frederick M. Thrasher, *The Gang* (Chicago, 1927), pp. 409–10.
32. H. C. Brearley, *Homicide in the United States* (Chapel Hill, N.C., 1932), pp. 149–51.
33. Ibid., table 10, pp. 209–16.
34. *Time*, April 16, 1928.
35. Barnes, op. cit., p. 129.
36. *Nation*, February 8, 1928.
37. *Time*, Oct. 27, 1930.
38. Landesco, op. cit., p. 183.
39. Humbert S. Nelli, *Italians in Chicago 1890–1930* (New York, 1970), pp. 132–40.
40. Kobler, op. cit., p. 89.
41. Lloyd Morris, *Postscript to Yesterday* (New York, 1947), pp. 78–79.
42. Lloyd Lewis, "Chicago's Booze War," *New Republic*, March 13, 1929.
43. Kobler, op. cit., p. 258.
44. Ray Tucker, "Seven Years of Prohibition," *New Republic*, June 8, 1927.
45. *New York Times*, January 18, 1930.
46. *Time*, July 21, 1930.
47. Arthur Kallett and F. J. Schlink, *100,000,000 Guinea Pigs* (New York, 1933), p. 152.
48. Izzy Einstein, *Prohibition Agent No. 1* (New York, 1932), pp. 258–59.
49. *Time*, April 22, 1929.
50. Ibid., June 13, 1930.
51. Sanford Bates, *Prisons and Beyond* (New York, 1937), p. 130; on conditions at Leavenworth, see Austin H. Merrick "Send Them Up," *Survey*, March 1, 1926.
52. David Burner, *Herbert Hoover* (New York, 1979).
53. *Time*, April 28, 1930, and April 13, 1931; *Nation*, April 30, 1930.
54. Emanuel H. Lavine, *The Third Degree* (New York, 1930), p. 4.
55. *Nation*, October 30, 1929.
56. Frank Tannenbaum, *Wall Shadows* (New York, 1922), pp. 106–107; *Survey*, September 1, 1926.
57. O. F. Lewis, "Delaware's Prison—A Paradox," *Survey*, July 2, 1921; *Time*, April 6, 1925.
58. Tannenbaum, op. cit., pp. 110–11.
59. Louis Berg, *Revelations of a Prison Doctor* (New York, 1934), p. 24.
60. Joseph E. Fishman, "The American Jail," *Atlantic*, December 1922; Bates, op. cit., pp. 50–53.
61. *Time*, May 13, 1929.
62. Thomas E. Gaddis and James O. Long, *Killer* (New York, 1970), pp. 189–93.
63. Robert E. Burns, *I Am a Fugitive from a Georgia Chain Gang* (New York, 1932), p. 256.
64. Beverley Nichols, *The Star-Spangled Manner* (London, 1928), p. 44.
65. Anne Morrow Lindbergh, *Hour of Gold, Hour of Lead* (New York, 1973), pp. 226–27.
66. *Time*, May 11, 1931, and August 24, 1931; Walker, op. cit., pp. 268–69.
67. *New Republic*, March 16, 1932.
68. Irey, p. 69; George Walker, *Kidnap: The Story of the Lindbergh Case* (New York, 1959), p. 23.
69. Mary Agnes Hamilton, *In America Today* (London, 1932), p. 116.

CHAPTER 25

1. Frank Lloyd Wright, *An Autobiography* (New York, 1943), p. 92.
2. Walter H. Kilham, *Raymond Hood, Architect* (New York, 1973), p. 32.
3. Wright, op. cit., p. 101.
4. Ibid., p. 107.
5. Finis Farr, *Frank Lloyd Wright* (London, 1962), p. 75.
6. Frank Lloyd Wright, *Modern Architecture* (Princeton, 1931), p. 16.

7. Wright, *Autobiography* p. 233.
8. Farr says Wright was not simply broke but deeply in debt, p. 172.
9. The Armory Show of 1913 is usually described as the watershed. But many visitors to it assumed that the modernistic works were a hoax. The few people who took European modernism seriously rejected (rightly) the American examples as being third-rate. Rudi Blesh, *Modern Art, USA* (New York, 1956), pp. 51–53, 83. It was the phenomenal growth of fine arts courses in the Twenties that created a large and educated American audience for art of all kinds. The Metropolitan Museum outdrew the Louvre and the London's National Gallery. Sixty new art museums were created in 1921–30, including the Museum of Modern Art and the Whitney Museum of American Art. The Guggenheim Foundation was established in 1924, and the Barnes Foundation, opened in 1922, held the biggest and probably best collection of post-Impressionist paintings in the world, even though few people ever saw it. On the growth of art museums and fine arts courses, see Frederick P. Keppel and R. L. Duffus, *The Arts in American Life* (New York, 1933), pp. 39, 46–47, 66–67; R. L. Duffus, *The American Renaissance* (1928), pp. 32–39.
10. Quoted in David Braider, *George Bellows and the Ashcan School of Painting* (Garden City, N.Y., 1971), p. 23.
11. Ibid., p. 20.
12. Kilham, op. cit., p. 79.
13. Bevis Hillier, *Art Deco* (New York, 1969), p. 69.
14. Calvin Robinson and Rosemarie H. Bletter, *Skyscraper Style* (New York, 1975), p. 12.
15. Harvard's Professor of Architecture, George Edgell, was lamenting as late as 1928, "The importance of color has been neglected, especially in the United States." G. H. Edgell, *The American Architecture of Today* (New York, 1928), p. 13.
16. Keppel and Duffus, op. cit., p. 115.
17. Kilham, op. cit., pp. 15–26, 92–94.
18. Ibid., p. 92.

CHAPTER 26

1. Veronica and Paul King, *The Raven on the Skyscraper* (London, 1925), p. 40; Stephen Spender, *A Briton in America* (New York, 1921), p. 22.
2. Ford Madox Ford, *New York Is Not America* (London, 1927), p. 33, 42.
3. Edmund Wilson, *The American Earthquake* (New York, 1932), p. 102.
4. *Business Week*, September 10, 1930.
5. *The Commonweal*, May 13, 1925.
6. Frank Lloyd Wright, *Modern Architecture* (Princeton, 1931), p. 97.
7. *Time*, Dec. 13, 1926.
8. Maurice R. Davie, *Problems of City Life* (New York, 1932), p. 19.
9. Elmer Davis, "Too Stately Mansions," *New Republic*, June 1, 1932.
10. From U.S. Bureau of the Census, *Census of Population* 1930, vol. 1, table 8, p. 14.
11. R. D. McKenzie, *The Metropolitan Community* (New York, 1933), see table 31, p. 73.
12. Davie, op. cit., p. 6.
13. Humbert S. Nelli, *Italians in Chicago 1890–1930* (New York, 1970), pp. 238–39.
14. See, for example, Harvey Zorbaugh, *The Gold Coast and the Slum* (Chicago, 1929), p. 82, with its "suicide map" of Chicago.
15. Caroline Ware, *Greenwich Village 1920–1930* (Boston, 1935), p. 422.
16. Clarence Darrow, *Crime: Its Cause and Treatment* (New York, 1922), p. 75.
17. Louis Wirth, *The Ghetto* (Chicago, 1928), pp. 197–98.
18. Zorbaugh, op. cit., p. 136.
19. Alfred Cahen, *Statistical Analysis of American Divorce* (New York, 1932), pp. 60–62, 115.
20. Davie, op. cit., p. 93.

21. McKenzie, op. cit., pp. 219–20.
22. Robert S. and Helen M. Lynd, *Middletown* (New York, 1929), pp. 31–34.
23. In Harold M. Stearns, ed., *Civilization in the United States* (New York, 1922), p. 13.
24. E.g., Davie, op. cit., p. 15.
25. Don S. Kirschner, *City and Country: Rural Responses to Urbanization in the 1920s* (Greenwich, Conn., 1970), Chap. 2.
26. From U.S. President's Research Committee on Recent Social Trends, *Recent Social Trends* (New York, 1933), pp. 1308–1309.
27. Paul Douglas, *Real Wages in the United States* (Boston, 1930), p. 487.
28. William A. Munro, *The Government of American Cities* (New York, 1926), pp. 1–2.
29. *Survey*, August 15, 1930.
30. McKenzie, op. cit., p. 314.
31. Harlan P. Douglass, *The Suburban Trend* (New York, 1925), p. 18.
32. Davie, op. cit., p. 200.
33. Edith Elmer Wood, *Recent Trends in American Housing* (New York, 1931), p. 9.
34. Ibid., p. 37.
35. "How Much House for a Dollar?" *Fortune*, April 1932.
36. "Housing: The Need," ibid., February 1932.
37. Jesse F. Steiner, *Americans at Play* (New York, 1933), table 1, p. 15; table 5, p. 25.
38. Ibid., p. 52.
39. Ibid., pp. 38, 41.
40. Robert A. Caro, *The Power Broker* (New York, 1974), pp. 143 et seq.
41. James Truslow Adams, *Our Business Civilization* (New York, 1929), pp. 137–38.
42. Davie, op. cit., p. 277.
43. Georges Duhamel, *America the Menace* (London, 1931), pp. 93–94.
44. Haven Emerson, "Are We Fostering the Unfit?" *Survey*, April 1, 1931.
45. Louis I. Dublin, *Health and Wealth* (New York, 1928), p. 15.
46. *Survey*, November 1, 1925; Davis, op. cit., p. 216.
47. On this medical mystery, see Dublin, op. cit., chap. 5.
48. Davie, op. cit., pp. 379–80; Robert L. Dickinson and Lura Beam, *A Thousand Marriages* (Baltimore, 1931), p. 41, report that of the 1,000 women examined 94 suffered from VD, and these were mostly middle-class women.
49. Dublin, op. cit., pp. 265–66.
50. Warren S. Thompson and P. K. Whelpton, *Population Trends in the U.S.* (New York, 1933), table 70, p. 249.
51. Joan Hoff Wilson, *Herbert Hoover* (Boston, 1975), p. 6.
52. U.S. President's Conference on Recent Economic Changes, *Recent Economic Changes* (New York, 1929), p. 43.
53. Haven Emerson, "Sweetness Is Death," *Survey*, October 1, 1924.
54. *Recent Economic Changes*, table 13, p. 42; advertising had almost nothing to do with the rise in sugar consumption, see Neil Borden, *The Economic Effects of Advertising* (Chicago, 1942), pp. 277–78.
55. Preston Slosson, *The Great Crusade and After* (New York, 1930), p. 156.
56. Pearce Bailey, "The Drug Habit in the United States," *New Republic*, March 16, 1921.
57. *Survey*, April 26, 1919.
58. John Palmer Gavit, "Uncle Sam Scores One on Opium," *Survey*, January 15, 1927.
59. Nicholas and Lillian Kopeloff, "The Drug Evil," *New Republic*, March 7, 1923.
60. Thomas S. Blair, "The Dope Doctor," *Survey*, April 3, 1920; Joseph P. Chamberlain, "Dope," ibid., September 6, 1919.
61. Morris Fishbein, *A History of the AMA* (Philadelphia, 1947), p. 320.
62. In Harold Stearns, ed., *Civilization in the United States* (New York, 1922), p. 447. The doctor who contributed to this compendium chose to remain anonymous.
63. William G. Shepherd, "The New Control of Surgeons," *Harper's*, February 1924.

64. *New Republic*, July 1, 1928.
65. Dublin, op. cit., pp. 55–56.
66. Davie, op. cit., p. 409.
67. Lynd and Lynd, op. cit., pp. 218–19.
68. Charles H. Judd, *Problems of Education in the United States* (New York, 1933), p. 15.
69. *Time*, September 17, 1923; see also Margaret A. Haley, "The Factory System," *New Republic*, November 12, 1924.
70. Edward A. Krug, *The Shaping of the American High School* (Madison, Wis., 1972), p. 46.
71. Judd, op. cit., table 32, p. 139.
72. *Recent Economic Changes*, table 1, p. 16; U.S. Dept. of the Interior—Office of Education Bulletin no. 15 "Statistics of Public High Schools 1927–1928," (Washington, D.C., 1929).
73. Douglas, op. cit., table 70, p. 201; Judd, op. cit., table 38, p. 160.
74. Lawrence A. Cremin, *The Transformation of the School* (New York, 1961), p. *viii*; Robert L. Church, *Education in the United States* (New York, 1976), pp. 344–52.
75. Krug, op. cit., pp. 107–109.
76. K. S. Cunningham and G. E. Philips, *Some Aspects of Education in the USA* (Melbourne, Australia, 1930), p. 69.
77. Krug, op. cit., pp. 117–18.

CHAPTER 27

1. *Time*, November 24, 1930; October 19, 1931.
2. Bernard Bellush, *Franklin D. Roosevelt as Governor of New York* (New York, 1955), p. 115.
3. Emanuel Lavine, *"Gimme": How Politicians Get Rich* (New York, 1931), pp. 38–41; *New Republic*, January 28, 1931.
4. Bleeker Marquette, "Housing Forward or Backward?" *Survey*, February 15, 1931.
5. Evans Clark, ed., *The Internal Debts of the United States* (New York, 1933), table 3, p. 13; Charles Merz, "Debts—Public and Private," *New York Times*, January 19, 1933.
6. Harris G. Warren, *Herbert Hoover and the Great Depression* (New York, 1959), p. 285.
7. *New Republic*, March 30, 1932.
8. *Time*, November 9, 1931.
9. Ibid., May 4, 1931.
10. Herbert Hoover, *Memoirs*, vol. 3, *The Great Depression* (New York, 1952), pp. 126–27.
11. Ferdinand Pecora, *Wall Street Under Oath* (New York, 1935), p. 232.
12. Forrest McDonald, *Insull* (Chicago, 1962), p. 293.
13. John T. Flynn, "What Happened to Insull," *New Republic*, May 4, 1932.
14. Mauritz Hallgren, *Seeds of Revolt* (New York, 1933), p. 228.
15. Quoted by McDonald, op. cit., p. 277.
16. John D. Black, *Agricultural Reform in the United States* (New York, 1929), pp. 9, 12, 40.
17. Ralph Borsodi, *Flight from the City* (New York, 1972), p. *xiii*.
18. Robert C. Cotner et al., *Texas Cities in the Great Depression* (Austin, Texas, 1973), pp. 11, 16.
19. *Time*, April 6, 1931.
20. *New York Times*, August 13, 1931.
21. Ibid., August 14, 1931.
22. Warren, op. cit., p. 177.
23. A. L. Schafer, "When Hunger Follows Drought," *Survey*, March 1, 1931; *Time*, January 19, 1931.
24. Edmund Wilson, *The American Jitters* (New York, 1932), pp. 86–97, describes some of these clashes.
25. Lement Harris, "An Arkansas Farmer Speaks," *New Republic*, May 27, 1931.

26. *New York Herald Tribune*, July 19, 1931.
27. John T. Commons et al., *History of Labor in the United States*, vol. 3 (New York, 1935), p. 92; *Time*, April 12, 1931; June 8, 1931.
28. Horace B. Davis, *Labor and Steel* (London, 1933), p. 60.
29. *Time*, October 5, 1931.
30. Edward F. Denison, *The Sources of Economic Growth in the United States* (New York, 1962), table 2, p. 17; Solomon Fabricant, *The Output of Manufacturing Industries 1899–1937* (New York, 1940), table 1, p. 44.
31. Mary Agnes Hamilton, *In America Today* (London, 1932), p. 86.
32. "No One Has Starved," *Fortune*, September 1932.
33. Niven Busch, *Twenty-One Americans* (New York, 1930), pp. 213–14.
34. Gertrude Springer, "Well-Advertised Breadlines," *Survey*, February 15, 1931.
35. Irving Bernstein, *The Lean Years* (Boston, 1959), p. 294.
36. Meridel Le Seuer, "Women on the Breadlines," *New Masses*, January 1932.
37. Hallgren, op. cit., pp. 4–5.
38. Henri Tescheraud, "The Art of Bumming a Meal," *American Mercury*, January 1925.
39. Louis Adamic, *My America 1928–1938* (New York, 1938), p. 279.
40. Gertrude Springer, "Ragged White Collars," *Survey*, November 15, 1931.
41. Stephen Spender, *A Briton in America* (New York, 1921), p. 143.
42. *New Republic*, December 31, 1930.
43. Gertrude Springer, "The Job Line," *Survey*, February 1, 1931.
44. U.S. President's Committee on Recent Social Trends, *Recent Social Trends* (New York, 1933), p. 1205.
45. Abraham Epstein, "Do the Rich Give to Charity?" *American Mercury*, May 1931; Robert W. Kelso, "Banker Control of Community Chest," *Survey*, May 1, 1932; Davis, op. cit., pp. 111–12.
46. Stuart Chase, *A New Deal* (New York, 1932), pp. 87–88.
47. Abraham Epstein, "Faith Cures for Unemployment," *American Mercury*, January 1931.
48. Bernstein, op. cit., pp. 288–89.
49. Quoted by Stuart Chase, *The Economy of Abundance* (New York, 1934), p. 127.
50. Cotner, op. cit., p. 125.
51. *Nation*, October 7, 1931.
52. Cotner, op. cit., p. 100.
53. Gilbert Seldes, *Years of the Locust* (Boston, 1933), p. 70.
54. Charles H. Trout, *Boston, the Great Depression and the New Deal* (New York, 1977), p. 60.
55. Ibid., pp. 93–94.
56. *Time*, July 20, 1931; Beulah Amidon, "Detroit Does Something About It," *Survey*, February 15, 1931; Charles Beard, ed., *America Faces the Future* (Boston, 1932), pp. 104–105.
57. Karl Borders, "Cashless Chicago," *Survey*, February 15, 1930; *Time*, September 21, 1931.
58. Seldes, op. cit., p. 208.
59. Pellush, op. cit., p. 134.
60. Roy Lubove, *The Professional Altruist* (Cambridge, Mass., 1965), p. 133.
61. Romasco, op. cit., p. 159.
62. Gertrude Springer, "The Lever of State Relief," *Survey*, January 15, 1932.
63. San Antonio was a typical example. See Cotner pp. 53–68.
64. Louis Francis Budenz, "Paterson Goes On Strike," *New Republic*, September 9, 1931; ibid., November 18, 1931.
65. *New Republic*, November 25, 1931.
66. Louis Stanley, "Danville: Labor's Southern Outpost," *Nation*, January 31, 1931; Tom Tippett, *When Southern Labor Stirs* (New York, 1931), p. 236; *Nation*, February 11, 1931.
67. Hallgren, op. cit., p. 51; *Time*, July 6, 1931.

68. Ibid., p. 69.
69. John W. Hevener, *Which Side Are You On?* (Urbana, Ill., 1978), p. 10.
70. Theodore Dreiser et al., *Harlan Miners Speak* (New York, 1932), pp. 66, 89; *New Republic*, September 19, 1931; June 1, 1932.
71. One of them wrote an account of his shooting: Boris Israel "I Get Shot," *New Republic*, October 21, 1931.
72. W. A. Swanberg, *Dreiser* (New York, 1961), pp. 387–89.
73. Commons, op. cit., p. 281.
74. See interview in the *New York Times*, December 6, 1921.
75. Ralph Chaplin, *Wobbly* (Chicago, 1948), p. 197.
76. Howard Scott et al., *Introduction to Technology* (New York, 1933), p. 16; "Technocracy" was originally coined in 1919 in an article by an engineer named William Henry Smyth with the title " 'Technocracy'—National Industrial Management" *Industrial Management* January-March, 1919.
77. William E. Akin, *Technocracy and the American Dream* (Los Angeles and Berkeley, 1977), pp. 211–16.
78. Edmund Wilson, *The American Jitters* (New York, 1932), p. 311.
79. Fred Beal, *Proletarian Journey* (New York, 1937), p. 77.
80. Sherwood Anderson, *Puzzled America* (New York, 1935), p. 46; see also Hamilton, op. cit., p. 111.
81. Irving Howe and Lewis Coser, *The American Communist Party* (New York, 1957), p. 257.
82. Benjamin Gitlow, *The Whole of Their Lives* (New York, 1948), pp. 156–62.
83. Eugene Lyons, *The Red Decade* (Indianapolis, 1941), p. 86.
84. Gitlow, op. cit., pp. 209–11.
85. Hallgren, op. cit., pp. 165–68, surveys the major clashes; for a vivid, eye-witness account of the Communist-led march on New York city hall in January 1931, see Wilson, op. cit., pp. 37–45.
86. Oakley Johnson, "After the Dearborn Massacre," *New Republic*, March 30, 1932; Allen Nevins and Frank Hill, *Ford: Expansion and Challenge* (New York, 1957), pp. 593–96.

CHAPTER 28

1. U.S. President's Conference, *Recent Economic Changes* (New York, 1929), table 23, p. 808.
2. Ernest Minor Patterson, "Taxation" supplement to *New Republic*, March 4, 1925.
3. U.S. President's Committee, *Recent Social Trends* (New York, 1933), table 2, p. 1287; table 12, p. 1306.
4. *Hammer v. Dagenhart*, 247 US 251 (1918).
5. *Bailey v. Drexel Furniture Co.*, 259 US 20 (1922).
6. *New Republic*, December 3, 1924.
7. Herbert Hoover, *Memoirs*, vol. 2, *The Cabinet and the Presidency* (New York, 1952), pp. 102–103.
8. The Gentleman at the Keyhole, "Big-Town Bob," *Collier's*, March 21, 1931.
9. Stuart Chase, *The Nemesis of American Business* (New York, 1931), p. 23.
10. New Republic, March 18, 1931; John Commons et al., *History of Labor in the United States*, vol. 3 (New York, 1935), p. 208; Robert S. Allen and Drew Pearson, *Washington Merry-Go-Round* (New York, 1931), pp. 67–68.
11. Abraham Epstein, "Freedom for the Aged," *New Republic*, April 23, 1930.
12. Commons, op. cit., pp. 385, 390.
13. E.g., Theresa Wolfson, "Trade Union Insurance—Promise and Realities," *Survey*, April 1, 1929; Roger Babson, *Fighting Business Depressions* (New York, 1932), pp. 92–94.
14. Hoover, op. cit., pp. 313–16.

15. Ibid., p. 53.
16. Charles Beard et al., *America Faces the Future* (Boston, 1932), reprints Swope's famous proposal along with his reply to his critics, pp. 160–85.
17. Ibid., pp. 196–264, for the text of the Chamber of Commerce plan.
18. U.S. Senate Subcommittee on Manufactures, *Unemployment Relief*, Seventy-second Congress, 1st Session (Washington, D.C., 1932); *Time*, January 11, 1932.
19. Herbert Hoover, *Memoirs*, vol. 3, *The Great Depression* (New York, 1952), pp. 2–4.
20. U.S. Bureau of the Census, *Historical Statistics of the United States* (Washington, D.C., 1957), pp. 243–44.
21. Herbert Feis, *Diplomacy and the Dollar* (Boston, 1933), pp. 89–90.
22. Theodore Joslin, *Hoover Off the Record* (New York, 1934), pp. 105–108.
23. *Time*, June 22, 1931.
24. Gene Smith, *The Shattered Dream* (New York, 1970), p. 72.
25. Bascom Timmons, *Portrait of an American* (New York, 1953), p. 314.
26. David Burner, *Herbert Hoover* (New York, 1979), p. 272.
27. John Brooks, *Once in Golconda* (New York, 1969), p. 140.
28. *Time*, Feb. 29, 1932.
29. Jordan Schwartz, *The Interregnum of Despair* (Urbana, Ill., 1970), p. 97.
30. Hoover, op. cit., p. 101.
31. *New York Herald Tribune*, January 15, 1932.
32. *New Republic*, August 26, 1931; *Nation*, April 15, 1931.
33. Schwartz, op. cit., p. 122; Howard Zinn, *La Guardia in Congress* (Ithaca, N.Y., 1956), pp. 217–18.
34. E. Cary Brown, "Fiscal Policy in the Thirties," *American Economic Reivew*, December, 1956.
35. Joslin, op. cit., p. 48.
36. Hoover, op. cit., p. 65.
37. Zinn, op. cit., p. 202.
38. *Congressional Record*, July 11, 1932, 75:15041.
39. Hoover, op. cit., p. 54.
40. W. W. Waters and William C. White, *B.E.F.* (New York, 1933), pp. 4–6.
41. Donald J. Lisio, *The President and Protest* (Columbia, Mo., 1974), pp. 56–60.
42. *Time*, January 18, 1932; Lisio, pp. 61–62.
43. Roger Daniels, *The Bonus March* (Westport, Conn., 1971), p. 79.
44. Waters, op. cit., p. 70.
45. Lisio, op. cit., pp. 73–81.
46. Gardner Jackson, "Unknown Soldiers," *Survey*, August 1, 1932.
47. "Not one man in twenty really expected to get the Bonus." Waters, op. cit., p. 32.
48. Lisio, op. cit., p. 178; Daniels, op. cit., pp. 149–50.
49. Daniels, op. cit., p. 152.
50. Hoover, op. cit., p. 227; Joslin, op. cit., p. 267.
51. Joslin, op. cit., p. 268.
52. Hoover, op. cit., p. 227; Daniels, op. cit., pp. 164–65.
53. *Time*, August 8, 1932.
54. Lisio, op. cit., pp. 210–12; Daniels, op. cit., pp. 170–78.
55. Hoover, op. cit., p. 230.
56. Oscar Handlin, *Al Smith and His America* (Boston, 1958), pp. 139–41.
57. Arthur Schlesinger, Jr., *The Crisis of the Old Order* (New York, 1957), p. 405.
58. *New York Herald Tribune*, January 8, 1932.
59. Frank Freidel, *Franklin D. Roosevelt: The Triumph* (Boston, 1956), pp. 308–309.
60. Freidel, p. 312.
61. Roy V. Peel and Thomas C. Donnelly, *The 1932 Campaign* (New York, 1935), pp. 21–22.

62. Hoover, op. cit., p. 218.
63. *New York Times*, October 20, 1932.
64. *Time*, October 10, 1932.
65. *New York Times*, September 24, 1932.
66. Stuart Chase, *A New Deal* (New York, 1932), p. 142.
67. *New Republic*, August 17, 1932.
68. David Shannon, *The Socialist Party of America* (New York, 1955), p. 187.
69. See, for example, the speech delivered at Detroit on October 27, 1932, reproduced in Hoover, pp. 273–76.
70. *Time*, Nov. 7, 1932.
71. William Allen White, "Herbert Hoover—The Last of the Old Presidents or the First of the New?" *Saturday Evening Post*, March 4, 1933.
72. Joslin, op. cit., p. 325.

CHAPTER 29

1. *Time*, January 21, 1929.
2. Ibid., December 9, 1929.

Bibliographical Essay

POLITICS

GENERAL

Harold U. Faulkner, *From Versailles to the New Deal* (New Haven, Conn., 1951), provides a useful survey of the major political developments. Dwight L. Dumond, *Roosevelt to Roosevelt* (New York, 1937), is written close to events, from a fervently pro-New Deal perspective. Karl Schriftgeisser, *This Was Normalcy* (Boston, 1948), is a florid and unreliable account of twelve years of Republican government. John D. Hicks, *Republican Ascendancy 1921–1933* (New York, 1963), is a standard account of the period; not as reliable as the parade of footnotes suggests. Edwin Emerson, *Hoover and His Times* (Garden City, N.Y., 1932), is an oddity: it is a political history that goes backward from 1928 to 1917. Abroad, L. Ethan Ellis, *Republican Foreign Policy 1921–1933* (New Brunswick, N.J., 1968), offers a dispassionate and accurate survey.

Alice Roosevelt Longworth, *Crowded Hours* (New York, 1935), is an insider's view of Washington by the gossipy, idiosyncratic wife of the Speaker of the House and daughter of Teddy Roosevelt. William Allen White, *Masks in a Pageant* (New York, 1928), contains impressionistic portraits of the leading political figures of the day by someone who knew all of them. What White had to leave out of this work he was able to include in *The Autobiography of William Allen White* (New York, 1946). Walter Lippmann, *Men of Destiny* (New York, 1927), is short and valuable. His later collection of similar pieces, *Interpretations 1931–1932* (New York, 1932), is equally trenchant. By way of contrast, Robert S. Allen and Drew Pearson, *Washington Merry-Go-Round* (New York, 1931), is gossipy but useful for period flavor; replete with malicious anecdotes. In the same vein is Irwin Hood Hoover, *Forty-Two Years at the White House* (Boston, 1934), by the former head usher.

Edmund W. Starling, *Starling of the White House* (New York, 1946), by the body-guard to four presidents is, however, far above the usual run of servants' memoirs.

There are two noteworthy accounts of state politics in the Twenties: J. Joseph Huthmacher, *Massachusetts People and Politics 1919–1933* (Cambridge, Mass., 1959), which shows how and why economic and ethnic pressures turned the Commonwealth from a Republican stronghold into a Democratic one before the New Deal; and T. Harry Williams, *Huey Long* (New York, 1969), which both sheds light on one of the most complex political figures of the period and provides a detailed account of political life in Louisiana.

Burl Noggle, *Teapot Dome* (Baton Rouge, La., 1962), is the standard account of the major political scandal of the Twenties and could hardly be done better. Emanuel H. Lavine, *"Gimme": How Politicians Get Rich* (New York, 1931), exposes the widespread corruption that flourished in New York City, including the courts and the schools. William B. Northrop and John B. Northrop, *The Insolence of Office* (New York, 1932), is the story of the Seabury investigation of corruption in those courts by two of the investigators. George Walsh, *Gentleman Jimmy Walker* (New York, 1974), is the story of an amiable crook, concentrating on his years as mayor of New York, 1926–1932. Robert A. Caro, *The Power Broker* (New York, 1974), has a long and useful section on New York State government in the 1920s. Charles E. Merriam, *Chicago* (New York, 1929), is the standard academic account of politics in Chicago in the same period.

WILSON

Volume two of Arthur Walworth, *Woodrow Wilson* (New York, 1965), is the standard general account of Wilson in his second term. Edith Bolling Wilson, *Memoirs* (Indianapolis, 1939), is, understandably, guarded and reveals little. Another firsthand account is Josephus Daniels, *The Wilson Era: Years of War and After, 1917–1923* (Chapel Hill, N.C., 1946), by Wilson's admiring, garrulous navy secretary. Gene Smith, *When the Cheering Stopped* (New York, 1964), offers a meticulous reconstruction of Wilson's last two years in the White House, vividly presented.

Denna F. Fleming, *The United States and the League of Nations* (New York, 1932), has long been a standard account. Some of the details have been amplified and clarified by more recent scholarship, but this remains the most satisfying general study. John A. Garraty, *Henry Cabot Lodge* (New York, 1953), is a very competent, if lackluster, biography of Wilson's chief antagonist. Ralph Stone, *The Irreconcilables* (Paducah, Ky., 1970), offers an alternative interpretation, excluding Lodge from the Irreconcilables and emphasizing the role of isolationist Progressives.

Wilson's attorney general, responsible for the odious "Red Scare," is the subject of Stanley Coben, *A. Mitchell Palmer: Politician* (New York, 1963), an excellent biography; both fair to the life and illuminating about the times. Zechariah Chafee, Jr., *Freedom of Speech* (New York, 1920), is the classic account of Espionage Act prosecutions. Louis F. Post, *The Deportations Delirium of Nineteen Twenty* (Chicago, 1923), by an official who fought the Red Scare fearlessly, is indispensable. Robert K. Murray, *Red Scare* (New York, 1964), is the best general account. William Preston, Jr., *Aliens and Dissenters: Federal Suppression of Radicals 1903–1933* (Cambridge, Mass., 1963), is careful in its scholarship, critical in its tone. John Higham, *Strangers in the Land* (New York, 1963), is an important study of nativism; the latter half is concerned with the years 1918–25.

HARDING

Wesley M. Bagby, *The Road to Normalcy: The Presidential Campaign and Election of 1920* (Baltimore, 1962), is a first-rate work which demolishes the myth of the "smoke-filled room." The first adequate biography of Harding was Andrew Sinclair, *The Available Man: The Life Behind the Masks of Warren G. Harding* (New York, 1965). It was followed three years later by Francis Russell, *The Shadow of Blooming Grove* (New York, 1968), which was concerned to a remarkable extent with Harding's mistresses. Both Sinclair and Russell were surpassed, however, by Robert K. Murray, *The Harding Era* (Minneapolis, 1969), a work of the highest distinction. Scrupulous and lively, it contains the only convincing biography of Harding. Murray's later volume, *The Politics of Normalcy* (New York, 1973), is a distillation of the 1969 work.

Samuel Hopkins Adams, *Incredible Era* (Boston, 1939), has long been surpassed by more scholarly and more detailed accounts of Harding's presidency. But it is still of value as the recollections of a journalist who knew Harding and many of those in his Administration. Another journalist's account is volume six of Mark Sullivan, *Our Times* (New York, 1935). Something of an eccentricity it is, despite being titled *The Twenties*, taken up almost entirely with the Harding Administration and Sullivan's interest in popular songs. Odder still is Harry M. Daugherty, *The Inside Story of the Harding Tragedy* (New York, 1932), a mixture of fact, fiction, and fairy tales.

Even Harding's severest critics applauded at least two of his appointments, and Joseph Brandes, *Herbert Hoover and Economic Diplomacy* (Pittsburgh, 1962), provides a useful account of Hoover's term as secretary of commerce. As for Hughes, the standard biography is Merlo Pusey, *Charles Evans Hughes*, two volumes (New York, 1951). A more recent study, concentrating on Hughes's service as secretary of state, is the perceptive Betty M. Glad, *Charles Evans Hughes and the Illusions of Innocence* (Urbana, Ill., 1966).

COOLIDGE

The famous biography by William Allen White, *A Puritan in Babylon* (New York, 1938), is sympathetic toward Coolidge the man, scathing toward Coolidge the President. Claude M. Fuess, *Calvin Coolidge: The Man from Vermont* (Boston, 1940), was long the most thorough and even-handed account, reliable, though not uncritical. It has been supplanted, however, by Donald R. McCoy, *Calvin Coolidge: The Quiet President* (New York, 1967), a first-rate biography of a figure who was and remains an enigma. As for *The Autobiography of Calvin Coolidge* (New York, 1933), it reveals little about his presidency, yet is remarkable among presidential memoirs for its brevity and humility.

C. Bascom Slemp, *The Mind of the President* (New York, 1926), is a collection of Coolidge's observations on a wide range of policy issues. Howard H. Quint and Robert H. Ferrell, eds., *The Talkative President* (Boston, 1964), is a record of Coolidge's off-the-record press conferences. Coolidge's Vice-President was Charles G. Dawes, a man who was involved in nearly all the major political events of his time. Dawes is the subject of an admiring biography: Bascom N. Timmons, *Portrait of an American* (New York, 1953). There is also some value in Charles G. Dawes, *Notes as Vice-President* (Boston, 1935), which touches on a remarkable variety of people and events. Another of the period's most able minor figures was Coolidge's friend Dwight Morrow, the subject of the fulsome biography by Harold Nicholson, *Dwight Morrow* (New York, 1935). As the authorized version, it omitted such details as Morrow's alcoholism, and in time Nicholson repudiated the work, claiming that Morrow really had "the mind of a master criminal."

The 1924 election was a dull affair from the Republican side and has thus excited little literary interest. The Democratic convention on the other hand is described in Robert K. Murray, *The 103rd Ballot* (New York, 1976), one of the essential works on the Democratic party in the Twenties. Kenneth C. MacKay, *The Progressive Movement of 1924* (New York, 1947), is a deeply sympathetic study of the third-party movement that year. Richard Lowitt, *George W. Norris: The Persistence of a Progressive, 1913–1933* (Urbana, Ill., 1971), fills in the gaps and corrects most of the errors in Norris's autobiography, *Fighting Liberal* (New York, 1945). LeRoy Ashby, *The Spearless Leader: Senator Borah and the Progressive Movement in the 1920s* (Urbana, Ill., 1972), is another able biography of a Progressive nonpareil.

HOOVER

Norman Hapgood and Henry Moscowitz wrote a campaign biography of Al Smith as the 1928 election approached: *Up from the City Streets* (New York, 1927), a work that revealed something of the admiration in which he was held by his followers, but little else. Nor did his autobiography, *Up to Now* (New York, 1928), give much away. Oscar Handlin, *Al Smith and His America* (Boston, 1958), is modest and impressionistic. Matthew and Hannah Josephson, *Al Smith: Hero of the Cities* (Boston, 1969), is a workmanlike biography.

Edmund A. Moore, *A Catholic Runs for President* (New York, 1956), is concerned almost entirely with the religious issue in the election. The standard account, Roy V. Peel and Thomas C. Donnelly, *The 1928 Campaign* (New York, 1931), is valuable, although highly idiosyncratic. Smith is presented as the good guy who lost. Allen J. Lichtman, *Prejudice and the Old Politics* (Chapel Hill,

N.C., 1979), is based on an exhaustive statistical study. It refutes the numerous interpretations that hold that the 1928 election marked a turning point in American politics.

The second volume of Hoover's *Memoirs*, titled *The Cabinet and the Presidency* (New York, 1951), is useful but unrevealing; volume three, *The Great Depression* (New York, 1953), is a long rebuttal. Theodore Joslin, *Hoover Off the Record* (Garden City, N.Y., 1934), is by Hoover's secretary. Plodding and pious, it is nevertheless useful. Eugene Lyons, *Herbert Hoover* (Garden City, N.Y., 1964), devotes most of its energies to defending its subject. David Hinshaw, *Herbert Hoover* (New York, 1950), is by a friend and coreligionist. It attempts, not always successfully, to explain Hoover by reference to his Quakerism. Ray Lyman Wilbur and Arthur Mastick Hyde, *The Hoover Policies* (New York, 1937), consists mainly of Hooverian utterances.

Martin L. Fausold and George T. Mazuzan, eds., *The Hoover Presidency* (Albany, N.Y., 1974), is a collection of essays, pro and con, of varying worth. A higher general standard is to be found in the four interpretive essays that comprise J. J. Huthmacher and Warren I. Susman, eds., *Herbert Hoover and the Crisis of American Capitalism* (Cambridge, Mass., 1973). Craig M. Lloyd, *Aggressive Introvert* (Columbus, Ohio, 1973), is a splendid study of Hoover's pioneering use of public relations methods to outflank his shyness, and the eventual disastrous consequences of these methods when he fell from public favor.

Joan Hoff Wilson, *Herbert Hoover: Forgotten Progressive* (Boston, 1975), stops short of being a full-scale biography, but it offers a reliable and persuasive account of the public Hoover. The same is true of David Burner, *Herbert Hoover: A Public Life* (New York, 1979), which contains a very sympathetic appraisal of Hoover's character. Herbert Corey, *The Truth About Hoover* (Boston, 1932), was one of the first full-length refutations of the false, and often absurd, attacks on Hoover's integrity. Albert U. Romasco, *The Poverty of Abundance: Hoover, the Nation and the Depression* (New York, 1968), treads a careful line. Critical of many of Hoover's policies, it portrays him as a decisive and, within limits, a creative figure. Harris Gaylord Warren, *Herbert Hoover and the Great Depression* (New York, 1967), is possibly the most satisfying account: thorough, fair, accurate, and witty. By way of contrast, Gene Smith, *The Shattered Dream: Herbert Hoover and the Great Depression* (New York, 1970), is entertaining, impressionistic, and slight.

W. W. Waters and William C. White, *B.E.F.* (New York, 1933), is coauthored by the principal leader of the bonus army; partial and on occasion plain wrong, it is nevertheless an invaluable eyewitness account. Roger Daniels, *The Bonus March* (Westport, Conn., 1971), is based on Pelham Glassford's papers. It is scrupulous about every detail in this sorry affair. Donald J. Lisio, *The President and Protest* (Columbia, Mo., 1974), is an astute and thoroughly researched history of the Bonus Expeditionary Force which does much to redeem Hoover's reputation.

Ray Lyman Wilbur, *The Memoirs of Ray Lyman Wilbur* (Palo Alto, Calif., 1960), contains a detailed account of his four years as Hoover's secretary of the interior.

Jordan A. Schwartz, *The Interregnum of Despair* (Urbana, Ill., 1970), is an important study of the efforts made by Congress to combat the Depression before the New Deal. Howard Zinn, *La Guardia in Congress* (Ithaca, N.Y., 1959), is an excellent account of a colorful, transitional figure.

Arthur M. Schlesinger, Jr., *The Crisis of the Old Order, 1919–1933* (New York, 1957), is very much a Democrat's theory of history, written with great artistry and verve. Its central figure from first page to last is Franklin D. Roosevelt. The earlier part of the period, up to Roosevelt's election as governor of New York, is the subject also of Frank Freidel, *Franklin D. Roosevelt: The Ordeal* (Boston, 1954). Freidel based his work on Roosevelt's papers. His second volume, *Franklin D. Roosevelt: The Triumph* (Boston, 1956), is the standard account of Roosevelt's governorship and his 1932 election to the presidency. Bernard Bellush, *Franklin D. Roosevelt as Governor of New York* (New York, 1955), takes an admiring view of the man, while acknowledging his limitations as governor.

Roy V. Peel and Thomas C. Donnelly, *The 1932 Campaign* (New York, 1935), is a more conventional work and a more detailed one than the account of the 1928 election. It takes a starry-eyed view of Roosevelt.

Socialists and Communists

David A. Shannon, *The Socialist Party of America* (New York, 1955), is still the standard general account. The biography of Debs by Ray Ginger, *The Bending Cross* (New Brunswick, N.J., 1949), is easy to admire; fully worthy of the man. Donald Drew Egbert and Stow Pearsons, eds., *Socialism and American Life* (Princeton, 1952), is a useful collection of studies. James Weinstein, *The Decline of Socialism in America 1912–1925* (New York, 1967), offers a detailed analysis of the internal politics of the Socialist party.

Theodore Draper, *The Roots of American Communism* (New York, 1957), is an indispensable account of the early years. James P. Cannon, *The First Ten Years of American Communism* (New York, 1962), provides an insider's view. So does Benjamin Gitlow, *The Whole of Their Lives* (New York, 1948), by one of the founders of the American Communist party. While Cannon and Gitlow became ex-Communists, Ella Reeve Bloor, *We Are Many* (London, 1941), is the autobiography of a true believer to the end; "Mother" Bloor was one of the CPUSA's most extraordinary figures. Another true believer was Elizabeth Gurley Flynn, whose autobiography, *The Rebel Girl* (New York, 1973), ends with 1927. Not yet a Communist party member, she was involved with many who were, and she herself was active in nearly all the radical causes of the time. Irving Howe and Lewis Coser, *The American Communist Party* (New York, 1962), is the standard (fiercely critical) history.

ECONOMICS

GENERAL

U.S. President's Conference on Unemployment, *Recent Economic Changes*, two volumes (New York, 1929), is one of the dozen most important studies of the period. U.S. Federal Trade Commission, *National Wealth and Income* (Washington, D.C., 1926), is, despite its limitations and eccentricities, an essential work. Paul F. Brissenden, *Earnings of Factory Workers 1899–1927* (New York, 1929), is a pioneering study, based on census returns. Paul H. Douglas, *Real Wages in the United States 1890–1926* (Boston, 1930), is another pioneering work, invaluable for its subject and period.

Harvey O'Connor, *Mellon's Millions* (New York, 1933), is a remarkably hostile biography of Andrew Mellon, yet diligently researched. David E. Koskoff, *The Mellons* (New York, 1979), is largely taken up with Andrew W. and treats him more kindly than O'Connor did.

Thomas C. Blaisdell, Jr., *The Federal Trade Commission* (New York, 1932), is a history of government's failure to regulate business in the Twenties. Harold L. Reed, *Federal Reserve Policy 1921–1930* (New York, 1930), is useful even though much of the material he needed had not yet been published. Elmus R. Wicker, *Federal Reserve Monetary Policy 1917–1933* (New York, 1966), acknowledges the failures but does not exaggerate them. Lester V. Chandler, *Benjamin Strong, Central Banker* (Washington, D.C., 1958), is both a valuable biography and an important contribution to economic history.

Herbert Feis, *The Diplomacy of the Dollar: First Era 1919–1932* (Baltimore, 1950), is an insider's account; terse, acidulous, and authoritative. Derek H. Aldcroft, *From Versailles to Wall Street 1919–1929* (London, 1977), is a highly critical, pedestrian account of the American role in the world economy, as is Joseph S. Davis, *The World Between the Wars* (Baltimore, 1975). E. E. Schattschneider, *Politics, Pressures and the Tariff* (New York, 1935), is a classic academic study based on exhaustive examination of the 1930 Hawley-Smoot tariff act.

AGRICULTURE

James H. Shideler, *Farm Crisis 1919–1923* (Los Angeles and Berkeley, 1957), is by far the best account of the onset of a crisis that lasted twenty years. Albert B. Genung, *The Agricultural Depression Following World War I* (Ithaca, New York, 1954), is valuable; by a senior USDA official in the Twenties. Andrew A. Bruce, *Non-Partisan League* (New York, 1921), sympathizes with the movement's aims, but is critical of its methods. Arthur Capper, *The Agricultural Bloc* (New York, 1922), vehemently states the farmer's case; by a founder member of the bloc. Lewis F. Carr, *America Challenged* (New York, 1929), is a personal, anecdotal survey of the rural depression. John D. Black, *Agricultural Reform in the United States* (New York, 1929), is the most exhaustive and authoritative study of the farm problem throughout the 1920s. Gilbert C. Fite, *George N. Peek and the Fight for Farm Parity* (Norman, Okla., 1954), is an able biography of the man who more than any other brought about the parity program. Edmund deS. Brunner et al., *American Agricultural Villages* (New York, 1927), is an unusually valuable study of farm life, based on 140 villages in every part of the United States.

LABOR

John R. Commons et al., *History of Labor in the United States 1896–1932*, four volumes (New York, 1935), has long been one of the standard works. Although leaden in style and organization, it is very thorough and very reliable. Volumes three and four are of the greatest value to an understanding of labor in the Twenties: Don D. Lescohier and Elizabeth Brandeis, *Working Conditions/ Labor Legislation*, and Selig Perlman and Philip Taft, *Labor Movements*. The best single-volume account is Irving Bernstein, *The Lean Years: A History of the American Worker 1920–1933* (Boston, 1960).

Len De Caux, *Labor Radical* (Boston, 1970), is an autobiography crammed with excellent eyewitness vignettes of labor leaders on both the Left and the Right in the Twenties. Fred E. Beal, *Proletarian Journey* (New York, 1937), is an utterly convincing account of working-class radicalism and union organizing in the period.

Robert H. Zieger, *Republicans and Labor 1919–1929* (Paducah, Ky., 1969), is useful, if lackluster. Edwin E. Witte, *The Government in Labor Disputes* (New York, 1932), is really a study of case law in labor disputes in the 1920s. Vaughn Davis Bornet, *Labor Politics in a Democratic Republic* (Washington, D.C., 1964), is an account of the role of labor in the 1928 election, It did not amount to much. Felix Frankfurter and Nathan Greene, *The Labor Injunction* (New York, 1930), is not only the standard work on its subject but a chamber of horrors.

The first thorough and impartial study of the Industrial Workers of the World is Paul F. Brissenden, *The IWW* (New York, 1920), by an enterprising investigator who knew most of the important figures in the IWW. John S. Gambs, *The Decline of the IWW* (New York, 1932), takes up where Brissenden leaves off. The most thorough, academic account is Melvyn Dubofsky, *We Shall Be All* (Chicago, 1973), but concentrates heavily on the IWW before 1919. *Rebels of the Woods: The IWW in the Pacific Northwest* (Eugene, Ore., 1967), is dispassionate, reliable, and illuminating. Robert L. Friedheim, *The Seattle General Strike* (Seattle, 1964), is an excellent account of an event shrouded in myth. William D. Haywood, *Bill Haywood's Book* (New York, 1929), traces an extraordinary life, from frontier cowboy to burial in the Kremlin wall. Ralph Chaplin, *Wobbly* (Chicago, 1948), is the absorbing autobiography of an IWW artist, poet, and organizer.

Interchurch World Movement, *Report on the Steel Strike of 1919* (New York, 1920), devotes as much attention to the conditions that prompted the strike as to the walkout itself. The IWM's later volume, *Public Opinion and the Steel Strike of 1919* (New York, 1921), is a useful supplement to the earlier report and covers far more than opinion. The organizer of the strike, William Z. Foster, wrote his own account, *The Great Steel Strike* (New York, 1927). Mary Heaton Vorse, *Men and Steel* (New York, 1920), describes life in the steel towns, and life among the strikers' families, with whom she lived during the strike. Charles Rumford Walker, *Steel: The Diary of a Furnace Worker* (Boston, 1922), is another unique and valuable personal account. David Brody, *Labor in Crisis: The Steel Strike of 1919* (Philadelphia, 1965), is useful in explaining the role of the AFL. Horace B. Davies, *Labor and Steel* (London, 1933), is a highly critical survey of conditions ten years after the strike, by a British expert on both labor and steel.

Winthrop D. Lane, *Civil War in West Virginia* (New York, 1921), provides a restrained, firsthand account of this epic struggle in the coalfields. Melvyn Dubofsky and Warren Van Tine, *John L. Lewis* (Chicago, 1977), is by far the best biography of Lewis, but its authors are deeply out of sympathy with their subject. Paul M. Angle, *Bloody Williamson* (New York, 1952), contains the most thorough, impartial account of the Herrin massacre. Theodore Dreiser et al., *Harlan Miners Speak* (New York, 1932), is a work with a double handicap: Dreiser's prose style and a party-line analysis. Yet the testimony the miners give is utterly convincing. John W. Hevener, *Which Side Are You On?* (Urbana, Ill., 1978), is a scholarly account of the miners' strikes in Harlan County in the early 1930s, with pertinent observations on social conditions and violence as industrialization moved into the mountains.

Tom Tippett, *When Southern Labor Stirs* (New York, 1931), is an account of the textile workers' strikes in the Piedmont in 1929–30 by one of the participants. Liston Pope, *Millhands and Preachers* (New Haven, Conn., 1942), began as a sociologist's account of religion in Gaston County. It is now accepted as a classic work on the lives of southern millworkers between the wars.

Sidney Howard and Robert Dunn, *The Labor Spy* (New York, 1924), is a well-documented account of one of the most pervasive and poisonous elements in labor relations before the New Deal. Milton J. Nadworny, *Scientific Management and the Unions 1900–1932* (Cambridge, Mass., 1955), is an able study of a contentious relationship. Elton Mayo, *The Human Problems of an Industrial Civilization* (New York, 1933), is a landmark in industrial relations research.

BUSINESS

Arthur F. Bentley, *Makers, Users and Masters* (Syracuse, N.Y., 1962), is a noted, but somewhat incoherent, critique of American capitalism at the end of World War I. Harry W. Payne, *Business Behavior 1919–1922* (Chicago, 1942), is a macroeconomic study of business behavior in the transition from war to peace. Alexander Dana Noyes, *The War Period of American Finance, 1908–1925* (New York, 1926), is one of the most cogent and readable economic histories of the period. Thomas Nixon Carver, *The Present Economic Revolution in the United States* (New York, 1926), is a famous paean to high wages and other enlightened business practices. Conversely, James Truslow Adams, *Our Business Civilization* (New York, 1930), even doubted business's ability to deliver the goods, and in *The*

Nemesis of American Business (New York, 1931) portrayed it as virtually a menace to American life. More influential, however, was his next critique, *A New Deal* (New York, 1932).

Charles C. Chapman, *The Development of American Business and Banking Thought 1913–1936* (New York, 1936), offers a useful narrative but very little analysis. Arthur Burns, *The Decline of Competition* (New York, 1936), is authoritative, concerned mainly with the major developments between the Sherman Anti-Trust Act and the New Deal. George Soule, *Prosperity Decade* (New York, 1947), is a standard economic history of the Twenties; knowledgeable and readable. A more technical, but equally valuable study, is Frederick C. Mills, *Economic Tendencies in the United States* (New York, 1932). Louis Galambos, *The Public Image of Big Business in America 1880–1940* (Baltimore, 1975), maintains that by 1930 the country had learned to love the large corporation.

Solomon Fabricant, *The Output of Manufacturing Industries 1899–1937* (New York, 1940), is the essential work on productivity, covering all the important industries and many of the minor ones. Harold Barger, *Outlay and Income in the United States, 1921–1938* (New York, 1942), is highly technical, yet innovative and important. Joseph L. Snyder, *Business Statistics*, 2nd ed. (New York, 1932), is useful.

Walter N. Polakov, *The Power Age* (New York, 1933), offers an energy consumption theory of the astonishing rise in productivity; in connection with which Gerald Forbes, *Flush Production* (Norman, Okla., 1942), Boyce House, *Oil Boom* (Caldwell, Idaho, 1936), and Samuel W. Tait, Jr., *The Wildcatters* (Princeton, 1946), are all useful and interesting.

Harry Jerome, *Mechanization in Industry* (New York, 1934), is an important study, concerned mainly with developments in the 1920s. Edward F. Denison *The Sources of Economic Growth in the United States* (New York, 1962) contains valuable insights into the variety of elements in the productivity boom of those years.

The high panjandrum of both high wages and high productivity has left his own (ghost-written) account: Henry Ford, *My Life and Work* (New York, 1923). As an account of his career, it is disingenuous. But as a picture of his mind at work, running largely on nineteenth-century homilies, it is Ford to a T. Samuel S. Marquis, *Henry Ford: An Interpretation* (Boston, 1923), is a shrewd psychological study by a man who knew Ford well, yet owed him nothing. Keith Sward, *The Legend of Henry Ford* (New York, 1948), is a hostile biography, fascinating but not always reliable. It needs to be read in conjunction with the much duller but far more authoritative Allen Nevins and Frank E. Hill, *Ford: Expansion and Challenge 1915–1933* (New York, 1957). On Ford as folk idol, Reynold M. Wik, *Henry Ford and Grass-roots America* (Ann Arbor, Mich., 1972), is invaluable. Charles Merz, *And Then Came Ford* (New York, 1929), is less a biography of Ford than an excellent social history of the Model T.

Alfred P. Sloan, Jr., *Adventures of a White Collar Man* (Garden City, N.Y., 1940), is the modest autobiography of the man who turned General Motors into the very model of a modern corporation. Far better, however, was his second attempt at autobiography, *My Years with General Motors* (Garden City, N.Y.,

1963). There is, unfortunately, no first-rate general social history of the automobile. James J. Flink, *The Car Culture* (Cambridge, Mass., 1975), aims at filling the bill, but despite its merits it eventually disappoints.

THE FIRST CONSUMER SOCIETY

Neil H. Borden, *Problems of Advertising* (New York, 1932), and *The Economics of Advertising* (Chicago, 1942), are probably the two most influential works ever written on the subject. They draw mainly on the advertising of the 1920s and early 1930s, and offer an expert's commentary on it. Frank Presbrey, *The History and Development of Advertising* (New York, 1929), presents it as the chief force for progress in a bewildered world. A diametrically opposed view is to be found in James Rorty, *Our Master's Voice* (New York, 1934), by a former advertising agency executive. James Playsted Wood, *The Story of Advertising* (New York, 1958), contains several useful chapters on the interwar years. Otis Pease, *The Responsibilities of American Advertising: Private Control and Public Influence, 1920–1940* (New Haven, 1958), is a probing and judicious account of the conflicts and compromises in what was advertising's most formative period. John Gunther, *Taken at the Flood* (New York, 1960), is a friendly biography of Albert D. Lasker, the most influential advertising man of the period. Stuart Ewen, *Captains of Consciousness* (New York, 1976), presents the consumer society as the child of the Twenties with advertising as the midwife. Riddled with errors of fact and logic, it is, alas, a poor book in pursuit of a good idea.

Stuart Chase and F. J. Schlink, *Your Money's Worth* (New York, 1927), is one of the pioneer works of consumerism. Arthur Kallett and F. J. Schlink, *100,000,000 Guinea Pigs* (New York, 1933), is the first consumer manifesto.

One of the fastest growing businesses of the Twenties was money-lending. Evans Clark, *Financing the Consumer* (New York, 1930), charts its growth. His later volume, *The Internal Debts of the United States* (New York, 1933), is equally important, an authoritative study of a problem which became a pressing problem in the wake of the 1929 crash. Jessica B. Peixotto, *Getting and Spending at the Professional Standard of Living* (New York, 1927), demonstrated that most professional people—the best-paid part of the labor force—were sliding inexorably into debt.

WALL STREET AND AFTER

Adolph A. Berle and Gardiner C. Means, *The Modern Corporation and Private Property* (New York, 1932), is the ground-breaking study on the post-Armistice separation of stock ownership from corporate control. James C. Bonbright and Gardiner C. Means, *The Holding Company* (New York, 1932), is the classic account of one of the other notable features of big business in the Twenties, a period which also saw the flourishing growth of investment trusts. John T. Flynn, *Investment Trusts Gone Wrong!* (New York, 1930), shows how easily they turned into shears for fleecing the unwary.

Ferdinand Pecora *Wall Street Under Oath* (New York, 1934) is an authoritative account of what the Senate Banking and Currency Committee found when it began turning over various stones following the crash. Clarence Barron, the founder of *Barron's Weekly*, was one man who knew all the major figures on Wall Street, and he diligently recorded their gossip. It became available soon after his death, in Arthur Pound and Samuel T. Moore, eds., *They Told Barron* (New York, 1930), an essential work for understanding Wall Street during the Big Bull Market. Richard D. Wyckoff, *Wall Street Ventures and Adventures* (New York, 1931), is another insider's account, but reveals very little of interest. William Z. Ripley, *Main Street and Wall Street* (Boston, 1927), is a professorial exposure of the shady side of the Street. Earl Sparling, *Mystery Men of Wall Street* (New York, 1930), contains brief portraits of a dozen of the more important figures of the big bull market. Far more reliable is John Brooks, *Once in Golconda* (New York, 1969), which is also far better written. There is also Frederick Lewis Allen, *The Lords of Creation* (New York, 1936), the latter half of which is devoted to Wall Street from armistice to New Deal, described in Allen's amiable style. Robert Sobel, *The Great Bull Market* (New York, 1968), is an excellent short account of the market and the crash, and the last chapter of Aaron M. Sakolski, *The Great American Land Bubble* (New York, 1932), covers the Florida land boom—and bust—which prefigured events on the stock market.

John Kenneth Galbraith, *The Great Crash: 1929* (Boston, 1955), is an ironic account, in which Galbraith's deep knowledge of economics is worn lightly. Gordon Thomas and Max Morgan-Witts, *The Day the Bubble Burst* (New York, 1979), is a lavishly detailed, gee-whiz account of the crash. Tom Schachtman, *The Day America Crashed* (New York, 1979), reads like fiction (not, in this case, a compliment).

On the transition from crash to Depression, Robert T. Patterson, *The Great Boom and Panic* (Chicago, 1965), blames both on the postwar inflation of money supply and credit. Lionel Robbins, *The Great Depression* (London, 1934), offers a macroeconomic analysis that also emphasizes the role of easy money policies. The monetarist interpretation of Milton Friedman and Anna J. Schwartz, *The Great Contraction 1929–1933* (Princeton, 1965), is stimulating and fruitful, even to those who do not agree with it. Peter Temin, *Did Monetary Forces Cause the Great Depression?* (New York, 1976), is a brilliant rebuttal to the monetarist analysis; Temin tries to find a middle way between monetarists and Keynesians.

On the most spectacular business crash of the Depression, Forrest McDonald, *Insull* (Chicago, 1962), has an absorbing story to tell, and tells it exceptionally well.

SOCIETY

GENERAL

The most important single source of material is U.S. President's Research Committee, *Recent Social Trends*, two volumes (New York, 1933); a mine of facts.

Frederick Lewis Allen, *Only Yesterday* (New York, 1931), created an entire genre of instant social history; as entertaining now as when it appeared half a century ago. William Leuchtenberg, *The Perils of Prosperity* (Chicago, 1958), is a slightly more academic version in the same vein. Preston W. Slosson, *The Great Crusade and After 1914–1928* (New York, 1930), is more conventional, old-fashioned social history; dull but reliable. J. C. Furnas, *Great Times* (New York, 1974), is a slight work that skates amusingly over the surface of the same events that Slosson covers. Isabel Leighton, ed., *The Aspirin Years* (New York, 1949), is a collection of specially written articles on some of the major developments; the standard is high, the result fascinating. Another useful compendium, with a more academic flavor, is John H. Braeman et al., eds., *Change and Continuity in 20th-Century America: The 1920s* (Columbus, Ohio, 1968).

Paul A. Carter, *Another Part of the Twenties* (New York, 1977), is a collection of short studies on a handful of subjects, such as feminism, advertising, business ideology. His earlier book, *The Twenties in America* (London, 1969), is intended for college students, but is a valuable introduction to the period for anyone interested in it. Frank Brookhouser, ed., *These Were Our Years* (Garden City, N.Y., 1959), is a collection of nostalgic pieces covering the entire interwar period. Francis Russell, *The Great Interlude* (New York, 1964), sticks to the Twenties; juxtaposes memories of a Boston boyhood with some of the memorable events and personalities of the time. Elizabeth Stevenson, *Babbits and Bohemians* (New York, 1967), is a slight effort, with far too many errors of fact. Jules Abels, *In the Time of Silent Cal* (New York, 1969), is more at home with the trivial than with the serious, and Allen Churchill, *The Year the World Went Mad* (New York, 1960), is an account of 1927 that is held together with exclamation marks. Paul Sann, *The Lawless Decade* (Cleveland, 1960), is a picture book.

Frederic L. Paxson, *Postwar Years: Normalcy 1918–1923* (Los Angeles and Berkeley, 1948), remains a useful account of the period from the Armistice to the death of Harding. Better in nearly every respect, however, is a more recent work, Burl Noggle, *Into the Twenties* (Urbana, Ill., 1974).

Edmund Wilson, *The Twenties* (New York, 1975), has been compiled from Wilson's notebooks. The result is one of the best memoirs of the period. It roams far beyond the New York literary scene. His earlier collection, *The Shores of Light: A Literary Chronicle of the Twenties and Thirties* (New York, 1952), contains a variety of good things, from glimpses of Fitzgerald to a night at Minsky's. Charles Merz, *The Great American Bandwagon* (New York, 1928), is an amused, and amusing, look at some of the changing social mores of the time. Louis Adamic, *My America 1928–1938* (New York, 1938), is another eyewitness account, but is only intermittently interesting. Ben Hecht, *A Child of the Century* (New York, 1954), contains nuggets on the Chicago literary renaissance, Hollywood between the wars, the Florida land boom, and the rising tide of recreational sex. H. L. Mencken, ed., *Americana 1925* (New York, 1925), can still delight the connoisseur.

Clifton Fadiman, ed., *Profiles from the New Yorker* (New York, 1938), is a work that is both delightful and valuable. Most of the people it describes—and not all were famous—are important to understanding the Twenties. Niven Busch, *Twenty-One Americans* (New York, 1930), performs a similar service.

SOCIAL PROBLEMS

Warren S. Thompson and Pascal K. Whelpton, *Population Trends in the United States* (New York, 1933), provides an authoritative commentary on the postarmistice census reports. Louis I. Dublin, *Health and Wealth* (New York, 1928), is an essential work. Alfred W. Crosby, Jr., *Epidemic and Peace* (Westport, Conn., 1976), is a medical history of unique value and interest. Morris Fishbein, *A History of the AMA 1847–1947* (Philadelphia, 1947), is the official history of organized medicine in the United States.

On the special provisions made for the needs of veterans, see Dixon Wecter, *When Johnny Comes Marching Home* (Boston, 1944), which is largely concerned with the returning AEF. It could hardly be bettered. James R. Mock and Evangeline Thurber, *Report on Demobilization* (Norman, Okla., 1944), is, by contrast, plodding, although sound.

Robert S. and Helen M. Lynd, *Middletown* (New York, 1929), is really an ethnography of Muncie, Indiana, as if it were an island in the South Seas visited by anthropologists. In its sober, understated way this brilliant study makes the usual stereotypical notions about the Twenties seem absurd. What it shows is a farm town that in one generation had become an industrial center. Harvey Zorbaugh, *The Gold Coast and the Slum* (Chicago, 1929), is an important, pioneering study of Chicago; based on the proposition that as the city grew, community declined. Louis Wirth, *The Ghetto* (Chicago, 1928), is an account of Chicago's Jewish ghetto in transition. For a general survey of what was happening to American cities, Maurice R. Davie, *Problems of City Life* (New York, 1932), is both exhaustive and unusually accurate. R. D. McKenzie, *The Metropolitan Community* (New York, 1933), provides a statistical analysis of the rapid growth of urbanization in the Twenties.

Caroline F. Ware, *Greenwich Village 1920–1930* (Boston, 1935), is a splendid, ground-breaking study of immigrant communities trying to adjust to city life. Humbert S. Nelli, *Italians in Chicago 1880–1930* (New York, 1970), is a useful modest study in similar vein. Michael Gold, *Jews Without Money* (New York, 1930), is really a memoir, not a novel. It provides a classic account of life among the urban poor before the welfare state. Edith Elmer Wood, *Recent Trends in American Housing* (New York, 1931), is a careful, highly critical work which shows that housing was a serious problem for half the population before the Depression.

Ralph Borsodi, *Flight from the City* (New York, 1929), describes one family's response to the urban crisis; a work famous in its day, Borsodi's book is mainly a manual of self-sufficiency. Harlan Paul Douglas, *The Suburban Trend* (New York, 1925), is one of the earliest serious studies of the flight to the suburbs. Don S. Kirschner, *City and Country: Rural Responses to Urbanization in the 1920s* (Westport, Conn., 1970), is an innovative study which confirms some of the conventional interpretations, and demolishes others. Alfred Cahen, *Statistical Analysis of American Divorce* (New York, 1932), was the first reliable study of the subject, and found urbanization to be the chief factor in the breakup of marriage.

T. J. Woofter, Jr., *Races and Ethnic Groups in American Life* (New York, 1933), found that the melting pot was largely a myth. Edith Abbott, *Immigration: Selected Documents and Case Records* (Chicago, 1924), is a collection which might have been called Ellis Island and After. Roy L. Garis, *Immigration Restriction* (New York, 1927), is by an acknowledged authority. Kate Holladay Claghorn, *The Immigrant's Day in Court* (New York, 1923), is a valuable, if melancholy, account of American justice at its lowest levels. Robert A. Divine, *American Immigration Policy 1924–1952* (New Haven, Conn., 1957), is a standard account of the rising barriers. Lawrence Guy Burton, *Immigration: Cultural Conflicts and Social Adjustments* (New York, 1930), attempts to counter the criticisms of the new immigration. Gerald Rosenblum, *Immigrant Workers* (New York, 1973), does the same.

On life at the very bottom of society there is Jim Tully, *Beggars of Life* (New York, 1924), a famous picaresque memoir of hobo life. The most reliable account, however, is Nels Anderson, *The Hobo* (Chicago, 1922), a work now considered a classic. William Z. Foster, *Pages from a Worker's Life* (New York, 1939), is an autobiography which rarely mentions Foster's conversion to Communism. It concentrates instead on telling vignettes of life among the very poor by someone who knew it from birth.

Mauritz Hallgren, *Seeds of Revolt* (New York, 1933), is an excellent, journalistic account of the many passive millions dispossessed of what little they had by the Depression. Gilbert Seldes, *The Years of the Locust: America 1929–1932* (Boston, 1933), is another of the essential works. Thomas Minehan, *Boy and Girl Tramps of America* (New York, 1934), is both riveting and depressing. Up to half a million teenagers had become nomads. Charles H. Trout, *Boston, the Great Depression and the New Deal* (New York, 1977), is valuable, although pedestrian in style and organization. The same is true of Robert C. Cotner et al., *Texas Cities and the Great Depression* (Austin, Texas, 1973). William E. Akin, *Technocracy and the American Dream* (Los Angeles and Berkeley, 1977), is an important, fair-minded account of one of the few grass-roots movements of the Depression. Edmund Wilson, *The American Jitters: A Year of the Slump* (New York, 1932), is a collection of pieces that show what a very good reporter Wilson was.

After winning the vote, women in the Twenties seemed unable to capitalize on a victory that was supposed to bring in the millenium, a disappointment ably examined in William L. O'Neill, *Everyone Was Brave* (Chicago, 1969), and J. Stanley Lemons, *The Woman Citizen: Social Feminism in the 1920s* (Urbana, Ill., 1973). William Henry Chafe, *The American Woman* (New York, 1972), is a useful survey of the major political, social, and economic changes affecting women after 1920.

Indians represent a unique social problem. Lewis Meriam et al., *The Problem of Indian Administration* (Baltimore, 1928), is exhaustive, authoritative, and critical.

On the struggle for civil liberties in the Twenties, Arthur Garfield Hayes, *Let Freedom Ring* (New York, 1937), is a report from the trenches.

Robert H. Bremner, *From the Depths* (New York, 1956), ably sets the scene for examining social reform in the Twenties. Clarke A. Chambers, *Seedtime of Reform: American Social Service and Social Action 1918–1933* (Minneapolis, 1963), shows that the reform impulse did not completely die out. But it makes melancholy reading all the same. Roy Lubove, *The Professional Altruist: The Emergence of Social Work as a Career, 1890–1930* (Cambridge, Mass., 1965), illuminates as it describes an important development.

SEX

Robert L. Dickinson and Lura Beam, *A Thousand Marriages* (Baltimore, 1931), is a pioneering study by a noted gynecologist. The sequel to this work, *The Single Woman* (Baltimore, 1934), is valuable but fails to organize the material as well as the earlier study does and offers a less incisive commentary. Katherine Bement Davies, *Factors in the Sex Life of 2200 Women* (New York, 1929), is another path-breaking study, based on responses from a highly educated part of the female population. G. V. Hamilton, *A Research in Marriage* (New York, 1929), is of some value even though it is based on a sample that is too small, too self-selected, and too well educated to be representative of anyone but the respondents. Ira S. Wile, ed., *The Sex Life of the Unmarried Adult* (New York, 1934), is not especially forthcoming about its ostensible subject, but it does reflect the range and nature of informed opinion on it at the time. Page Smith, *A Letter from My Father* (New York, 1975), is an extraordinary sexual memoir; exaggerated as all the recollections of a Don Juan inevitably are, it remains, nevertheless, a convincing account of a life devoted entirely to sex in the Twenties and after.

Margaret Sanger, *My Fight for Birth Control* (New York, 1931), offers auto-biography laced with mythology. Her later effort, *An Autobiography* (New York, 1939), is better in every respect. David M. Kennedy, *Birth Control in America* (New Haven, 1970), is an important contribution to American social history. This biography of Margaret Sanger counteracts the extravagant praise she excited while doing complete justice to her remarkable achievements.

Howard B. Woolston, *Prostitution in the United States* (New York, 1921), sets the scene. Willoughby Cyrus Waterman, *Prostitution and Its Repression in New York City 1900–1931* (New York, 1932), is valuable. Walter C. Reckless, *Vice in Chicago* (Chicago, 1933), is an important, unsensational study of commercial sex in the Twenties.

Victor F. Calverton, *The Bankruptcy of Marriage* (New York, 1928), is an impassioned defense of the "new morality." Its justifications of sexual freedom have a very contemporary ring.

BLACKS

John Hope Franklin, *From Slavery to Freedom: A History of Negro Americans*, 3rd. ed. (New York, 1967), is the standard general account, with some odd omissions, e.g., no mention of jazz. Herbert Seligmann, *The Negro Faces America* (New York, 1920), admirably sets the scene. E. Franklin Frazier, *The Negro Family*

(Chicago, 1939), is a sociological classic, concerned mainly with the effects of urbanization on black families after World War I. Harold Gosnell, *Negro Politicians* (Chicago, 1935), is an important study of the politicalization of urban blacks.

Chicago Commission on Race Relations, *The Negro in Chicago: A Study of Race Relations and a Race Riot* (Chicago, 1922), is exhaustive and a landmark in what has since become a continuing series of official inquiries into the lives of black people in American cities. This was the first and more or less established the pattern. Carl Sandburg, *The Chicago Race Riot, July 1919* (New York, 1919), is a short, impressionistic account of life on the South Side. William M. Tuttle, Jr., *Race Riot: Chicago in the Red Summer of 1919* (New York, 1970), is a valuable work. Like Sandburg, Tuttle uses the riot as a starting point for a wider examination on life in the fast-growing urban black community. Walter White, *Rope and Faggot* (New York, 1929), is an important study, informed by White's courageous personal investigation of 41 lynchings.

E. David Cronon, *Black Moses* (Madison, Wis., 1955), is a sympathetic biography of Marcus Garvey. Theodore G. Vincent, *Black Power and the Garvey Movement* (Berkeley, 1972), is littered with Marxist clichés but is a valuable account of early black nationalism despite that.

Gilbert Osofsky, *Harlem: The Making of a Ghetto* (New York, 1968), is reliable and well written. Alain Locke, ed., *The New Negro* (New York, 1925), is a collection that touches on all the major developments; and a work which, whatever its defects, was in itself a part of the phenomenon it set out to describe. Nathan Irvin Huggins, *Harlem Renaissance* (New York, 1973), places the black artistic emergence of the Twenties in the historical context of the artist's life in America; deftly and imaginatively done.

Langston Hughes, *The Big Sea* (New York, 1940), is one of the most consistently interesting and illuminating memoirs to come out of the Twenties. Claude McKay, *Home to Harlem* (New York, 1928), is less a novel than a series of vignettes of black life in Harlem and on the railroads.

Sterling D. Spero and Abram L. Harris, *The Black Worker* (New York, 1931), is an important and pessimistic study.

THE SOUTH

George B. Tindall, *The Emergence of the New South 1913–1945* (Baton Rouge, La., 1967), plods along but brings together a vast amount of material. Frank Tannenbaum, *Darker Phases of the South* (New York, 1924), provides an impressionistic, brief account of the Klan, mill villages, prisons, and tenancy. Edwin Mims, *The Advancing South* (New York, 1926), is a survey of liberalism, higher education and the higher culture as they existed—northern doubts notwithstanding—in the South circa 1925. Twelve Southerners, *I'll Take My Stand* (New York, 1930), is the famous Agrarian Manifesto. It is largely an extension of the Civil War. Virginius Dabney, *Liberalism in the South* (Chapel Hill, N.C., 1932), takes a decidedly optimistic view. W. J. Cash, *The Mind of the South* (New York, 1941), is a work of classic stature on the post-Reconstruction South. It is at its most vivid when covering the 1920s and early 1930s.

Ku Klux Klan

John Moffatt Mecklin, *The Ku Klux Klan* (New York, 1924), is an indispensable study of the Klan revival. Arnold S. Rice, *The Ku Klux Klan in America* (Washington, D.C., 1962), is concerned chiefly with the Klan in the Twenties. Kenneth T. Jackson, *The Ku Klux Klan in the City 1915–1930* (New York, 1967), is an important social history, and a powerful corrective to many long-established, simplistic notions concerning the Klan. David M. Chalmers, *Hooded Americanism* (New York, 1965), provides a state-by-state account of the Klan between the wars. Charles C. Alexander, *The Ku Klux Klan in the Southwest* (Paducah, Ky., 1965), and Emerson H. Loucks, *The Ku Klux Klan in Pennsylvania* (Harrisburg, Pa., 1936), are both of considerable value.

Prohibition

Every general history of prohibition has followed the approach (and anecdotes) of Charles Merz, *The Dry Decade* (New York, 1931). Andrew Sinclair, *The Era of Excess* (New York, 1964), is the most thorough account, presenting it as largely a struggle between city and country. Herbert Asbury, *The Great Illusion* (Garden City, N.Y., 1950), is particularly valuable for its account of prohibition in New York city. Thomas M. Coffey, *The Long Thirst* (New York, 1975), is an entertaining volume, telling the tale in terms of the personal roles of more than a dozen individuals. To my mind, the best work of all is Norman H. Clark, *Deliver Us from Evil* (New York, 1976), a book that is subtle, iconoclastic, and fair; splendid in every way.

The personal accounts by Mabel Walker Willebrandt and Roy Asa Haynes are little more than government dry propaganda dignified by being placed between hard covers. Izzy Einstein, *Prohibition Agent No. 1* (New York, 1932), is of some interest, but is repetitious and superficial. Frederic Van de Water, *The Real McCoy* (New York, 1931), is an engaging biography of the first rum-runner. The other side's story is Malcolm F. Willoughby, *Rum War at Sea* (Washington, D.C., 1964), the official Coast Guard history of a thankless enterprise.

Paul C. Conley and Andrew A. Sorensen, *The Staggering Steeple* (Philadelphia, 1971), is a brief account of the role of the churches. Joseph R. Gusfield, *Symbolic Crusade* (Urbana, Ill., 1963) is a study of the temperance-prohibition movement from a sociological perspective. Lewis L. Gould, *Progressives and Prohibitionists* (Austin, Texas, 1973), is a provocative study of the dry Progressives of Texas. Norman H. Clark, *The Dry Years: Prohibition and Social Change in Washington* (Seattle, 1965), is a fine example of local history illuminating a national phenomenon. James H. Timberlake, *Prohibition and the Progressive Movement 1900–1920* (Cambridge, Mass., 1963), is a work essential to understanding the background to the Prohibition Amendment.

Stanley Walker, *The Night Club Era* (New York, 1933), is, considering its subject, surprisingly down-to-earth; based on Walker's own extensive observations. Kenneth Allsop, *The Bootleggers* (London, 1961), is useful in parts but often credulous and awestruck. Jimmie Lewis Franklin, *Born Sober: Prohibition in Oklahoma, 1907–1959* (Norman, Okla., 1971), is a lackluster regional study.

CRIME AND PUNISHMENT

H. C. Brearley, *Homicide in the United States* (Chapel Hill, N.C., 1932), is one of the best studies of its kind and is still in print. John Landesco, *Organized Crime in Chicago* (Chicago, 1929), is a landmark work in criminology. Courtenay Terrett, *Only Saps Work* (New York, 1930), explains the principles—if that is the word—on which dozens of rackets operated. Frederick M. Thrasher, *The Gang* (Chicago, 1927), is an important study that unearthed 1,300 gangs in and around Chicago. Emanuel H. Lavine, *The Third Degree* (New York, 1930), covers a wide variety of police, and criminal, practices. Clarence Darrow, *Crime: Its Cause and Treatment* (New York, 1922), is essential to understanding the foremost criminal lawyer of the time, and is as germane to the subject now as when it was written. Gene Fowler, *The Great Mouthpiece* (New York, 1931), is a biography of the first of a new breed of lawyers, William Fallon, whose rise went hand in hand with that of big-time mobsters. George Waller, *Kidnap: The Story of the Lindbergh Case* (New York, 1960), is a thorough, reliable account of the "crime of the century."

Clarence Darrow, *The Story of My Life* (New York, 1932), is a strangely impersonal autobiography. Arthur Weinberg, ed., *Attorney for the Damned* (New York, 1957), contains long extracts from the transcripts of some of Darrow's most important cases. Irving Stone, *Clarence Darrow for the Defense* (Garden City. N.Y., 1941), is biography going on hagiography. Thomas E. Gaddis and James O. Long, *Killer* (New York, 1970), is based on the autobiography of Carl Panzram, a criminal psychopath given to anal rape and murder, executed in 1931. Panzram's autobiography was too explicit and horrifying to be published until recent years. Danny Ahern, *Confessions of a Gunman* (London, 1930), sheds light on the mentality of the small-time mobster who was likely to end up dead in the trunk of a car. Clifford R. Shaw, *The Jack-Roller: A Delinquent Boy's Own Story* (Chicago, 1930), is a classic autobiography of a delinquent—later criminal—career. Ernest Booth, *Stealing Through Life* (New York, 1929), is an autobiographical account of an unsuccessful life of crime. Chic Conwell, *The Professional Thief* (New York, 1937), is a famous work by a thief who "retired" in 1933 after twenty years of stealing.

John Kobler, *Capone* (New York, 1971), is a rarity among books on famous gangsters—restrained and coherent. Elmer L. Irey, *The Tax Dodgers* (Garden City, N.Y., 1949), is—with ghostly help—by the man who put Capone in prison.

Eliot Ness and Oscar Fraley, *The Untouchables* (New York, 1957), would be more convincing were it not for the dime-novel style.

Lewis E. Lawes, *Life and Death in Sing Sing* (New York, 1929), is by the model warden of a (then) model prison. Sanford Bates, *Prisons and Beyond* (New York, 1937), is by the first director of the Federal Bureau of Prisons, a man modest about his achievements. Harry Elmer Barnes, *Battling the Crime Wave* (Boston, 1931), was a criminologist's case for prison reform. Harry L. Best, *Crime and the Criminal Law in the United States* (New York, 1930), contains an exhaustive statistical survey of the prison population of the 1920s. Frank Tannenbaum, *Wall Shadows* (New York, 1922), is the result of a personal survey of seventy jails and prisons, supplemented by Tannenbaum's own experience as a convict. Louis Berg, *Revelations of a Prison Doctor* (New York, 1934), shows convincingly how bad even the "good" prisons were. Robert E. Burns, *I am a Fugitive from a Georgia Chain Gang* (New York, 1932), is the most celebrated account of prison life in America; the years have not diminished its force. Nathan F. Leopold, *Life Plus 99 Years* (Garden City, N.Y., 1958), contains, in the first half of the book, an excellent firsthand account of prison life between the wars. Kate Richards O'Hare, *In Prison* (New York, 1923), is a uniquely valuable memoir of women in prison by an Espionage Act prisoner who later became the *grande dame* of penal reform. Robert Joyce Tasker, *Grimhaven* (New York, 1928), is another remarkable memoir, written inside San Quentin.

SACCO AND VANZETTI

B. Flexner and C. Burlingham, eds., *The Sacco and Vanzetti Case: Transcript of the Record of the Trial and Subsequent Proceedings*, six volumes (New York, 1929), provides the basic materials. There is a skillfully edited, shorter version, with useful explanatory notes: Osmond K. Fraenkel, *The Sacco-Vanzetti Case* (New York, 1931). Marion D. Frankfurter and Gardner Jackson, eds., *The Letters of Sacco and Vanzetti* (New York, 1930), is absorbing and moving. Felix Frankfurter, *The Case of Sacco and Vanzetti* (Boston, 1927), is the summary of the case which did most to turn it into a *cause célèbre*. Jeanette Marks, *Thirteen Days* (New York, 1929), is an eyewitness account of the last days of the Sacco and Vanzetti Defense Committee.

Herbert B. Ehrmann, *The Case That Will Not Die* (New York, 1969), is the most thorough and persuasive vindication of Sacco and Vanzetti by one of their lawyers. Roberta Strauss Feurlicht, *Justice Crucified* (New York, 1977), is shrill and didactic, but contains important details which have come to light only in recent years. John Dos Passos, *Facing the Chair* (Boston, 1927), set the pattern for all later accounts that portrayed them as the victims of a frame-up.

Francis Russell, *Tragedy in Dedham* (New York, 1962), is highly readable but on the basis of very shaky evidence concludes that Sacco was guilty. David Felix, *Sacco-Vanzetti and the Intellectuals* (Bloomington, Ind., 1965), offers the case for the prosecution, plus contempt for the intellectuals.

G. Louis Jougin and Edmund H. Morgan, *The Legacy of Sacco and Vanzetti* (New York, 1948), is a remarkable study, first of the case, then of its impact on American law and literature.

RELIGION

Norman F. Furniss, *The Fundamentalist Controversy 1918–1933* (New Haven, Conn., 1958), is an excellent account of a heated and complicated issue. Maynard Shipley, *The War on Modern Science* (New York, 1927), is a hostile study of Fundamentalism, as is the more famous Harry Elmer Barnes, *The Twilight of Christianity* (New York, 1929). Ray Ginger, *Six Days or Forever* (Boston, 1958), is a lively and complete report on the Dayton trial, putting it firmly in its social and historical setting. Lawrence Levine, *Defender of the Faith* (New York, 1965), is a scrupulously fair account of William Jennings Bryan's last ten years of life, 1915–25.

Robert Moats Miller, *American Protestantism and Social Issues 1919–1939* (Chapel Hill, N.C., 1958), is thorough, perceptive, generous, and witty. Donald B. Meyer, *The Protestant Search for Political Realism 1919–1941* (New York, 1963), is a study of Protestant ministers and ex-ministers who tried to express their faith through social and political action. Kenneth K. Bailey, *Southern White Protestants in the 20th Century* (New York, 1964), contains several useful chapters on the Twenties. Liston Pope, *Millhands and Preachers* (New Haven, Conn., 1942), is a sociologist's study of religion in North Carolina between the wars. Paul C. Conley and Andrew A. Sorenson, *The Staggering Steeple* (Philadelphia, 1971), examines the role of the churches in Prohibition.

On the changing fortunes of revivalism, William G. McLoughlin, Jr., *Billy Sunday Was His Real Name* (Chicago, 1955), is a workmanlike biography of one of its major figures. Bernard A. Weisberger, *They Gathered at the River* (Boston, 1958), is useful. Tom Driberg, *The Mystery of Moral Re-Armament* (London, 1964), tried to account for Frank Buchman. Lately Thomas, *Storming Heaven* (New York, 1970), is a fascinating biography of the turbulent Aimee Semple McPherson.

EDUCATION AND YOUTH

Charles H. Judd, *Problems of Education in the United States* (New York, 1933), relates changes in the schools to changes in postwar society. Heinrich E. Bucholz, *Fads and Fallacies in Present-Day Education* (New York, 1931), is scathing. William A. Smith, *Secondary Education in the United States* (New York, 1932), offers a useful survey of the major developments. K. S. Cunningham and G. E. Philips, *Some Aspects of Education in the USA* (Melbourne, Australia, 1930), is by two Australian educators and offers an objective, fair-minded appraisal. Lawrence A. Cremin, *The Transformation of the School* (New York, 1957), is *the* history of Progressive education. Edward A. Krug, *The Shaping of the American High School 1920–1941* (Madison, Wis., 1972), is an unusually reliable survey, covering every aspect of public high school development. Ben B. Lindsey and Wainwright Evans, *The Revolt of Modern Youth* (New York, 1928), is by exceptionally knowledgeable and sympathetic observers of high-school-age youth.

Paula S. Fass, *The Damned and the Beautiful* (New York, 1973), is a useful study of college youth in the Twenties, but gives them a highly inflated role in society at large. Robert Cooley Angell, *The Campus* (New York, 1928), is a sociologist's thoroughly pessimistic appraisal of undergraduates. Abraham Flexner, *Universities: American, English, German* (New York, 1930), considers mainly—and roundly condemns—the American variety. Jessica B. Peixotto, *Getting and Spending at the Professional Standard of Living* (New York, 1927), is valuable both as a commentary on middle-class aspirations and on academic life.

Morse Adams Cartwright, *Ten Years of Adult Education* (New York, 1935), provides a brief survey of an important development.

LINDBERGH

Kenneth S. Davis, *The Hero* (Garden City, N.Y., 1959), is an adequate biography, of the kind that leans heavily on the rhetorical question and a fence of exclamation marks. Leonard Mosley, *Lindbergh* (Garden City, N.Y., 1976), offers the most skillful organization of the known facts, without penetrating the shell of Lindbergh's personality. Brendan Gill, *Lindbergh Alone* (New York, 1977), is a sympathetic, highly speculative essay.

Charles A. Lindbergh, *"We"* (New York, 1927), is modest and laconic; concerned mainly with his early years as a pilot before the Paris flight. His later, *The Spirit of St. Louis* (New York, 1953), is an account worthy of the event.

On the other major episode involving aviation in the Twenties, Burke Davies, *The Billy Mitchell Affair* (New York, 1967), provides an excellent account.

COMMUNICATIONS MEDIA

Noel F. Busch, *Briton Hadden* (New York, 1949), is an engrossing biography of the cofounder of *Time*. James Boylan, ed., *The World and the 20's* (New York, 1973), is a worthy tribute to a great newspaper. Frank Luther Mott, *American Journalism: A History* (New York, 1962), is thorough and readable. Cleveland Amory and Frederic Bradlee, *Cavalcade* (New York, 1960), contains a diverting selection from *Vanity Fair*. Laurence Greene *The Era of Wonderful Nonsense* (Indianapolis, 1939), is a collection of newspaper sensations of the Twenties. W. A. Swanberg, *Citizen Hearst* (1961), contains a conscientious, unsensational account of the gutter press at its most unrestrained. Gene Fowler, *Skyline: A Reporter's Reminiscences of the 1920s* (New York, 1961), is an anecdotal account of journalism in New York by one of Hearst's ace reporters.

On periodicals, Theodore Peterson, *Magazines in the 20th Century* (Urbana, Ill., 1964), is devoted in large part to the phenomenal growth of magazine publishing in the period.

Karl A. Bickel, *New Empires* (Philadelphia, 1930), is concerned with radio and newspapers. William Peck Banning, *Commercial Broadcasting Pioneer* (Cambridge, Mass., 1946), is an insider's account of one of the most important of the early radio stations, WEAF, New York. Eric Barnouw, *A Tower in Babel* (New York, 1966), is the definitive account of broadcasting between the wars.

William Manchester, *Disturber of the Peace* (New York, 1952), is a pious biography of H. L. Mencken. Mencken's own autobiographical trilogy is *Happy Days* (New York, 1940), *Newspaper Days* (New York, 1941), and *Heathen Days* (New York, 1943).

Jazz

Gunther Schuller, *Early Jazz* (New York, 1968), is, for anyone with a serious interest, by far the best introduction, with an emphasis on jazz from the armistice to 1933. Richard Hadlock, *Jazz Masters of the Twenties* (New York, 1974), is another superior introduction, containing an unusually good discography. Rudi Blesh, *Shining Trumpets* (New York, 1958) is inclined to be dogmatic, yet remains one of the most important accounts of jazz before the 1920s.

Nat Hentoff and Albert McCarthy, eds., *Jazz* (New York, 1959), is a collection of authoritative articles on the evolution of jazz. Hugues Panassié, *The Real Jazz*, rev. ed. (New York, 1960), is a standard introduction by one of the first important French jazz scholars. Martin Williams, *Jazz Masters of New Orleans* (New York, 1967), is mainly a collection of short vivid biographies of the leading figures. Louis Armstrong, *Satchmo: My Life in New Orleans* (New York, 1954), is a delight.

Milton "Mezz" Mezzrow and Bernard Wolfe, *Really the Blues* (New York, 1946), is an autobiography that is beyond any doubt the most authentic account of what it was like to be a jazz musician in the Twenties. Nat Shapiro and Nat Hentoff, eds., *Hear Me Talkin' to Ya* (New York, 1955), is a highly evocative history of jazz told entirely by the people who made it. Frederic Ramsey, Jr., and Charles Edward Smith, *Jazzmen* (New York, 1939), is a valuable compendium, based on interviews with many of the leading jazz musicians of the Twenties. Alan Lomax, *Mister Jelly Roll*, 2nd. ed. (Los Angeles and Berkeley, 1973), has an absorbing story to tell. It is hard to imagine that anyone interested in American music would not be moved by it.

Films

Paul Rotha, *The Film Till Now* (New York, 1947), and Lewis Jacobs, *The Rise of the American Film* (New York, 1939), are two of the standard accounts which deal largely with films of 1915–33. David Robinson, *Hollywood in the Twenties* (New York, 1968), is a lively, perceptive introduction to the silent screen at its peak. Robert W. Henderson, *D. W. Griffith: His Life and Work* (New York, 1972), does justice to a great artist. Lillian Gish, with Ann Pinchot, *The Movies, Mr. Griffith and Me* (London, 1969), is a splendid, often shrewd, account of all three.

Gary Carey, *Lost Films* (Greenwich, Conn., 1970), contains stills and plot synopses of thirty major films from the 1920s, since irretrievably lost, thanks to nitrate stock. David A. Yallop, *The Day the Laughter Stopped* (London, 1976), attempts to elevate a private tragedy into one of the cataclysmic events of the twentieth century; nevertheless, a valuable work on Hollywood in its silent heyday. King Vidor, *A Tree Is a Tree* (New York, 1953), is an engaging autobiography by one of the more important directors of the period. Alexander Walker, *The Shattered Silents: How the Talkies Came to Stay* (London, 1978), is an important, accurate account of the advent of sound.

Andrew Bergman, *We're in the Money* (New York, 1972), offers a lively, lapidary account of movies from 1929 to 1939. Ben M. Hill, *The Best Remaining Seats* (New York, 1961), is an enthusiastic history of the swift rise, and equally swift descent, of the great picture palaces.

Charles Chaplin, *My Autobiography* (London, 1968), is an indispensable work on the period by its greatest star.

SPORT

Paul Gallico, *A Farewell to Sport* (New York, 1937), is, despite the florid flourishes and occasional inaccuracy, one of the best books ever written about professional athletes. Alison Danzig and Pete Brandwein, eds., *Sports' Golden Age* (New York, 1948), contains contributions on all the major sports and most of the minor ones. Grantland Rice, *The Tumult and the Shouting* (New York, 1954), is devoted mainly to the champions of the Golden Age, most of whom Rice knew well.

Harold Seymour, *Baseball: The Golden Age* (New York, 1971), is the most authoritative account. Robert W. Creamer, *Babe* (New York, 1974), is a work of the highest distinction, in a field where even adequate biographies are as rare as a triple-play. Marshall Smelser, *The Life That Ruth Built* (New York, 1975), is not only a splendid biography but also a fine history of the game between the wars, always alert to its place in modern American life. Kal Wagenheimer, *Babe Ruth: His Life and Legend* (New York, 1974), is useful.

Nat Fleischer, *Fifty Years at Ringside* (New York, 1958), manages to be both anecdotal and authoritative. Jack Dempsey and Barbara Piatelli Dempsey, *Dempsey* (New York, 1977), is a surprise and a delight. Gene Tunney, *A Man Must Fight* (Boston, 1932), sticks entirely to his ring career. Randy Roberts, *Jack Dempsey: The Manassas Mauler* (Baton Rouge, La., 1979), combines scholarship with a scintillating style.

Frank DeFord, *Big Bill Tilden* (New York, 1977), tells a strange story exceedingly well.

Herbert Warren Wind, *The Story of American Golf* (New York, 1956), is an excellent survey of the game up to World War II.

Jessie F. Steiner, *Americans at Play* (New York, 1933), is a valuable work that corrects any notion that Americans were becoming a nation of spectators.

ART AND ARCHITECTURE

Milton W. Brown, *American Painting from the Armory Show to the Depression* (Princeton, 1955), provides a first-rate introduction; unhappily the excellent text is let down by the reproductions. Frederick P. Keppel and R. L. Duffus, *The Arts in American Life* (New York, 1933), made no great claims for them, but was optimistic. R. L. Duffus, *The American Renaissance* (New York, 1928), surveys the remarkable postwar interest in the fine arts.

Three useful, broader surveys are John I. Baur, *Revolution and Tradition in Modern American Art* (Cambridge, Mass., 1951); Rudi Blesh, *Modern Art, USA* (New York, 1956); and Sam Hunter, *American Art of the 20th Century* (New York, 1973).

Irma B. Jaffe, *Joseph Stella* (Cambridge, Mass., 1970), is workmanlike and well illustrated. Constance Rourke, *Charles Sheeler* (New York, 1938), stresses Sheeler's pioneering efforts in photography alongside his painting. Lloyd Goodrich and Doris Bry, *Georgia O'Keefe* (New York, 1970), is superbly illustrated. Emily Farnham, *Charles Demuth: Behind a Laughing Mask* (Norman, Okla., 1971), is an awkward but enthusiastic biography. David Braider, *George Bellows and the Ashcan School of Painting* (Garden City, N.Y., 1971), is a short, workmanlike account of Bellows's short, workmanlike career.

Bevis Hillier, *Art Deco* (New York, 1968), is the best introduction to the last of the total styles. Unfortunately, it contains no American examples. Martin Battersby, *The Decorative Twenties* (New York, 1969), is useful.

Frank Lloyd Wright, *An Autobiography* (New York, 1943), is by the greatest artist in any medium that the United States has produced. It deals, therefore, as much with his spirit as with his buildings. Henry-Russell Hitchcock, *In the Nature of Materials* (New York, 1942), contains drawings and photographs of all Wright's buildings up to 1941, an indispensable accompaniment to the autobiography. Norris Kelly Smith, *Frank Lloyd Wright* (Englewood Cliffs, N.J., 1966), is a study of the architectural content of Wright's buildings; somewhat disappointing. Herbert Jacobs, *Frank Lloyd Wright* (New York, 1965), must be one of the very few biographies of an architect written by a client; probably the only. The best biography of Wright is Finis Farr, *Frank Lloyd Wright* (New York, 1962).

G. H. Edgell, *The American Architecture of Today* (New York, 1928), is an exceptionally instructive survey, lavishly illustrated. W. A. Starrett, *Skyscrapers and the Men Who Build Them* (New York, 1928), is an engagingly individualistic account of all aspects of these huge enterprises. G. E. Kidder Smith, *A Pictorial History of American Architecture*, volume 1 (New York, 1976), contains many excellent illustrations of the architecture of the interwar years. So too does Walter C. Kennedy, *The Architecture of Choice: Eclecticism in America 1880–1930* (New York, 1974). John Burchard and Albert Bush-Brown, *The Architecture of America* (London, 1967), has a useful section on the years 1913–33.

Frank Lloyd Wright, *Modern Architecture* (Princeton, 1931), is stimulating, impassioned, and an education in how to look at modern buildings. R. W. Sexton, *The Logic of Modern Architecture* (New York, 1929) is a short guide to the modernist's faith; particularly valuable for its inclusion of interiors and furnishings. Don Vlack, *Art Deco Architecture in New York 1920–1940* (New York, 1974), is useful; illustrations better than the text. Cervin Robinson and Rosemarie H. Bletter, *Skyscraper Style: Art Deco in New York* (New York, 1975), is well written, well illustrated.

Walter H. Kilham, *Raymond Hood, Architect* (New York, 1973), is a competent, admiring biography.

LITERATURE

Mark Schorer, *Sinclair Lewis* (New York, 1961), is one of the best biographies of recent times. Carlos Baker, *Ernest Hemingway* (New York, 1969), is the standard, lavishly detailed, more or less official biography. Arthur Mizener, *The Far Side of Paradise* (Boston, 1959), is a well-written, reliable, and sympathetic life of Fitzgerald. Andrew Turnbull, *Scott Fitzgerald* (London, 1962), is part biography, part memoir; a sensitive and graceful account. Matthew J. Bruccoli, *Scott and Ernest* (New York, 1977), firmly sets right a wide variety of mistaken stories about the most famous literary friendship of the Twenties. Nancy Milford, *Zelda* (New York, 1970), tells the sad story of Fitzgerald's wife.

James Thurber, *The Years with Ross* (Boston, 1959), is a charming, convincing memoir. Dale Kramer, *Ross and the New Yorker* (Garden City, N.Y., 1951), does justice to its twin subjects.

Arthur and Barbara Gelb, *O'Neill* (New York, 1964), is a fascinating biography; invaluable not only in regard to O'Neill, but as a history of American theater in its golden age. Mardi Valgemae, *Accelerated Grimace: Expressionism in the American Drama of the 1920s* (Carbondale, Ill., 1972) is an important study of a cultural watershed. Jack Poggi, *Theater in America: The Impact of Economic Forces* (Ithaca, N.Y., 1968), is also an important study, concerned chiefly with Broadway in the Twenties. Joseph Wood Krutch, *The American Drama Since 1918* (New York, 1939), is a splendid guide.

Alfred Kazin, *On Native Grounds* (New York, 1943), is one of the seminal works of modern American literary criticism; concerned mainly with writers in the Twenties. Irene and Allen Cleaton, *Books and Battles: American Literature 1920–1930* (Boston, 1937), is stimulating, knowledgeable, and often amusing. Frederick J. Hoffman, *The Twenties: American Writing in the Postwar Decade* (New York, 1955), attempts to portray the period through a close study of its literature, much of which he considers naive. Bernard De Voto, *The Literary Fallacy* (Bloomington, Ind., 1944), is a famous commentary on the literature of the Twenties; a useful counterpoint to the hundred volumes of praise. Allen Churchill, *The Literary Decade* (Englewood Cliffs, N.J., 1971), is merely anecdotal.

Dale Kramer, *Chicago Renaissance* (New York, 1966), is a skillful introduction to a score of major literary figures from the years around World War I. Louis

Cowan, *The Fugitive Group* (Baton Rouge, La., 1959), is a careful, modest study. Burton Rascoe, *A Bookman's Daybook* (New York, 1929), casts narrow but bright beams of light down the byways of literary culture in the Twenties.

On the Lost Generation, there are three excellent inside accounts: Ernest Hemingway, *A Moveable Feast* (New York, 1961); Matthew Josephson *Life Among the Surrealists* (New York, 1962); and Malcolm Cowley, *Exile's Return* (New York, 1951).

Daniel Aaron, *Writers on the Left* (New York, 1977), is a remarkably objective study of the unhappy affair between literature and political leftism between the wars. Frederick J. Hoffman, *Freudianism and the Literary Mind* (Baton Rouge, La., 1957), is a pathbreaking study. Max Eastman, *Love and Revolution* (New York, 1964), is an absorbing and indispensable account of life on the literary Left.

Alice Payne Hackett, *60 Years of Bestsellers* (New York, 1956), is a valuable guide to changing literary taste.

BOHEMIA

Joseph Freeman, *An American Testament* (New York, 1936), an autobiographical account of the life of one young literary bohemian torn, as many were, between the demands of art and revolution. Albert Parry, *Garrets and Pretenders* (New York, 1933), is the standard work on American bohemianism. Emily Hahn, *Romantic Rebels* (Boston, 1966), is a useful supplement to Parry. Edward Lueders, *Carl Van Vechten and the Twenties* (Albuquerque, N.M., 1955), is an episodic appraisal of a literary and music critic famous in his time and a leading fixture in both Harlem and Greenwich Village. Hutchins Hapgood, *A Victorian in the Modern World* (New York, 1939), is the autobiography of an upper-class bohemian.

HOME THOUGHTS FROM ABROAD

Ford Madox Ford, *New York Is Not America* (London, 1927), is by a noted English man of letters who adored New York. Philip Guedalla, *Conquistador* (London, 1927), is a highly atmospheric record of travels in America by a writer famous in his day. Mary Agnes Hamilton, *In America Today* (London, 1932), is an at times trenchant assessment of the state of the union in 1932. Sisley Huddleston, *What's Right With America?* (London, 1930), concludes that almost everything was right with America; a portrait so flattering that even the patriot might have trouble recognizing it. Beverley Nichols, *The Star-Spangled Manner* (London, 1928), contains incisive sketches of his meetings with a dozen notable figures, from Coolidge and Mellon to Anita Loos and Charlie Chaplin. Harold Spender, *A Briton in America* (London, 1921), offers the impressions of a visitor who was fascinated by everyday life in the United States. George Harmon Knoles, *The Jazz Age Revisited* (Palo Alto, Calif., 1955), is a useful survey of contemporary British writing on America in the Twenties.

Andre Siegfried, *America Comes of Age* (New York, 1927), made a great splash when it first appeared; one of those impressionistic surveys which is at one moment astute, the next moment stunningly wrong. Georges Duhamel, *America, the Men-*

ace (London, 1931), is by a Frenchman who liked Americans while detesting American life. Henri Dubreuil, *Robots or Men?* (New York, 1930), is the most remarkable of the foreign visitors' accounts, by a French metal worker. Objective and perceptive, this book offers many unexpected observations on working-class life.

Hugh Grant, *An Australian Looks at America* (London, 1928), is by an Australian labor leader who found little that he liked. Ernst Toller, *Which World, Which Way?* (New York, 1929), records the cross-country travels of a German Socialist.

INTERPRETATIONS

Joseph Wood Krutch, *The Modern Temper* (New York, 1929), and Walter Lippmann, *A Preface to Morals* (New York, 1929), are brilliant accounts of the moral crisis of the Twenties.

Gilbert Seldes *The Seven Lively Arts* (New York, 1924), is one of the notable critical works of the era, casting a mantle of acclaim around humble popular diversions. Howard Mumford Jones, *The Bright Medusa* (Urbana, Ill., 1952), examines the obsession with youth and art. Harold M. Stearns, ed., *Civilization in the United States* (New York, 1922), did not find much. Nor did the contributors to Ernest Gruening, ed., *These United States* (New York, 1923).

Ralph Borsodi, *This Ugly Civilization* (New York, 1929), is a famous critique of factory-dominated existence, and raised the banner of self-sufficiency. The spirit that informs it, however, is more Nietzsche than *Whole Earth Catalog*. Stuart Chase's *Men and Machines* (New York, 1929) attempted to assess the balance of an issue that was hotly argued all through the Twenties. His earlier, *The Tragedy of Waste* (New York, 1925), even had the temerity to challenge the belief that the United States was rich, efficient, and hard-working.

John B. Watson, *Behaviorism*, rev. ed. (New York, 1925), is an important work in various ways, not least as a guide to how Americans saw themselves; a work vastly more accessible than modern psychology monographs. David Shakow and David Rapaport, *The Influence of Freud on American Psychology* (Cleveland, 1968), is a useful introduction rather than a complete study; concerned largely with the interwar years.

Robert M. Crunden, *From Self to Society, 1919–1941* (Englewood Cliffs, N.J., 1972), is an interesting short account of changing social values. Robert H. Elias, *"Entangling Alliances with None"* (New York, 1973), explores the development of privatism in the Twenties. James Gilbert, *Designing the Industrial State* (Chicago, 1972), is an ambitious but not entirely successful attempt to survey the development of "collectivist" thought. Even more ambitious is Gilbert M. Ostrander, *American Civilization in the First Machine Age* (New York, 1970), which tries to say something important about concurrent changes in demography and industrialization. Its emphasis is on the first post frontier generation.

Morris Markey, *This Country of Yours* (Boston, 1932), is an account of the travels of a noted reporter who toured the country in search of its Depression-wracked soul and found "a wilderness, crying for a voice."

INDEX